Walking
Switzerland

a Lonely Planet walking guide

Clem Lindenmayer

Walking in Switzerland

1st edition

Published by

Lonely Planet Publications
Head Office: PO Box 617, Hawthorn, Vic 3122, Australia
Branches: 155 Filbert St, Suite 251, Oakland, CA 94607, USA
10 Barley Mow Passage, Chiswick, London W4 4PH, UK
71 bis rue du Cardinal Lemoine, 75005 Paris, France

Printed by
Colorcraft Ltd, Hong Kong

Photographs by
Clem Lindenmayer

Front cover: Signpost below Rigi-Kulum Summit

Published
May 1996

National Library of Australia Cataloguing in Publication Data

Lindenmayer, Clem.
    Walking in Switzerland.

    1st ed.
    Includes index.
    ISBN 0 86442 327 6 (pbk.).

    1. Walking – Switzerland – Guidebooks. 2. Switzerland –
    Guidebooks. I. Title. (Series: Lonely Planet walking guide).

914.940473

text © Clem Lindenmayer
maps © Lonely Planet
photos © photographers as indicated 1996
climate charts compiled from information supplied by Patrick J Tyson, © Patrick J Tyson, 1996

Clem Lindenmayer

Clem has lived and walked in Switzerland on and off during the last 10 years. Although quite familiar with other mountain regions of the world, he feels a special affection for the rugged beauty of the Alps. Clem researched and authored Lonely Planet's *Trekking in the Patagonian Andes*, and has helped update other Lonely Planet travel guidebooks to Western Europe and China. Some day he might even get a real job.

From the Author

My wife, Romi Arm (who accompanied me on many of the walks in this book) gets a Swiss kiss for her help with the research.

The following regional tourist offices were kind enough to provide me with free walking maps for my research: Davos-Platz, Hasliberg, Mendrisio, Poschiavo, Samnaun, Frutigen, Château d'Oex and Thusis. Thanks as well to all the tourist offices who answered my queries.

The following organisations also provided me with important information: Schweizerische Vereinigung der Stahler und Mineraliensammler; Swiss Hiking Federation (SAW/FSTP); Schweizerischer Fischereiverband (FVB); Swiss Alpine Club (SAC); Swiss Mountain Guide Federation; Bergsteigerzentrum Grindelwald; Schweizer Postautodienst; Swiss Friends of Nature; Swiss Society for the Protection of Nature; Swiss Youth Hostel Association.

Thanks also to Patagonia Inc. for their assistance.

Mark Honan's *Switzerland – a travel survival kit* published by Lonely Planet was an invaluable reference for my work. An extra big thank-you goes to Tita and Walo Bänziger, who lent me their house in Bächli/Toggenburg while I spent months and months and months writing up my notes.

From the Publisher

This, the first edition of *Walking in Switzerland*, was edited by Frith Pike with assistance from Kristin Odijk, Rachel Scully and Susan Noonan. Thanks also to Michelle

Glynn for the Ötzi aside and Kathrin Franke for German translation.

Andrew Smith prepared the maps with help from Richard Stewart, Indra Kilfoyle and Geoff Stringer. Andrew was also responsible for design and layout with assistance from Margaret Jung. Thanks to Simon Bracken and Andrew Tudor for the cover design, and to Reita Wilson, Indra, Geoff Stringer and Margaret Jung for the illustrations. Colour wraps were prepared by Andrew Smith and Geoff Stringer.

Disclaimer

Although the author and publisher have done their utmost to ensure the accuracy of all information in this guide, they cannot accept any responsibility for any loss, injury or inconvenience sustained by people using this book. They cannot guarantee that the tracks and routes described here have not become impassable for any reason in the interval between reseach and publication.

The fact that a trip or area is described in this guidebook does not necessarily mean that it is a safe one for you and your walking party. You are ultimately responsible for judging your own capabilities in light of the conditions that you encounter.

Warning & Request

Things change – prices go up, schedules change, good places go bad and bad places go bankrupt – nothing stays the same. So if you find things better or worse, recently opened or long since closed, please write and tell us and help make the next edition better.

Your letters will be used to help update future editions and, where possible, important changes will also be included in a Stop Press section in reprints.

We greatly appreciate all information that is sent to us by travellers. Back at Lonely Planet we employ a hard-working readers' letters team to sort through the many letters we receive. The best ones will be rewarded with a free copy of the next edition or another Lonely Planet guide if you prefer. We give away lots of books, but, unfortunately, not every letter/postcard receives one.

Contents

Map Legend

BOUNDARIES

▬·▬·▬·▬·▬ .... International Boundary

▬··▬··▬··▬·· .... Regional Boundary

ROUTES

▬▬▬▬▬▬ .... Freeway

▬▬▬▬▬▬ .... Highway

▬▬▬▬▬▬ .... Major Road

▬ ▬ ▬ ▬ ▬ ▬ .... Unsealed Road or Track

▬▬▬▬▬▬ .... City Road

▬▬▬▬▬▬ .... City Street

+++++++++++++++ .... Railway

▬▬▬▬▬▬ .... Underground Railway

▬·▬·▬·▬· .... Tram

▬ ▬ ▬ ▬ ▬ ▬ .... Walking Track

•••••••••••••••• .... Walking Tour

▬ ▬ ▬ ▬ ▬ ▬ ▬ .... Ferry Route

+++++++++++++++ .... Cable Car, Chair Lift
or Funicular

AREA FEATURES

.... Parks

.... Forest

.... Mountain Range

.... Beach or Desert

.... Built-Up Area

.... Reef

.... Market

HYDROGRAPHIC FEATURES

.... Coastline

.... River, Creek

.... River Flow

»» ⠀⠀⠀»‖ .... Rapids, Waterfalls

.... Lake, Intermittent Lake

.... Glacier

.... Canal

.... Swamp

SYMBOLS

✪ CAPITAL	.... National Capital	
◉ Capital	.... Regional Capital	
🌑 CITY	.... Major City	
● City	.... City	
● Town	.... Town	
● Village	.... Village or Hamlet	
■ ▼	.... Place to Stay, Place to Eat	
⚚ ♟	.... Cafe, Pub or Bar	
✉ ☎	.... Post Office, Telephone	
❶ ❾	.... Tourist Information, Bank	
◒ ℗	.... Transport, Parking	
🏛 ♠	.... Museum, Youth Hostel	
🏕 ⚑	Caravan Park, Camping Ground	
❶ ➕	.... Church, Cathedral	
☪ ✡	.... Mosque, Synagogue	
卍 卐	Buddhist Temple, Hindu Temple	
✚ ★	.... Hospital, Police Station	

◔	℗	.... Embassy, Petrol Station
✈	✝	.... Airport, Airfield
▭	✿	.... Swimming Pool, Gardens
❖	🐘	.... Shopping Centre, Zoo
⚜	⊓	... Winery or Vineyard, Picnic Site
←	A25	One Way Street, Route Number
🏛	⚑	.... Stately Home, Monument
🏠	◙	.... Castle, Tomb
⌂	⌂	.... Cave, Hut or Chalet
▲	❋	.... Mountain or Hill, Lookout
×1400 m	⛺	.... Spot Height, Shelter
)(	◎	.... Pass, Spring
🏖	⚑	.... Beach, Surf Beach
	∴	.... Archaeological Site or Ruins
		.... Ancient or City Wall
⟿	⇐	.... Cliff or Escarpment, Tunnel
		.... Train Station

Note: not all symbols displayed above appear in this book

Introduction

Switzerland is such a tiny country, and yet there's so much of it! Switzerland lies at the cultural and linguistic crossroads of western Europe, and it's fascinating that such a small country should have such great regional variation. Some patient person once worked out that Switzerland has around 5000 individual valleys. In fact virtually, every region in the country has its own unique style of architecture, its own traditional dress, its own local customs, even its own kind of cheese – it's own special charm. Switzerland has four main national languages, but everywhere you go the local people speak a different dialect. The only thing that scarcely seems to change are the flower boxes in the windows, all full of bright red geraniums.

Although less than 15% of the Alps actually lie within Switzerland, providence has given the country rather more than its fair share of the great Alpine scenery. With few real exceptions, the Swiss Alps have the highest peaks, the largest glaciers, the deepest valleys and the loveliest mountain lakes. Indeed, Switzerland has some of the most beautiful and spectacular mountain scenery found anywhere on earth.

One of the most appealing aspects of walking in the Swiss countryside is the mixture of cultural and natural elements, which sometimes blend smoothly together but just as often present a dramatic contrast. A quaint old farmhouse sits amongst gentle flowery meadows grazed by tinkling cows, while a high waterfall tumbles down the sheer rock walls of a nearby snowcapped peak to meet a gushing glacial torrent far below in the valley – such scenes typify the Swiss Alps.

This guidebook offers a broad selection of suggested walks in virtually every region of the country. It includes many of Switzerland's most classic hiking routes – of which there are dozens – but the selection is far from complete. Most of the suggested routes are day walks that can be done by anybody with minimal experience. The book also details longer trips where walkers stay overnight in huts or mountain hotels high up in the Swiss Alps.

Facts about the Country

HISTORY
The Ice Ages
Beginning around one million years ago, the earth experienced a repeated cycle of Ice ages, with extended cold intervals following climatically warmer periods. When the last Ice age reached its peak around 25,000 years ago, the Alps were covered by a vast sheet of ice. Huge glaciers sprawled down from the mountains, smothering most of today's Switzerland under icy masses up to 1000 metres deep. The Ice-age glaciers' slow but enormous force carved out and deepened the mountain valleys to give them a characteristically glacial U-shaped appearance.

Mountainsides were sheared to create bare sheer rock walls – the Matterhorn's classic pyramid form is the finest such example in the Alps. Where the glaciers melted, great quantities of rock rubble transported within the ice built up to form high walls. These glacial moraines acted as natural dams, impounding rivers to create the large bodies of water such as lakes Geneva, Maggiore and Constance along with numerous other smaller lakes.

The earliest undisputed evidence of human habitation of the Alps has been found in the Alpstein massif in north-eastern Switzerland. Here, in limestone caves (known as the Wildkirchlihöhlen) situated at 1500 metres above sea level, remains of a Palaeolithic hunter-gatherer culture dating from a warmer interglacial period some 100,000 years ago have been found. Archaeologists surmise that the first humans may well have reached the Alpine region much earlier still, but any evidence of this has probably since been erased by intervening glaciations.

Higher areas of the Jura and Alpine foothills were the only significant snow-free areas in this Ice-age landscape and were mostly covered by an open tundra-type vegetation. This higher ground nevertheless supported a surprising variety of creatures, including the so-called mega-fauna. These large animals – such as hairy mammoths, giant elk and cave bears – had become extinct by around 15,000 years ago, as the first Mesolithic (or middle Stone-age) hunters began to recolonise the now slowly warming lowlands. Cave paintings found at the Kesserloch (near Schaffhausen) dating from around 10,000 years ago depict frigid-climate animals such as reindeer – an indication that the gradual post-glacial warming had still only just begun.

Early Inhabitants
The Ice ages left behind a landscape highly favourable to human settlement, with new broadened valley floors enriched by fertile moraines and low, easily crossed mountain passes. Following the valleys of the Rhône and the Danube, Neolithic (late Stone-age) farmers began arriving in the present-day Swiss Mittelland about 6000 years ago. These settlers cleared and burnt the forests, creating a new environment in which other migratory plant and animal species could gain a foothold.

These primitive farming cultures found suitable sites for settlement around the large lowland lakes and rivers. Remains of pile-dwellings – raised houses on stilts – have been found in submerged or buried sites around the shores of lakes Zürich and Constance. With the arrival of the metal-working culture some 5000 years ago the Alps became an importance source of copper, since ore deposits were most easily discovered and worked from the exposed-rock mountainsides. The sensational discovery of the mummified body of a prehistoric man – the now famous 'Ötzi' – on the continental divide in the nearby Tirolean Alps proves that trans-Alpine routes were already well established at this time.

The Celts & Romans
In the 1st century BC, the area of modern Switzerland was largely inhabited by Celtic

tribes (the word 'Alps' is of Celtic origin). The most important of these were the Helvetians, in the Swiss Mittelland, and the Rhaetians, in today's Graubünden. The Celts increasingly came into conflict with the expanding Roman Empire until they were largely subdued by the Roman generals Tiberius and Drusus during their remarkable Alpine campaign around 15 BC. Under Caesar's successor, Augustus, all of the area of today's Switzerland was brought under Roman control.

The Romans built paved roads and established major regional centres such as Helvetiorum (Avenches) and Augusta Rauricorum (Augst). A process of assimilation began, which gradually produced a 'Gallo-Roman' culture. While the Swiss Mittelland and parts of the Alpine foothills had permanent agricultural settlements, few of the higher Alpine valleys were inhabited year-round, being visited only during the warmer months of summer for hunting, mining etc.

The Settlement of the Alps

From the 5th century onwards German-speaking tribes with their herds of cattle began pushing southwards into the area of today's Switzerland. In the western regions these Germanic newcomers were quickly assimilated into the Latinised-Celtic population, but in the east they supplanted this culture completely. Modern Switzerland's French/German linguistic division can be traced back to that time.

The moist climate in the Alps and their foothills makes this ideal grazing country, and the German-speaking cattle-herders gradually spread out into the Alpine valleys. A typical feature in the settlement of many high valleys was that the farmers first made use of the upper reaches, where glaciers had levelled out the terrain. Such upper valleys were often accessible only by way of an Alpine pass, this being less dangerous than the gorges at the bottom of the valley.

Origins of the Swiss Confederation

In the early medieval period the Habsburg kingdom (centred in modern-day Austria) sought to bring the profitable trade route over the Passo del San Gottardo under its control. To this end the Habsburgs forcefully subjugated the German-speaking forest communities around the shores of Lake Lucerne. These 'Inner Swiss' refused to accept domination by the Habsburgs, however, and in 1291 they formed a military pact to assert their independence. In a struggle epitomised by the legend of Wilhelm Tell, the Habsburgs were permanently expelled.

Originally consisting of Uri, Schwyz and Nidwalden, by 1383 Bern, Glarus, Lucerne, Zug and Zürich had joined this first loose Swiss Confederation. Throughout the subsequent centuries Switzerland further expanded its territory by military conquest and by the admission of other neighbouring communities or 'cantons'. Despite often bitter inter-cantonal rivalry, the Swiss Confederation has proven cohesive enough to withstand the last 700 years of European history.

The Walser Migrations

The uppermost part of the Valais – the area near the source of the Rhône River known as Goms – was one of the first large Alpine valleys to be settled. From around 800 AD, German-speaking farmers of the Bernese Oberland began migrating over the Grimselpass and Lötschenpass to Goms, draining highland moors and clearing mountain forests for pastures and agriculture. This was a bold and novel undertaking for these early times, and – although Celtic tribes had inhabited the Rhône Valley from at least 1000 BC – the first serious attempt by medieval farmers to establish permanent settlements above 1500 metres in the Alps. The settlers developed sound methods of highland farming, such as driving their grazing stock up to the high pastures in summer so that the valleys could be cropped or mown for winter feed.

In Goms the practice of passing on the family farm to a single heir forced sons to seek out new lands, and by the end of the

12th century these Walsers (from the German *Walliser*, meaning Valaisan) had colonised all important side valleys of the Upper Valais. The Walsers now began to migrate out of the Rhône Valley basin, driving their herds south and eastwards across Alpine passes and introducing the dairy-farming culture to wide areas of the central Alps. Due to their expertise in colonising hitherto unproductive highland valleys, the Walsers were favoured by feudal landholders, who offered them freedom from bondage and hereditary rights of land use (though usually not ownership) as a reward for opening up new territories.

The Walser migrations lasted for several centuries, and by the end of the Middle Ages even the highest valleys of the Swiss Alps had been penetrated by Walser settlers. The Walsers were not always welcome, however, often being regarded with suspicion by the local population. Large numbers of Walsers put down roots in Romansch-speaking regions of today's Graubünden. As a response to the continual influx of Walser colonists, a law was passed in the Val Lumnezia in 1457 prohibiting the acquisition of property by non-Romansch-speaking peoples.

Today some 150 towns and villages – widely dispersed in a 300-km long arc stretching across the central Alps as far Tirol – are known to be original Walser settlements. Numerous localities have names that betray their Walser origins: Valsesia near Monte Rosa in northern Italy, Valzeina in the Prättigau region of Graubünden, and the Grosses Walsertal in Austrian Vorarberg to name a few.

The Trans-Alpine Pass Routes

There are around a dozen major north-south pass routes in the Swiss Alps, including the Bernina, Splügen, San Bernardino, Lucomagno (Lukmanier), San Gottardo (St Gotthard), Simplon and Grande St Bernard, as well as many east-west passes such as the Col de Jarman, Furka, Susten and Klausen. These important transport and communication routes have been crossed regularly for

thousands of years. The Romans laid down the first well-graded and paved routes across the Alps which allowed the transportation of much greater quantities of cargo by teams of pack animals.

The mountains presented the road builders with numerous hindrances. Bridges were needed to span the numerous streams, narrow gorges made it necessary to make a high detour, and Alpine moors had to be filled out with rock. Particularly difficult obstacles in the Alpine terrain were slippery ice-polished slabs caused by glacial action – a problem that was overcome by chiselling grooves or steps into the rock.

In the Middle Ages the route over the Simplonpass was the shortest and lowest route between Milan and Paris, but after the construction in the 13th century of the legendary Teufelsbrücke – the 'Devil's Bridge' spanning a gorge of the Reuss River known as the Schöllenen – the Passo del San Gottardo (St Gotthard Pass) developed into the most important trans-Alpine route in the central Alps. The increased availability of explosives from the middle of the 17th century made it practicable to blast a safe-transit route along even the steepest cliff faces. This not only made pass transport and travel easier, but helped open up some previously inaccessible highland areas to regular summer grazing.

The control of the most important pass routes brought considerable power and prosperity, and the privileges of this profitable trade were jealously guarded. The notorious Kaspar Jodok von Stockalper (1609-91), otherwise known as the 'King of the Simplon', was able to amass a phenomenal fortune by monopolising the pass trade in the Valais.

It may at first seem odd that more cargo was actually transported in winter than in summer. The reason for this was that most of the mule drivers (*Säumer* in German, *mulattieres* in French) were mountain farmers, who in summer were simply too busy to work on the pass routes. In winter the otherwise idle farmers had to work hard to keep the passes open. A trail was laid on the mule paths after the first snow, and this had to be stamped flat by mules, horses or oxen after every new fall. This produced a hard, icy surface over which large quantities of goods could be transported on sleds; travellers actually preferred the softer winter snows to the bumpy summer ride. The dangers of avalanches were often extreme, however, and whole mule teams were sometimes claimed by the 'white death'.

Commodities with a high value-to-weight ratio were the preferred cargo. Products exported south across the passes included hard Swiss cheeses and livestock; while wine, rice, salt, spices and leather were typical north-bound goods. The expansion of road and rail routes during the 19th century finally led to the decline and eventual abandonment of the age-old muleteer profession. Today traces of the mule trails that for hundreds of years served as the sole travel and transport routes can still be seen throughout the Swiss Alps. In recent years these old routes have been rediscovered and restored as paths for recreational walking.

Exploration & Tourism in the Swiss Alps
Monks and the clergy were the first true pioneers of Alpine exploration. The earliest recorded ascent of a prominent peak in Switzerland took place in 1387, when six priests scaled the 2132-metre Pilatus – and were promptly thrown into jail for breaking a law specifically prohibiting climbing this peak. Pastor Nicoline Sererhard was the first to climb Graubünden's 2964-metre Schesaplana in 1740. The agile Benedictine monk Placidus à Spescha (1752-1833) of Disentis/Mustèr made first ascents of more than 30 summits over 3000 metres in Graubünden and Central Switzerland, including the Rheinwaldhorn (3402 metres) and the 3327-metre Oberalpstock (Piz Tgietschen). A landmark summit of Central Switzerland, the 3238-metre Titlis, was first scaled in 1744 by two monastic brothers from Engelberg.

The Romantic period produced a wave of interest in the Alps, which for the first time came to be regarded as more than just an awesome and forbidding barrier. From the mid-1700s onwards, Europe's intellectuals, including the philosopher Jean-Jacques Rousseau, his fellow-Genevan and naturalist Horace Bénédict Saussure, and Wolfgang von Goethe flocked to the Swiss Alps for poetic inspiration, scientific studies – or just to have a good look. After developing a fascination for the Alps on his first visit in 1775 (aged 26), Goethe undertook a longer second journey that took him up the Rhône Valley across the Furkapass, then down the Reuss and across Lake Lucerne, where he climbed the Rigi.

English-speaking visitors also came in droves. The poet Lord Byron toured the Bernese Oberland in the early 1800s. His compatriot, the landscape artist William Turner, visited Switzerland six times between 1802 and 1844, producing thousands of drawings and sketches as well as some important watercolour and oil paintings. Charles Dickens made lengthy trips to the Swiss Alps in the 1840s. In his classic *A Tramp Abroad*, the American writer Mark Twain describes his travels in the Bernese Oberland during the 1890s, including his crossing of the Gemmipass on foot taking several arduous days.

The so-called 'heyday of mountaineering' in the Alps was dominated by the British. In 1855 Grenville and Christopher Smyth conquered the highest summit of the Swiss Alps, the Dufourspitze in the Monte Rosa massif, and several years later the journalist Sir Leslie Stephen made various first ascents in the Bernese and Valaisan (Pennine) Alps. In 1861 the acclaimed English physicist John Tyndall scaled the 4505-metre Weisshorn, before turning his attention to the Bündner, Bernese and Vaud Alps. The summit of 4479-metre Matterhorn was first reached in 1865 by a party of seven led by Edward Whymper. On the descent tragedy struck, and four of Whymper's climbers fell to their deaths.

Promoted largely by wealthy British tourists, Switzerland led the development of Alpine tourism. Known as the 'Belle Epoche', the period between 1880 and 1914

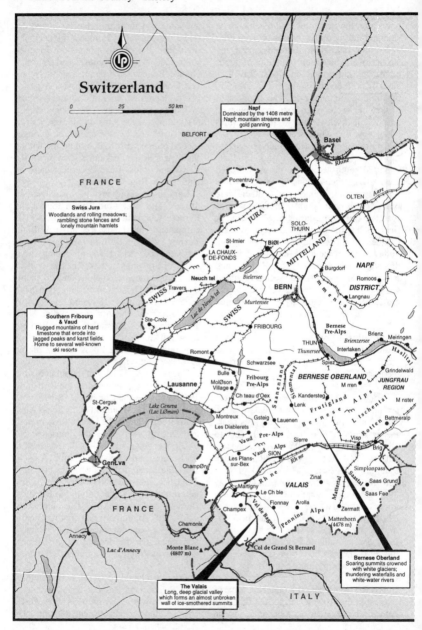

Switzerland

0   25   50 km

Napf
Dominated by the 1408 metre Napf; mountain streams and gold panning

Swiss Jura
Woodlands and rolling meadows; rambling stone fences and lonely mountain hamlets

Southern Fribourg & Vaud
Rugged mountains of hard limestone that erode into jagged peaks and karst fields. Home to several well-known ski resorts

Bernese Oberland
Soaring summits crowned with white glaciers; thundering waterfalls and white-water rivers

The Valais
Long, deep glacial valley which forms an almost unbroken wall of ice-smothered summits

FRANCE

BELFORT

Porrentruy

DelÉmont

OLTEN

Basel

Rhine

Aare

JURA

SOLO-THURN

MITTELLAND

NAPF
DISTRICT

St-Imier

LA CHAUX-DE-FONDS

BiÉl

BERN

Burgdorf

Romoos

Langnau

Emmental

Neuchâtel

Travers

Bielersee

Lac de Neuchâtel

Murtensee

SWISS

SWISS

FRIBOURG

THUN

Thunersee

Bernese
Pre-Alps

Brienzersee

Brienz

Meiringen

Interlaken

Haslital

Ste-Croix

Romont

Schwarzsee

Fribourg
Pre-Alps

BERNESE OBERLAND

Grindelwald

Bulle

MolÉson
Village

Spiez

Mürren

JUNGFRAU
REGION

Lausanne

Château d'Oex

Kandersteg

Münster

St-Cergue

Lake Geneva
(Lac LÉman)

Montreux

Gsteig

Lauenen

Lenk

Saanenland

Simmental

Frutigland

Bernese
Alps

Lötschental

Bettmeralp

Les Diablerets

Vaud
Pre-Alps

Sierre

Visp

Rotten

Brig

GenÉva

ChampÉry

Les Plans-sur-Bex

Vaud
Alps

SION

Rhône

Simplonpass

Saas Grund

Martigny

Le Châble

Fionnay

Arolla

Zinal

VALAIS

Mattertal

Saastal

Saas Fee

FRANCE

Champex

Val de Bagnes

Pennine
Alps

Zermatt

Matterhorn
(4478 m)

Annecy

Lac d'Annecy

Chamonix

Monte Blanc
(4807 m)

Col de Grand St Bernard

ITALY

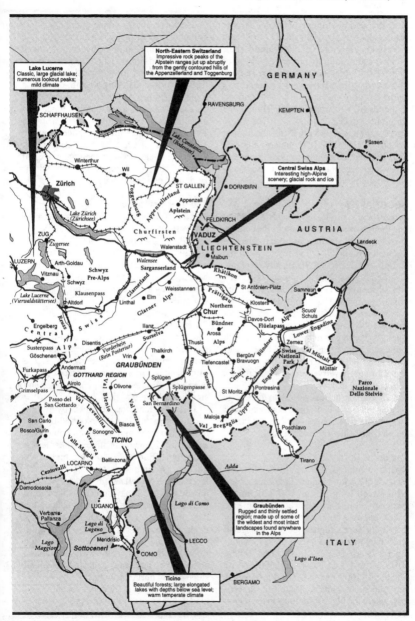

saw the establishment of many Alpine resorts (such as Grindelwald, St Moritz and Zermatt) which have maintained their premier status until the present day. Most of Switzerland's classic old funiculars and cog railways date from those years. A pioneering achievement of this early 'railway tourism' in the Swiss Alps was the completion of the Jungfraujoch cog railway in 1912, whose upper station is at 3454 metres – the highest in Europe. Since WWII, mountain cable cars have proliferated rapidly, providing summer and winter access to areas otherwise reachable only on foot.

GEOGRAPHY

Switzerland's surface area totals 41,285 sq km, though by some calculations the country would be about six times as large (or the size of Great Britain) if – God forbid! – all the bumps were ironed out. Politically speaking, the often rugged Swiss landscape is divided into 26 cantons and half-cantons, which are self-governing and have considerable autonomy in domestic affairs. Their borders don't always follow natural or 'logical' divisions (such as mountain ranges or rivers), with numerous isolated enclaves and other irregularities which hint at the jealous inter-cantonal rivalry during Switzerland's 700-year long history.

Switzerland can be divided into three basic geographical regions arranged from north-west to south-east in progressively broader bands: the Jura, the Mittelland and the Alps.

The Swiss Jura

Taking in around 10% of the country, the Swiss Jura is a low chain of limestone mountains stretching some 150 km north-eastwards along the French border from near Lake Geneva as far as the city of Basel. Only the Swiss Jura's highest peaks manage to reach much more than 1500 metres, including La Dôle (1677 metres), Mont Tendre (1679 metres), Le Chasseron (1606) and Le Chasseral (1607 metres). The Jura extends west and southwards well into French territory, where the highest summits in the region are found.

The Swiss Jura is younger and much less complex geologically when compared to the Alps, with high rolling plateaux of mixed meadows and forest (largely beech and red spruce) being its most typical landscapes. This is prime dairying country, and the region is known for its soft, full-flavoured cheeses. Although it has a moist climate and experiences intensely cold winters (which in some areas pushes the timberline down to 1200 metres), the Jura has no glaciers at all. On its south-eastern edge the mountains fall away often quite abruptly into the Mittelland, making ideal lookout peaks.

The Swiss Mittelland

The Swiss Mittelland (sometimes called the Swiss Plateau or the Swiss Midlands) extends right across the country from Lake Geneva to Lake Constance, forming an undulating, roughly 80-km-wide basin hemmed in between the Jura and the Swiss Alps. Taking in large parts of Fribourg, Bern, Lucerne and Zürich cantons, the Swiss Mittelland makes up only around 30% of Switzerland's area, yet over 75% of the country's population and almost all of its industry is based here. Embracing both French and German-speaking areas, the Mittelland is also Switzerland's true cultural heartland, with most of its major cities and significant historical sites.

This is a landscape typified by rolling cornfields pastureland interspersed by high hills. Altitudes within the region range from as little as 350 metres to almost 1000 metres, and in other European countries might even qualify as 'mountain terrain'. The rock layers of the Mittelland lie more or less flat, however, without having been subjected to the folding and uplifting that produced the Alps and the ranges of the Jura. Drained by the large tributaries of the Rhine such as the Sarine (Saane), the Aare, the Emme, the Reuss and the Limmat, the Swiss Mittelland is divided by numerous valley basins which slope gently north-eastwards.

The Mittelland's sheltered location and moderate altitudes produce a mild climate, which – together with its fertile soils com-

REGIONAL GUIDE

Region	Duration of Walks	Grade of Walks	Distance of Walks	Comments
Bernese Oberland	1-3 days	easy-difficult	7-26 km	With its soaring summits crowned with gleaming-white glaciers and thundering waterfalls that spill into sheer-sided glaciated valleys, the Bernese Oberland offers a full-spectrum Alpine experience.
Central Switzerland	1/2-3 days	easy-moderate	7.5-31 km	In early summer sweeping fields of wildflowers carpet the mountainsides, and walkers can enjoy arguably the most splendid Alpine flora found anywhere in the Swiss Alps.
Swiss Jura	1/2-3 days	easy-moderate	12-25 km	The word Jura originates from an ancient Celtic term meaning 'mountains of forest', and the word still aptly describes this region in which forests of mainly fir and spruce clothe the higher slopes above thick stands of beech.
Southern Fribourg and Vaud	1/2-4 days	easy-difficult	13-52 km	The moist climate prevailing in Southern Fribourg and Vaud make this some of the choicest dairying country in Switzerland.
The Valais	1 hr-2 days	easy-difficult	7-19 km	With most of Switzerland's peaks above 4000 metres, the Valais is a mountaineer's dream.
Ticino	1/2-3 days	easy-difficult	10-25 km	Ticino's climate favours the cultivation of Mediterranean species such as figs and oranges, and has produced a rich native flora. Chestnuts thrive in the mountains, often forming beautiful forests.
Graubünden	3 hr-4 days	easy-difficult	8.5-37 km	Spread over Europe's major drainage systems, Graubünden waters flow into the North, Black and Mediterranean seas, giving this pivotal Alpine canton an unusually complex geography.
North-Eastern Switzerland	1/2-2 days	moderate-difficult	9-34 km	The mountains of North-Eastern Switzerland offer some of the most varied and interesting walking in the country.

posed largely of ancient moraine deposits left behind by Ice-age glaciers – makes this region the 'breadbasket' of the nation. Although agricultural development is intensive, large pockets of fir, spruce and beech forest lie scattered throughout the Mittelland. Roads and motorways, railways and power lines, rivers and canals crisscross this region from all directions. Largely because of its built-up nature and less interesting contours, no walks in the Swiss Mittelland have been included in this guidebook.

The Swiss Alps

Separating northern and southern Europe, the Alps form a sort of crescent-shaped ridge that sweeps around from the Mediterranean Riviera in the west to near Vienna in the east. The Swiss Alps are in the rather more elevated central-western part of this great mountainous arc.

The Swiss Alps account for around 60% of Switzerland's territory. They form a geographically complex area centred at the pivotal Gotthard region (which is named after the one of the great trans-Alpine passes, the Passo del San Gottardo), where western Europe's three main watersheds converge. Four of Switzerland's largest rivers, the Rhône, the Reuss, the Rhine (especially the Vorderrhein) and the Ticino have their source at the Gotthard region.

The Rhône-Gotthard-Vorderrhein line, which stretches along the two great longitu-

RURAL ARCHITECTURE

A remarkable feature of the Swiss countryside is the diversity in traditional architecture. Local architectural styles reflect cultural influences as much as the local topography and the availability of certain building materials, and developed gradually over a period lasting centuries. Traditional houses in rural regions of German-speaking Switzerland tend to be wood based; while the French, Italian and Romansch Swiss generally build in stone. Also rather different is the traditional settlement pattern, with German Swiss often living in scattered settlements of independently organised farms, while the Latin cultures show a preference for clustered villages in which farming, social and leisure activities are organised communally. One unifying thing that changes little from canton to canton, however, are the ubiquitous flower boxes filled with bright-red geraniums that adorn houses.

Appenzell Style

The typical houses of the Appenzellerland and the Toggenburg are wooden constructions with a shingled exterior. Their low ceilings (which never bothered their Appenzeller occupants who generally have a lower physical stature) give them a quaint 'doll's house' character. A narrow overhanging canopy runs above the windows along the front of the building between each floor. Until fairly recently many rural households relied on additional income from weaving and embroidering, and many houses in this region have extensions with larger windows that provide more natural light. Rural scenes are frequently painted on the house façade in a traditional naive style.

Bernese Style

The grandiose wooden architecture of the Bernese Oberland gradually developed between 1600 and 1850, and is a testimony to the prosperity and self-confidence of the Alpine dairy farmers, who saw no need to imitate the stone houses of the urban gentry. With their enormous overhanging roofs, the massive Bernese farmhouses are recognisable to English speakers as the much imitated 'Swiss chalet' style. Typically, ornate designs are carved and/or painted onto the wooden exterior along with biblical and folk sayings. Some of the finest examples of the Bernese Oberland style can be seen in the Simmental or the Hasliberg area of the Haslital.

Engadine (Bündner) Style

The standard structural form in (formerly) Romansch-speaking regions of Graubünden, the Engadine (or Bündner) style integrates farmhouse, barn, cowshed and granary within a single large building. The massive stone walls can be up to 1.5 metres thick, and are traditionally adorned with so-called *sgraffito* – geometric or floral designs which are scratched into the exterior rendering before it sets. Some of the best examples are the grand old houses of the Val Müstair or Lower Engadine, many having been originally built by local mercenaries who returned from foreign wars much the richer.

Fribourg Style

The most striking feature of the houses in the Fribourg Pre-Alps is their disproportionately large roofs. Rows of elaborately arranged shingles protect the structure from the moist climate of the region, while the single-storey base of the farmhouse seems to hide below the wooden canopy. In many of the farmhouses and alp huts in the Fribourg Pre-Alps the

chimney can be sealed off with an external wooden board that keeps out rain and snow.

So-called *poyas* – colourfully painted scenes on exterior wooden panels similar to those seen on Appenzell houses – typically depict the annual driving of cattle up to the highland pastures.

Jura Style

Built for the severe Jurassian winters, the mountain farmhouses of the Jura are generally stone structures with shingled roofs, with roofed forecourts accessible via large arched gateways.

It may seem surprising that stone is the almost universal building material in an area with such abundant forests. This was due to the historical dominance of Basel, which forbade the use of wood for building since it was needed to fire the city's iron-smelting works.

Ticino Style

Typically, houses in the Ticino are small, square dwellings with thick drystone walls and heavy slab-rock roofs. Space is arranged vertically, with a ground-floor kitchen below the living room and bedrooms which are accessible only via an outside stairway. The sunny side of the house often has a grape-vine arbour for summer shade. Hay barns and milking

sheds are unattached, and usually situated in the fields well away from the village. In the northern part of Ticino a style know as the 'Gotthard house' developed, which blended the wood-based styles typical of regions north of the Alps with the local stone-based architecture.

Valaisan Style

The heavy timber houses of Valaisan farms and villages present another of Switzerland's romantic architectural styles. Traditional Valaisan-style buildings are constructed of larch, whose durable reddish timber gradually blackens as it weathers centuries of exposure to the elements, and roofed with heavy stone slabs three or four cm thick. Typically buildings are single-purpose structures with barn, granary and living quarters as separate wooden constructions. Striking features of the small, square Valaisan granaries are rounded

stone plates fixed between the wooden pillars and the upper building to keep out thieving rodents. Medieval Walser immigrants from Goms in the upper Valais were responsible for introducing the heavy-timber houses to many parts of Graubünden and Ticino. ■

dinal valleys of the Rhône and the Rhine rivers, divides the Swiss Alps into northern and southern sections. On the northern side are the Vaud, the Bernese, the Central Swiss and the Glarner Alps, while to the south the mighty Valaisan (Pennine) and the Bündner Alps form the continental divide. The Rhône and Rhine valleys themselves form a kind of intermediate zone very much hemmed in by high solid-rock mountains on either side.

The western half the Swiss Alps is especially high and rugged, with many classic peaks – such as the Eiger, the Schreckhorn and the Lauteraarhorn of the Bernese Oberland; and the Matterhorn, the Weissmies, the Dent Blanche and the Grand Combin in the Valais – rising well above 4000 metres. Despite steady glacial recession since the mid-1800s, the Swiss Alps remain the most intensely glaciated part of the Alpine chain. Of the 10 largest glaciers in the Alps, eight lie entirely within Swiss territory. Glaciers cover around 1300 sq km – or slightly more than 3% – of Switzerland's surface.

On their northern and southern sides, the Swiss Alps are fringed by a wide band of lower and often heavily forested foothills, the Pre-Alps (Voralpen, préalpes). While dwarfed by the major summits of the Alps proper, these Pre-Alpine ranges can reach surprising heights, sometimes approaching 2500 metres.

The Formation of the Alps

The formation of the Alps began around one hundred million years ago. At this time, Africa, under the unimaginably powerful forces of plate tectonics, began to drift north towards Europe, slowly pushing its way across the ancient Tethys Ocean, the shallow predecessor of the Mediterranean Sea. The African continent advanced like a giant bulldozer, causing the intervening seafloor to buckle and uplift under the enormous stress. As this process continued, a peninsula running east to west was formed, dividing the emerging Mediterranean Sea into northern and southern branches.

New rivers – such as the once-mighty 'proto-Reuss' which must have flowed somewhere through the middle of that ancient Switzerland – cut their way along mountain fault lines, eroding vast amounts of gravel and sand onto the surrounding seafloor. On both sides of the young Alpine range, these deposits gradually accumulated to reach thousands of metres in depth, finally filling in the northern branch of the early Mediterranean Sea and creating the broad Lombardy Plain in today's northern Italy. The cement-like amalgam rocks (known in German as *Nagelfluh)* that are especially widespread in the Pre-Alpine ranges consist of alluvial-marine deposits originating from that latter stage in the Alps' formation. A final phase of mountain-building pushed up the ranges of the Jura, the Alpstein and the Pre-Alps.

This whole process was accompanied by a great amount of folding and sandwiching of the different rock types. Some regions were pushed far northwards, while others – such as the central massifs of the western Alps – were scarcely moved at all. (If shifted back to its original ancient site, for example, St Moritz would be on the same latitude as the city of Bologna in Italy.) Today the fossilised remains of sea creatures can be found in ancient marine sediments throughout the northern Alps. In places molten magma spilled up from beneath the limestone crust, creating areas with granite-based rocks. Where this marine limestone occurs, underground caverns may form; the most notable are those at Beatus on Lake Thun and the Höllach caves in the Muotatal, which form the largest cave system in Europe.

Mountain Phenomena
Mountain Landslides Throughout the Alps the Ice-age glaciers sheared past mountainsides leaving behind high, almost vertical walls. As any engineer will tell you, these steep rock faces are structurally unstable, and occasionally whole mountainsides collapse into the valley. In the past such 'mountainslides' (known in German as *Bergsturz*, or as *éboulement* in French) have obliterated entire villages in the Swiss Alps.

Some particularly unfortunate examples

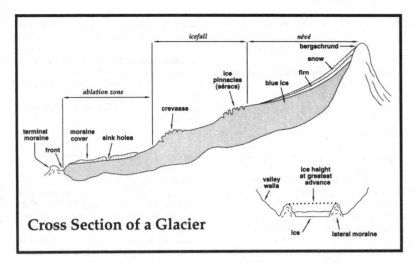

Cross Section of a Glacier

of mountain landslides include Ticino's Val Bavona in 1594, the Rossberg landslide of 1806 at Goldau in Central Switzerland, and at Elm in the Glarnerland in 1881. A recent and comparatively minor landslide occurred in 1992 in the Mattertal just north of Randa; fortunately nobody came to harm, but the devastation is still quite apparent. Very often the fallen debris dams the valley to create a new lake, as is the case with the Tchingelsee in the Bernese Oberland, which resulted from a relatively small landslip in 1950.

The Alps' largest ever mountainslide occurred some time between 15,000 and 10,000 years ago, immediately following the last Ice age. In this so-called Flimser Bergsturz an estimated 15 cubic km of rock material collapsed along a 15-km section of

Glaciers

At high altitudes most precipitation falls as snow rather than as rain. In areas where so much snow falls that it cannot melt away completely during the short summer, so-called névés and glaciers form. 'Valley' glaciers, best typified by Switzerland's mighty Grosser Aletschgletscher, are the largest kind of glacier. These great slow-motion 'rivers of ice' move at an extremely slow yet immensely powerful pace, grinding and shearing away at their supporting rock base and transporting large volumes of debris (or moraine) out of the mountains.

'Shelf' glaciers form elongated icy strips, or nestle within rounded cirques, which themselves are formed by this same pattern of erosion by snow and ice. The French word névé (German: *Firnfeld*) is used to describe a high-Alpine snowfield. As the older snow moves downslope, pushed by the weight of new snow further uphill, it becomes compacted and gradually turns into a glacier. Névés often lie at the head of a glacier, constantly feeding it with new ice.

Like glaciers over the world, Switzerland's areas of perpetual ice and snow have receded markedly over the last 150 years. The country's glaciers have lost around one third of their surface area. Glaciologists calculate that if this trend continues at the present rate, many smaller glaciers will have thawed out completely by the end of the second decade of the next century. ■

the Rein Anteriur (Vorderrhein) River. This debris was gradually eroded to produce the interesting Ruin' Aulta gorges of the Rein Anteriur in Graubünden.

Another large mountainslide occurred in September 1714 above Derborence in the lower Valais, when a cliff face of the Diablerets collapsed, crushing whole forests and Alpine pastures under great masses of rubble. Obvious signs of major instability such as eerie cracking noises accompanied by occasional falling rocks were heeded by most of the local herders, so the number of human deaths was relatively low. More catastrophic was the Rossberg mountainslide of 1806, in which 40 million cubic metres of material thundered down without warning on Goldau, wiping out the entire village.

Ice Avalanches Steep glaciers, known as icefalls, regularly send large blocks of ice – some the size of a house – crashing down mountainsides. The volumes of ice released by ice avalanches, however, are vastly greater and far more catastrophic. Ice avalanches generally occur after a long, hot summer when the rock beneath the glacier warms up so much that its frozen bond with the ice dissolves. One such ice avalanche occurred on the 11 September 1895 near Kandersteg in the Bernese Oberland at 5 am. A colossal chunk of ice suddenly broke off from the Altelsgletscher, smothering the Alpine pastures of Spittelmatte and Winteregg directly below the glacier under some four million cubic metres of ice debris. This disaster killed six herders and their cattle, and the mass of ice took five years to melt.

A more curious and tragic disaster caused by an ice avalanche took place in the Valais in the early 1870s, several decades after the entire lower section of the Glacier du Giétro had collapsed into the Val de Bagnes to dam the river. By 1818 the impounded waters were threatening to break out and flood the lower valley, but (just as the lake was being drained in order to avert the danger) the ice wall suddenly gave way, killing 35 people as an icy wave engulfed villages downstream.

Today an artificial reservoir, the Lac de Mauvoisin, occupies this site.

Lakes & Reservoirs Natural and artificial water bodies cover roughly 5% of Switzerland's surface area, providing some of the most picturesque scenery on offer. Most water bodies (from large lakes to small Alpine tarns) were formed by the action of glaciers, which gouged out deep troughs or left depressions at the terminal moraine which then flooded as the ice receded.

Switzerland also has many lakes of less natural origin, most built as storage reservoirs for hydroelectricity. High precipitation levels and excellent so-called heads of water (the altitude difference between reservoir and power station) make Switzerland ideal territory for hydroelectric development. Hydroelectricity makes up some 60% of Switzerland's total power-generating capacity.

Dams are seen or passed along many walking routes, and it's hard not to admire the engineers' work as you look up to an impressive curved-concrete dam wall built across a deep mountain ravine. Switzerland has already reached 90% of its hydroelectric potential, however, and many Swiss environmentalists are determined to prevent the remaining 10% from being developed. Regional electricity companies and conservationist groups are currently locking horns over hydroelectric projects planned for the Central Valais and south-western Graubünden.

Erratic Blocks Erratic blocks are large boulders left 'stranded' by Ice-age glaciers, and typically stand incongruously in valley pastures or forests. These isolated giants are often composed of different rock types than those found locally, and therefore a reliable indication of the ancient glacial flow paths. In past centuries many of these great Ice-age relics were blown apart and used as building material, but in Switzerland most erratic blocks are now protected by law.

Karst Formations Karst is a greyish type of

limestone rock. In many places throughout the Swiss Alps, jagged slab-like formations known as karst fields (*Karrenfelder* in German) are found. These form when water containing carbonic acid (as in rainwater) seeps through the limestone, slowly dissolving it, and have been likened to petrified glaciers. A particularly interesting phenomenon encountered in ranges composed of karst are so-called doline depressions. These form when a large subterraneous cavern produced by water seepage collapses into itself, leaving a broad hollow where water may accumulate to create a lake. The Alpstein massif, and the ranges around the Thunersee and Brienzersee (Lake Thun and Lake Brienz), the Swiss Jura and the Fribourg and Vaud Pre-Alps generally have the best examples of karst formations.

Hanging Valleys Walkers may often observe that a higher, gently sloping side valley drops away precipitously or flows through a tight gorge where it meets the main valley. Such mountain landscapes were formed as Ice-age glaciers gouged out and deepened the main valley, leaving the mouth of the side valley 'hanging' high above the new valley floor. Immediately after the Ice-age glaciers receded, the side-valley stream would have met the main valley as a high waterfall, but in most cases the stream has gradually cut its way back into the side valley to form an often narrow gorge. Examples of hanging valleys are the Gasterntal in the Bernese Oberland, the Safiental in Graubünden's Surselva region or the lateral valleys of the Rhône Valley.

CLIMATE

The Alps provide Europe's most marked climatic division, largely cutting off the north of the continent from the milder conditions prevailing around the Mediterranean Sea. Conversely, the Alps shelter the Mediterranean from the periodic intrusions of cold Arctic air that produce starkly lower than average temperatures on the northern side of the range.

Several climatic regions overlap in Switzerland, and the country has rather a complex weather pattern. Summer weather is influenced by four main wind currents. Northerly airstreams bring frigid Arctic air masses into the Alps, usually producing snowfalls. The warm and moist southerlies bring rainfall, but the bad weather normally doesn't last for very long. In summer north-easterly winds are dry and warm (but cold in winter). Easterlies are generally responsible for longer periods of wet weather.

Most areas above around 1200 metres (or 1500 metres in Ticino) are covered by a thick blanket of snow at least from January to March. The mid-winter snowline even drops down into the Swiss Mittelland, although during the last few decades the snow cover has rarely stayed more than a week or so at such low altitudes.

Snow and rainfall levels can vary radically over relatively short distances in the Swiss Alps. For example, the Jungfraujoch has an annual precipitation – most of it falling as snow – exceeding 4000 mm, while the Central Valais, just 40 km to the south-west, only receives around 500 mm.

Weather

Certain seasonal weather phenomena occur in Switzerland with surprisingly regularity, such as the 'sheep's cold', a chilly spell that comes in mid-June, or the 'St Martin's summer', a warm period around the first week in November. Switzerland generally enjoys an extended run of stable weather in mid-autumn (familiar to English speakers as the Indian summer), which can bring day after day of fine, settled conditions.

Below is a brief outline of regional climate and weather patterns in Switzerland. See also Weather Information in the Facts for the Visitor chapter.

The Northern Swiss Alps The northern side of the Alps lies in the path of the oceanic westerly airstreams, which bring frequent alternations between high-pressure and low-pressure systems. These regions have moist climates with heavy winter snowfalls and appreciable summer rain. On the windward

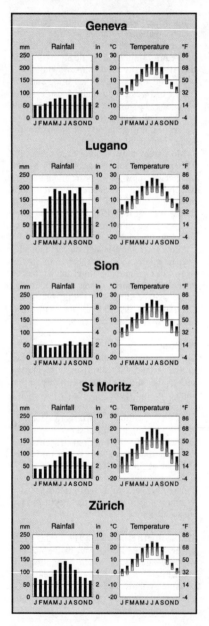

sides of the mountains where cloud build-up frequently occurs, precipitation levels are considerably higher than on their leeward sides, which lie within the 'rain-shadow' of the mountains.

In places, warm southerly air is repeatedly ducted through 'Föhn valleys' (see boxed text), which consequently enjoy annual temperatures well above the regional averages. Due to the amount of moisture in the air, summers can be unpleasantly humid. Summer thunderstorms are very prevalent on the northern side of the Alps, particularly in the mountains of the Bernese Oberland and Central Switzerland.

From autumn until early winter a heat inversion occurs in northern Switzerland, when colder temperatures are recorded in the lowlands than at higher altitudes. A thick layer of fog often builds up over the Swiss Mittelland, which visitors often mistake for overcast conditions. Above a maximum altitude of 1300 metres, however, the sun may be clothing the mountains in glistening autumn light.

The Swiss Jura The Swiss Jura is cooled by the westerlies, and as a consequence average temperatures are decidedly lower than at identical altitudes in the Alps. Annual precipitation on the Jura's upper slopes averages 1500 mm, with high summer rainfall due to frequent and often heavy thunderstorms. The Swiss Jura experiences frigid winters with positively 'Siberian' temperatures, which in places drop below 40° C.

The Longitudinal Valleys The longitudinal valleys of the inner Swiss Alps comprise the Rhône Valley in the Valais, most of Graubünden's upper Rhine valley and the Engadine. These regions have a very pronounced 'continental' type of climate, with major seasonal and daily temperature variation. Summer days are typically warm – often rising above 30° C – while night temperatures can be decidedly chilly.

Enclosed by high mountains on either side, the longitudinal valleys receive substantially less precipitation (whether rain or snow) than regions situated directly on the southern or northern side of the Alpine chain. The longitudinal valleys are also rather more sheltered from storms, and the drier conditions tend to hinder the development of the heavy summer thunderstorms. Solar radiation is very intense in the longitudinal valleys, but walkers tend to feel the summer heat much less due to the lower humidity levels.

Ticino The Gotthard massif is a particularly important Alpine barrier, and ensures Switzerland's southernmost canton, Ticino, has a surprisingly mild climate. Affectionately known as the 'sunroom of Switzerland', Ticino lies within the Mediterranean's climatic sphere of influence – a fact strongly reflected in its local vegetation. The northernmost part of Ticino around the Gotthard massif itself is a partial exception, however, and tends to hold in bad weather for longer. Summer thunderstorms are somewhat less frequent than on the northern side of the Alps, but once the rainclouds break the downpours can be incredibly heavy.

MOUNTAIN AND ALPINE FLORA OF SWITZERLAND

Several Ice ages over the last million years repeatedly forced cold-resistant highland plants to move down to lower areas in order to survive. Following the last Ice age, new plants steadily re-colonised the Alps, so the Alpine flora actually consists of relatively recent arrivals. For this reason there are few highly specialised plants in the Swiss Alps.

In the mountains the growing season (essentially the snow-free period) becomes shorter with increasing altitude, and therefore Alpine plants take longer to recover from any setback in their growth cycle. Walkers should always consider this, and take particular care to avoid damaging the fragile flora of the Alps.

VEGETATION ZONES

As they hike up from valley floor to mountain summit, walkers will note that the vegetation changes in stages, becoming progressively smaller in stature and more sparsely distributed. Swiss botanists distinguish four rough vegetation zones: lowland, montane, subalpine and Alpine. These vary considerably due to the local microclimate, exposure to the elements or even human alteration of the ecosystem. In Ticino the vegetation zones are up to 300 metres higher.

The lowland zone reaches up to 600 metres, and is the warmest, most agriculturally productive and densely populated zone. It includes most of the Swiss Mittelland as well as larger valleys of the Jura, the Alps and Ticino. In especially mild areas typical southern plants such as maize, chestnuts, figs and oranges can be grown.

The montane zone takes in areas up to about 1200 metres. In the montane zone animal husbandry is already more important than agriculture, and broad-leaf forests of beech, elm, maple, linden (lime), oak and birch predominate. Ticino's beautiful horse-chestnut forests (known locally as *selva*) also lie with the montane zone.

The subalpine zone goes up to roughly 1700 metres, and is largely covered by coniferous forests. Lower down the most common tree species tends to be the red (Norway) spruce *(Picea excelsa)*, which higher up gives way to larch *(Larix decidua)*, arolla pine *(Pinus cembra)* or other highland conifers such as mountain pine *(Pinus montana)* and Scots (Scotch) pine *(Pinus sylvestris)*.

The Alpine zone begins at timberline, although exactly where this lies is not always directly obvious. The upper line of the forest can vary considerably, with isolated stands of trees even managing to survive well above it. Fields of Alpine heathland that include small semi-prostrate shrubs like dwarf mountain pine, juniper and Alpine rhododendrons (alpenroses) often extend upwards far above the last trees. The rich highland meadows (called *Alpen* or *Matten* in German, and *alpe* or *alpage* in French) form the basis of dairy farming in the Alps, and are subject to regular summer grazing. They are surprisingly rich in species, with many native grasses and well over 100 common wildflower plants. Non-flowering mosses, fungi and lichen or loose, unvegetated talus and scree slopes present the upper limit of the Alpine zone.

MOUNTAIN TREES

Some 25% of the Swiss Alps and Pre-Alps are covered by forest. Alpine forests play a vital role in preventing avalanches, and as early as 1200 AD the highland Swiss planted trees on bare mountain slopes for winter protection. The average treeline (timberline) in the Swiss Alps varies widely – from 1700 up to 2300 metres above sea level. Many tree species are essentially Eurasian that is, they range from western Europe into Siberia. Some of the trees most commonly encountered in the mountains of Switzerland are described below.

European Larch *(Larix decidua)*

European Larch Unique amongst the Swiss conifers, the European larch *(Larix decidua)* is a deciduous tree that turns a striking golden colour before the first autumn storms strip the needles from the branches. If needles fall into a lake, an interesting phenomenon may sometimes be observed where they are rolled together to form 'larch balls'. In order to thrive larch demands sunny and dry conditions, and is therefore very common in areas with a 'continental' climate such as the Valais or Graubünden. This highland species grows right up to the treeline, often in beautiful open stands with a heather underbrush. Larch wood is harder and more weather resistant than any other type of timber, and for centuries it has been a favoured building material in mountain communities.

Beech The beech *(Fagus sylvatica)* is the most abundant broad-leaf tree in Switzerland. Preferring moist locations in the montane zone, beech form almost pure-stand forests in every region except for the Engadine and Central and Upper Valais. The trees are easily identified by their smooth, pearl-grey bark. They often attain a height of 45 metres and an age of 300 years. Beech forests are rich ecosystems and make attractive areas for walking. The oily beech nuts provide an important source of food for many birds and animals, particularly squirrels, pheasants and wild boar. The oval-shaped leaves of the beech are light green in spring, dark green in summer and golden brown in autumn, when they fall in a thick carpet over the forest floor. When they cover foot tracks, beech leaves can create a slippery (and potentially dangerous) walking surface.

Arolla Pine *(Pinus cembra)*

Arolla Pine Like the larch, the arolla pine *(Pinus cembra)* is a true high-mountain tree that grows only at upper elevations, and is rarely found below 1300 metres. Arolla pine has a similar form to other mountain pines (such as *Pinus montana*), but uniquely it has five needles on each bunch rather than the two of other Swiss mountain pine species. The purplish-brown cones contain resinous edible nuts that provide an important food source for birds, squirrels and foxes. The arolla pine can withstand the extreme conditions well above the normal forest line, with the highest specimens found in the Valais at 2850 metres! Under the harsh conditions of these high-altitude environments the tree takes on a twisted and weathered form, yet may live to a thousand years of age with a 1.5-metre-thick trunk.

Mountain Pine Another larger high-mountain conifer is the mountain pine *(Pinus montana)*. This tree can grow to 20 metres in height, and frequently occupies rocky ground or stabilised talus slopes where it may form pure stands. The mountain pine has oval-shaped cones with two-needle branchlets.

Red Spruce The red spruce *(Picea excelsa*, also called Norway spruce) is a densely foliated conifer whose cones point downwards. Foresters and farmers have favoured this useful and fast-growing tree for centuries, and as a result the red spruce is ubiquitous throughout northern Switzerland, where it forms closed forests at altitudes of up to 1800 metres. Perhaps due to its (over) representation in the forests of Switzerland, in recent decades the red spruce has shown itself to be particularly susceptible to damage by acid rain and the bark beetle.

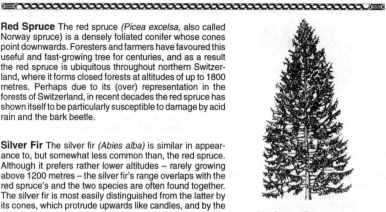

Red Spruce *(Picea excelsa)*

Silver Fir The silver fir *(Abies alba)* is similar in appearance to, but somewhat less common than, the red spruce. Although it prefers rather lower altitudes – rarely growing above 1200 metres – the silver fir's range overlaps with the red spruce's and the two species are often found together. The silver fir is most easily distinguished from the latter by its cones, which protrude upwards like candles, and by the slight whitish tinge to its branches and trunk.

Sweet Chestnut The sweet chestnut *(Castanea sativa)* is assumed to have been brought by the Romans to Ticino, where these attractive trees form whole forests. It is a large tree with slightly serrated and elongated leaves. It develops hairy capsules that split open in autumn to release the ripe brown nuts. Rich in carbohydrates, sweet chestnuts were the staple food for many mountain-dwellers in Ticino, who would bake bread using flour ground from the dried nuts. Sadly, Ticino's chestnut forests are threatened by a fungus of American origin that attacks the tree's roots and shoots.

Fruit of the Sweet Chestnut
(Castanea sativa)

Sycamore Maple The mountain maple *(Acer pseudoplatanus)* is one of Switzerland's loveliest trees. Sometimes reaching an age of 500 years and a height of 40 metres, its characteristic form is a broadly spread crown above a thick and gnarled old trunk. The mountain maple prefers moist sites between the high-montane and Alpine zones, where it frequently colonises old screeslides. Being a particularly hardy tree it is often planted along roadsides, and in autumn its large leaves turn a striking reddish golden yellow.

Sycamore Maple
(Acer pseudoplatanus)

ALPINE HEATHLAND PLANTS

Alpenroses or Alpine Rhododendrons Known as alpenroses in Switzerland, Alpine rhododendrons typify the high-Alpine landscape perhaps more than any other species of plant. Two species of rhododendron grow in the Swiss Alps, the rust-leaved alpenrose *(Rhododendron ferrugineum)* and the hairy alpenrose *(Rhododendron hirsutum)*, often forming lovely rolling Alpine heaths up to 2500 metres. Easily the most common is the rust-leaved alpenrose, which favours the acidic soils typical for Switzerland's mountain regions. The flowers of the rust-leaved alpenrose are dark red. The much less common hairy alpenrose has bright-red blooms and grows in limestone soils; the undersides of its leaves are green.

Both species of alpenroses are protected in most Swiss cantons, but picking highland wildflowers anywhere in the Alps shows bad form.

Dwarf Pine *(Pinus mugo)*

Dwarf Pine The dwarf pine *(Pinus mugo)* grows mostly above the treeline, typically forming semi-prostrate thickets up to two metres high on exposed Alpine slopes. It has thick deep-green needles in tufts of two. Being well adapted to harsh conditions, this large, hardy shrub has been successfully planted in coastal land-stabilisation programmes. The dwarf pine can also be found down to 1500 metres, however, where it grows to be a largish tree of up to 20 metres and looks rather similar to the mountain pine. Due to the often isolated nature of its distribution, the dwarf pine has developed into several subspecies.

Dwarf Willows Some of the most interesting plants of the Alpine heaths are the half-dozen or so dwarf willows *(Salix* species) which grow in the sheltered sites over 1500 metres above sea level and can be found up to 2500 metres or more. The lesser willow *(Salix herbacea)* has pale green thinly serrated leaves about two cm in length. It's one of the smallest trees in the world, rarely exceeding five cm in height. The blunt-leaved willow *(Salix retusa)* has small, shiny leaves and may reach 80 cm or more, often growing up larger rocks which remain warm after nightfall.

Bilberry A relative of cultivated blueberries, the bilberry *(Vaccinium myrtillus)* is a heavily branched shrub reaching up to half a metre in height. It is a true Alpine species whose natural distribution is generally well above 1500 metres, often growing interspersed with larch or mountain pine forest if not above the treeline itself. The berries begin ripening from early August in Ticino, and somewhat later on the northern side of the Alps. Rich in vitamin C, their tangy flavour tempts many a walker to stop and pick. In autumn the leaves turn a rusty-red hue, giving a melancholic feel to the highland slopes.

ALPINE WILDFLOWERS
The Alps have a florescent diversity and splendour equalled by few other mountain regions of the world. Amateur botanists can delight in learning to recognise the scores of different species of Alpine flora. Each species comes into bloom at a particular time (and/or at different elevations), so from spring to midsummer (from May to late July) the Alpine slopes always offer something interesting. There are numerous species of anemone, buttercups, daisies, gentians, lilies and orchids to name a just few.

A brief selection including some of the author's favourite Alpine wildflowers appears below.

White Crocus
(Crocus vernus)

Edelweiss The Edelweiss *(Leontopodium alpinum)* is so characteristic of the Alpine flora that the Swiss tourist authorities – despite a prior claim by their Austrian neighbours – recently declared it the national emblem; ironically, the Edelweiss actually originates from Central Asia. Preferring sunny and remote mountainsides up to 3500 metres, the Edelweiss blooms from July to September. The entire plant, including the delicate star-shaped flowers, is covered with a white felt-like coating that protects it against dehydration. The edelweiss is quite rare nowadays, and although walkers often still can't resist picking it, this 'true' Alpine flower is strictly protected in all Swiss cantons.

White Crocus One of the mountain world's real early bloomers is the white crocus *(Crocus vernus)*, an Alpine saffron species. Beginning in March at its lowest elevations of around 1000 metres, this hardy plant pops its purplish-white flowers straight through the melting spring snows, and until other later species come into flower whole fields are dominated by the white crocus. Such a sight is enough to fill every springtime walker's heart with the joy.

Bearded Bellflower Another resident of the Alpine zone is the bearded bellflower *(Campanula barbata)*, which grows up to 2600 metres above sea level. Blooming throughout the summer, its bell-shaped lilac-blue flowers and elongated leaves are covered with coarse, stiff hairs. The bearded bellflower prefers slightly acid soils and is fairly common on mountain pastures.

Globeflower Favouring very moist or even waterlogged sites, the globeflower *(Trollius europaeus)* grows to 60 cm in height and is commonly seen along meandering streams in the highland pastures. Blooming in early summer, with its cupped, yellow flowers it bears a passing resemblance to some buttercup species.

Yellow Alpine Pasqueflower Reasonably common on mountain meadows is the yellow Alpine pasqueflower *(Pulsatilla sulphurea)*, a pretty Alpine anemone. The plant grows to about 25 cm and produces a large, single six-petal flower that blooms from late spring until midsummer. The flower matures into a white, hairy ball that looks vaguely like the head of a dandelion.

Spring Gentian Spring gentians *(Gentia verna)* are one of the most attractive and widely spread smaller Alpine wildflowers. These are those shy sparkles of violet-blue hiding amongst the Alpine herbfields or pastures. Spring gentians grow close to the ground in clusters and are best seen from April to early June.

Yellow Gentian The yellow gentian *(Gentiana lutea)* has an appearance quite unlike other Alpine gentian species, which are mostly small with bluish flowers. A single plant may reach 70 years of age, each season producing new a thick succulent stem up to 100 cm high which dies back again in autumn. The yellow gentian has long leathery cupped leaves and bunched bright yellow flowers. For centuries an astringent essence has been produced from the roots for medicinal purposes.

Bearded Bellflower *(Campanula barbata)*

| Globeflower *(Trollius europaeus)* | Yellow Alpine Pasqueflower *(Pulsatilla sulphurea)* | Spring Gentian *(Gentia verna)* | Yellow Gentian *(Gentiana lutea)* |

Purple Gentian
(Gentiana purpurea)

Purple Gentian Another of the well-represented Alpine wildflowers of the genus *Gentiana*, the purple gentian *(Gentiana purpurea)* has fleshy bell-shaped velvet-purple coloured flowers clustered at the end of the single stem up to 60 cm high. The purple gentian is found sporadically on mountain pastures and in Alpine heaths, and its roots contain bitter medicinal substances similar to those of the yellow gentian.

Glacier Buttercup Numerous species of buttercup grow in the Swiss Alps, but the rare glacier buttercup *(Ranunculus glacialis*, also called the glacial crowfoot) is probably the most hardy Alpine wildflower of all. Seldom seen below 2000 metres, the glacier buttercup can survive at elevations of well over 4000 metres, establishing itself on scree slopes, moraine rubble or crevices in cliffs. The glacier buttercup has five white petals which gradually turn pink.

Thorny Thistle Rather common in the Swiss Alps, the thorny thistle *(Cirsium spinosissimum)* is often the first larger plant encountered as you descend from the bare high-Alpine slopes into the vegetation line. Growing up to 50 cm tall, the thorny thistle has a pale yellow crown with long spiny leaves. In autumn it dies back and starts to decay, giving off an odour distinctly reminiscent of sour socks.

Martagon Lily *(Lilium martagon)*

Martagon Lily The Martagon lily *(Lilium martagon)* has mauve petals curled back in a form reminiscent of a sultan's turban. Although not especially common the Martagon lily is one of the Alps' most flamboyant Alpine wildflowers, and blooms in June and July.

Alpine Poppy The Alpine poppy *(Papaver alpinum*, sometimes called the Rhaetian poppy) is rare and is found only in the northern Alps at elevations above around 2000 metres. The flower buds hang in a 'nodding' position before opening out into attractive white blooms.

Alpine Aster *(Aster alpinus)*

Noble Wormwood Although not especially common, noble wormwood *(Artemisia mutellina)* is found throughout the ranges of Central Switzerland. It is a small, delicate plant with numerous little yellow flower buds that typically grows on steep, rocky mountainsides. When rubbed between the fingers the plant gives off an intense, aromatic odour. The noble wormwood has medicinal properties (an infusion made from the leaves is a cure for stomach upsets) and its bitter essence is the flavouring used in Vermouth.

Alpine Aster The Alpine aster *(Aster alpinus)* is a small daisy-like wildflower found only in limestone regions, typically on cliffs or well-drained mountain slopes. It blooms throughout the summer months and the flowers have elongated bluish petals radiating around a strikingly yellow centre.

FAUNA OF SWITZERLAND'S ALPINE REGION

As with the flora, many animals that now inhabit the Alpine region migrated there after the Ice ages. Some, such as the snow hare and snow grouse, came from Arctic regions, while others, like the marmot, were originally inhabitants of Central Asia. Certain noxious animals have recently established themselves in Switzerland, most notably the enok (or 'marten dog') from eastern Asia. Other less than welcome newcomers are the racoon and musk rat, which were inadvertently introduced from North America. Conservationists are concerned that these intruders may excessively prey upon or compete too heavily with the native fauna.

Below is a list of native fauna of interest to walkers. It's educational to note how many species of native animal became extinct in Switzerland – many have since been reintroduced.

LARGE PREDATORS

Brown Bear Switzerland's last brown bear *(Ursus arctos)* was shot in the Engadine village of S-charl in September 1904.

Being true symbols of wilderness, bears demand a habitat of extensive forest with steep-sided slopes (preferably cliffs) as a protective retreat. Other needs are a local vegetation rich in berries and roots, and an abundance of small prey (like marmots) or larger animals to supply plenty of carrion.

Having now enjoyed protection for more than half a century, western Europe's populations of wild bears have increased dramatically. With small but resilient populations of brown bears existing in the adjoining Trentino region of Italy, the expectation that individual animals will one day wander across the border to re-establish Switzerland's bear populations is not unreasonable. Whether through migration or by artificial reintroduction, it's likely that in the next 10 years or so bears will again live and breed in the wilds of the Swiss Alps.

Brown Bear *(Ursus arctos)*

Wolf The situation regarding Switzerland's wolves is similar to that of its bears, but unfortunately there is less public sympathy for wolves. Persecuted to extinction in the 19th century, wolves have occasionally remigrated into Swiss territory, and – not being protected by law – these new arrivals have soon been shot by local hunters.

Lynx The largest native European cat species, the lynx *(Lynx lynx)* reaches a maximum length of 1.5 metres from its head to the tip of its tail. This handsome feline has pointed ears ending in paintbrush-like tufts, a spotted ginger-brown coat and a short thick tail with a black tip. Originally found throughout the Swiss Alps, the lynx had been completely wiped out by the beginning of the 20th century. From 1970 onwards, however, lynx have been progressively re-released into the wild, and the animals are once again part of the natural ecosystem. With a territorial range of up to 300 sq km, lynx typically prey on deer or chamois, although smaller mammals are also taken. They present absolutely no danger to humans.

Lynx *(Lynx lynx)*

Red Fox *(Vulpes vulpes)*

SMALL PREDATORS

Red Fox The red fox *(Vulpes vulpes)* is found throughout Switzerland and is often seen by walkers. This intelligent opportunist can adapt to widely varying environments – from remote Alpine to densely populated urban – although it thrives best in areas of mixed field and forest. The fox may dig its own burrow, but prefers to enlarge an existing rabbit warren and may even co-inhabit the burrow of a badger. In April or May the vixen – don't call her a bitch! – produces a litter of up to six whelps, which she takes with her on the hunt after just one month. Mice are the staple prey of foxes in Switzerland, but they will eat anything from frogs to beech nuts.

Foxes are the main carrier of rabies (see the Health section in Facts for the Walker), and until the early 1980s Switzerland's fox populations were drastically culled in order to minimise the number of infected animals. This unfortunate practice was ended after it was demonstrated that regular immunisation using baits laced with rabies vaccine was a more effective method of combating the disease.

Stoat This smallest predator hunts rabbits, mice or birds. Living in the Swiss Alps up to an elevation of 3000 metres, the stoat *(Mustela erminea)* has a reddish brown summer coat that turns snow-white for the winter season (when the animal is referred to as an ermine). The stoat kills its prey by biting deeply into the back of the head with its sharp teeth. For better observation of their surroundings, stoats often stop and sit up on their hind legs in a 'begging' position.

Marten Cousins of weasels and stoats, several species of these small omnivorous hunters live in Switzerland. The adaptable stone marten *(Martes foina)* is brown except for a white patch on the collar, and ranges from lowland areas to well above the treeline. The stone marten has settled in urban areas, where it may nest in the crevices of buildings or disused pipes etc. The tree marten *(Martes martes)* is almost identical to the stone marten, but inhabits undisturbed montane forests. An excellent climber, the tree marten preys mainly on squirrels and mice, but also feeds on nuts, berries, insects and birds. In winter, marten are hunted or trapped in cages for their pelts.

Stoat *(Mustela erminea)*

Marten *(Martes foina)*

Badger Despite its being a member of the stoat and marten family, the badger *(Meles meles)* is more an omnivorous scavenger, as much accustomed to feeding on seeds and fruits as snails, birds or small mammals. Badgers are outstanding diggers, building surprisingly complex burrows, with several entrances and sleeping chambers. A social animal, the badger lives in family groups, visiting and overnighting in neighbouring burrows. Legendary for its cleanliness, the badger leaves no remains of its prey after feeding and – hikers take note! – carefully buries its excrement in neat funnel-shaped holes.

Although they produce small litters only sporadically, badgers have few natural enemies and reach a comparatively old age. In past decades, however, badger numbers have been severely reduced by hunting in order to control the spread of rabies. This, along with the badger's decidedly nocturnal habits, make it fairly unlikely that you'll see one in the wild.

Badger *(Meles meles)*

LARGE HERBIVORES

Ibex A true mountain species, ibex *(Capra ibex)* have an outstanding adaption to the Alpine environment. These long-horned beasts normally stay well above the treeline, moving to the warmer south-facing mountainsides in winter. Ibex are related to domesticated goats, and will occasionally breed with farm animals if unable to find a mate in the wild. Once relentlessly exploited for the (supposed) medicinal properties of the flesh and horns, by the early 1900s there were no ibex left in Switzerland. Since the animal's gradual reintroduction into the wild from a single small pure-blood population of Italian origin, numbers have increased so much that seasonal hunting of ibex is once again permitted.

Less timid and/or more curious than chamois, ibex are the most frequently sighted game animal in the Alps. Feeding on Alpine herbs, grasses and lichens, ibex are typically seen in small herds on craggy mountain ridgetops, from where they can survey the surrounding slopes. As long as walkers stay on their downhill side, ibex will generally allow you to approach within a reasonable distance.

Ibex *(Capra ibex)*

Chamois A member of the antelope family, the chamois *(Rupicapra rupicapra)* is another animal characteristic of the Alpine zone. Adapted to the mountain environment at least as well as the ibex, chamois are excellent climbers and jumpers, with spread hooves to avoid sinking into the snow. The animals have shorter crook-shaped horns and a reddish-brown summer coat with a black stripe along the spine. Their diet consists of lichen, grass, herbs or pine needles.

Although generally shy, chamois are quite abundant in Alpine regions and mountain walkers have an excellent chance of spotting them. The Swiss wildlife authorities are currently concerned about a previously unknown disease that gradually causes blindness in chamois. As their sight worsens, the animals drop out of the herd and ultimately die of starvation.

Chamois *(Rupicapra rupicapra)*

Red Deer *(Cervus elaphus)*

Red Deer Red deer *(Cervus elaphus)* are Switzerland's largest wild animals and range in forests and Alpine meadows up to 2800 metres. This is another species that was eradicated from the Swiss Alps, although natural restocking soon occurred through migrations from neighbouring Austria. Without its natural predators (the bear, wolf and lynx) red deer numbers have now increased so much that – despite continual cullings by hunters – they compete to the detriment of other native hooved mammals. The animals have a reddish-brown summer coat, and every year the stags develop impressive antlers that are shed in spring. The stags' formidable mating roar can often be heard from as far as several km away.

Roe Deer
(Capreolus capreolus)

Roe Deer Being active during the day, roe deer *(Capreolus capreolus)* are quite frequently seen in forested terrain right up to the treeline. Deer numbers were actually much lower in the 19th century than today, and they can be hunted legally in all parts of Switzerland. Roe deer eat shoots, buds, berries or fungi.

Wild Boar Wild boar *(Sus scrofa)* mostly inhabit areas of deciduous forest, feeding largely on beech nuts and acorns, but may sometimes move up to Alpine pastures at over 2000 metres. During plentiful seasons the sows produce abundant litters, but a severe winter can decimate the herd. Although not often seen by walkers, wild boar are much more common in Switzerland than is realised. Wallowing holes and turned-up ground left by foraging animals are an unmistakable indication of their presence. Wild boar are unpopular with farmers, whose crops they sometimes raid; foresters, on the other hand, value wild boar highly, since they destroy tree pests and prepare the ground for natural seeding.

SMALLER MAMMALS & RODENTS

Alpine Marmot Alpine marmots *(Marmota marmota)* live in colonies of around 50 individuals. These large rodents prefer sunny grassy slopes between 1300 and 2700 metres. In June females give birth to two to four young, who reach maturity within just two months. Marmots build extensive burrow systems, and with the first snowfalls seal off the burrow entrance with grass and stones before beginning a long winter hibernation. During this time they survive exclusively on fat reserves built up over the summer.

Marmots are extremely alert and wary, and at the slightest sign of danger let out a shrill whistling sound to warn other members of the colony, who immediately head for the underground shelter. Due to their slim and agile form in spring and early summer, marmots are most easily observed in the autumn when slowed down by their heavy fat reserves. A pair of binoculars and a discreet manner of approach are the best tricks for observing marmots in the wild.

Affectionately called *Mungg* in Swiss German, in the past marmots provided many a meal to mountain families and are sometimes still hunted for food.

Alpine Marmot *(Marmota marmota)*

Snow Hare The snow hare *(Lepus timidus)* inhabits the Alpine zone from 1600 metres right up to 3400 metres. Being somewhat smaller than the lowland subspecies, in summer the snow hare has reddish-brown fur with white-tinged ears and tail, but in winter the entire coat turns snowy white. Widely distributed throughout the Alps, the snow hare typically feeds on twigs and grasses found in Alpine heathlands. Snow hares are solitary and nocturnal creatures, and are therefore seen only sporadically.

Red Squirrel Unlike in Britain, where the red squirrel *(Sciurus vulgaris)* has become rather scarce due to competition from the larger introduced North American grey squirrel, these small arboreal rodents are quite common in the coniferous forests of Switzerland up to an altitude of 1800 metres. Eluding the eyes of earth-bound humans, this shy creature rarely leaves the treetops, where it largely feeds on pine or beech nuts. In autumn squirrels bury the nuts as food reserves, but the winter snows make it hard for them to locate all these storage spots. Since some seeds stay in the ground to germinate, squirrels make an important contribution to the regeneration of their forest habitat.

BIRDS

Golden Eagle Although sometimes called the 'king of the Alps', the golden eagle *(Aquila chrysaetos)* was once rather less common in the Alpine zone, but took refuge in the mountains to escape human persecution in its original lowland habitat. With a wingspan of up to 2.5 metres, the bird can frequently be observed gliding around the highest peaks seeking its prey. Marmots are the bird's staple food, but it also regularly attacks larger animals trapped in snowdrifts or injured by falls. The golden eagle is now fully protected throughout Switzerland, with some 300 breeding pairs. Its population levels in the Swiss Alps have reached saturation point, and the birds have now begun spreading back down into the Mittelland.

Lammergeier With a wingspan measuring up to 2.8 metres and a body length of more than one metre, the lammergeier *(Gypaetus barbatus)* is Europe's largest bird of prey. This 'bearded vulture' was mercilessly persecuted as a supposed predator of sheep, and finally became extinct in Switzerland in 1886. Having been reintroduced into the wild only in the last decade, the bird still occupies a tenuous niche in the Alpine habitat.

The lammergeier typically preys on marmots or hares, but finds plenty to eat during the long Alpine winter when animals are killed by avalanches or fall to their death due to icy conditions. In March, when such carrion is most plentiful, the vulture raises its brood. Living in strongly bonded pairs, lammergeiers generally nest on exposed cliff ledges to allow for better takeoff. The birds vigorously defend their territory – an area as large as 80 sq km – against intruding fellow species, and territorial fights commonly end in the death of one of the birds.

The plumage of the bearded vulture is slate black in colour apart from a darker stripe by its eyes. Unlike other vulture species, its head is completely covered with feathers, with a tuft of bristle-like plume under the chin. Even from a relatively close distance, the lammergeier is hard to distinguish from the golden eagle.

Golden Eagle *(Aquila chrysaetos)*

Lammergeier *(Gypaetus barbatus)*

Alpine Jackdaw
(Pyrrhocorax pyrrhocorax)

Snow Grouse
(Lagopus mutus)

Alpine Jackdaw The Alpine jackdaw *(Pyrrhocorax pyrrhocorax)* has pitch-black feathers and a yellow beak. A relative of the common crow, this hardy opportunist is an ever-present companion throughout the mountains. Alpine jackdaws are often seen swooping around mountain-top restaurants in search of discarded food scraps, but walkers should refrain from deliberately feeding them. The birds normally feed on worms, insects or berries.

Snow Finch Like the snow grouse, the small white-black-brown coloured snow finch *(Montifringilla nivalis)* is an exclusively Alpine bird. Never venturing below the treeline even in winter, it nests in very high sites up to 3000 metres – anywhere from sheltered nooks in mountain huts to crevices on the north wall of the Eiger. Normally eating insects and seeds, the snow finch (which is really a member of the sparrow family) has a tendency to scrounge for food scraps around sites frequented by humans.

Snow Grouse The snow grouse *(Lagopus mutus)* is a true mountain species well adapted to the Alpine zone. In winter the bird digs itself an insulating cavity in the snow, wandering the exposed, snow-free slopes in search of food during the day. Like the stoat and the mountain hare, the snow grouse camouflages itself for the winter by turning from a sprinkled brown to a snowy-white colour. With the sprouting of the mountain vegetation in spring, the snow grouse feeds on the protein-rich new shoots, moving progressively up the mountainside as the summer awakens.

REPTILES
Snakes All of Switzerland's eight native species of snake are endangered and protected by law. Two species of viper, *(Vipera aspis)* and *(Vipera berus)*, are venomous, although their bite is fatal only in extremely rare cases. Snakes are fairly uncommon in northern Switzerland and they keep very much to themselves even south of the Alps. Being cold-blooded, snakes go into a seasonal torpor during the winter months, so your best chance of seeing them is in spring when they're still in a slow and sluggish state.

Lizards Easily mistaken for a snake is the copper-coloured slowworm *(Anguis fragilis)*, a common legless lizard that prefers a moist environment close to forest clearings. The spotted brown mountain lizard *(Lacerta vivipara)* grows to a length of 15 cm, and can live up to an altitude of 3000 metres.

Slowworm *(Anguis fragilis)*

CONSERVATION & THE ALPINE ENVIRONMENT

Switzerland's natural habitats, particularly its Alpine environment, are under assault from a myriad of sources.

Every year the forests become a little bit sicker. The phenomenon of forest dieback (or *Waldsterben*) is a complex reaction to the environmental impact of ozone, nitrous oxide and other pollutants from industrial sources and motor vehicles. The myth of fresh Alpine air is illustrated by the following: readings consistently show that the average level of air pollution in Basel is actually lower – at least on weekends – than that on the Jungfraujoch. Acid rain seriously damages trees' foliage and stunts growth, and in some parts of Switzerland has produced soil with the consistency of greasy putty. Lichen species that grow on tree trunks – one of the best so-called bio-indicators – are disappearing noticeably.

Global warming, now scarcely disputed by Swiss climatologists, is clearly evident in the steady recession of Switzerland's glaciers and névés. Glaciers act as a giant frozen reservoir of fresh water, and since glacial meltwater accounts for a considerable part of the summer flow of the large rivers that drain the Swiss Alps – such as the Rhine and the Rhône – this will have undesirable consequences for everything from hydroelectricity production, river navigation and agriculture (particularly in the parched Central Valais). The lower level of permafrost in the Swiss Alps, currently at around 2400 metres, is gradually moving upwards, causing instability and landslides on the thawing mountainsides.

For several decades now, foresters have noted a small but significant 'upward creep' of the treeline in the Swiss Alps – another effect of gradual rising average temperatures. Exotic evergreen plants originally from warmer climes appear to have gained a major foothold in the broadleaf forests of Ticino, where their presence was previously quite marginal.

Another worrying problem is the continuing plague of bark beetles in Swiss forests. These insects weaken trees by boring under the bark to feed on the sap, leaving the trunk exposed and causing fungal rot. Walkers may often notice black-plastic traps positioned in forest areas throughout Switzerland in order to control the spread of the bark beetle.

The further expansion of the already dense road system is a major worry to Swiss conservationists. New motorways are planned for the Central Valais and Goms regions, and some 200 km of new 'access' tracks are bulldozed and blasted in Alpine regions every year. Switzerland has a 28-tonne limit for road freight, compared with 40 tonnes in countries of the European Union (EU). Even Swiss who are strongly 'pro-Europe' are concerned that pressure from the EU for greater heavy-vehicle transit rights via Switzerland could bring higher traffic volumes. (This has been the experience of Switzerland's Alpine neighbour, Austria, which has seen an almost 50% increase of trucks on the Brenner Pass route since that country joined the EU.)

Use of the Alps as a prime recreation zone often conflicts with its role as a last stronghold for many species of animals and plants. Alpine tourism, most particularly the skiing industry, has turned many once quiet and charming mountain villages into sprawling holiday centres. New lifts with an ever-greater carrying capacity are being installed: in the 10 years from 1980 to 1990 the *hourly* carrying capacity of Switzerland's mountain cableways increased from 267,000 to 425,000 people! The sheer numbers of visitors (including walkers) contributes to the ecological degradation.

In view of the increasing stress on the Alps, Europe's six Alpine countries – Austria, France, Germany, Italy, Slovenia and Switzerland – signed the Alpine Convention in 1991. The Alpine Convention aims to minimise or reduce the environmental damage caused by tourism and motor traffic in the Alps. Unfortunately, the signatories' varying interpretations of the convention and unwillingness to compromise on certain issues has limited its effectiveness.

In a 1994 referendum the Swiss people voted in favour of the 'Alpine Initiative', which aims to force freight off the busy motorways and onto the railways. Heavy trucks that currently transit Switzerland will be transported on special 'piggy-back' shuttle trains. As part of the so-called NEAT project, over the coming decades Switzerland will invest billions of francs on new railway tunnels through the Simplon and Gotthard massifs.

Meanwhile, walkers can make a worthwhile contribution to conservation in the Alps by using public rather than private transport where possible. See also the Looking after the Environment section in the Facts for the Walker chapter.

PEOPLE

Switzerland marks the division between the western and eastern Alps, and hence the cultural border between Latin-based (French, Italian and Romansch) and Germanic peoples. Switzerland has a population of some 6.8 million (164 inhabitants per sq km), of which around 18% are foreign citizens. German-speaking Swiss account for 66%, francophone Swiss for 18%, Italian speakers for 10% and Romansch for just 1% of the population.

Despite sharing all the trappings of the nation-state, Switzerland's three main ethnic groupings don't actually mix a great deal. Many French Swiss (Suisses Romandes) know Paris better than Zürich, and – in spite of their latent anti-German prejudices – the German Swiss (Deutschschweizer) grudgingly orient themselves towards their powerful northern neighbour. The Italian Swiss (Svizzeri Italiani) complain that their northern compatriots treat them virtually as if they *were* Italians, but most of them do seem to drive Fiats!

French and German Swiss often jokingly refer to their cultural and geographical divisions as the Rösti Graben (French: fossé de röschti). In recent years, however, fundamental differences have emerged between French Swiss and German Swiss regarding the future of their country within Europe. The former are overwhelmingly in favour of Switzerland joining the EU, while a thin but resolute majority of German Swiss reject EU membership or even the 'compromise solution' of the European Economic Space (of which Norway is a member). It seems somewhat ironic that such a pivotal European country should be so 'anti-Europe'.

In terms of lifestyle, of course, the real contrasts within Swiss society are urban/rural not French/German. Traditional farming is still very much alive and well in Switzerland (albeit only with the support of massive state subsidies on agriculture). Many of the country's most celebrated folk traditions and activities – from yodelling and playing the Alp horn to competitive sports like body wrestling and flag swinging – are still widespread in the rural regions.

LANGUAGE

Switzerland has four official languages – German, French, Italian and Romansch. Easily the most important of these, both in its population and regional coverage, is German.

Swiss German

The term Swiss German (or *Schwyzter-*

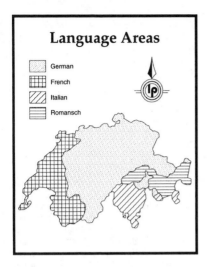

Language Areas

- German
- French
- Italian
- Romansch

words over their High German counterparts. The usual word for 'bicycle' is *vélo* (not *Fahrrad)*, an icecream is a *Glace* (not a *Sahneneis)*, and a station platform is usually called a *Perron* (rather than a *Bahnsteig)*. English words have increasingly come into vogue as well.

German Swiss have no trouble understanding High German, though at times you may come across people who slip back into dialect because their High German has become a little rusty. If you don't understand, just say *Bitte, sprechen Sie Hochdeutsch?* (Excuse me, do you speak High German?) Unless you plan to stay a few years (or are writing a master's thesis in linguistics), there's really no point trying to learn *Schwytzertütsch*. You can impress your walking companions, however, by using the Swiss German greetings, *Grüezi* (formal) or *Hoi* (informal – use for children), when you meet others along the way.

High German

Pronunciation Unlike English or French, German has no real silent letters. You pronounce the **k** at the start of the word *Knie* (knee), the **p** at the start of *Psychologie* (psychology), and the **e** at the end of *ich habe* (I have). One distinctive feature of German is that all nouns are written with a capital letter.

tütsch) describes the group of Alemannic dialects spoken throughout the German-speaking regions of Switzerland. Unlike the status of regional dialects in neighbouring Austria and Germany, in Switzerland dialects are used for verbal communication, even in quite formal situations.

Swiss German is perhaps best described as a sub-language, with a somewhat different grammar and vocabulary to standard (or 'High') German. There are also very significant regional variations between the half-dozen or so main Swiss German dialects. Hardly anyone ever writes in Swiss German and, apart from witty advertising slogans or 'folksy' poetry, everything from cookbooks to the house rules in Swiss mountain huts is written in High German.

To outsiders familiar with High German, *Schwyztertütsch* can sound like a ridiculous parody of it, due to the many dialects. The Bernese talk in slow melodic tones quite reminiscent of the soft mooing of their cows, while the strong gutteral dialect spoken around Zürich has been unkindly likened to the sound made by someone with a severe throat infection. In everyday usage there is a preference for foreign (especially French)

Vowels As in English, vowels can be pronounced long, like the 'o' in 'pope', or short, like the 'o' in 'pop'. As a rule, German vowels are long before one consonant and short before two consonants: the **o** is long in the word *Dom* (cathedral), but short in the word *doch* (after all).

a	short, like the 'u' in 'cut', or long, as in 'father'
au	as in 'vow'
ä	short, as in 'act', or long, as in 'hair'
äu	as in 'boy'
e	short, as in 'bet', or long, as in 'day'
ei	as in 'aisle'
eu	as in 'boy'
i	short, as in 'in', or long, as in 'see'

ie	as in 'see'
o	short, as in 'pot', or long, as in 'note'
ö	like the 'er' in 'fern'
u	like the 'u' in 'pull'
ü	similar to the 'u' in 'pull' but with stretched lips

Consonants Most German consonants sound similar to their English counterparts. One important difference is that **b**, **d** and **g** sound like 'p', 't' and 'k', respectively, at the end of a word.

b	normally like the English 'b', but as 'p' at end of a word
ch	like the 'ch' in Scottish *loch*
d	like the English 'd', but like 't' at the end of a word
g	normally like the English 'g', but as 'k' at the end of a word, or 'ch' in the Scottish *loch* at the end of a word when after 'i'
j	like the 'y' in 'yet'
qu	like 'k' plus 'v'
r	can be trilled or guttural, depending on the region
s	normally like the 's' in 'sun', but like the 'z' in 'zoo' when followed by a vowel
sch	like the 'sh' in 'ship'
sp/st	the **s** sounds like the 'sh' in 'ship' when at the start of a word
tion	the **t** sounds like the 'ts' in 'hits'
ß	like the 's' in 'sun' (written as **'ss'** in this book)
v	as the 'f' in 'fan'
w	as the 'v' in 'van'
z	as the 'ts' in 'hits'

Basics

Hello.
Guten Tag.
Hello. (in southern Germany)
Grüss Gott.
Goodbye.
Auf Wiedersehen.

Bye bye.
Tschüss.
Yes.
Ja.
No.
Nein.
Please.
Bitte.
Thank you.
Danke.
That's fine/You're welcome.
Bitte sehr.
Sorry. (Excuse me/Forgive me.)
Entschuldigung.
Just a minute!
Ein Moment!

Language Difficulties

Do you speak English?
Sprechen Sie Englisch?
Does anyone here speak English?
Spricht hier jemand Englisch?
I (don't) understand.
Ich verstehe (nicht).
Please write that down.
Können Sie es bitte aufschreiben?
How much is it?
Wieviel kostet es?

Small Talk

What is your name?
Wie heissen Sie?
My name is ...
Ich heisse ...
Where are you from?
Woher kommen Sie?
I'm from ...
Ich komme aus ...
How old are you?
Wie alt sind Sie?
I'm ... years old
Ich bin ... Jahre alt.

Getting Around

What time does (the) next ... arrive/leave?
Wann fährt (das/der) nächste ... an/ab?

the boat	*das Boot*

the bus (city)	*der Bus*
the train	*der Zug*
I would like ...	*Ich möchte ...*
a one-way ticket	*eine Einzelkarte*
a return ticket	*eine Rückfahr-karte*
1st class	*erste Klasse*
2nd class	*zweite Klasse*

Finding Your Way

Can you show me (on the map)?
Können Sie mir (auf der Karte) zeigen?
I'm looking for ...
Ich suche ...
Where is the bus stop?
Wo ist die Bushaltestelle?
Where is the tram stop?
Wo ist die Strassenbahn-haltestelle?

far/near	*weit/nahe*
Go straight ahead.	*Gehen Sie geradeaus.*
Turn left.	*Biegen Sie links ab.*
Turn right.	*Biegen Sie rechts ab.*

Around Town

I'm looking for ...	*Ich suche ...*
a bank	*eine Bank*
the city centre	*die Innenstadt*
the ... embassy	*die ... Botschaft*
my hotel	*mein Hotel*
the market	*den Markt*
the police	*die Polizei*
the post office	*das Postamt*
a public toilet	*eine öffentliche Toilette*
the telephone centre	*die Telefon-zentrale*
the tourist office	*das Verkehrsamt*

Signs

Open	*Offen*
Closed	*Geschlossen*
Camping Ground	*Campingplatz*
Entrance	*Eingang*
Exit	*Ausgang*

Full/No Vacancies	*Voll/Besetzt*
Guesthouse	*Pension/Gästehaus*
Hotel	*Hotel*
Information	*Auskunft*
Police	*Polizei*
Police Station	*Polizeiwache*
Train Station	*Bahnhof (Bf)*
Rooms Available	*Zimmer Frei*
Toilets	*Toiletten (WC)*
Youth Hostel	*Jugendherberge*

Walking

Is this the trail/road to ...?
Ist das der Weg/die Strasse nach ...?
Which trail goes to ...?
Welcher Weg führt nach ...?
Is the trail steep/wide/ narrow?
Ist der Weg steil/breit/eng?
How many kilometres to ...?
Wieviele Kilometer sind es bis ...?
Where are you going?
Wohin gehst Du?
Do you know this area well?
Kennst Du Dich hier gut aus?
Is the trail safe?
Ist der Weg sicher?
Where can I hire a guide/ tent?
Wo kann ich hier einen bergführer/ein Zelt mieten?
Is there a camp site nearby?
Gibt es dort in der Nähe einen Zeltplatz?
Can we camp here?
Dürfen wir unser Zelt hier aufbauen?
I'm lost.
Ich habe mich verlaufen.
Do I need a guide?
Brauche ich einen Bergführer?
What's that animal called?
Wie heisst dieses Tier?
What's that plant called?
Wie heisst diese Pflanze?

Weather

It's raining/frosty/snowing.
Es regnet/friert/schneit.
It's hot/cold/cloudy.
Ist heiss/kalt/bewölkt.
What will the weather be like tomorrow?
Wie wird das Wetter morgen sein?

Some Useful Words

alp hut	*Alphütte*
alp track	*Alpweg*
Alpine garden	*Alpengarten*
Alpine rhododendron	*Alpenrose*
arolla pine	*Arve/Zirbe*
avalanche	*Lawine*
backpack	*Rucksack*
beech	*Buche*
bilberry	*Heidelbeere*
bridge	*Brücke*
buttercup	*Hahnenfuss*
cable car	*Luftseilbahn*
cairn	*Steinmännchen*
camping ground	*Zeltplatz*
chair lift	*Sessellift*
chamois	*Gemse*
cirque	*Kar/Felszirkus*
contour	*Höhenlinie*
cornice	*Wächte*
crampons	*Steigeisen*
crossing	*Übergang*
direction	*Richtung*
dormitory	*Massenlaer/ Touristenlager*
east	*Ost*
edelweiss	*Edelweiss*
fog	*Nebel*
forest	*Wald*
gap	*Furgge/Scharte*
gentian	*Enzian*
glacier	*Gletscher*
gondola lift	*Gondelbahn*
gorge/ravine	*Schlucht*
hanging glacier	*Hängegletscher*
hill	*Hügel*
hut	*Hütte*
ibex	*Steinbock*
icepick	*Eispickel*
lake	*See*
larch	*Lärche*
lynx	*Luchs*
map	*Landkarte*
maple	*Ahorn*
marmot	*Murmeltier*
moraine	*Moräne*
mountain guide	*Bergführer*
mule path	*Saumpfad*
north	*Nord*

outlet	*Auslauf*
pasqueflower/ anemone	*Anemone*
path/trail	*Pfad/Wanderweg*
peak/summit	*Gipfel*
Pre-Alps	*Voralpen*
red spruce	*Rottanne/Fichte*
reservoir	*Stausee*
ridge	*Grat*
river	*Ufer*
rockfall	*Steinschlag*
saddle	*Joch/Sattel*
scree/talus	*Geröll*
signpost	*Wegweiser*
silver fir	*Weisstanne*
slope	*Hang*
snow	*Schnee*
snowfield	*Firn*
snowfree	*aper*
spring/fountain	*Quelle/Brunnen*
stream	*Bach*
sweet chestnut tree	*Kastanienbaum*
elder	
the (Swiss) Alps	*die (Schweizer) Alpen*
thunderstorm	*Gewitter*
torrent	*Tobel/Wildbach*
tourist office	*Verkehrsbüro*
tower	*Turm*
valley	*Tal*
walking map	*Wanderkarte*
waterfall	*Wasserfall*
west	*West*

Accommodation

Where is a cheap hotel?
Wo ist ein billiges Hotel?
What is the address?
Was ist die Adresse?
Do you have any rooms available?
Haben Sie noch freie Zimmer?

I would like ...	*Ich möchte ...*
a single room	*ein Einzelzimmer*
a double room	*ein Doppelzimmer*
a room with a bathroom	*ein Zimmer mit Bad*

to share a dorm   *einen Schlafsaal*
                        teilen
a bed   *ein Bett*

How much is it per night/per person?
Wieviel kostet es pro Nacht/
   pro Person?
Can I see it?
Kann ich es sehen?
Where is the bathroom?
Wo ist das Bad?

Shopping
How much is it?
Wieviel kostet es?
I would like to buy ...
Ich möchte ... kaufen.
I'd like a film for this camera.
Ich möchte einen Film fü diese Kamera.
Could you lower the price?
Können Sie den Preis reduzieren?

bookshop	*Buchhandlung*
camera shop	*Fotogeschäft*
chemist/pharmacy	*Apotheke*
department store	*Warenhaus*
laundry	*Wäscherei*
market	*Markt*
newsagency	*Zeitungshändler*
supermarket	*Supermarkt*

Food
breakfast	*Frühstück*
lunch	*Mittagessen*
dinner	*Abendessen*

I would like the set lunch.
Ich hätte gern das Tagesmenü.
Is service included in the bill?
Ist die Bedienung inbegriffen?
I am a vegetarian.
Ich bin Vegetarierin (f)/
   Vegetarier (m).

bakery	*Bäckerei*
grocery	*Lebensmittel*
delicatessen	*Delikatessen*

restaurant   *Restaurant/*
                Gaststätte

Health
I'm ...	*Ich bin ...*
diabetic	*Diabetikerin (f)/*
	Diabetiker (m)
epileptic	*Epileptikerin (f)/*
	Epileptiker (m)
asthmatic	*Asthmatikerin (f)/*
	Asthmatiker (m)

I'm allergic to antibiotics/penicillin.
Ich bin gegen Antibiotika/
   Penizillin allergisch.

antiseptic	*Antiseptikum*
aspirin	*Aspirin*
condoms	*Kondome*
constipation	*Verstopfung*
contraceptive	*Verhütungsmittel*
diarrhoea	*Durchfall*
medicine	*Medizin*
nausea	*Übelkeit*
sunblock cream	*Sunblockcreme*
tampons	*Tampons*

Emergencies
Help!	*Hilfe!*
Call a doctor!	*Holen Sie einen*
	Arzt!
Call the police!	*Rufen Sie die*
	Polizei!
Go away!	*Gehen Sie weg!*

Time & Dates
today	*heute*
tomorrow	*morgen*
in the morning	*morgens*
in the afternoon	*nachmittags*
in the evening	*abends*

Monday	*Montag*
Tuesday	*Dienstag*
Wednesday	*Mittwoch*
Thursday	*Donnerstag*
Friday	*Freitag*
Saturday	*Samstag/Sonnabend*
Sunday	*Sonntag*

Numbers

0	*null*
1	*eins*
2	*zwei (zwo* on phone or public announcements)
3	*drei*
4	*vier*
5	*fünf*
6	*sechs*
7	*sieben*
8	*acht*
9	*neun*
10	*zehn*
11	*elf*
12	*zwölf*
13	*dreizehn*
14	*vierzehn*
15	*fünfzehn*
16	*sechzehn*
17	*siebzehn*
18	*achtzehn*
19	*neunzehn*
20	*zwanzig*
21	*einundzwanzig*
30	*dreissig*
40	*vierzig*
50	*fünfzig*
60	*sechzig*
70	*siebzig*
80	*achtzig*
90	*neunzig*
100	*hundert*
1000	*tausend*
one million	*eine Million*

Swiss French

Although in past centuries strong so-called 'provincial' dialects existed in the French-speaking regions of Switzerland, today a more or less standard form of French is spoken throughout the country. Some important departures from standard French still persist, however. For example, the Swiss French term for 'post box' is *case postale* rather than *boîte postale*, a female waiter is addressed as *sommelière* instead of *serveuse*, and a *gymnase* is a place you go to gain an education, not to work off excess body fat. Suisse Romande, as the language is called in Switzerland, is also identifiable to other French speakers by its slower pace and slight accent.

Pronunciation

French has a number of sounds which are difficult for Anglophones to produce. These include the distinction between the 'u' sound (as in *tu*) and 'oo' sound (as in *tout*). For both sounds, the lips are rounded and projected forward, but for the 'u' the tongue is towards the front of the mouth, its tip against the lower front teeth, whereas for the 'oo' the tongue is towards the back of the mouth, its tip behind the gums of the lower front teeth.

During the production of nasal vowels the breath escapes partly through the nose and partly through the mouth. There are no nasal vowels in English; in French there are three, as in *bon vin blanc*, 'good white wine'. These sounds occur where a syllable ends in a single 'n' or 'm'; the 'n' or 'm' is silent

The standard 'r' of Parisian French is produced by moving the bulk of the tongue backwards to constrict the air flow in the pharynx while the tip of the tongue rests behind the lower front teeth. It is similar to the noise made by some people before spitting, but with much less friction.

Basics

Hello.
 Bonjour.
Goodbye.
 Au revoir.
Yes.
 Oui.
No.
 Non.
Please.
 S'il vous plaît.
Thank you.
 Merci.
You're welcome.
 Je vous en prie.
Excuse me.
 Excusez-moi.
Sorry. (Excuse me/Forgive me.)
 Pardon.

Language Difficulties

Do you speak English?
Parlez-vous anglais?
Does anyone speak English?
Est-ce qu'il y a quelqu'un qui parle anglais?
I understand.
Je comprends.
I don't understand.
Je ne comprends pas.
Just a minute.
Attendez une minute.
Please write that down.
Est-ce-que vous pouvez l'écrire?

Small Talk

What is your name?
Comment appelez-vous?
My name is ...
Je m'appelle ...
Where are you from?
Vous venez d'où?
I am from ...
Je viens de (d') ...
How old are you?
Quel age avez-vous?
I am ... years old.
J'ai ... ans.

Getting Around

What time does the next ... leave/arrive?
À quelle heure part/arrive le prochain ...?

boat	*bateau*
bus (city)	*bus*
train	*train*

I would like ...   *Je voudrais ...*
  a one-way ticket   *un billet aller simple*
  a return ticket   *un billet aller retour*

1st class	*première classe*
2nd class	*deuxième classe*

Finding Your Way

Where is the bus/tram stop?
Où est l'arrêt d'autobus/de tramway?

I want to go to ...
Je veux aller à ...
I am looking for ...
Je cherche ...
Can you show it to me (on the map)?
Est-ce que vous pouvez me le montrer (sur la carte)?

far/near   *loin/proche*
Go straight ahead.   *Continuez tout droit.*
Turn left.   *Tournez à gauche.*
Turn right.   *Tournez à droite.*

Around Town

I'm looking for ...   *Je cherche ...*
  a bank   *une banque*
  the city centre   *le centre-ville*
  the ... embassy   *l'ambassade de ...*
  my hotel   *mon hôtel*
  the market   *le marché*
  the police   *la police*
  the post office   *le bureau de poste*
  a public toilet   *des toilettes*
  the railway station *la gare*
  a public telephone   *une cabine téléphonique*
  the tourist information office   *l'office de tourisme/le syndicat d'initiative*

Walking

Is this the trail/track to ...?
C'est la chemin pour aller à ...?
Which trail goes to ...?
Je prends quel chemin pour aller à ...?
Is the trail steep/ wide/narrow?
Est'ce que ce chemin est raide/ large/ étroit?
How many kilmoetres to ...?
Combien de kilomètres à ...?
Where are you going?
Où allez-vous?
Do you know this area well?
Vous connaissez bien cette région?
Is the trail safe?
Est-ce que le chemin est sauf?

Where can I hire a guide/tent?
Où puis-je louer un guide/une tente?
Is there a camp site nearby?
Y a-t-il un camping tout près?
Can we camp here?
Nous pouvons camper ici?
Can we stay here tonight?
Nous sommes permis à rester ici ce soir?
I'm lost.
Je suis perdu(e).
Do I need a guide?
Est-ce qu'il faut un guide?
What's that animal called?
Qu'est-ce que c'est cet animal?
What's that plant called?
Qu'est-ce que c'est cette plante?

Weather

It's raining/frosty/snowing.
Il pleut/gèle/neige.
It's hot.
Il fait chaud.
It's cold.
Il fait froid.
It's cloudy
Le temps est couvert.

Some Useful Words

alp hut	*chalet (de alpage)*
alp track	*chemin de alpage*
Alpine garden	*jardin alpin*
Alpine rhododen-dron	*rhododendron des Almrausch Alpes*
arolla pine	*arolle/Pine Mediterranéen*
avalanche	*avalanche*
backpack	*sac à dos*
beech	*hêtre/foyard*
bilberry	*myrtille*
bridge	*pont*
buttercup	*renoncule*
cable car	*téléphérique*
cairn	*cairn*
camping ground	*camping*
chair lift	*tété-siège*
chamois	*chamois*
cirque	*cirque*
contour	*contour*
cornice	*corniche*
crampons	*crampons*
crossing	*passage*
direction	*direction*
dormitory	*dortoir*
east	*est*
edelweiss	*étoile des Alpes*
fog	*brouillard*
forest	*forêt/bois*
gap	*brèche*
gentian	*gentiane*
glacier	*glacier*
gondola lift	*télécabine*
gorge/ravine	*gorge*
hanging glacier	*glacier suspendu*
hill	*colline*
hut	*cabane*
ibex	*bouquetin*
icepick	*piolet*
lake	*lac*
larch	*mélèze*
lynx	*lynx*
map	*carte*
maple	*érable*
marmot	*marmotte*
moraine	*moraine*
mountain guide	*guide de montagne*
mule path	*chemin muletier*
north	*nord*
outlet	*issue*
pasqueflower/ anemone	*anémone*
path/trail	*sentier/chemin*
peak/summit	*sommet/cime*
Pre-Alps	*Préalpes*
red spruce	*épicéa/sapin rouge*
reservoir	*réservoir*
ridge	*crête*
river	*rive*
rockfall	*chute de pierres*
saddle	*col/selle*
scree/talus	*éboulis*
signpost	*poteau indicateur*
silver fir	*sapin blanc*
slope	*pente*
snow	*neige*
snowfield	*névé*
snowfree	*dénudé*
spring/fountain	*source/fontaine*

stream	*ruisseau*
sweet chestnut tree elder	*marronnier*
the (Swiss) Alps	*les Alpes (suisses)*
thunderstorm	*orage*
torrent	*torrent*
tourist office	*office du tourisme*
tower	*tour*
valley	*vallée*
walking map	*carte pédestre*
waterfall	*chute*
west	*ouest*

Accommodation

Where can I find a cheap hotel?
Où est-ce que je peux trouver un hôtel bon marché?
What is the address?
Quelle est l'adresse?
Do you have any rooms available?
Est-ce que vous avez des chambres libres?

I would like ...	*Je voudrais ...*
a single room	*une chambre à un lit*
a double room	*une chambre à deux*
a room with shower and toilet	*une chambre avec douche et WC*
to stay in a dorm	*coucher dans un dortoir*
a bed	*un lit*

How much is it per night/per person?
Quel est le prix par nuit/ par personne?
Can I see it?
Est-ce que je peux la voir?
Where is the bathroom/ shower?
Où est la salle de bain/douche?

Shopping

How much is it?
C'est combien?
I'd like to buy ...
Je voudrais ...

Do you accept credit cards?
Est-ce que je peux payer avec carte de crédit?
Could you lower the price?
Vous pouvez baisser le prix?

bookshop	*librairie*
camera shop	*boutique de photographe*
chemist/pharmacy	*pharmacie*
laundry	*blanchisserie*
market	*marché*
newsagency	*papeterie*
supermarket	*supermarché*

Food

breakfast	*petit déjeuner*
lunch	*déjeuner*
dinner	*dîner*

I would like the set lunch.
Je prends le menu.
I am a vegetarian.
Je suis végétarien (m)/végétarienne (f).

bakery	*boulangerie*
cake shop	*pâtisserie*
cheese shop	*fromagerie*
delicatessen	*charcuterie*
grocery	*épicerie*
restaurant	*restaurant*

Health

I'm ...	*Je suis ...*
diabetic	*diabétique*
epileptic	*épileptique*
asthmatic	*asthmatique*
anaemic	*anémique*
constipated	*constipé(e)*

I'm allergic to antibiotics/penicillin.
Je suis allergique aux antibiotiques/à la pénicilline.

antiseptic	*antiseptique*
aspirin	*aspirine*
condoms	*préservatifs*
contraceptive	*contraceptif*
diarrhoea	*diarrhée*
medicine	*médicament*

sunblock cream	*crème solaire*
tampons	*tampons hygiéniques*

Emergencies

Help!	*Au secours!*
Call a doctor!	*Appelez un médecin!*
Call the police!	*Appelez la police!*
Leave me alone!	*Fichez-moi la paix!*

Time & Dates

today	*aujourd'hui*
tomorrow	*demain*
yesterday	*hier*
in the morning	*le matin*
in the afternoon	*l'après-midi*
in the evening	*le soir*

Monday	*lundi*
Tuesday	*mardi*
Wednesday	*mercredi*
Thursday	*jeudi*
Friday	*vendredi*
Saturday	*samedi*
Sunday	*dimanche*

Numbers

0	*zéro*
1	*un*
2	*deux*
3	*trois*
4	*quatre*
5	*cinq*
6	*six*
7	*sept*
8	*huit*
9	*neuf*
10	*dix*
11	*onze*
12	*douze*
13	*treize*
14	*quatorze*
15	*quinze*
16	*seize*
17	*dix-sept*
18	*dix-huit*
19	*dix-neuf*
20	*vingt*
21	*vingt-et-un*
22	*vingt-deux*
30	*trente*
40	*quarante*
50	*cinquante*
60	*soixante*
70	*soixante-dix*
80	*quatre-vingts*
90	*quatre-vingt-dix*
100	*cent*
1000	*mille*
one million	*un million*

Swiss Italian

The differences between standard Italian and the Ticinese dialects are relatively small. In northern Ticino certain Romansch-sounding expressions are often used, such as *Bun di* instead of *Buongiorno* ('Hello') or *Buona noc* (pronounced 'nockh') instead of *Buona notte* ('Goodnight').

Pronunciation

Italian is not difficult to pronounce once you learn a few easy rules. Some of the more clipped vowels and stress on double letters require a little practice. Stress usually falls on the second last syllable. When a word has an accent the stress falls on that syllable.

Vowels Vowels are generally more clipped than in English.

a	like the second 'a' in 'camera'
e	like the 'ay' in 'day', but without the 'i' sound
i	as in 'see'
o	as in 'dot'
u	as in 'too'

Consonants The pronunciation of many Italian consonants is similar to that of English. The following sounds depend on certain rules:

c	like 'k' before **a**, **o** and **u**; or like the 'ch' in 'choose' before **e** and **i**
ch	a hard 'k' sound

g	a hard 'g' as in 'get' before **a** and **o**
gh	a hard 'g' as in 'get'
gli	like the 'lli' in 'million'
gn	like the 'ny' in 'canyon'
h	always silent
r	a rolled 'r' sound
sc	like the 'sh' in 'sheep' before **e** and **i** or a hard sound as in 'school' before **h, a, o** and **u**
z	like the 'ts' in 'lights' or 'ds' in 'beds'

Basics

Hello.
Buongiorno/Ciao.
Goodbye.
Arrivederci/Ciao.
Yes/No.
Sì/No.
Please.
Per favore/Per piacere.
Thank you.
Grazie.
You're welcome.
Prego.
Excuse me/Sorry
Mi scusi/Perdoni.

Language Difficulties

Do you speak English?
Parla inglese?
Does anyone speak English?
C'è qualcuno che parla inglese?
I (don't) understand.
(Non) Capisco.
Just a minute!
Un momento!

Small Talk

What is your name?
Come si chiama?
My name is ...
Mi chiamo ...
Where are you from?
Da dove viene/Di dove sei?
I am from ...
Vengo da/Sono di ...
How old are you?
Quanti anni ha?
I'm ... years old.
Ho ... anni.

Getting Around

What time does the ... leave/arrive?	*A che ora parte/ arriva ...?*
boat	*la barca*
bus	*l'autobus*
train	*il treno*
first	*il primo*
last	*l'ultimo*
I would like ...	*Vorrei ...*
a one-way ticket	*(un biglietto di) solo andata*
a return ticket	*(un biglietto di) andata e ritorno*
1st class	*prima classe*
2nd class	*seconda classe*

Finding Your Way

Where is ...?
Dov'è ...?
I want to go to ...
Voglio andare a ...
Can you show me (on the map)?
Me lo puo mostrare (sulla carta/pianta)?

far/near
lontano/vicino
Go straight ahead.
Si va sempre diritto.
Turn left ...
Gira a sinistra ...
Turn right ...
Gira a destra ...

Around Town

I'm looking for ...	*Sto cercando ...*
a bank	*un banco*
the church	*la chiesa*
the city centre	*il centro (città)*
the ... embassy	*l'ambasciata di ...*
my hotel	*il mio albergo*
the market	*il mercato*
the museum	*il museo*
the post office	*la posta*

a public toilet — *un gabinetto/ bagno pubblico*

the telephone centre — *il centro telefonico/ SIP*

the tourist information office — *l'ufficio di turismo/ d'informazione*

I'm lost.
Sono perso(a).
Do I need a guide?
Si ha bisogno di una guida?
What's that animal called?
Come si chiama quest'animale?
What's that plant called?
Come si chiama questa pianta?

Signs

Camping Ground — *Campeggio*
Youth Hostel — *Ostello per la Gioventù*

Entrance — *Ingresso/Entrata*
Exit — *Uscita*
Full/No Vacancies — *Completo*
Guesthouse — *Pensione*
Hotel — *Albergo*
Information — *Informazione*
No Smoking — *Vietato Fumare*
Open/Closed — *Aperto/Chiuso*
Police — *Polizia/Carabinieri*
Police Station — *Questura*
Telephone — *Telefono*
Toilets — *Gabinetti/Bagni*

Weather

It's cloudy/cold/frosty/hot.
È nuvoloso/freddo/gelido/caldo.
It's raining.
Piove.
It's snowing.
Nevica.
What will the weather be like tomorrow?
Come sarà il tempo domani?

Walking

Is this the trail/road to ...?
Questo è il sentiero giusto per ...?
Which trail goes to ...?
Quale sentiero va a ...?
Is the trail steep/ wide/narrow?
Questo sentiero è ripido/largo/stretto?
How many kilometres to ...?
Quanti chilometri a ...?
Where are you going?
Dove va?
Do you know this area well?
Conosce bene questa zona?
Is the trail safe?
Questo sentiero non è pericoloso?
Where can I hire a guide/tent?
Dove posso noleggiare una guida/tenda?
Is there a camp site nearby?
C'è un campeggio qui vicino?
Can we camp here?
Si può campeggiare qui?

Some Useful Words

alp hut — *chalet alpino*
alp track — *sentiero alpino*
Alpine garden — *giardino alpino*
Alpine rhododendron — *rododendro delle Alpi*
arolla pine — *pino mediterraneo*
avalanche — *valanga*
backpack — *zaino*
beech — *faggio*
bilberry — *mirtillo*
bridge — *ponte*
buttercup — *ranuncolo*
cable car — *funicolare*
cairn — *tumolo (di pietre)*
camping ground — *campeggio*
chair lift — *seggiovia*
chamois — *camoscio*
contour — *contorno*
cornice — *cornicione*
crampons — *ramponi*
crossing — *passagio*
direction — *direzione*
dormitory — *dormitorio*
east — *este*
edelweiss — *stella alpina*
fog — *nebbia*
forest — *foresta*
gap — *spazio vuoto*

gentian	*genziana*
glacier	*ghiacciaio*
gondola lift	*gondola*
gorge/ravine	*gola/burrone*
hanging glacier	*ghiacciaio sospeso*
hill	*collina*
hut	*baita*
ibex	*stambecco*
icepick	*piccozza da alpinisti*
lake	*lago*
larch	*larice*
lynx	*lince*
map	*carto*
maple	*acero*
marmot	*marmotta*
moraine	*morena*
moutain guide	*guida di montagne*
mule path	*sentiero di mula*
north	*mord*
outlet	*scarico*
pasqueflower/ anemone	*anemone*
path/trail	*sentiero*
peak/summit	*cima/sommità*
red spruce	*abete rosso*
reservoir	*bacino idrico*
ridge	*cresta/crinole*
river	*fiume*
rockfall	*caduta di pietre*
saddle	*sella*
scree/talus	*ghiaione*
signpost	*palo indicatore*
silver fir	*abete bianco*
slope	*pendio*
snow	*neve*
snowfield	*nevaio*
snowfree	*denudato*
spring/fountain	*sorgente/fontana*
stream	*ruscello*
sweet chestunut tree elder	*castagno*
Swiss Alps	*Alpi svizzeri*
thunderstorm	*oragio*
torrent	*torrente*
tourist office	*officio del turismo*
tower	*torre*
valley	*valle*
walking map	*carta Pedestre*
waterfall	*cascata*
west	*ovest*

Accommodation

Where is a cheap hotel?
  Dov'è un albergo che costa poco?
What is the address?
  Cos'è l'indirizzo?
Do you have any rooms available?
  Ha camere libere?

I would like ...	*Vorrei ...*
a single room	*una camera singola*
a double room	*una camera per due*
a room with a bathroom	*una camera con bagno*
to share a dorm	*un letto in dormitorio*
a bed	*un letto*

How much is it per night/ per person?
  Quanto costa per la notte/ ciascuno?
Can I see it?
  Posso vederla?
Where is the bathroom?
  Dov'è il bagno?

Shopping

How much is it?
  Quanto costa?
I'd like to buy ...
  Vorrei comprare ...
Do you accept credit cards?
  Accetta la carta di credito?
Could you lower the price?
  Può farmi lo sconto?

bookshop	*libreria*
camera shop	*negozio di abbigliamento*
chemist/pharmacy	*famacia*
laundry	*lavanderia*
market	*mercato*
newsagency	*edicola/cartolaio*
supermarket	*supermercato*

Food

breakfast	*prima colazione*
lunch	*pranzo/colazione*
dinner	*cena*

I would like the set lunch.
Vorrei il menu turistico.
Is service included in the bill?
È compreso il servizio?
I am a vegetarian.
Sono vegetariano/a.

bookshop	*libreria*
camera shop	*fotografo*
chemist/pharmacy	*farmacia*
laundry	*lavanderia*
market	*mercato*
newsagency	*edicola*
supermarket	*supermercato*

Health

I'm ... *Sono ...*
   diabetic *diabetico/a*
   epileptic *epilettico/a*
   asthmatic *asmatico/a*

I'm allergic ... *Sono allergico/a ...*
   to antibiotics *agli antibiotici*
   to penicillin *alla penicillina*

antiseptic	*antisettico*
aspirin	*aspirina*
condoms	*preservativi*
contraceptive	*anticoncezionale*
diarrhoea	*diarrea*
medicine	*medicina*
sunblock cream	*crema solare/latte solare*
tampons	*tamponi*

Time & Dates

What time is it?
Che ora è/Che ore sono?

today	*oggi*
tomorrow	*domani*
yesterday	*ieri*
in the morning	*di mattina*
in the afternoon	*di pomeriggio*
in the evening	*di sera*

Monday	*lunedì*
Tuesday	*martedì*
Wednesday	*mercoledì*
Thursday	*giovedì*
Friday	*venerdì*
Saturday	*sabato*
Sunday	*domenica*

Numbers

0	*zero*
1	*uno*
2	*due*
3	*tre*
4	*quattro*
5	*cinque*
6	*sei*
7	*sette*
8	*otto*
9	*nove*
10	*dieci*
11	*undici*
12	*dodici*
13	*tredici*
14	*quattordici*
15	*quindici*
16	*sedici*
17	*diciassette*
18	*diciotto*
19	*diciannove*
20	*venti*
21	*ventuno*
22	*ventidue*
30	*trenta*
40	*quaranta*
50	*cinquanta*
60	*sessanta*
70	*settanta*
80	*ottanta*
90	*novanta*
100	*cento*
1000	*mille*
one million	*un milione*

Emergencies

Help!	*Aiuto!*
Call a doctor!	*Chiama un dottore/ un medico!*
Call the police!	*Chiama la polizia!*
Go away!	*Vai via!* (inf)/*Mi lasci in pace!*

Romansch

Although the language is only spoken by around 1% of the population, hikers are likely to hear people speaking Romansch during their visit to Switzerland. This is because the Romansch-speaking regions, which lie entirely within the canton of Graubünden, have some of the nicest and most spectacular walks in the country.

Originating from the common Latin spoken by the original Roman settlers, Romansch was widely spoken throughout the medieval kingdom of Rhaetia, which once covered most of today's Graubünden. Due to the steady encroachment of the German, the relative number of Romansch speakers has fallen dramatically over the last hundred years or so. One major problem facing the survival of the language is that Romansch is divided into five main dialect groups, and, unlike other minority languages in Switzerland, it has neither a cultural, educational nor commercial centre. One step towards saving the language has been the development of a standard Romansch language, called Rumantsch Grischun, which incorporates elements of each regional form. Even in areas of Graubünden where German has been spoken for centuries, local place names still show an unmistakable link with the Romansch past. Below is a short list of useful words to get you started.

map	*charta topografica*
mountain	*montagna/munt*
mountain guide	*guid da muntogna*
mountain hut	*chamoua*
path/track	*senda/via*
peak/summit	*piz/culm*
post office	*uffizi postal*
Rhaetian Railways	*Viafer retica*
ridge	*cresta*
river	*flum*
rock	*crap*
shore/bank	*riva*
signpost	*mussavia*
slope	*spunda/costa*
snow	*naiv*
snowfield	*vadret*
spring/fountain	*fontauna*
stream/brook	*dutg*
Swiss National Park	*Parc Naziunal Svizzer*
Switzerland	*Svizra*
tourist office	*biro da traffic*
train station	*staziun da viafer*
valley	*val/vallada*
village	*vischnanca/vitg*
Walser route	*senda Gualser*
waterfall	*cas da aua*
east	*ost/orient*
west	*vest/occident*
north	*nord*
south	*sid*

Some Useful Words

alp hut	*tegia d'alp*
(Alpine) pasture	*pastgira (d'alp)*
backpack	*loulscha/satgados*
bridge	*punt*
camping ground	*campadi*
castle/fort	*chastè*
church	*baseglia*
farmhouse	*chassa da pur*
fence	*saiv*
field	*chomp/fuus*
forest	*guaud*
glacier	*glatscher*
gorge	*chavorgia*
Graubünden	*Grischun*
lake	*lai*

Animals

Alpine jackdaw	*curnagl*
badger	*tais*
bird	*utschè*
chamois	*chamutsch*
cow	*vatga*
fish	*pesch*
goat	*chaura/zila*
ibex	*capricorn*
marmot	*muntanella*
marten	*fiergna*
snow grouse	*urblauna*
snow hare	*lieur alva*
stoat	*mustaila*

Plants

arolla	*schember*	mushroom	*bulieu*
chestunut tree	*chastagner*	red spruce	*pign*
edelweiss	*stailalva*	silver fir	*aviez*
larch	*laresch*	tree	*planta/pumer*

Facts for the Walker

VISAS & ENTRY REQUIREMENTS

Citizens of many Western European countries don't require a passport to enter Switzerland; a national identity card is generally sufficient. Citizens of Australia, Canada, Hong Kong, New Zealand, Singapore, South Africa and the USA do not need a visa for stays of less than three months.

MONEY

The Swiss franc (Sfr), called *Schweizer Franken* in German or *franc suisse* in French, is one of the world's most important international currencies. Unfortunately for foreign tourists (and the Swiss hotel industry), the franc has steadily advanced to become Europe's strongest currency, which can make holidaying in Switzerland an expensive proposition.

New Swiss-franc banknotes with incredibly intricate designs, including holograms that make them absolutely 'non-counterfeitable', are currently being issued. These new banknotes will be in full circulation by 1997, and will come in 10, 20, 50, 100, 200 and 1000 franc denominations. There are coins for five, 10, 20 and 50 centimes (or *Rappen* in German), as well as for one, two and five francs.

Exchange Rates

UK£1	=	Sfr1.80
DM1	=	Sfr0.80
FF10	=	Sfr2.35
ASch10	=	Sfr1.15
IL1000	=	Sfr0.74
US$1	=	Sfr1.16
C$1	=	Sfr0.85
A$1	=	Sfr0.86
NZ$1	=	Sfr0.77
S$1	=	Sfr0.82

All major travellers' cheques are accepted, though you may want to stick to those from American Express, Visa or Thomas Cook because of their 'instant replacement' policies. Credit cards give somewhat greater financial freedom than travellers' cheques, and allow you to get a cash advance at most banks. Automated teller machines (ATMs) in Switzerland are generally open 24 hours a day and give you ready access to your credit card or bank account back home for a surprisingly reasonable fee – but check with your bank first. Eurocheque cards can also be used in ATMs.

Some travellers to Switzerland, particularly those who return regularly, open a post office postcheque account *(Postcheckkonto*, or *compte de cheque postal)*. This is a convenient alternative, since post offices are open longer and are found even in the smallest towns.

Budgeting

The rock-solid Swiss franc makes Switzerland one place to watch your scarce monetary resources, and – surprise, surprise – the best way of saving money in Switzerland is to head for the hills.

Accommodation is cheaper (if more rudimentary) in the mountains. Dormitories (such as in mountain huts and youth hostels) are available for a fraction of the cost of a room in even a lower-budget hotel, and organised camping grounds are cheaper still.

Although prices at mountain restaurants generally compare favourably with those in Swiss cities, picnicking on some Alpine meadow will always work out a less expensive and more enjoyable alternative. Buy food and other supplies for your walk at a larger supermarket rather than a small grocery store near the trailhead – supermarket prices are generally significantly cheaper.

Depending on whether you intend basing yourself somewhere or will be continually moving around the country, rail and other transport passes can save you money (see the Getting Around chapter). Of course, hitchhiking will bring your per-km costs down to (almost) nil.

Even after heeding these basic saving tips, however, the most thrifty walker would be unrealistic to budget for much less than Sfr50 per day for travel in Switzerland – but don't worry, you're getting the best country for walking that money can buy.

WHEN TO GO

The walking season in Switzerland starts in mid-spring (May/June), and – depending on autumn snowfalls – can continue right until the end of November.

In general, the lower the area, the longer its walking season. In the high-Alpine zone above 2500 metres the snow-free period can differ quite a bit from season to season, with the most dramatic variations in autumn. While in warmer years newly fallen snow will melt away repeatedly until the winter begins in late November, in colder years the snow may already start to accumulate from early October.

Although each month has its own particular attractions and disadvantages, the recommended time for walking is from mid-August until late October, when the weather is generally cooler and more settled.

Spring

Spring officially begins in late March, but at that time skiers are still whizzing down the slopes of the Alps and the snow-free area is below 1000 metres. In June the sections of the path in higher areas may still be snow-bound, though not necessarily impassible. Alpine wildflowers, most notably alpenroses, are at their prime in mid to late June. In June the days reach their maximum length, with over 15 hours of sunlight.

Summer

Summer only really gets under way towards the end of June. Particularly in the Alps, thunderstorms occur with great frequency until about mid-August. The hot, humid weather at this time of year can make walking a sticky and uncomfortable affair. The sun can be surprisingly penetrating, but

swimming in lakes and rivers is a major compensation. The moisture in the air makes for hazy conditions in midsummer, and while this often cuts out the fine Alpine views, the mist-shrouded peaks develop an enchanting atmosphere. The unpredictable midsummer weather can makes mountain walking uncertain, and at times hikers might have to sit out a few days of bad weather before continuing.

Autumn

Autumn begins in late September, and typically brings long periods of fine, settled weather. The brilliant golden and red colours of the forests and Alpine heathland give this season a special flavour. Autumn is perhaps the best time for walking in the Swiss Jura or the ranges of southern Ticino (Sottoceneri), when a carpet of thick fog covers the lowlands of the Swiss Mittelland and the Lombardy Plain of Italy, while the mountain heights bask in balmy sunshine.

Unfortunately, many postbus and mountain-transport services stop running in late October, making access to these areas difficult even though the weather conditions may still be suitable well after then. Remember also that at this time of the year any major deterioration in the weather is liable to bring snowfalls down to 1500 metres or lower.

November is a highly unpredictable time for walking. The daylight period is getting rather short (around nine hours), so late-autumn walkers should get an early start and plan their routes carefully. By the time the winter begins in late December, the only areas free of snow and ice are in lowland regions.

Winter

Winter lasts from late December until late March and presents the mountain landscape from an altogether different aspect. Winter walking, led by people fed up with the rat race of the ski slopes, has gained a modest following over recent years. Nowadays virtually all mountain resorts keep some of their walking trails open throughout the winter.

More adventurous is winter walking on

uncleared snow paths. To avoid sinking into the often deep snow, winter walkers use snowshoes made of rigid netting supported by a frame which fits onto each boot. Winter walking can be hard going and takes a while getting used to – as does the frustration of not being able to ski effortlessly down every snow slope you come to.

Obviously, conditions at this time of year are more extreme, and due to the danger of avalanches it's generally not advisable to walk above the forest line without a qualified mountain guide. Wild animals shelter in the snow-bound mountain forests during winter, and are highly sensitive to any kind of disturbance due to their seasonally low energy reserves. For this reason winter walkers should keep to main pathways and avoid making unnecessary noise.

For organised weekend and longer winter walking trips, contact Gabriella Lohner (☎ 081-61 10 29), Bova 11, 7432 Zillis or Fair Travel (☎ 01-984 05 47), Forchstrasse 112, 8132 Egg.

Weather Information
Given that Switzerland has one of the most complex weather patterns anywhere on the planet, the country has a surprisingly accurate weather forecasting service.

Tourist offices or mountain huts (when staffed) have the latest weather information. The recorded telephone weather report (updated five times daily) in German, French or Italian on ☎ 162; and the special Alpine weather report on ☎ 157 12 62 18 (Sfr0.86 per minute) are particularly useful for hikers. For non-recorded, personal advice in English regarding the weather in any part of Switzerland you can call ☎ 157 52 62 0 (Sfr2.13 per minute). You can also call the office of the national weather bureau (Landeswetterzentrale) in Zürich on ☎ 01-252 76 44.

The information in television and newspaper weather reports is graphic, so the basics are readily grasped even if you don't understand a word of German or French. Switzerland's German-language television service (DRS) broadcasts its excellent weather report called *Meteo* at the end of the main evening news at around 7.55 pm. The Zürich *Tages Anzeiger* newspaper is available all over Switzerland; it also has an excellent daily weather report with a four-day forecast that includes isobar maps and colour charts.

WHAT TO BRING
Since mountain accommodation is abundant and the routes generally short, few walkers in Switzerland bother carrying camping gear such as tents, sleeping bags, portable stove etc. Equipment that you maybe/definitely can't do without is listed below.

General Clothing
Continental Europeans often prefer wearing special walking breeches. The legs of breeches are tapered to just above the knees, and are less restrictive than full-length pants. Long socks protect the lower legs.

Warm Weather Wear Midsummer conditions in the Swiss Alps can be surprisingly hot, so walkers at this time of the year often prefer to wear lighter clothing such as shorts and a short-sleeved shirt – but use a UV sunblock for exposed limbs. It's a good idea to wear a broad-rimmed hat for maximum protection from the sun.

Cold Weather Wear Especially on longer walks or those that take you high up into the mountains, carrying plenty of warm clothing is essential. A thick woollen sweater or 'fibrepile' garment will keep the body warm even when wet. Walkers who intend doing overnight trips in the mountains might consider taking a down jacket. Also take gloves and a woolly cap.

Wet Weather Wear It is vital that walkers carry a completely windproof and waterproof rain-jacket at all times. It should be properly seam-sealed and have a hood to keep the rain and wind off your head. Nowadays, most experienced hikers prefer garments made from Gore Tex or a similar 'breathable' fabric. A pair of waterproof overpants is also highly recommended. Plastic ponchos – or other cheap solutions – just won't do, however, as they tear easily, catch on branches and blow around in the wind.

Trekking Stocks First popularised by Reinhold Messner, twin lightweight trekking stocks are standard equipment for many walkers in the Alps, yet some mountaingoers find them more of a nuisance than an additional support whilst ascending and descending. Similar in appearance to ski stocks, trekking stocks have a fold-away 'telescopic' design, which makes them easy to strap onto even small day packs. All good mountain-sports shops stock stocks, but expect to pay at least Sfr80 per pair.

Backpack A small, light pack is the way to go. Depending on the sort of walks you intend doing, a day pack with a 20-litre capacity may be large enough to suit your needs. At least one outside pocket (preferably on the top or the rear side) makes it easier to grab your camera or snacks like that bar of chocolate.

Backpacking Shops

Switzerland is a comparatively expensive country, so it's unlikely you'll want to buy much in the way of walking gear here. If you do forget to bring any essential item – your sunglasses, your compass, your boots! – finding a replacement is never a problem except in the most out-of-the-way places.

Particularly recommended are the Transa shops in Switzerland's larger German-speaking cities, which offer a broad range of travel, hiking and mountaineering gear. The Intersport chain also has numerous stores selling outdoor equipment in just about every larger centre. A list of shops selling such equipment follows:

Basel
    Eiselin Sport Ecke Gundeldinger/Falkensteinerstrasse 66, Basel (☎ 061-331 45 39)
    Transa, Leonhardsgraben 8, 4051 Basel (☎ 061-261 59 86)

Bern
    Kost Sport, Freie Strasse 51, 4001 Basel (☎ 061-261 22 55)
    Eiselin Sport, Monbijoustrasse 20, 3001 Bern (☎ 031-381 76 76)
    Transa, Speichergasse 39, 3011 Bern (☎ 031-312 12 35)

Geneva
    Charles Sports, 23 quai des Bergues, 1201 Geneva (☎ 022-731 59 60)
    Ski-Montagne-Sport Coquoz, rue Villereuse 10, 1201 Geneva (☎ 022-735 23 21)

Lausanne
    Passe Montagne Bourgeois, avenue d'Echallens 40, 1004 Lausanne (☎ 021-625 25 55)
    Yosemite, Blvd de Grancy, 1006 Lausanne (☎ 021-617 3100)

Lucerne
    Bannwart Sport, Weggisgasse 14, 6004 Lucerne (☎ 041-410 45 3)
    Eiselin Sport, Obergrundstrasse 70, 6003 Lucerne (☎ 041-22 12 17)

Zürich
    Bächtold Sport, Rämistrasse 3, 8001 Zürich (☎ 01-252 09 34)
    Eiselin Sport, Stampfenbachstrasse 138 (☎ 01-362 48 28)
    Spatz, Hedwigstrasse 25 (☎ 01-383 38 38)
    Transa, Josefstrasse 59, 8005 Zürich (☎ 01-271 90 40)
    Trottomundo, Rindermarkt 6, 8001 Zürich (☎ 01-252 87 65)

TOURIST OFFICES

There is some kind of tourist office in every city, town and village in Switzerland; in the smallest places the post office and/or the train station gives out basic tourist information. Lists of accommodation in all price ranges, tourist maps and other (usually free) literature – including suggested walks in the area – are often available in English. Many local tourist authorities produce and sell special walking maps covering their own regions.

The Swiss national tourist authority has recently been renamed Switzerland Tourism (Schweiz Tourismus, Suisse Tourisme). The head office (☎ 01-288 11 11) is in Zürich at Bellariastrasse 38, CH-8027 Zürich. Switzerland Tourism's main offices abroad include:

Australia
    Switzerland Tourism, 203-233 New South Head Rd, PO Box 193, Edgecliff, NSW 2027 (☎ 02-328 7925)

Belgium/Luxembourg
   Suisse Tourisme, Avenue Brugmann 24, B-1060 Bruxelles (☎ 02-345 54 45)
Canada
   Switzerland Tourism, 96 The East Mall, Etobicoke, Toronto, Ont M9B 6K1 (☎ 416-695 2090)
France
   Suisse Tourisme, Porte de la Suisse, 11 bis, rue Scribe, F-75009 Paris (☎ 1-44 51 65 51)
Germany
   Schweiz Tourismus, Kaiserstrasse 23, D-60311 Frankfurt/Main (☎ 069-256 00 10)
Hong Kong
   Switzerland Tourism, Admiralty Centre, Tower 2, 8th Floor, 18 Harcourt Rd, Hong Kong (☎ 00852-2821 8290)
Israel
   Switzerland Tourism, c/o Swissair, 1 Ben Yehuda St, 63801 Tel Aviv (☎ 03-511 66 66)
South Africa
   Switzerland Tourism, c/o Swissair, Swiss Park, 10 Queens Road, Parktown, POB 3866, Johannesburg 2000 (☎ 011-484 19 86)
UK
   Switzerland Tourism, Swiss Centre, Swiss Court, London W1V 8EE (☎ 01711-734 1921)
USA
   Switzerland Tourism, Swiss Center, 608 Fifth Ave, New York, NY 10020 (☎ 212-757 59 44)
   Midwest Region: Switzerland Tourism, 150 N Michigan Avenue, Chicago, IL 60601 (☎ 312-630 58 40)
   Western Region: Switzerland Tourism, Suite 1570, 222 Sepulveda Blvd, El Segundo, CA 90245 (☎ 310-335 5980)

USEFUL ORGANISATIONS
Mountain Clubs
Swiss Alpine Club The Swiss Alpine Club (Schweizer Alpenclub, Club Alpin Suisse, Club Alpino Svizzero, or SAC) is Switzerland's main mountain club. Although the club is mainly oriented to mountaineering and Alpine ski-touring, most members are also keen walkers. The SAC publishes climbing guidebooks to all parts of Switzerland in German, French and Italian. Non-resident foreigners are welcome to join the SAC. Members receive large discounts on all SAC publications and pay lower fees when overnighting in SAC huts (or huts belonging to other clubs with reciprocal rights). The Swiss Alpine Museum at the SAC's national office (listed following)

covers the history of Alpine mountaineering and cartography, and has an impressively comprehensive collection of relief maps.

For further information contact the Schweizer Alpenclub (SAC) (☎ 031-351 36 11), Helvetiaplatz 4, Bern or write to: SAC, Postfach, 3000 Bern 6.

Other Mountain Clubs Italian-speaking Ticino has two large independent (ie non-SAC) mountain clubs, the Federazione Alpinista Ticinese (FAT) and the Società Alpinistica Ticinese (SAT), which together outnumber the SAC both in terms of local membership and the number of mountain huts they have. Contact the Società Alpinistica Ticinese (☎ 091-44 84 21) at via Vela 2, 6830 Chiasso; and the Federazione Alpinista Ticinese at via San Gottardo 160, 6517 Arbedo.

The Swiss Hiking Federation
The Swiss Hiking Federation (called Schweizerische Arbeitsgemeinschaft für Wanderwege (SAW) in German, Fédération Suisse de Tourism Pédestre (FSTP) in French or L'ente Svizzero Pro Sentieri (ESS) in Italian) is a national organisation that promotes recreational walking in Switzerland. The SAW/FSTP oversees the construction, maintenance and waymarking of all official hiking routes. Together with its affiliated associations, the SAW/FSTP organises a vast number of guided walking tours – programmes are available from the federation itself or tourist offices.

The SAW/FSTP publishes the *Wander Revue Sentiers*, a bimonthly magazine about hiking with German and French editions. The magazine is available for free reading on Swiss trains, but copies are pilfered so quickly that keen readers usually prefer to subscribe. The SAW/FSTP also produces high-quality walking maps (see under Maps below), which *Revue* subscribers can purchase for a substantial discount.

For further information, contact Schweizer Wanderwege (☎ 061-601 15 35), Im

Hirshalm 49, CH-4125, Riehen. Some important regional hiking associations affiliated with the SAW/FSTP are as follows:

Basel
Wanderwege beider Basel, Rütlistrasse 51, 4051 Basel (☎ 061-272 50 58)
Bern
Berner Wanderwege (BWW), Nordring 10a, Postfach, 3000 Bern 25 (☎ 031-332 33 42)
Fribourg
Association Fribourgeoise de Tourisme Pédestre, c/o UFT, case postale 921, 1700 Fribourg 1 (☎ 037-24 56 44)
Geneva
Association genevoise de tourisme pédestre, c/o section genevoise du TCS, Quai Gustave-Ador 2, 1211 Genève 3 (☎ 022-736 58 67)
Glarus
Glarner Wanderwege, Tourismusverband Glarnerland, Raststätte, 8867 Niederurnen (☎ 058-21 21 25)
Graubünden
Bündner Wanderwege (BAW), Kornplatz 12, 7000 Chur (☎ 081-23 70 24)
Lucerne
Luzerner Wanderwege, Himmelrichstrasse 55, 6010 Kriens (☎ 041-42 23 63)
Neuchâtel
Association Neuchâteloise de Tourisme Pédestre (ANTP), FNT, rue du Trésor 9 (Place des Halles), 2001 Neuchâtel (☎ 038-25 17 89)
St Gallen
Kantonal St Gallische Wanderwege, Säntisstrasse 3, 9030 Abtwil (☎ 071-31 38 60)
Schwyz
Schwyzer Wanderwege, Steineggstrasse 9, 8853 Lachen (☎ 055-63 33 80)
Solothurn
Solothurner Wanderwege, Allmendstrasse 48, 4500 Solothurn (☎ 065-22 06 15)
Ticino
Associazione Ticinese per i Sentieri Escursionistici (ATSE), c/o Ente Ticinese per il Tourismo, Case postale 1441, 6501 Bellinzona (☎ 092-25 70 56)
Uri
Arbeitsgemeinschaft Urner Wanderwege, Pfistergasse 9, 6460 Altdorf (☎ 044-1 18 70)
Valais
Association Valaisanne de Tourisme Pédestre, Rue des Creusets 31, Case postale 23, 1951 Sion (☎ 027-22 20 17)
Vaud
Association Vaudoise de Tourism Pédestre, Place Grand-St-Jean 2, 1003 Lausanne (☎ 021-323 10 84)

Zürich
Zürcher Wanderwege (ZAW), Eggweg 5, 8620 Wetzikon (☎ 01-930 20 36)

Guides & Mountaineering Schools

The Swiss Mountain Guide Federation (Schweizerischer Bergführerverband/Association des Guides de Montagne de la Suisse), c/o Skischule, Promenade 157, CH-7260 Davos Dorf, is the professional organisation for accredited mountain guides in Switzerland. The Federation lists all mountain guides who work in Switzerland, whether individually or in association with a mountaineering school.

Switzerland's top schools of mountaineering are all affiliated with the Swiss Association of Mountaineering Schools (Schweizer Verband der Bergsteigerschulen, Association Suisse de Écoles d'Alpinisme) (☎ 044-6 77 70), Postfach 141, CH-6490 Andermatt. As well as running regular instruction courses in rock and ice-climbing techniques, the schools act as agencies for qualified mountain guides. They also organise guided trekking tours and glacier hikes for walkers who may not feel completely confident by themselves in the high Alps. Details such as prices, dates and the level of experience required are outlined in each mountaineering school's summer guiding programme (normally published annually). The 21 schools affiliated with the Swiss Association of Mountaineering Schools are listed below:

Bernese Oberland
Grindelwald: Bergsteigerzentrum Grindelwald, CH-3818 (☎ 036-53 52 00)
Kandersteg: Bergsteigerschule Kandersteg, CH-3718 (☎ 033-75 22 10)
Meiringen: Bergsteigerschule Rosenlaui, CH-3860 (☎ 036-71 35 37)
Unterbach: Bergsteigerschule Meiringen-Haslital, CH-3857 (☎ 036-71 25 93)
Central Switzerland
Andermatt:Alpine Sportschule Gotthard-Andermatt, CH-6490 (☎ 044-6 77 88)
Andermatt:Bergsteigerschule Uri, Mountain Reality, CH-6490 (☎ 044-6 77 70)
Engelberg: Bergsteigerschule Engelberg, CH-6390 (☎ 044-6 72 75)

Isenthal: Bergsteigerschule Montanara, CH-6461 (☎ 044-6 92 59)

Graubünden

Disentis-Mustèr: Alpine Bergsportschule Surselva, CH-7180 (☎ 081-947 49 39)

Flims-Dorf: Bergsteigerschule Mountain Fantasy, CH-7017 (☎ 081-83 22 21)

Klosters: Bergsteigerschule Alpintour, CH-7520 (☎ 081-69 36 36)

Pontresina: Bergsteigerschule Pontresina, CH-7504 (☎ 082-6 64 44)

North-Eastern Switzerland

Glarus: Alpinschule Tödi, CH-8750 (☎ 058-61 70 75)

Valais

Ausserberg: Alpinschule Ausserberg, CH-3938 (☎ 028-23 09 03)

Fiesch: Bergsteigerschule Fiesch, CH-3984 (☎ 028-71 25 77)

Riederalp: Bergsteigerschule Riederalp, CH-3987 (☎ 028-27 24 07)

Saas Fee: Bergsteigerschule Saas Tal, CH-3906 (☎ 028-57 23 48)

Saas Grund: Bergsteigerschule Weissmies, CH-3910 (☎ 028-57 14 44)

Verbier: École d'Alpinisme La Fantastique, CH-1936 (☎ 026-31 64 22)

Zermatt: Bergführerbüro Zermatt, CH-3920 (☎ 028-67 34 56)

Vaud Alps

Leysin: École d'Alpinisme Leysin, CH-1854 (☎ 025-34 18 46)

Swiss Friends of Nature

The Swiss Friends of Nature (Naturfreunde Schweiz, Amis de la Nature Suisse) are associated with the international body founded to promote environmentally responsible tourism. Apart from organising numerous outdoor tours and courses – from mountaineering and canoeing to animal watching and botanical walks – the Swiss Friends of Nature run almost 100 hostels (see Accommodation below). The Swiss Friends of Nature can be contacted at: Naturfreunde Schweiz (☎ 031-301 60 88), Pavillonweg 3, Postfach, Bern 3001.

The Swiss Society for the Protection of Nature

The Swiss Society for the Protection of Nature (Schweizer Bund für Naturschutz, Ligue Suisse pour la Protection de la Nature) was the earliest nationally based conservation lobby in Switzerland, and has a history going back to the first decade of the 1900s. Since then the society has been instrumental in the establishment of many nature reserves throughout the country, including the Swiss National Park. The society puts out a monthly magazine with French and German editions.

For more information contact: Schweizer Bund für Naturschutz (☎ 061-312 74 42), Postfach, Wartenbergstrasse 22, 4020 Basel.

Swiss Jura Association

The Swiss Jura Association (Schweizerischer Juraverein, Association du Jura Suisse) is a regional conservation group affiliated with the SAW/FSTP (see above). The association exists to promote sustainable recreation in the Swiss Jura. It annually publishes a free German/French booklet titled *Verpflegungs-und Unterkunftsmöglichkeiten längs der Jurahöhenwege/Possibilités de Ravitaillement et de Logement le long des Chemins des Crêtes*, which gives accommodation possibilities throughout the region.

For more information write to: Schweizerischer Juraverein, Postfach 233 (PC 46-406-1), 4600 Olten.

Swiss Youth Hostel Association

The Swiss Youth Hostel Association (Schweizer Jugendherbergen, Auberges de Jeunesse Suisse, Alberghi Svizzeri per la Gioventù) is affiliated with the International Youth Hostel Federation (IYHF), which runs thousands of other youth hostels worldwide. Membership is open to anyone. It's probably cheaper and more convenient to join in your own country, but the annual membership fee in Switzerland is Sfr20 for juniors (under 19 years of age) and Sfr30 for seniors.

The association organises a whole range of summer and winter outdoor programmes lasting up to a week, including walking and rafting trips or courses in scuba-diving and mountaineering. The association also produces a dozen or so excellent brochure-maps in separate French and German versions which detail a selection of 'thematic' walks in Swiss landscapes, including walks along rivers, over mountain passes, through gorges or in the Alpine foothills. These brochure-maps are very worthwhile and available free of charge at Switzerland's larger youth hostels.

For more information you can contact the Swiss Youth Hostel Federation's national office: Schweizerischer Jugendherbergen, (☎ 01-360 14 14), Schaffhauserstrasse 14, Postfach, CH-8042 Zürich. The regional office for French-speaking Switzerland is: Auberges de Jeunesse Suisses (☎ 039-23 78 51), Siège romand, Ave Léopold-Robert 65, CH-2300 La Chaux-de-Fonds .

BUSINESS HOURS

Shops are generally open from 8 am to 6.30 pm Monday to Friday, and to 4 or 5 pm on Saturday. In larger cities many shops (particularly supermarkets and department stores) stay open over the midday break, but otherwise shops close for 1½ to two hours from around noon. In country areas, shops are often closed on Wednesday (or just Wednesday afternoon). Banks are almost always open Monday to Friday from 8.30 am until 4.30 pm.

Public holidays fall on New Year's Day, 1 January; Good Friday; Easter Sunday and Monday; Ascension Day; National Day, 1 August; Whit Sunday and Monday; Christmas Day, 25 December; and Boxing Day, 26 December. Some cantons observe their own special holidays and extra religious days, for example, 2 January, 1 May (Labour Day), and Corpus Christi.

POST & TELECOMMUNICATIONS
Post

Switzerland's postal service (PTT) is extremely efficient. Post offices are generally open Monday to Friday from 8 am to noon and from 2 to 6.30 pm; and Saturday from 8 until 11 am, but in larger cities the central post office stays open throughout the midday break. The minimum postal rates for mail not exceeding 20 gm are: Sfr0.70 within Switzerland, Sfr1.00 within Europe, and Sfr1.80 to all other countries.

Poste-restante mail can be sent to any Swiss post office, and is held for a period of 30 days; there is no charge for this service. In villages and very small towns, the local post office often serves as a tourist office and gives out basic information. The PTT also operates the extensive network of postbuses which leave (at least where there is no train station) from the local post office.

Telephone

The national telephone service (Telecom-PTT) is one of the best in Europe, and direct dialling is standard for all overseas calls. Almost all public telephones will take both coins and a Taxcard (plastic 'smart' card), available from post offices for Sfr10 or Sfr20. The minimum charge for a local call is Sfr0.40.

The country code for Switzerland is 41. To call Switzerland from abroad, drop the initial zero from the area code; eg for Bern dial ☎ 41 31, *preceded* by the overseas access code of the country you're calling from. The overseas access code *from* Switzerland is 00. The telephone number for local enquiries is ☎ 111, but a minimum fee of Sfr1.60 is now charged for each enquiry call.

The network of mobile telephones (called *Natel* in German and French) covers large parts of the Swiss Alps, and local walkers or climbers sometimes even take their own phone with them into the mountains.

The telephone numbers in certain regions are currently being changed. Area codes are being simplified and (most) new numbers are to have seven digits. The new telephone numbers in Ticino, Graubönden, Central Switzerland and North-eastern Switzerland are given in this guidebook, but the revised numbers for other regions (including the Brenese Oberland, Solothurn and parts of Vaud Canton) are due to change in late 1996.

TIME

Swiss time is one hour ahead of GMT/UTC. The daylight-saving period ('summer time') is now the same all over western Europe, and begins at midnight on the last Saturday in March (put clocks forward one hour), and ends on the last Saturday in October.

ELECTRICITY

Absurdly, three different power plug variants are used in Switzerland, with two or (more commonly) three round pins. The standard continental European type plug is compatible with most – but not all – Swiss electrical sockets. Where the socket is connected to an electrical cord, sawing off the socket rim is sometimes a simple way of solving the problem – it's not as dangerous as it sounds, but using an adapter plug is a less radical method.

The electric current in Switzerland is 220 V, 50Hz. Most appliances designed for 240 V will handle 220 V quite well, but travellers from North America will need a step-down transformer – this may be integrated in your appliance, so read the instructions.

BOOKS

Most books are published in different editions by different publishers in different countries. As a result, a book might be a hardcover rarity in one country while it's readily available in paperback in another. Fortunately, bookshops and libraries search by title or author, so your local bookshop or library is best placed to advise you on the availability of the following recommendations.

Travel Guidebooks

Switzerland by Mark Honan (Lonely Planet Publications, Melbourne) is, like all Lonely Planet guidebooks, thoroughly updated and republished regularly. It includes information on travel and has numerous accurate city and regional maps. Without wanting to seem biased, we think it's the best all-round travel guidebook available on Switzerland.

Off the Beaten Track in Switzerland by Kenneth Loveland & John Marshall (Moorland, Ashborne) focuses on some of the less-visited regions of Switzerland.

Switzerland at its Best by Robert S Kane (Passport Books, Lincolnwood, Illinois) is another quality travel guidebook.

Camping 96 by Swiss Camping Association (SCA, or Verband Schweizer Campings/ Association Suisse de Campings) is an an-

nually published guide to organised camping grounds (mostly affiliated with the SCA).

Guide Camping Führer 1996 by the Touring Club of Switzerland (TCS) is similar to the above, covers TCS-affiliated camping grounds and is updated every year.

Walking Guidebooks

Some of the best English-language walking guides to Switzerland are published by Cicerone Press, 2 Police Square, Milnthorpe, Cumbria, LA7 7PY, UK. Most of Cicerone's titles on Switzerland were written by Kev Reynolds, whose books include: *The Valais, The Bernese Alps, Central Switzerland, Walks in the Engadine, Walking the Jura High Route, Walking in Ticino* and *The Alpine Pass Route*. Another Cicerone guidebook is *The Tour of Monte Rosa* by CJ Wright. Unfortunately Cicerone maps are a bit sketchy.

Other English-language titles dedicated to walking in Switzerland are as follows:

Walking Switzerland the Swiss Way by Marcia & Philip Lieberman (The Mountaineers, Seattle, 1987). This book describes 'inn-to-inn' walks in many parts of the country. The first section covers day walks in the Valais, Bernese Oberland and Engadine, while the second section describes longer walks with overnight accommodation.

The booklet *Downhill Walking in Switzerland* by Richard & Linda Williams (Old World Travel, Tulsa, USA) outlines descent walks all starting out from high points that can be easily reached by public transport or mountain cableway.

Walking in Switzerland by Brian Spencer (Moorland, Ashbourne, UK, 1986) describes walks around 10 resort centres in the Swiss Alps. The text is accompanied by sketch maps.

Footloose in the Swiss Alps by William Reifsnyder (Sierra Club Books, San Francisco, 1986) is one of the best English-language guides to Switzerland, with well-detailed walks and maps of places throughout the Swiss Alps.

Adventuring in the Alps by William &

Marylou Reifsnyder (Sierra Club Books, San Francisco, 1986) takes in the whole area of the Alps, and therefore the selection of walks within Switzerland is limited.

Guidebooks in German & French

Switzerland's largest publisher of walking guidebooks is Kümmerly + Frey (K + F), Hallerstrasse 6-10, 3001, Bern (☎ 031-301 36 66). K + F has dozens of regional guides that cover every part of Switzerland; all are published in German, but many also appear as French-language titles. K + F's *Grosser Wander-Atlas der Schweiz*, titled *Le Grand Atlas Suisse des Promenades* in French, outlines excursions on foot all over Switzerland.

The Swiss outdoors publisher Werd-Verlag, Postfach, 8021 Zürich, has a number of worthwhile titles, including *40 Lohnende Bergtouren*, *40 Panorama Wanderungen* and *40 Wanderungen am Wasser*, which have suggestions for walking in many parts of Switzerland. The Ott Verlag in Thun puts out thematic guidebooks detailing cultural, historical or natural walks, such as *Auf den Spuren der Kelten und Römer* and *Wanderungen zu den schönsten Naturschutzebieten*.

The Swiss Alpine Club (SAC) publishes guidebooks on all of the country's mountain areas, but these are mainly intended for hardy Alpinists rather than humble walkers. An exception is the SAC's publication *Wandern Alpin*, titled *Randonnées en altitude* in French, which describes over 80 easy, moderate and strenuous mountain walks throughout Switzerland.

Other good publishers of German-language guides are Bergverlag Rother, Landshuter Allee 49, D-80637 Munich, and Bruckmann Verlag, Postfach 20 03 53, D-8003 Munich. Bruckmann's *Die Schönsten Bergwanderungen der Schweiz* by Rose M Kaune & Gerhard Bleyer is recommended.

General

For a good overall run-down on Switzerland there is *Switzerland – Land, People, Economy* by Aubrey Diem (1991). Another general title giving an insight into the country is *Why Switzerland?* by Jonathan Steinberg. Mark Twain's entertaining European travelogue *A Tramp Abroad* has been a classic for a hundred years or more; the author spent considerable time journeying through Switzerland.

Alpine Travel & Exploration

The literature left behind by the pioneers of the Swiss Alpine travel and exploration takes up whole bookshelves. Larger libraries are likely to stock any of the titles listed below.

Early Travellers in the Alps by Gavin R de Beer (first published in 1930) is essentially the history of early Alpine exploration and travel from the early 1700s until the late 19th century. This book recounts the experiences of people such as the Genevan naturalist Horace Bénédict Saussure, who made several scientific journeys into the mountains of the Valais. Numerous woodcuts and engravings of people and scenery are featured. De Beer is also the author of a dozen or so interesting titles dealing with travel in Switzerland, including *Escape to Switzerland* (Penguin, 1945) and *Alps and Men* (London, 1932).

Scrambles Amongst the Alps by Edward Whymper was first published in 1871. Whymper made first ascents of several important peaks in the Valaisan Alps, and a climbing party under his leadership was the first to reach the summit of the Matterhorn. Whymper's classic work provides a good introduction to the Victorian era of mountaineering in the Alps.

The Playground of Europe by Leslie Stephen (first published in 1871). As president of the British Alpine Club, Stephen made countless climbing excursions to Switzerland, and these accounts of his ascents, traverses and pass-crossings in the Alps make excellent reading.

Wandering Among the High Alps by Alfred Wills (first published in 1939) is recommended reading for anyone interested in the heyday of mountaineering.

A History of Mountaineering in the Alps by Claire Eliane Engle (first published in 1953) traces the beginnings of mountaineering, from the first scientific ascents by 17th-century naturalists through Alpinism's 'golden years' in the 1800s to its gradual popularisation after WWII.

Natural History

The Alpine Flowers of Britain and Europe by Christopher Grey-Wilson & Marjorie

Edelweiss
(*Leontopodium alpinum*)

Purple Bellflower
(*Campanula* species)

Primrose
(*Primula vulgaris*)

Leopard's Bane
(*Doronicum grandiflorum*)

Alpine Buttercup
(*Ranunculus alpestris*)

Alpine Marigold
(*Chrysanthemum alpinum*)

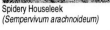

Spidery Houseleek
(*Sempervivum arachnoideum*)

Fairy Foxgloves
(*Erinus alpinus*)

Moss Campion
(*Silene acaulis*)

All photos taken by Clem Lindenmayer

CLEM LINDENMAYER

CLEM LINDENMAYER

CLEM LINDENMAYER

Top: Ibex are typically seen in small herds on craggy mountain ridgetops.
Middle: Sonogno (Ticino) is known for its charming stone houses and as a base for outstanding walks into the surrounding mountains.
Bottom: The Surenenpass (Central Switzerland) offers an undisturbed mountain landscape.

Blamey is a standard field guide covering the Alpine and subalpine flora in mountain regions of western Europe (chiefly Britain, Scandinavia, Iberia and the Alps).

Our Alpine Flora by Elias Landolt (SAC, Bern) is a translation from the original German (there's also a French edition). Landolt's compact hard-cover work is a comprehensive English-language field guide to plants of the Swiss Alps. It's full of drawings and colourplates depicting some 500 species – just about every Alpine wildflower or shrub you're likely to want to identify on your walks. This book is thoroughly recommended, though at around Sfr46 (somewhat cheaper for SAC members) it's a bit pricey.

Alpenblumen/Fleures Alpines (Editions MPA Verlag) is a much cheaper multilingual field guide which describes 64 of the most common Alpine flowers in German, French, Italian and English.

Alpenpflanzen (Arboris Verlag, Bern) is an inexpensive guidebook to Swiss Alpine flora, showing the most commonly seen wildflowers in detailed colour photos, making identification quick and easy. Unfortunately, the main text is in German only, but plants' common names are also shown in French and English.

Geschützte Landschaften der Schweiz (Das Beste/Reader's Digest) is a German-language coffee-table book featuring Switzerland's 100 most significant nature reserves. This excellent publication contains some superb larger-format colour shots of natural environments all over the country. It is stocked by virtually all larger public libraries in German-speaking Switzerland.

Guide du naturaliste dans les Alpes by JP Schaer (Délachaux et Niestlé, Neuchâtel-Paris) is a general field guide in French covering Alpine geology, flora and fauna.

A Guide to the Minerals of Switzerland by Max Weibel (Interscience Publishers, London, first published in 1966). Some of the most interesting minerals in the world are found in Switzerland, and this book is probably still the best work available for amateur crystal-seekers. It provides a general overview of individual minerals and their regional occurrences as well as many tips for collectors.

MAPS

Surveying and cartography is something (else) the Swiss excel in; their maps are veritable works of precision, if not of art. The national mapping authority is the Bundesamt für Landestopographie (BL or Office Fédéral de Topographie (OFT) in French), whose central office is at Seftigenstrasse 264, CH-3084 Wabern (☎ 031-54 91 11).

The BL/OFT produces three standard topographical series covering the whole country, which are scaled at 1:25,000, 1:50,000 and 1:100,000. These maps show often quite complex geographical features extremely accurately and with astonishing detail, combining the use of contour lines and shading together with a highly skilled 'artistic' representation of important features such as gorges, mountain cirques or exposed rock ridges; this gives readers a clear and immediate impression as to the 'lie of the land'. The BL/OFT updates its maps on a regular six to seven-year cycle.

Due to the painstaking and expensive work involved in their production, Swiss maps are not cheap to buy. Prices per sheet for the BL/OFT's standard topographical maps are Sfr12 for the 1:25,000 series and Sfr13.50 for sheets scaled at 1:50,000. A peculiarity of BL/OFT maps is that they don't include a legend on the sheet itself, but explanatory brochures *(Zeichenerklärung, légend des signes)* are available free at all points of sale.

The BL/OFT produces a free fold-up catalogue outlining its various map series (including the SAW/FSTP 'T' series – see below). Larger bookstores invariably have a wide – though not always complete – selection of Swiss topographical, walking and travel maps. Public libraries also stock maps, but non-residents of Switzerland may not always be entitled to borrow them. (It is, however, usually possible to make photocopies in the library itself.) Library maps must be returned in a reasonable state of repair, so take particular care to protect them from wind, rain or fingers greased with smelly Appenzell cheese. A transparent map-holder (available from good backpacking stores) allows you to look at the relevant section of the route without having to con-tinually unfold the map.

Given the small and compact nature of the Swiss Alps, walkers can often get away with buying just a few sheets – depending entirely, of course, on where they'll be walking. Don't even consider using any topographical map with a scale greater than 1:100,00 for serious navigation in the moun-tains. Maps at the still lower scale of 1:50,000 – or even 1:25,000 – are the pre-ferred ones, however.

General Travel & Transport Maps

The *Rail-map Switzerland* (or *Bahn-Karte Schweiz/Carte Ferroviaire Suisse)* produced by the Swiss Federal Railways (SBB/CFF) and scaled at 1:301,000 clearly shows all rail, ferry and postbus lines as well as the numerous funiculars, cog railways and cableways; importantly, the respective time-table code of each service is included (see the Getting Around chapter).

One of the best road maps is the 1:301,000 *Schweiz/Suisse TCS*, published by Kümmerly + Frey (K + F) in association with the Touring Club der Schweiz (TCS), Switzerland's largest car club. K + F's 1:400,000 *Quick Map* includes street maps of all major Swiss cities. Orell Füssli also puts out a good road map, the *Strassenkarte Schweiz*, scaled at 1:303,000, as well as a 1:350,000 tourist map called *Touristenkarte Schweiz*.

For general use, the BL/OFT publishes a 1:300,000 map of Switzerland, the *Generalkarte der Schweiz/Carte général de la Suisse*, as well as a somewhat more detailed set of four 1:200,000 sheets cover-ing the whole country. These maps are good for basic orientation, but due to their rela-tively high scales are quite unsuitable for serious navigation.

Although they have limited value as walking maps, larger-scale regional maps often give a worthwhile overview of the hiking possibilities within the area. The best of these are K + F's 1:120,000 *Holiday Map* series, which covers the Bernese Oberland, Ticino, Graubünden and the Valais.

Walking Maps

A wide range of specially produced walking maps are available in Switzerland. These are contoured topographical maps that indicate features of particular interest to walkers – walking routes, mountain huts or inns, public cableways, minor train stations, postbus stops etc – more clearly than standard topo-graphical maps. Foot tracks are generally shown as (continuous or dotted) red lines.

With few exceptions, the maps referred to and/or recommended in this guidebook are walking maps rather than the BL/OFT's standard topographical series. The latter always make viable alternatives, however, virtually all Swiss walking maps are ulti-mately drawn from existing BL/OFT base references anyway.

SAW/FSTP Walking Maps In association with BL/OFT, the Swiss Hiking Federation (SAW/FSTP, see under Useful Organisations above) produces a series of 1:50,000 walking maps based on the national mapping authority's standard topographical series. SAW/FSTP maps are distinguishable by their orange (rather than green) covers and a 'T' after the grid number, eg *Jungfrau (264 T)*. On the whole they are the cheapest and best-quality walking maps available in Swit-zerland, and are updated regularly.

The SAW/FSTP 'T' series corresponds to the 1:50,000 national grid, so there's no overlap between individual sheets. Importantly, SAW/FSTP maps are printed on durable paper more resistant to water, wind and wear than the paper used for most com-mercial (especially K + F) walking maps. At the time of writing some 20 sheets in the SAW/FSTP 'T' series still hadn't been pub-lished, but it's expected that all 78 maps will be available by early 1999.

The standard retail price for SAW/FSTP walking maps is Sfr21.50, but SAW/FSTP members and subscribers can order them at the reduced rate of Sfr17.50 per sheet.

Other Walking Maps Apart from the national-grid SAW/FSTP walking maps and standard BL/OFT sheets, a wide assortment of other maps has been specially produced for walkers by commercial publishers, local tourist authorities or even cantonal sections of the SAW/FSTP. Often, these walking maps are actually preferable, especially where they give single-sheet coverage to the area or route that you're interested in.

By far the largest commercial publisher of walking maps in Switzerland is Kümmerly + Frey (K + F), which has the entire country covered in several dozen overlapping sheets at various scales. Most K + F maps are scaled at 1:60,000, and although these show rather less detail than most other walking maps they are quite accurate enough to be used for serious navigation by walkers. K + F's 1:60,000 sheets sell for Sfr24.80.

Another important commercial publisher of walking maps is Editions MPA Verlag, CH-1054 Morrens. MPA produces high-quality 1:25,000 and 1:50,000 sheets which mainly concentrate on the French-speaking regions of Switzerland. MPA maps usually indicate average walking times in both directions for each stage of a route. MPA's 1:25,000 walking maps cost around Sf18.50 (varying a bit depending on size) and its 1:50,000 sheets cost between Sfr23 and Sfr28. Other smaller commercial publishers of walking maps include Orell Füssli, Schaad + Frey and Baeschlin.

Local tourist authorities often produce their own local walking maps (partly as a way of promoting the region). These generally cover the area surrounding their resort or valley, and can be very useful indeed. Depending on their size and quality, tourist-office walking maps normally cost between Sfr12 and Sfr18.

In some cantons, associations affiliated with the SAW/FSTP also produce walking maps. The most active of these is the Kantonal St-Gallische Wanderwege, which has brought out a small series of excellent

1:50,000 and 1:25,000 walking maps covering most parts of the canton of St Gallen.

NOMENCLATURE

Switzerland is a multi-ethnic country, and naturally this is reflected in its nomenclature. Topographical maps and trail signposts always show place names in the language predominant in that area (although unofficial signs painted on rocks and trees often betray the ethnic origins of the non-locals who wrote them). Where two linguistic regions converge, such as the Pass da Sett/Septimerpass in Graubünden, maps (and sometimes signposts) give both place names.

Walkers may sometimes notice that somewhat different versions of the same place name exist, such as Lauchbühl/Loichbiel (near Grindelwald) or Kreuzboden/Chrizbode (in the Saastal). This is particularly common in German-speaking regions, where local pronunciation of a place name in the local dialect is different to standard (High) German. Most interesting are place names consisting of two languages, as frequently occurs along the linguistic borders, where French/German combinations like Vieille Rossmatte or Le Steffelbletz (in eastern Fribourg Canton) frequently come up. Note also that valleys very often carry quite a different name to the stream that flows through them; for example, the Val de Travers in the western Jura is drained by a river known as L'Areuse.

HEALTH

It's easy to underestimate the strenuousness of mountain walking. Routes in the Swiss Alps commonly involve ascents of 1000 metres or more, so a good level of physical fitness is essential. The best way to prepare yourself for your walking holiday is to undertake some regular (vigorous) exercise shortly before you arrive in Switzerland. Otherwise take things very easy during the first week or so.

Health & Travel Insurance

Health costs are expensive in Switzerland, and since non-residents on holiday there do *not* have free medical coverage you are strongly urged to take out some kind of travel insurance. Travel agents can advise you on the most appropriate travel-insurance package, but be sure that you will be covered for all outdoor pursuits you undertake during your trip. Some policies specifically exclude 'dangerous activities' such as paragliding or roped mountaineering, but sometimes even hiking may not be covered. Also check whether the policy covers ambulances or an emergency flight home.

Medical Kit A small, straightforward medical kit is a wise thing to carry. A possible kit list includes:

Aspirin or Panadol – for pain or fever

Antihistamine (such as Benadryl) – useful as a decongestant for colds, allergies, to ease the itch from insect bites or stings or to help prevent motion sickness. Antihistamines may cause sedation and interact with alcohol so care should be taken when using them.

Kaolin preparation (Pepto-Bismol), Imodium or Lomotil – for stomach upsets

Antiseptic such as Betadine, which comes as impregnated swabs or ointment, and an antibiotic powder or similar 'dry' spray – for cuts and grazes

Calamine lotion – to ease irritation from bites or stings

Bandages and Band-aids – for minor injuries

Scissors, tweezers and a thermometer (note that mercury thermometers are prohibited by airlines)

Insect repellent, sunscreen, chap stick and water purification tablets

Mountain Safety & Emergencies

First a sobering statistic: in some summers, the fatalities involving walkers account for almost 50% of all deaths resulting from 'mountain recreation accidents'. The remainder lose their lives pursuing more obviously dangerous activities – mainly roped mountaineering, rock-climbing and paragliding. Unlike other mountain sports, however, where the objective risks are far higher, most walker deaths are directly attributable to tiredness, carelessness and inadequate clothing or footwear. Falls resulting from a slide on grass, autumn leaves, scree, or iced-over paths are one of the most common hazards.

Where possible don't walk in the mountains alone. Two is considered the minimum number for safe walking in the mountains, and having at least one additional person in the party will mean someone can stay with an injured walker while the other seeks help. Properly inform a responsible person – a family member, hut warden, hotel receptionist etc – of your plans, and avoid altering your specified route. Under no circumstances should walkers leave the marked trails in foggy conditions. With some care, most walking routes can be followed in fog, but otherwise wait by the path until visibility is clear enough to proceed.

The standard Alpine distress signal is six whistles, six calls, six smoke puffs – ie six of whatever sign you can make – followed by a pause equalling the length of time taken by the calls before repeating the signal again. Emergency communications in the Swiss Alps are very good indeed. All SAC huts (and virtually all other club huts) are equipped with a telephone, as are all mountain hotels and restaurants. Some walkers even take their own mobile telephone (or *Natel*) with them into the mountains – 'high-status safety'.

Emergency Rescue The Swiss air search-and-rescue organisation, REGA, is a division of the Swiss Red Cross. REGA helicopters can reach almost every part of Switzerland within 15 minutes, and each year they carry out hundreds of emergency flights for mountaineers, skiers and walkers in distress. For REGA sponsors (annual rate Sfr30/70 per person/family) all costs of search and/or emergency evacuation are waived, but people without appropriate insurance cover may be asked to contribute to the rescue costs. Note that REGA sponsorship is not a replacement for standard travel and health insurance. For more information, contact REGA (☎ 01-385 85 85), Mainaustrasse 21, CH-8008 Zürich.

The REGA's 24-hour emergency telephone number is ☎ 01-383 11 11.

Water

Water oozes, bubbles or gushes forth at mountain springs throughout the Swiss Alps, and finding safe drinking water somewhere along the route is seldom a problem. Livestock and wildlife in Switzerland do not carry any particularly nasty diseases (such as the dreaded giardiasis), but drinking faecally contaminated water anywhere is likely to give you a bout of the 'runs' (see the Diarrhoea section below).

Throughout the mountains, drinking fountains are the most reliable source of potable water. Generally a trough hewn out of a log or rock slab and filled by piped spring water, drinking fountains can be found along most well-transited paths and walkways. Mountain huts below 2500 metres (or so) usually have a drinking trough for guests and passing walkers, but this is not always the case at higher elevations where running water is often in scarce supply. Towns and village squares often have fountains of running water. If the water is not of drinking quality, this will usually be indicated by *Kein Trinkwasser* or *eau non potable* signs.

When deciding whether to trust the water from a particular stream, remember that water flowing through a heavily visited area should always be treated with suspicion – avoid drinking from streams near mountain huts or downstream from any dwelling. It's advisable to carry a water bottle on longer walks to fill up at obviously reliable sources. Throughout Switzerland, bottled mineral water is cheaply available in still and carbonated forms.

Water Purification It's unlikely you'll have to drink water from a suspect source, but the simplest way of purifying water is to boil it vigorously for five minutes. Remember that water boils at a progressively lower temperature the higher up you go, so noxious bacteria are less likely to be killed. Simple filtering will not remove all dangerous organisms, so if you cannot boil water it should be treated chemically. Chlorine tablets (Puritabs, Steritabs or other brand names) will kill many but not all pathogens, including giardia and amoebic cysts. Iodine is very effective in purifying water and is available in tablet form (such as Potable Aqua), but follow the directions carefully and remember that too much iodine can be harmful.

Minor Medical Problems

Blisters Blisters are an (almost) inevitable part of walking, and can occur even with properly worn-in boots. Steep descents are a typical cause of blisters, causing the toes and/or heels to rub continually against the inside of the boot as you go down. Since blisters quickly turn your walking holiday into an excursion of agony, it's worth doing all you can to avoid getting them in the first place. Be sure to wear in new boots well before attempting lengthy walks, and protect susceptible parts of your feet as soon as – if not before – the skin starts to get tender. Swiss druggists and pharmacies sell 'second skin' type sticking plasters that both prevent and treat blisters; one such locally made brand is Compeed.

Diarrhoea While a change of water, food or climate may give travellers a case of the runs, Switzerland's high standard of hygiene means that serious diarrhoea – which is caused by contaminated food or water – is fairly uncommon. If diarrhoea does hit you, however, fluid replacement is the mainstay of management. Weak black tea with a little sugar, soda water, or soft drinks allowed to go flat and diluted 50% with water are all good. With severe diarrhoea a rehydrating solution is necessary to replace minerals and salts. Commercially available oral rehydration salts (ORS) are very useful. You should stick to a bland diet as you recover.

Lomotil or Imodium can be used to bring relief from the symptoms, although they do not actually cure the problem.

Fungal Infections The high humidity that typically accompanies hot summer weather in Switzerland creates ideal breeding conditions for fungi. Fungal infections most commonly effect walkers between the toes (athlete's foot). Another common walkers' complaint is 'crotch rot', a painful rash in the groin-to-buttocks area caused by the combination of rubbing and sweating as you walk; simple solutions include wearing comfortable, non-abrasive clothing and keeping clean. Ringworm (which is a fungal infection, not a worm) is picked up from infected animals or by walking on damp areas like shower floors.

Heat Exhaustion At high altitude the sun can beat down on you with great intensity and midsummer conditions in Switzerland can be surprisingly hot. Dehydration or salt deficiency can cause heat exhaustion, so ensure that your body gets sufficient liquids. Salt deficiency is characterised by fatigue, lethargy, headaches, giddiness and muscle cramps, and in this case salt tablets may help. One way walkers can avoid the heat is by getting an early start, then taking it easy during the hottest part of the day.

Knee Pains Long, steep descents put a heavy strain on the knees, since the leg has to bend more sharply in order to compensate for the lower step. As weight is transferred onto the bent knee, the kneecap is pulled backwards against the joint, which can be uncomfortable to say the least.

Walkers can reduce knee strain by developing a proper technique of descent. Take short, controlled steps with the legs in a slightly bent position, placing your heels on the ground before the rest of the foot. Mountain paths usually negotiate very steep slopes in numerous switchback curves to avoid a much steeper direct descent. Trekking stocks (see under What to Bring) distribute much of the load off the legs and knees (albeit at the expense of the arms), but their long-term use tends to gradually reduce a walker's surefootedness. Many walking routes in Switzerland give you the option of making your descent by some mechanical means, such as a cable car, funicular railway etc.

Sunburn A great many walks described in this guidebook take you well above 2000 metres. At that altitude you can get sunburnt surprisingly quickly, even in overcast weather. Despite being very painful and unpleasant, sunburn permanently damages your skin and increases your risk of later developing skin cancer. Sunburn is a particular problem in early summer (June), since the sun's intensity is then greatest and large snowdrifts remain to reflect the UV radiation back up at you. Protect your skin by wearing a broad-rimmed hat and keeping your limbs and face either covered up or well smeared with a good sunblock – a recommended local brand is Piz Buin. A robust pair of sunglasses with UV lenses is more or less essential. Calamine lotion is good for mild sunburn.

Serious Medical Problems

Altitude Sickness The potentially fatal condition called Acute Mountain Sickness (AMS) is caused by the lack of oxygen and the lower atmospheric pressure at high altitudes. This prevents the lungs from passing enough oxygen into the blood.

There is no hard and fast rule about when 'true' cases of AMS can occur: although fatal cases of AMS at altitudes as low 3000 metres have been documented, it more typically occurs from 3500 metres upwards. Older people and those with high blood pressure often have an increased reaction to altitude.

The classic warning signs of AMS are headaches, nausea, dizziness, a dry cough, insomnia, breathlessness and loss of appetite. Mild altitude problems will generally abate after a day or so but if the symptoms persist or become worse the only treatment is to descend – even 500 metres can help. Breathlessness; a dry, irritating cough (which may progress to the production of pink, frothy sputum); severe headache; loss of appetite; nausea, and sometimes vomiting are all danger signs. Increasing tiredness, confusion, and lack of coordination and balance are real danger signs. Any of these symptoms individually, even just a persistent headache, can be a warning.

Few walks described in this guidebook take you above 3000 metres, and although you may well 'feel the altitude' after ascending, the real risk of AMS to walkers in Switzerland is fairly remote.

If you have reason to believe you may be susceptible to AMS take the following precautions:

Ascend slowly with frequent rests.
Drink extra fluids – in the mountains moisture is more easily lost as you breathe; certain symptoms of body dehydration are easily mistaken for AMS.
Eat light, high-carbohydrate meals for more energy.
Avoid alcohol as it may increase the risk of dehydration.
Avoid taking sedatives.

Encephalitis In Switzerland ticks are carriers of bacterial and viral encephalitis diseases, which may become serious if not detected early. Both types of encephalitis initially appear with influenza-like symptoms, and can effect the skin, nervous system, muscles or the heart, often causing headaches and sore joints. Only a very low percentage of people bitten by ticks develop either form of encephalitis, and most make a quick and full recovery. Some, however, have lasting health problems and occasionally the disease is actually fatal. Treatment is usually with antibiotics, but inoculations are available for those particularly at risk.

Read the Insects section below for instructions on what to do about tick bites.

Hypothermia Hypothermia (also known as exposure) is a real and ever-present threat to mountain walkers anywhere. Hypothermia occurs when the body loses heat faster than it can produce it, causing the core temperature to fall.

It is surprisingly easy to progress from very cold to dangerously cold due to a combination of wind, wet clothing, fatigue and hunger, even if the air temperature is above freezing. Key signs of hypothermia include exhaustion, slurred speech, numb skin (particularly toes and fingers), shivering, irrational or violent behaviour, lethargy, stumbling, dizzy spells, muscle cramps and violent bursts of energy. Irrationality may

take the form of a sufferer claiming they are warm and trying to take off their clothes.

To treat hypothermia, first get the person out of the wind and/or rain, remove their clothing if it's wet and replace it with dry, warm garments. Give them hot liquids – not alcohol – and some simple sugary food. Do not rub the victim but place them near a fire or in a warm (not hot) bath. This should be enough for the early stages of hypothermia, but if it has gone further it may be necessary to place the victim in a warm bed or sleeping bag and get in with them.

Death by hypothermia is certainly no new phenomenon in the Alps. Archaeologists believe that 'Ötzi' – the mummified prehistoric man found in glacial ice in the Tyrolean Alps – probably died of hypothermia after being caught high up in the mountains by a summer storm. Indeed, sudden thunderstorms can easily drench ill-prepared walkers in cold and heavy downpours.

Watch for signs of impending bad weather and descend or seek shelter if things start to look dicey. Walkers should always carry a totally waterproof rain-jacket (and preferably overpants) no matter how good the weather appears when they set out. Also carry basic supplies, including food containing simple sugars to generate heat quickly and lots of fluid to drink.

Rabies Rabies is present in Switzerland, but its spread is rigorously contained through the immunising of native animals, most particularly foxes, which are the prime carrier of the virus. The only part of the country where recent cases of rabid animals have been registered is the eastern Swiss Jura between Olten and Delémont.

Rabies is caused by abrasive contact with an infected animal, so any bite, scratch or even lick from a warm-blooded, furry animal should be cleaned immediately and thoroughly. Scrub with soap and running water, and then clean with an alcohol solution. If there is any possibility that the animal is infected, medical help should be sought immediately. Even if the animal is not rabid, all bites should be treated seriously as they can become infected or can result in tetanus. A rabies vaccination is now available and should be considered if you are in a high-risk category – for example, you work with animals.

DANGERS
Avalanches
Snow avalanches are essentially a winter phenomenon, but on certain high-Alpine routes very early in the walking season there may sometimes still be a significant risk from avalanches. Even experienced mountaineers often have trouble assessing avalanche danger, so walkers are advised to consult the local tourist office, mountain hut or school of mountaineering for advice. Paths that cross potential avalanche paths are normally closed until summer snow melt renders them safe.

Black Ice
Particularly in autumn, water trickling across the path can quickly freeze to form a thin sheet known as black ice. Often looking more like damp earth or an innocuous puddle, black ice can be extremely treacherous and tricky to cross. Where the problem is very severe, wearing ice-spurs – 'mini-crampons' that fit simply onto your walking boots – is recommended. Ice-spurs are available from outdoor equipment stores (from around Sfr80).

Glaciers
With their unstable ice and deep crevasses, glaciers make extremely dangerous obstacles. For this reason inexperienced walkers should never venture onto the ice unless guided by someone with a sound knowledge of glacier travel. For safe glacier travel all members of the party are tied onto a rope to prevent falling into hidden crevasses. Glacier travel is most uncertain in spring, because at that time the crevasses are generally snowed over and not immediately obvious. Walking on snow and ice requires well-insulated footwear. Rock debris (known as moraine) accumulates on the

glacier's surface, and can be very tiring to walk on.

In some places, however, walking routes do lead across harmless sections of a glacier (where crevasses cannot form because the ice runs smoothly over a flat-rock base). Such routes are marked – usually with stakes and/or the orange or red cones used by road maintenance crews – in early summer by the local mountain-hut warden or other person responsible for waymarkings. Two simple and obvious rules apply here: *don't leave the marked route*, and *if you lose your way, turn back immediately*.

The Hunting Season
Recreational game hunting is popular in all of Switzerland's mountain cantons, especially Graubünden. Depending on local bylaws, the open season on chamois, ibex and deer is for a limited – usually four-week – period between September and October. Although the danger should not be overstated, shooting accidents have occasionally occurred after walkers – but more often other hunters! – strayed into the line of fire. It's a good idea to keep your wits about you on autumn walks, particularly if you leave the marked trails. Interestingly, during the hunting season Switzerland's canny hooved fauna seeks refuge in and around the numerous nature reserves scattered throughout the country, so this can actually be a good time to see wild animals.

Rockfall
The danger presented by rockfall *(Steinschlag* in German or *chute de pierres* in French) is most acute in the sparsely vegetated high-Alpine zone, where continual melting and freezing produces brittle crags and unstable slopes. Mountaineers are most at risk from falling rocks, but rock fall sometimes also causes serious injury or even death to unwary walkers.

Sections of path most obviously exposed to rock fall lead through steep and eroding mountainsides, or below cliffs fringed by heavy fields of talus. Don't hang around in such places any longer than necessary and keep a watchful eye for 'movements' above as you pass. If you accidentally send a loose chunk of rock into motion, shout out a loud warning to any walkers who may be below you. Chamois or ibex sometimes dislodge rocks, so animal watchers should take special care to keep well clear of the fall-path. In Switzerland, especially dangerous sections of path (or road) have warning signs posted along the way.

Snakes

Switzerland has two species of venomous snake (see Reptiles in the Facts about the Country chapter), which can deliver a painful rather than a fatal bite. To minimise your chances of being bitten always wear boots, socks and long trousers when walking through undergrowth where snakes may be present. Don't put your hands into holes and crevices, and be careful when collecting firewood.

In the unlikely event of someone being bitten, keep the victim calm and still, wrap the bitten limb tightly, as you would for a sprained ankle, and then attach a splint to immobilise it. Then seek medical help, if possible with the dead snake for identification. Don't attempt to catch the snake if there is even a remote possibility of being bitten again. Tourniquets and sucking out the poison are now comprehensively discredited.

Thunderstorms & Lightning

Thunderstorms accompanied by intense electrical activity commonly occur in summer in Switzerland as a result of heavy cloud build-up. This phenomenon, most pronounced in higher mountain regions, produces often quite localised thunderstorms which can sweep across neighbouring ranges surprisingly quickly. The dangers posed by the sudden wet, windy conditions brought by summer storms are dealt with above (see Hypothermia). To minimise the risk of being struck by lightning, however, walkers should note the basic safeguards outlined below.

In open areas where there is no shelter, find a depression in the ground and take up a crouched-squatting position with your feet together. Do *not* lie flat on the ground – if lightning strikes close by the voltage difference between your head and feet can reach several thousand volts. Avoid contact with metallic objects – do *not* use an umbrella!

Never seek shelter under objects which are isolated or higher than their surroundings (such as trees or transmission-line poles), as these are far more likely to get zapped. Isolated buildings and trees at the edge of a forest are other key targets for lightning bolts. If you find yourself in a forest of regularly high trees, you are relatively safe as long as you keep a fair distance from each tree and away from any overhanging branches.

Lightning prefers to strike exposed mountain summits and ridges. Mountaineers should seek out a concave formation in a rock wall, avoiding direct contact with the rock itself. Keep a good distance from ice-axes and crampons. If you happen to be swimming or standing in a lake or river when a thunderstorm approaches, get out of the water at 'lightning' speed. Anglers should quickly pack away their fishing rods. Swiss mountain huts are always fitted with lightning rods and therefore offer safe shelter during thunderstorms, but don't touch externally connected objects like the telephone or water taps.

Should anyone actually be struck by lightning, immediately begin first-aid measures such as mouth-to-mouth resuscitation and treatment of burns. Get the patient to a doctor as quickly as possible.

ANNOYANCES & INCONVENIENCES
Insects

Ticks are found throughout Switzerland up to an altitude of 1200 metres, and typically live in underbrush at the forest edge or beside walking tracks. The tick will crawl onto a passing animal or person, embedding its head in the host's skin in order to suck its blood. In Switzerland ticks are carriers of encephalitis diseases, so check your body carefully after walking through a potentially tick-infested area, and remove the parasites as soon as possible. While a good insect repellent will often stop ticks from biting, Swiss medical authorities now strongly discourage using oil, alcohol or the heat of a flame to persuade ticks to let go, as this may actually release encephalitis pathogens into the bloodstream. The recommended removal method is to grab the insect's head with a pair of tweezers – or better still with a specially designed tick-removal instrument sold cheaply in local pharmacies – then pull the tick out slowly without 'levering' or twisting the hand.

Apart from ticks, insects merely have nuisance rating in Switzerland. Horse flies are worst around streams in hot weather from early June to mid-July, but only occasionally do they become really bothersome – except, that is, to poor, defenseless cows. Horse flies' only virtue is their dim-wittedness, which makes it relatively easy swat them dead.

In spring and summer you'll often pass beehives on lower-elevation walks. The local bee breeds seem mild-mannered enough, however, and wasps generally agree to leave you alone if you do the same to them. Bee and wasp stings are usually painful rather than dangerous, and can be treated with calamine lotion or ice packs to reduce the pain and swelling.

Military Shooting Ranges

As the saying goes, 'it's never quiet in the mountains'. It is surprising how much shooting practise the Swiss army seems to need, and some of the nicest Alpine valleys are periodically used as artillery or shooting ranges. Although the Federal Military Department (Eidgenössisches Miltär Departement (EMD) in German, Departement Militaire Fédéral (DMF) in French) is more sensitive to environmental criticism than in the past, new shooting ranges have been set up in remote areas even in recent years.

Military shooting exercises may last a couple of days or several weeks, and military sentries ensure that unauthorised people keep well outside of the danger zone. Firing is generally interrupted at intervals to allow walkers to pass through (especially where no nearby alternative route exists), but in some cases access may not be permitted at all. In practice, exercises seldom seriously interfere with walkers' plans, though it's still advisable to note shooting dates. Information sheets with maps *(Schiessanzeigen, avis de tir)* showing the firing ranges are displayed in local post offices and at all entry points to the area.

If you happen to come across a (possibly) unexploded shell, the obvious advice is don't touch it; inform the EMD/DMF on ☎ 155 12 00.

Below is a list of EMD/DMF information offices which can be contacted for the most current situation regarding shooting exercises within their respective regions:

Airolo ☎ 094-88 25 25 (Val Leventina, northern Ticino)

Andermatt ☎ 044-6 02 05 (Uri Canton)

Bern ☎ 031-324 25 25 (Bern Canton and the eastern Swiss Jura)

Bière ☎ 021-809 56 11 (western Lake Geneva and western Swiss Jura)

Brig ☎ 028-23 51 23 (Upper Valais)

Bure ☎ 066-65 56 55 (Jura Canton)

Chamblon ☎ 066-65 56 55 (central Swiss Jura)

Chur ☎ 081-23 35 13 (Graubünden, except for the Hinterrhein region – see below)

Fribourg ☎ 037-20 82 08 (Fribourg Canton and eastern Lake Geneva)

Glarus ☎ 058-61 57 57 (Glarus Canton)

Hinterrhein ☎ 081-62 15 85 (the valleys of the Hinterrhein Rein Anteriur) and Val Mesolcina in Graubünden)

Lucerne ☎ 041-41 20 42 (central Swiss Mittelland and Central Switzerland except for Uri Canton)

Monte Ceneri ☎ 091-95 80 97 (Ticino except for Airolo region – see above)

Petit-Hongrin ☎ 029-4 44 54 (Vaud Alps)

St Gallen ☎ 071-28 27 07 (north-eastern Switzerland except for Glarus Canton and St Galler Oberland – see above)

Sargans ☎ 081-725 11 22 (St Galler-Oberland)

St Maurice ☎ 025 65 91 11 (Lower Valais)

Sion ☎ 027-31 35 31 (Central Valais)

Zürich ☎ 01-739 32 40 (Zürich and Schaffhausen cantons)

THE WALKS

Switzerland has some 3500 individual marked trails, with a combined length of well over 50,000 km! Walking routes may follow old aqueducts, stone-laid mule tracks, pilgrim trails or even ancient Roman roads.

The walks described in this guidebook are a varied selection taken from an almost endless number of possibilities, and introduce Switzerland's most famously scenic places. Not surprisingly, they are overwhelmingly in Alpine regions, and many lead through nature reserves. Except for high-level routes that may be undertaken when snow covers paths early or late in the season, none of the walks involves the use of mountaineering skills or equipment.

Official walking routes are generally very well maintained. From time to time the path may have to be re-routed, such as when bridges are washed away or foot tracks are made impassable by flooding, landslides and avalanches. New sections of trail are constantly been laid down, particularly where a busy road forms the only walking route.

In this guidebook Switzerland's 26 cantons have been grouped into eight regional chapters. Note here that where a walking route crosses from one region into another, it appears in the regional chapter considered most appropriate – this usually means in the region from which you set out. Route descriptions generally begin and end at a train station, postbus (PTT) stop, or the upper station of a mountain railway or cableway.

The Walking Bases sections in this guidebook provide basic information on places that (may) serve as convenient bases for hikes within each region. These sections complement the information given in the description of each featured walk, but are not intended as a comprehensive list covering every regional village, town or city.

Route Markings

Paths in Switzerland are exceptionally well waymarked, with signposts at important junctions. While you may still occasionally see paint markings in 'non-standard' colours, all official walking routes are now marked in either yellow, white-red-white, or white-blue-white. Despite a fair bit of overlap,

these colour codes essentially indicate a route's altitude – lowland, Alpine or high-Alpine rather than its difficulty alone. A single walk may variously follow yellow, white-red-white or even white-blue-white marked routes in places. A further explanation follows:

Markings in yellow indicate a low-level walking route *(Wanderweg* or *sentier)*, such as those in the Swiss Mittelland, the Jura and the ranges of the Alpine foothills. Yellow route markings are metal plates along with painted diamonds and squares on rocks, trees, posts or buildings to show the way. Yellow-marked routes generally follow cut paths, alp tracks or even sealed roads, but in places they may lead cross-country over short sections of untracked farmland.

Red-white-red markings indicate that you are on a mountain route *(Bergweg* or *sentier de montagne)* that leads above the treeline. While walking at higher altitudes requires better weather conditions and calls for greater caution, white-red-white marked routes are not necessarily more strenuous than yellow-marked routes.

Markings in white-blue-white indicate high-level Alpine routes *(alpine Routen* or *itinéraires alpins)*. Such routes may traverse barren rock ridges, or cross scree slopes, snowfields and even glaciers; stone cairns sometimes replace the paint markings completely. White-blue-white marked routes are intended for experienced mountain walkers rather than roped-up mountaineers, however, and generally have fixed cables or other safety constructions to secure the most exposed sections. Few of the walks described in this guidebook follow white-blue-white marked routes, and those that do include an easier alternative.

Walking Times & Standards

The length of a walk is always measured in time rather than distance, although a comparison of the two is often helpful in gauging a route's difficulty. The walking times given in this guidebook are based on the author's own measurements, with consideration given to normal variation in walking pace – these may differ a bit with the 'official' times shown on signposts. Note that walking times never include rest stops.

The walking standards used in this guidebook rate the overall 'seriousness' of a walk, and are based on a combination of factors such as strenuousness, path condition, overall length and en-route shelter options. Bear in mind that both walking times and standards can vary considerably according to factors such as weather and snow conditions.

Walks have been graded as *easy*, *moderate* or *difficult*, as outlined below:

Easy walks can be done by virtually anyone, and a minimal level of fitness is needed. They are short in distance and follow well-marked and graded paths with gentle gradients and modest climbs or descents.

Moderate walks call for appreciably more experience and better physical condition. They are best attempted after you have completed at least several easy walks.

Difficult walks are physically demanding, and generally lead through high-Alpine terrain where some experience of mountain walking is advisable. Steep ascents and/or descents on poorly formed trails are typical hindrances, while snow may lie along parts of the route well into summer. Robust footwear and proper wet-weather clothing is utterly essential. Route markings may normally be still quite good, but walkers nevertheless require a basic level of navigational ability.

Trail Etiquette

Walking is a very casual affair, of course, but observing a few simple rules of etiquette will keep you in good stead with other walkers.

Except on very busy routes, it's considered impolite not to greet others you pass along the trail – see the language section for a few expressions. The custom on narrow paths is that ascending walkers have right of way over those going down. Always leave farm gates as you found them. In summer low-voltage electric fences are set up to control stock on the open Alpine pastures; where an electric fence crosses a path it usually has a hook that can be easily unfastened to allow walkers to pass through without getting zapped.

Taking care of the environment is more than just polite – also see the Looking after the Environment section.

Activities en Route

It goes without saying that activities such as bird and animal watching or identifying Alpine wildflowers are integral to walking in Switzerland. A few other en-route activities are introduced below.

Crystalling During their geological formation, conditions in the Alps were particularly suitable for the formation of rock crystals *(Bergkristalle, cristals de roches)* and the Swiss Alps are famous for their fine smoky quartz and amethyst types. Rock crystals were created around 18 to 20 million years ago in a prolonged process, whereby water is heated and pressurised by subterranean forces. As it seeps through rocks fissures, the water first dissolves quartz out of the rock, then gradually re-deposits it in a pure crystalline form along the sides of the rock. The largest and most perfectly formed crystal 'plates' can be worth tens of thousands of dollars, and are often on display in local museums and shop windows.

Crystal hunters *(Strahler, cristalliers)* are among Switzerland's keenest mountain-goers, with many hundreds of amateur enthusiasts and professionals, who can sometimes be spotted digging (or blasting) their way into the crystal fissures. To prospect for crystals you must have a licence issued by the local authorities in the canton concerned.

The national organisation of crystal hunters is called the Schweizerische Vereinigung der Stahler und Mineraliensammler (SVSM), (Association Suisse des Cristalliers et Collectionneurs de Minéraux (ASCM)) (☎ 032-42 36 28), Postfach 71, 2500 Biel 8 Mett. The SVSM publishes an introductory guide to crystalling (crystal-hunting in Switzerland in German and French editions titled *Mineralien sammeln* or *La Recherche de Minéraux*, as well as a dual-editions quarterly magazine titled *Schweizer Strahler* or *Le Cristallier Suisse*.

Fishing Many of Switzerland's highland lakes and rivers are continually restocked with (rainbow, brown and lake) trout. Other fish common in Swiss waters are salmon, pike, carp, and grayling. Fishing permits are required in all parts of Switzerland, and are issued by the cantonal or local authorities. The length of the fishing season, the closed season for each species, the minimum sizes and the maximum catches all vary somewhat between regions or cantons.

Hobby anglers are represented by the Schweizerischer Fischereiverband (FVB) (☎ 031-381 32 52), Postfach 8218, 3011 Bern. The *Schweizer Fischerkalendar* published annually by WEKA Verlag, Zürich, costs Sfr25 and has useful information (in German) on fishing in Switzerland. The German-language *Petri-Heil* is Switzerland's largest magazine for anglers.

Mushrooming Switzerland has many edible varieties of mushrooms such as the delicious aromatic ceps *(Boletus edulis)* and chanterelles *(Cantharellus melanoxerus)*, a small yellow forest fungi. Although the regulations differ between individual cantons, mushrooming is strictly controlled throughout Switzerland. The maximum amount of wild mushrooms you may pick anywhere is two kg per person per day, but many cantons allow no more than one kg – which is quite enough anyway. There are many closed days, and fines are imposed for infringement of bylaws.

To protect the environment and your own health, exercise discretion when mushrooming. Avoid disturbing the ground around the stem unnecessarily, and remove any earth or plant matter immediately. Several deadly toadstool species grow in Switzerland, so never pick a mushroom you can't identify – just one poisonous mushroom is often enough to contaminate the whole lot. If in any doubt whatsoever, seek the advice of the mushroom identification service *(Pilzkontrollstelle)* offered free by local councils (ask at tourist offices).

Photography The Swiss countryside is so eminently photogenic that you may find yourself taking more shots than you planned (or budgeted) for. Using a UV filter protects the camera lens from scratching, and for outdoor shots invariably gives somewhat better results. For the much harsher light conditions typically encountered in snow or on large bodies of water, a polarising filter is recommended – don't overuse the polariser, though, as it darkens the photos and sometimes gives them a bluish or greenish tinge. A roll of Kodakchrome costs around Sfr19, and Kodak Gold around Sfr8.

Swimming In the sweaty weather of midsummer, cool mountain lakes and rivers can be an irresistible place for a refreshing splash. Even lowland lakes and rivers in Switzerland are exceptionally clean by European standards, and up in the hills they are of drinking-water quality. Common sense says to check the water temperature before you take the plunge – some higher Alpine lakes stay *very* chilly throughout the hottest weeks of July and August. With its southerly climes and wild waters, Ticino is unquestionably the best place for swimming. Topless bathing is now widely accepted, but skinny dipping (ie nude bathing) is OK only in less frequented swimming spots.

Long Walks

So-called long walks are multi-day walking trips that consist of several or more shorter sections which can often be undertaken as individual day hikes. Most long walks follow a thematic route – an historical pass crossing, the circumnavigation of a major mountain massif, the traverse of a culturally interesting valley etc – and there's something rather satisfying about doing the entire walk from start to finish. A number of long walks have been created in recent years particularly to commemorate Switzerland's 700th anniversary in 1991. These include the Trekking 700 in Ticino, the Waldstätterweg around Lake Lucerne and the Stern 91/Étoile 91, a 'star' of seven main routes which lead from all parts of Switzerland to meet at the Rütli meadow on Lake Lucerne.

The Alpine Herders

The annual tradition of driving cattle up to graze on the highland pastures for the summer dates back thousands of years in the Alps. Until quite recently it was usual for many mountain families to spend several months in virtual isolation up in the mountains. Feeding on nourishing Alpine herbs and grasses, the animals produce high-quality milk. Since the milk needed to be processed quickly to avoid spoiling, the technique of cheese-making was perfected early by the Alpine Swiss.

The animals are driven up into the mountains between late May and late June – this is always a festive occasion (called *Alpenaufzug* in German). Farmers often dress up in their traditional regional costumes, play music and adorn their cows with flowers and coloured ribbons; each animal is refitted with its own large cowbell suspended from a thick leather collar. The older animals, having made the same annual journey perhaps 10 times or more, know the way and guide the herd.

Once the cattle are up on the high pastures, the Alpine herders have little rest. Despite modern technical aids their days are still very hard. The work begins around 5.30 am and continues until 9 pm, when the cowhands can finally bed down in the (often quite primitive) alp hut. Daily tasks include fetching and milking the cows, processing the milk into cheese or butter and looking after the fragile mountain pastures. As the grass is eaten down the herds are driven from meadow to meadow, grazing only for a short period on the uppermost pastures. ■

The Alpine Pass Route The 340-km Alpine Pass Route (Alpenpassroute in German, Itinéraire des Cols Alpestres in French) is Switzerland's classic long walk. The east-to-west route takes you right across the country, from Sargans near the Liechtenstein border to Montreux on Lake Geneva, crossing 16 mountain passes that introduce some of the Swiss Alps' highest and most spectacular scenery. The middle sections of the Alpine Pass Route – especially those in the Bernese Oberland's Jungfrau Region – are the most popular. With rest days and time off for bad weather, walking the entire length of the Alpine Pass Route takes around four weeks.

This guidebook covers the Alpine Pass Route in full, with each section described as a day walk in its respective chapter; Cicerone Press also publishes an English-language guidebook to the Alpine Pass Route.

The Haute Route As its French name suggests, the Haute Route goes through some of the highest – as well as the most scenic – country accessible to walkers anywhere in the Alps. Leading from the mountain centre of Chamonix in France through the Valais to Zermatt, it's better known as a classic ski-mountaineering route than a long-distance walk. The summer route differs quite a bit

from the winter one, and takes around two weeks to complete. Like the Alpine Pass Route, the Haute Route mainly involves 'pass hopping', though it demands a higher level of fitness, with very long ascents and descents on just about every section. Recommended is the guidebook *Chamonix to Zermatt – the Walker's Haute Route* by Kev Renyolds (Cicerone Press).

The Jura High Route The approximately 180-km Jura High Route (Chemin des Crêtes du Jura in French, Jurahöhenweg in German) runs from Geneva to Basel via the often highest ridgetops of the Swiss Jura. The route has its own special marking of yellow-red diamonds, and takes around 10 days to complete.

Again, Cicerone Press has published a guidebook, *The Jura High Route*, covering this long walk.

Tour Wildstrubel The Tour Wildstrubel circumnavigates the Wildstrubel massif on the Bern/Valais cantonal border. The route leads from Kandersteg via Adelboden, Lenk, Crans-Montana and Leukerbad; the sections in the Bernese Oberland correspond to those of the Alpine Pass Route.

Monte Rosa Circuit Leading right around Switzerland's loftiest mountain massif, Monte Rosa, the 160-km Monte Rosa Circuit is a newly established international long walk. The route goes via Zermatt; Grächen; Saas Fee; and the Italian towns of Macugnagna, Gressoney and St-Jacques, and takes around 10 days. There are some quite demanding sections, and even a pass crossing where walkers inexperienced in glacier travel will require the services of a qualified mountain guide.

Kümmerly + Frey has produced a special 1:50,000 walking map, *Tour Monte Rosa*, with multilingual notes (including English) on the reverse side.

The Tour des Combins This is an eight to 10-day international circuit hike leading around the ice-encrusted 4000-metre peaks of the Grand Combins massif in the Lower Valais. Traditionally, the village of Verbier is the start of the walk. The route leads up through the Val de Bagnes over the Fenêtre de Durand to Barasson into the Val Pelline in Italy. From here it returns into Swiss territory via St-Rhémy and the Col du Grand St-Bernard, and follows the Val d'Entremont back to Verbier.

The Tour du Mont Blanc The Tour du Mont Blanc is a five or six-day walk circumnavigating the mighty Mont Blanc massif, which boasts the highest mountains and most glaciated scenery in Europe. Most of the walking route leads through Italy and France, with only about 1½ days spent on the Swiss side of the frontier.

The Grosser Walserweg For centuries Germanic Walsers migrated from Goms, venturing often far beyond their Valaisan homeland to settle formerly untouched highland valleys. The Grosser Walserweg (or 'Great Walser Trail') starts in Zermatt and stretches as far as Tirol in Austria, leading through valleys and over passes in northern Italy, Ticino, Graubünden and Liechtenstein, thus linking all important valleys and villages first settled by Walsers.

Side branches and route alternatives make it hard to state the exact length, so – depending on which way you go – this long walk might take four weeks or more of solid hiking to complete. A few walks featured in this guidebook coincide with sections of the Grosser Walserweg. For further interest, see the guidebook *Der Grosse Walserweg* (Beneteli Verlag, Bern, 1991), with multilingual text in German, French, Italian and English.

The Trekking 700 This is another of the long routes established to commemorate Switzerland's 700th anniversary. The Trekking 700 starts off from the village of Mesocco, in Graubünden's Italian-speaking Valle Mesolcina, and leads east-to-west across northern Ticino via the towns of Biasca, Sonogno and Fontana to terminate in the Val Formazza (Pomatal) in Italy. This week-long pass-hopping tour gives hikers some of the very best walking that the southern Swiss Alps have to offer.

ACCOMMODATION

In most parts of Switzerland walkers will find a wide choice of accommodation options. Tourist offices always have current lists of accommodation in all price brackets; sometimes a small booking fee and/or a deposit on the price of the room is charged. Except in the case of the most basic mattress-room accommodation (such as in mountain huts), breakfast is invariably included in the price. Lower-budget places normally give the standard 'continental' breakfast consisting of bread and jam with a pot of coffee or tea, but more up-market hotels generally offer a breakfast buffet. In most towns and villages a low, middle and high-season rate applies. Rates at budget hotels scarcely vary, but in better hotels the seasonal price variation is generally at least 20%.

Organised Camping

Organised camping grounds offer the cheapest and arguably the best value in places to stay. Camping grounds are often sited along a riverside or by a lake, and amenities are generally excellent; most have a pay laundry – otherwise difficult to find even in larger towns – and some offer basic cooking facilities. Tent sites cost from Sfr3 per night, with an additional charge of around Sfr5 per adult camper. Most camping grounds also have on-site caravans (trailers) costing around Sfr20 per night, and some offer dormitory accommodation (from around Sfr12).

Wild Camping

Although at times you may spy walkers making a sly camp in some forest clearing or beside an Alpine lake, camping outside organised camping grounds – so-called 'wild' camping – is officially prohibited in Switzerland. In practice this rule is not strictly enforced provided wild campers are discreet and leave the site as they found it. Those camping off-limits should at least observe the following basic rules:

Exercise great circumspection when choosing a camp site; keep well away from official walking routes, farmhouses or mountain huts, and if possible ask permission first before pitching the tent.

Don't light a campfire except at established fireplaces.

To spare the fragile mountain vegetation, don't camp longer than one night at any one place.

Practise hygiene: defecate well away from lakes and streams and dispose properly of your bodily wastes.

Leave the site just as you found it – take all your rubbish with you.

Alp Huts

The most basic places to stay in the mountains are the 'alp huts' – the simple dwellings of the Alpine herders (and their families) who spend their summers high up in the Alps. On the more popular routes alp hut owners often cater to walkers passing by, and supplement their normal income by offering simple meals and refreshments. Many alp huts have milk and cheese for sale, and at some you can even sleep in the straw for as little as Sfr4 per night. Conditions in alp huts can be very spartan, however, with a rustically pungent cowshed often serving as the communal sleeping quarters and a spring-water fountain providing the only place for

that icy-cold wash. Alp huts give walkers a real taste (and smell) of what life in the high mountains is all about.

Mountain Huts

Although there are still a few minor gaps in the national network, Switzerland probably has the most extensive and best maintained system of mountain huts *(Berghütten, cabanes de montagne, capanni di montagne)* anywhere in the world. Most of these huts are owned by the Swiss Alpine Club (SAC) or some other mountain club (see Useful Organisations above).

Simple dormitories or 'mattress rooms' *(Massenlager, dortoirs, dormitori)* are the standard sleeping arrangement in all mountain huts, although occasionally rooms are also available. Huts always supply plenty of woollen blankets, so carrying a sleeping bag is unnecessary, though for reasons of hygiene walkers are expected to bring their own 'youth-hostel'-type sleeping sheet. Most mountain huts in Switzerland – with the partial exception of Ticino – do not have a kitchen for the use of guests, although cooked meals are then available at fairly reasonable prices. An evening meal – simple dishes like stew, cheese fondue or *Rösti* are cooks' favourites – generally costs around Sfr15, and breakfast about Sfr10 per person. Few mountain huts have showers, but there are usually basic facilities for (cold-water) washing. Snack foods, softdrinks, beer and wine are on sale in virtually all huts, even when they are unstaffed.

Overnighting fees vary quite a bit depending on hut ownership, remoteness, and facilities. SAC members and members of mountain clubs with reciprocal rights pay a much lower rate when staying at SAC huts. Rates range from Sfr10 to Sfr14 for adult club members (or members of another mountain club with full reciprocal rights) to Sfr14 to Sfr26 for non-members. Children usually pay half the adult rate, but the definition of 'child' varies from under 12 to 16 years of age. Additional fees are payable if you use the hut's fuel (gas or wood) for cooking or heating. Fees can be paid to the resident warden, or dropped into the hut's honesty box in a special envelope provided. You can also bank the fee directly into the hut's own postcheque account (at any post office in Switzerland) using one of the special green deposit slips that you'll surely find in the hut. Remember this is an honesty system that relies on your goodwill – don't 'forget' to pay.

Unfortunately, none of the mountain clubs in English-speaking countries enjoy reciprocal rights with the SACs, but those that do are as follows: the Deutscher Alpenverein, the Club Alpin Francais, the Club Alpino Italiano, the Federación Española de Montañismo, the Club Alpin Belgique, the Österreichischer Alpen Club and the Österreichischer Alpenverein.

Most huts are staffed only during the warmer months; when the Swiss flag and/or the local cantonal flag is flying it means the resident warden is present. Club-owned huts are always left unlocked, with access to at least the main dining room and a dormitory. Even in summer it's relatively uncommon to find a hut completely full, though it certainly does happen from time to time (such as when school groups or guided mountaineering tours pass through). In such circumstances you probably won't be turned away, but if things are really tight you may have to sleep on the floor. In July, August or September, walking parties of three people or more are advised to reserve a berth.

Finally, please observe the following basic rules when staying at mountain huts:

Contact the warden as soon as you arrive. If there is no warden present, register your name in the logbook immediately – otherwise you may be suspected of trying to avoid payment.

Boots are not to be worn in the dormitories – leave them in the vestibule by the entrance. Most huts provide slippers to wear inside.

Be careful with fire – don't take burning candles into the dormitories.

Smoking is prohibited inside the huts.

Be very quiet in the dormitories – walkers and mountain climbers often go to bed very early to ensure an early start.

Mountain Hotels & Restaurants

In popular walking areas mountain hotels and restaurants also offer accommodation for walkers. Mountain hotels and restaurants are often situated at the upper station of a cableway, funicular or cog railway, and not infrequently offer exceptionally good value in rooms and/or dormitories. Hot showers – something walkers greatly appreciate after a sweaty day's hiking – are usually available, sometimes for an additional fee. The average price per person for a room (including a continental breakfast with freshly brewed coffee) is around Sfr40, and for a bed in the dormitory Sfr25 (also with breakfast). Because these places often cater mainly for winter tourists, getting a bed at mountain hotels and restaurants is seldom a problem.

Youth Hostels

The Swiss Youth Hostel Association runs almost 80 youth hostels in cities, towns and villages throughout the country. Although some regions – most notably Ticino – are rather poorly covered, youth hostels often make ideal bases for walks within a region.

Youth hostels offer accommodation mainly in small dormitories, but increasingly hostellers have a choice of paying a bit more for their own (double or family) room. Less than half of the youth hostels in Switzerland have cooking facilities for hostellers. Note that some youth hostels cater mainly to groups and may be booked out at various times. Reception is usually closed between 9 am and 5 pm, and priority is given to hostellers under 25 years of age. Overnighting fees vary considerably, but the average charge is around Sfr24 including breakfast; most offer a 10% discount on each additional night you stay.

For more information on the Swiss Youth Hostel Association see Useful Organisations.

Friends of Nature Hostels

The Swiss Friends of Nature (Naturfreunde Schweiz, Amis de la Nature Suisse) runs some 100 hostels throughout the country. Each hostel (known as Naturfreundehaus in

German or Maison des Amis de la Nature in French) is located in a mountain region or close to a nature reserve. Prices and conditions are similar to those of Swiss youth hostels. The hostels are open to everyone, although members receive a large discount. For more information on the Swiss Friends of Nature see Useful Organisations above.

Private Rooms

Similar to English bed-and-breakfast establishments, places offering private rooms are most easily found through the local tourist office. They normally only have a small number of beds costing around Sfr40 per person per night – comparable in price to budget hotels.

Hotels & Pensions

In valley towns and villages, hotels and pensions are the main form of accommodation. Prices vary considerably depending on the region or time of year, but the rate for a simple room with washbasin and external shower and toilet typically start at around Sfr35 or Sfr40. Breakfast is usually served from around 7 am, but walkers keen to make that 'Alpine start' can usually arrange for an earlier sitting.

Holiday Apartments

Self-contained holiday apartments can be found in and around just about every tourist resort in the country. Apartment accommodation is probably best suited to families or walking groups who need a walking base for a week or two. (Since this book features walks in all parts of Switzerland, however, the assumption is that readers will not want to tie themselves to one particular place.) Tourist offices always have listings of locally available holiday apartments.

FOOD

Cheese and potatoes form the basis of many traditional Swiss dishes. These tend to be simple to prepare and are therefore often standard on the menu in mountain huts and restaurants.

To all Swiss, cheese *fondue* is the classic winter dish. To make fondue, Gruyères and other cheeses, like Emmentaler, are slowly melted into a mixture of white wine, kirsch (cherry brandy) and garlic. Cubes of chopped bread are dipped on long forks into this aromatic, bubbling brew – truly food of the gods. Fondue is cold-weather fare, and the Swiss themselves seldom eat it between June and September – except in the mountain huts and restaurants, that is, where fondue is a kind of Alpinists' staple.

Originally a typical dish of Valaisan herders who toasted their own cheeses over an open campfire, *raclette* is now second only to fondue in the (cholesterol-choked) hearts of the Swiss. Raclette's main attraction seems to be that it keeps everyone contentedly busy laying slices of well-seasoned cheese on a tiny tray, garnishing it with pickles and other spices, then sliding the whole lot under a special griller where it melts into a delicious messy mass.

Rösti is made from grated potatoes, which are pan-fried with butter, bacon or – yet again! – cheese to form a cohesive crisply browned cake. Rösti is such a symbol of German-Swiss cuisine, that the language barrier which supposedly divides the German-speaking rösti-eaters from their French-speaking compatriots is known colloquially as the 'Rösti Trench'. Nonetheless, this simple and tasty dish is enjoyed by people on both sides of the country.

A dish typical for Switzerland's Italian-speaking regions, *polenta* invariably has a place on the menu in Ticino's *grotti* – small restaurants set in a garden surroundings. Polenta is made from coarsely ground maize meal, which – at least according tradition – is slowly boiled in a large cauldron over a small fire. The yellow, porridge-like mixture has to bubble away for several hours before it's ready to serve with white wine, mushrooms, garlic and parmesan cheese.

Trail Food

Many of the walks described in this guidebook pass by mountain restaurants, which serve simple meals and refreshments. When staffed, most – but by no means all – mountain huts prepare hot evening meals; cut lunches can also be ordered and snack foods are available for the day's walk (see also Mountain Huts above). Many en-route farms and alp huts sell milk and cheese.

For economy, greater variety and safety, however, it's essential to carry some of your own food on all walks. The kind of trail food and how much of it you bring will depend on the walk's length, but some tried-and-true favourites include:

fruit – fresh and dried
mixed nuts
cheese – try local Emmentaler, Gruyères and (smelly) Appenzell types
Bündnerfleisch (or *pulpa* in Romansch) – smoked, air-dried beef that originates from Graubünden
wholemeal bread – great variety available in supermarkets, including organic loaves
Müesli – that nourishing mix of breakfast cereals originally invented (though not perfected) by the Swiss
chocolate – Swiss chocolate is smooth on the palate, easy on the wallet, but hard on the waistline
Gly-Coramin – a kind of chewy sweet (sold without prescription in pharmacies) that Swiss walkers often eat on long strenuous hikes. Apart from glucose, Gly-Coramin contains Nicethamid, a mild stimulant that promotes breathing and increases the body's uptake of oxygen. The Bolivians have their coca leaves, the Swiss have their Gly-Coramin.

LOOKING AFTER THE ENVIRONMENT

The Swiss are particularly environmentally conscious, and walkers should aim to follow their example by heeding these cardinal rules of conduct in the mountains.

All rubbish, including cigarette butts, sweet wrappers and tampons, should be carried out in your pack – not dumped, buried or hidden under some rock.

Don't pick Alpine wildflowers – they really do look lovelier on the mountainsides. Animal watchers should approach wildlife with discretion. Moving too close will unnerve wild animals, distracting them from their vital summer activity of putting on fat for the long Alpine winter.

Always keep to the marked path, and don't short-cut corners. Mountain farmers will be grateful if you refrain from stepping off paths that lead across Alpine fields and meadows.

Be thoughtful regarding where and how you dispose of your bodily wastes. Use proper toilets where they are available (such as at mountain huts and restaurants), otherwise go well away from the path and bury your scat properly.

Many people take pet dogs with them on walks. Dogs must be kept on a leash where the path leads through forest (which provide natural shelter for wildlife during the day), past farmland with newly born lambs or calves or into nature reserves. Note that dogs are not allowed at all in the Swiss National Park and some nature reserves.

Take special care with fire – only light fires in established fireplaces. Walkers who camp out in the mountains should read the notes under Wild Camping above.

Getting There & Away

Particularly for long-distance air travellers en route to Switzerland, it may well work out cheaper and/or more convenient to fly into a major European city like Frankfurt or Milan, then take a connecting flight or a train.

AIR

Switzerland's two main international airports are at Zürich and Geneva. Bern and Lugano airports also take some international flights. The nearby French city of Mulhouse serves as the international airport for the Basel region.

These days so many cut-price or discount deals are available, that few travellers end up paying the full fare on their air ticket. Official cut-price (advance-purchase, Apex, or off-peak) tickets can be purchased directly from the airline or its agent; airlines offer various other discounts to passengers who qualify for a youth, student or senior citizen reduction. Unofficial cut-price air tickets can be bought from a travel agent (which orders tickets in bulk and can therefore offer heavy discounts with a lower profit margin).

Return tickets usually work out substantially cheaper than two one-ways. So-called 'open jaw' returns, by which you can travel into one city and out of another, save you having to backtrack to your point of entry. Round-the-World (RTW) tickets may sometimes work out cheaper than an ordinary return ticket.

Note that fares quoted in this book should be used as a guide only, as they are subject to change.

To/From the UK

London is one of the world's major centres for discounted fares. You should be able to find a flight that beats the equivalent fare by rail.

One of the best and biggest sellers of discount air tickets in London is Trailfinders (☎ 0171-938 3999) at 194 Kensington High St, London W8. Other large competitors include STA (☎ 0171-937 9962) at 74 Old Brompton Rd, London SW7, and Campus Travel (☎ 0171-938 2188), 174 Kensington High St, London W8. Recommended for cheaper flights to Switzerland is Bluewheel Limited (☎ 0181-202 0111), 417 Hendon Way, London, NW4 3LH. Also look for ads in *Time Out*, the *Evening Standard* and *Exchange & Mart*, or free magazines and newspapers like *TNT*, *Southern Cross* and *Trailfinder*.

Depending on when you travel, you should be able to pick up a cut-price return air ticket – say, London/Geneva or Manchester/Zürich – for little more than £100. Charters are often very cheap (around £70 return), but these flights are intended for short visits and don't give you long (maximum two weeks) in Switzerland.

The aggressively competitive discount carrier British Midland has recently entered the London/Zürich route which should push down airfares considerably.

To/From Continental Europe

Athens is a good centre for cheap fares; shop around the travel agents in the backstreets between Syntagma and Omonia squares. Amsterdam is another recognised centre for cheap tickets: try Budget Air (☎ 020-627 12 51), ICL Reizen (☎ 020-620 51 21), Malibu Travel (☎ (020-623 68 14), or the student agency, NBBS (☎ 020-624 09 89).

STA outlets in important transport hubs include: Voyages et Découvertes (☎ 1-42 61 00 01), 21 Rue Cambon, Paris; SRID Reisen (☎ 069-43 01 91), Berger Strasse 118, Frankfurt; and ISYTS (☎ 01-32 21 267), 2nd Floor, 11 Nikis St, Syntagma Square, Athens.

To/From the USA

Numerous airlines have trans-Atlantic flights. Some of the larger agents selling

84

cut-price tickets are STA, Council Travel and Access International. The *New York Times*, the *LA Times*, the *Chicago Tribune* and the *San Francisco Chronicle Examiner* have travel sections advertising cheap flights. It's unlikely you'll pay more than around US$600 for your air ticket even for high-season travel.

To/From Canada

Travel CUTS has offices in all major cities. Scan the budget travel agents' ads in the *Toronto Globe & Mail*, the *Toronto Star* and the *Vancouver Province*. Swissair flies daily except Monday and Tuesday from Toronto and Montreal to Zürich.

To/From Australia & New Zealand

No airline flies direct into Switzerland from Australia or New Zealand. STA and Flight Centres International are major dealers in cheap air fares. Round-the-World (RTW) tickets cost as little as A$1800, and may work out cheaper than an ordinary return ticket.

Travel sections of Saturday newspapers in the capital cities have advertisements for cheap fares. Return fares to Europe on mainstream airlines cost between A$1600 (low season) and A$2500 (high season). Flights to/from Perth are a couple of hundred dollars cheaper.

From New Zealand the lowest airfares to Europe are often routed via North America.

To/From Hong Kong

Hong Kong is the discount air-ticket capital of Asia, and its bucket shops are at least as unreliable as those of other cities. Ask the advice of other travellers before buying a ticket. Many of the cheapest fares from South-East Asia to Europe are offered by Eastern European carriers. STA is one of Hong Kong's largest sellers of discount tickets.

TRAIN

Given the time taken up in getting to and from an airport (not be mention customs and baggage delays), the *real* travel time by (fast) train often turns out to be insignificantly longer than by plane. Unfortunately, rail is not as competitive against air travel as it ought to be – the return fare from London to Zürich is around £130.

Switzerland can be reached by direct international trains from Amsterdam, Hamburg, Milan, Munich, Paris, Rome and Vienna. Its leading cities are accessible by Europe's high-tech ultra-rapid trains. French TGV trains run from Paris to Lausanne and Geneva. Italian Pendolino tilt-trains run from Milan and/or Rome to Zürich, Geneva and Basel (via Bern). German ICE trains connect Berlin and Hamburg with Zürich (via Basel). New express 'hotel trains' run nightly in either direction between Zürich and Hamburg.

European Rail Passes

Eurail Passes can only be bought by residents of non-European countries, and are valid for unlimited rail travel on national (and certain private) railways in all western European countries *except* Britain. Inter-Rail passes (limited to travellers under 26 years) allow unlimited travel similar to Eurail passes but also cover most central European countries.

For people primarily interested in walking in Switzerland, however, European railpasses are unlikely to work out cheaper than buying a normal train ticket to Switzerland then using a national railpass (see the Getting Around chapter).

CAR & MOTORBIKE

Switzerland is connected to its European neighbours by modern motorways. An important tunnel if approaching from the south is the Grand St-Bernard between Aosta (Italy) and Bourg St-Pierre.

The minor roads are more fun and scenically more interesting but special care is needed when negotiating mountain passes. Some, such as the N5 (E21) route from Champagnole (in France) to Geneva are not recommended if you have not had previous experience of driving in the mountains.

All vehicles driving on motorways in

Switzerland must display a special sticker (known as a *vignette*) on the windscreen. It costs Sfr30 per calendar year, and fines are imposed on drivers caught using the motorways without a current vignette.

Vehicles registered abroad can be driven within Switzerland for up to 12 months. Foreign driving licences are also valid for a period of one year, but you may find it useful to obtain an International Driving Permit from your motoring organisation. The Green Card, the international third-party insurance certificate, is not compulsory in Switzerland as long as you already have third-party insurance. If you intend driving across Europe to Switzerland it's a good idea to get a Green Card (issued by your vehicle insurer) before leaving.

HITCHING

Seasoned hitchers will usually confirm that pairs of either two women or a man and woman make the safest and most successful combination for getting lifts. A woman hitching on her own is taking a risk. Organised 'hitching agencies', such as Allostop-Provoya in France and Germany's Mitfahrzentrale, can usually arrange a ride with someone going your way – but they charge a fee, including your share of the driver's petrol (gasoline) costs.

Don't waste time hitching out of urban areas: take public transport to the main city exit route. In all countries it's illegal to hitchhike on motorways or their entry/exit roads, but service stations can be very good places to pick up a ride. Look presentable and cheerful, and make a cardboard sign indicating your intended destination in the local language. Never hitch where drivers can't stop in good time or without causing an obstruction.

Although many travellers hitchhike, it's not a totally safe way of getting around. How and where to hitchhike is discussed in this book but it isn't necessarily recommended.

Getting Around

Switzerland has a difficult topography for road and railway construction. Mountain routes invariably take a long winding course with repeated sections of tunnel, so travel times are often much longer than they look on the map. A journey by train from the Lower Engadine to the Lower Valais would take you all day.

Virtually all walks included in this book are accessible by public transport, which is the most environmentally friendly way of getting around. Standard rail and bus fares are very expensive in Switzerland, but numerous special tickets and passes are available which reduce public transport costs dramatically.

All train, bus, ferry and mountain cableway routes are numerically coded, and appear in that numerical order in public transport timetables.

TRAIN

The Swiss Federal Railways (whose German/French initials are SBB/CFF) form the backbone of the national transport system. Switzerland also has some 65 privately owned railways – more than any other country in Europe – which are well integrated into the national network. Virtually all Swiss trains have separate 2nd and 1st-class sections and most have smoking and non-smoking compartments.

Switzerland's two busiest and most important rail lines are the Zürich-Lugano line – the so-called 'Gotthard' railway – and the Geneva-St Gallen line crossing the Swiss Mittelland via Fribourg, Bern and Zürich. On both lines fast, direct Intercity trains run in either direction at hourly intervals. Other major rail lines include the Bern-Brig-Domodossola – the so-called 'Lötschberg/Simplon' railway – and the Lausanne-Brig and the Zürich-Chur lines. The flagship of Switzerland's tourist trains is the famous *Glacier Express*, which takes 7½ hours to run the scenic route between St Moritz and

Zermatt, giving a continually changing Alpine panorama.

Travel Information

There is often more than one viable public-transport route for getting to and from your walk. Especially where several train and/or bus connections are involved, travelling via a longer route may actually work out faster – though probably more expensive if you don't have a pass. Station staff, even at out-of-the-way train stations, speak English and have computers that quickly calculate the best train and bus connections to/from anywhere in the country; print-outs show your departure and arrival times.

For railway information anywhere within Switzerland call ☎ 157 33 33.

Train Tickets

Children between six and 16 years of age travel at half-price; with a Family Card (available without charge from Switzerland Tourism offices abroad or for Sfr20 within the country) all children under 16 years accompanied by at least one parent travel free. All train tickets allow you to break your journey, but advise the conductor before your ticket is punched.

Small stations in the most out-of-the-way places are often staffed sporadically, but standard tickets can usually be purchased from the conductor on the train. However, an increasing number of regional lines (especially those of smaller, privately owned railways) now operate on a 'self-control' basis without a regular conductor. Whenever this system applies, passengers must have a valid ticket *before* boarding the train, or risk paying a fine of Sfr50. On self-control train services a yellow 'eye' pictogram is displayed prominently inside and/or outside each carriage.

Walkers may want to send their luggage ahead to the town or village at the end of the walk. If you have a rail pass or a valid ticket (such as a circuit ticket) from the place you are sending your luggage you will usually only be charged a flat charge of Sfr10 for this service.

Half Fare Card The Half Fare Card costs Sfr85 for one month or Sfr150 for a full year. It allows you to purchase half-price tickets for all trains, postbuses, ferries, suburban trams and buses as well as many forms of mountain transport (see below).

Single Tickets Single train tickets for distances over 87 km are valid for two days.

Return tickets Return tickets give a discount of 20% compared to the price of two singles. Return tickets are only valid for two days unless the overall distance exceeds 87 km, in which case they are valid for one month. A 2nd-class return ticket from Zürich airport to Interlaken costs Sfr102 (or Sfr51 with the Half Fare Card).

Circuit Tickets A circuit ticket *(Rundfahrt-Billet* or *billet circular)* also brings a 20% discount. Circuit tickets allow you to travel via a circuitous route, stopping at numerous places before returning to your starting point, so walkers may find them a cheaper alternative to rail passes. Postbuses, ferries and most forms of mountain transport (see below) can be included on your ticket. As long as you complete the journey within one month, your itinerary can be as long or as complicated as you like.

Swiss Card The Swiss Card is valid for one month and allows you travel to and from the Swiss border (or airport) and during your stay it serves as a Half Fare Card (see above). It costs Sfr130 (2nd class) or Sfr160 (1st class).

GENERAL PASSES
General passes are especially worthwhile if you intend travelling around the country a fair bit rather than basing yourself somewhere during your walking holiday. Note that on some important private railways –

most notably the Furka-Oberalp-Bahn (FOB) between Brig and Disentis or the Brig-Visp-Zermatt (BVZ) railway in the Valais – SBB/CFF and European rail passes are not valid, although they will get a 50% fare reduction.

Day Pass
Standard day tickets are only worthwhile if you intend travelling virtually to one end of the country and back again within a single day (which leaves little opportunity for walking). From time to time, however, the SBB/CFF offers special day-ticket deals, typically in the months of May and November or on summer Sundays; these give very good value indeed, and are worth looking out for. Recent short-term SBB/CFF deals have included a Sfr15 day pass allowing unlimited travel on all slower regional trains, and a Sfr20 day ticket valid for all trains (apart from a few private lines) after 9 am.

Swiss Pass
The Swiss Pass gives unrestricted travel by rail, postbus and ferry within a period of up to one month. It also gets you major reductions on many forms of mountain transport.

Swiss Flexi Pass
The Swiss Flexi Pass gives you three days of unlimited travel by rail, postbus and ferry within a 15-day period. The Swiss Flexi Pass otherwise offers the same reductions as the Swiss Pass.

Regional Passes
For walkers who prefer to base themselves within one region, regional passes are often a cost-saving alternative. They can be purchased in major cities and the respective regional train stations.

Most regional passes are valid for a 15-day and/or a seven-day period. They generally give a number of days of unlimited travel, plus other days of travel at half-price within the period and region of validity. Holders of the Swiss Card, Swiss Pass or the Half Fare Card can buy the regional passes for a considerable reduction. Regional passes are normally only on offer during the summer season (from the start of May until the end of October).

A regional pass generally covers all regional mountain transport, although it may only get you a 50% or a 25% reduction on some postbus, cable-car, chair lift, funicular and cog-railway services. Synoptic maplets clearly indicate the services that allow unlimited travel and those that only offer a fare reduction.

The regional passes available in Switzerland are listed below.

Berner Oberland Only a 15-day regional pass is available, which costs Sfr175 (Sfr140 concession). It fully covers all regional rail lines, lake ferries as well as most postbuses and most mountain transport in the Bernese Oberland. The pass gives free travel on the Niederhorn, Brienzer Rothorn, Niesen, Schynige Platte, First and Grosse Scheidegg services, but only a 25% reduction on Stockhorn cable car, the Hahnenmoospass chair lifts and the Jungfraujoch railway. The 50% reduction also applies on certain connecting postbus and rail lines that run well outside the Bernese Oberland (including services to Bern, Montreux and Brig).

Lake Lucerne Known as the Tell-Pass, this regional pass costs Sfr160 (Sfr128 concession) for 15 days or Sfr116 (Sfr58 concession) for a seven-day period. The Tell-Pass gives unlimited travel for five days (or two days), plus 10 days (or five days) of travel at half-price on the Lake Lucerne ferries, and many – but not all – railway services around the shore; it includes the Jochpass lifts as well as the Pilatus and (both) Rigi cog railways. On other postbus and rail services within a broader area of southern Central Switzerland it costs half-price.

Montreux This is a seven-day pass costing Sfr77 (Sfr61 concession) that allows three days' unlimited travel and four days' travel at 50% reduction on ferries on eastern Lake Geneva and regional railways as far as Lausanne, Bulle and Lenk, including the

(MOB) Rochers de Naye and Les Pléides cog railways. A 50% reduction applies on certain peripheral ferry and postbus services; and a 25% reduction on the Moléson, La Braye, Videmanette and Glacier des Diablerets cableways.

Lower Valais & Southern Vaud This is a seven-day pass costing Sfr54 (Sfr43 concession) that allows three days' unlimited travel and four days' travel at 50% reduction within the 'Chablais' region centred around the town of Aigle. It covers train and bus services to Montreux, St-Gingolph, Champery, Leysin, Les Diablerets and Bex. Fares on postbus services to Les Plans-sur-Bex, Col des Mosses, Château d'Oex and Gstaad are half-price; the Berneuse gondola lift and several other cableways have a 25% reduction.

Fribourg A one-day regional pass called the Fri-Pass is available costing Sfr25 (or Sfr12.50 for holders of a Half Fare Card only). The Fri-Pass gives unlimited travel on Fribourg Canton's regional (GFM) rail and bus network. It also includes connecting bus services to Boltigen (Bernese Oberland) and to Vevey (on Lake Geneva). The Fri-Pass does not include chair lifts or cable cars.

Southern Ticino Two seven-day regional passes are offered in southern Ticino. These give unlimited travel either for the full period, or for three days within seven days. The zones covered by the two passes overlap considerably.

The full seven-day pass for the Locarno region costs Sfr76 or Sfr50 with three unlimited days of travel; it includes Lago Maggiore ferries as well as rail and postbuses in the Valle Maggia and Val Verzasca. There is only a 50% reduction on some postbus services, and only a 25% reduction on the Cardada/Cimetta lifts.

The full seven-day pass for the Lugano region costs Sfr92 or Sfr70 with only three free days. The pass gives unlimited travel on the Monte Lema gondola lift and ferries on Lago di Lugano. There is a 50% reduction on all other mountain transport as well as on most regional postbuses; a 25% reduction applies for the Monte Generoso cog railway.

Graubünden This regional pass is only available for a 15-day period and costs Sfr120 (Sfr100 with Half Fare Card only). It gives five days' unlimited travel, plus 10 days' travel at half-price travel on all Rhaetian Railways lines as well as the Palm Express postbus between St Moritz and Lugano in Ticino. Fares on other regional postbuses and connecting postbus and rail services to Bellinzona (in Ticino), Andermatt/Brig, and Zürich are half-price during the period of validity.

Appenzellerland/Toggenburg A regional pass to this area costs Sfr95 (Sfr75 concession) for 15 days or Sfr75 (Sfr60 concession) for a seven-day period. It gives unlimited travel on five days (or three days) on all public transport and mountain lifts within the region between Lake Constance (Bodensee) and the Walensee (Lake Walen). Outside the selected days of travel full-price fares must be paid. It includes free travel on the Säntis, Hoher Kasten, Ebenalp, Gamsalp and Chäserugg cableways.

POSTBUS

With their melodic three-note bugle horns, the yellow and red postbuses are one of the characteristic sights and sounds of the Swiss countryside. Operated by the post and telecommunications authority, or PTT, Switzerland's postbuses run some 700 different routes with a combined length of more than 8500 km – twice that of the national rail network. Since virtually every mountain valley with road access can be reached by scheduled postbus, they are an indispensable means of public transport for walkers.

Postbuses leave from train stations or (where there's no railway) the local post office, and schedules are synchronised with trains. Regional timetables are available in yellow booklets free of charge at post offices, train stations or tourist offices; all postbus routes are numbered, and are listed according to their numerical code.

For a flat rate of Sfr12 hikers can send their unaccompanied luggage ahead to any destination which has a proper post office and pick it up later – even a few days later – when they've finished the walk; bicycles can also be transported on many (but not all!) postbus routes. A surcharge (usually Sfr5) must be paid by each adult passenger on certain tourist routes (such as the Flüelapass), and prior reservation (at least one hour before travel) is necessary for some of the PTT's smaller minibus services or very popular routes – indicated by an 'R' symbol at the top of the timetable. Seats can be reserved by telephone or in person through the local train station or post office.

The Half Fare Card and other (Swiss) general and most regional passes get you the full 50% reduction. Regional postbus passes, which give unlimited travel for up to seven days on all postbus lines within areas such as the Lower Engadine or Schwyz Canton can also be quite good value.

The postbus information service, Schweizer Postautodienst/Service des Cars Postaux suisses, publishes an excellent two-part bilingual guide in German and French called *Erlebnis Postauto/Fascination Car Postal.* It gives numerous suggestions for excursions and walks using postbuses in all parts of Switzerland, and is available free of charge from Postauto Schweiz (☎ 031-386 65 65), 3030 Bern.

CAR

The use of a private vehicle to get to the start of any walk is unnecessary in Switzerland. Actually, it's not particularly environmentally considerate either, since cars are the main cause of the high levels of ozone, nitrous oxide and other pollutants regularly recorded in Alpine regions (see Conservation & the Alpine Environment in the Facts about the Country chapter) and any increase in motor traffic will worsen the problem further. In any case, cars are a less practical option for getting to and from walks given the excellent standard of public transport.

Apart from circuit routes, motorists will always be inconvenienced by having to return to their parked car. Walkers driving in Switzerland are advised to leave vehicles at the youth hostel, hotel or local train station.

Die-hard drivers should note that many smaller backroads in the Alps are strictly closed to all but authorised (forestry and agricultural) traffic, and anyone caught driving on them without a special permit is likely to be fined. To drive on motorways in Switzerland your car must have a special vignette – rental cars normally come with this annually renewable sticker.

MOUNTAIN TRANSPORT

The Swiss Alps probably have a higher concentration of mountain lifts than anywhere else in the world. At the last tally, there were no less than 283 mountain cableways, funiculars and cog railways providing direct access to Alpine resorts or panoramic peaks. (These figures don't include the vast number of small, private utility-only cableways used by mountain dwellers to transport goods to and from their isolated mountainside farmlets or the great proliferation of winter-only ski tows.)

While 'purist' walkers may find such mountain transport unsightly or superfluous, on a hot day your attitude tends to be more approving as you (and that weighty pack) are hauled up from the sweaty depths of the valley to the cool upper slopes at the start of your hike.

Most of the mountain lifts are privately owned, and this makes fares expensive with limited concessions. You'll generally pay between Sfr12 and Sfr16 for a one-way cable-car ride that carries you up 1000 or so vertical metres. Frequently, private lifts will give you some sort of reduction for your Swiss Pass or Half Fare Card, but less often for Inter-Rail and almost never for Eurail passes. Many mountain communities rely almost solely on a funicular or cable car for basic access, however, and in such cases the service is heavily subsidised and fares are only a fraction of what similar privately run services charge.

For lowlanders unfamiliar with the various 'artificial means of ascent', here is a brief explanation. A cog-railway or rack-railway *(Zahnradbahn, chemin de fer à crémaillère)* is a steeper-gradient narrow-gauge railway with a rack between the tracks into which a cogwheel grips as the train climbs or descends. The term 'cableway' can apply to several kinds of mountain lift. A funicular railway *(Standseilbahn, funiculaire, funivia)* is an inclined track on which a pair of counter-balancing cars are drawn by cables. A cable car *(Luftseilbahn, téléphérique, funivia)* is a carriage taking up to 70 passengers suspended from a – hopefully! – extremely robust cable, also with a counter-balancing twin that goes down when it goes up. A gondola lift *(Gondelbahn, télécabine)* is a continuously running cable onto which four-or six-person compartments are hitched. A chair lift *(Sesselbahn, télésiège, seggiovia)* is similar, but passengers ride on an unenclosed 'chair' secured only by a safety bar.

BICYCLE

Cycling is the next-best thing to walking, and Switzerland is one place where it's not at all difficult to combine the two activities. Although somewhat outside the scope of this guidebook, plenty of walking routes can actually be done by mountainbike (MTB). Since there is sometimes friction between walkers and mountainbikers, however, cooperation between both is called for. Mountainbikers please note that certain paths are strictly out of bounds to MTBs. Special cycling maps *(Velokarten* or *cartes cyclistes)* indicating road and MTB routes are available (from Kümmerly + Frey among other publishers) for most parts of Switzerland. Tourist offices often produce brochures detailing local (mountain)biking routes.

Larger train stations also have touring and MTB bikes for hire, which can be returned to other larger stations. Bikes can be transported on slower regional trains, and it's actually railway policy to allow cyclists to personally load their own precious two-wheeler onto the train.

HITCHING

Given the relatively high cost of public transport (along with most other things!) in Switzerland, some travellers may decided to thumb their way around. These days hitchhiking is a relatively uncommon means of travel in Switzerland – with the notable exception of Italian-speaking Ticino – but the universal rules of hitching seem to apply here. If possible choose a spot where vehicles can easily pull over, such as a roadside layby. Rides are much easier to get on less transited backroads, and especially in bad weather, drivers will often stop to offer walkers a lift. Hitchhiking is not permitted on motorways.

BOAT

Ferry boats operate on all of Switzerland's larger waterbodies, such as lakes Constance, Geneva, Lucerne, Lugano, Maggiore, and Neuchâtel and Zürich. Most ferries cater to tourists, and services are most frequent during the busy summer season from around May to late September, but a few run during the winter months. Rail passes are generally also good for travel by boat. The one-year Swiss Navigation Boat Pass costs Sfr30 and entitles the bearer to 50% off fares of all ferry services operated by SBB/CFF.

Bernese Oberland

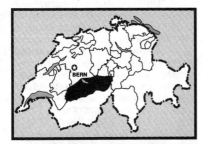

Bernese Oberland
With stunning white glaciers, soaring summits and white-water rivers, the Bernese Oberland includes walks from one to three days in duration (seven to 26 km), graded from easy to difficult. Walks include: the Stockhorn Circuit, Kleine Scheidegg (part of the Alpine Pass Route), the Chrinepass and the Wildstrubel Traverse.

Forming a 100-km-long strip extending westwards from the Col du Pillon as far as the summit of the Titlis, the German-speaking region of the Bernese Oberland (Berner Oberland) takes in almost half of the mountains along the northern edge of the Swiss Alps. Moving west to east, these southern 'uplands' of Bern Canton become progressively higher, peaking (both in terms of altitude and scenery) at the 4000-metre giants of the Jungfrau Region. Known as the Bernese Alps (Berner Alpen in German), this is the highest range anywhere within the great Alpine chain that does not form part of the main continental divide itself.

The Bernese Alps separate Bern Canton from the Valais, and apart from a small area fringing the Fribourg and Vaud Alps they are drained by direct tributaries of the Aare River. Long side valleys such as the Simmental, the Kandertal, the Lütschental and the Haslital reach southwards deep into the highest mountains. The range presents a formidable geographical and cultural barrier, with only half a dozen or so high-Alpine passes serving as crossing points between the two cantons. Although these passes have been used since prehistoric times, their altitude and steepness render them unviable for modern roadways, yet routes from the Bernese Oberland into the Valais make ideal walking tours.

With its soaring summits crowned with gleaming-white glaciers, thundering waterfalls that spill into sheer-sided glaciated valleys and white-water rivers rushing through wild gorges, the Bernese Oberland offers a 'full-spectrum Alpine experience'. The region also has plenty of rural mountain charm, with large wooden Bernese-style farmhouses and barns embellished by ornate designs or proverbs on their façades. Walkers stroll across the rich dairying pastures to the tinkling of cowbells, greeting highland farmers who still mow their mountainside meadows using traditional hand-held scythes.

Serviced by an astonishingly well-developed network of trains, postbuses, lake ferries, mountain cableways, funiculars and cog railways, probably no mountain region in the world is so easily accessible as the Bernese Oberland. With thousands of km of well-marked walking routes crisscrossing the mountains, the network of pathways is even thicker – the hiking is as splendid as it is varied.

Around the Brienzersee & Thunersee

The region surrounding the Brienzersee and Thunersee (Lake Brienz and Lake Thun) offers a wonderful variety of walking possibilities. This lovely lakeland landscape of idyllic mountain hamlets, historic castles, rich dairying country and panoramic mountaintops gives magnificent watery views from almost every vantage point. The southern slopes of the Thunersee are gentle and fertile, with orchards and vineyards thriving in the mild microclimate of the lakeshore. The Brienzersee, on the other hand, has a steeper shoreline fringed by high sunny terraces and rugged ranges.

Surrounded by mountains reaching well over 2000 metres, the Brienzersee and Thunersee mark a transition point between the much lower ranges of the Bernese Pre-Alps and the stupendously high summits of Bernese Oberland. These deep-water lakes were formed by the ancient Aaregletscher, the ices of which gouged out a deep trough within the mountainous landscape. The height of both lakes differs only slightly – being little more than 550 metres above sea level – and immediately after the Ice ages they were connected by a narrow strait. Over the following millennia, however, a broad alluvial plain gradually formed (where the city of Interlaken now stands) as enormous volumes of mountain rubble were deposited by the Lütschine River.

The region has a great deal of tourist infrastructure, with excellent rail connections and a dozen or so ferryboats that ply the lakes in summer. Mountain railways and funiculars provide effortless access to a number of popular lookout summits.

WALKING BASES
Interlaken

As suggested by its name, the small city of Interlaken is situated 'between lakes' at around 570 metres on a three-km wide alluvial plain called Bödeli that divides the Brienzersee from the Thunersee. The original town is on the northern bank of the Aare River, and has interesting old buildings including the 15th-century town hall. Interlaken's central location has made it the leading tourist centre of the Bernese Oberland, and it makes a good base for walks in the area – if you don't mind a bit of commuting. The walk around the north-eastern shore of the Thunersee to the extensive limestone

cave system of the Beatushöhlen makes worthwhile outing. A funicular goes up directly from Interlaken to Harder Kulm (1322 metres), from where a panoramic walking route follows the ridgetops high above the Brienzersee as far as the 1965-metre Blasenhubel.

Interlaken has over half a dozen camping grounds, including the *Sackgut* (☎ 036-22 44 34) by the river. The private *Balmer's Herberge* (☎ 036-22 19 61) offers cheap hostel-type dormitory accommodation and camping close to the centre of town. There's an official *youth hostel* (☎ 036-22 43 53) at nearby Bönigen on the Brienzersee. A good budget place to stay is the *Hotel Aarburg* (☎ 036-22 26 15) on the northern side of the river. Interlaken's tourist office (☎ 036-22 21 21) is at Höheweg 37.

There are two train stations, Interlaken West and Interlaken Ost. Trains run hourly between Lucerne and Interlaken-Ost (via the Brünigpass), and there are more frequent connections from Bern via Spiez. Interlaken is the changing point for the private BOB trains to Lauterbrunnen and Grindelwald.

Brienz

Brienz is the centre of the Swiss woodcarving industry and the main town on Lake Brienz. There is organised camping by the lake at the *Camping Aaregg* (☎ 036-51 18 42) and the homy *youth hostel* (☎ 036-51 11 52) is in a traditional large old wooden Bernese Oberland house. Two lower-budget places to stay are the *Löwen am See* (☎ 036-51 11 31) and the *Hotel Sternen am See* (☎ 036-51 35 45). The tourist office (☎ 036-51 32 42) is in the centre of town. Brienz is on the Interlaken-Lucerne rail line, with hourly trains in either direction. There are postbuses to Axalp and the historic steam-driven trains run from Brienz up to the Brienzer Rothorn (see Other Walks).

Spiez

The attractive town of Spiez lies about midway along the south-western shore of the Thunersee almost opposite the Justistal. There is a *youth hostel* (☎ 033-54 19 88) at the nearby village of Faulensee. The *Hotel Krone* (033-54 41 31) near the train station and the *Hotel Bären* (☎ 033-54 38 15) have rooms at rates not unreasonable for the Bernese Oberland. Spiez is an important rail junction for trains of the Montreux-Oberalp-Bahn (MOB) line. Spiez is the transit point for train travellers to/from Bern, Interlaken, Brig (in the Valais) and the Fribourg and Vaud Alps in western Switzerland (via Zweisimmen). Of course Spiez can be reached by the Thunersee lake ferries from Interlaken or Thun.

Thun

The small historic city of Thun is at the northern end of the Thunersee where the Aare flows out of the lake. Thun has an attractive old quarter dominated by the medieval castle on a prominent outcrop. A recommended budget place to stay is the *Hotel Bio Pic* (☎ 033-22 99 52) at Bälliz 54. The tourist office is in the train station (☎ 033-22 23 40). In summer lake ferries run regularly around the lake, stopping at Spiez, Beatenbuch and Interlaken.

THE JUSTISTAL

Rail passengers travelling around the southern shore of the Thunersee are often struck by the interesting geological form of the Justistal. Like a miniature Alpine valley with perfect 'textbook' proportions, the Justistal descends from a remarkable horseshoe-shaped pass between two parallel ranges that reach up to 2000 metres. The steep-sided mountains surrounding the Justistal nurture small colonies of ibex and chamois, while the grassy valley basin is given over to dairy farming. Each September the so-called Kästeilet takes place, when the season's cheese produce is ceremonially distributed to the sharefarmers in the valley.

This most rewarding circuit walk takes you from the Niederhorn, another of the Bernese Oberland's great lookout points, and follows the ridgeline forming the Justistal's eastern rim before descending via the narrow trough of the valley floor.

Maps

Walkers have a choice of either of the following walking maps: the SAW/FSTP sheet *Interlaken (254 T)* or Schaad + Frey's *Wanderkarte Thuner-und Brienzersee*, both at a scale of 1:50,000. Kümmerly + Frey's special 'Holiday Map' titled *Thunersee* scaled at 1:33,333 also covers the Justistal.

Walking Times & Standard

This is a medium-length day walk. The use of mountain transport obviates making the exhausting climb up to the Niederhorn on foot. The path is as well signposted and waymarked as any popular walking route in Switzerland. Note that there is no running water on the Güggisgrat ridge on the first part of the walk, so in hot weather carry some liquid refreshment.

The Justistal walk is rated *easy*, and covers 16 km.

Places to Stay

At Beatenberg, there is a *Friends of Nature hostel* (☎ 033-43 42 91 or 036-41 11 18). The *Hotel Beatus* (☎ 036-41 15 28) and the *Hotel Waldegg* offer rooms at prices not unreasonable for the region. Most recommended is the *Berghaus Niederhorn* (☎ 036-41 11 97, open from June to October) near the upper chair-lift station at 1932 metres which has rooms and dormitory accommodation.

For accommodation suggestions in Thun, Spiez and Interlaken see Walking Bases.

Getting to/from the Walk

The start of the hike is the upper station of the Beatenberg-Niederhorn chair lift (1932 metres), which operates daily at least until around 5 pm from the end of May to the end of October. The lower chair-lift station at Beatenberg can be reached directly by hourly postbus from Interlaken West train station. You can also catch one of the Thunersee ferries or the frequent postbuses which run along the northern shore of the lake (between Interlaken and Thun) to Beatenbucht. From Beatenbucht the old funicular railway built in 1889 travels up to

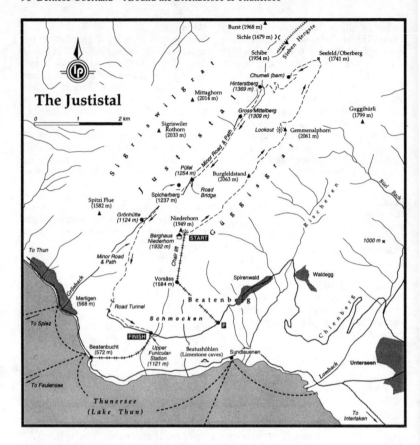

The Justistal

Schmocken/Beatenberg at approximately half-hourly intervals between the end of May and mid-November (with a reduced service until mid-December). From the upper funicular station it's 15 to 20 minutes' walk to the lower chair-lift station. Postbuses run all year round and are synchronised with the funicular service. Boats on the Thunersee only operate from the end of May until the last Sunday in October. Integrated tickets that included the postbus, boat, funicular and chair lift are available; the standard concessions apply.

The walk finishes either at the upper funicular station or the lower chair-lift station, from where the same postbus/cablecar/ferry options apply. The last bus to Interlaken West leaves Beatenberg some time before 8 pm.

Private vehicles are best left at the car park near the lower chair-lift station.

Route Directions: Niederhorn to Beatenberg (via the Justistal)

(16 km, 4½ to 5½ hours)

Up on the slopes below the telecommunications tower on the **Niederhorn** (1949 metres) you get the first spectacular views across

Top: Nowhere else in the Alps do glaciers descend as far down into the valley as at Oberer Grindelwaldgletscher.

Bottom: The Rosenlaui Gletscherschlucht is accessible only via an amazing walkway that leads past thundering waterfalls and churning whirlpools.

CLEM LINDENMAYER

CLEM LINDENMAYER

CLEM LINDENMAYER

CLEM LINDENMAYER

Top:	The Bachsee set against the peaks of the Wetterhorn and the Schreckhorn.
Middle Left:	A walker ventures high up in the Upper Simmental.
Middle Right:	The ornate wooden architecture of the Bernese Oberland.
Bottom:	For centuries the Gemmipass was the most-transited summer crossing route between the Bernese Oberland and the Valais.

Interlaken and the Thunersee to the icy giants of the Bernese Oberland. From the upper chair-lift station take the wide path leading north-eastwards along the grassy mountainsides (one of the most popular paragliding take-off points). The white-red-white marked route follows along the undulating ridgetop of the Güggisgrat past weathered dwarf pines.

On your left the land falls 600 metres down to the meandering stream in the Justistal, and the classic U-shaped pass of Sichle (1679 metres) forms the end of the valley ahead. Continue over the 2063-metre **Burgfeldstand** (whose shape supposedly resembles a ruined castle), skirting on around occasional rock outcrops to reach **Gemmenalphorn** at 2061 metres, 1¼ to 1½ hours from the Niederhorn. This lookout point makes a scenic – though sometimes all too popular – spot for a rest.

Drop down steeply leftwards on a stepped pathway to avoid cliffs on the Gemmenalphorn's northern side, then resume the northward traverse along the main ridge. The route makes its way on through light forest and scattered clumps of Alpine rhododendrons towards the impressive sloping karst rock slabs of the Sieben Hengste to meet a signposted junction at the hollow of **Seefeld-Oberberg** (1741 metres). Descend south-west below a few alp huts into a gradually broadening gully, passing the barnyard of **Chumeli** before you come to another old barn. Here cut leftwards into the trees and follow a winding foot track quickly down to reach **Hinterstberg**, 1⅓ to 1⅔ hours on. This farmhouse/restaurant lies at 1369 metres at the uppermost part of the Justistal and offers light refreshments.

Walk on gently down the narrow road through the green pastures past the farmlets of **Gross Mittelberg** and **Püfel** (1254 metres). From down here you can appreciate the enclosed nature of the Justistal, which is bordered on either side by high craggy ranges. After crossing the gurgling Grönbach the route begins a somewhat steeper descent through pockets of damp spruce forest, passing by the old hamlet of

Spicherberg (1237 metres) to arrive at a road intersection near the **Grönhütte** (1124 metres) after 50 minutes to one hour.

Turn left here and follow the bitumen out of the Justistal. The road contours around the steep-sided and heavily wooded slopes through a 300-metre long tunnel, before coming back out onto the long terrace of **Beatenberg**. Continue past scattered holiday houses and farms high above the Thunersee to reach the upper funicular station (1121 metres) after 50 minutes to one hour. The car park at the chair lift is a further 15 to 20 minutes' walk on up the road.

THE STOCKHORN CIRCUIT

The compact range culminating in the 2190-metre Stockhorn is a unique botanical and geographical area which forms a small nature reserve. The Stockhorn has the richest Alpine flora in the Bernese Oberland, with several species of wildflowers that are found in few other parts of the region and various botanical trails winding around its upper slopes.

Underground streams drain much of this small limestone massif, and in certain places water seeping through the porous rock has formed caverns. Filling natural funnel-like sinkwells on the Stockhorn's northern slopes are the Oberstockensee and Hinterstockensee, two small lakes with subterraneous outlets, whose deep trout-stocked waters attract anglers.

Although it leads through a very small area, this walk is surprisingly long and varied. On a threshold between the Bernese Oberland and the Swiss Mittelland, the summit of the Stockhorn is a natural lookout offering super Alpine vistas. The village of Erlenbach (im Simmental) at the foot of the Stockhorn has some wonderful examples of massive-roofed Bernese wooden architecture and a striking medieval church with frescoes originating from the 14th and 15th centuries.

Maps

Recommended is the 1:50,000 SAW/FSTP sheet *Gantrisch (253 T)* and either Schaad +

The Stockhorn

Frey's *Wanderkarte Gantrisch* or Editions MPA Verlag's *Berner Oberland Ost* are (two other 1:50,000 walking maps covering the Stockhorn area).

Walking Times & Standard

This is a straightforward day walk that makes use of a cable car to shorten the route. The initial section from Chrindi to the Stockhorn summit nevertheless involves an often steep climb of around 550 altitude metres. Waymarkings never let you down, and there are no routefinding difficulties. The walk is best from mid-June to mid-July when the wildflowers are at their most lovely. Autumn, when there are fewer visitors, is another nice time to visit the Stockhorn.

The walk is rated *easy*.

Places to Stay

In Erlenbach, the *Hotel Stöcki* (☎ 033 81 21 26) has rooms at prices somewhat above-average. There is a *Friends of Nature hostel* (☎ 033-22 83 67) three km south-west of Erlenbach at Feldmöser (1342 metres). There is other accommodation in the nearby town of Spiez (see Walking Bases).

Restaurant Stockhorn (☎ 033-81 21 81,

open late May to early November) at the upper cable-car station just below the Stockhorn summit has a small mattress room for walkers. The *Berggasthaus Oberstockenalp* (☎ 033-81 14 88, open July to mid-October) in a large old converted barn at 1776 metres has a large cosy dormitory.

Getting to/from the Walk

The Stockhorn Circuit begins and ends at Chrindi (1640 metres), the intermediate station on the Erlenbach-Stockhorn cable car (Stockhornbahn). The lower station of the Stockhornbahn can be reached on foot in 15 minutes from Erlenbach (im Simmental) train station by walking up a winding laneway before turning left along the main road through the village. One-day fishing permits for the Stockhorn can be purchased at the cable car ticket office.

The Stockhornbahn operates half-hourly from mid to late May at least until the first week of November. Various concessions apply and the last downward cable car leaves Chrindi at around 5.30 pm. The walk can be shortened by around 1½ hours by taking the cable car from Chrindi up to the upper station at the Restaurant Stockhorn.

Erlenbach (im Simmental) can be reached by hourly trains from Spiez (see Walking Bases); rail routes from western Switzerland run via Zweisimmen. Note that express trains don't stop in Erlenbach. Private vehicles can be left free of charge at the car park immediately below the Stockhornbahn cable-car station in Erlenbach.

Route Directions:
Chrindi-Stockhorn-Chrindi

(9 km, 3¼ to 4½ hours)

The cable car from Erlenbach heaves you up over 900 vertical metres to the intermediate station of **Chrindi** (1640 metres) just above the **Hinterstockensee**. This turquoise lake lies within an enclosed basin completely surrounded by high peaks, and often remains icebound into early summer. Walk a short way down past an interesting karst rock formation, then follow an alp track off to the right. This ascends the steep grassy slopes

past the alp huts of **Oberbärgli** to a ridgetop saddle below the Chummli, before traversing westwards around the mountainside high above the lake to reach a signposted intersection directly under the cableway.

Continue up steeply again past a jumping ramp for paragliders to the **Restaurant Stockhorn** (see Places to Stay), joining the crowds for the final climb via a stepped path leading quickly up to the 2190-metre summit of the Stockhorn, 1¼ to 1¾ hours from Chrindi. Up here you get a full-spectrum Alpine panorama that includes some 200 peaks stretching from the Titlis to Mont Blanc. The Thunersee (Lake Thun) is visible far below to the east, while the land drops away to the north of the Stockhorn directly into the Bernese Mittelland.

Drop back down to the junction below the cableway, taking the right-hand (west) branch that descends steadily in occasional twists to reach the **Berggasthaus Oberstockenalp** (1776 metres, see Places to Stay) after 35 to 45 minutes. Head on across the little grassy shelf along a partially stone-laid foot track, ignoring trails diverging to the left and right. The route brings you gently down through scattered coniferous forest to the **Oberstockensee**, another small lake occupying a trough with no apparent outlet. The Oberstockensee is fed only by two tiny inlet streams and the lake's given water level of 1665 metres actually varies quite a bit depending on rainfall.

Make your way around to the western side of the Oberstockensee, rising briefly to the cottage of **Speetbärgli**. The path sidles on around the slopes, before climbing away to a grassy saddle at 1799 metres, 35 to 45 minutes from Oberstockenalp. Cut down over green pastures to a route intersection at the first alp huts of **Vorderstockenalp**. Here take the path that branches gently away leftwards (not the way going off more sharply to the left), and contour around eastwards over herbal meadows before coming to a small gap in the ridge between the Cheibenhorn and the Mieschflue.

The route now heads back down via a small spur towards a tiny forested peninsula in the Hinterstocksee to meet the broad walkway running around the lake. Turn left here and continue around past the farmlet of **Hinterstockenalp** (1616 metres), arriving back at the Chrindi cable-car station after a final 40 to 50 minutes. Keen downhill walkers can make the descent back to Erlenbach on foot in around two hours.

OTHER WALKS
The Brienzer Rothorn
Marking the meeting point of the cantons of Lucerne, Obwalden and Bern, the Brienzer Rothorn rises up abruptly from the town of Brienz (see Walking Bases) at the north-eastern end of the Brienzersee. The mountain's 2349-metre summit presents visitors with an almost unsurpassed Alpine panorama that embraces the long chain of peaks stretching eastwards from Les Diablerets as far west as the Säntis. The Brienzer Rothorn is directly accessible from Brienz itself via another of Switzerland's classic cog railways, whose old steam-driven locomotives puff their way up inclines of up to 25%.

A spectacular walk leads quickly from the upper train station (2244 metres) to the Brienzer Rothorn. Two equally popular route alternatives exist: either make a long sidling descent around the northern side of the range via Chäseren and Schäri to the Brünigpass (1002 metres), or continue eastwards along the ridgetop to Schönbüel (2012 metres), from where two cable cars carry you down via Turren to Obsee (752 metres) near Lungern. Both the Brünigpass and Lungern are on the Interlaken-Lucerne rail line.

The average walking time to the Brünigpass is 4½ hours, or around three hours to Schönbüel. Walkers can also reach the heights of the Brienzer Rothorn by cable car from Sörenberg (itself accessible by postbuses running between Lungern and Schüpfheim) on the other side of the range.

The *Berghotel Rothorn Kulm* (☎ 036-51 12 21) near the summit of the Brienzer Rothorn has various standard rooms as well as a large dormitory. The only available walking map that (fully) shows the route(s)

on a single sheet is Kümmerly + Frey's 1:40,000 sheet *Flühli Sörenberg*. Together the SAW/FSTP's *Escholzmatt (244 T)* and *Interlaken (254 T)* also cover the walk.

The Hinterburgseeli
The Hinterburgseeli is a lovely little lake sitting in a forested hollow of a high terrace above the south-eastern corner of the Brienzersee below the 2320-metre Axalphorn. A very pleasant and easy route leads eastwards from the modest winter sports resort of Axalp (1535 metres) to the Hinterburgseeli (1514 metres), then descends gently along the edge of the sloping terrace of Hinterburg to the hamlet of Furen (963 metres) at Züün. From here walkers can either head on smoothly down eastwards to Meiringen (see Walking Bases), or drop down northwards directly into the Haslital to the train station at Hirssi.

The average walking time to Hirssi is four hours, or around five hours to Meiringen. Axalp is accessible by up to five daily postbuses from Brienz (see Walking Bases); the last bus leaves Brienz at around 4.30 pm. The *Sporthotel Axalp* (☎ 036-51 16 71) offers nice rooms and has a large dormitory. The 1:50,000 walking maps *Wanderkarte Oberhasli* produced by the local tourist authorities covers the route.

The Niesen
The 2362-metre Niesen forms a final triangular-shaped outcrop at the northern end of the sharp and narrow range separating the valleys of the Kandertal and the Emmental, whose rivers meet at the foot of the mountain just before entering the Thunersee. Occupying this unique position, the Niesen is one of the region's prime lookout points, and – inevitably – has long been made accessible by a two-stage funicular railway from the village of Mülenen in the Kandertal. The summit gives grand views across the valleys of the Central Bernese Oberland to the main ranges of the Alps. A very enjoyable four-hour downhill route leads from the Niesen over broad spurs along the east side of the range via Oberniesen (1813 metres),

Hubelweid (1513 metres) and Eggweid (1371 metres) to the town of Frutigen at 780 metres in the Kandertal.

The *Berghaus Niesen-Kulm* (☎ 033-76 11 13) at 2343 metres by the upper funicular station has rooms and dorms. Both Mülenen and Frutigen are on the main Spiez-Kandersteg rail line. The most detailed walking map covering this route is the 1:25,000 sheet titled *Frutigen* published by the local tourist authorities.

The Hohgant

The limestone ranges culminating at the 2197-metre Hohgant are an extension of the Niederhorn's Güggigrat ridge. The Hohgant-Seefeld area forms an interesting nature reserve that (by Bernese Oberland standards) is relatively inaccessible and almost without mountain lifts. A rewarding walk leads up northwards from the village of Habkern (1055 metres), which is accessible from Interlaken West/Ost by regular daily postbus. The route leads via Wildegg to the natural lookout on top of the Hohgant, from where the descent can be made via Luterschändi to Bumbach (913 metres); there are postbuses from Luterschändi to Wiggen on the Bern-Langnau-Lucerne rail line). Schaad + Frey's 1:50,000 walking map *Wanderkarte Thuner-und Brienzersee* covers the area, but for better detail use the standard topographical series map *Beatenberg* scaled at 1:25,000.

The Jungfrau Region & Haslital

Stretching eastwards from the 2970-metre Schilthorn to meet Central Switzerland at the Jochpass, the Jungfrau Region and Haslital form the eastern Bernese Oberland. Dominated by the staggeringly sheer rock faces of the Eiger, Münch and Jungfrau – arguably the Alpine world's most famously scenic threesome – and the almost equally impressive 'horned' summits of the Schreckhorn, Lauteraarhorn, and Wetterhorn, this is a region of true superlatives. Presenting a seemingly ubiquitous backdrop, these awesome mountains are identifiable in the distance from places far outside the Bernese Oberland. The heart of the eastern Bernese Alps is an icebound wilderness only properly accessible to experienced mountaineers (or at least fit, professionally guided walkers). The lower surrounding ranges, however, have some classic routes that can be undertaken by just about anybody.

The Jungfrau Region is drained by the glacial-grey Lütschine River, which divides into the two branches of the Weisse Lütschine of the Lauterbrunnental and Schwarze Lütschine of the Lütschental. In these twin upper valleys are Lauterbrunnen (with two nearby mountain villages of Wengen and Mürren perched on high terraces either side of it) and the large centre of Grindelwald. Not surprisingly, the Jungfrau Region is the most heavily touristed part of the Swiss Alps, and after savouring the magnificent views for a while some walkers may register the urge to head for wilder places.

The area to the east of the 1962-metre Grosse Scheidegg lies within the valley basin of the Haslital, and forms the easternmost corner of the Bernese Oberland. At the uppermost reaches of the Aare River, the Haslital is unlike any other valley in the Bernese Oberland, penetrating deeply into the mountains as far as the 2165-metre Grimselpass. This pass was the first (or final) stage of the historically important trans-Alpine routes going over the Nufenen (Novena) and Simplon passes. The Urbachtal, a side valley of the Haslital, is one of the most wild and interesting areas of the region.

WALKING BASES
Meiringen

Situated at 595 metres in the lower Haslital, since early medieval times Meiringen was favoured as a transit point for the travel and trade routes across the Susten, Grimsel, Grosse Scheidegg and Joch passes. Two popular short day walks from Meiringen go to the nearby Reichenbach Falls (famous as the place where the fictional Sherlock Holmes fell to his death) and the spectacular Aare Gorge (Aareschlucht).

Meiringen's nearest camping ground is *Aareschlucht* (☎ 036-71 53 96) on the road to Innertkirchen (regular postbuses); there are several others around Innertkirchen. The local *youth hostel* (☎ 036-71 17 15) is 10 minutes' walk from the centre of town. The *Victoria* (☎ 036-71 10 33) and the *Hirschen* (☎ 036-71 18 12) are two good lower-budget hotels in Meiringen. Meiringen has one of Switzerland's top mountaineering schools, the Bergsteigeschule Rosenlaui (☎ 036-71 35 37) and a helpful tourist office (☎ 036-71 43 22).

Meiringen is midway on the Lucerne-Interlaken Ost rail line, with approximately hourly trains in either direction via the Brünigpass. Important postbus connections go to Andermatt and Grindelwald (via the Grosse Scheidegg).

Grindelwald

Nestled below the peaks of the Eiger, Münch and Jungfrau, Grindelwald (1034 metres) is perhaps the most scenic (and touristy) town in the Swiss Alps. World-famous is the cog railway tunnelled through the Eiger's north face to the 3454-metre saddle of the Jungfraujoch, where there is an observatory and weather station (known as the Sphinx). There are many wonderful walks in the mountains surrounding Grindelwald, including routes over the Kleine Scheidegg, Grosse Scheidegg and the Faulhornweg (all featured in this guidebook); also of great interest to walkers are the Unterer Grindelwaldgletscher and Oberer Grindelwaldgletscher, two impressive glaciers that descend far down into the valley.

There are four local camping grounds, including the *Aspen* (☎ 036-53 11 24) and the *Gletscherdorf* (☎ 036-53 14 29). There is dormitory accommodation at the *youth hostel* (☎ 036-53 10 09, open from June to the end of October), the *Mountain Hostel* (☎ 036-53 39 00) and the *Friends of Nature hostel* (☎ 036-53 13 33). Grindelwald has a tourist office (☎ 036-53 12 12) and the local

school of mountaineering, the Bergsteigerzentrum (☎ 036-53 12 22), is a good source of advice, and organises guided walks and sells maps and books.

Grindelwald is reached from Interlaken by regular trains of the Berner-Oberland-Bahn (BOB) running via Zweilütschinen.

Lauterbrunnen

The stretched-out village of Lauterbrunnen lies at 797 metres in the deep glacial trough of the upper Lauterbrunnental. An easy two-hour walk from Lauterbrunnen goes up to the end of the transitable road at Stechelberg (910 metres) past numerous waterfalls plummeting over the cliffs into the valley. Lauterbrunnen has two good camping grounds nearby; best is the *Camping Schützenbach* (☎ 036-55 12 68) which also offers low-budget accommodation in dormitories and rooms. The *Alpenhof* (☎ 036-55 12 02) at Stechelberg is a Friends of Nature hostel. Lauterbrunnen's least expensive place to stay is the *Hotel Horner* (☎ 036-55 16 73). The tourist office (☎ 036-55 19 55) is near the train station.

Lauterbrunnen is accessible by at least hourly trains from Interlaken Ost. The cog railway via Wengen and the Grosse Scheidegg connects Lauterbrunnen with Grindelwald.

Mürren

Mürren (1638 metres) is a car-free resort catering mainly to the well-to-do wintersports set. Situated high up on the western side of the Lauterbrunnental, the village looks directly out across the valley towards the sheer rock walls of the Eiger, Münch and Jungfrau. A popular day excursion goes up to the Schilthorn, a 2970-metre lookout peak accessible either via a steep foot track or by the Mürren-Schilthorn cable car. One of the less expensive hotels in Mürren is the *Hotel Regina* (☎ 036-55 14 21). The *Pension Suppenalp* (☎ 036-55 17 26) above the village has a budget rooms and a dorm. The tourist office (☎ 036-55 16 16) is in the sports centre. Mürren is accessible by a funicular and mountain train combination from Lauterbrunnen.

Wengen

This pleasant village is perched almost 500 metres above the trough of the Lauterbrunnental. Like Mürren on the opposite side of the valley, Wengen is one of Switzerland's dozen or more car-free mountain resorts. A number of places offer dormitory accommodation including the *Massenlager Bären Garni* (☎ 036-55 14 19) and *Eddy's Hostel* (☎ 036-55 39 50) which have the lowest rates. The *Hotel Edelweiss* (☎ 036-55 23 88) has the cheapest rooms in Wengen. The tourist office (☎ 036-55 14 14) is just up around the corner from the train station. Wengen is reached by cog railway from Lauterbrunnen.

THE GROSSE SCHEIDEGG
(Section 6 of the Alpine Pass Route)

The gentle 1962-metre pass known as the Grosse Scheidegg ('great watershed') divides Meiringen from Grindelwald in the Jungfrau Region. It is another of the eastern Bernese Oberland's classic and extremely popular walks, offering ever-changing scenery that builds up to its highlight around the Grosse Scheidegg itself. The route first leads up through the Reichenbachtal below the limestone needles of the Engelhörner, a side valley of the Haslital, past the Rosenlauigletscher, whose roaring meltwaters have carved out an amazing gorge. At the head of the Reichenbachtal stands the 3701-metre Wetterhorn, whose massive and overpowering grey-rock walls will bring a shiver of awe even to well-seasoned Alpine walkers.

Maps

One of the best walking maps available detailing the route over the Grosse Scheidegg is the excellent small 1:50,000 sheet *Wanderkarte Oberhasli* published by the local tourist authorities. The Editions MPA Verlag walking map *Berner Oberland Ost* also scaled at 1:50, 000 covers a larger area and is useful for many other walks in the region; Kümmerly + Frey's 1:60,000 sheet *Jungfrau-Region Oberhasli* is similar. Alternatively, you can use two 1:50,000 SAW/FSTP sheets, *Sustenpass (255 T)* and *Interlaken (245 T)*.

Walking Times & Standard

Going the whole way from Meiringen to Grindelwald in one day makes a very long and tiring hike. With so much lovely scenery to savour, it's recommended that walkers stop off for the night at one of the several cosy guest houses and hotels passed en route.

The Grosse Scheidegg walk involves a long and mostly gently rising approach to the pass totalling over 1350 altitude metres, with a much steeper 950-metre descent to Grindelwald. Since the recent construction of several new sections of path, the route now follows graded foot tracks rather than the road for most of the way. The walk can be safely undertaken by walkers with a minimum of experience, but beware of summer thunderstorms which can break very suddenly; don't forget to pack your rainjacket. The Grosse Scheidegg is normally crossed between the beginning of June and late September, when there is a postbus service and plenty of en-route accommodation.

The walk over is rated *easy* and covers some 21 km.

Places to Stay

The *Hotel Schwendi* (☎ 036-71 28 25) has very reasonable rates for simple rooms. The *Gasthaus Zwirgi* (☎ 036-71 14 22) a short way up has a mattress room for walkers. The *Hotel Rosenlaui* (☎ 36-71 29 12, open June to October) has more comfortable rooms as well as small dormitories (showers available).

The *Chalet Schwarzwaldalp* (☎ 036-71 35 15, open March to mid-November) at 1454 metres has the best value in dormitory accommodation on the whole route. The *Berghotel Grosse Scheidegg* (☎ 036-53 12 09, open early June to October) right on the pass height offers rooms and dormitory accommodation; due to a shortage of water

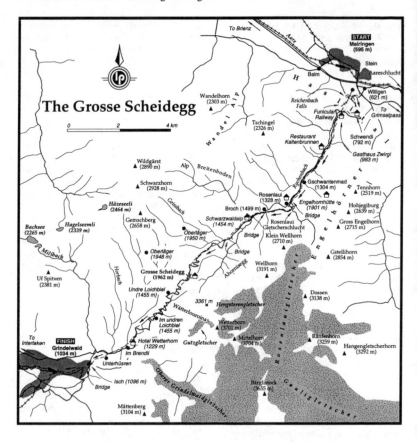

The Grosse Scheidegg

however, washing facilities are very basic. Halfway down to Grindelwald the *Hotel Wetterhorn* (☎ 036-53 12 18, open May to late November) has simple rooms and dormitories.

Places to stay in Meiringen and Grindelwald are given in the respective Walking Bases sections.

Getting to/from the Walk

The walk sets out from Meiringen and ends in Grindelwald; for access to both towns see Walking Bases. From June until late September postbuses run along the road between

Meiringen and Grindelwald. There are bus stops at many places along the way, so if you get tired or lazy opting out is a simple matter. The last bus leaves Grosse Scheidegg for Grindelwald shortly after 5.30 pm.

Route Directions: Meiringen to Grindelwald

(21 km 6½ to 9 hours)

From the Meiringen railway station, signposts point along the main road and quickly lead you south-east across the swift, milky waters of the Aare River to the village of **Willingen**. Here, 50 metres above the Hotel

Tourist, turn right onto a bitumened lane. This leads up beside restored old Bernese houses and continues as a grassy track bordered by stone walls and raspberry bushes to meet a road. Follow the road a short way uphill, then leave off to the right along a partially stone-laid path. The route goes up steeply through forest and pasture, recrossing the road a number of times before coming to the hamlet of **Schwendi**. Head on up via Tannenhubel (where a trail to the Reichenbach Falls diverges) to reach the **Gasthaus Zwirgi** at 983 metres, 1¼ to 1½ hours from Meiringen.

Find the path at the left of the road. Often within earshot of the rushing Rychenbach stream, it goes through forest and clearings from where you get the first views of the high snowcapped peaks ahead, then crosses the road once more at two sharp curves. From here the road itself provides the main walkway until you reach the **Restaurant Kaltenbrunnen** (rooms and refreshments) after 30 to 40 minutes. Not far up from the restaurant (near where a signposted trail branches off to the Engelhornhütte) follow a foot track leading off right into the forest.

Taking a course close to the Rychenbach, the path again crosses the road several times while the valley broadens and flattens out. Don't cross at the first road-bridge, but continue five minutes along the grassy flats beside the stream, where another bridge leads across to **Gschwantenmad**, 30 to 40 minutes after leaving Kaltenbrunnen. A nice spot for a rest-stop, Gschwantenmad (1304 metres) is just a scattering of old barns and farmhouses. From here there are superb views of the adjacent jagged peaks of the Engelhörner range and the Rosenlauigletscher plus the Wellhorn and Wetterhorn farther upvalley.

From Gschwantenmad, a new walking route continues 15 to 20 minutes along the opposite (true right) bank of the stream through pleasant forest, returning to the road on a bridge a short way before you reach **Rosenlaui** (1328 metres, see Places to Stay). Well worth visiting here is the **Rosenlaui Gletscherschlucht**, a few minutes up from the hotel. This deep and very narrow glacial gorge is accessible only via an amazing walkway that leads past thundering waterfalls and churning whirlpools.

Near the entrance to the Gletscherschlucht, pick up the path immediately above the road. This gravelled walking track takes you past **Broch** (where the road crosses to the other side of the Rychenbach), and continues along the southern side of the stream, passing a footbridge leading over to **Schwarzwaldalp** (1454 metres, see Places to Stay) after 30 to 40 minutes. This is the end of the road for all but authorised local traffic and postbuses.

The route doesn't cross the footbridge at Schwarzwaldalp, but follows the trail up away from the stream through patches of forest until it comes out onto open fields of wildflowers after 20 to 25 minutes. Clinging to the walls of the Wetterhorn directly above you are the spectacular hanging glaciers of the Hengsterengletscher, from which large chunks of ice continually break off and crash down onto the cliffs. Make your way around to the right, crossing a small wooden bridge over the milky stream coming down from these glaciers, then head up a vehicular track to meet the road once again a further five to 10 minutes on.

From now on the path climbs up steadily beside the road, cutting off numerous bends; white-red-white markings on the bitumen, trees or fence posts indicate these short cuts. Well-spaced benches along the way provide plenty of excuses to sit and admire the magnificent views of the 3701-metre Wetterhorn, whose striking north face appears breathtakingly near. After 1½ to two hours you reach **Grosse Scheidegg** at 1962 metres (see Places to Stay), where views and altitude culminate. The Grosse Scheidegg offers splendid vistas across Grindelwald to the Kleine Scheidegg.

The initial descent from the Grosse Scheidegg is rapid and often steep. Follow the road a few paces on from the Berghotel, then continue down through mixed pasture and Alpine heathland. As before, the well-graded path short-cuts the many sharp curves in the road, dropping down through **Undre Loichbiel** (1455 metres, shown on some maps and signposts as Unterlauchbühl) then descending beside the road to reach the **Hotel Wetterhorn** after one to 1½ hours. The hotel looks out towards the impressive Oberer Grindelwaldgletscher.

A short way below the hotel, follow a signposted vehicle track off left through the forest. Head down past **Im Brendli**, then continue westwards along a marked walking trail which crosses several streams as it contours the hillside via **Underhüsren** (also called Unterhäusern), **Im Stutz** and **Isch**. At Isch walk down to a small lane which leads around right to rejoin the main Grindelwald-Grosse Scheidegg road at the village church after 30 to 40 minutes. From here **Grindelwald** train station is 10 to 15 minutes' stroll down through town.

For the following section of the Alpine Pass Route (Grindelwald to Lauterbrunnen) refer to the Kleine Scheidegg walk.

THE FAULHORNWEG

The high-level panoramic route from the Schynige Platte via the 2680-metre Faulhorn to First well deserves its reputation as one of the Bernese Oberland's great classic walks. The Faulhornweg leads through the geologically interesting range separating the Jungfrau Region from the Brienzersee, with fine examples of twisted and overlayed rock strata and karst fields as well as some of the most dramatic ridge formations you're likely to find anywhere in the Swiss Alps. Constant companions are the towering north faces of four of Europe's most famous peaks, the Wetterhorn, Eiger, Münch and Jungfrau.

Maps

Recommended is the SAW/FSTP sheet *Interlaken (254 T)*, scaled at 1:50,000. Other good options are either *Berner Oberland Ost* published by Editions MPA Verlag, or Kümmerly + Frey's *Jungfrau-Region Oberhasli*. Less recommended is the 1:25,000 *Wanderkarte Grindelwald* published by Schad + Frey, as it is rather sketchy and shows the route right at the edge of the sheet.

Walking Times & Standard

The Faulhornweg gives you a full day's hiking, which can be broken into two more leisurely stages by staying overnight somewhere en route (see Places to Stay). The white-red-white marked route leads entirely above the treeline at elevations mostly over 2000 metres. Although the walk uses mountain transport to avoid any really heavy climbing and has no real difficulties, it involves a gradual rise totalling around 600 altitude metres that may get you puffing and makes a rather tiring day. The route passes through mostly rocky terrain, so you'll need well-fitting boots – nothing too light. There is little running water on this ridgetop walk, so unless you carry your own water the only sources of liquid refreshment are the several restaurants along the route.

The final section of this trail between the Hotel Welterhorn and First is a popular winter walking route and is snow-cleared.

The walk has been given a *moderate* rating and covers 15 km.

Places to Stay

The *Restaurant Schynige Platte Kulm* (☎ 036-22 34 31, open from early June to late October) near the upper station of the cog railway has rooms and dorms, but is a bit on the expensive side. At the saddle of Männdlenen (2344 metres) is the *Weberhütte* (☎ 036-53 44 64, open July to the end of September), a private restaurant/mountain hut with a small mattress room for walkers.

The *Hotel Faulhorn* (☎ 036-53 10 25, open late June to late October) has 16 rooms and a large dormitory. Rates are surprisingly reasonable. The *Berghaus Bort* (☎ 036-53 17 62) at the middle station of the First-Bahn gondola lift (1570 metres, see below) also has mattress-room accommodation. Various small emergency huts along the route grant water-tight shelter, but are not intended for overnight use.

See Walking Bases for accommodation in Grindelwald and Interlaken.

Getting to/from the Walk

The start of the hike is Schynige Platte (1987

metres), which is accessible by the historic narrow-gauge cog railway from Wilderswil on the Interlaken to Grindelwald line of the Berner Oberland-Bahn (BOB). Trains run up to Schynige Platte at approximately 40-minute intervals until around 5 pm from about early June until the middle of October, although the period of operation varies somewhat from year to year depending on weather and snow conditions. For information call ☎ 036-22 85 44. The walk up to Schynige Platte from Wilderswil is a gruelling four-hour climb and is not recommended.

The walk terminates at First (2167 metres), from where the over five-km-long First-Bahn – Europe's longest gondola lift – takes you down into Grindelwald (see Walking Bases). The First-Bahn runs daily from late May to mid-late October; the last downhill ride is around 5.30 pm.

Slightly cheaper combined tickets for walkers are available which include the Schynige Platte and First-Bahn as well as the BOB trains from Grindelwald back to Interlaken; various concessions are also available.

Route Directions: Schynige Platte to First

(15 km, 4¾ to 6¼ hours)
The old cog railway hauls walkers up some 1400 altitude metres to the Schynige Platte station (1987 metres) in around 40 minutes. From this superb natural lookout you get the first of the day's breathtaking views across to the great white summits of the Jungfrau Region. Before setting off it's worth visiting Schynige Platte's **Alpengarten** (open from mid to late June until mid-September), which shows typical Alpine flora in simulated landscapes such moors, rock cliffs and screeslides.

Walk north-east along an alp track over rolling pastures past the alp hut of **Oberberg**, heading gently upwards above the green basin of Inner Iselten to reach **Louchera** (shown on some signposts as Laucheren) at 2020 metres. (Not far on from the Schynige Platte station the **Panoramaweg**, a some-

what longer alternative route diverges left and leads via the 2069-metre **Oberberghorn** to Louchera, giving outstanding views down to Interlaken and the Brienzersee). Head around scree-slopes on the western side of the **Loucherhorn** (2230 metres) to cross over a low grassy crest. The way dips and rises as it sidles on through two gaps in rocky spurs on the mountain's southern flank before coming to **Egg**, a wide grassy pass at 2067 metres strewn with boulders and Alpine herbs, 1¼ to 1½ hours from Schynige Platte.

Egg opens out northwards into the Sägistal, a tiny valley completely enclosed by ridges and without an above-ground outlet. Filling the lowest point within the basin, the waters of the small Sägistalsee (1935 metres) seep away subterraneously. Skirt up the Sägistal's southern side below the precipitous Inri Sägissa, before swinging around south-west above the raw, talus-choked gully of Bonera (or Hühnertal). The route picks its way on up through an interesting landscape of rough karst slabs to arrive at the **Weberhütte** (2344 metres, see Places to Stay) on the little saddle of **Männdlenen**, one to 1⅓ hours on.

Make a rising traverse about a broad ledge between stratified cliffs to gain the ridge of Winteregg, following white-red-white markings and metal posts on north-eastwards. A short distance past a minor turn-off at 2546 metres, take a signposted foot track leading up left along the main range to arrive at the top of the 2680-metre **Faulhorn**, one to 1⅓ hours from Männdlenen. Just below the summit stands the historic **Hotel Faulhorn** (see Places to Stay), which first opened for business in 1832 and is the oldest and highest mountain hotel in the Alps. These lofty heights enjoy a stunning Alpine panorama dominated by the grand trio of the Eiger, Münch and Jungfrau.

Descend the rounded, sparsely vegetated ridge to the little col of **Gassenboden** (2553 metres), then drop down eastwards past an emergency shelter into the tiny grassy basin of the **Bachsee** (2265 metres). The tranquil waters of this picturesque lake contrast

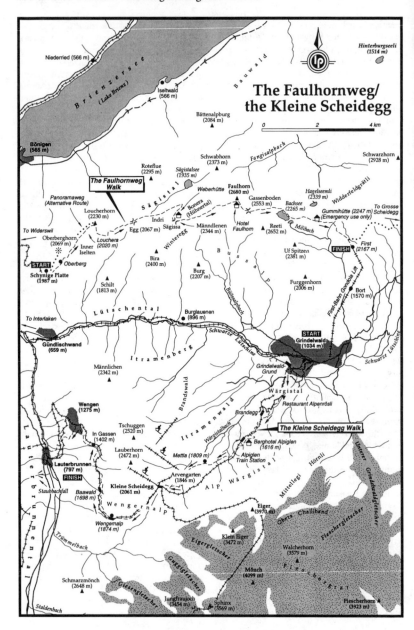

The Faulhornweg/
the Kleine Scheidegg

starkly with the imposing, ice-shrouded peaks of (from left to right) the Wetterhorn (3071 metres), the Schreckhorn (4078 metres) and the Finsteraarhorn (4274 metres) which rise up directly behind it – yet another of the Swiss Alps' marvellous views!

Head on around the northern shore of the Bachsee, climbing gently past a smaller, slightly lower lake. A wide and well-trodden path now sidles gradually down through Alpine pastures high above the marshy Milibach streamlet to the distant tinkling of cowbells, reaching the upper gondola-lift station at **First** (2167 metres) 1½ to two hours after leaving the Hotel Faulhorn. First looks straight across to the narrow, snaking icefall of the Oberer Grindelwaldgletscher, and – unless you continue on foot to the Grosse Scheidegg, which adds another 1½ hours or so to the walk – this is the last high-level viewing point for what has been a particularly scenic walk.

THE KLEINE SCHEIDEGG
(Section 7 of the Alpine Pass Route)
The Kleine Scheidegg lies in the shadow of the Eiger, whose stunning 1800-metre high north face is at once the most notorious and captivating of any in the Alps. This broad saddle of the comparatively low Männlichen range dividing the two upper branches of the Lütschine River makes a natural lookout with incredible close-range views taking in Switzerland's most famous peaks. Excursions to the Kleine Scheidegg have long been popular, and Goethe and Byron hiked over the pass whilst visiting the Jungfrau Region in the early 1800s. Today the Kleine Scheidegg is accessible from both sides by way of a busy mountain railway running between Grindelwald and Lauterbrunnen, with a large station on the pass height itself from where trains continue up to the 3454-metre Jungfraujoch.

Although the Bernese Oberland definitely offers wilder routes than this, the Kleine Scheidegg is unquestionably one of the most scenic in the Swiss Alps – well worth the day's walk despite the hoards of international tourists and the relatively physically unchallenging terrain.

Maps
Best maps for this walk are either *Berner Oberland Ost* published by Editions MPA Verlag at a scale of 1:50,000 or the SAW/FSTP's 1:50,000 sheet *Interlaken (245 T)*. Otherwise, you can use the 1:60,000 Kümmerly + Frey sheet *Jungfrau-Region Oberhasli*, Schad + Frey's special 1:50,000 walking map *Wanderkarte Thuner-und Brienzersee* or the 1:40,000 *Wanderkarte Lauterbrunnental* produced by the local tourist authorities. Least recommended is Schad + Frey's *Wanderkarte Grindelwald* scaled at 1:25,000, which is very sketchy and cuts off the last part of the route.

Walking Times & Standard
Done in its entirety, the hike over the Kleine Scheidegg takes up a full day's energetic walking. Although it involves climbs and descents that both total more than 1000 metres, the route has absolutely no technical difficulties and can therefore be undertaken by anyone in reasonable health.

The walk is rated *easy*, and covers 18 km.

Places to Stay
Most recommended is the *Berghotel Alpiglen* (☎ 036-53 11 30), which has standard rooms and dormitory accommodation (showers available). At Kleine Scheidegg, the *Bahnhof Restaurant* (☎ 036-55 11 51) right beside the station platform also has a dorm.

See also Walking Bases for places to stay in Grindelwald, Wengen and Lauterbrunnen.

Getting to/from the Walk
The walk sets off from Grindelwald and ends at Lauterbrunnen (or alternatively Wengen); access details to all three places are covered under Walking Bases. Since the walk largely traces the line of the Wengeneralp Bahn (WAB) narrow-gauge cog railway, hikers can cop out by boarding the train at either of the several well-spaced train stations passed en route.

Route Directions: Grindelwald to Lauterbrunnen

(18 km, 5¾ to 7¼ hours)

From the main Grindelwald railway station, follow a signposted laneway leading down beside the Hotel Regina then past the Hotel Glacier to reach the Grindelwald-Grund railway station after 15 to 20 minutes. Most trains to the Kleine Scheidegg and the Jungfraujoch leave from here.

Cross the road bridge and walk 50 metres to the right. After taking a bitumened pedestrian laneway up left, ascend steeply past holiday cottages to meet a broad road, then continue on to cross the WAB rail lines via an underpass. Signposts direct you on across a smaller road to the Restaurant Alpenrösli, from where a path leads up beside the Sandbach stream. Take this often steep foot track up through the forest, recrossing the road briefly about halfway before you pass under a tiny arched-stone rail bridge. The route now climbs up close to the train lines, again dipping under a small rail tunnel just before reaching the **Berghotel Alpiglen** (see Places to Stay), two to 2½ hours from Grindelwald-Grund. The Berghotel stands at 1616 metres under the north face of the Eiger a short way down from the Alpiglen train station.

The path recrosses the rail lines a short way above the hotel, climbing more gently now past clusters of weather-beaten mountain pines and the farmhouses in the hollow of **Mettla** (1809 metres). Make your way on up to the ski lifts of **Arvengarten**, where you meet the 'Weg 2000' (a path contouring the mountainsides at roughly 2000 metres) before sidling up around the slopes below the rail line to arrive at the **Kleine Scheidegg** (2061 metres, see Places to Stay) after 1⅓ to 1⅔ hours.

This minor pass provides a tremendous close-range vantage point for the savage ice and rock walls of the Eiger, Münch and Jungfrau that soar almost 2000 metres above you. From the bustling Kleine Scheidegg train station walkers can opt to make the return trip by cog railway up to the Jungfraujoch – but don't expect the ticket price to be much cheaper compared to the extremely expensive fare charged from Grindelwald itself!

Head smoothly down along the broad path to the left of the train line, dipping under the tracks shortly before you come to the station of **Wengernalp** at 1874 metres. There are more wonderful vistas ahead that include the Gspaltenhorn and Schilthorn beyond where the land plunges away into the deep glacial trough of the Lauterbrunnental. An alp track leads on around northwards through pockets of Alpine forest to cross the railway yet again, whereafter a well-formed roadway winds around the slopes via **In Gassen** (1402 metres) to reach the car-free mountain resort of **Wengen** (1275 metres, see Walking Bases) after 1½ to two hours.

From Wengen train station, follow the signposted walking track back under the rail lines onto a narrow road. The route soon begins a steep descent in short spirals through tall forests of spruce and maple, twice crossing the railway in quick succession. There are occasional glimpses through the foliage upvalley towards the 3785-metre Lauterbrunner Breithorn and the long spectacular Staubbachfall cascade. Drop on down through open slopes to cross the raging torrent of the Weisse Lütchine on a footbridge a short way before coming out at the main street in **Lauterbrunnen** (797 metres, see Walking Bases) after a final 40 to 50 minutes.

For the following section of the Alpine Pass Route, see the Sefinenfurgge walk (Lauterbrunnen to Griesalp) below.

THE SEFINENFURGGE
(Section 8 of the Alpine Pass Route)

As the lowest point in the high craggy ridge extending from the Gspaltenhorn to the Schilthorn, the 2612-metre pass known as the Sefinenfurgge (sometimes shown as 'Sefinenfurke' on signposts or maps) leads out of the Jungfrau Region into the Frutigland. Walkers crossing the Sefinenfurgge will savour more of the eastern Bernese Oberland's best scenery, without having to share it with (quite) as many people as on other routes.

Maps

The 1:40,000 *Wanderkarte Lauterbrunnen-tal* produced by the local tourist authorities, and the 1:60,000 Kümmerly + Frey walking map *Jungfrau-Region Oberhasli* both show the whole route in a single sheet but are not particularly well detailed. The 1:50,000 SAW/FSTP sheet *Jungfrau (264 T)* is therefore recommended, despite the fact that it misses most of the first short section of the walk between Grütschalp or Lauterbrunnen and Mürren; this area is on the adjoining sheet *Interlaken (254 T)*.

Walking Times & Standard

Despite the use of the Lauterbrunnen-Grütschalp funicular, this is a long day's walk that can be shortened somewhat by staying overnight somewhere en route. Much of the climb to the Sefinenfurgge is steady and gradual, but there are some steeper sections before and after the pass with very loose rock on the path. The climb to the pass totals almost 1200 altitude metres, and the descent to Griesalp is slightly more than this.

The walk is rated *moderate*, and is 21 km long.

Places to Stay

The *Restaurant-Pension Spielbodenalp* (☎ 036-55 14 75, open from May to October) at 1790 metres, around 40 minutes from Mürren has a simple mattress dorm (no showers). About one hour farther on at Poganggen (2039 metres) you'll find the *Rotstockhütte* (☎ 036-55 24 64, open from June to October), a typical mountain hut belonging to a local skiing club. It's a pleasant spot, but conditions are basic. The only other en-route accommodation is at the alp huts of *Obere Dürreberg* (no telephone, open from mid-June until late September), on the other side of the Sefinenfurgge, where walkers can sleep on straw in the loft. It's

very cheap with plenty of pungent and rustic 'atmosphere'.

Also see the respective Walking Bases sections of this chapter for accommodation in Lauterbrunnen, Mürren and Griesalp.

Getting to/from the Walk

Although some people may prefer to set out from Lauterbrunnen (see Walking Bases) itself, the recommended place to start the walk from is the upper station of the Lauterbrunnen-Grütschalp funicular railway. The funicular runs at least half-hourly; the Half Fare Card and Swiss Pass are valid.

For transport details from the end of the walk at Griesalp see Walking Bases.

Route Directions: Grütschalp to Griesalp

(21 km, 6 to 8 hours)
In seven minutes the Lauterbrunnen-Grütschalp funicular hauls you from around 800 metres straight up to the glacial shelf high above the valley at 1489 metres. The way from Grütschalp to Mürren is easy and very scenic, so don't even consider taking the railway.

From the upper station at **Grütschalp**, cross over the train tracks and walk along the broad path running just above the rail lines. The gradient is fairly smooth, causing no distraction from the glorious panorama taking in all the great summits of the Jungfrau Region, including the Jungfrau, Münch and Eiger to your left. After passing the **Winteregg** station (1578 metres) and restaurant, the route swings south-eastwards, with a clear view of the Breithorn in front of you at the head of the Lauterbrunnental, and continues on to reach the terminal station at the edge of **Mürren** (see Walking Bases) after 50 minutes to one hour.

Alternatively, you can walk up from Lauterbrunnen by taking the well-marked walkway that leaves off right, 250 metres uphill from the lower funicular station. This route rises briefly beside the channelled

Gryfenbach stream, then swings left to ascend diagonally through occasional clearings in the tall mixed forest. You pass by the picnic tables at Staubbach about halfway before meeting the Grütschalp-Mürren railway at **Mittelberg** (1620 metres) a short way before you get to Mürren. This lengthens the walking time by two to 2½ hours.

Follow the main street up right through the village to about 500 metres past the Schilthorn cable car (Schilthornbahn) station. Here a right-hand trail leaves the road, skirting up across sunny hay-making meadows

dotted with quaint old wooden barns as it brings you around into a small grassy basin. Cross the Schiltbach and walk a few paces over to the **Restaurant-Pension Spielbodenalp** (see Places to Stay) at 1790 metres, around 40 minutes from Mürren train station.

Head over to the foot of a steep ridge, and begin climbing this in (often exposed) switchbacks leading up to a signposted trail junction at **Bryndli** (2020 metres). Sitting benches along this stretch offer a welcome respite and the chance to take in more of the

wonderful vistas. Taking the right branch, sidle around the flower-covered mountainsides high above the Sefinental, a wild Alpine valley beneath the striking form of the 3436-metre Gspaltenhorn, to reach **Poganggen** after 1¼ to 1¾ hours. At 2039 metres in this rocky basin lies the **Rotstockhütte** (see Places to Stay).

Make your way upvalley over terrain strewn with debris washed down by a mountain torrent, passing numerous piles of stones laboriously collected to keep these rough pastures open. The path rises steadily on through grassed-over moraine mounds, before zigzagging up more steeply through eroding shale. These slopes are often snowbound well into summer, but walkers generally arrive at the 2612-metre **Sefinenfurgge** one to 1⅓ hours after leaving the Rotstockhütte. Although just a crack in the saw-blade ridge between the Hundshorn and the Bütlasse, this pass gives a fine view south-west towards the Blüemlisalp massif. Looking back you'll see the 2970-metre Schilthorn and its lower castle-like neighbour, the Birg (2677 metres), both with cable-car stations on their summits.

Drop directly down the steep, loose-rock sides below the pass, where fixed cables, railings and steel ladderways give added confidence. The descent continues over bare talus slopes above a streamlet, following this down through gradually thickening vegetation to reach the rustic alp huts of **Obere Dürreberg** (see Places to Stay) at 1995 metres after 50 minutes to 1¼ hours.

The route now crosses the stream, winding its way down grassy fields that look over to the perpetual snows of the Blüemlisalp, before coming onto a dirt road at the neat farmhouse of **Bürgli** (1620 metres). Walk on right across the Dürreberg stream, then take a marked path running down left through the trees past **Bundstäg** to an attractive riverside clearing by the Gamchibach. Here cross the bridge to pick up a wide track leading on through more light forest via **Dündenessli**, passing by some interesting 'glacier pots' – enormous rock cavities formed by pressurised, silt-laden water flowing beneath Ice-age glaciers. A few paces down is the small village of Griesalp (1408 metres, see Walking Bases), 1¼ to 1¾ hours from Obere Dürreberg.

Alpine Pass Route walkers can now turn to the Hohtürli walk (Griesalp to Kandersteg) in the Frutigland section of this chapter.

OTHER WALKS
The Urbachtal

The Urbachtal is one of the few really wild Alpine valleys left in the Bernese Oberland, and is probably more often visited by mountaineers than by walkers. This is largely because extensive glaciers and impressive peaks reaching well over 3000 metres completely surround the upper valley area, forming a formidable barrier that only experienced climbers can breach; walkers are obliged to return from the valley via the access route.

From Innertkirchen (625 metres), five km from Meiringen, a road leads up to lovely open plains along the Urbachtal's middle reaches. From there a well-marked path climbs steadily on up through the valley to reach the Gaulihütte, an SAC-run hut at 2205 metres, after six to seven hours. The ascent totals 1600 altitude metres and requires good physical fitness. Recommended walking maps are either of the following: the locally produced *Wanderkarte Oberhasli*, Editions MPA Verlag's *Berner Oberland Ost* or the SAW/FSTP sheet *Interlaken*, all at a scale of 1:50,000.

The Upper Haslital & Grimselpass

The 2165-metre Grimselpass was an established trade route for centuries, though nowadays tourists vastly outnumber the mule trains. This moderate walk starts at the village of Guttannen (1049 metres), and leads through the upper Haslital between craggy giants to reach the Grimselpass after four or five hours. Although the landscape of the upper valley has been altered for hydroelectricity production, it has kept its wild and intensely glaciated feel.

The route mostly avoids the pass road,

following the still-transitable romantic old mule trail in places. Due to the (slight) danger of avalanches, it's not advisable to do this walk before early August. The Grimsel Hospiz, overlooking the Grimselsee a short way below the pass, and the hotels *Grimsel-Passhöhe* (☎ 036-73 11 37) and *Grimsel-Blick* (☎ 036-73 11 26) on the pass itself, have accommodation. There are several daily postbuses running between Andermatt and Meiringen (reservation obligatory). Use either of these 1:50,000 walking maps: *Wanderkarte Oberhasli, Berner Oberland Ost*, or both of the SAW/FSTP sheets *Sustenpass (255 T)* and *Nufenenpass (265 T)*.

The Grindelwald Glaciers

Virtually in Grindelwald's backyard, the two fascinating glaciers known as the (upper) Oberer Grindelwaldgletscher and the (lower) Unterer Grindelwaldgletscher tumble down from a vast system of icefalls and perpetual snowfields clothing the great summits high above the town. Nowhere else in the Alps do glaciers descend so far down into the valley as at Grindelwald. Today the snout of the Oberer Grindelwaldgletscher reaches down to around 1250 metres, although just 200 years ago it approached the 1000-metre level.

A suggested walk leads up from the Hotel Wetterhorn to the Oberer Grindelwaldgletscher, stopping for a look at the ice grottoes. From here the route climbs up to Halsegg, before contouring via Breitlouwina to Pfingstegg at 1391 metres (where a cable car runs down to Grindelwald). From Pfingstegg you can continue directly down past the Berghaus Marmorbruch to the gorge below the Unterer Grindelwaldgletscher. Recommended is the spectacular side trip to the Berghotel Stieregg (1702 metres) along a path cut into ledges high above the Unterer Grindelwaldgletscher, but sturdy footwear and sureness of step are necessary for this section. Very fit and keen walkers can go farther still to the SAC's Schreckhornhütte (2529 metres).

The average walking time from the Hotel Wetterhorn to the Berghaus Marmorbruch is three hours; the return walk to the Berghotel Stieregg takes an extra three hours. There are regular postbuses from Grindelwald to the Oberer Grindelwaldgletscher (most of them continuing up to the Grosse Scheidegg). The *Berghotel Stieregg* (☎ 036-53 17 66) offers mattress-room accommodation. Use either the 1:50,000 SAW/FSTP sheet *Interlaken (254 T)* or the 1:50,000 walking map *Berner Oberland Ost* published by Editions MPA Verlag.

The Sulsseewli

The Sulsseewli is an Alpine tarn lying at 1920 metres high above the junction of the Lauterbrunnental and the Lütschental. From the upper funicular station at Grütschalp (1496 metres) the route gently rises around through the forest to Sousläger, there crossing the Sousbach stream and climbing up to a contouring path that brings you over the Sulsbach to the Sulsseewli. The nearby private Lobhornhütte offers a splendid lookout point for the enormous white summits of the eastern Bernese Oberland.

The descent can be made by dropping down to the scattered hamlet of Sulwald (1081 metres), from where a private cableway runs down to the Isenfluh, or by continuing over the Tschingel ridge to the tiny village Saxeten (1003 metres). The average walking time from Grütschalp to the Sulsseewli is two hours; the descent to Sulwald takes no more than two hours, or around three hours to Saxeten. From Isenfluh there are postbuses every one or two hours to Lauterbrunnen until around 5.30 pm. Postbuses run from Saxeten to Widerswil three times daily, the last leaving at around 4.30 pm; reservations are advisable (call ☎ 036-71 32 05). The 1:50,000 SAW/FSTP sheet *Interlaken* best covers the walk.

The Upper Lauterbrunnental

The upper Lauterbrunnental is enclosed on three sides by massive summits presided over by the 3785-metre Lauterbrunner Breithorn. The sides of this upper valley are hung with glaciers and icefalls, and this unique area forms a nature reserve. From the end of the road at Stechelberg (910 metres) a rewarding five to six-hour circuit can be made via Obersteinberg to the little Alpine lake of Oberhornsee (2065 metres). From here you can continue up to the Schmadrihütte (2262 metres), before descending via Schwand to Schürboden (1379 metres). The last leg back to Stechelberg leads along the river past Trachsellauenen (1201 metres).

Apart from the Schmadrihütte, there are quite a few mountain hotels and a Friends of Nature hostel in the upper Lauterbrunnental area with rooms and dormitory accommodation. The postbuses run hourly from Lauterbrunnen (see Walking Bases) to Stechelberg all year round. The last bus returns to Lauterbrunnen around 5.30 pm. The 1:50,000 SAW/FSTP walking map *Jungfrau (264 T)* and the 1:40,000 *Wanderkarte Lauterbrunnental* both cover the upper Lauterbrunnental.

The Frutigland

Lying between the Wildstrubel and the Schilthorn, the Frutigland forms the central part of Bernese Oberland. This compact region comprises the Kandertal and its large side valleys, the Engstligental and the Kiental, and is enclosed by long, high ranges that branch northwards from the main chain of the Berner Alps. Although average elevations are somewhat lower than in the neighbouring Jungfrau Region, the Frutigland has at least as much of the classic scenery that 'sums up' the Swiss Alps.

Routes resounding with the cheerful clang of cowbells lead up to the Alpine meadows dotted with brilliant blue lakes before a backdrop of high snow-capped ranges. One of the true jewels of the Frutigland is the Oeschinensee, a large high-Alpine lake in the Blüemlisalp massif. Situated right on the Löschberg rail corridor, the Frutigland is easily accessible both from northern Switzerland as well as from the Valais, so there are no acceptable excuses for leaving this region out!

WALKING BASES
Griesalp

This tiny village lying at 1408 metres in the upper Kiental consists of a cluster of less than a dozen houses and hotels at the end of the transitable road through the valley. Griesalp is a walking base for the Höhtürli, Sefinenfurgge and Kientaler Höhenweg routes covered in this chapter. Another excellent walk from Griesalp goes up to the 1965-metre Abendberg, from where the descent can be made into the valley of Spiggengrund. A short way from the village are some interesting 'glacier pots' formed by pressurised water flowing beneath ancient Ice-age glaciers.

Griesalp has four places to stay, all offering rooms and dormitory accommodation at reasonable prices: most recommended is the *Berghaus Griesalp* (☎ 033-76 12 31). There is also a nearby *Friends of Nature hostel* (☎ 033-76 23 09) at Gorneren (1570 metres). The nearest tourist office (☎ 033-76 10 10) is in Kiental, a small town some six km down the valley. There are postbus connections to Griesalp from Reichenbach (on the Spiez-Kandersteg rail line) via Kiental several times daily between late May and early to mid-October. Outside this period the postbus only runs as far as Kiental. Reservations are advisable (call ☎ 033-71 22 93). This is the steepest postbus route in Europe!

Kandersteg

Just a small village before the construction of the Lötschberg railway, the town of Kandersteg (1176 metres) lies in the upper Kandertal. Although Kandersteg has little in the way of historical interest, it is an appealing and very scenic place that makes an ideal base for hikes in the central Bernese Oberland, including the Höhtürli (Oeschinensee), Bunderchrinde and Gemmipass/Rote Chumme walks featured in this guidebook. A popular and simple day walk from

Kandersteg leads down along the banks of the Kander to the Blausee, a beautiful crystal-clear lake in a riverside nature reserve.

Good lower-budget places to stay include the *Hotel Zur Post* (☎ 033-75 12 58), the *Hotel-Pension Spycher* (☎ 033-75 13 13) and the *Pension Edelweiss* (☎ 033-75 11 94). The *Restaurant Rendez-vous* (☎ 033-75 13 54) at the lower Kandersteg-Oeschinen chair-lift station offers dormitory accommodation and runs the local *camping ground*. The town has a tourist office (☎ 033-75 22 33) and a mountaineering school, the Bergsteigerschule Kandersteg (☎ 033-75 22 10). Kandersteg is just north of the Lötschberg tunnel on the Bern-Valais rail corridor, through which car-carrying trains continue south to Brig. Train connections are regular, and all but a few international expresses stop here.

Adelboden

Adelboden is situated at 1348 metres in the upper Engstligental, and although a bit touristy it is a pleasant enough place with all the modern conveniences. The town's central St Anton church dates from the 15th century. A popular local walk is the Engstligentaler Höhenweg, a panoramic route leading along the eastern slopes of the valley to (or from) the town of Frutigen.

Accommodation within the village area is not cheap. The least expensive places are the tiny *Pension Bel-Air* (☎ 033-73 22 62) and the *Pension Bodehüttli* (☎ 033-73 37 00). The *Pension Schermtanne* (☎ 033-73 10 51) three km outside Adelboden has dormitory accommodation. There are two summer camping grounds at Adelboden, the *Camping Albo* (☎ 033-73 12 09) and the *Camping Bergblick* (☎ 033-73 14 54). Adelboden's tourist office (☎ 033-73 22 52) is near the town church. There are hourly postbuses (until around 9.30 pm) to Adelboden from Frutigen, a town on the Lötschberg rail line with hourly train connections from Bern and Brig.

THE HOHTÜRLI
(Section 9 of the Alpine Pass Route)

Walking over the 2778-metre Hohtürli, or 'high doorway', which links the upper valley of the Kiental with Kandersteg, is one of the Bernese Oberland's classic hikes. This walk takes you high into the mountains past the mighty Blüemlisalp massif, then down via the Oeschinensee. Regarded by some as Switzerland's most beautiful Alpine lake, the Oeschinensee (1578 metres) was formed thousands of years ago, when unstable mountainsides below the Dolderhorn collapsed across the Öschibach stream. The lake has no visible outlet, but drains away subterraneously before re-emerging as a natural stream about halfway down to Kandersteg.

Maps

Which maps you decide to buy may depend on which other walks you plan to do in the region. Two of SAW/FSTP's 1:50,000 sheets cover the walk: *Jungfrau (264 T)*, and *Wildstrubel (263 T)*. You can also use either of the following two 1:60,000 Kümmerly + Frey walking maps: *Jungfrau-Region Oberhasli* or *Saanenland-Simmental-Kandersteg*. Another option is Editions MPA Verlag's *Berner Oberland West*, scaled at 1:50,000, though the route is a bit close to the edge of this map for comfort.

Walking Times & Standard

As long you get off to a fairly early start, completing the walk over the Hohtürli in a single day is quite realistic, although you might consider staying overnight somewhere on the way to better enjoy the magnificent surroundings.

The walk involves a long haul with an altitude gain of some 1370 metres, and therefore requires good physical condition. The final ascent to the Hohtürli is very steep and loose in places. There is little reliable water after Bundalp, so take enough for the sweaty climb. The downhill section from the Hohtürli is easier going – unless you're walking the other way.

The walk is rated *difficult*, and it covers 15 km.

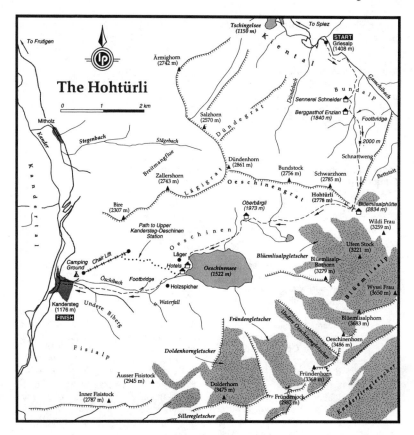

The Hohtürli

0   1   2 km

To Frutigen

Mitholz

Tschingelsee (1150 m)

To Spiez

START
Griesalp (1408 m)

Ärmighorn (2742 m)

B u n d a l p

Sennerei Schneider

Berggasthof Enzian (1840 m)

Footbridge

Salzhorn (2570 m)

2000 m

Schnattweng

Stegenbach

Stägebach

Dündenhorn (2861 m)

Bundstock (2756 m)

Schwarzhorn (2785 m)

Bettstatt

Breitmannflue

Zallershorn (2743 m)

Hohtürli (2778 m)

Blüemlisalphütte (2834 m)

Bire (2307 m)

Oberbärgli (1973 m)

Wildi Frau (3259 m)

Path to Upper Kandersteg-Oeschinen Station

Läger

Ufem Stock (3221 m)

Blüemlisalpgletscher

Blüemlisalp-Rothorn (3279 m)

Camping Ground

Chair Lift

Hotels

Oeschinensee (1522 m)

Wyssi Frau (3650 m)

Öschibach

Footbridge

Holzspicher

Kandersteg (1176 m)

FINISH

Undere Biberg

Waterfall

Fründengletscher

Undere Oeschinengletscher

Blüemlisalphorn (3683 m)

Oeschinenhorn (3486 m)

F i s i a l p

Doldenhorngletscher

Äusser Fisistock (2945 m)

Dolderhorn (3475 m)

Fründenhorn (3368 m)

Fründenjoch (2987 m)

Inner Fisistock (2787 m)

Silleregletscher

Places to Stay

At Bundalp, the *Sennerei Schneider* (☎ 033-76 12 64, open early June to late September) offers very good value in dormitory accommodation. It's a typical Bernese Alpine dairy, where you can watch the daily cheese-making. Just above at 1840 metres is the *Berggasthof Enzian* (☎ 033-76 11 92, open from May to late September). Along with a cosy restaurant, it has a dormitory (with shower) for up to 90 walkers.

If the altitude doesn't bother you, the *Blüemlisalphütte* (☎ 033-76 14 37) just above the Hohtürli at 2834 metres, is the

most scenic place to spend a night. This SAC hut is always open, but only staffed from late June until mid-October.

On the other side of the Hohtürli at 1980 metres is the *Berghaus Bärgli* (no telephone, open mid-July to late August) at Ober-öschinenalp. It's simple and cheap with a small dormitory. On the western side of the Oeschinensee, are the *Hotel Oeschinensee* (☎ 033-75 11 19) and the *Berghaus Oeschinensee* (☎ 033-75 11 66). Both offer rooms and dormitories at reasonable rates, and are open from May to October.

For accommodation in Griesalp and

Kandersteg, see Walking Bases above in this section.

Getting to/from the Walk

For the walk over the Hohtürli you set out from Griesalp, and end up in Kandersteg. Public transport access to both places is given in the Walking Bases sections of this chapter.

Route Directions: Griesalp to Kandersteg

(15 km, 6 to 8½ hours)

From the Berghaus in Griesalp (see Walking Bases), make your way upvalley through field and forest (retracing your last steps if you walked over the Sefinenfurgge to Griesalp). When you get to the bridge over the Gamchibach, follow the right-hand path (signposted 'Blüemlisalphütte') winding up through the trees beside a cascading stream to meet a surfaced road. Short-cut steeply on over the high Alpine pastures of **Bundalp**, passing the Sennerei Schneider (see Places to Stay) shortly before reaching the Berggasthof Enzian at **Oberi Bund** (1840 metres, see Places to Stay) after one to 1⅓ hours.

Head 500 metres up the (now dirt) road, then turn off right onto a marked foot track. This quickly cuts across the grassed-over slopes, then begins climbing very steeply up a badly eroding ridge of old moraines, eventually connecting with a larger rocky spur. The strenuous ascent continues along the left side of this ridge – in many places ladders or stairways with fixed cables provide the only way up – finally arriving at the tiny 2778-metre platform of the **Hohtürli**, 2¼ to 3½ hours from Oberi Bund. The Blüemlisalphütte (see Places to Stay) stands just 60 metres farther up the ridge, and grants stunning views of the Blüemlisalp peaks and the crevassed icy mass of the Blüemlisalpgletscher from a breathtakingly close vantage point.

Descend in spirals around to the right through loose talus, before following a narrow shelf past icefalls at the lower tip of the adjacent Blüemlisalpgletscher. The path leads on along the crest of a high lateral moraine ridge left by the receding glacier, with a murky meltwater lakelet visible below, then drops down rightwards through the first wildflowers to reach **Oberbärgli** at 1973 metres after 1¼ to 1¾ hours.

Walk down a short way to the edge of a precipice, where the magnificent emerald-coloured **Oeschinensee** comes into sight, and climbs down via stepways safeguarded by cables. Continue down and bear right to cross a footbridge, after which a well-cut trail begins a traverse of the lake's steep northern sides. Across the Oeschinensee, sheer cliffs adorned with waterfalls drop down from the towering glacier-clad peaks directly into the lake. Frequent resting benches along this stretch are ideal for contemplating the outstanding natural scenery.

The way leads down to a tiny cove with a pebble beach, where – in hot weather only – walkers may be tempted to go in for a dip. Head a short distance on around through lovely tall stands of spruce to reach the hotels at the lake's western shore (see Places to Stay), 50 minutes to one hour after you left Oberbärgli. (From here a shorter 20 to 25 minute alternative route goes to the upper Kandersteg-Oeschinen chair-lift station, which brings you the rest of the way down to Kandersteg.)

Make your way on down left along the dirt service track, picking up a foot trail off right just as you pass a high waterfall coming down from the Dolderhorn. This leads along forested slopes above the Öschibach, before coming onto a sealed road just down from the lower chair-lift station. Follow the bitumen a short way around to the left to arrive in **Kandersteg** (see Walking Bases) after 50 minutes to one hour. The train station, at 1176 metres, is a short walk down across the river.

The Alpine Pass Route continues below in the Bunderchrinde walk (Kandersteg to Adelboden).

THE BUNDERCHRINDE
(Section 10 of the Alpine Pass Route)

Although it's relatively short in distance as the crow flies, Kandersteg and Adelboden are separated by a surprisingly high and craggy range. The 2385-metre gap of the Bunderchrinde is one of the few crossing routes between the two towns and makes a perfect day-long ramble. On its eastern flank the range has a classic tiered form, with a broad intermediate terrace between high cliffs fringed by screeslides. These precipitous crags are popular with local rock-climbers, though walkers on the Bunderchrinde route are far more numerous.

Maps

Best are the special 1:25,000 walking map titled *Wanderkarte Kandersteg* (although it just cuts out Adelboden) or the 1:50,000 SAW/FSTP sheet *Wildstrubel (263 T)*. Two other walking maps, the 1:50,000 *Berner Oberland West*, produced by Editions MPA Verlag, and Kümmerly + Frey's 1:60,000 *Saanenland-Simmental-Kandersteg*, make quite good alternatives.

Walking Times & Standard

The Bunderchrinde is a rather lengthy day walk that can be broken up into a longer and a shorter stage by staying overnight en route. This is quite a good mountain path marked with white-red-white painted stripes. The going may get quite strenuous, with many sections of loose rock or scree. The ascent is 1200 altitude metres with a similar descent.

The walk is rated *moderate* and covers a distance of 16 km.

Places to Stay

The only place to stay on the way is the *Berghaus Bonderalp* (☎ 033-73 17 16, open mid-June to mid-September) at Vordere Bunder (1755 metres), which offers cheap dormitory accommodation.

For places to stay in Kandersteg and Adelboden see Walking Bases.

Getting to/from the Walk

See Walking Bases for access to Kandersteg and Adelboden.

Route Directions: Kandersteg to Adelboden

(16 km, 5 to 6¾ hours)

From the train station in Kandersteg (see Walking Bases above), walk below the rail underpass then continue southwards along a bitumened lane. This briefly runs beside the rail lines, before leading off rightwards past the landing ground of the Kandersteg paragliding school. A broad path leads on along the banks of the Kander River, passing the Pfadfinder Zentrum (an international scouting and guiding centre) a few paces before you come to a road bridge, 20 to 25 minutes from Kandersteg.

A signpost here directs you off right along an initially vague foot track that goes over the riverside meadows for five to 10 minutes, before branching right to begin a long and steep ascent up the partially forested valley sides. The route soon meets a surfaced road and follows this for short sections, cutting out the numerous switchback curves as it climbs on beside the Alpbach stream to reach **Usser Üschene** at 1595 metres after a further one to 1⅓ hours. Here the pretty Üschene valley opens out below the spectacular terraced cliffs of the Grosser Lohner.

Make your way left across the green pastures for 10 minutes to the road, and proceed to a signpost a few paces farther upvalley. The route first zigzags up beside a gravel-filled stream, then moves left to climb steeply through the cliffs past a small waterfall. Rising to a high shelf, the trail turns right then traverses undulating slopes before coming to the farmstead of **Alpschele** at 2095 metres, one to 1⅓ hours farther on. Alpschele looks across to the white-topped summits of the Balmhorn and Altels towering above the sheer-walled Gasterntal, one of the Bernese Oberland's most classic glacial valleys. Basic refreshments are for sale here.

Continue up towards an obvious grassy saddle on the Alpschengrat, doubling back left when you get to the track turn-off to Obere Allme on your right. The well-trodden path now cuts up across talus slopes to arrive at the **Bunderchrinde** after 40 to 50 minutes. This narrow 2385-metre pass is merely a gap in the ridge between interesting layered-rock crags. There are views of all the previously mentioned sights, and the Oeschinensee is now clearly identifiable slightly downvalley behind Kandersteg. To the west is the Albristhorn, with the village of Adelboden immediately below.

Descend in spirals through a scree-filled gully, before easing steadily over to the right to avoid more broken-up terrain. The route turns right at a dirt road and follows this for a short distance to the **Berghaus Bonder-alp**, 45 minutes to one hour from the pass. This alp restaurant at 1755 metres offers dormitory accommodation, refreshments and its own cheeses.

From below the Berghaus, take the signposted foot track which cuts across the grassy slopes to the left. Drop down through forest, crossing minor roads a number of times before coming out onto a broader road just before a bridge over the Bunderlebach after 30 to 40 minutes. The road leads on another 20 to 30 minutes past the scattering of holiday chalets and restaurants at **Bunderle** to cross the Engstlige stream just before intersecting with the Unter dem Birg turn-off.

Turn right and walk over a second road bridge (crossing the Allebach) to the main Adelboden-Frutigen road. From here a steep pedestrian laneway leads up beside houses for 15 to 20 minutes to the centre of Adelboden (see Walking Bases above).

For the following section of the Alpine Pass Route (Adelboden to Lenk), refer to the Hahnenmoospass walk in this chapter.

THE GEMMIPASS & ROTE CHUMME

For centuries the 2322-metre Gemmipass was the most-transited summer crossing route between the Bernese Oberland and the Valais. After the widening of the amazing winding mule path cut into cliffs high above Leukerbad in the early 1700s, the Gemmi

became the only significant pass for travel and transport between the two cantons. Each year in late July the traditional Schäferfest takes place on the Gemmipass. Originally a festive meeting of shepherds from the Valais and the Bernese Oberland, today flocks of people and sheep turn up to eat raclette (and grass) around the shores of the Daubensee.

This walk doesn't lead down into the Valais however, but continues over the 2628-metre gap of the Rote Chumme through an impressive glaciated landscape to the broad green bowl of Engstligenalp, one of the largest expanses of high-Alpine pastures in the Bernese Oberland. In ancient times Engstligenalp was covered by a lake, which was gradually filled in by rubble washed down from the slopes of the surrounding mountains.

Maps

The recommended map for this walk is the 1:50,000 SAW/FSTP sheet *Wildstrubel (263 T)*. Reasonable alternatives are Editions MPA Verlag's 1:50,000 *Berner Oberland West* or *Kümmerly + Frey's Saanenland-Simmental-Kandertal*, which is scaled at 1:60,000.

Walking Times & Standard

This two-day hike takes you well up into the exposed terrain of the high-Alpine zone and is therefore a serious undertaking. Higher up the waymarkings are white-red-white painted stripes. You will need fine and stable weather conditions – watch out for thunderstorms! There is plenty of heavy climbing and some steep descents.

The walk is rated *moderate to difficult* and covers 26 km.

Places to Stay

The *Berghotel Schwarenbach* (☎ 033-75 12 72, open from March to October) at 2061 metres has basic rooms and a dormitory (with showers). On the Gemmipass at 2322 metres is the *Hotel Wildstrubel* (☎ 027-61 12 01, open June to October), which has hotel-style beds as well as sleeping space in dormitories for 150 people.

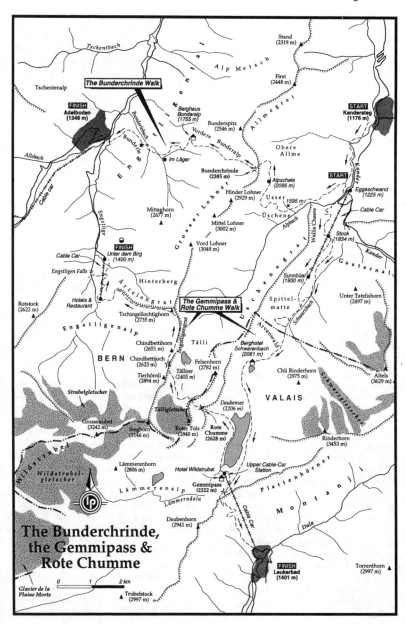

The Bunderchrinde,
the Gemmipass &
Rote Chumme

0   1   2 km

*Glacier de la
Plaine Morte*

At Engstligenalp, the *Berghaus Bärtschi* (☎ 033-73 13 73, open early June to mid-October) offers simple rooms and dormitory accommodation (with showers). The nearby *Hotel Engstligenalp* (☎ 033-73 22 91, open mid-June to late October) offers a range of rooms as well as dorms (with use of shower), but is a little on the expensive side.

Getting to/from the Walk

The walk begins from Kandersteg (see Walking Bases above). Stage 1 can be shortened by around three hours by taking a postbus/cable-car combination from Kandersteg train station. There are 10 or so daily postbuses to Eggeschwand, from where the cable car up to Sunnbüel runs half-hourly; the last upward car leaves well before 6 pm.

The walk finishes at Engstligenalp, from where a cable car carries you down to Unter dem Birg. It runs half-hourly until 6 pm (until 5 pm before mid to late June and after mid-September). Half-hourly postbuses run from Unter dem Birg to Adelboden until 5 pm. Otherwise, Adelboden is a pleasant one hour's walk from Unter dem Birg.

Route Directions – Stage 1: Kandersteg to Berghotel Schwarenbach

(15 km, 4¼ to 5½ hours)

From Kandersteg train station, head below the railway bridge following a bitumened lane upvalley first alongside the tracks then off to the right past the landing ground of the Kandersteg paragliding school. A gravelled walkway leads on along the banks of the Kander River, passing the Pfadfinder Zentrum (an international scouting and guiding centre) just before you come to a road bridge. Here take a right-hand path that cuts up gently through riverside meadows (past the route leading off right up to the Bunderchrinde) crossing the Alpbach on a footbridge to meet the main Kandersteg-Gasterntal road not far up from the cable-car station at **Eggeschwand**, 30 to 40 minutes from Kandersteg.

Go 300 metres uphill to a tight curve in the road, where a signpost directs you straight ahead into the forest. A broad track now takes you on a long spiralling ascent up the steep slopes below the interesting tilted sediments of the Wallis Cheere. As you gain altitude occasional avalanche clearings bring good views down to the upper Kandertal, and after 1½ to two hours the path passes above the middle cable-car station at **Stock** (1834 metres).

As the gradient evens out the trail sidles around the side of an abrupt precipice, through the trees to your left the land falls away directly into the flat-bottomed Gasterntal, a classic glacial trough-valley. The local wildflowers here are particularly varied, and many of the Alpine plants growing beside the way are identified with individual nameplates. Walk on past the roaring Schwarzbach, and begin rising gently into the Alpine pastures of **Spittelmatte**. These rolling slopes were the site of a tragedy in September 1895, when the lower section of a glacier on the 3629-metre Altels (the nearby peak to the south-east) suddenly collapsed into the valley, crushing herders and their cattle under millions of tonnes of ice.

Not far on the walking route merges with a wider alp track coming from the upper cable-car station at **Sunnbüel** (1930 metres), and follows this past a dairy farm fringed by the trees of the Arvenwald. Continue up across the cantonal border into the Valais, climbing around to the left over stabilised moraines to reach the **Berghotel Schwarenbach** (see Places to Stay), 1¼ to 1¾ hours from Stock. This building is a former customs post on the old frontier that separated the once independent Valais from the Swiss Confederation, and stands at 2061 metres above a tiny greenish lake.

Bearing left past a turn-off just beyond the hotel, make your way up the steady incline to reach a little bay at the northern end of the **Daubensee** after 30 to 40 minutes. Filling a long undrained basin at 2206 metres, the Daubensee is the highest of the Bernese Oberland's larger natural lakes. High-tension power lines running along the western shore are an unfortunate intrusion into the otherwise splendid Alpine scenery.

Stroll on 30 to 40 minutes around the lake's grassy eastern shores to the cable-car station at the **Gemmipass** (2322 metres, see Places to Stay). The view extends southwards to the mountains of the Matterhorn region, while mighty cliffs sweep down from the pass to Leukerbad, a modern resort at 1401 metres. Leukerbad is reachable in 1¼ to 1¾ hours via an exhilarating old mule trail cut into the rock face as well as by cable car.

Stage 2: Gemmipass to Engstligenalp
(11 km, 4½ to 6¼ hours)

Backtrack a short way, then take a trail down to cross the Lämmerndalu stream on a wooden footbridge near where it enters the Daubensee. Head on around the western shore, climbing high over scree-slopes before swinging left away from the lake. Paint markings guide you on up through a long rocky-grassy gully that ends with a steep ascent of switchbacks to arrive at the **Rote Chumme** (2628 metres) after 1½ to two hours. This barren gap near a striking monument-like rock column marks your return into Bernese territory. Before you lies the heavily glaciated upper valley of Tälli, whose most interesting features are the receding ices of the Tälligletscher and a small lake, the Tällisee. Small herds of ibex may sometimes be spied loitering around this seemingly inhospitable area.

Drop down to the left over loose moraines and snowdrifts often lingering well into July to cross the freezing stream, then cut back rightwards up the well-trodden scree-slopes above the Tällisee to another pass crossing, the 2623-metre **Chindbettijoch**, just 30 to 40 minutes on. At the signposted junction a few paces down from here you get a nice view of the Engstligenalp.

Continue around to the right below the Chindlibetthorn to begin a surprisingly easy and spectacular high traverse along the **Engstligengrat**. Following this bare ridge, the route steers past the odd rock outcrop as it rises over a broad hump before cutting left across the scree-slopes under the 2735-metre

Tschingellochtighorn. Head down along the sharper and grassier spur of the **Ärtelengrat** to where it peters out above sheer cliffs falling straight into the upper Engstligental. A short and milder descent leftwards over hillside meadows brings you down to the hotels at Engstligenalp (1954 metres, see Places to Stay) after 1¼ to 1¾ hours.

Engstligenalp is a wide grassy bowl enclosed on almost every side by the domineering form of the Wildstrubel and high craggy ridges running off that massif. From here you can take the cable car – or better, the very steep mule trail down via the **Engstligen Falls** – to the postbus stop at **Unter dem Birg** (1400 metres).

THE HAHNENMOOSPASS
(Section 11 of the Alpine Pass Route)

The 1956-metre Hahnenmoospass links Adelboden in the Engstligental with Lenk in the Simmental. In medieval times the broad grassy pass height was the common meeting place of the local Alpine herders from both valleys, who held annual wrestling competitions there. More recently, the upper Engstligental has seen modest development for winter skiing, but the gentle nature of this area has not been lost.

Maps

The recommended walking maps are the 1:25,000 *Wanderkarte Lenk*, or the 1:50,000 sheet *Wildstrubel (263T)* published by the SAW/FSTP. Kümmerly + Frey's walking map *Saanenland-Simmental-Kandertal* at a scale of 1:60,000 also shows the route.

Walking Times & Standard

This is a medium-length day walk, that can be stretched out or shortened at will by staying overnight en route or by taking one of the transport options along the way. Although the walk involves a total climb of around 1000 altitude metres (with a descent of some 800 metres), the going is relatively unstrenuous, making this a mountain walk suited to any reasonably fit person.

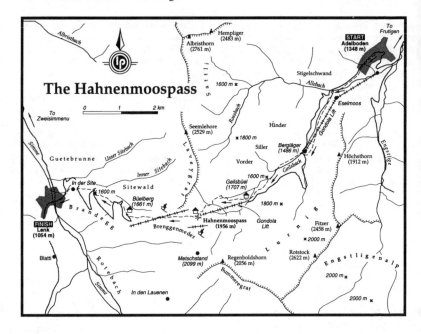

The Hahnenmoospass

The Hahnenmoospass has been given an *easy to moderate* rating, and covers 13 km.

Places to Stay

At Geilsbüel, the *Restaurant Geilsbrüggli* (☎ 033-73 21 71) has a dormitory for walkers. On the pass height itself, the *Berghotel Hahnenmoospass* (☎ 033-73 21 41), open mid-June to mid-October) offers simple rooms and dormitory beds (with shower) for quite reasonable rates. More expensive is the *Hotel Büelberg* (☎ 030-3 15 60, open early June to late October) at Büelberg, which only has rooms.

For places to stay in Adelboden and Lenk, see under Walking Bases.

Getting to/from the Walk

The Hahnenmoospass walk leaves from Adelboden and finishes at Lenk; for access details to both places see Walking Bases above.

The walk can be shortened by taking any of the following forms of public or mountain transport. There are seven daily postbuses from Adelboden via Berglägger to Geilsbüel; you can also take the gondola lift from Adelboden-Oey to Berglägger, which in summer operates daily until around 5 pm. From Geilsbüel a gondola lift runs up to the Hahnenmoospass until around 5.30 pm. Finally, some four public minibuses run between Büelberg and Lenk each day.

Route Directions: Adelboden to Lenk
(13 km, 3½ to 4½ hours)

From the church clock tower walk gently uphill along the main road out of town, heading left at a fork near the Pension Schermtanne. Immediately after crossing the Allebach stream, a signposted path on your right ducks below the concrete road bridge and crosses the Geilsbach, 25 to 30 minutes from Adelboden. The route continues up the eastern side of the stream, crossing a farm track before it climbs away left under a gondola lift to meet a bitumened road. Here turn right and cross the river to reach the **Bergläger** gondola station (1486 metres) after a further 30 to 40 minutes.

Follow the gravelled road 700 metres upvalley, then take a trail leading off left. This crosses the stream on a small footbridge and makes its way up through pockets of damp, mossy forest; before coming out at another surfaced road, 30 to 40 minutes on from Bergläger. Just over the rise is **Geilsbüel** (1707 metres), with a hotel/restaurant and cable car running up to the Hahnenmoospass.

The climb to the pass is easy and straightforward, and goes along a narrow bitumened road from just above the cable-car station. The route winds up through the grassy rolling basin, with a few short cuts to avoid curves in the road, and arrives at the 1956-metre **Hahnenmoospass** after 40 to 50 minutes. There is a mountain hotel here (with refreshments and accommodation), as well as some great views south-eastwards to the Wildstrubel massif.

Dropping to the right, follow an alp track down the attractive open slopes giving more wonderful views across the upper valley of the Simmental to the Weisshorn and glaciers that drain the Plaine Morte. The gravelled lane crosses under a winter ski-tow about halfway before reaching a bitumened road at the large **Hotel Büelberg** (see Places to Stay), 30 to 40 minutes from the pass. Büelberg lies at 1661 metres and looks directly down to Lenk, 600 metres below.

The route continues rightwards from below the hotel, crossing and briefly following the roadway as it descends through flowery Alpine meadows to **Brandegg** (1536 metres). Here a signposted old mule trail leads on steeply down to the right alongside a forested gully, twice recrossing the road before coming out at a bridge over the Innere Sitebach stream, 45 minutes to one hour on. **Lenk** train station is now just 10 minutes' walk down to the left. (For information on Lenk, see Walking Bases above).

For the next section of the Alpine Pass Route (Lenk to Lauenen), refer to the Trüttlisbergpass walk in the Saanenland & Simmental section of this chapter.

OTHER WALKS
The Kiental Höhenweg

This roughly three-hour route begins with a chair-lift ride from the village of Kiental up nearly 500 altitude metres to Bamslauenen (1408 metres). From here a path traverses high along the largely forested western slopes of the Kiental valley before descending to Griesalp (see Walking Bases). The route passes high above Switzerland's youngest (natural) lake, the Tschingelsee, which formed after a landslide in 1950 dammed the Gornerewasser stream. The route is covered by the 1:50,000 Kümmerly + Frey walking map *Saanenland-Simmental-Kandertal* or the two 1:50,000 SAW/FSTP sheets *Jungfrau (264 T)* and *Interlaken (254 T)*.

The Lötschberg Nordrampe

The Lötschberg Nordrampe trail is the Bernese Oberland's counterpart to the Lötschberg Südrampe in the Valais. Although less grandiose, it follows a similar high-level panoramic route beside the rail lines. The 4½-hour walk begins at the upper station of the Kiental-Ramslauenen cable car (1409 metres), and sidles around below the 2129-metre Gehrihorn to Chüeweid (1468 metres). From here the path makes a gently dropping southward traverse of the slopes high above the Kandertal via Schlafegg, before descending past tunnel loops of the Lötschberg rail line to the tiny lake of Blausee beside the Kander River. The final section continues along the banks of the river to Kandersteg (see Walking Bases). The 1:25,000 walking map *Wanderkarte Frutigen* produced by the local tourist authority covers the route well.

The Gasterntal

Beyond the narrow Chluse ravine above Kandersteg lies the Gasterntal, one of the Alps' most classic glacial trough-valleys. This tiny hanging valley has been filled in and flattened out by the accumulation of some 200 metres of glacial and alluvial debris to create a flat and surprisingly broad valley floor with only a slight gradient over its roughly eight-km length. Having been sheared by the Kanderfirn glacier, the rock walls enclosing the Gasterntal rise almost vertically to culminate in summits over 3500 metres high. Until several decades ago the valley was inhabited all year round, but today the Gasterntalers move down for the winter, when the area is visited only by infrequent parties of ski-mountaineers.

The Gasterntal is accessible only from the Kandertal or via the Lötschenpass (see below), and forms a wild and beautiful nature reserve. An easy 2½-hour walk leads up from Kandersteg (see Walking Bases) via the Chluse to the tiny village of Selden at 1537 metres. From Selden walkers can make the four to five-hour return hike up to a lookout at the snout of the Kanderfirn. The *Hotel Steinbock* (☎ 033-75 11 62) and the *Hotel Gasterntal-Selden* (☎ 033-75 11 63) in Selden, and the *Berggasthaus Heimritz* (☎ 033-75 14 34) one km up the valley all have rooms and dormitory accommodation and are open throughout the main walking season. The small access road into the valley is closed to unauthorised traffic, but the private Autoverkehr Kandersteg-Gasterntal (☎ 033-71 11 72) operates a regular shuttle minibus service from Kandersteg to Selden. Reservations are essential. The excellent 1:25,000 walking map titled *Wanderkarte Kandersteg* covers the whole valley well.

The Lötschenpass

The 2690-metre Lötschenpass forms the Bern/Valais cantonal border, and despite its relatively high altitude has been a preferred Alpine crossing since prehistoric times. The pass height itself was once the scene of bloody battles between the rival powers of Bern and the Valais, and before the construction of the Gemmipass mule trail the Lötschenpass was the most important connection between the Bernese Oberland and the upper Valais. Today the Lötschberg railway tunnel passes directly under the Lötschenpass, though walking is definitely the

more scenic – if somewhat longer – alternative to taking the train.

This classic pass crossing is nevertheless a serious undertaking unsuited to hikers inexperienced in mountain walking. From Selden (see the Gasterntal walk) the route climbs steeply southwards via Gfällalp, largely following the remains of the ancient mule track. About midway along the ascent the route crosses a small glacier; this section is well marked in summer and avoids dangerous crevasses – keep to the markings. From the pass height the route drops down into the Lötschental (see the Valais chapter) either via Kümmenalp to Felden or via Laucheralp to Wiler.

The Lötschenpass can be crossed in a very long day, but this is unnecessary as there are very good accommodation options en route. Combining the Lötschenpass with the previously mentioned Gasterntal walk from Kandersteg is highly recommended. The following places en route all offer mattress-room accommodation: the *Berghaus Gfällalp* (☎ 033-75 11 61) one hour above Selden, the *Lötschpasshütte* (☎ 077-28 43 02) right on the pass height, the *Berghaus Lauchern* (☎ 028-49 12 50) well down on the Valais side, and the *Gasthaus Kummenalp* (☎ 028-49 12 80) at 2083 metres. The best map to use is the special 1:25,000 sheet *Wanderkarte Kandersteg*, published by Verlag Egger and available in Kandersteg. The SAW/FSTP sheet *Jungfrau (264 T)* is also very good.

The Saanenland & Upper Simmental

West of the Wildstrubel massif the Bernese Alps have decidedly less impressive heights than their Alpine neighbours of the eastern Bernese Oberland, with only a few of the higher summits – such as the Oldenhorn and the Wildhorn – breaching the 3000-metre mark. The region is typified by high glaciated plateaus of up to 2800 metres that fall away abruptly northwards, and lovely upper valleys that always seem to begin at a large spectacular waterfall: the Simmenfälle, Engstligenfall, Geltenschuss and Iffigfall.

The Saanenland, in the Bernese Oberland's westernmost corner, is drained by the Saane (Sarine in French), which flows westwards through Fribourg and Vaud cantons before entering the Aare near Biel/Bienne. Divided from the rest of Bern Canton only by the low and indistinct Saanenmöser watershed, the Saanenland is the only German-speaking area in the upper valley. The Simmental, on the other hand, is a long side valley that meets the Aare at the Thunersee.

Although the Saanenland and upper Simmental are rather less popular than the central and eastern Bernese Oberland, the lower average height of the mountains in this region allows (unroped) walkers to venture high up amongst the loftiest summits on foot. There are some excellent trans-Alpine routes leading over the main range into the Valais.

WALKING BASES
Lenk
Lenk lies at 1054 metres in the upper Simmental, and has long been known for its sulphurous thermal baths which were first developed in 1688. The fire in 1878 destroyed most of the original village, and today Lenk is a pleasant though modern tourist resort. There's not much budget accommodation in town, but the cheapest places to stay are the *Hotel Alpenruh* (☎ 030-2 10 64) and the *Hotel Alpina* (☎ 030-3 10 57). Campers can go to the *Camping Hasenweid* (☎ 030-3 26 47) or the *Seegarten* (☎ 030-3 16 16). Lenk's tourist office (☎ 030-3 15 95) is just across the bridge from the train station.

Lenk is accessible by train via a branch line of the private Montreux-Oberland Bahn (MOB) from Zweisimmen. From the southern Jura and the Lake Geneva region, you can take the MOB railway via Saanen-Gstaad, although from the lower Valais a rail/postbus combination via either the Col du Pillon or the Col des Mosses may be

quicker. Zweisimmen is best reached from German-speaking Switzerland, Ticino or the northern Jura via Spiez (on the Brig-Bern line).

Lauenen
This pleasant and unspoilt village at 1241 metres has many fine examples of wooden architecture typical for the Bernese Oberland, such as the early 16th century St Petrus church with its quaint shingled steeple. There are several hotels in the village offering budget rooms. The nearest *youth hostel* (☎ 030-4 13 43) is at Saanen-Gstaad. Lauenen has a small supermarket and a tourist office (☎ 030-5 33 30). From late June to mid-October there are around 10 daily buses between Lauenen and Gstaad; the last bus from Lauenen leaves around 6 pm.

Gsteig
Gsteig (1189 metres) is a quaint old village in this forgotten south-west corner of the Bernese Oberland. Like nearby Lauenen, it has been mostly overlooked by tourist developers and also has nice wooden buildings. Of interest are the newly restored village church built in 1453 and the 18th-century Hotel Bären (☎ 030-5 10 33), which has rooms. There is no supermarket as such, but basic supplies can be bought at the local general store. Gsteig has a nearby camping ground, the *Camping Heiti* (☎ 030-5 10 29) and a tourist office (☎ 030-5 12 31). There is a *youth hostel* (☎ 030-4 13 43) in nearby Saanen-Gstaad.

From late June to late September postbus connections between Les Diablerets and Gstaad (via the Col du Pillon) meet at Gsteig, where you often have to change. There are about a dozen daily postbuses between Gstaad and Gsteig. The last postbus from Gsteig to Gstaad departs before 7 pm; the last bus to Les Diablerets leaves around 5 pm.

THE TRÜTTLISBERGPASS
(Section 12 of the Alpine Pass Route)
The 2038-metre Trüttlisbergpass leads out of

the Simmental into the Saanenland in the south-western corner of the Bernese Oberland. This relatively low crossing point between Lenk and Lauenen is one of the easier Alpine passes in the region. Beautiful unspoilt highland meadows interrupted by interesting limestone protrusions surround the quiet pass heights on both sides. The walk gives excellent views of the upper Lauenental, making this a very pleasant outing indeed.

Maps

A good locally available walking map is the *Wanderkarte Lenk* scaled at 1:25,000 and produced by the local tourist authorities. Also recommended is the 1:50,000 SAW/FSTP sheet, *Wildstrubel (263T)*. The 1:50,000 Editions MPA Verlag walking map *Berner Oberland West* shows the route accurately, but cuts off much of the western Bernese Alps to the south.

Walking Times & Standard

The Trüttlisbergpass is a medium-length day walk, although some Alpine Pass Route hikers choose to combine it with the much shorter Chrinepass walk (see below). The ascent to the pass and the descent to Lauenen are long but fairly mild.

The Trüttlisbergpass has been rated *easy to moderate* and covers 15 km.

Places to Stay

There is no en-route accommodation at all. See Walking Bases for places to stay in Lenk and Lauenen.

Getting to/from the Walk

The walk begins in Lenk and finishes in Lauenen (see Walking Bases).

Route Directions: Lenk to Lauenen

(15 km, 4½ to 6 hours)

From Lenk railway station go west across the bridge up beside the small park to where a signpost points you off right. Follow this road out of the village, turning left onto a

smaller road just before the bridge, then continue up beside the Wallbach stream. Just past the lower station of the Betelberg chair lift a wide track branches off right into the cool, damp forest and leads alongside the stream, which it soon crosses on a footbridge.

Walk a short way on to the **Wallbach-schlucht**, climbing steel ladders and stone stairways through this gorge past mossy cascades and small water-eroded ponds, then recross and ascend steeply away from the stream. The path comes out of the forest to meet the chair lift just above the **Gasthaus Wallegg** (restaurant only), 45 minutes to one hour from Lenk. Head 100 metres directly up then dip back into the forest along an old vehicle track that rises gradually against the contour to cross the Wallbach once more after another 40 to 50 minutes.

Make your way up to a dirt road and follow this a short way upvalley to where a signposted path departs off right. The path cuts up across the open slopes, passing several old barnyards to reach **Obere Lochberg** at 1910 metres after 50 minutes to one hour. Continue on over the lovely rolling pastures dotted with patches of Alpine heath, from where interesting karst (limestone) formations on the opposite side of the valley come into view. You'll arrive at the broad **Trüttlisbergpass** at 2038 metres after a further 45 minutes to one hour. From here the Hahnenmoospass is visible back towards the north-east, and to the south-east lie the peaks of the Wildstrubel.

Walk around left to a trail junction (where the path to Stübenli diverges), then descend right along a broad grassy spur, coming to **Vordere Trütlisberg** (1818 metres), a farmhouse at the end of a rough alp track. Apart from the odd marked short cut, the route follows this road down to reach a bitumened road at **Flueweid** after 45 minutes to one hour.

Head on gently down through **Flue**, an open shelf at 1480 metres from where the picturesque Tungelschuss and Geltenschuss waterfalls can be seen at the head of the Lauenental, before turning left off the main

The Trüttlisbergpass & the Chrinepass

The Trüttlisbergpass Walk

The Chrinepass Walk

4 km

START Lenk (1054 m)

To Zweisimmen

Simme

Oberlaubhorn (1999 m)

Iffigbach

Wallbachschlucht

Gasthaus Wallegg

Flöschhore (2079 m)

Betelberg Chair-Lift

Mülkerblatte (1935 m)

Pöntzal

Rohrbach

Weidli

Wistätthorn (2362 m)

Obere Lochberg (1910 m)

Abläch

Chlingbach

Stübleni (2109 m)

Iffighore (2378 m)

Turbach

Horemäder Trüttlisberg

Tube (2106 m)

Trüttlisbergpass (2038 m)

Rothorn (2276 m)

Niesehorn (2776 m)

Schnidehorn (2937 m)

Tungelgletscher

Giferspitz (2541 m)

Lauenehore (2477 m)

Vordere Trüttlisberg (1818 m)

Flue (1480 m)

Zwischenbächen

Tungelschuss

Follhore (2195 m)

Geltenschuss

Hahnenschritthorn (2833 m)

Dürrischürt (1936 m)

Schneitbächli

Mittbach

Louibach

Lauenensee (1381 m)

Brüeschergat

Bode

FINISH Lauenen (1241 m)

START

Sattel (1400 m)

Ski Lift

Brüchli (1457 m)

Chrinepass (1659 m)

The Chrinepass Walk

Mutthore (2312 m)

Spitzhorn (2806 m)

Louibach

To Gstaad

Hohi Wispile

Chrine

Walliser Wispile (1982 m)

Längmatte (1452 m)

Saane

Feutersoey (1130 m)

To Col du Pillon

FINISH Gsteig (1184 m)

road at **Zwischenbächen** (shown on some maps as 'Zwüschbäche') onto a gravelled lane. This crosses several streams as it makes its way over to the right through field and forest to meet another surfaced road at **Bode**, 30 to 40 minutes on.

Continue left a short way, then take the first dirt track leading off left. Follow this back down to the **Mülibach**, from where well-marked trails and lanes fringed with wild raspberry bushes bring you down beside the stream to reach the main valley road near the **Lauenen** post office after a further 20 to 30 minutes.

For the next section of the Alpine Pass Route (Lauenen to Gsteig) refer to the Chrinepass walk below.

THE CHRINEPASS
(Section 13 of the Alpine Pass Route)
The Chrinepass (shown on some signposts as 'Krinnenpass') is a mere low point in a small ridge dividing the Lauenental and upper valley of the Saane. While it lacks some of the majestic scenery of other routes in the region, the Chrinepass makes a gentle and easy day walk.

Maps
The 1:50,000 SAW/FSTP sheet *Wildstrubel (263T)* and the 1:50,000 Editions MPA Verlag walking map *Berner Oberland West* both cover the route.

Walking Times & Standard
This is a short day walk that is often done together with the previous Trüttlisbergpass hike. The Chinepass involves a quite modest climb and drop to Gsteig and, although the path has occasional muddy sections, there are no real difficulties.

The seven-km walk has an *easy* rating.

Places to Stay
The Chrinepass has en-route accommodation. Places to stay in Lauenen and Gsteig are covered under Walking Bases.

Getting to/from the Walk
The walk begins at Lauenen and Gsteig (see Walking Bases).

Route Directions: Lauenen to Gsteig
(7 km, 2¼ to 2¾ hours)
Walk 500 metres south along the road out of the village, enjoying magnificent views of the tiny upper valley of the Geltenbach and glaciated peaks behind, then take a signposted path down across a small wooden bridge over the turgid glacial waters of the Louibach. Make your way up beside a tiny sidestream to a gravelled road and continue right past several houses to where a foot trail goes up left. The route ascends gently over open slopes scattered with graceful old maples to reach a farm track at **Sattel** (1400 metres) near the end of a ski lift, 40 to 50 minutes from Lauenen.

Follow the road on across a stream, then (first ignoring a side track up right to Hohi Wispile) leave off right across vegetated old moraine mounds. The path sidles above **Brüchli**, an attractive farmlet cradled in a small grassy basin enclosed by forested hills, before climbing on through the spruce trees to arrive at the 1659-metre **Chrinepass** after a further 40 to 50 minutes. Although little more than an indistinct dip in this low ridge, the pass offers nice views down to Gsteig in the upper Saanental and across the Col du Pillon towards the Les Diablerets massif.

Drop down 200 metres to meet a dirt track at a farmhouse, and follow this on through the tiny open valley, crossing the stream before coming onto a broader sealed road. The route leads down this road, leaving the sharper curves at paint-marked short cuts, to reach a turn-off on the left (signposted 'Gsteig/Post'), 30 to 40 minutes from the pass. From here descend left alongside a small stream until the path brings you back onto the bitumen. Continue on down past occasional chalets to the main Gstaad-Col du Pillon road, then walk left a short way to the **Gsteig** post office after a further 20 to 30 minutes.

For the next section of the Alpine Pass Route (Gsteig to Col des Mosses) refer to the

Col des Andérets walk in the Southern Fribourg & Vaud Alps chapter.

THE WILDSTRUBEL TRAVERSE

Combining some of the best features of high-Alpine landscapes, this long and varied hike leads across the Bernese Alps into the Valais. The route explores the interesting raw and heavily glaciated massif of the 3243-metre Wildstrubel, a landmark dividing the central and western Bernese Oberland. At the western foot of the Wildstrubel lies the Plaine Morte, a 'dead plain' that forms a large expanse of permanent snow filling a rocky depression. The meltwaters of the Plaine Morte flow into the Rhône and the snowfield once belonged to the Valais, although – much to the exasperation of the thirsty southern canton – the area has been part of Bern Canton for more than a century. The final section of the walk follows a breathtakingly spectacular path alongside the old Bisse du Ro, a three-km long aqueduct built to transport water to the central Valais resort of Crans-Montana.

Maps

Two 1:50,000 national-grid walking maps cover the route: the SAW/FSTP sheet *Wildstrubel (263 T)* and the adjoining *Montana (273)*, which has been published independently by Editions MPA Verlag. A fair single-sheet alternative is Kümmerly + Frey's 1:60,000 *Saanenland-Simmental-Kandersteg*, although this special map misses the village of Crans-Montana by a hair's breath.

Walking Times & Standard

The Wildstrubel Traverse is a three-day walk through often rugged high-Alpine terrain. The route is suited only to walkers with a very good level of fitness and perhaps some experience of mountain hiking. While fairly well marked, the newer Tierberg section of the route is less prominent. There is loose rock in many places and some areas above 2500 metres are likely to remain snow-covered well into July. The path along the

Bisse du Ro is not for walkers who suffer from vertigo, but is quite safe. It's unlikely that conditions will be suitable for walking in these mountains after mid-October.

The walk is rated *moderate to difficult*, and covers a total distance of around 24 km.

Places to Stay

Right at the start of the walk is the *Hotel Simmenfälle* (☎ 030-3 10 89), offering mid-range rooms. The *Gasthaus Rezliberg* (☎ 030-3 12 86), near the Sibe Brünne, has a 12-person bunkhouse (no showers). North of the lake outlet at the Fluesee is the small private *Flueseelihütte* (call ☎ 030-3 22 73 for information and reservations), which has sleeping space for just 14 people; this is a basic self-catering style hut, with no resident warden.

The two *Wildstrubelhütten* (☎ 030-4 33 39), at 2793 metres are the only other en-route accommodation options, until you reach Crans-Montana/Sierre. These are SAC-run huts with plenty of bunk space and a resident cook/warden.

For places to stay in Lenk and Sierre, see the relevant Walking Bases sections of the Bernese Oberland and Valais chapters respectively.

Getting to/from the Walk

The walk begins at the Hotel Simmenfälle at Oberried near the head of the Simmental. Postbuses to the hotel leave Lenk roughly hourly until around 6 pm (until around 5 pm after mid-September). The walk ends in Crans-Montana, a large winter-sports resort above Sierre (Siders) in the central Valais. Regular public buses connect Crans-Montana with Sierre, but taking the funicular is a nicer way of getting down.

Stage 1: Hotel Simmenfälle to Flueseelihütte

(4 km, 2½ to 3 hours)

Just up from Hotel Simmenfälle, a signposted path leads off to the right up through a gorge to the thundering falls known as the **Simmenfälle** and continues a short way back to the road. Follow this on upvalley beside the cascading river through field and forest to reach the **Gasthaus Rezliberg** (1405 metres, see Places to Stay) after 50 minutes to one hour. At the nearby **Sibe Brünne** a spring bubbles forth from the cliffs in many – the name supposes seven – streamlets forming the source of the Simme.

Turn left at the junction 50 metres beyond the Gasthaus and cut directly across the paddock to where the route commences a steep ascent. Although the slopes above appear impassable due to several rows of sheer buttresses, a well-cut foot track (with occasional fixed chains to hold onto) picks its way up through gaps in the rock. After 1½ to two hours of steady climbing, you finally rise out of the cliffs to reach the **Flueseeli** at 2045 metres. This lovely emerald-green lake dips into a terrace under the Wildstrubel's north-western flank. On the far side of the fields of raw scree come right down to the water, while lush pastures fringe the Flueseeli's outer shores. The **Flueseelihütte** (see Places to Stay) is a few minutes away across the outlet stream.

Stage 2: Flueseelihütte to Wildstrubelhütten

(7 km, 3¼ to 4½ hours)

Walk back over the lake outlet and on over grassy meadows past a boggy tarn to the top of the small ridge running off right to the **Flueseehöri** (2133 metres). This point grants a stark view of the grey glaciated landscape ahead, with a heavy meltwater cascade splattering down from the Rezligletscher. A military installation stands out clearly near the summit of the Weisshorn (2947 metres).

Continue left up this rocky spur to a poorly indicated fork at around 2250 metres. The left branch is a rough walking route that goes up through loose frost-shattered rubble and unstable screeslides to the 3243-metre western peak of the **Wildstrubel**. The stunning summit panorama is particularly fine looking south and south-west across the Glacier de la Plaine Morte towards the Valais

Alps or the strikingly close Wildhorn (3247 metres). Although it's quite strenuous, there are no real difficulties given fine weather and normal summer snow conditions. The return trip takes about four hours.

Take the right branch leading some way on up to reach the **Rezligletschersee** at 2261 metres, 50 minutes to one hour from the Flueseelihütte; the snout of the glacier that formed this turgid lake overhangs the barren rock just above it. Crossing wild glacial streams on sturdy footbridges, follow the path around the Rezligletschersee over debris-strewn slabs looking down towards Lenk. Stone cairns and the familiar red and white paint splashes guide you on over a gravelly stream bed into the tiny upper valley of Tierberg.

After rising some distance along the lightly vegetated northern slopes, dip down left and make your way up through the moraine-filled gully below the long icy ledge of the Tierberggletscher. Zigzags lead up over a persistent snowdrift to **Tierbergsattel** at 2654 metres, 1⅓ to 1⅔ hours from the Rezligletschersee. Directly below you lie several sparkling little lakes called the Rawilseeleni, and farther behind the Rawilpass, an historic trans-Alpine route. The fit and agile can make the worthwhile side trip to the **Tierberghöhle**, a cave that once sheltered prehistoric visitors to these mountains. Head around north-eastwards from just below the Tierbergsattel, climbing over loose scree to reach the rock opening on a grassy ledge below the craggy ridge.

Drop down to the right to the **Rawilseeleni**, where you meet a more prominent path (coming up from Iffigenalp) near the middle station of a military cable car (not shown on topographical maps). Head up left between the lakes and begin a steep spiralling climb up the western flank of the Weisshorn below the line of cables to arrive at the **Wildstrubelhütten** (2793 metres, see Places to Stay) after one to 1¼ hours. The newer main building and the original stone hut erected in 1927 stand on a levelled-out terrace not far down from the summit of the Weisshorn.

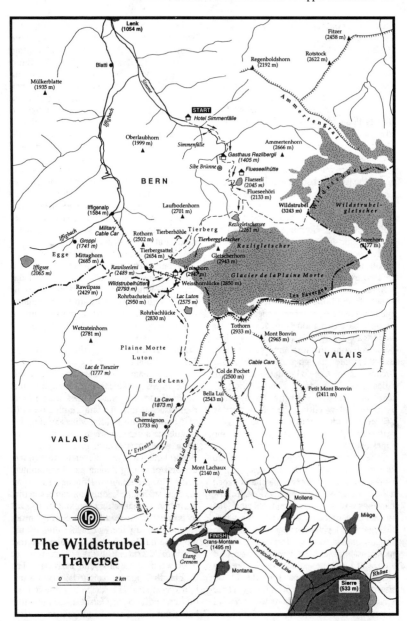

Lenk
(1054 m)

Fitzer
(2458 m)

Rotstock
(2622 m)

Regenboldshorn
(2192 m)

Blatti

Mülkerblatte
(1935 m)

Ammertengrat

START
Hotel Simmenfälle

Simmenfälle

Oberlaubhorn
(1999 m)

Gasthaus Rezlibergli
(1405 m)

Ammertenhorn
(2666 m)

Flueseelihütte

BERN

Sibe Brünne

Flueseeli
(2045 m)

Flueseehöri
(2133 m)

Wildstrubel
(3243 m)

Wildstrubel-
gletscher

Laufbodenhorn
(2701 m)

Iffigenalp
(1584 m)

Rezligletschersee
(2261 m)

Tierberhöhle Tierberg

Schneehorn
(3177 m)

Rezligletscher

Military
Cable Car

Iffigbach

Rothorn
(2502 m)

Tierbergsattel

Groppi
(1741 m)

Egge

Mittaghorn
(2685 m)

Rawilseeleni
(2489 m)

Tierbergg
(2654 m)

Tierberggletscher

Gletscherhorn
(2943 m)

Glacier de la Plaine Morte

Iffigsee
(2065 m)

Wildstrubelhütten
(2793 m)

Weisshorn
(2947 m)

Weisshornlücke
(2850 m)

Les Faverges

Rawilpass
(2429 m)

Rohrbachstein
(2950 m)

Lac Luton
(2575 m)

Rohrbachlücke
(2830 m)

Wetzsteinhorn
(2781 m)

Tothorn
(2933 m)

Mont Bonvin
(2965 m)

VALAIS

Plaine Morte

Luton

Lac de Tseuzier
(1777 m)

Er de Lens

Col de Pochet
(2500 m)

Cable Cars

Petit Mont Bonvin
(2411 m)

La Cave
(1873 m)

Bella Lui
(2543 m)

Er de
Chermignon
(1733 m)

L' Ertentse

Bella Lui Cable Car

VALAIS

Bisse du Rô

Mont Lachaux
(2140 m)

The Wildstrubel
Traverse

Vermala

Mollens

Miège

0   1   2 km

FINISH
Crans-Montana
(1495 m)

Étang
Grenom

Montana

Funicular Rail Line

Sierre
(533 m)

Rhône

Stage 3: Wildstrubelhütten to Crans-Montana

(13 km, 3¾ to 5 hours)

From the main hut, head up around to the right over patches of old snow to the **Weisshornlücke**, the obvious low point in the bare rock ridge at approximately 2850 metres, where the broad snow basin of the Glacier Plaine la Morte comes into view. Except for its northern edge, the Plaine Morte has no dangerous crevasses and draws cross-country skiers even in midsummer.

Make your way south-east (in the direction of the Rohrbachstein, the square-shaped peak with a large cross mounted on its summit) to a narrow gap at around 2830 metres, which mountaineers know as the **Rohrbachlücke**. Continue across the cantonal border into the Valais, descending easily over firm scree-slopes to reach **Lac Luton**, a lake set in barren surroundings at 2575 metres, after 50 minutes to one hour.

Make your way down through the rocky slopes of the **Plaine Morte Luton**, which is sparsely vegetated with hardy species of buttercups, past two tunnels in low moraine mounds evidently built to drain tiny lakes. When you come to a fork almost two km on, take the route that goes eastwards in the direction of the Col de Pochet. The cut path sidles above cliffs, passing interesting rock columns before sinking to another signposted intersection at the head of the tiny **L'Ertentse** valley, 40 to 50 minutes on. The Bella Lui cable car is visible high on the ridges over to the left.

Take the trail signposted 'Bisse du Ro/Crans-Montana' down the steep slopes daubed with wildflowers to meet a dirt road at the **Er de Lens** on the valley floor. Yellow markings now lead a few minutes along the true left bank of the stream to a bridge. Cross (disregarding a path that branches up left to Crans-Montana) and descend along an alp track, passing the dilapidated old slate-roof cottage at **La Cave** a short way before you get to the Alpine pastures of the **Er de Chermignon** after 40 to 50 minutes. There is an emergency shelter here for wayward winter skiers.

Follow the dirt road down across the stream and continue five minutes to pick up an unmarked but obvious foot track leading off left up into the forest. The path climbs slightly below loose cliffs – keep moving here as there is some risk of rockfall – then begins a long contouring traverse around the moutainside beside the **Bisse du Ro**, an historic aqueduct that brings water to Crans-Montana. This route has been cut into the cliff face, with some exhilarating sections on wooden walkways secured by fixed cables and safety rails mounted onto sheer rock, and finally comes out onto a rough roadway after one to 1½ hours.

The well-signposted last part of the walk leads eastwards around the slopes past villas and holiday chalets, crossing or following roads and tiny aqueducts before arriving at the artificial lake Étang Grenom after 25 to 30 minutes. The upper funicular station is a further 10 to 15 minutes' walk on through the centre of **Montana** township. Although more oriented to winter tourism, this modern resort is quite lively during the summer months.

OTHER WALKS

The Rawilpass

The 2429-metre Rawilpass is another classic route crossing the Bernese Alps into the Valais. From Iffigenalp (1584 metres) the route ascends in long spirals up the precipitous northern sides of the Mittaghorn to the Blattihütte (2029 metres), then climbs on more gently past a tarn to the Rawilpass. Beyond the pass the route leads through the expanse of rolling Alpine meadows known as the Alpage de Rawil, before descending to the dam wall of the Lac de Tseuzier reservoir. From here you can either continue on foot or by postbus via Anzère down to Sion, or head around eastwards via Er de Chermignon and the Bisse du Ro to Crans-Montana (see the Wildstrubel Traverse walk).

Between early June and early to mid-October there are up to eight daily postbuses to Iffigenalp from Lenk (see Walking Bases) until around 5.15 pm. Outside these times the buses run only on demand (minimum five passengers or equivalent fare paid; call ☎ 030-3 14 12). The walk can be shortened by taking the postbus directly from Barrage du Rawil down to Sion. The *Berghotel Iffigenalp* (☎ 030-3 13 33, open June to mid-October) at Iffigenalp offers rooms and dormitory accommodation. The route is covered by two 1:50,000 SAW/FSTP sheets: *Wildstrubel (263 T)* and *Montana (273 T)*.

The Iffigsee

The Iffigsee (2065 metres) is the source of the Iffigbach, a large sidestream of the Simme River. Embedded in a sink fringed by screeslides at the base of the 3247-metre Wildhorn, this delightful little Alpine lake is highly regarded among well-tramped walkers of the Bernese Oberland. The way to the Iffigsee starts at Iffigenalp (see the Rawilpass walk above), and leads smoothly up to the alp huts of Groppi (1741 metres) before beginning the steeper climb along the ridge of Egge to reach the lake. A popular continuation to the route goes around the northern slopes of the Nieselhorn via a minor watershed (just south of point 2377 metres) Lauenen in the upper Lauenental (see below).

The walking time from Iffigenalp to Lauenen averages five hours. The *Wildhornhütte* (☎ 030-32 38 82), a SAC-run mountain hut, is 45 minutes from Iffigsee off the route. Use the 1:50,000 SAW/FSTP's walking map *Wildstrubel (263 T)*.

The Upper Lauenental

This long return day walk from Lauenen explores the valley area above the village. Once destined for hydroelectric development, today the wild upper Lauenental is a nature reserve. The ascent route goes via the Lauenensee, a forest-fringed moor lake on a terrace above the valley, to the *Geltenhütte* (☎ 030-3 23 82), an SAC-run hut at 1985 metres. The return can be made via the Rohr swamp. There is a road as far as the

Lauenensee, which is accessible by postbus and private car (high parking fees apply), making a shorter version of this walk possible. The best walking map is the 1:50,000 SAW/FSTP sheet *Wildstrubel (263T)*.

Col du Sanetsch

Together with the Grimselpass, the Gemmipass and the Rawilpass, the 2242-metre Col du Sanetsch (also called Col de Sénin) is one of four Alpine crossings from the Bernese Oberland into the Valais which is snow-free in summer. Although the area has been developed for hydroelecticity, the Col du Sanetsch remains a scenic and quite popular walking route. From Gsteig (see Walking Bases) the way follows the road south-east to the lower station of the (electricity company) cable car. A path climbs very steeply under the cables to point 2002 metres (which marks the Bern/Valais cantonal border), then crosses Alpine meadows to meet a road at the Barrage du Sanetsch (the dam wall of the Lac de Sénin reservoir) at 2040 metres. After continuing on or near the road to the Col du Sanetsch, the route descends via Tsanfleuron and Glarey to the hamlet of Grand Zour (1437 metres), from where the once-daily (!) postbus passing at approximately 4.30 pm takes you on down to Sion (see Walking Bases in the Valais chapter).

The average walking time from Gsteig to Grand Zour is 5½ hours, which can be shortened dramatically by riding the cable car to the upper station (2062 metres), or by taking the postbus directly from the Barrage du Sanetsch. There are two en-route places to stay with rooms and dormitory accommodation: the *Auberge du Barrage du Sanetsch* (☎ 030-5 12 32) at the Lac de Sénil, and the *Hôtel du Sanetsch* (☎ 027-36 11 61) at Tsanfleuron. Two SAW/FSTP walking maps cover the route: *Wildstrubel (263 T)* and *Montana (273 T)*

Central Switzerland

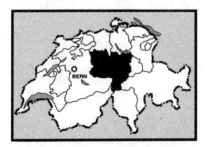

Central Switzerland
The Central Swiss Alps are packed with interesting high-Alpine scenery and glacial rock and ice. The Alps include walks from half-day to three days in duration (7.5 to 31 km), graded from easy to moderate. Walks include: Bürgenstock Felsenweg, the Klausenpass and the Fuorcla da Cavardiras.

Together the cantons of Lucerne, Uri, Schwyz, Unterwalden and Zug form Central Switzerland, the country's geographical and cultural heartland. Clustered around the beautiful Lake Lucerne, this region is of special significance to all Swiss people, who trace their national origins back to 1271, when the original three cantons of Uri, Schwyz and Nidwalden signed a pact on a lakeside meadow, the famous Rütli. Central Switzerland also has a special place in Swiss legend, since the folk hero Wilhelm Tell supposedly hailed from the southern shores of Lake Lucerne. Rather less virtuously, this was the principle birthplace of the Swiss mercenaries, who – at once feared and loathed – sold their fighting skills on the foreign battlefields of Europe in centuries past.

With the exception of Lucerne, these are small, lightly settled cantons whose economic mainstays – alongside tourism – are agriculture and animal husbandry. The

'Inner Swiss' *(Innerschweizer)*, as the German-speaking people of this region are known, are generally rather conservative with a strong sense of independence. Here the upholding of traditions often takes precedence over modern needs.

Although sometimes likened to neighbouring Bern Canton (or even the Glarnerland), Central Switzerland has a physical character rather different to both. The northern section of this region (chiefly in Lucerne Canton) lies outside the basin of the Reuss River, and takes in a good part of the undulating landscape of the Swiss Mittelland that includes the Napf District. Of greater interest to walkers is the southern half of Central Switzerland, a geographically more complicated area that embraces the lower (but nonetheless quite impressive) ranges of the Alpine foothills around Lake Lucerne as well as the much taller peaks of the Central Swiss Alps.

Although many parts of Central Switzerland are relatively unprosperous by Swiss standards, scenically speaking the region is a veritable treasure house. Here and there quaint rustic alp huts rest amongst fastidiously tended pastures before a grandiose backdrop of high snowcapped peaks. In early summer sweeping fields of wildflowers carpet the mountainsides, and walkers can enjoy arguably the most splendid Alpine flora found anywhere in the Swiss Alps.

The Napf District

Beginning roughly 20 km west of Lucerne, the Napf District forms a striking, circular formation surrounding the 1408-metre Napf. Numerous streams radiate from this summit, and – were this not Switzerland – casual map readers might easily assume the Napf District to be a large extinct volcano. On closer inspection, however, a definite ridgeline can be made out running roughly north-south right through the area to form the Lucerne/Bern cantonal border.

As is typical for much of the Alpine foothills, these ranges are composed of coarse sediments (known in German as *Nagelfluh*), but in the Napf District the rock also contains traces of gold. The precious metal is washed down into the streams, and this alluvial gold has been extracted by the panning method for centuries. The Ice-age glaciers did not cover the Napf, but left it as an island within the ice and consequently the area has a fairly gentle topography. Being very thinly settled, the Napf District is ringed only by small villages, each with its own minor cul-de-sac access road, but remaining quite without traffic thoroughfares.

WALKING BASES
Langnau
Lying at the south-western edge of the Napf District in Bern Canton, Langnau is the regional centre of the Emmental – the valley from where the genuine bubbly 'Swiss' cheese originates. Langnau is also known for its traditional pottery, and has a pleasant old town. In all seasons walks along the Emme River are an attractive proposition. Langnau's *youth hostel* (☎ 035-2 45 26) is at Mooseggstrasse 32; it closes from late September until mid-October. The *Hotel Bahnhof* (☎ 035-2 14 95) offers the cheapest rooms in town; otherwise contact the local tourist office (☎ 035-2 42 52). Langnau is about halfway along the Bern-Lucerne rail line, with express and (slower) regional trains passing by at alternate half-hourly intervals in either direction. Regular postbuses run from Langnau to Frankhaus, and via Lüderenalp (at 1144 metres on the Napf's western side) to the village of Wasen several times on Sunday only.

OVER THE NAPF
This delightful little walk from Romoos to Frankhaus is perhaps the nicest way to the top of the Napf. As its German name implies, the Napf resembles an upturned bowl and is sometimes called the 'Rigi of the Emmental'. The mountain's 1408-metre summit makes an ideal lookout point that grants a fantastic panorama stretching north across the Mittelland as far the Jura and southwards to the icy giants in the Jungfrau Region.

From the grassy upper ridgetops tiny valleys open out in all directions through the low hills clothed by dense forests of spruce and beech. The Napf District is the only part of Switzerland where the traditional method of making charcoal is still practised. The logs are meticulously stacked into a high rounded mound and covered with green branches; a small chimney opening in the otherwise airtight 'kiln' ensures only a gradual smouldering occurs. This modest industry (supplying fuel for Swiss barbeques) is centred around the village of Romoos, and in autumn smoke hangs over the surrounding valleys.

Maps
Kümmerly + Frey's 1:60,000 walking map *Emmental-Oberaargau* covers the route on a single sheet. Otherwise you'll need two 1:50,000 SAW/FSTP sheets: *Escholzmatt (244 T)* and *Willisau (234 T)*.

Walking Times & Standard
This is a short day walk with no real difficulties. The Napf District is a high point at the edge of the Swiss Mittelland and therefore tends to catch passing rain clouds, making it one of the wettest parts of the country – don't forget your waterproofs.

The walk is graded *easy*.

Places to Stay
The only place to stay in Romoos is the *Hotel Kreuz* (☎ 041-480 13 51), a lovely old shingled building with rooms in the medium price range. On the Napf itself is the *Hotel Napf* (☎ 035-6 54 08), which is presently run only as a restaurant.

For places to stay in Langnau see Walking Bases above.

The Napf

0   1   2 km

Getting to/from the Walk

The walk begins at Romoos (791 metres), which is accessible by postbus from the small town of Wolhusen. There are around eight scheduled buses daily from Wolhusen, the last leaving around 6.45 pm. From late May to mid-October you can take one of the two morning postbuses which continue on from Romoos to Holzwegen, thus shortening the walk by just over one hour. Wolhusen is on a railway junction of the main Bern-Langnau-Lucerne and the small Langenthal-Wolhusen lines.

The end of the walk is the tiny village of Frankhaus, from where there are a dozen or so daily postbuses to Langnau (trains to Bern or Lucerne); the last bus leaves Frankhaus at about 7.45 pm.

Route Directions: Romoos to Frankhaus

(14 km, 3½ to 4½ hours)
Walk along the street past the Hotel Kreuz,

turning right at a fork near the edge of Romoos. Bear right again at a sawmill and follow the road over a small bridge, before climbing on around to a farmhouse on the ridgetop. Here the pre-Alpine ranges of the Schrattenfluh and Hohgant come into sight beyond the green rolling hills. A rough vehicle track now leads westwards along the crest of the grassy ridge to reach **Holzwegen** (1079 metres, see Places to Stay) after one to 1⅓ hours.

Cross a broad road here and continue along another well-graded vehicle track past the restaurant. Head up right on a signposted path soon after you pass a gravel quarry, and ascend steeply through the forest back to the top of the ridge. The route rejoins the road a short way on, rising and dipping as it follows the grassy heights above deeply eroded gorges to pass by the farmlets of **Änzi** (1347 metres) and **Stechelegg** (1315 metres).

A last climb through pockets of spruce forest brings you up to the hotel/restaurant on the summit of the **Napf** (1408 metres, see Places to Stay), 1⅓ to 1⅔ hours on from Holzwegen. In clear conditions the little grassy summit plateau offers tremendous views in all directions. To the north across the Mittlelland lie the ranges of the Jura, while before you to the south stand the great snowcapped peaks of Central Switzerland and the Bernese Oberland.

Take the signposted foot track that drops in steep spirals down the Napf's heavily wooded southern slopes to meet a forestry road, then follow this quickly down beside the stream to reach **Mettlenalp** at 1051 metres after 30 to 40 minutes. There is a restaurant here and one late-afternoon bus to Langnau on Sunday only. The last section of the walk follows the bitumen down through the quiet upper-valley area of the Frankhusgraben past sporadic old Bernese farmhouses to arrive at the tiny village of **Frankhaus** (with regular postbuses to Langnau) after a further 40 to 50 minutes.

Around Lake Lucerne

The beautiful 114-sq-km Lake Lucerne is Switzerland's classic large glacial lake, with fjord-like arms branching off in all directions. As indicated by its German name (Vierwaldstättersee or 'lake of the four forest cantons'), Lake Lucerne is fronted by the cantons of Lucerne, Uri, Unterwalden and Schwyz. This large waterway provided a natural transport route between these cantons, and for centuries – until the opening of the Gotthard railway in the late 1800s – cargo on the Gotthard route was shipped across the lake rather than carted over land.

Lake Lucerne lies at 434 metres above sea level and is ringed by numerous lookout peaks of the Alpine foothills, many of them rising up directly from the irregular shoreline. The lake was formed during the last Ice age by the massive Reuss Glacier, which once protruded far out into the Swiss Mittelland, gouging a deep trough into the landscape. Lake Lucerne is now gradually filling up again as its many inlet rivers continuously wash in large volumes of rock and sand. Due to its large size, Lake Lucerne acts as a reservoir of warmth, and enjoys a mild climate – an effect that is enhanced by the warm southerly Föhn winds that frequently blow down from the Alps.

Although there are some heavily settled areas scattered around the lakeshore, in most places nature reserves front the waterline. The nicest places to stay are on Lake Lucerne's more isolated eastern shores. More than 20 ferries (including five old historic steamers) ply the lake in summer, stopping off at all larger lakeside towns. The Waldstätterweg walking route leads the whole way around the Lake Lucerne, and there are some excellent hikes in the surrounding mountains.

WALKING BASES
Lucerne
Lucerne's beautiful old town and scenic location on a northern arm of Lake Lucerne ensures it a place on most tourist itineraries. Unlike other large centres in Switzerland, Lucerne (Luzern in German) is a true 'Alpine city'. Lying so close to the high mountains, there are majestic views stretching southwards to the Pilatus, the city's chief landmark, and the 3238-metre Titlis. Lucerne's Gletschergarten is a fascinating introduction to Switzerland's glacial past, and its museum has very good relief models of the Alpstein (Säntis), Bernina and other Swiss mountain massifs. An easy and short walk directly out of Lucerne goes up from Grütsch over the Sonnenberg ridge to the Chrüzhöchi (775 metres), then down via the interesting gorge at Ränggloch to Obernau, from where there are buses back to Lucerne.

Lucerne has two camping grounds, the *Steinibachried* (☎ 041-340 35 58) at the little bay of Horw, and the *Lido* (☎ 041-370 21 46). There is a large local *youth hostel* (☎ 041-420 88 00). The *Hotel Linde* (☎ 041-410 31 93) and the *Hotel Schlüssel* (☎ 041-210 10 61) have budget rooms. Lucerne's tourist office (☎ 041-410 71 71) is near the train station at Frankenstrasse 1.

There are at least hourly trains from Lucerne to Interlaken, Bern, Zürich and Geneva (via Interlaken or Langnau).

Weggis

The small resort town of Weggis lies within an enclave of Lucerne Canton stretching along the great lake's eastern shore to include Vitznau. Famous for its mild, sunny climate, Weggis is a horticultural paradise and was long a major supplier of garden produce to the city of Lucerne. The valley station of the Rigi Kaltbad cable car is in Weggis. A recommended budget place to stay is the *Hotel-Restaurant Viktoria* (☎ 041-390 11 28), overlooking the lake promenade. Weggis' tourist office (☎ 041-390 11 55) is next to the ferry landing jetty. Apart from the Lake Lucerne boats, regular postbuses connect Weggis to Küssnacht am Rigi (from where there are trains on to Lucerne and Zürich) and Schwyz (via Gersau).

Vitznau

The affection-inspiring old holiday resort of Vitznau lies on the isolated central-eastern banks of Lake Lucerne at the foot of the Rigi. Vitznau is the starting point of the historic Vitznau-Rigi-Bahn, built in 1871 as Europe's first cog railway. Vitznau has a local *camping ground* (☎ 041-397 12 80) and there is a *youth hostel* (☎ 041-828 12 77) at Rotschuo, several km east around the lake towards Gersau. The cheapest place to stay is the *Hotel Schiff* (☎ 041-397 13 57), while Vitznau's grand old *Parkhotel* (☎ 041-397 01 01) is an up-market option. Vitznau has a tourist office (☎ 041-398 00 35).

Gersau

Gersau was a self-governing independent republic for over 500 years, but today this tiny town on the lakeshore belongs to Schwyz Canton. In a tradition that goes back to republican times, Switzerland's Sinti and Roma (otherwise known as Gypsies) meet each year in Gersau for the Feckerchilbi, a festival lasting several days. There is budget accommodation at the *Hotel Adler* (☎ 041-

828 11 66) and the *Hotel Schäfli* (☎ 041-828 11 63). Gersau has a small tourist office (☎ 041-828 12 20). Ferries run across the lake to Lucerne, and there are postbuses to Schwyz.

THE BÜRGENSTOCK FELSENWEG

Sometimes called the 'little brother of the Rigi', the Bürgenstock is a high limestone ridge forming a peninsula that reaches across Lake Lucerne almost as far as the adjacent shore. Some thousands of years ago the Bürgenstock was an island, but alluvial debris washed out of the surrounding mountains gradually created a broad fertile plain connecting the Bürgenstock to the 'mainland'. Although its upper heights reach a relatively modest 1127 metres at the indistinct peak of Hammetschwand, the Bürgenstock arguably shows Lake Lucerne from the most beautiful angle, with superb views across the lake to the Pilatus, Lucerne and the Rigi itself.

Today the Bürgenstock has regained its island status in quite a different sense. Atop the Bürgenstock is a privately owned and self-contained luxury resort – itself called Bürgenstock – with palatial hotels, boutiques, magnificent gardens and a golf course. The famous entrepreneur Franz Josef Bucher-Durrer began building Bürgenstock village in 1870. To impress his well-to-do guests, Bucher-Durrer then constructed the so-called Felsenweg, a panoramic 'precipice walkway' cut into the cliff face.

The Felsenweg, along with an impressive lift mounted onto the side of the sheer rock walls to take walkers up to the Hammetschwand, was completed in 1905. Over the following decades, however, the route gradually deteriorated, eventually becoming unsafe and impassable. After its thorough restoration in 1971, the Felsenweg now forms part of the long Waldstätterweg which circumnavigates Lake Lucerne.

Maps

Either of the following two 1:60,000 Kümmerly + Frey walking maps are recommended: *Luzern* or *Schwyz-Zug-Vierwald-stättersee*; the latter covers all of Lake Lucerne along with a large swathe of the Alps in Central Switzerland, so it's probably best. The SAW/FSTP sheets *Rotkreuz (235 T)* and *Stans (245 T)* intersect right along the walking route, so they're less preferable.

Walking Times & Standard

Despite its spectacular route, this simple and short half-day hike has very mild ascents and downhill sections, and can be done by all walkers. The Felsenweg is cut into high, sheer cliffs which some people may find unnerving or giddying, but it is perfectly safe.

This is an *easy* walk of just 7.5 km.

Places to Stay

Needless to say, there's nothing less than five-star accommodation in Bürgenstock village, but the *Pension Trogen* (☎ 041-610 13 41) about 1.5 km away has cheaper rooms. In Ennetbürgen the *Hotel Kreuz* (☎ 041-620 13 17) opposite the post office has standard-price rooms. For places to stay

in other towns around Lake Lucerne see Walking Bases.

Getting to/from the Walk

The walk begins at Bürgenstock, a ritzy resort high above Lake Lucerne. The easiest (and most romantic) way of reaching Bürgenstock is to take a lake ferry to Kehrsiten-Bürgenstock (462 metres), then the funicular directly from the landing jetty up to Bürgenstock (874 metres). From the end of May until late September there are about a dozen daily boats from Lucerne or Flüelen to Kehrsiten-Bürgenstock. Outside these times the ferry service and funicular run much less often, and from the last Sunday in October until after the first week of April neither operates at all. Once the ferries and funicular stop running, the best access is by postbus (maximum of four daily) from Stansstad (on the Lucerne-Engelberg rail line) to the village of Kehrsiten, from where the steep walk up to Bürgenstock takes a good 40 minutes.

The village of Ennetbürgen, at the end of the walk, is also serviced by the Lake Lucerne ferries. Postbuses running between

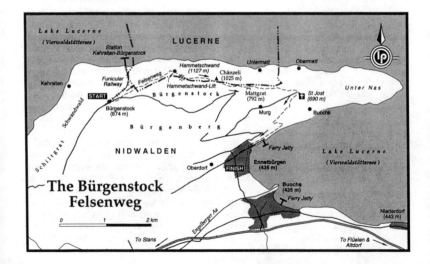

Seelisberg (near the start of the Weg der Schweiz walk) and Stans (on the Lucerne-Engelberg rail line) also pass through Ennetbürgen quite frequently.

The best place to leave private vehicles is the train station in Stansstad.

Route Directions: Bürgenstock to Ennetbürgen

(7.5 km, 2 to 2½ hours)

From the upper funicular station at Bürgenstock walk east along the road lined with German luxury cars past the Palace Hotel, then turn left onto a broad gravelled walkway. The path mainly contours along the side of the ridge above heavily forested cliffs that drop over 400 metres straight down to the lake. Frequent breaks in the trees offer lovely views across Lake Lucerne to the Pilatus behind you, the tilted form of the Rigi ahead and northwards as far as the Zugersee (Lake Zug) behind Lucerne.

'After 30 to 35 minutes you come to the **Hammetschwand-Lift**. Resembling a building crane, this 160-metre structure has been fixed onto the cliff face and is the highest free-standing lift in Europe. Before you go on it's worth riding up to the lookout on the **Hammetschwand** (1127 metres) for a fuller panorama stretching around from the Swiss Mittelland to the main peaks of the Central Swiss Alps in the south. The Hammetschwand is within a tiny enclave belonging to the municipality of Lucerne, making it the highest point in the 'city'.

Head on through a series of short tunnels blasted into the vertical rock walls, with sturdy steel railings and frequent sitting benches for the giddy. The Felsenweg passes under a final tunnel-gate just before terminating at a junction, after which the white-red-white marked path (signposted 'Waldstätterweg') continues east along the wooded crest of the ridge via **Chänzeli** (1025 metres) to reach **Mattgrat**, 25 to 30 minutes on. The several houses here at the end of a gravelled road look down over open slopes towards the village of Ennetbürgen in a cove of Lake Lucerne.

Make your way on gently up past a small

private cableway (which services the isolated farmlet of Untermatt on the lakeshore), bearing left at a fork not far before you get to the historic chapel of **St Jost** after 20 to 25 minutes. Situated at 690 metres on a grassy pasture high above the blue waters of the lake, this tiny whitewashed church was erected in 1733 as the final resting place of a medieval hermit who lived beneath a nearby granite boulder. During a recent renovation original frescos were discovered under the interior plaster.

Cut diagonally down over the green fields past an enormous barnyard to some scattered farmhouses, then take a signposted path that doubles back briefly left alongside an overgrown fence. After crossing a minor road the route steers right again and sidles along the lightly forested lakeside to meet an asphalted street at the edge of **Ennetbürgen**. Follow this straight down past the ferry dock to arrive at the village centre, 40 to 50 minutes from St Jost.

THE RIGI HÖHENWEG

Marking a natural division between the lower and flatter Swiss Mittelland and the high snow-daubed summits of the Alps proper, the Rigi is perhaps the most classic panorama mountain in Switzerland. The Rigi's tilted 'beret' form rises up between Lake Lucerne and the Zugersee (Lake Zug), and is a familiar landmark to the countless rail and road travellers who whiz past the mountain every day.

Culminating at the northernmost summit of Rigi-Kulm (1797 metres), the Rigi itself is really a short range made up of numerous minor peaks that provide superb lookout points in all directions. Like most of the Alpine foothills, the Rigi is composed of cement-like marine sediments filled with coarse rounded stones that were laid down by the so-called proto-Reuss River some 80 million years ago. The instability of this amalgam rock (called *Nagelfluh* in German) was responsible for the catastrophic Rossberg landslide of 1806, which wiped out the village of Goldau at the eastern foot of the Rigi.

The Rigi has been an extremely popular destination for day excursionists since the very beginnings of Alpine tourism. Already by the early 19th century hundreds of sight-seers were making the pilgrimage up to the Rigi each day – many hauled up by sedan-chairs or on horseback. In 1871 the world's first mountain railway, the Vitznau-Bahn, was built from Lake Lucerne up to the main Rigi summit. Soon after, a second private Rigi railway was constructed from Arth-Goldau on the other side of the mountain. Yet another section of railway, the Rigi-Scheidegg-Bahn, was built along the Rigi's panoramic ridgetop, but it never turned a profit and was eventually closed. Today the Rigi Höhenweg follows the embankment of this long-defunct rail line for much of the way, giving marvellous views.

The Rigi is not for those seeking that solitary Alpine challenge, however, and walkers can expect gentle gradients and plenty of company. The Rigi is nonetheless an outstanding area for walking, and should not be disregarded simply because of its thoroughly developed tourist infrastructure.

Maps

The recommended walking map is the SAW/FSTP sheet *Rotkreuz (235 T)* scaled at 1:50,000. Another good option is Orell Füssli's 1:50,000 *Kanton Schwyz*. Kümmerly + Frey's 1:60,000 walking map *Schwyz-Zug-Vierwaldstättersee* takes in the whole of Lake Lucerne (and is also useful for the nearby Bürgenstock Felsenweg walk).

Walking Times & Standard

Although the Rigi Höhenweg is only a short day hike, it's well worth spending a night up on the mountain at one of the many reasonably priced hotels. Making use of the Rigi's various 'mechanical means of ascent' to reach the upper slopes of the mountain, the walk has no steep climbs or descents, though at times the views themselves may have you gasping for breath. The mountain's relatively low height (averaging 1500 metres) and sunny aspect makes this an almost year-round route. Apart from the short Felsenweg

section (which becomes dangerously icy and is therefore closed), the Rigi Höhenweg can also be done as a winter walk since snow is regularly cleared from the path.

The Rigi Höhenweg is rated *easy* and covers 10 km.

Places to Stay

The slopes of the Rigi are dotted with numerous hotels, many of which have cheap mattress rooms. Places to stay en route that offer both rooms and dormitory accommodation (with showers) are the *Rigi-Kulm Hotel* (☎ 041-855 03 12) at the Rigi-Kulm train station, the *Hotel Rigi-Staffel* (☎ 041-855 02 05) near the Rigi-Staffel station, the *Hotel Rigi-First* (☎ 041-859 03 10) at First, the *Gasthaus Unterstetten* (☎ 041-855 01 27) down a short turn-off from the rail bridge at Unterstetten, and the *Berghotel Rigi-Scheidegg* (☎ 041-828 14 75) which is at Rigi- Scheidegg. The *Berggasthaus Rigi-Burggeist* (☎ 081-26 21 21) at the upper chair-lift station below Rigi-Scheidegg has a mattress room.

See also Walking Bases for places to stay in Gersau and Vitznau.

Getting to/from the Walk

The Rigi Höhenweg begins at the Rigi-Kulm station, just below the mountain's main summit, and finishes at Rigi-Scheidegg, a lower summit on the Rigi range (some four km south-east as the crow flies). Two cog railways run up to Rigi-Kulm: the Vitznau-Bahn from the Lake Lucerne resort of Vitznau (see Walking Bases), and the Rigi-Bahn from Arth-Goldau. Arth-Goldau is on the main rail line between Ticino and Basel/Zürich, and provides the easiest access. (Arth-Goldau's Bergsturzmuseum dealing with the 1806 Rossberg landslide is worth a visit.)

The finish of the walk is Rigi-Scheidegg, from where there are two mechanical descent options. Best is the cable car down to the Chräbel station on the Rigi-Bahn line to Arth-Goldau. The Gschwänd-Burggeist chair lift down to Gschwänd is not quite as good. There are only occasional buses from

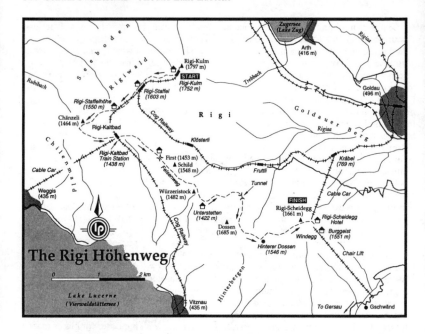

The Rigi Höhenweg

0   1   2 km

Lake Lucerne
(Vierwaldstättersee)

Gschwänd to Gersau, but if you don't mind going the extra distance on foot (roughly 1½ hours) it's a pleasant and well-marked walk down to Gersau.

Long jealous rivals, the Rigi's two private mountain railway companies have recently merged. They now offer a range of combined ticket options that integrate the several local mountain cableways with Lake Lucerne ferries. If you want to visit the Rigi as a return day trip from one of the larger cities, the SBB/CFF also offers special package deals.

Route Directions: Rigi-Kulm to Rigi-Scheidegg

(10 km, 2¾ to 3¼ hours)

Both the Vitznau and Arth-Goldau cog railways terminate at the **Rigi-Kulm** train station (1752 metres), from where the 1797-metre summit is only a few minutes' walk on uphill. The panorama from this highest of the Rigi's various summits is quite stunning.

With views stretching westwards over Lake Lucerne to the city of Lucerne and northwards across the Zugersee (Lake Zug) down into the Swiss Mittelland, from here the Rigi seems surrounded by water.

Walk back to the Rigi-Kulm station and take the broad bitumened footpath down beside the terraced precipice at the Rigi's northern edge, crossing over the train tracks at the station of **Rigi-Staffel** (1603 metres, see Places to Stay). Follow the rail lines on to **Rigi-Stafelhöhe**, before continuing ahead south-west along the ridge path (signposted 'Gratweg') to reach **Chänzeli** after 50 minutes to one hour. This dramatic outcrop at 1464 metres is arguably the most scenic lookout point of the Rigi range. From where you stand the land drops away 1000 metres into Lake Lucerne, which appears as a watery landscape of long fjord-like arms and peninsulas.

Descend very gently south-east past the romantic St Michael's chapel and an old spring fountain to the train station of **Rigi-Kaltbad** on the Vitznau rail line. A pedestrian road brings you on through the scattered chalets and modern hotels of this car-free resort, sidling up the lightly forested slopes to the saddle of **First** (1453 metres, see Places to Stay), 30 to 40 minutes on. Here proceed right onto the **Felsenweg**, a path cut into cliffs that quickly traverses the mountainsides below the 1454-metre Schild. The Felsenweg gives more wonderful views across the lake towards Lucerne and the Bürgenstock.

Where you come to another dip on the main Rigi range, head on along the broad winding path that contours around the hill tops. This ideal walkway is actually the old Scheidegg-Bahn route, a rail line that originally linked Rigi-Kaltbad with Rigi-Scheidegg and ceased operating in 1931. Continue across the old rail bridge at **Unterstetten** (1422 metres, see Places to Stay), climbing almost imperceptibly through a short tunnel and around above a little Alpine valley to reach a signpost at **Hinterer Dossen**, 50 minutes to one hour from First.

Go off to the left up over herb fields to an escarpment, following the foot track on along the edge of the cliffs before easing over right to reach the tiny plateau of **Rigi-Scheidegg** at 1658 metres after 20 to 25 minutes. These open tops mark the end of the main Rigi range, and give yet another classic vista southwards to Central Switzerland's highest ice-capped Alpine summits around the Titlis and south-east towards the Glarner Alps. The upper station of the Kräbel-Scheidegg cable car is a few minutes' walk on along the road from here. The Geschwänd-Burggeist chair lift is 10 to 15 minutes' walk directly down the slopes.

OTHER WALKS
The Grosser Mythen
Rising up like two rock noses directly to the east of the small city of Schwyz, the 1899-metre Grosser Mythen and the 1811-metre Kleiner Mythen are key landmarks of this

minor cantonal capital. While climbing the Kleiner (small) Mythen makes a challenging hike, the way to the top of the Grosser Mythen is a simple and scenic route that has gained considerable popularity. The summit offers quite outstanding vistas of Lake Lucerne and the Urner Alps.

The walk is best done from the upper station of the Rickenbach-Rotenfluh cable-car station at 1529 metres. From Rotenfluh a mild descent leads down to Holzegg (1405 metres), from where a very steep zig-zagging path cut into the cliffs (with fixed cables in places) goes up to the Grosser Mythen. After returning to Holzegg, you can either take the cable car down to Brunni (1089 metres; postbus to Einsiedeln), walk back to Rotenfluh, or – most recommended – continue on foot around the northern side of the mountain to the impressive gap of Zwüschet Mythen (1438 metres), before descending steeply back to Schwyz.

The total walking time from Rotenfluh to Schwyz (via Zwüschet Mythen) is around five hours. The climb to the Grosser Mythen requires some sure-footedness, but is quite safe in good conditions. Throughout summer both the Rickenbach-Rotenfluh and the Brunni-Holzegg cable cars run half-hourly until 6.30 pm. The *Restaurant Holzegg* (☎ 041-811 12 34) at the upper gondola-lift station has rooms and a dorm.

Use either Orell Füssli's *Kanton Schwyz* or the SAW/FSTP sheet *Lachen (236 T)*, both scaled at 1:50,000.

The Pilatus
Another of Central Switzerland's classic panoramic lookouts, the six-peak Pilatus juts up abruptly from the south-eastern shore of Lake Lucerne, dominating the views looking southwards from the city of Lucerne. Although the mountain was probably sacred to the early lakeside Celtic settlers, it owes its biblical name to a medieval saga in which Pontius Pilate found his last resting place on the summit.

Dragons, witches and demons were thought to inhabit the raw upper slopes of the Pilatus. For centuries, climbing the mountain was strictly forbidden because it was believed this would bring ruin upon the surrounding populace. A group of six monks were prosecuted for climbing it in 1387. Today the Pilatus has completely lost its former mystery, with numerous walking routes, a cog railway and a gondola lift going up to hotels on the summit. To complete the desecration, powerful spotlights now illuminate the mountain at night to impress foreign tourists. The Pilatus does, however, still make a tremendously scenic place for walking.

The most popular ascent to the Pilatus on foot follows the 2½-hour so-called Bandweg route from Fränkmünt (1416 metres), which is accessible by the gondola lift from the town of Kriens. The Bandweg ascends very steeply through stages of cliffs past the historic little chapel at Klimsensattel (1869 metres), climbing on via steel ladders through the Chriesiloch to the lower summits of Oberhaupt (2106 metres) and Esel (2120 metres). From here the historic cog railway built in 1889 goes down to Alpnachstad on Lake Lucerne – it runs at a gradient of up to 48%, the steepest of any railway in the world. The main 2128-metre Pilatus summit is a short climb on, and gives a stupendous panorama down to the great lake.

A most worthwhile five-hour continuation of the walk follows a high-level path southwest along the top of the craggy range via the Tomlishorn (2128 metres) to the Mittaggüpfi at 1916 metres. The descent leads on past Trochenmattegg (1461 metres), then down through the lovely highland valley of the Eigental to the little village of Eigental (1017 metres), from where there are at least four daily buses to Lucerne (until about 5.30 pm).

This walk requires sure-footedness and a head for lofty heights! There are two midrange to up-market hotels on the Pilatus' summit, the *Hotel Bellevue* and the *Hotel Pilatus Kulm*; they have the same reception (☎ 041-670 12 55). Eigental also has several places to stay. The recommended walking map is the special 1:50,000 *Wanderkarte Nidwalden und Engelberg*, produced by the Nidwaldner Wanderwege.

The Stanserhorn

Only slightly less popular than the other great lookout peaks around Lake Lucerne, the 1897-metre Stanserhorn stands just to the south of the Bürgenstock. Falling away abruptly on its eastern and western flanks, the Stanserhorn grants more of the fine watery views for which the Lake Lucerne region is famous. The Stanserhorn's standard walk is a three-hour climb from the small ski resort of Wirzweli (1220 metres).

The route winds up across the pastures via the hamlet of Ober Holzwang (1415 metres) to the gap of Chrinnen at 1719 metres, from where a final steep ascent leads to the summit. The descent can be made on foot, or by the cable-car/funicular combination to the town of Stans. (Originally a three-stage funicular dating from 1893 ran the whole way up, but when the engine-room and hotel at the upper station were destroyed by fire in 1970 the two higher sections were replaced by the cable car.)

Wirzweli is accessible by cable car from near Dallenwil, which like Stans is on the Lucerne-Engelberg rail line. The *Hotel Kurhaus* (☎ 041-628 14 14) in Wirzweli has rooms and a dorm. Use either the *Wanderkarte Nidwalden und Engelberg* or the SAW/FSTP sheet *Stans (245 T)*, both scaled at 1:50,000.

The Weg der Schweiz

Forming part of the Waldstätterweg walking route, which was opened in 1991 for Switzerland's 700th anniversary, the 35-km Weg der Schweiz (or 'Swiss Path') leads around the Urnersee (Lake Uri) from Rütli to Brunnen. The route has 26 sections, each representing one of Switzerland's cantons; these are arranged according to when the canton joined the Swiss Confederation and their length is based on the canton's population.

This easy route follows a well-marked and contoured walkway taking in some really lovely scenery. With a total walking time of 12 hours, the Weg der Schweiz is best done in two stages, although you can start or finish the walk at various places (accessible by ferry, postbus or train) along the way. A special walking map *Weg der Schweiz* is available at a scale of 1:25,000; it has route descriptions in English, French, German, and Italian.

The Central Swiss Alps

South of Lake Lucerne the lower ranges of the Alpine foothills rise up gradually as they merge with the Alps proper. These are the Central Swiss Alps, which stretch eastwards from the high peaks around the 3238-metre Titlis to the snowy crowns of the Clariden (3267 metres) and Tödi, and southwards as far as the continental divide. Most of the interesting high-Alpine scenery lies within the 'Gotthard canton' of Uri, whose borders more or less correspond to the rugged catchment area of the upper Reuss River. Jutting deep into the Alps along the valley of the Reuss, half of Uri consists of glacial rock and ice. Large side valleys, most notably the Schächental, Maderanertal, Meiental and Göschener Tal, intersect with the Reuss on either side.

The southern half of Uri forms the so-called Urner Oberland in the pivotal Gotthard region. Apart from being the north-south watershed, the Gotthard massif marks a geographical division between the eastern and western Alps. The historic route over the Passo del San Gottardo leads up alongside the Reuss through the Schöllenen, a perilous gorge below Andermatt. From the Middle Ages until the opening of the Gotthard railway this was the most important trans-Alpine crossing in the central Alps. Four other key passes provide well-transited road links from Uri into adjacent cantons: the 1948-metre Klausenpass into the Glarnerland, the 2224-metre Sustenpass into the Bernese Oberland's Haslital, the 2044-metre Oberalppass into Graubünden's Surselva region, and the Furkapass into Goms in the upper Valais.

Also of interest to walkers is the valley of the Engelberger Aa in Unterwalden (the col-

lective term for the two half-cantons of Nidwalden and Obwalden). The 35-km long river descends from the glaciers of the Titlis, flowing through a wild gorge in its central section.

WALKING BASES

Altdorf

Altdorf (447 metres) is the capital of Uri Canton. Although much of the town was reconstructed after a disastrous Föhn-storm fire in 1799, a few buildings of real historical interest remain, including the St Karl monastery. According to folklore, the Tell memorial in the town square marks the spot where Wilhelm shot the arrow through an apple sitting on his son's head. Altdorf is a stop on the Alpine Pass Route, and a number of excellent walking routes lead north-east across the mountains overlooking Lake Lucerne into the interesting valley of Muotatal in Schwyz Canton (see the Chinzig Chulm walk).

Tenters can go to the *Camping Altdorf* (☎ 041-870 85 41) between Flüelen and Altdorf. There is no real budget accommodation in Altdorf, so try to avoid staying here. The least expensive place is the *Hotel Bahnhof* (☎ 041-870 10 32) near the railway station; better is the *Hotel Tourist* (☎ 041-870 15 91) in nearby Flüelen. Altdorf's tourist office (☎ 041-870 02 88) is in the centre of town just behind the Tell monument.

Although Altdorf is on the busy Gotthard rail corridor, only very occasional regional trains from Arth-Goldau stop here, so it's necessary to disembark at nearby Flüelen and take one of the regular public buses from there.

Engelberg

Engelberg (1004 metres) is a large but surprisingly pleasant mountain resort that lies directly below the 3238-metre Titlis, Central Switzerland's most inspiring Alpine peak.

Engelberg has been the region's most important monastic centre since medieval times, and its main historical feature is the large Benedictine monastery. The main building dates from the 18th century, and can be visited on regular daily tours. A short and pleasant day walk from Engelberg leads down past waterfalls in the gorges of the Engelberger Aa to the small train station at Obermatt. A somewhat longer hiking route goes up to the Lutersee, a picturesque tarn at 1700 metres. Engelberg is also the starting/finishing point for the Benediktusweg, Surenenpass and Jochpass walks featured in this guidebook.

There is an organised local camping ground at the *Eienwäldli* (☎ 041-637 19 49). Hotel accommodation is rather expensive; but Engelberg has a *youth hostel* (☎ 041-637 12 92), 10 minutes' walk from the train station. The hotels *Bänklialp* (☎ 041-637 34 34) and *St Jakob* (☎ 041-637 13 88) have cheaper dormitories. Two medium-range places to stay are the *Gasthaus Heimat* (☎ 041-637 13 32) and the *Hotel Engel* (☎ 041-637 53 10). Engelberg has a tourist office (☎ 041-637 37 37) and a top school of mountaineering, the Bergsteigerschule Engelberg (☎ 041-887 12 75).

Engelberg is most easily reached on the approximately hourly trains from Lucerne via Stans; the trip takes a little more than one hour. The best way of travelling between Engelberg and the Bernese Oberland by train is the cog railway to/from Interlaken via Meiringen and the scenic Brünigpass with a change at Hergiswil.

Andermatt

Andermatt is situated at 1436 metres immediately north of the Gotthard massif in the Urner Oberland. Although it has a fascinating historical past as an important post servicing the trans-Alpine trade and transport routes, today Andermatt is a modern mountain resort with little in the way of interesting places to visit. The town does make a very convenient and central walking base, however, with hiking routes leading literally in all directions. Along with the Urschner Höhenweg and the Unteralptal and Gemstock hikes (see Other Walks below), popular walks from Andermatt go over the 2108-metre Passo del San Gottardo via the original old muleteers' trail and up to the Oberalppass (see the Graubünden chapter).

Andermatt's *Lager Zgraggen* (☎ 041-887 16 58) has cheap mattress-room accommodation. The *Hotel Bergidyll* (☎ 041-887 14 55) is a good budget place to stay and the *Hotel Badus* (☎ 041-887 12 86) has rooms in the mid-range. There is a *youth hostel* (☎ 041-887 18 89) at the nearby village of Hospental. Andermatt has a tourist office (☎ 041-887 14 54) and two leading schools of mountaineering, the Alpine Sportschule Gotthard- Andermatt (☎ 041-887 17 88) and the Bergsteigerschule Uri Mountain Reality (☎ 041-887 17 70).

Andermatt is a minor transport hub for the Gotthard region. Trains of the private Furka-Oberalp-Bahn (FOB) railway running between Disentis in Graubünden and Brig in the Valais pass through Andermatt almost hourly; the *Glacier Express* also passes Andermatt. From Zürich or other places in northern Switzerland access is via Göschenen (see below). Trains run at least hourly between Göschenen and Andermatt. The 'self control' system applies – passengers caught without a valid ticket pay a fine. From late June until late September postbuses run between Andermatt and Meiringen (via Göschenen and the Sustenpass), Oberwald in the Valais (via the Furkapass), and Airolo (via the Passo del San Gottardo). Each of these postbus routes has three daily departures in either direction, the last leaving Andermatt in the mid-afternoon. The PTT surcharge applies and reservations are strongly advisable (call ☎ 041-887 11 88).

Göschenen

The village of Göschenen lies at 1106 metres on the upper Reuss where the lovely Göschener Tal meets the main valley. A classic 1½-hour walk from Göschenen leads up to Andermatt via the legendary Teufelsbrücke, a bridge over the gorge of Schöllenen. Göschenen has a *youth hostel* (☎ 041 885 11 69) and the *Hotel Gotthard* (☎ 041-885 12 63) has lower-budget rooms. There is also a small local tourist office (☎ 041-885 11 80). Both the Gotthard railway and motorway disappear into long tunnels at Göschenen, so it's the last stop north of the Alps before passengers emerge in Ticino. Faster trains don't stop here, but there are hourly connections from Lucerne and Zürich with a change at Arth-Goldau.

THE KLAUSENPASS
(Section 3 of the Alpine Pass Route)

The 1948-metre Klausenpass is situated at the northern foot of the mighty ice-crowned peak of the Clariden. The pass connects the Glarnerland with Uri Canton and has been in active use as a crossing point since ancient times. The way over the Klausenpass leads through Urner Boden, the largest single expanse of Alpine pastures in Switzerland. Although it lies east of the watershed, Urner Boden fell into the hands of the Urner graziers long ago, and has remained a part of the Uri Canton ever since. These rich green meadows spread out along the valley and are the property of Switzerland's biggest sharefarming cooperative.

Towering more than 1000 metres above the Urner Boden is the craggy Jegerstock range, whose tiered slopes have rows of classically formed Alpine terraces that run along the range almost as far as the pass itself. The really great views open out on the western side of the Klausenpass, however, where the walk follows balconies high above the Schächental. The Klausenpass was the first in the Central Swiss Alps to be upgraded for motorised traffic, and the pass road was opened to through-traffic in 1899. In most places the walking route manages to keep a respectable distance from the well-transited road, leaving you to view the magnificent scenery along the way with surprisingly little disturbance.

Maps

The 1:50,000 SAW/FSTP sheet *Klausenpass (246T)*, properly covers the route. An acceptable alternative is Kümmerly + Frey's *Kanton Uri*, also at a scale of 1:50,000, but this walking map leaves off the area between Linthal and the Glarus/Uri cantonal border.

Walking Times & Standard

Although fanatically fit walkers might manage to do the whole stretch in a single day, anyone out to enjoy this walk will have to put up for the night somewhere en route.

The walk almost invariably follows broad paths or walkways and presents no real difficulties, although there is some wheezy climbing from Linthal up to Braunwald and from the village of Urnerboden to the Klausenpass. The walk can be shortened by taking the Braunwald-Bahn (funicular) or a postbus somewhere along the way (see Getting to/from the Walk).

The walk is rated *easy to moderate* and has a total distance of approximately 40 km.

Places to Stay

On Stage 1 of the walk, Braunwald has several better hotels and a *youth hostel* (☎ 058-84 13 56) some way above the village. On the road a few km before Urnerboden are the *Gasthaus Sonne* (☎ 055-21 21 11, open all year) and the *Gasthaus Klausenpass*, both offering rooms and dorms (with shower). The village of Urnerboden has several pensions with rooms and dorms, the cheapest of which is the *Hotel Wilhelm Tell* (☎ 058-84 14 17).

If you want to stay overnight on Stage 2 of the walk, the recommended place is the *Hotel Klausenpasshöhe* (☎ 041-879 11 64) 20 to 25 minutes on from the pass. The hotel has rooms and a large dormitory (with shower) for reasonable rates. In Spirigen the *Gasthaus St Anton* (☎ 041-879 11 41) has no dorm but well-priced rooms. Bürglen has a few budget pensions, including the *Hotel Tell* (☎ 041-870 22 04) and the *Hotel Adler* (☎ 041-870 11 33).

For accommodation in Linthal and Altdorf see Walking Bases in the relevant chapters.

Getting to/from the Walk

The walk begins in Linthal and finishes in Altdorf; transport details to both places are given under the respective Walking Bases sections.

From Linthal you can take the (Braunwald-Bahn) funicular up to Braunwald, thus shortening the walk by at least one hour. The Braunwald-Bahn runs at least every 30 or 40 minutes during the day until just before 7 pm, then several times until around 10.30 pm. This is a community-run service with (cheaper) subsidised fares.

Since the walking route touches the road repeatedly, you can shorten the walk (or opt out completely) at your pleasure by catching a postbus. From late June to late September there are four postbus connections between Linthal and Altdorf/Flüelen via the Klausenpass. Reservations are advisable (call Linthal ☎ 058-84 12 03 or Flüelen ☎ 041-870 21 36), and a fare surcharge applies on the stretch between Urnerboden and Urigen. All other postbus services to/from Flüelen and to/from Linthal go only as far as Urigen and Urnerboden respectively.

Stage 1: Linthal to Urnerboden Village

(13 km, 4 ¼ to 5 ½ hours)

From Linthal railway station walk a short distance downvalley, then follow signposts a few minutes up left across the railway tracks to the lower funicular station of the Braunwald-Bahn. Taking the funicular avoids almost 600 vertical metres of steep path and is the recommended means of ascent.

If you decide to walk up anyway, pick up the trail to Braunwald above the car park between the lower station and the old apricot-coloured hotel building. The path ducks under the funicular tracks and heads on for 10 to 15 minutes through the forest of beech and maples to merge with a right-hand trail coming up from Rüti. Make your way on up over steeply sloping clearings to cross back under the funicular tracks, then continue ascending in sharp switchbacks past a romantic old church just before you come onto a broad walkway after a further 40 to 50 minutes.

Turn right and quickly follow the wide path around to the left above the Hotel Niederschlacht. On the right is the turn-off to **Braunwald**, a scattered mountain resort

sitting on a terrace high above the valley. Although completely modern, the village is car-free and a pleasant enough place. Braunwald has a better tourist infrastructure than Linthal, including a local tourist office, a youth hostel and even a small cinema. (If you arrive here on the Braunwald-Bahn, take the road down past below the lower station of a gondola cableway and make a right turn at the intersection above the Hotel Niederschlacht.)

The route leads on westwards over undulating pastures browsed by jingling cows, with the 2717-metre Ortstock providing an impressive mountain backdrop. Keeping to the main track, head on across two cascading streams of the Brummbach, then swing around to the left and contour through patches of forest before coming out onto a high grassy shelf. Bear right (ignoring a walking trail from Linthal to Rietberg that crosses the track here) and continue a short way on to reach **Nussbüel**, one to 1 ⅓ hours from Braunwald. This hamlet lies at 1248 metres and has a restaurant overlooking the Linthtal.

The track narrows after Nussbüel, sidling for 10 to 15 minutes across long clearings to an intersection. Take the right-hand branch, which now begins a rough rising-traverse along the steep wooded slopes, leading across a small avalanche gully then over open meadows to meet a gravelled road near a holiday cottage after a further 30 to 45 minutes. This spot lies directly below the looming crags of the Ortstock, and offers the first clear views across Urner Boden to the Klausenpass.

Turn left and follow the road down to the stone farmhouse of Vorder Stafel (1399 metres). Here leave off to the right along an alp track, contouring the mountainside to where a paint-marked (but unsignposted) trail goes down on your left, 300 metres before Hinter Stafel. The path cuts down diagonally across pastures to reach the Klausenpass road after 35 to 45 minutes. Here, near the borderstone marking the Glarus/Uri cantonal division, is a local postbus stop.

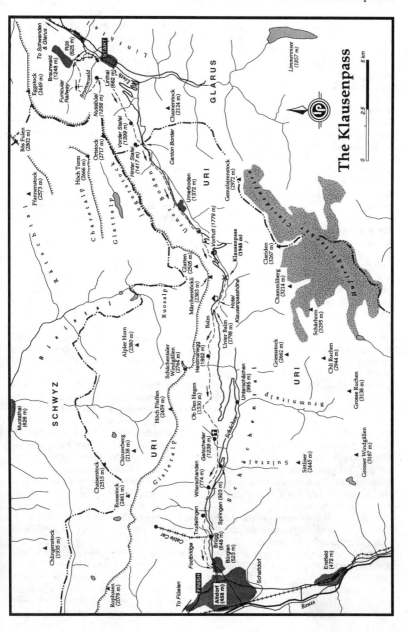

The Klausenpass

The remainder of Stage 1 runs on or close to the main road, which at times can get quite busy. Nevertheless, the broad open river plain of the Urner Boden makes for easy walking, with outstanding scenery including the Jegerstock range on your right and the snowfields of the Clariden towards the head of the valley. The route passes by the Gasthaus Sonne and the Gasthaus Klausenpass, climbing gently to arrive at the small village of **Urnerboden** after one to 1⅓ hours. Sitting at 1372 metres on a partially forested hillock of ancient glacial moraines, Urnerboden's slightly elevated position gives more nice views over the rich, green valley.

Stage 2: Urnerboden Village to Altdorf
(27 km, 6 to 8 hours)

Stay on the bitumen for two km, gradually rising up to a scattered stand of spruce trees, where the road begins its steep ascent at a sharp bend. From here a walking trail marked with the familiar white-red-white painted stripes leads directly up the slopes, following the road for two brief stretches as it short-cuts the numerous switchback curves to return to the road above **Vorfrutt** (1779 metres), 1¼ to 1¾ hours from Urnerboden. Turn around here for a last look back across Urner Boden.

Continue 500 metres along the road past an interesting drinking fountain hewn out of a single stone block to the next hairpin bend. Here a poorly marked trail makes its way up beside the tiny stream to arrive at the **Klausenpass** after a further 25 to 30 minutes. The pass height lies at 1948 metres below an impressive square pinnacle of the Märcherstöckli, and has a restaurant/kiosk beside a spacious car park.

Walk down a few paces to a yellow signpost just below the tiny chapel, and take the path that drops down between the main road and the meandering brook (not the more obvious broad vehicle track that contours around the left side of the valley). Make your way on past an idyllic farmlet set in front of a small waterfall, then cross hillsides strewn with Alpine rhododendron bushes below the

Hotel Klausenpasshöhe. For refreshments or accommodation, use the short, steep side-track branching up to the hotel, but otherwise continue gently down to meet the main road again at **Unter Balm** (1798 metres), 30 to 40 minutes from the pass. To your left the land falls away dramatically into the deep glacial trough of the Schächental.

Follow the Klausenpass road a short way uphill (ignoring a lower variant that leads down via Unterschächen), before heading left along a gravelled farm track. The route soon bears right at a fork and rises slightly against the contour past quaint wooden alp huts and barns before it reaches the hamlet of **Heidmanegg** (1862 metres), 30 to 40 minutes from Unter Balm. As you look directly over to the magnificent glacier-clad peaks of the Chammliberg and Schärhorn, these high south-facing terraces are ablaze with wildflowers until midsummer.

The now somewhat rougher alp track makes a sidling descent across the open slopes to end at the tight bend of a sealed road after 25 to 30 minutes. Visible below is the village of Unterschächen, while towards the mouth of the valley stands the prominent rump of the Grosser Windgällen and still farther off the Uri-Rotstock. Turn left and walk down the bitumen for 15 to 20 minutes to **Ob Den Hegen** (1530 metres), there taking a marked trail that steeply short-cuts beside a streamlet, then continue on downhill to pick up a signposted foot track that brings you to **Getschwiler**, after another 25 to 30 minutes. Getschwiler's small 16th-century church has an altar-piece painted by Flemish artist Denys Calvaert.

A broad stock-driving lane now serves as an easy walkway, dropping steadily down the hillside for 25 to 30 minutes to come out at **Spiringen**. This small village lies at 923 metres on the Klausenpass road. Since the route ahead mainly follows the road, many walkers might now prefer to take a postbus directly on to Altdorf or Flüelen.

Go 200 metres down the road to Spiringen's large old wooden Schulhaus, where a well-graded trail leads on gently down through areas of light forest to meet the main road again at **Witerschanden** after 25 to 30 minutes. Follow the road down two km past **Trudelingen** to where a signposted path leaves off to the right. The route climbs a short way to **Sigmanig**, then continues quickly down left along a concrete road to reach **Brügg** (648 metres), 30 to 40 minutes from Witerschanden.

Walk right 200 metres past the **Kinzig cable-car station** and pick up a track along the mostly steep northern banks of the stream. The path constantly rises and dips as it passes through forest patches and occasional farmyard gardens, crossing over to the Schächen on a footbridge just before it reaches the village of **Bürglen** at 523 metres, after 30 to 45 minutes. The birthplace of Switzerland's legendary folk hero Wilhelm Tell, Bürglen's historic buildings include the 13th-century Meierturm and the Wattigerturm, which houses the Tell-Museum. (For places to stay in Bürglen see the Places to Stay section above.)

The final part of the walk leads down beside the village church then along the main road past the historical museum and the St Karlin monastery to arrive at the centre of **Altdorf** after 25 to 30 minutes; (for more information see Walking Bases above). The train station is a further 15 to 20 minutes' walk left (south-west) down Bahnhof-Strasse, but most trains stop only in nearby Flüelen.

The Alpine Pass Route continues below in the Surenenpass walk (Altdorf to Engelberg).

THE SURENENPASS
(Section 4 of the Alpine Pass Route)

Linking Altdorf in Uri Canton with the Obwalden enclave of Engelberg, the Surenenpass has been a significant crossing route since the 13th century. Despite its long history of use, the Surenenpass was never developed for motorised traffic, and offers a marvellous undisturbed mountain landscape that is relatively rare for the region. At one time Engelberg controlled the whole of the rich highland pastures known as Surenen as far as the pass height itself. Over the centu-

ries, however, the neighbouring Urner herders were more able to assert their claim to these 'outer Alps' against Engelberg's weaker monastic administrators – not unlike what happened in the Urner Boden area. Today the forest line below Surenen marks the Obwalden/Uri cantonal border.

With constantly changing scenery that shows the mountains from every angle, this wild walk has more dramatic Alpine atmosphere than any other pass-crossing in the Central Swiss Alps. After climbing below a line of the incredible grassy-jagged pillars on the sides of the Brunnistock, the route leads down past the impressive, perfectly rounded amphitheatre at Gritschen, then onward directly under the imposing 3238-metre form of the Titlis – believed in medieval times to be the highest of the Helvetian summits. The Surenenpass is a very spectacular hike indeed.

Maps

Either of two 1:50,000 walking maps can be recommended for the Surenenpass: the *Wanderkarte Nidwalden und Engelberg* published by the Nidwaldner Wanderwege or the SAW/FSTP's *Stans (245T)* scaled at 1:50,000. This latter sheet just cuts off Altdorf – which is on the SAW/FSTP's adjoining *Klausenpass (246 T)* – but includes all of Stage 2 from Brüsti.

Walking Times & Standard

If you go the entire distance on foot in a single day, the Surenenpass is a very long and strenuous walk. The hike can be moderated by overnighting somewhere en route, or by using public transport to avoid Stage 1. This entails taking the bus from the centre of Altdorf to Attinghausen then riding the cable car up to Brüsti (1525 metres), thus shortening the walk by around three hours. The walk can be further shortened by taking the Fürenalp cable car (see below).

The ascent to the pass is quite exposed to the elements and takes you up some 750 altitude metres (or a total of more than 1800 metres if you don't take the cable car up from Attinghausen). The descent involves a drop of around 1200 altitude metres and is very drawn out. The hike is nevertheless recommended to all walkers with reasonable common sense and good physical fitness. The appropriate wet-weather clothing and sturdy, well worn-in boots are absolutely indispensable. The optimum time for a Surenenpass crossing is from mid to late June until early October.

For seven or eight days each summer the Swiss military carries out shooting exercises at Surenen, and occasionally walkers may have to wait an hour or so before being given the all-clear to continue through the area. For the current situation call the EMD/DMF's regional information office in Andermatt on ☎ 044-6 02 05.

The hike has been given a *moderate to difficult* rating, and has a total length of 28 km (if walked from Altdorf).

Places to Stay

There are many overnighting options along this route. The *Gasthaus Krone* (☎ 041-870 10 55) in Attinghausen offers rooms and dormitory accommodation. The *Berggasthaus Brüsti* (☎ 041-870 10 77) at the upper cable-car station also has rooms and a dorm (no shower). Beyond the Surenenpass is the *Restaurant Blackenalp* (☎ 041-871 20 01, open mid-June to late September), with simple refreshments (including alp-made cheese) and inexpensive sleeping in a rustic loft. Farther down are the *Berggasthaus Stäfeli* (☎ 041-870 37 29, open May to October) offering nice six-person dorms and the *Restaurant Alpenrösli* with a simpler dorm.

For accommodation in Altdorf and Engelberg see Walking Bases.

Getting There & Away

The (more or less optional) Stage 1 of the walk begins in Altdorf, while the resort of Engelberg is the finish of the walk. Access to both places is covered above under Walking Bases.

The recommended start of the walk is Brüsti (1525 metres), reached by cable car from the village of Attinghausen. Buses run regularly to Attinghausen from the centre of Altdorf. In summer the cable car runs half-hourly from around 7 am, with a lengthy midday break; no concessions are offered. The cable car takes you up over 1000 altitude metres in two sections. Before embarking at the unstaffed lower station, push the yellow button and listen to the intercom for the intermediate-station operator's answer; once inside the cable car, press another yellow button for confirmation.

A minor route variant involves turning off right at Stalden and taking the small cable car from Fürenalp down to Herrenrütiboden (1080 metres). In summer the Fürenalp cable car operates until 5 pm (6 pm on weekends).

Stage 1: Altdorf to Brüsti

(6 km, 2¾ to 3¾ hours)

For those determined to walk every step of the Alpine Pass Route, the walk description begins from Altdorf railway station. From the station follow the walking route (signposted 'Brüstli Seilbahn') south-east, turning right at the Gasthaus Walter Fürst through underpasses below the railway and motorway. Continue over the fast-flowing **Reuss** to the village of **Attinghausen**, then up past the supermarket to reach the Brüsti cable car after 30 to 40 minutes.

The path up to Brüsti leaves from near the lower cable-car station, leading up to the right of a stream which it crosses to reach the intermediate cable-car station after 20 to 30 minutes. Here a wide track ascends the steep slopes in switchback curves through mixed pasture and forest before reaching **Höchiberg** (1420 metres) after 1½ to two hours. **Brüsti** is another 20 to 30 minutes on from here.

Stage 2: Brüsti to Engelberg

(22 km, 5½ to 7 hours)

From the upper cable-car station at 1525 metres, take the broad foot track leading right past Brüsti's scattering of houses. Follow a prominent ridge which soon leads out of the trees over grassy slopes dotted with Alpine rhododendrons to **Grat**. The path continues along this increasingly sharp

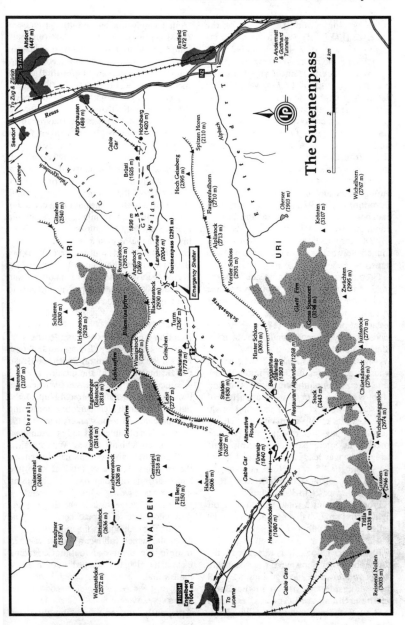

ridge, giving wonderful views of the Urnersee (Lake Uri) down to the right, the tiny upper valley of Waldnacht far below on the left, and the impressive craggy walls of the Brunnistock in front of you. Climb on over the open tops of the **Angistock** before descending slightly to reach **Langschnee** (2004 metres), after 1½ to two hours.

The final ascent to the pass is straightforward, if rather strenuous. Various welltrodden routes cut across the course talus slopes from Langschnee (which as its name suggests remains snow-covered well into summer) before ascending in zigzags through steep and loose rock to arrive at the **Surenenpass** (2291 metres), 45 minutes to one hour on. The view from the pass is dominated by the majestic hump of the Titlis (3238 metres) to the south-west. Immediately below are the sparkling Seewen tarns.

Drop down leftwards more gently past a small emergency shelter, sidling on over wildflower meadows terraced by centuries of cattle grazing to reach the alp huts and restaurant of **Blackenalp** (1773 metres, see Places to Stay) after 50 minutes to one hour. Blackenalp looks up towards the 2887-metre Wissigstock and 2930-metre Blackenstock, whose craggy sides fall away into a superb semi-circular amphitheatre with 250-metre-high walls in the tiny side valley of Gritschen. Make your way on along an alp track past Blackenalp's romantic little chapel standing amongst the rolling green pastures to cross the Stierenbach on a narrow stone bridge. The way leads above the left bank of the stream for 1.5 km, before recrossing to reach a signposted junction at **Stalden** (1630 metres), another 25 to 30 minutes on.

From this point a route variant goes off right across broad balconies high above the valley to Fürenalp (1840 metres), from where a cable car runs down to Herrenrütiboden (see below). Recommended is the left-hand branch, however, which quickly brings you down beside a gushing waterfall then alongside the stream to the **Berggasthaus Stäfeli** at 1393 metres (see Places to Stay). With small waterfalls spilling down

from hanging glaciers on the 3198-metre Gross Spannort up to the left, walk on smoothly down into the mixed forest marking the Uri/Obwalden cantonal border past the **Restaurant Alpenrösli** (1258 metres, see Places to Stay).

Head on down directly beneath the graceful outline of the Titlis, whose ice-crowned summit towers more than 2000 metres above you. As the valley begins to open out, follow a path off left over moist river flats to rejoin the road not far up from the lower cable-car station at **Herrenrütiboden** (1080 metres), one to 1¼ hours from Stäfeli. Continue 500 metres along the bitumen, before turning right onto a narrow laneway. This takes you through pleasant farmland and scattered holiday chalets, leading on past the large historic monastery to reach the centre of **Engelberg** (1004 metres, see Walking Bases) after a further one to 1¼ hours.

Alpine Pass Route hikers can now prepare for the walk over the Jochpass (Engelberg to Meiringen) described below.

THE JOCHPASS
(Section 5 of the Alpine Pass Route)
The walk over the 2207-metre Jochpass brings you out of Central Switzerland into the Haslital region of the eastern Bernese Oberland. The northern side of the pass (belonging to the half-canton of Nidwalden) has been intensively developed for skiing and tourism, and some walkers may find the proliferation of cableways and mountain restaurants here a bit off-putting. With the Titlis reflecting its majestic 3238-metre form on the still blue waters of the Trüebsee, the Engelberg side of the Jochpass is not without its charms, however, while just beyond the pass another gorgeous lake, the Engstlensee, dips into beautiful Alpine herbfields. The real highlight though is the second stage of the walk, which follows a high-level panoramic route far above the Gental, a classically glacial U-shaped side valley of the Haslital.

Maps
Apparently, the only walking map that

covers the route over the Jochpass in one sheet is *Wanderwege Engelberg*, produced by the Engelberg tourist authority at a scale of 1:50,000. You can also use two 1:50,000 SAW/FSTP sheets, *Stans (263T)* and *Sustenpass (255T)*, or even combine two other excellent 1:50,000 walking maps, the *Obwaldner Wanderkarte* and the *Wanderkarte Oberhasli*, which have been published by local tourist authorities.

Walking Times & Standard

If you insist on going the whole way up and over the Jochpass on foot (rather than using one or more of the mountain lifts) it's a very long and exhausting day's hiking. Breaking the walk up into two shorter stages with a night spent en route is a much better option.

The route itself is quite easy to follow and presents few difficulties. Due to the area's popularity and the large amount of tourist infrastructure, water from even the smallest streams along the first part of the walk from Engelberg to the Jochpass should be treated as suspect. Carry water or buy liquid refreshments at the various restaurants along the way. Depending on seasonal snow conditions, the Jochpass can normally be crossed from at least early to mid-June until late October.

The walk is rated *moderate* and covers a total distance of some 29 km.

Places to Stay

Due to its length, this walk is probably best done in two shorter days. The *Hotel Trübsee* (☎ 041-637 13 71, open all year) near the Trüebsee, and the *Berghaus Jochpass* (☎ 041-637 11 87, open June to late September), on the pass height itself, both have rooms and dormitories (including use of hot showers). At Engstlenalp the *Hotel Engstlenalp* (☎ 033-24 11 11 61, open mid-June to mid-October) with medium-range rooms. There are also hotels and guesthouses in the village of Reuti.

For accommodation in Meiringen see Walking Bases in the Bernese Oberland chapter.

Getting to/from the Walk

This route sets out from Engelberg and terminates in Meiringen; refer to the respective Walking Bases sections for access details to/from these towns.

Mountain cableways run from Engelberg right up to the Jochpass. Riding the gondola lift up to Trüebsee is a pleasant idea in hot weather and shortens the hike by around two hours, but taking the Trüebsee-Jochpass chair lift on up to the pass rather defeats the idea of walking. Most rail passes get you a moderate discount on the gondola lift, but the chair lift gives no concessions. The lower station of the Engelberg-Trüebsee gondola lift is a pleasant 10-minute walk from the train station downstream along the left bank of the river. It operates throughout the day until around 6 pm from May until mid-November.

A good alternative for walkers based in Meiringen is to catch a postbus to Engstlenalp, then simply walk Stage 2 from Engstlenalp back to Meiringen. Postbuses run between Engstlenalp and Meiringen some five times daily. From late May to late September the last bus leaves Meiringen at approximately 4.15 pm (otherwise at around 2.15 pm) and returns from Engstlenalp at approximately 5.15 pm (otherwise around 4.15 pm).

The walk can also be (further) shortened by taking the cable car from Reuti down to Meiringen. The Reuti-Meiringen cable car is a public-transport service with very reasonable fares and offers all of the usual ticket concessions. In addition, there are a dozen or so daily postbuses from Reuti to Brünig-Hasliberg (with regular rail connections to Lucerne and Interlaken).

Stage 1: Engelberg to Engstlenalp

(10 km, 4 to 4¾ hours)

From the train station walk 20 metres around to the right, where a pedestrian laneway goes off left between rows of trees to cross to a small road bridge spanning the Engelberger Aa. Climb up past the Hotel Bänklialp into the trees, bearing right at a fork before you come out of the forest. The route continues

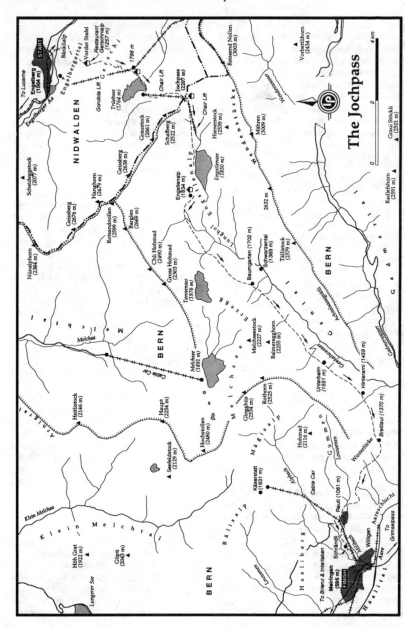

The Jochpass

along a gravelled alp track through the rolling grassy fields of **Vorder Stafel** to reach the **Restaurant Gerschnialp** at 1257 metres after 40 to 50 minutes. Take the signposted foot track up leftwards along a slight ridge past winter ski tows on the pastures of **Gerschi**. As you near the lightly wooded higher slopes, commence a steep ascent in tight zigzags underneath the Engelberg-Trüebsee gondola lift to reach the upper station and restaurant at 1796 metres on a high terrace overlooking the Engelbergertal, a further 1¼ to 1½ hours on.

A wide, graded walkway now leads gently down around the southern shore of the Trüebsee, a delightful lake embedded in a broad basin at the foot of the majestic 3238-metre Titlis to the Trüebsee-Jochpass chair lift (1771 metres). Just before the lower station, begin a winding climb below the cableway to the right of a grassy spur to arrive at the Jochpass (2207 metres, see Places to Stay) after 1¼ to 1½ hours. The pass itself is relatively unspectacular, and somewhat overdeveloped.

Continue south-west, initially along the line of yet another chair lift. The path leads through grassy meadows to meet a dirt road beside the **Engstlensee**, an attractive Alpine lake popular with anglers. Peaks of the Wendenstöcke rise spectacularly above the Engstlensee from its opposite shore. Follow an alp track as it leads away from the lake to reach the tiny scattered village of **Engstlenalp** (1834 metres, see Places to Stay), 50 minutes to one hour from the Jochpass. Dairy products including goats' cheese are on sale here.

Stage 2: Engstlenalp to Meiringen
(19 km, 4¼ to 5¼ hours)

From just below the hotel, take the path signposted 'Melchsee/Hasliberg' *(not* 'Schwarzental/Meiringen') that leads off right along a dirt road. Make your way past old wooden barns (whose distinctive style indicates that you're now in Bern Canton) and signposted trails going off right to Tannenalp and Melchsee. The route now begins its long but generally easy traverse high

above the Gental, a beautiful Alpine valley with a typically U-shaped glacial form, passing through **Baumgarten**, one to 1¼ hours on. This hamlet sits perched at 1702 metres on a prominent terrace sheltered from winter avalanches.

Leave Baumgarten via the access road coming up from Schwarzental, picking up the path again at the first bend. The way gently rises and dips across flowery mountainside pastures for 50 minutes to one hour to reach the lone alp hut of **Unterbalm** (1551 metres). With the mighty snow-clad summits of the Schreckhorn, the Finsteraarhorn and the Wetterhorn group ahead in the distance, make your way on to meet a dirt road at **Hinterarni** (1459 metres). This sidles on smoothly down the slopes overlooking the village of Innertkirchen at the junction of three mountain valleys before intersecting with a broader sealed roadway at **Breitlaui** (1370 metres) after another 50 minutes to one hour.

Climbing slightly, the route follows the bitumen to **Winterlücke**, from where you get a glimpse of the Brienzersee (Lake Brienz) far beyond Meiringen. From here the route mainly follows the road, with a few signposted short cuts leading down through the forest, to reach **Reuti** (1061 metres) after 30 to 40 minutes. The village has fine old wooden houses built in the typical style of the Bernese Oberland. The Hasliberger Dorfweg, a marked walking route from Reuti to Hohfluh offers a fuller introduction to local architecture.

The way down to Meiringen leaves off left just after the road bridge a short distance before Reuti. A steep foot track spirals down through the oak and linden forests, in places below the cable car, and comes out onto a road at the upper part of **Meiringen** (see under Walking Bases in the Bernese Oberland chapter) after 45 minutes to one hour. From here continue rightwards through a stone gateway, following yellow route markings for 10 or 15 minutes to the train station.

THE FUORCLA DA CAVARDIRAS
The roughly 2650-metre high pass known by

its Romansch name of Fuorcla da Cavardiras connects canton Uri's Maderanertal with the Surselva region along the Rein Anteriur (Vorderrhein) in Graubünden. The Fuorcla da Cavardiras gives breathtaking views across the broad icy névé of the Brunnifirn towards the 3328-metre Oberalpstock (familiar to the Romansch-speaking dwellers on the other side as Piz Tgietschen). This is relatively remote country by the standards of the Swiss Alps, and walkers will probably meet no more than a handful of other people along the route.

The way up to the Fuorcla leads up through the Brunnital, a charming Alpine valley well known for its rock crystals. Here amateur crystal-seekers – so-called *Strahler* – can often be seen digging into promising-looking rock fissures in the surrounding mountainsides. The yellow gentian *(Gentia lutea)* grows abundantly on these highland slopes and in late summer you may also see locals collecting this wildflower's roots, which produce a highly astringent 'medicinal' extract that gives certain brands of high-alcohol liqueur their mouth-puckering aftertaste.

Maps

Two 1:50,000 sheets published by the SAW/FSTP cover the route, *Klausenpass (246 T)* and *Disentis (256 T)*. Either of Kümmerly + Frey's walking maps, *Surselva* scaled at 1:60,000 or the 1:50,000 sheet *Kanton Uri*, can be also used.

Walking Times & Standard

The Fuorcla da Cavardiras is an overnight hike that might even be stretched out by an additional day to give a maximum of three short days' walking time. The walk follows a generally very good and well-marked path, though on the approach to the Fuorcla da Cavardiras there is some minor rock scrambling and the final section to the Camona da Cavardiras leads briefly over a harmless icy corner of the Brunnifirn – keep to the markings here. Walkers must carry food and basic supplies as meals are generally not available at the Camona da Cavardiras; the last chance

to buy groceries is the village of Bristen in the Maderanertal.

This walk is rated *moderate to difficult*, and has total length of around 31 km.

Places to Stay

The *Gasthaus Wehrebrücke* (☎ 041-883 11 19) in Bristen has rooms and dormitory accommodation at well below-average rates. The *Berggasthaus Legni* (☎ 041-883 11 43, open mid-May to mid-November) between Bristen and Balmenschachen also has a cheap mattress room for walkers. At Balmenegg (1349 metres) is the historic *Berghotel Maderanertal* (☎ 041-883 11 22, open from June to October), in a grand old Victorian-era building, which – despite extensive renovations – may be forced to close in the near future due to low guest numbers.

The *Hinterbalmhütte* (☎ 041-883 13 29), is a private mountain hut at 1817 metres in the Brunnital. There is a main building with self-catering facilities and dormitory, as well as half a dozen or so small cabins nearby for rent. The friendly farmer/warden is present from around early June to October, but the hut is otherwise left open. The SAC-owned *Camona da Cavardiras* (☎ 081-947 57 47), a self-catering type hut standing at 2649 metres almost on the Fuorcla da Cavardiras is better placed for walkers. The warden is present in July, August and September; but the camona is never locked.

For accommodation in Disentis see Walking Bases in the Graubünden chapter.

Getting to/from the Walk

The walk starts from the lower station of the Golzern cable car at Platten, two km upvalley from the village of Bristen. You can get there by a postbus combination from Erstfeld train station (on the main Gotthard rail axis), with a change at Amsteg. There are up to eight postbus connections from Erstfeld to Platten per day throughout the walking season. The last bus leaves Erstfeld just before 5.30 pm.

The end of the walk is Disentis (see Walking Bases in the Graubünden chapter),

CLEM LINDENMAYER

CLEM LINDENMAYER

CLEM LINDENMAYER

Top Left: Walkers cross the Brunnibach on an arched-stone footbridge over a tiny gorge.
Top Right: The Rigi – a short range made up of numerous minor peaks that provide superb lookout points.
Bottom: The Hinterbalmhütte (1817 metres) – a private mountain hut in the Brunnital.

Built against the cliffs at the Einsiedelie are a quaint hermit's cottage and tiny stone church. Reclusive monks have lived here since the early 17th century.

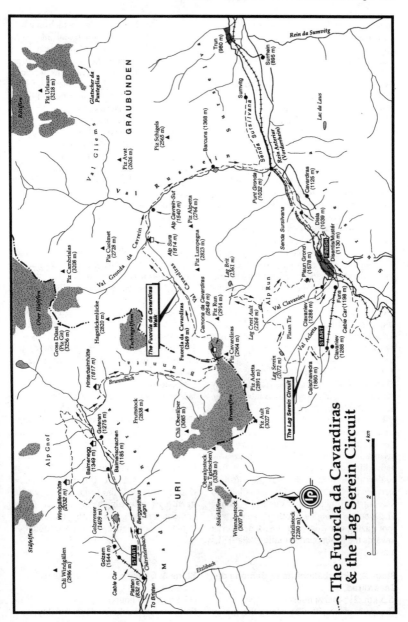

The Fuorcla da Cavardiras & the Lag Serein Circuit

though the final section can be shortened by taking a postbus from Punt Gronda to Disentis. There are four buses daily, the last leaving Punt Russein around 3.30 pm.

Stage 1: Platten to Hinterbalmhütte
(8.5 km, 3¼ to 4 hours)
From the lower cable-car station at Platten (832 metres), follow the bitumen 600 metres upvalley, turning left along a dirt track (signposted 'Balmenschachen'). This small road soon takes you down over the milky-white glacial waters of the Chärstelenbach and on past the **Berggasthaus Legni** (see Places to Stay) to recross the stream. Head through pockets of fir trees along the gentle floor of the Maderanertal before coming to the locality of the **Balmenschachen** at 1185 metres after around 1½ hours.

Don't cross the stream here, but go right a few steps to pick up a short-cut trail. This leads quickly alongside the river and returns to the road not far before you get to the farmlet of **Guferen** (1275 metres). There are some nice views into the head of the valley, where small glaciers cling to the 3234-metre Schärhorn. Walk across the footbridge, passing a broad track going up left to **Balmenegg** (see Places to Stay), and continue along the true right bank of the Chärstelenbach through occasional grassy meadows to reach a signposted intersection, 50 minutes to one hour on.

Recross the Chärstelenbach for the last time, doubling back right in a sometimes steep climb to meet the Brunnibach at a small ravine. Secured in places by steel fences, the path skirts the stream for a way before cutting up left over slopes of Alpine heath to arrive at the **Hinterbalmhütte** (see Places to Stay) at 1817 metres after one to 1⅓ hours. The wooden-shingled hut occupies a scenic spot gazing out west over the Maderanertal towards the ice-capped summits of the Titlis massif.

Stage 2: Hinterbalmhütte to Camona da Cavardiras
(5.5 km, 2½ to 3¼ hours)
The path makes its way along the grassy

slopes into the **Brunnital**, which starts to reveal itself as an attractive and interesting Alpine valley. Cross the Brunnibach on an arched-stone footbridge at a tiny gorge, climbing gently past a thundering waterfall onto flat and open highland meadows after 40 to 50 minutes. At the termination of the valley, hanging glaciers spill down from the Brunnifirn over barren rock walls.

Recross the stream and continue above its eastern banks for about one km, gradually rising away to the left. The white-red-white marked path leads on up through increasingly steep and rocky terrain (with the odd fixed chain to hold on to) to reach a natural lookout on a green ridgetop after one to 1⅓ hours. There are good views of the upper valley from here.

Sidle a short way on around the loose slopes, then climb as before through broken rock and slabs to a large square cairn beside the **Brunnifirn**, 30 to 40 minutes on. The glacier's glassy, in places heavily crevassed surface sweeps around to cover much of the 3328-metre Oberalpstock (Piz Tgietschen). A difficult alternative route to Disentis used by mountaineers leads up across the Brunnifirn via an obvious gap between Piz Ault (3027 metres) and Piz Cavardiras (2964 metres).

An arrow points you down onto the harmless uncrevassed edge of the ice, from where the hut comes into sight. Head left (roughly eastwards) across the **Fuorcla da Cavardiras** marking the Uri/Graubünden cantonal border, then over snow gullies and moraine mounds to arrive at the **Camona da Cavardiras** (2649 metres, see Places to Stay) after just 15 to 20 minutes. Looking directly out across the Brunnifirn as well as north-east towards the Tödi massif, the camona offers some of the nicest high-Alpine scenery you'll see from any mountain hut.

Stage 3: Camona da Cavardiras to Disentis
(17 km, 4 to 5 hours)
Follow route markings down quickly via a

rock ridge to cross a small permanent snow-field, then descend on left over eroding slopes into the grassy basin at the uppermost end of the **Val Cavardiras**. From here a graded foot track continues down along the northern side of the rubble-choked stream past a lonely alp hut, and rises on through a high grassy gully before dropping down steeply again to reach **Alp Sura** (1814 metres) after 1¾ to 2¼ hours. Here, where the Val Cavardiras and the Val Gronda da Cavrein merge, stands an alp hut in the shelter of rock blocks.

Wander over the moist herb fields and pick up an old mule trail shortly after crossing the Cavardiras stream just above the confluence. The route winds its way down over slopes of bilberries and alpenroses, crossing and recrossing the stream on stone footbridges before meeting a good farm track at **Alp Cavrein-Sut** (1540 metres) after 25 to 30 minutes, where you enter the main **Val Russein**.

Head over the bridge, turning right onto the valley road running down beside river flats past the very small hydroelectric reservoir at **Barcuns** (1368 metres). The white tops of the Medels massif can be made out in the distance ahead. The road leads more steeply on through light forest before coming out at **Punt Gronda** (1032 metres) on the main Trun-Disentis road, one to 1¼ hours from Alp Cavrein-Sut. From here go 300 metres right (west), crossing the Russein stream via the roofed wooden pedestrian bridge (the original road bridge built in the 1860s) to the postbus stop.

Walkers now continuing on foot to Disentis can take the signposted **Senda Sursilvana** running down under the rail lines. Stroll down along the narrow road to a hairpin curve, then follow a right-hand path marked with yellow diamonds. The way rises and dips through hay fields and patches of forest, passing the tiny settlement of Cavardiras with its quaint church perched high on the adjacent side of the valley before coming to the hamlet of **Disla** (1039 metres). Here leave the main Senda route and make your way up along a country lane beside the

lovely old Romansch farmhouses and chapel, crossing back over the rail lines below the Pension Schuoler. Walk on left down the main road to arrive in **Disentis**, 50 minutes to one hour from Punt Gronda. For information on Disentis see Walking Bases in the Graubünden chapter.

OTHER WALKS
The Chinzig Chulm
The 2073-metre Chinzig Chulm (also called 'Kinzigpass') is a pass leading out of the Schächental over into the heavily forested Muotatal, one of the nicest larger valleys of Schwyz Canton. The Chinzig Chulm gives fine views of the nearby horned Rosstock and Kaiserstock peaks as well as southwards to the Urner Alps. From the upper cable-car station at Biel-Kinzig (1627 metres), the route climbs up along a steep spur before sidling around eastwards below the main ridge to the pass. The descent takes you down through the lovely Hürlital via the restaurant at Lipplisbüöl (1194 metres) to the hamlet of Hinterthal (623 metres) on the main road through the valley of the Muotatal. An alternative route from just below the Chinzig Chulm departs up left (north-west) and leads via the Seenalper Seeli (1719 metres), an attractive tarn in a tiny side valley. The Hölloch, Europe's largest limestone cave system, is just 1.5 km from Hinterthal.

The average walking time is three hours (four hours via the Seenalper Seeli). The cable car to Biel-Kinzig operates half-hourly until 7.30 pm between late May and the end of September. The lower cable-car station at Brügg (see the Klausenpass walk) can be reached by frequent public-bus connections from Flüelen (via Altdorf – see Walking Bases). From Hinterthal there are roughly hourly postbuses to Schwyz (with train connections to Lucerne and Zürich) at least until 7 pm. Hikers can use either of three 1:50,000 walking maps covering the route on a single sheet: the SAW/FSTP's *Klausenpass (246 T)*, or Orell Füssli's *Kanton Schwyz*, or Kümmerly + Frey's *Kanton Uri*.

The Golzernsee

The Golzernsee is a natural lake set amongst meadows and light Alpine forest on the northern slopes of the Maderanertal. A rewarding day or overnight circuit can be done from Bristen (see the Fuorcla da Cavardiras walk above), where the cable car connects to a high route running past the Golzernsee to the SAC's *Windgällenhütte* (☎ 041-885 10 88) at 2032 metres. A side trip to a lookout at the Stäfelfirn, a snowfield above the hut is also worthwhile. The descent/return to Bristen is made via Balmenegg then along an easy path down beside the river.

The recommended walking map is Kümmerly + Frey's *Kanton Uri* at a scale of 1:50,000. Refer also to the map Fuorcla da Cavardiras/Lag Serein Circuit in this chapter.

The Göschener Tal

The Göschener Tal is an impressively enclosed side valley of the Reuss River that meets the main valley at the village of Göschenen. The head of the Göschener Tal is blocked by the icy giants of the Winteregg massif, including the Sustenhorn (3503 metres), the Dammastock (3630 metres) and the Galenstock (3583 metres). Apart from mountaineering tours, only one (difficult) walking route leads out of this 'dead end' valley, so circuit or return walks are offered. A large part of the upper-valley area is covered by the (hydroelectricity) reservoir known as the Stausee Göscheneralp, but this detracts little from the area's scenic beauty.

A particularly interesting feature of the Göschener Tal is the Sandbalmhöhle, the largest rock-crystal cave in Switzerland, which has quarzite, calcite and chlorite formations. The Sandbalmhöhle can be reached by first following the path towards Voralphütte then turning off left (the return time from the path turn-off is 2½ hours). Another thoroughly scenic five-hour return hike from the Stausee Göscheneralp leads up through the tiny Chelenalptal (valley) to the *Kehlenalphütte* (☎ 041-885 19 30), an SAC-run mountain hut at 2350 metres. Excellent

day or overnight walks can also be made to three other SAC huts in the Göschener Tal area, the *Salbithütte* (☎ 041-885 14 31), the *Voralphütte* (☎ 041-887 04 20) and the *Bergseehütte* (☎ 041-885 14 35).

The *Campingplatz Gwüest* (☎ 041-885 13 18) offers organised camping in the valley, and the *Berggasthaus Dammagletscher* (☎ 041-885 16 76) near the dam wall has rooms and a dormitory. There are three postbuses daily from Göschenen to Göscheneralp until 4 pm; seat reservation is compulsory (call ☎ 041-885 11 80). The Göschener Tal is covered by Kümmerly + Frey's 1:50,000 walking map *Kanton Uri* or the SAW/FSTP sheet *Sustenpass (236 T)*.

The Urschner Höhenweg

The broad highland valley of the Ursental descends from the 2431-metre Furkapass to Andermatt (see Walking Bases). The Urschner Höhenweg is a 5½-hour high-level route leading eastwards from the small village of Tiefenbach (2106 metres) via the hamlets of Tätsch, Ochsenalp, Lochbergbach, Lipferstein and the Lütersee, a crystal-clear Alpine lake at 1976 metres, before descending to Andermatt. Largely following sunny terraces high above the Ursental at around 2000 metres, the Urschner Höhenweg gives constant views southwards to the mountains of the Gotthard region. The route is well marked and of an easy-to-moderate standard.

From late June until late September postbuses running between Oberwald in the Upper Valais and Andermatt (via the Furkapass road) pass by Tiefenbach three times daily. The last bus leaves Andermatt around 2.30 pm and reservation is compulsory (☎ 041-887 11 88).

Use the SAW/FSTP's *Sustenpass (236 T)* or K + F's *Kanton Uri*, both scaled at 1:50,000.

The Unteralptal & Gemstock

The Unteralptal is a romantically wild valley that stretches southwards from Andermatt (see Walking Bases) into the Gotthard massif. The first part of the walk leads up smoothly through the Unteralptal (following a road with restricted vehicle access) to the SAC's *Vormigelhütte* at 2044 metres. More experienced mountain-goers can continue on via the lovely highland tarns of Gefallen then steeply up beside a tiny glacier to the upper Andermatt-Gemstock cable-car station on top of the Gemstock. The glorious panorama from the 2961-metre summit takes in a myriad of major peaks in the Swiss Alps.

The last scheduled cable car back to Andermatt leaves the Gemstock station at around 4.30 pm. The walk can be done in one day, but two shorter stages with a night spent at the Vormigelhütte is a better option. The best single-sheet walking map is K + F's 1:50,000 *San Gottardo*.

The Benediktusweg

The Benediktusweg is an easy and popular 3½-hour walk leading along the eastern slopes of the Walenstöcke through light forest and Alpine meadows to the Bannalpsee, a very pleasant (although artificial) lake at 1587 metres. The Benediktusweg begins at the upper station of the Brunni (Ristis) cable car (1605 metres) above Engelberg (see Walking Bases). The route heads northwards via Chruteren (1563 metres) to Walenalp (1665 metres). Here you can opt for the somewhat harder (but recommended) way to the Bannalpsee going up right over the ridge of Walegg (1943 metres), or follow the main route around to the lake via the hamlet of Firnhütt (1406 metres). A cable car from the Bannalpsee takes you down to Fell near Oberrickenbach, from where there are four or five daily postbuses to Wolfenschiessen (on the Lucerne-Engelberg rail line).

Both the Engelberg-Brunni and the Fell-Bannalpsee cable cars run half-hourly through the summer at least until 5 pm. The *Berghaus Bannalpsee* (☎ 041-628 15 56) near the dam wall and the *Berghaus Urnerstaffel* (☎ 041-628 15 75) some 1.5 km away at Bannalp each offer rooms and dorms. For walking maps use either the SAW/FSTP sheet *Stans (245 T)* or the *Wanderkarte Nidwalden und Engelberg*, both scaled at 1:50,000.

The Melchsee & Tannensee

In the geographical heart of Switzerland, the Melchsee and Tannensee are two attractive lakes that lie embedded in a lovely grassy basin. The Melchsee area offers easy, laid-back walking and is extremely popular with families. From the small ski resort of Melchsee-Frutt (1936 metres), a suggested easy three to four-hour return route leads south around the shores of the Melchsee, then up (on foot or by chair lift) to the minor lookout peak of the Balmeregghorn (2255 metres). From here continue down along the Erzegg range past the Tannensee, from where the walk back to Melchsee-Frutt can be made via Tannen and the Bonistock (2168 metres), or directly around the lake's northern side and through the grassy basin.

The walk can be very easily extended by climbing eastwards over the low range to Engstlenalp (see the Jochpass walk). Another alternative is to head up west past the tarn of Blausee to the 2480-metre Hochstöllen, then down to Hohsträss (2119 metres); from here a cable car descends to Wasserwendi (with hourly postbuses to Brünigpass train station).

Melchsee-Frutt is accessible by cable car from Stöckalp (1081 metres) at the head of the Melchtal. Between mid-June and the last Sunday in October postbuses run up to seven times daily to Stöckalp from Sarnen on the Lucerne-Interlaken rail line; the last bus leaves Sarnen around 4.30 pm. Two places to stay in the Melchsee area are the *Berghaus Bonistock* (☎ 041-669 12 30) and the *Berggasthaus Tannalp* (☎ 041-669 14 67, open until the end of June, then from mid-October), which is an official youth hostel. Two good 1:50,000 walking maps cover the Melchsee on one sheet: the *Obwaldner Wanderkarte* produced by the local tourist authorities or *Kanton Schwyz* published by Orell Füssli.

The Swiss Jura

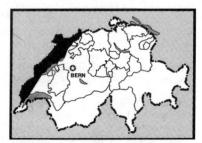

The Swiss Jura
The Swiss Jura is home to woodlands and meadows, rambling stone fences and lonely mountain hamlets. The Jura includes walks from half-day to two days in duration (12 to 25 km), graded from easy to moderate. Walks include: the Weissenstein, Le Creux du Van Poëta Raisse and Mont Tendre.

km-wide basin of the Swiss Mittelland, the gentle summits of the Jura make outstanding natural lookout points. (According to local legend, God, having just finished the painstaking task of building the Alps, created the Jura as an afterthought so that the splendour of the original work could be viewed from a suitable distance.)

The word Jura originates from an ancient Celtic term meaning 'mountains of forest', and the word still aptly describes this region in which forests of mainly fir and spruce clothe the higher slopes above thick stands of beech. Walkers accustomed to the grandiose high-mountain scenery of the Alps sometimes find the rolling tree-covered ranges of the Swiss Jura monotonous and unspectacular. To be sure, you won't find any glaciers here and few peaks rise very far above the treeline, yet the Swiss Jura often surprises in its variety of landscapes.

The chain of low mountains known as the Jura extends some 150 km north-east along the Swiss-French border. From its highest summits near Lake Geneva, the Swiss Jura gradually drops in height before petering out at Basel. Spanning six cantons – Vaud, Neuchâtel, Bern, Jura, Solothurn and Basel – the region takes in around 10% of Switzerland's area. The Swiss Jura is overwhelmingly French-speaking, with a relatively small German-speaking area at its most north-easterly end between Solothurn and Basel.

The Jura is a limestone range with much lower elevations as well as a simpler and more recent geological formation than the Alps themselves. Throughout the region water seeping through the porous and soluble calcium-based rock has formed subterranean streams, limestone caverns, karst fields and rugged gorges. For walkers this often means there is little (safe) drinking water available. Separated only by the 80-

The Northern Swiss Jura

The Northern Swiss Jura stretches from the Vue des Alpes pass (between Neuchâtel and La Chaux-de-Fonds) north-eastwards as far as Basel. Although generally lower in height and rather narrower than farther to the south, here the Jura range rises up rather more abruptly out of the Swiss Mittelland. The countryside on the northern side of the Jura range is a beautiful landscape of woodlands and rolling meadows renowned for horsebreeding. Despite the region's very moist climate large parts of this region – particularly in the Franches Montagnes district – are completely without above-ground rivers and streams, since the water disappears immediately into the limestone ground.

WALKING BASES

St-Imier

St-Imier lies at 793 metres in the Vallon de St-Imier of the Bernese Jura. Although the town traces its origins back to an early medieval hermit who first took up residence here, St-Imier was largely destroyed by fires in the 19th century. One of the few buildings to escape the flames was the old St Martin church built of hewn-stone blocks. St-Imier has long been a centre of the Jurassian watchmaking industry, and the internationally renowned Longines firm is based here.

There is a nearby *Friends of Nature hostel* (☎ 039-41 37 48) at 1257 metres at Mont Soleil. The *Hôtel de la Fontaine* (☎ 039-41 29 56) and the *Hôtel de l'Eruel* (☎ 039-41 22 64) have rooms at somewhat above-average rates. The tourist office (☎ 039-41 26 63) is at Rue du Marché 6. The express trains from Biel to Le Locle (via La Chaux-de-Fonds) stop at St-Imier every two hours, and there are slower train connections (often with a change at Sonceboz) at least hourly.

Solothurn

The capital of Solothurn Canton, this city sits at 432 metres at the southern foot the main Jura range. Solothurn is Switzerland's most Baroque city, boasting quite a number of superb 18th-century buildings built in local marble, including the St Ursus cathedral, the Baseltor and the Jesuit church. Solothurn has many fine museums, including the Jurassisches Museum dealing with the Swiss Jura. Solothurn makes a charming base for walks into the nearby Weissenstein hills.

The Solothurn *youth hostel* (☎ 065-23 17 06) is excellent and very central. Two lower-range hotels are the *Kreuz* (☎ 065-22 20 20) and the *Nelson* (☎ 065-22 04 22). The Solothurn tourist office (☎ 065-22 19 24) is near the cathedral on Kronenplatz. The private RBS railway links Solothurn with Bern (note that the 'self control' system applies on these trains). The best train connections from cities east of Solothurn go via Olten, and there are regular trains via Neuchâtel and Biel. In summer tourist boats run along the Aare between Biel and Solothurn.

THE WEISSENSTEIN

Standing, so to speak, in Solothurn's backyard, the round-topped 1397-metre summit of the Röti in the Weissenstein range is one of the Swiss Jura's most popular panoramic points. The views from the Röti are particularly dramatic in autumn, when a thick layer of high-level fog hangs over the Swiss Mittelland. The Weissenstein – whose name means 'white stone' in German – consists of a durable marble which provided an ideal building material for many of Solothurn's grand old Baroque edifices. This delightful little walk crosses the Weissenstein's open tops before bringing you down via the Einsiedelei, a romantic hermitage below the limestone cliffs of a tiny gorge.

Maps

The 1:50,000 walking map *Solothurn und Umgebung* produced by the local tourist authority is recommended. You can also use either of the following 1:60,000 Kümmely + Frey sheets: *Kanton Solothurn*, or *Delsberg Prun-trut Biel Solothurn*, or *Emmental Oberaargau*, or *Berner Jura Laufental Seeland*.

Walking Times & Standard

Since the setting-off point is already quite high, this simple half-day walk involves only moderate ascents although there are some steep downhill sections. The Weissenstein can normally be visited from at least May until mid-November, although mid-autumn is generally agreed to be the nicest time of the year for this hike.

This is an *easy* walk of 12 km.

Places to Stay

The *Hotel Oberbalmberg* (☎ 065-77 19 05) at the start of the walk has rooms at somewhat above average rates. The *Hotel Kurhaus Weissenstein* (☎ 065-22 02 64) at 1284 metres has mid-to-upper range accommodation as well as a dormitory for walkers; a hotel has stood on this site since 1828.

For places to stay in Solothurn see Walking Bases above.

The Weissenstein

Getting to/from the Walk

This walk begins at Oberbalmberg, a tiny mountain resort above Solothurn (see Walking Bases). For most of the year there are postbuses to Oberbalmberg almost hourly from Solothurn; the last bus leaves Solothurn train station at around 7.45 pm. The walk ends in Solothurn.

Route Directions: Oberbalmberg to Solothurn

(12 km, 3¾ to 4½ hours)

A signpost near the postbus stop at **Oberbalmberg** (1078 metres) points you past the large **Hotel Oberbalmberg** (see Places to Stay). Head past winter ski tows and climb quickly over a low crest onto steep forested hillsides looking out towards the village of Günsberg. This 'geological path' sidles slightly upwards around the slopes past fossils of ancient marine fauna, then climbs more steeply up through the forest to **Nesselbodenröti** (1290 metres).

Here you leave the yellow-marked route for a less prominent trail going up right along the ridge. This comes out of the trees onto open pastures leading quickly on up to the wooden cross and surveying triangle on the

Röti at 1397 metres, one to 1¼ hours from Oberbalmberg. This green rounded summit makes a superb natural lookout, and on clear days there are truly uplifting views south to the giant peaks of the Bernese Oberland as well as north towards the lower ripples of the Black Forest in Germany.

Make your way on down south-westwards along the broad grassy tops and cross over a low rib in the ridge. The route descends gently along a dirt track to a minor saddle, then follows a gravelled walkway up to the **Kurhaus Weissenstein** (1284 metres, see Places to Stay), which has a scenic open balcony. Drop down to the road, taking a signposted path leaving off right just down from the Bergrestaurant Sennhaus. This brings you smoothly down through the forest to cross under the chair lift (going from the hotel to the train station at Oberdorf) shortly before you reach **Nesselboden** (1057 metres), 40 to 50 minutes after leaving Röti.

Go left across the road and continue along a broad foot track, which gradually steepens to begin a very sharp descent in stepped switchback curves down the south-facing slopes of mixed conifers. The route leads down via **Stigenlos** (805 metres) to meet a gravelled forest track and follows this south-east to intersect with a larger road at **Falleren** (559 metres). Walk along the bitumen past fields and houses, bearing left at a large Y-junction to take a left-hand turn-off after another 300 metres.

A signpost a short way on directs you off right onto a farm track running along the edge of a clearing to pass a large restaurant, 1⅓ to 1⅔ hours on from Nesselboden. A few paces on at the upper end of the little gorge known as the **Verenaschlucht** is the interesting **Einsiedelei** (493 metres). Here, built against the cliffs stands a quaint hermit's cottage and tiny stone church where reclusive monks have dwelled in relative isolation since the early 17th century.

Follow the broad well-cut path alongside the tiny stream through beech and oak forest, and cross small footbridges before coming onto a road at **Wengistein** (455 metres.)

Yellow diamonds and signposts now guide you along residential streets to a busy Y-intersection. Here cut rightwards across the park past the round corner tower of the original city walls, dipping under an arched gateway into the old town and continuing down cobblestone laneways to the Baroque cathedral at the centre of **Solothurn** after 30 to 40 minutes. The train station is a further 10 to 15 minutes' walk down the cobblestone laneway of Kroneng, across the pedestrian bridge spanning the Aare, then left along Hauptbahn- hofstrasse.

LE CHASSERAL VIA LA COMBE GRÈDE

Rising up from the vineyards around the Bielersee (Lake Biel), the main Jura range forms a long hump of beautiful subalpine meadows culminating in the 1607-metre summit of Le Chasseral. A familiar walking area for lovers of the Bernese Jura, Le Chasseral gives splendid vistas of the main Alpine massifs in whose centre the Eiger, Mönch and Jungfrau can be easily identified.

On the western side of Le Chasseral is La Combe Grède, a wild limestone gorge that has cut its way into the stratified sedimentary rock leaving imposing, almost vertical cliffs that reach 300 metres or more above the tiny stream. The luxuriant forests surrounding the gorge were once exploited for charcoal production, but today the area is protected by the Parc Jurassien de la Combe Grède – a true 'Jurassic Park' without the dinosaurs! Reintroduced populations of chamois and marmots now thrive on the slopes around Le Chasseral, while La Combe Grède provides an important habitat for endangered species of ground-dwelling birds including the capercaillie.

Maps

The most suitable walking map is SAW/FSTP's *Vallon de St-Imier (232 T)*; a reasonable alternative is the 1:60,000 Kümmerly + Frey walking map *Chasseral Neuchâtel Val de Travers Ste-Croix*, though it cuts off just north of St-Imier.

Walking Times & Standard

This is a full day's walk that can be stretched out over two leisurely day stages by over-nighting at the Hôtel Chasseral. You could also finish the walk at the hotel by taking a bus back to St-Imier or by riding the chair lift down to Nods.

The often steep climb up to Le Chasseral totals more than 800 altitude metres which includes a section of stairways and steel ladders. The railings along the path are dis-mantled in late autumn (mid-November), but in ice-free conditions the path remains quite passable as long as you take some care. Note that there is no drinking water en route between the Hôtel Chasseral and Orvin.

The walk is rated *easy to moderate*.

Places to Stay

For places to stay in St-Imier see Walking Bases. The *Hôtel de la Combe Grède* (☎ 039-41 29 39) with lower-budget rooms. is in nearby Villeret. The *Hôtel Chasseral* (☎ 038-51 24 51) has various rooms and a large, reasonably priced dormitory (showers available).

Some distance off-route is the *Cabane Jurahaus*, a small hut at 1320 metres run by the Swiss Friends of Nature, 1.5 km north-east along the range from the Crête du Chasseral.

In Orvin at the end of the walk are the *Maison Bethel* (☎ 032-58 12 84), which has budget rooms and a dormitory, and the *Hôtel de la Crosse-de-Bâle* (☎ 032-58 12 15) which has doubles. The nearest *youth hostel* (☎ 032-41 29 65) is in Biel.

Getting to & from the Walk

The start of the walk proper is the village of Villeret. Since only slower trains from Biel to La Chaux-de-Fonds stop at Villeret it may be more convenient to take an express to nearby St-Imier (see Walking Bases), about 30 minutes' walk from Villeret. The walk terminates at the village of Orvin (669 metres), from where there are around a dozen direct postbuses to Biel each day. The last bus leaves Orvin at about 7 pm on weekdays and Sunday, and at around 6 pm on Saturday.

The walk can be turned into a much shorter semi-circuit by taking a bus from the Hôtel Chasseral back down to St-Imier. Between late June and the beginning of

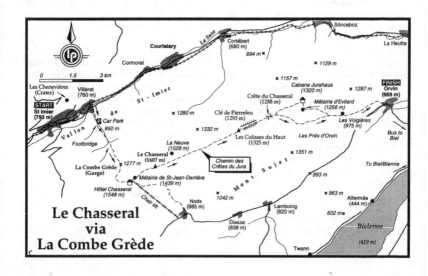

Le Chasseral
via
La Combe Grède

October there are three daily buses from the hotel, but there is otherwise at least one bus each day. From the Hôtel Chasseral you can also descend on foot or by direct chair lift to the village of Nods (885 metres), from where there are more frequent and regular postbuses to Neuveville on the Biel-Neuchâtel rail line.

Private vehicles can be left free of charge at the small car park just up from Villeret below La Combe Grède.

Route Directions: St-Imier to Orvin
(24 km, 5¼ to 6¾ hours)

From St-Imier train station follow the 'tourism pédestre' signs eastwards out of town along Rue Tivoli and Rue Neuve, then take a short stairway down right to reach the **Villeret** train station (760 metres) after 25 to 30 minutes. Walk down through the village, turning left along the main road to the **Hôtel de la Combe Grède** (see Places to Stay). A laneway leads up right past quaint old houses and barns onto open fields to reach a car park by the stream at the foot of the Jura range after a further 15 to 20 minutes.

A short way on a signposted trail leads off right straight across a footbridge and continues through the forest to the start of **La Combe Grède**. Following the bed of the stream (which in places flows subterraneously) where there is no formed path, make your way on up into the gorge proper to begin the steeper ascent via cut-rock stairways and several steel ladders. The route goes up past tumbling cascades under the high overhanging limestone cliffs before coming out onto a gently sloping shelf at a springwater pipe spilling into a wooden trough. Head up quickly through a small wildflower meadow to reach a signposted trail junction at 1277 metres, 1¼ to 1½ hours from the car park.

Ignoring side tracks running off to the left and right, climb on south-west through clearings before you leave the forest for open herb fields grazed by herds of jingling cows. The path now cuts up leftwards between the tight bend of a bitumened road, making a steeply rising traverse up the grassy slopes above the

Métairie de St-Jean-Derrière to arrive at the **Hôtel Chasseral** (1548 metres, see Places to Stay) after 40 to 50 minutes. From here, on top of the main Jura range, you get a sweeping view down across the waters of Lac de Neuchâtel, the Bielersee and Lac de Morat in the Swiss Mittelland to the great mountain chain of the Alps, which rise up like a glistening white wall extending from the Säntis in the east to Mont Blanc in the west.

Walk 15 to 20 minutes along the road to the rather hideous telecommunications tower on the 1607-metre summit of **Le Chasseral**. Follow red-yellow diamonds and 'Chemin des Crêtes' signs (which both indicate you are now on the Jura High Route) north-eastwards over the treeless tops of the range, with cultivated fields down on your right and the high rolling tableland of the Swiss Jura over to the left. The path makes a smooth traversing descent along the ridge to reach the old barn of **Les Colisses du Haut** at 1325 metres after one to 1¼ hours.

Continue easily along the broad grassy ridgetop past **Clé du Pierrefeu** to a car park at **Crête du Chasseral** (1288 metres), where a well-transited road crosses the range. Leave the Jura High Route at a signpost 200 metres on, cutting down rightwards through pastures to join a narrow farm track coming from the Métairie d'Evilard. The route proceeds down this steadily improving roadway past occasional holiday chalets of **Les Prés d'Orvin**, before turning off left at a sharp bend. Make your way through **Les Voigières** (975 metres) along an old mule path lined by ageing oaks to cross the (now bitumened) road. The foot track leads a way on through the forest, before dropping on down rightwards to reach the village square in **Orvin** at 669 metres) after a final 1½ to two hours.

OTHER WALKS
The Étang de la Gruère
Lying at around 1000 metres in the Franches Montagne district of southern Jura Canton, the Étang de la Gruère is one of the loveliest highland peat bogs in Switzerland. This area has vegetation more typical of climes farther

north. The moor is mostly covered by a tea-coloured lake with several tiny armlets, whose waters drain subterraneously towards Tramelan. The originally much smaller pond was enlarged by monks during the 17th century in order to provide water power for a nearby sawmill. Throughout the first half of the 20th century conservationists fought a long battle to save this unique moor from destruction by peat cutting, and today the Étang de la Gruère is protected within a small nature reserve. While within the reserve don't leave the paths as the peaty ground is easily damaged.

This very short and easy day walk leads from the small town of Saignelégier (where the famous Marché-Concours horse market takes place in early August) via the hamlet of Les Cerlatez to the Etang de la Gruère. The walk can be continued via Le Cernil to Tramelan. There is a *youth hostel* (☎ 039-51 17 07) at Bélmont close to Saignelégier. Saignelégier can be reached by train either from Neuchâtel via La Chaux-de-Fonds, or from Basel and Biel via Delémont. There are train connections from Tramelan to Biel and Basel via Tavannes. Both the 1:50,000 SAW/FSTP sheet *Clos du Doubs (222 T)* and Kümmerly + Frey's 1:60,000 *Delsberg Pruntrut Biel Solothurn* cover the route.

The St Peterinsel

The St Peterinsel is an 'island' in the Bielersee (Lake Biel) connected to the shore by a narrow three-km-long spit. Once completely surrounded by water, the St Peterinsel became a peninsula only after the level of the lake was lowered. Today the whole area forms an interesting nature reserve protecting the aquatic birdlife and fauna. The philosopher Rousseau lived here in the 1760s, and the house in which he resided is now a museum. The St Peterinsel can be visited as a very easy three-hour return walk from the village of Erlach, or as part of a boat trip on the Bielersee. The nearest train station is at Neuveville, from where there are occasional postbuses to Erlach and (in summer) regular boats to the St Peterinsel. You don't really need a map,

of course, but the St Peterinsel is covered by the 1:50,000 SAW/FSTP sheet *Vallon de St-Imier (232 T)*.

Mont Soleil

Steep forested slopes rise up immediately north of St-Imier (see Walking Bases) before easing into a broad undulating plateau that culminates in the rounded 1288-metre summit of Mont Soleil. This small mountain-top gives excellent views south-westwards to the Fribourg Alps, south towards Le Chasseral as well as eastwards down along the stretched-out Vallon de St-Imier. There is a large solar energy 'farm' on Mont Soleil. Less than one km to the east is Les Chenevières, a 400-metre wide crater which geologists believe was formed by the impact of a very large meteorite some 10,000 years ago.

From St-Imier a 2½ to three-hour circuit walk can be made via Mont Soleil to the hamlet of Le Sergent (1182 metres), then down past Les Chenevières back to St-Imier.

A funicular railway goes up 350 vertical metres to the scattered village of Mont Soleil, which cuts around one hour off the walking time. The 1:50,000 SAW/FSTP sheet *Vallon de St-Imier (232 T)* covers the route in one sheet. (Although it does not clearly show Les Chenevières, the crater is an unmistakeable feature on the map.)

Montagne de Moutier

This is another easy and very pleasant day walk through a typically Jurassian landscape of rolling grassy plateaus dotted with old farmhouses and stone fences. The route leaves from the small industrial town of Choindez in Jura Canton and climbs south-west via the village of Vellerat (which recently 'seceded' from Bern to Jura Canton), following paths on to a country inn near the saddle of La Combe (1043 metres). From here farm tracks continue up through the gently undulating highland pastures of the Montagne de Moutier to the hamlet of Les Clos (1105 metres). The descent leads south-east through the Basse Montagne to

Moutier (529 metres), the 'capital' of the Bernese Jura.

The average walking time is four hours. Trains running between Basel and Biel stop at Choindez. From Moutier there are direct hourly trains to both Solothurn and Basel. Kümmerly + Frey's 1:60,000 *Delsberg Pruntrut Biel Solothurn* covers the walk on a single sheet.

The Southern Swiss Jura

The Southern Swiss Jura lies within the cantons of Vaud and Neuchâtel. Characterised by extensive areas of highland plateau and small upland valleys with rambling stone fences and lonely mountain hamlets, this region has some of the most typical and romantic Jurassian landscapes. With average altitudes of around 1000 metres culminating in the 1679-metre summit of Mont Tendre the Jura range is much broader and rather more elevated here than in areas farther to the north. The two major Aare tributaries, the Orbe and Areuse, rise as large springwater streams, cutting their way through the main Jura range in deep gorges. The Southern Swiss Jura experiences extremely cold winters and, once the snow falls, becomes a veritable mecca for cross-country skiers.

WALKING BASES
St-Cergue
St-Cergue (1044 metres) sits below the 1677-metre La Dôle at the end of the broad plateau-like western end of the Jura range. It is a pleasant little town typical of the French-speaking Swiss Jura. St-Cergue is the start of the Jura High Route (Chemin des Crêtes du Jura), a walking (and cross-country skiing) route leading north-east along the highest ranges of the Swiss Jura. Its first stage goes to the Col du Marchairuz via the ruins of the medieval cloisters at d'Oujon.

Tenters can go to the *Camping St-Cergue*

(☎ 022-360 18 98), one km out of the village. The cheapest places to stay in St-Cergue are the *Auberge Communale Les Cheseaux* (☎ 022-360 12 88) and the *Hôtel-Bar Le Treplin* (☎ 022-360 26 66). St-Cergue has a small tourist office (☎ 022-360 26 20).

The town can be reached on the narrow-gauge Nyon-La Cure mountain railway. Trains leave (from outside Nyon station) hourly until around 10.30 pm. As the train winds its way steeply up into the Jura there are nice views across Lake Geneva.

Ste-Croix
Ste-Croix (1088 metres) is a nice old typically Jurassian town in the north of Vaud Canton. Ste-Croix has long been famous for its mechanical music boxes, whose fascinating history is dealt with in the local CIMA museum. The town is a stop along the Jura High Route long walk that continues northeastwards via the 1607-metre summit of Le Chasseron. A short nearby hike goes down through the Gorges de Covatanne to the village of Vuiteboeuf (from where there are postbuses to Yverdon).

Ste-Croix has a *youth hostel* (☎ 024-61 18 10) and the *Hôtel Beau-Séjour* (☎ 024-61 21 50) has simple rooms at standard rates. A better hotel is *La France* (☎ 024-61 38 21). The local tourist office (☎ 024-61 27 02) is at Rue de l'Industrie 2. Ste-Croix can be reached in 40 minutes from the small city of Yverdon-les-Bains at the southern end of Lac Neuchâtel on another of the Swiss Jura's romantic old mountain railways. Postbuses also run roughly every two hours to the village of Buttes at the terminus of the Val de Travers rail line, from where there are at least hourly trains to Neuchâtel.

Môtiers
Môtiers lies at 737 metres at the foot of the Jura range in the Val de Travers of Neuchâtel Canton, and is a charming little town with fine 18th buildings. The French philosopher Jean-Jacques Rousseau lived in political exile here between 1762 and 1765, (where he wrote his book *Promenades Solitaires*). His stay is commemorated by Môtiers'

Rousseau Museum. Worth visiting are the Vieux Château on a hill above Môtiers and the old asphalt mines nearby. Môtiers has several small food stores, but no supermarket or bank.

The only places to stay in Môtiers are the *Hôtel National* (☎ 038-61 40 23) with standard rooms and rates, and the *Hôtel de Six Comunes* (☎ 038-261 20 00), which offers medium-range accommodation. There is a camping ground in nearby Fleurier, *A Belle Roche* (☎ 038-61 42 62, open from May to the end of September). Môtiers is on the Val de Travers rail line, with hourly trains from Neuchâtel.

LE CREUX DU VAN VIA POËTA-RAISSE

This combines two of the most interesting features of the Val de Travers: the gorge known as the Poëta-Raisse and the Creux du Van. The Poëta-Raisse was formed over thousands of years, as water flowing down from the Jura tablelands cut its way into the limestone rock. Belying its name meaning 'terrible ravine' in the local Jurassian dialect, the Poëta-Raisse is a romantically wild gorge of small waterfalls and gentle mossy pools, accessible by way of an intriguing stepped pathway.

One of Switzerland's most impressive geological landscapes, the Creux du Van is a limestone cirque with sheer 200-metre high cliffs. The area around this amazing semi-circular amphitheatre forms Switzerland's oldest nature reserve, which was established in 1870. For over a hundred years, the animals in the reserve have enjoyed strict legal protection and lack the timidity of wildlife elsewhere. The local fauna includes chamois, ibex and even lynx, which have all been reintroduced since being hunted out in past centuries.

The Creux du Van's French name roughly translates as 'wind funnel' and the grassy meadows above the precipice are windswept and treeless. The existence of permafrost under the talus debris at the base of the rock walls (at just 1200 metres above sea level) indicates the severity of the winter in the Jura. Only low stunted conifers, some 200 years old, and plant species otherwise found above the treeline grow here.

Maps

The 1:50,000 SAW/FSTP sheet *Val de Travers (241 T)* is the recommended walking map. Another option is Kummerly + Frey's *Chasseral Neuchâtel Val de Travers Ste-Croix*, scaled at 1:60,000.

Walking Times & Standard

This is a longish day hike which can be easily broken up into two fairly short and leisurely days. The route follows well-graded trails, alp tracks or roads virtually the whole way, although in places paths can be a bit muddy. It is fairly well signposted and marked (with yellow diamonds) and requires little navigation. A drystone wall provides a reassuring saftey fence around the abrupt precipice of the Creux du Van.

The walk is rated *easy*, although it has a relatively long overall distance of 21 km.

Places to Stay

For places to stay in Môtiers see Walking Bases. The *Chalet La Combaz* (☎ 024-71 11 53) has a small dormitory (showers available). Excellent value and most recommended is the *Café-Restaurant Les Rochat* (☎ 024-73 11 61, open all year) which has a 30-person mattress room for walkers (showers available). The *Restaurant La Baronne* (☎ 038-55 13 91) has a dorm in an upstairs hay loft with basic conditions and very cheap rates. At the Creux du Van is the *La Soliat* (☎ 038-63 31 36), a charming restaurant at 1386 metres which has a large bunkroom (showers available).

Unfortunately, Noiraigue, at the end of the walk, has little or no suitable accommodation available.

Getting to/from the Walk

This walk starts off at Môtiers and finishes in Noiraigue. Both places are on the Val de Travers rail line, and easily accessible from the city of Neuchâtel.

From the end of May until mid-September postbuses also run between Couvet (in the

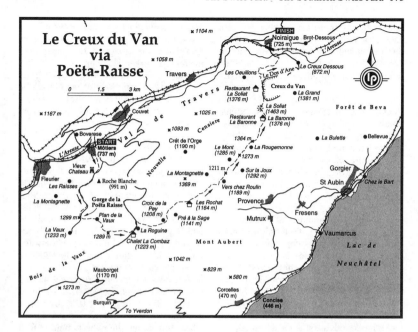

Le Creux du Van
via
Poëta-Raisse

Val de Travers) and Yverdon (on Lake Neuchâtel), and stop at the Chalet La Combaz; some walkers might prefer to set out from La Combaz, leaving out the first section of the walk.

Route Directions: Môtiers to Noiraigue (21 km, 5 to 6 hours)

From the railway station in Môtiers (see Walking Bases above) walk past the Hôtel des Six Comunes on the main road, then proceed straight along a street leading quickly out of town. A large red-and-white painted Swiss cross stands out on a mountain cliff face ahead. At a fork near the edge of the forest bear right onto a logging road running up beside the Poëta Raisse (which flows underground in places).

The route crosses the stream a number of times and continues as a well-cut foot track to an open cavern, where the **Gorge de la Poëta Raisse** begins. A series of cut-stone stairways and boarded walkways brings you

up steeply beside tiny waterfalls to reach a signposted intersection at the end of the gorge, one to 1½ hours from Môtiers.

Head left over a footbridge, making your way on up through a little gully past an old barn to meet a surfaced road. Turn left and climb gently 500 metres to where the Jura High Route crosses the road at the crest of the range. Take the left-hand trail off into the forest, before dropping down a short way across open paddocks to arrive at the **Chalet La Combaz** at 1223 metres (see Places to Stay), on the Couvet-Yverdon road, after 40 to 50 minutes.

Follow the bitumen 500 metres around to the left to the next postbus stop. Here leave off right along a gravelled track and continue past a farmhouse with a traditional high wooden-shingle roof, keeping to the dirt lane until this ends at another house, the **Croix de la Pey**. Here jump over a stile and cut down right across a small flowery meadow to meet a rough road, making your way on through mixed Jurassian forest to connect with another road. Turn right and walk a short distance downhill to reach the **Restaurant Les Rochat** (see Places to Stay) at 1164 metres, 40 to 50 minutes on from La Combaz.

Pick the marked path just down from Les Rochat. The route rises and dips through stands of broadleaf trees and wide clearings before coming out at a surfaced roadway. Follow a foot trail up left beside the road for two km to a signposted track turn-off, and ascend gently to reach a little saddle between low hills after 45 minutes to one hour. From here there is a nice view towards the rounded summit of La Soliat slightly east of north.

Head quickly around right through two gates, then branch off left and sidle the slopes above the rolling grassy basin to the rustic **Restaurant La Baronne** (see Places to Stay) at 1376 metres. An old vehicle track climbs 500 metres around left to where a line of rock markings guides you straight up right to the 1463-metre top of **La Soliat**, after 30 to 40 minutes. In fine weather the panorama from La Soliat extends as far as the Savoy Alps in Italy.

Just a few paces on is the **Creux du Van**, the highlight of the walk. A path runs around the precipitous rim beside a stone fence built to keep livestock (and people) a healthy distance from the cliff face. A tiny enclosed valley forms a forest wilderness stretching away immediately below the impressive 200-metre walls. To get the best-angle view of the Creux du Van head up around to the right (east), before doubling back to the cirque's lower side at the edge of the woods. From here a path cuts a few hundred metres left across the pastures to the restaurant at **La Soliat** (see Places to Stay).

Follow the well-graded foot track known as the Sentier des Contours that descends steeply through the forest in increasingly broad switchback curves into the clearing of **Les Oeuillons** (1014 metres). A narrow dirt road begins just below the restaurant here, and sidles rightwards down the slope to intersect with a bitumened roadway near a row of defensive tank obstacles. Make your way on easily down past the hamlet of **Vers chex Joly** and cross the Areuse on a bridge to arrive at the village of **Noiraigue** (725 metres) after one to 1¼ hours. Noiraigue lies on the flat floor of the steep-sided Val de Travers at the upper end of the Gorges de l'Areuse. Its name means 'black waters', a reference to the river's dark, peat-stained waters.

MONT TENDRE

At 1679 metres Mont Tendre is the most elevated point in the Swiss Jura. Despite its relative height, the mountain has a mildly contoured topography of gently rolling, lightly forested hills. Its slopes are criss-crossed by old drystone fences, many of which were built centuries ago and once served as lines of demarkation between farms or local communities. Mont Tendre stands above the fiord-like Lac de Joux, the largest lake within the Jura range, and its smaller companion Lac Brenet. Lying at around 1000 metres, both lakes owe their existence to thick deposits of glacial silt which formed an almost watertight seal in the otherwise very porous Jurassian limestone. With no above-ground outlet, the lakewater drains away into subterraneous channels which flow to the surface at the Grotte de l'Orbe. This powerful spring forms the source of the Orbe River. Once the most polluted lake in Switzerland, the water quality in the Lac de Joux has improved dramatically over the last decade or so and the lake has now regained its natural crystal-clear state.

Maps

Kümmerly + Frey's 1:60,000 special Jura walking map *Lausanne La Côte St-Cergue Vallée de Joux* fully covers the route. Two 1:50,000 SAW/FSTP sheets are otherwise necessary: *Vallée de Joux (250 T)* and *La Sarraz (251 T)*.

Walking Times & Standard

Mont Tendre makes a moderately long day hike that has a steady but mostly gentle ascent of almost 700 altitude metres.

Although otherwise fairly straightforward, the route crosses many forest tracks and farm roads, so keep a continual watch for waymarkings. Lower down the route is yellow-marked, but on Mont Tendre's upper slopes the markings are white-red-white.

The walk has been given an *easy to moderate* rating.

Places to Stay

The only place to stay en route is the *Alpage et Buvette du Mont Tendre* (☎ 071-22 60 27) at 1646 metres on the upper slopes of Mont Tendre, where the friendly proprietor lets walkers sleep amongst the haystacks in the barn free of charge. Return the favour by ordering a meal or refreshment. In May the restaurant is based at the Chalet Neuf du Mont Tendre (1513 metres), but from late June until late October it moves one km up the road to the Chalet du Mont Tendre (1646 metres).

All of the villages around the Lac de Joux have hotel accommodation. Le Sentier at the end of the walk has a *camping ground* (☎ 021-845 51 74) and the *Hôtel de Ville* (☎ 021-845 52 33) offers rooms of various standards at quite reasonable rates. In the village of Le Lieu halfway along the western side of the lake is the similarly named *Hôtel de Ville* (☎ 021-841 12 22) with a few very low-budget rooms. There is a *youth hostel* (☎ 021-843 13 49) in the nearby town of Vallorbe. The Vallée de Joux tourist office (☎ 021-845 62 57) is in Le Sentier.

Getting to/from the Walk

The walk begins at Le Pont, a village that lies between the Lac de Joux and the Lac Brenet. Le Pont is best accessible by train on the Le Day-Le Brassus rail line that runs along the Vallée de Joux. Le Day itself is on the Lausanne-Vallorbe rail line, and from Lausanne there are hourly connections to Le

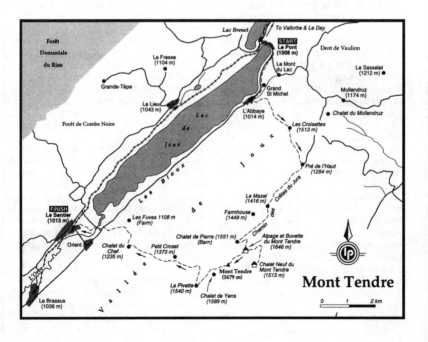

Pont until at least 8.30 pm. The village of Le Sentier at the end of the walk is on the same rail line.

The walk can be shortened slightly by taking a bus from Le Pont to L'Abbaye.

Route Directions: Le Pont to Le Sentier
(25 km, 5¼ to 6½ hours)

From the Le Pont train station walk along the lakeside promenade and take the path leading around the reedy shoreline of **Lac de Joux** past holiday houses to the village of **L'Abbaye** after 35 to 40 minutes. At the local bus stop a signpost directs you a short way up a laneway to a lumberyard, then briefly left to where a foot track climbs away rightwards. Carefully follow yellow markings up along tracks in the forest, before cutting on up through attractive hillside meadows to meet a dirt road. Turn left here and make your way quickly on to meet a bitumened road at **Les Croisettes** (1513 metres) after a further one to 1⅓ hours.

Cross the cattle grid and immediately break away left onto a farm track, continuing between the two branches when you come to a fork. The route goes over lovely rolling herb fields to intersect with another surfaced road at the **Pré de l'Haut** (1284 metres). After following this south-west until the bitumen ends just before a farmhouse, head off right along an alp track that leads through typical lightly forested Jurassian countryside. A signposted trail at **Le Mazel** (1416 metres) departs left through a turnstile and sidles gently up the slope via a long grassy clearing to the lone barnyard of **Chalet de Pierre** at 1551 metres, 1¼ to 1½ hours from Les Croisettes.

Another vehicle track brings you up over the crest of the broad treeless range to the **Alpage et Buvette du Mont Tendre** (1646 metres, see Places to Stay), from where a white-red-white marked path guides you quickly on along the open rocky ridge to reach the top of **Monte Tendre** after 30 to 40 minutes. The 1679-metre summit is crowned by a prominent surveying triangle and in clear conditions gives nice views of the surrounding Jura as well as classic vistas across Lake Geneva towards the mightiest snow-capped peaks in the western Alps.

Descend gently south-west along the right-hand side of the range over snowdrifts persisting well into summer to the **Chalet de Yens** at 1589 metres. Make your way on gently down to a signposted path junction beside an ancient stone fence and turnstile at **La Pivette** (1540 metres). Here drop down northwards past a track going off right to Les Bioux, following yellow diamonds down through small pockets of trees to join a graded lane at the farmhouse of **Petit Croset** (1373 metres). The route rolls along through more mixed field and forest for a way, edging downwards again as the Lac de Joux comes into view before reaching a surfaced road at **Chalet du Chef** (1235 metres), 1¼ to 1½ hours from Mont Tendre.

Walk down the bitumen to a farm gate, and take a short-cut track off left to **Les Fuves** (1108 metres). After continuing down to meet the main road one km from the village of Orient, head directly across the Orbe and pick up an (unsignposted) path just after the bridge. This leads left across a riverside meadow to a sawmill, then on to the right through the woods to terminate below the railway at **Le Sentier** (1013 metres, see Places to Stay) after a final 40 to 50 minutes. Here the Rue de la Sagne can be quickly followed to the train station.

OTHER WALKS
La Dôle

The second-highest and most south-westerly summit in the Swiss Jura, the 1677-metre La Dôle rises up surprisingly steeply between Lake Geneva and the French border. The open tops offer a full Alpine panorama sweeping across the great lake to the Mont Blanc, Dents du Midi and Les Diablerets massifs. La Dôle has long been a popular lookout point, its earliest and most distinguished visitors having included the philosopher Jean-Jacques Rousseau and the young Goethe. Today there is a television tower on the mountain, an aerial navigation and weather station on its main peak, and the northern slopes have been developed for winter sports, yet La Dôle is nonetheless worthy of the energetic climb required to reach its summit.

La Dôle can be ascended in a relatively easy four-hour semi-circuit from La Givrine (1290 metres), a small station on the Nyon-La Cure rail line. From La Givrine the route heads south-west across green rolling hills to the chair lift at Couvaloup de Crans, then climbs past the alp hut of Reculet Dessus (1479 metres) to meet a path sidling the main ridge running south-west to the summit. The descent route goes back along the main ridge to the Col de Porte (1559 metres), before traversing gently south-east down to another small saddle. Continue through a tiny valley past the farmlet of Le Vuarne (1319 metres), dropping on down through narrow clearings to reach a road leading down to the attractive town of St Cergue (see Walking Bases).

Either of two good walking maps can be used: the 1:50,000 SAW/FSTP sheet *St Cergue (260 T)* or Kümmerly + Frey's 1:60,000 *Lausanne-La Côte-St Cergue-Vallée de Joux*.

Le Chasseron

Rising up sharply from the Val de Travers, the 1606-metre Le Chasseron is the third highest peak in the Swiss Jura. The mountain's eastern sides are an attractive gently sloping plateau of highland pastures overlooking the Lac de Neuchâtel. Le Chasseron is best reached from the town of Ste-Croix (see Walking Bases), from where a section of the long-distance Jura High Route leads along the grassy ridges to the summit. From here walkers can continue down to Môtiers via the Poëta Raissa or ahead to the road at La Combaz (see the Chasseral walk).

The *Hôtel du Chasseron* (☎ 024-61 23 88) just below the summit of Le Chasseron has panoramic rooms and a dormitory. The best walking maps covering the route are the 1:25,000 *Carte d'Excursions Ste-Croix les Rasses* produced by the local tourist authority, the 1:50,000 SAW/FSTP sheet *Val de Travers (241 T)* or Kümmerly + Frey's

Chasseral Neuchâtel Val de Travers Ste-Croix scaled at 1:60,000.

Les Gorges de l'Areuse

One of the nicest walks in the Neuchâtel Jura leads from the village of Boudry up through the fascinating, wild Gorges de l'Areuse to Noiraigue, where the small Areuse River snakes its way through a mysterious and surprisingly narrow chasm. Following close to the rail lines past the station at the old milling hamlet of Champ de Moulin Dessous, the path leads up along stone stairways and over little stone bridges and past tumbling waterfalls in the damp, dark depths below the limestone cliffs. The walk is quite easy and can be completed in around three hours. Boudry is on the Yverdon-Neuchâtel rail line. Kümmerly + Frey's 1:60,000 walking map *Chasseral Neuchâtel Val de Travers Ste-Croix* covers the route in a single sheet. Two SAW/FSTP sheets are otherwise needed: *Val de Travers (241 T)* and *Avenches (242 T)*.

Les Ponts-de-Martel to La Brévine

This walk in the Neuchâtel Jura leads from the highland moors in the upper valley of the Grand Bied to the village of La Brévine near the French border in the remote Vallée de la Brévine. Although it lies only slightly above 1000 metres – much lower than many mountain valleys of the Alps – winter temperatures in the Vallée de la Brévine regularly fall below 30° C. Known as the 'Swiss Siberia', La Brévine is the coldest place in the country – but only in winter, since average summer temperatures are as mild as elsewhere in the Jura. This region has a 'Nordic' type of vegetation typified by heathland and forests of birch.

The walk sets off southwards from the village of Les Ponts-de-Martel (1009 metres) to Brot-Dessus across the marshy bed of an ancient lake, the peaty ground of which is partly exploited and partly protected within a small nature reserve. The route continues westwards high above the Val de Travers cross the crest of the Crête de Sapel before descending through scattered woodlands to La Brévine (1043 metres), where there are two or three places to stay.

The average walking time is 4½-hours. Les Pont-de-Martel is the terminus of the small private railway from La Chaux-de-Fonds, which can be reached by frequent trains from Neuchâtel and Biel. From La Brévine there are some five daily postbuses (until around 5.30 pm) to Fleurier, from where there are hourly train connections to Neuchâtel.

The Saut & Côtes du Doubs

Rising in France, the Doubs River drains virtually all of the northern Jura before flowing on into larger rivers of the Rhône basin. The Doubs forms a lengthy part of the Franco-Swiss border, and even flows briefly through Switzerland before re-entering the French Jura at the village of Brémoncourt. As is typical in the limestone areas of the Jura, the Doubs' water level rises and falls fairly dramatically depending on recent rainfall. In many places the river has cut out gorges. An easy four to five-hour route follows the southern (ie Swiss) side of the Doubs between the Lac des Brenets and the small riverside hamlet of Maison Monsieur, a wild stretch of the river that lies in Neuchâtel Canton.

To reach the start of the walk take one of the tourist boats that leave from the village of Les Brenets every 45 minutes from May until late October. The 20-minute boat trip takes you through the attractive gorges of the Lac des Brenets to the Saut du Doubs, where the waters of the lake plummet 27 metres into the artificial reservoir of Lac de Moron. The route leaves from the landing jetty, passing by the falls before it sidles high around the steep-sided Lac du Moron. After a short, steep descent at the dam wall, the way leads on for hours through little mossy gorges, quiet riverside flats and anglers' cottages of the Côtes du Doubs to the tranquil hamlet of Maison Monsieur.

Les Brenets can be reached on the private narrow-gauge railway from Le Locle, which is itself accessible by a 50-minute train ride from Biel/Bienne. Some three daily postbuses run from Biaufond via Maison Monsieur to the regional centre of La Chaux-de-Fonds, from where there are train connections to Neuchâtel and Biel. There are only two places to stay en route: the *Hôtel du Saut-du-Doubs* (☎ 039-32 10 70), near Saut du Doubs landing jetty with a few double rooms; and the attractive *Auberge de la Maison-Monsieur* (☎ 039-28 60 60) at Maison Monsieur with cheaper dormitory accommodation only.

When waters are low the Doubs can be easily crossed, so it may be a good idea to carry a passport or identity card in case of border control. Kümmerly + Frey's *Chasseral Neuchâtel Val de Travers Ste-Croix* covers the route on a single walking map. Two SAW/FSTP sheets are otherwise needed for the walk: *Le Locle (231 T)* and *Vallon de St-Imier (232 T)*.

Southern Fribourg & Vaud

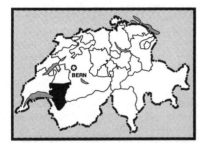

The southern part of Fribourg (Freiburg) Canton is an extensive area of Alpine foothills whose higher summits push up well beyond the treeline, often surpassing the 2000-metre level. The southernmost part of Vaud Canton is a mountainous region sandwiched – almost as an enclave – between the Bernese Oberland to the east, the Valais to the south and Fribourg to the north. Except for German-speaking communities living along Fribourg's cantonal border with Bern, this is a francophone region.

The moist climate prevailing in Southern Fribourg and Vaud make this some of the choicest dairying country in Switzerland. Beginning in the 14th century, steadily rising demand for hard, durable cheeses gave rise to an important dairy industry centred in these Alpine foothills. Local cheeses, particularly Sbrinz and Gruyères types, were exported to many parts of western Europe. Cheese-making brought widespread pros-

perity to the local farmers, and the 'Fribourg' style of rural architecture (which is also common in the southern Vaud) gradually developed. These graceful houses with their high roofs of wooden shingles are a typical feature of the countryside.

Together the compact ranges of southern Fribourg and Vaud form an unexpectedly interesting and varied region for walking. Five routes are featured in this chapter.

The Fribourg & Vaud Pre-Alps

The pre-Alpine ranges of cantons Fribourg and Vaud (called the Préalpes romandes in French, or the Freiburger und Waadtländer Voralpen in German) form an often rugged band of mountains sweeping south-west from the Fribourg Mittelland across the districts of Gruyères and Pays d'Enhaut as far as Lake Geneva. Unlike most other areas of the Alpine foothills, these mountains are composed of hard limestones that frequently erode into jagged peaks and interesting karst fields. With their sheer rock faces and craggy peaks, the Fribourg and Vaud Pre-Alps excite the attentions of many a mountain rock-climber. Despite their modest height when compared with the 'true' Alpine summits to the south, the ranges of this area offer some splendidly scenic walks.

WALKING BASES
Schwarzsee
The name of both the lake and the holiday locality scattered around the reedy shoreline, Schwarzsee (called Lac Noir by francophone Swiss) lies at 1046 metres in the north-eastern Fribourg Pre-Alps. The Schwarzsee's dark waters are set before a backdrop of high limestone peaks with remarkable jagged summits that rise up dramatically

from more softly contoured grassy hills. The local people here speak an earthy dialect similar to neighbouring regions of Bern Canton, although the Schwarzsee is on the linguistic border and walkers are likely to hear as much French spoken as German.

The local camping ground at Schwarzsee is *Seeweid* (☎ 037-32 11 58), which also offers mattress-room accommodation. Schwarzsee has a Friends of Nature hostel, the 49-bed *Naturfreundehaus Chalet Aurore* (☎ 037-32 11 23). Other lower-budget places to stay are the *Hotel Gypsera* (☎ 037-32 11 12) at Schwarzsee, and the *Hotel Kaiseregg* (☎ 037-39 11 05) in nearby Plaffeien. The Schwarzsee tourist office (☎ 037-32 13 13) at Gyspera has other accommodation options.

Schwarzsee is accessible from Fribourg (on the main Geneva-Bern-Zürich-St Gallen rail line) by direct GFM public buses via Plaffeien around 10 times per day. The last bus leaves Fribourg train station at roughly 6.45 pm; it's a pleasant one-hour trip through green rolling hills.

Château d'Oex

The small town of Château d'Oex (968 metres) is the centre of the Pays d'Enhaut district, and has been developed into a resort for both summer and winter outdoor sports. There are some excellent day and overnight hikes in the nearby mountains, particularly around the Vanil Noir (2389 metres) to the north and the Gummfluh (2458 metres) to the south, as well as easy day walks along the Sarine River.

The *Au Berceau* (☎ 029-4 62 34) by the river has organised camping, and there is a local *youth hostel* (☎ 029-4 64 04). The *Hôtel La Printanière* (☎ 029-4 61 13) and *Buffet de la Gare* (☎ 029-4 77 17) both have budget rooms. Château d'Oex has a helpful tourist office (☎ 029-4 77 88).

Château d'Oex is on the Montreux-Oberland-Bahn (MOB) rail line that links Lake Geneva with Spiez (via Zweisimmen) in the Bernese Oberland; departures are at least hourly. If you are travelling to or from Fribourg a rail/bus combination via Montbovon

and Bulle is necessary. Regular postbuses also run between Le Sépey and Château d'Oex via the Col des Mosses.

Col des Mosses

This modest winter-sports resort lies on the broad grassy Col des Mosses (1445 metres), a low pass marking the continental watershed between the Rhine basin (on its northern side) and the catchment area of the Rhône to the south. The Col des Mosses has a general store as well as a tourist office (☎ 025-55 14 66), and serves as a convenient base for walks in the nearby Tour de Famelon and around Pic Chaussy. The village is also a stop on the long Alpine Pass Route walk.

The local camping ground is *La Toundra* (☎ 025-55 20 45), and for dormitory accommodation try the *Hôtel Les Fontaines* (☎ 025-55 12 12). The *Resthôtel Keller* (☎ 025-55 16 31) has medium-range rooms. Postbuses between Château d'Oex and Le Sépey (a station on the Aigle-Les Diablerets rail line) run via the Col des Mosses. In summer there are five buses in either direction each day; the last bus leaves for Château d'Oex a little after 6 pm.

Montreux

Montreux is situated on the eastern Lake Geneva shoreline – an area known as the 'Swiss Riviera' that enjoys marvellous vistas across the water towards the Mont Blanc massif. Popular with well-to-do foreign (especially British) tourists since the mid-1850s, the city boasts many grand old hotels and villas. The Château de Chillon, a famously picturesque medieval castle, stands on the lakeshore several km to the south.

The Rochers de Naye, a classic 2042-metre lookout peak is directly accessible from Montreux by a cog railway. A scenic three to four-hour high-level traverse route leads down from the Rochers de Naye summit via the Col de Jarman and Le Molard (1703 metres) to the upper station of the cog railway at Les Pléiades (1360 metres). Montreux is also the termination of the two-week long Alpine Pass Route.

In Montreux-Territet are the local *youth hostel* (☎ 021-963 49 34) and the *Hôtel Villa Germaine* (☎ 021-963 15 28) at 3 Ave de Collonge with lower-budget rooms. The Montreux tourist office (☎ 021-963 12 12) is on the lakefront near the Place du Marché.

Montreux is on the main Lausanne-Brig rail line with hourly express trains; slower regional trains pass through Montreux approximately half-hourly. Running through numerous tight curves and tunnels, the private Montreux-Oberland-Bahn (MOB) connects Montreux with Spiez via the towns of Château d'Oex, Saanen, Gstaad and Zweisimmen in the Vaud and Bernese Pre-Alps.

From the end of May until late September numerous ferries link Montreux with resorts around Lake Geneva, including villages and towns on the lake's French (southern) shoreline. Outside the summer tourist season boats run far less frequently.

THE KAISEREGG

Towering more than 1100 altitude metres above the dark waters of the Schwarzsee, the 2185-metre Kaiseregg is one of the most prominent peaks of the northern Fribourg Pre-Alps. The summit stands just west of the Fribourg/Bern cantonal border, and makes an excellent lookout point with a panorama including the Swiss Mittelland, the surrounding jagged ranges of the Alpine foothills and higher main summits of the Alps to the south. This walk leads over the Kaiseregg into the Simmental, a valley renowned for its fine examples of Bernese wooden architecture.

Maps

The best available walking map is *Schwarzseegebiet Plasselb und Jaun* produced at a scale of 1:25,000 by the local tourist authorities. Also very good is the 1:50,000 SAW/FSTP sheet *Gantrisch (253 T)*. Covering the same area is Schaad + Frey's 1:50,000 walking map titled *Wanderkarte Gantrisch* which shows the topography

in less detail but is nevertheless of use to hikers.

Walking Times & Standard

This walk is a longish day walk without the option of staying somewhere en route. The route is generally in condition from at least early June until late October, and is marked in white-red-white or yellow-diamond markings (on lower sections). The climb to the Kaiseregg summit totals just over 1100 altitude metres and requires some heavy legwork, but is nevertheless recommended to anyone with reasonable fitness. The descent involves a drop of around 1200 altitude metres, and includes an extended steep and rocky section.

The Swiss military (EMD/DMF) holds shooting exercises in the Geissalp and Walop areas for short periods in the summer and autumn. At such times walkers may have a short wait before the sentries give the all-clear to pass through. To check on the current situation call the EMD/DMF's regional information office in Fribourg on ☎ 037-20 82 08. The walk is rated *moderate* and covers a distance of around 14 km.

Places to Stay

For accommodation options in Schwarzsee, see Walking Bases above. There is no other accommodation until you get to Boltigen, at the end of the walk, where the *Hotel Bären* (☎ 030 -3 60 66) is one of several local hotels which offer standard rooms.

Getting to/from the Walk

Walkers can set off either directly from the Gyspera postbus stop at Schwarzsee (see Walking Bases), or take the chair lift from Gyspera up to Riggisalp (1493 metres). The chair lift runs from mid-June until the end of October and takes some of the grunt and wheeze out of the long climb up to the Kaiseregg.

Walkers who climb the Kaiseregg as a day trip from Fribourg may find the Fri-Pass (see the Getting Around chapter) an economical public transport option.

Motorists arriving via Bern should exit the

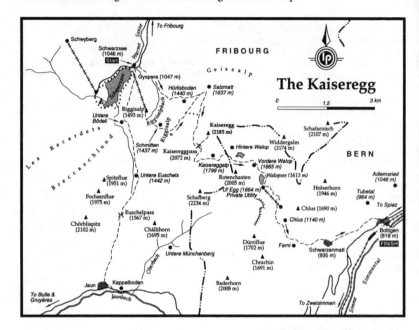

The Kaieregg

N12 at Düdingen; vehicles can be parked at the free car park in Schwarzsee-Gyspera. From Boltigen you can take the postbus over the Jaunpass to Jaun (accommodation available), from where a pleasant three-hour walk leads north over the Euschelpass (1567 metres) back to Schwarzsee.

Route Directions:
Schwarzsee/Riggisalp to Boltigen
(14 km, 4¾ to 7 hours)
If you have the time, it's worth doing the easy two-hour walk around the lovely shore of the Schwarzsee (follow the 'Seerundgang/Tour du Lac' signs). Walkers starting out directly from Schwarzsee can take the signposted foot track 200 metres east of **Gyspera** (1047 metres), which leads up beside the Riggisalpbach. The path soon crosses to the stream's true right (ie eastern) bank, ascending steadily over rich Alpine pastures to the jingling of cowbells. Climb on past the alp hut of **Hürlisboden** (1440 metres) to arrive

at the farmhouse of **Salzmatt**, at 1637 metres on a broad col looking down into the pleasant green upper valley of Geissalp, after 1½ to two hours.

From the upper chair-lift station at **Riggisalp** (1493 metres) walk a short way south along a rough gravelled track, then take a left-hand turn-off leading down into the grassy bowl to **Schmitten** (1437 metres). This large alp hut is a typical Fribourg-style construction with a high, wooden-shingled roof. Fresh milk, cheese and basic refreshments are available here. Follow a yellow-marked trail up past the barn past a tiny tarn nestling in a rounded crater-like trough, before sidling up along steep slopes above the Riggisalp. The route passes under a winter ski tow (from where some walkers short-cut directly up the slope to rejoin the path on the ridge – see below), to reach **Salzmatt**, 50 minutes to one hour from the upper chair-lift station.

Continue southwards up a spur coming

down from the Kaiseregg, breaking away to the right not long after you pass the upper end of the ski tow. The path makes a rising traverse along the mountainside herbfields through occasional wooden stiles, before snaking up steeply in switchbacks through broken rock to come out onto the saddle of the **Kaisereggpass** (2072 metres) after one to 1⅓ hours. These green lawns offer a nice place for a short rest before making the final ascent

The 20 to 30-minute return walk up to the wooden cross atop the 2185-metre **Kaiseregg** skirts north-east along the rocky southern side of the ridge over rocky slopes covered with stinging nettles. The summit panorama includes the Schwarzsee and the surrounding jagged ranges of the Fribourg and Vaud Pre-Alps, while to the north the land plummets away into the Swiss Mittelland, where the cities of Bern and Fribourg can be made out. Standing out in the distant south are the snow-topped mountains between the Les Diablerets and the Wildstrubel massifs.

After signing your name in the summit logbook, backtrack to the Kaisereggpass and begin descending south-east. The white-red-white marked path winds down around to the right through raw karst rock into a basin of grassed-over moraines enclosed by the craggy peaks to meet a vehicle track at the alp hut of **Kaisereggalp** (1799 metres).

Follow this rough road on down through a stone fence marking the Fribourg/Bern cantonal border, then immediately (ie just before you get to the farmlet of **Hintere Walop**) continue rightwards around past a small, shallow lake to reach **Vordere Walop** (1665 metres), 50 minutes to one hour on.

Make your way quickly on over a slight crest, where the emerald-green waters of the **Walopsee** come into sight. The often muddy route leads high around the lake's steep eastern side along slopes scattered with dotted gentians to a small square barn just before the upper station of a utility cableway at **Uf Egg** (1664 metres). Here leave off left and begin dropping down into the spruce forest in numerous steep spirals beside

impressive overhanging rock walls. One to 1⅓ hours on from Vordere Walop, the path comes out at **Chlus** (1140 metres, shown on some signposts as 'Klus'), where the terrain softens into gentle open pastures.

Proceed smoothly down through this little valley along the narrow road via the hamlet of **Farni** (ignoring a diverging path here signposted 'Tubetal/Adlemsried/Boltigen') to **Schwarzenmatt** (935 metres). Turn off left along a bitumened laneway leading quickly out of the village, following sporadic yellow diamonds gradually down past a milking shed amongst meadows fringing the Simmental to meet a road. About 150 metres down from here take a foot track going off left down beside a stream to arrive at the main road in **Boltigen** (see Places to Stay) after a final 30 to 40 minutes. The village has some good examples of the grandiose Bernese-style wooden architecture. Boltigen's train station (818 metres) is a further five minutes along to the right past the tourist office.

THE COL DE CHAUDE
(Section 15 of the Alpine Pass Route)
The walk over the 1621-metre Col de Chaude is a long but thoroughly enjoyable ramble through the high rolling hills of the Vaud Pre-Alps. The route takes you from Col des Mosses to the resort city of Montreux on the Lake Geneva shoreline. Under the influence of this large body of water, the steep upper slopes below the Rochers de Naye enjoy a milder climate and are covered by luxuriant mixed broadleaf forests. The Col de Chaude is the final section of the long Alpine Pass Route.

Maps
Either the Editions MPA Verlag's 1:50,000 walking map *Alpes Vaudoises* or the 1:50,000 SAW/FSTP sheet *Rochers de Naye (262 T)* can be used for this hike. Readers should also refer to the 'Vaud Pre-Alps' map in this chapter.

Walking Times & Standard
Following a sunny and relatively low course,

the walk can generally be undertaken from early May until late November. The route is a bit too long to be done comfortably in a single day, but unfortunately the few better en-route accommodation options are near the start and finish of the hike. Apart from the length itself, the walk presents no real difficulties, however, and leads along little-transited roads or forest tracks for much of the way. The route markings are mainly yellow diamonds.

The route is rated *easy to moderate*, and covers a total distance of some 27 km.

Places to Stay

The *Hôtel-Restaurant La Lécherette* (☎ 029-4 62 59) is one of several places in the village of La Lécherette that has budget rooms. The *Chalet de Chaude*, just east of the Col de Chaude, offers rustic sleeping in the hay loft. At the hamlet of Sonchaux, roughly 2½ hours before Montreux, the *Auberge de Sonchaux* (☎ 021-963 44 67, open May to October) offers good-value mattress-room accommodation (showers available). See Walking Bases for places to stay at the Col des Mosses and in Montreux.

Getting to/from the Walk

The walk begins at the Col des Mosses and terminates at Montreux; access to both places is covered in Walking Bases above.

Route Directions: Col de Mosses to Montreux

(27 km, 8 to 11 hours)

From the Col des Mosses post office head a few minutes along the busy highway to a bitumened road on your left. Follow this under the power transmission lines then right along a short side road and up the grassy slope along a wire fence to a vehicle track. The track rises slightly to meet a larger gravel road at a bend. Here go right along the edge of the forest, gently descending beside a barn to a main road and continuing right past the military barracks to reach the tiny resort village of **La Lécherette** (1379 metres) after 40 to 50 minutes.

Pick up the route at the small road behind the La Lécherette post office (signposted 'La Sia/Les Moutins'). Head up past a small chapel then along a path on past houses to meet another surfaced road. Turn left and continue onto slopes high above the Lac de L'Hongrin reservoir with unusual double-curved dam walls. Painted route markings lead on past the restaurant at **Col Sonlomont** (1503 metres) to a car park at the end of the road, from where a short foot track cuts up the grassy slope to reach the **Linderrey** farm-house at 1669 metres after two to three hours. There are clear views westwards from here to the adjacent Rochers de Naye.

Drop down in zigzags through steep pastures to meet the L'Hongrin valley road and follow this right across the bridge to the farmhouse at **La Vuichoude d'en Bas**. From here an old mule track leads left up grassy slopes to a farmlet then through light forest to the **Chalet de Chaude** (1475 metres, see Places to Stay) at the head of this tiny valley. The Chalet is a traditional stone-built homestead with a graceful wooden-shingle roof. From above the barn-yard continue along the bitumen road to reach the **Col de Chaude** at 1621 metres, 1½ to 2 hours from La Vuichoude. The village of Villeneuve on Lake Geneva is visible from here. A steep signposted path directs you off right up the Rochers de Naye, from where there are fine views of the lake. Descend the road from the Col, cutting off a section of curves on a steep foot track, to reach a narrow grassed-over road leading off right after one to 1½ hours. This climbs slightly through the forest for 30 to 40 minutes to meet another surfaced road at the **Auberge de Sonchaux** (1261 metres, see Places to Stay), from where the Dents du Midi and the mountains of the Savoy range are visible behind Lake Geneva.

Head northwards along the road which passes directly below the Auberge for 15 minutes, then take a steep path down through the trees to a gravelled vehicle track. Turn right and continue in a long gradual descent through tall broadleaf forest to a bitumened road and follow this down left into the village of **Glion** (708 metres), 1¼ to 1½ hours from

Sonchaux. From Glion station walkers can opt to take the cog railway directly down to Montreux or the funicular railway down to Montreux-Territet (look out for the 'Gare PTT' sign).

Walk down the road through the village, then turn right onto a stepped path descending steeply through the trees to Rue de Temple in the upper part of **Montreux** (see Places to Stay). From here continue right across the bridge over the Baye de Montreux, following the Rue de la Gare on down to reach the main train station (396 metres) after a final 40 to 50 minutes.

If you've just finished walking the entire Alpine Pass Route, your arrival in Montreux is something to celebrate!

OTHER WALKS
The Vanil Noir

Forming a natural division between Fribourg's Gruyères district and the Pays d'Enhaut of the Vaud, at 2389 metres the Vanil Noir is one of the loftier summits of the Pre-Alps. Precipitous rock buttresses on both sides give this range rather a striking aspect, and have spared the Vanil Noir from the (often excessive) skiing development of other Pre-Alpine areas. Having been severely overgrazed by sheep in the past, today the Vanil Noir is protected in one of the wildest nature reserves in the region. It is a botanically rich area which also has free-roaming herds of ibex and chamois.

The range is most easily accessible from Château d'Oex (see Walking Bases). The most popular walk is a four to five-hour circuit from the guesthouse at Ciernes Picat (1168 metres). There is no public transport to Ciernes Picat, but you can walk there from Flendruz (four km east of Château d'Oex) in around one hour. The route climbs up to Paray Dorena (1674 metres), then traverses the steep slopes below the Vanil Noir to Oussanna (1513 metres), an alp hut at the base of the wild Vallon de Mortey. The descent leads alongside the stream back to Ciernes Picat. Recommended for this walk

is the special 1:25,000 walking map entitled *Pays d'Enhaut* produced by local tourist authorities.

A more ambitious (very long day or overnight) hike goes up through the Vallon de Mortey to the summit of the Vanil Noir. The descent leads via the Chalet de Bounavaux (a restaurant at 1620 metres) to the village of Grandvillard, from where there are various train/postbus connections via Bulle to Fribourg. There is a mountain hut at *Les Marrindes* (1868 metres) in the Vallon de Mortey, and at Bounavaux walkers can sometimes sleep in the hay loft.

The Swiss military (EMD/DMF) carries out regular shooting exercises on the western (Fribourg) side of the Vanil Noir throughout summer and autumn, but the area remains open to walkers. For more information call the EMD/DMF regional information office (☎ 037-20 82 08). For this longer walk use either the SAW/FSTP sheet *Rochers de Naye (262 T)* or Editions MPA Verlag's *Alpes Vaudoises*, both scaled at 1:50,000.

The Gummfluh

Standing opposite the Vanil Noir in the Pays d'Enhaut district is the Gummfluh. The craggy 2458-metre main summit itself is difficult to get to on foot and is best left to the Alpine rock-climbers, but the area has many good walking routes. A popular walk from Château d'Oex (see Walking Bases) leads upstream along the forested southern banks of the Sarine to Gérignoz, before heading up into the tiny valley of the La Gérine to the lookout on La Videmanette (2130 metres). Shorter route variants involve taking a cable-car/chair-lift combination from Château d'Oex up to La Montagnette (1625 metres) and/or the Rougemont-La Videmanette gondola lift. The walk continues southwards around the eastern flank of the Gummfluh to the Col de Jable (1884 metres), then sidles down westwards to the postbus stop at L'Evitaz on the Château d'Oex-Col des Mosses road. The best walking map is the 1:25,000 *Pays d'Enhaut* published by the local tourist authorities.

The Col de Jarman

Situated just north of the Rochers de Naye, the 1512-metre Col de Jarman connects the Gruyères and Pays d'Enhaut districts with Lake Geneva. For centuries this low pass was an important transport route for muleteers, whose pack animals carried Gruyères cheeses westwards and wines from the Lake Geneva region eastwards. Known as the Route du fromage, this mule trail lost all economic importance after the opening of the (MOB) railway tunnel (which passes almost directly below the Col de Jarman) around the turn of the century.

Walking east to west, the old route runs from Montbovon (797 metres) through the Vallée des Allières, then snakes its way up steeply to the pass. The descent leads via Les Avants (968 metres), from where various paths continue down to Montreux (see Walking Bases). The *Restaurant Le Manoïre* (☎ 021-964 63 30) on the Col de Jarman has basic accommodation. The 1:50,000 walking map *Hautes de Montreux* produced by the local tourist authorities and the 1:50,000 SAW/FSTP sheet *Rochers de Naye (262 T)* both cover the walk.

The Moléson

Only just managing to break the 2000-metre barrier, the Moléson might not be spectacularly high. Cableways and a ski village dominate the mountain's northern slopes, so it's hardly wilderness country either. As a final north-western ripple in the Fribourg Pre-Alps, however, the Moléson does give some very worthwhile panoramas taking in Lake Geneva, the Swiss Mittelland as far as the Jura and the western Alps.

A pleasant and simple three-hour Moléson circuit starts at Plan-Francey (1520 metres), accessible by cable car from the resort of Moléson-Village. The route first contours along a 'botanical path' (with nameplates identifying numerous local wildflowers) to Gros Moléson at 1529 metres, before sidling westwards and ascending to the cable-car station and observatory on the Moléson's 2002-metre summit. A nice descent route follows the ridgeline southwards, then drops

off rightwards via Tremetta (1689 metres) and Gros Plané (1476 metres) back to Plan-Francey.

Moléson-Village has a *Friends of Nature* hostel (☎ 021-948 73 07), and the *Hôtel-Restaurant Plan-Francey* (☎ 029-6 10 42) offers rooms and dormitory accommodation. The 1:25,000 sheet *Moléson-Rochers de Naye* published by Editions MPA Verlag is the most detailed walking map to the Moléson area. A good alternative is the SAW/FSTP's 1:50,000 *Rochers de Naye (262 T)*.

Fribourg's GFM-network buses run from Bulle via Gruyères to Moléson-Village some seven times a day. The last bus leaves Bulle around 4.15 pm and returns from Moléson shortly before 5 pm. Bulle is best reached by regular (GFM) bus from Fribourg, or by rail from both Montreux and Château d'Oex via Montbovon.

The Vaud Alps

South of the Col des Mosses, the lower Alpine foothills give way to the Vaud Alps (Alpes Vaudois in French). Although they make up only a tiny part of the Swiss Alps, these ranges are full of topographical and scenic surprises. Cornered by the deep trough of the lower Swiss Rhône on their western and southern sides, the Vaud Alps drop away into the Rhône Valley with an often staggering abruptness. The region is primarily geared towards the skiing industry (which easily tops dairying as the mainstay of the local economy), with half a dozen well-known mountain resorts.

The only especially high mountains in the Vaud Alps are the Muverans and Les Diablerets, which run along the cantonal border with the Valais. These two massifs form an interesting range – essentially a south-western continuation of the Bernese Alps – which boasts several landmark 3000-metre summits and some quite outstanding Alpine landscapes. The Tour des Muverans (described below) is one of Switzerland's lesser known classic walks.

WALKING BASES
Les Diablerets
This village, lies at 1151 metres at the foot of the Diablerets massif just to the west of the Col du Pillon in the Ormond-Dessus district. A popular short walk from the village leads up to Lac Retaud (1685 metres), and a gondola lift goes up directly from Les Diablerets to La Marnèche (see the Col des Andérets).

The nearest camping is *La Murée* (☎ 021-801 19 08), three km downvalley at the village of Vers l'Église. A less expensive place to stay in Les Diablerets is the *Auberge de la Poste* (☎ 025-53 11 24); otherwise enquire at the local tourist office (☎ 025-53 13 58). Les Diablerets is best reached from Aigle on the hourly trains (via Le Sépey), or by postbus from Gstaad in the western Bernese Oberland (via the Col du Pillon).

Leysin
Perched on sub-Alpine slopes below the Tour d'Aï, Leysin (1315 metres) looks out southwards to the Muveran, the Dents du Midi and Mont Blanc massifs. In early July Leysin hosts a rock festival featuring popular musicians. Leysin has a helpful tourist office (☎ 025-34 22 44) and a top school of mountaineering, the École d'Alpinisme Leysin, CH-1854 (☎ 025-34 18 46).

Leysin's *Club Vagabond* (☎ 025-34 13 22) has budget rooms and dormitory accommodation. There is camping at *Sémiramis* (☎ 025-34 11 48). Another cheaper place to stay is the *Hôtel Bel-Air* (☎ 025-34 13 39). Leysin is accessible by the cog railway from Aigle, a small town south of Montreux on the main Lausanne-Brig rail line.

Villars
Essentially a winter ski resort, Villars (1253 metres) lies at the northern foot of the Muveran massif and has superb views towards the Dents de Midi, Mont Blanc and the Glacier du Trient. The cheapest place to stay in Villars is the *Hôtel Les Papillons*

(☎ 025-35 34 84). Otherwise ask at the tourist office (☎ 025-35 32 32). Villars can be reached via the private (BVB) mountain railway from Bex, a town on the main Rhône Valley rail line. There are regular postbuses to Villars from Aigle. Between early July and mid to late September postbuses run three times daily between Villars and the village of Les Diablerets (via the 1778-metre Col de la Croix).

THE COL DES ANDÉRETS
(Section 14 of the Alpine Pass Route)
The 2034-metre Col des Andérets is a slight pass in the ranges above the Col du Pillon watershed, where the Rhine and Rhone river systems converge. Leading from the village of Gsteig in the German-speaking Bernese Oberland through the francophone Ormont-Dessus district to the Col des Mosses, the way over the Col des Andérets transcends Switzerland's linguistic division. This is frontier country from yet another aspect, since here the higher peaks of the Bernese and Vaud Alps go over into the – still quite rugged – Alpine foothills to the north. This lovely walk takes you through a picturesque landscape of gentle mountain pastures, high moors, Alpine heathland and isolated little hamlets perched high above the valley opposite the 3000-metre peaks of the Diablerets massif.

Maps
The best option is Kümmerly + Frey's *Grand St Bernard-Dents du Midi-Les Diablerets*, a 1:60,000 walking map. The 1:50,000 FSTP/SAW sheet *Rochers de Naye* covers the entire route but doesn't show much of the interesting mountainous area immediately to the south. The Editions MPA Verlag walking map *Alpes Vaudoises*, scaled at 1:50,000, includes most of the Vaud Alps area, but unfortunately leaves out the first two km of the route from Gsteig.

Readers should also refer to the Vaud Pre-Alps map in this guidebook.

Walking Times & Standard
The Col des Andérets can be tackled as a

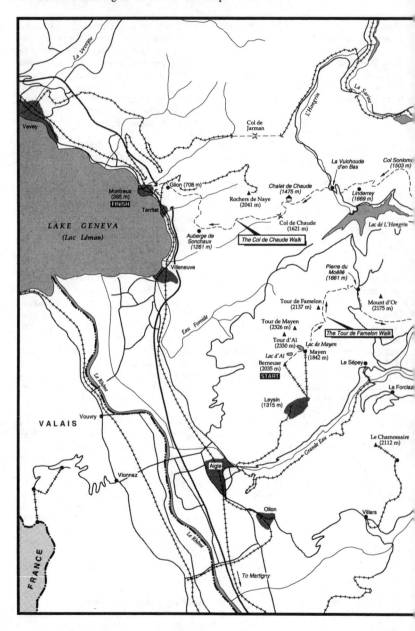

La Veveyse

Vevey

Col de Jarman

L'Hongrin

La Sarine

La Vuichoude
d'en Bas

Col Sonlome
(1503 m)

Glion (708 m)

Chalet de Chaude
(1475 m)

Linderrey
(1669 m)

Montreux
(395 m)
FINISH

Rochers de Naye
(2041 m)

Territet

LAKE GENEVA
(Lac Léman)

Col de Chaude
(1621 m)

Lac de L'Hongrin

Auberge de
Sonchaux
(1261 m)

The Col de Chaude Walk

Villeneuve

Pierre du
Moëllé
(1661 m)

Eau Froide

Tour de Famelon
(2137 m)

Mount d'Or
(2175 m)

Tour de Mayen
(2326 m)

The Tour de Famelon Walk

Tour d'Aï
(2330 m)

Lac de Mayen

Lac d'Aï

Mayen
(1842 m)

Le Sépey

Berneuse
(2035 m)
START

Le Rhône

La Forclaz

Leysin
(1315 m)

VALAIS

Vouvry

Le Chamossaire
(2112 m)

Grande Eau

Aigle

Vionnaz

Ollon

Villars

Le Rhône

FRANCE

To Martigny

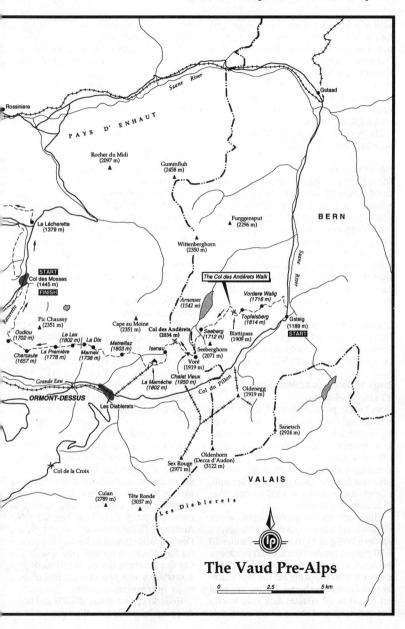

The Vaud Pre-Alps

Rossinière

Saane River

Gstaad

PAYS D' ENHAUT

Rocher du Midi
(2097 m) ▲

Gummfluh
(2458 m) ▲

Furggensput
(2296 m) ▲

BERN

La Lécherette
(1379 m)

Wittenberghorn
(2350 m) ▲

Saane River

START
Col des Mosses
(1445 m)
FINISH

The Col des Andérets Walk

Armensee
(1542 m)

Vordere Walig
(1716 m)

Pic Chaussy
(2351 m) ▲

Cape au Moine
(2351 m) ▲

Col des Andérets
(2034 m)

Seeberg
(1712 m)

Topfelsberg
(1814 m)

Gsteig
(1189 m)
START

Oudiou
(1702 m) ●

Le Lex
(1802 m)

La Dix
(1802 m)

Metreillaz
(1803 m)

Isenau

Blattipass
(1909 m)

Chersaule
(1657 m)

La Première
(1778 m)

Mamex
(1738 m)

Seeberghorn
(2071 m)

Voré
(1919 m)

Reverete

Grande Eau

La Mamèche
(1802 m)

Chalet Vieux
(1950 m)

Col du Pillon

Oldenegg
(1919 m) ▲

ORMONT-DESSUS

Les Diablerets

Sanetsch
(2924 m)

Col de la Croix ✝

Oldenhorn
(Decca d'Audon)
(3122 m) ▲

Sex Rouge
(2971 m) ▲

VALAIS

Culan
(2789 m) ▲

Tête Ronde
(3037 m) ▲

Les Diablerets

0   2.5   5 km

relatively long day walk, but may be best done in two shorter day stages with an overnight break en route (in La Marnèche or Les Diablerets). The first section of the route involves some initially quite steep climbing. Stage 2 is mostly easy high-level walking along mountainside terraces, whose unsheltered south-facing aspect makes them rather exposed to the summer sun.

The walk is rated *easy to moderate*, and has a total distance of 23 km.

Places to Stay

The only place to stay en route is the *Restaurant d'Isenau* (☎ 025-53 12 93) by the upper cable-car station at La Marnèche, where Stage 1 ends. It's open from early June to the end of September and charges very reasonable rates for rooms and dormitory beds. Showers are available.

For accommodation in Gsteig, Col des Mosses and Les Diablerets see Walking Bases in the Bernese Oberland chapter and above in this section.

Getting to/from the Walk

The walk begins at Gsteig and finishes at the Col des Mosses; access details to both places are covered above under Walking Bases.

Stage 1: Gsteig to La Marnèche

(11 km, 3 to 4 hours)

From Gsteig post office walk down to the upper side of the Hotel Viktoria, where a road departs up left. Follow this around to the right, crossing a stream before heading up left on a foot track (simply signposted 'Bergweg') along the steep ridge through mixed forest and clearings to reach **Schopfi**, a farmhouse and barn at 1502 metres, after 45 minutes to one hour.

Climb left up the grassy slopes, where red-white-red marker stakes lead the way to **Vordere Walig** at 1716 metres, a further 20 to 30 minutes on. An alp track runs just above this small cluster of farms, which sits high above the valley looking out towards graceful peaks to the south-east. Follow this road left for 20 to 30 minutes as it rises briefly then curves around above a very small side

valley to the isolated dairy farmlet of **Topfelsberg** at 1814 metres.

The road peters out a short way on, and the route continues as a neatly trodden foot track. This path quickly sidles along the hillside before making a short, steep ascent rightwards to reach the 1909-metre **Blattipass** after another 10 to 15 minutes. From the grassy tops of this small pass you get fine panoramas stretching from the Diablerets and the Spitzhorn in the south to the Wittenberghorn in the north.

Cut down towards the west through sporadic stands of spruce trees, orienting yourself by paint markings wherever the way becomes indistinct, soon meeting a trail coming up from the right. Turn left and contour high above the Arnensee across rolling slopes strewn with rhododendron bushes, passing the alp huts of **Ober Stuedeli** before dropping down to the isolated farmstead of **Seeberg** (1712 metres), 25 to 30 minutes from the Blattipass.

Follow the path quickly up left over mountain heathland to a saddle in a small side ridge. Head on across the green pastures of the tiny upper valley, then climb gently past a shallow tarn to reach the small col of **Voré** (1919 metres) after 30 to 40 minutes. The stone fence at Voré marks the border between the francophone canton of Vaud and German-speaking Bern. The col itself gives a tremendous view southwards across the Col du Pillon to the adjacent Sex Rouge and Oldenhorn peaks of Les Diablerets.

Walk five minutes diagonally up the open hillside to your right to the **Chalet Vieux**, at the end of a dirt road. The chalet overlooks the Arnensee, and sells milk and cheese as well as light refreshments. The route now continues along the road, rising steadily to cross the slight crest of the **Col des Andérets** (2034 metres), from where the Dents du Midi as well as the far-off peaks of the Savoy Alps move into view ahead. The Col des Andérets lies on the Rhine/Rhône watershed where two of western Europe's major river systems converge.

Head down past winter ski-lifts and begin dropping leftwards into the open basin on

Top: The Matterhorn viewed from the Grindjisee (2334 metres), 40 to 50 minutes walk from Sunnegga on the Sunnegga to Riffelalp walk.
Bottom: House at Alpe Chaude in the Vaud Alps. Together, the compact ranges of southern Fribourg and Vaud form an unexpectedly interesting and varied range for walking.

CLEM LINDENMAYER

CLEM LINDENMAYER

Top: Kühmad Church in Lötschental. Despite its inaccessibility, Celtic visitors ventured into Lötschental as early as 800 BC.

Bottom: Autumn colours in the Lötschental. An arduous route through the Quertalschlucht (an avalanche-prone gorge) was once the only access.

short-cut trails that lead off the road to the farmyard of **Isenau**. The road heads on down around the slopes to the left to reach the upper cable-car station at **La Marnèche** (1802 metres), 45 minutes to one hour from Voré. There is a large restaurant here with rooms and dormitory accommodation. The gondola lift connects La Marnèche with the skiing resort of Les Diablerets in the valley below, and generally runs from early June to early October.

Stage 2: La Marnèche to Col des Mosses

(12 km, 3 to 4 hours)

The route from La Marnèche to the Col des Mosses mostly leads along gently undulating terraces high above the valley, offering easy and very scenic walking.

Proceed 50 metres along the road, then take a yellow-marked foot track off right down through meadows to a rustic farmhouse. The path continues across a small stream before beginning a diagonal traverse up slopes below the Cape au Moine to reach **Metreillaz** (also called Meitreile) after 30 to 40 minutes. This small hamlet sits at 1803 metres on a ridgetop looking out across the valley. There are more great views to your left of the Muveran, Diablerets and Dents du Midi massifs.

Pick up paint markings (avoiding a more obvious walking track that departs down left) and make your way across the flowery hillsides ahead, gradually descending to meet an alp road at the farmlet of **Marnex** (1738 metres). The route now contours along a rough vehicular track through the small cluster of wooden alp buildings at **La Dix**, before continuing as a foot path that rises and dips slightly to reach a sealed road not far on from **Le Lex** (1802 metres, shown on most maps as Le Lé), 50 minutes to one hour from Metreillaz.

Continue westwards along the road fringed by raspberry bushes and thickets of stinging nettles, soon passing the locality of **La Première**. After you come to another small group of dwellings at **Chersaule** (1657 metres) the road makes a sharp bend

and begins its descent into the valley. Here follow a farm track (signposted 'Les Mosses') leading around through pleasant spruce forest to a clearing on the low ridge of **Oudiou**, 50 minutes to one hour on. The Col des Mosses is now clearly visible ahead at the end of the small La Raverette valley.

Pass through a farm gate, then dip leftwards back into the trees and descend quickly to a road. The road winds through the forest for a while, then begins dropping steadily across open slopes to arrive at the mountain resort of **Col des Mosses** (1445 metres, see Walking Bases) after a final 50 to minutes to one hour.

For the next (and last) stage of the Alpine Pass Route refer to the Col de Chaude walk in the Fribourg & Vaud Pre-Alps section.

THE TOUR DE FAMELON

The grey limestone mountains immediately south-west of the Col des Mosses form a compact and geologically fascinating range culminating at the 2137-metre Tour de Famelon. In this area natural weathering has left deeply fluted formations and jagged outcrops in the karst rock, while glacial action has produced several impressive mountain cirques. Archaeologists have recently established that this craggy range served as a kind of enormous open-air temple for the pre-Christian Celtic tribes who inhabited the south-eastern shores of Lake Geneva some 2500 years ago. Sacrilegiously, today the northern side of the range is used by the Swiss military as a shooting range, although the southern side of the Tour de Famelon lies within a nature reserve.

Maps

The most detailed walking map covering the route is *Leysin – Les Mosses*, published at a scale of 1:25,000 by Editions MPA Verlag. Excellent alternatives are the SAW/FSTP's *Rochers de Naye (262 T)* or the MPA sheet *Alpes Vaudoises*, both scaled at 1:50,000. Kümmerly + Frey's 1:60,000 walking map *Grand St Bernard-Dents du Midi-Les Diablerets* is another reasonable larger-scale alternative.

Readers should also refer to the Vaud Pre-Alps map in this guidebook.

Walking Times & Standard

This is a roughly four-hour day walk that takes a fairly straightforward route. Using a gondola lift to gain virtually all of the necessary height, the walk involves little climbing. The descents are also very undemanding, so this is a walk that can be done by anyone with a minimal level of fitness. The path passes through sporadic sections of rocky or very muddy terrain, so wearing reasonably protective footwear will be an advantage. Surprisingly, the route is less well marked than most other popular routes in Switzerland, though it would be pretty hard to get lost.

The walk is rated *easy to moderate*.

Places to Stay

There is no en-route accommodation, but for places to stay in Leysin and the Col des Mosses see Walking Bases above.

Getting to/from the Walk

The walk begins from the upper gondola-lift station of Berneuse at 2035 metres above the mountain resort of Leysin (see Walking Bases). The gondola lift operates from late May until the last Sunday in October. The one-way fare is rather expensive considering the distance, but you can walk up to Berneuse in around 1½ hours.

The end of the walk is the Col des Mosses (see Walking Bases).

Route Directions: Berneuse to Col des Mosses

(13 km, 3½ to 4½ hours)

In the gondola lift you sail up from Leysin (1315 metres) to the minor peak of **Berneuse** (2035 metres) in just over five minutes. This natural lookout grants superb views to the west across Lake Geneva as well as the Dents du Midi and Les Diablerets massifs to the south. The futuristic-looking revolving restaurant here overlooks a small winter skifield; in summer the rich Alpine pastures contrast starkly with the raw rock walls of a precipitous spur descending from the Tour d'Aï (2330 metres).

Take the signposted foot track leading north-east along the left side of the ridge, before dropping diagonally down to meet an alp road at the eastern shore of **Lac d'Aï**. At 1892 metres near this shallow reedy tarn is a cluster of rustic barns with wooden-shingled roofs. The route traces the winding road gently down the grassy mountainsides hopping with marmots, bearing right at a fork to reach the dairy farmlet and upper gondola-lift station at **Mayen** (1842 metres) after 25 to 30 minutes.

Drop down a few steps to the **Lac de Mayen**, a small lake at the termination of a rocky gully coming down from the 2326-metre Tour de Mayen, then ascend leftwards along a low ridge onto slopes scattered with yellow gentians to a signpost on a rounded grassy spur. Follow white-red-white markings right (north), traversing slanting terraces below a craggy cirque before climbing over a crest. The path now sidles through rock rubble along the base of an impressive 200-metre high precipice under the 2137-metre Tour de Famelon, then descends into a basin of semi-forested karst fields.

Skirt past these interesting formations eroded into the rugged grey rock, before rising out onto a broad grassy ridge. A rough alp track leads eastwards past several red-roofed wooden barns in the direction of the 2175-metre Mont d'Or, the northern sides of which are covered with large screeslides. Where the alp track swings away left, continue down a foot track to reach a road at **Pierre du Moëllé** (1661 metres), 1½ to two hours from the Lac de Mayen. There is a restaurant on this low-pass beside an enormous three-storey rock block into which tunnels have been built to create a military bunker.

Walk south down the bitumen to the first hairpin bend, then turn off left along a forestry track. Contour along slopes of spruce and maples, bearing right at a minor fork before dropping down to meet another road. The walking route continues off to the right at a neat wooden farmlet a few paces uphill, sidling on down north-eastwards through moist pastures and mixed forest. There are some rather muddy cow-trodden sections, and the yellow-diamond waymarkings are a bit indistinct and vague in places. After coming onto a bitumened lane, make your way down past holiday houses to reach the main Le Sépey-Col des Mosses road (at the 1368-metre point) after one to 1¼ hours. There is a postbus stop here.

Take a signposted laneway off right from the main road and make your way up through the narrow upper valley below the 2351-metre Pic Chaussy. Not far on the lane briefly meets the road, before turning away again to reach a large holiday chalet. Here cut directly ahead over the grassy lawns on a well-worn walking pad, soon coming onto another narrow bitumened lane that brings you back onto the road at the small mountain resort of **Col des Mosses** (1445 metres, see Walking Bases) after a final 30 to 40 minutes.

THE TOUR DES MUVERANS

The Muverans massif stands immediately west of the Diablerets massif. This is the last range before the Rhône River finally breaks northwards out of its enclosed valley at the so-called Coude du Rhône. Its highest peak is the 3051-metre Grand Muveran, a spectacular dolomite summit that regularly attracts Alpine rock-climbers. On the Muverans' southern and western sides where the range fringes the Valais, the land plummets some 2500 metres into the Rhône Valley.

The Muverans lie in a transitional zone between the drier climate of the Valais and the moister oceanic climate of Vaud Alps. The Muverans area is one of the wilder parts of the Swiss Alps, and has two important nature reserves at Derborence and the Vallon de Nant. Derborence was the site of two great mountain landslides in 1714 and 1749, when the southern face of Les Diablerets – the 'devil's mountain' – crashed catastrophically into the valley. Isolated and largely abandoned since then, today the Derborence area harbours ancient – almost pristine – forests found nowhere else in Switzerland. The Vallon de Nant has healthy populations of snow grouse, marmots, stoats, chamois, and ibex.

The Tour des Muverans follows a high-level route right around the impressive peaks of the massif, passing below mountain cirques and through interesting karst landscapes. The walk grants some breathtaking vistas into the depths of the Rhône Valley and beyond to the icy giants of Mont Blanc and the Pennine Alps. Few other longer walks in Switzerland can offer such outstanding and varied Alpine scenery.

Maps

The most detailed walking map available is a special 1:25,000 sheet titled *Coude du Rhône* and published by Editions MPA Verlag. This map actually features the Tour des Muverans, and although very good it only includes the route between Anzeindaz and the Pas de Cheville (literally) by a hair's breadth, cutting out all of the Diablerets massif. The 1:50,000 SAW/FSTP walking map *St Maurice (272 T)* covers the entire route (with plenty of space around it). Kümmerly + Frey's 1:60,000 sheet *Grand St Bernard-Dents du Midi-Les Diablerets* is another reasonable larger-scale alternative.

Walking Times & Standard

The Tour des Muverans is a four-day route that can be done in less time by fitter hikers who don't mind walking longer days. The best time to undertake the Tour des Muverans walk is from late July until late September.

The route is well signposted and marked (in the standard red-white-red colours used for all mountain paths). The circuit's lowest and highest points are 1100 metres and 2600 metres. The stages follow rather an up-and-down course with a few sustained (but not really strenuous) climbs and descents. The route also crosses a large permanent snowfield, and until about late July old winter snowdrifts will probably cover the path in many places. Walking on snow for long becomes rather chilly underfoot, so stout, well-insulated footwear is desirable.

A number of the en-route mountain huts have cooking facilities for self-caterers, so bring some lightweight food to cook if you intend staying at these huts. There are *no* shops en route (including at Les Plans-sur-Bex and Derborence), but refreshments, snacks and meals are available in most of the huts.

The Swiss military (EMD/DMF) conducts regular shooting exercises throughout the summer along the section of the route between the Col du Demècre and the Col des Perris Blancs. The exercises never run for more than two consecutive days, and walkers can generally pass through the area without (major) delays. For the current situation call the regional EMD/DMF information office in St-Maurice on ☎ 025 65 91 11.

The Tour des Muverans has been given an overall rating of *moderate to difficult*; the walk has a combined distance of some 52 km.

Places to Stay

There are plenty of overnight options along the Tour des Muverans, so hikers can walk at their own pace. Most of the mountain huts have a permanent resident warden in summer. Meals and snacks are also available from a number of restaurants en route.

In Pont de Nant, the *Auberge Communale* (☎ 025-68 14 67, open from mid-May to late October) has lower-budget rooms and a dormitory (with use of shower).

At Anzeindaz (1876 metres) are two large private mountain inns, the *Refuge Giacomini* (☎ 025-68 22 18, open from mid-April to late October) and the *Refuge de la Tour* (☎ 025-68 11 47, open late May until the end of October). Both places have restaurants serving meals as well as offering rooms and dormitory accommodation (showers available). Prices are fairly standard, although the Refuge Giacomini is slightly cheaper.

At Derborence, the *Auberge de Lac* (☎ 027-36 71 89, open April to November) at 1449 metres, and the *Auberge du Godet* (☎ 027-3615 58, open mid-June until mid-October) some way below the village at 1370

metres, both offer good-value dorm accommodation (with showers). The latter also has rooms.

The next en-route place to stay is the 50-bed *Cabane Rambert* (☎ 027-27 11 22), an SAC-run hut at 2580 metres. The overnight rates are in the upper range for Swiss mountain huts.

Roughly midway along Stage 3 is the *Cabane de Fenestral* (☎ 026-46 31 97), a 45-bed mountain hut on the Col de Fenestral belonging to the Ski-Club de Fully. The Cabane de Fenestral is mainly equipped for self-caterers, but the warden/cook is resident from early July to late August and on weekends. At other times the hut is left open. The local ski club also owns the nearby 60-bed *Cabane de Sorgno* (☎ 026-46 31 97), around 20 minutes' walk down from the Lac Superior de Fully at 2064 metres. Overnight rates at both these huts are quite reasonable.

The 60-bed *Cabane de Demècre* (☎ 026-46 10 19, always open), is a privately owned mountain hut at 2361 metres on the Col du Demècre. Only drinks and refreshments are sold, but there is a kitchen for self-caterers. This pleasant and inexpensive hut is a recommended place to stay. Less than one hour on (though just off Stage 4 of the route) is the Chalet Neuf (☎ 026-67 13 10), a restaurant that also offers very cheap dormitory accommodation.

The last en-route place to stay is the 60-bed *Cabane de la Tourche* (☎ 025-65 26 65), an SAC hut at 2198 metres, which also has surprisingly cheap mattress-room accommodation.

Getting to/from the Walk

The route description assumes hikers will start/finish at Les Plans-sur-Bex (1095 metres) on the Vaud side of the Muveran massif, although there are several other access possibilities so opting out along the way is no problem.

Les Plans-sur-Bex can be reached by a 25-minute postbus ride from the town of Bex. There are up to eight postbuses in either direction daily. The last leaves Bex train station at around 6.30 pm, returning from

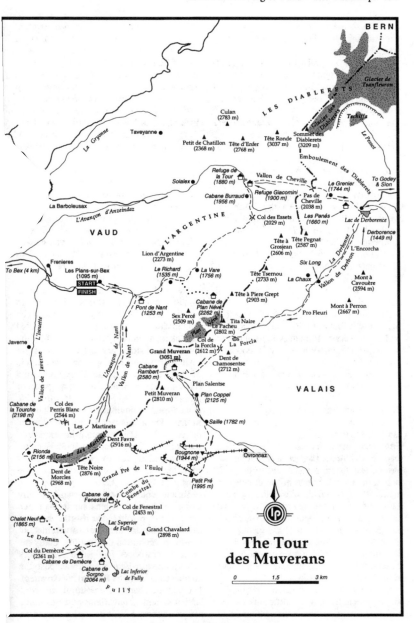

BERN

LES DIABLERETS

Glacier de Tsanfleuron

Glacier de Diablerets

Tschiffa

Le Pecoi

To Godey & Sion

Culan (2783 m)

Taveyanne

Petit de Chatillon (2368 m)

Tête d'Enfer (2768 m)

Tête Ronde (3037 m)

Sommet des Diablerets (3209 m)

Eboulement des Diablerets

La Gryonne

Solalex

Refuge de la Tour (1880 m)

Vallon de Cheville

Le Grenier (1744 m)

Cabane Burraud (1956 m)

Refuge Giacomini (1900 m)

Pas de Cheville (2038 m)

Lac de Derborence

Les Penés (1660 m)

Darborence (1449 m)

La Barboleusaz

L'Avançon d'Anzeindaz

Col des Essets (2029 m)

L'Encorcha

L'Derbont

VAUD

L'ARGENTINE

Tête à Grosjean (2606 m)

Tête Pegnat (2587 m)

Six Long

Vallon de Derbon

Mont à Cavouère (2594 m)

Lion d'Argentine (2273 m)

Le Richard (1535 m)

La Vare (1756 m)

Tête Tsernou (2733 m)

La Chaux

Mont à Perron (2667 m)

Frenieres

Les Plans-sur-Bex (1095 m)

To Bex (4 km)

START

FINISH

Pont de Nant (1253 m)

Tête à Piere Grept (2903 m)

Pro Fleuri

Cabane de Plan Névé (2262 m)

Sex Percé (2509 m)

Plan Névé

Le Pacheu (2802 m)

Tita Naire

Javerne

L'Iouette

Vallon de Javerne

Vallon de Nant

L'Avançon de Nant

Col de la Forcla (2612 m)

Grand Muveran (3051 m)

La Forcla

Dent de Chamosentse (2712 m)

VALAIS

Cabane Rambert (2580 m)

Plan Salentse

Cabane de la Tourche (2198 m)

Col des Perris Blanc (2544 m)

Petit Muveran (2810 m)

Plan Coppel (2125 m)

Les Martinets

Saille (1782 m)

Rionda (2156 m)

Glacier des Martinets

Dent Favre (2916 m)

Grand Pré de l'Euloi

Bougnone (1944 m)

Ovronnaz

Dent de Morcles (2968 m)

Tête Noire (2876 m)

Petit Pré (1995 m)

Cabane de Fenestral

Combe du Fenestral

Col de Fenestral (2453 m)

Chalet Neuf (1865 m)

Le Dzéman

Lac Superior de Fully

Grand Chavalard (2898 m)

Col du Demècre (2361 m)

Cabane de Demècre

Cabane de Sorgno (2064 m)

Lac Inferior de Fully

Fully

The Tour des Muverans

0   1.5   3 km

Les Plans-sur-Bex at about 7 pm. Bex is on the Lausanne-Brig line, and most trains stop there.

There are several other possible starting/finishing points. Some people set out from Derborence (1449 metres), which is accessible by just two daily postbus connections to/from Sion (see Walking Bases) via the village of Aven between late June and late September. Outside this time there is no service at all. The last bus connection to Derborence leaves Sion at approximately 2 pm, and returns at around 4.30 pm.

Bougnone (1944 metres, see Stage 3) above the village of Ovronnaz (1350 metres) also provides access to the Tour des Muverans. There are up to eight daily postbuses from Sion (via Leytron) to Ovronnaz all year round. The last bus leaves Sion shortly after 6.30 pm and returns from Ovronnaz not long after 7.30 pm. From Ovronnaz a chair lift runs up to Bougnone between early July and early September until 4.30 pm daily.

The Refuge Giacomini at Anzeindaz (see Stage 1 and Places to Stay) also operates a taxi shuttle service from the village of Gryon on the private Bex-Villars (BVB) mountain railway.

Private vehicles can be parked at Pont de Nant, Derborence or Ovronnaz.

Stage 1: Les Plans-sur-Bex to Derborence

(15 km, 4¾ to 5½ hours)
From the post office take the minor road leading south-east past chalets among the pastureland to cross the Avançon de Nant stream on a small bridge just after entering the forest. A foot track follows the southern bank of the river, before crossing again and climbing over a small sidestream to reach the hamlet of **Pont de Nant** (1253 metres, see Places to Stay) after 25 to 30 minutes. Pont de Nant has an Alpine garden established by the University of Lausanne, and is the start of the Tour des Muverans.

The route leads north-eastwards along a rough vehicle track into a little side valley. Make your way on above the southern side

of a stream through mixed meadows and patches of forest past a side path going up to the SAC's Cabane de Plan Névé to the alp hut of **Le Richard** (1535 metres). Continue eastwards, climbing up beside the now tiny stream away from the last scatterings of low trees. The route eases into gentle meadows just before coming to the **La Vare** at 1756 metres, 1⅓ to 1⅔ hours from Pont de Nant. This mountain farmlet has a restaurant and looks south-west towards the 3051-metre Grand Muveran.

Follow the white-red-white markings on smoothly up through a strip of grassy pastures within a narrow elongated basin hemmed in between the main Muveran massif and the craggy ridge of L'Argentine. The path picks an easy way on up through white cliffs to arrive at the **Col des Essets** at 2029 metres after one to 1¼ hours. This pass height looks across to the craggy peaks on the adjacent Les Diablerets massif.

Descend gently northwards for 20 to 25 minutes, passing the **Cabane Barraud** (a private locked hut at 1956 metres) to reach **Anzeindaz** (see Places to Stay), a scattered hamlet in a broad grassy bowl. Take the signposted alp track just up from the **Refuge de la Tour**, soon crossing to the northern side of the burbling streamlet. The route now rises up at an agreeably easy gradient through the lovely highland valley to arrive at the **Pas de Cheville** (2038 metres) after a further 35 to 40 minutes. This gentle pass lies on the Vaud/Valais cantonal border at the foot of Les Diablerets' main 3209-metre summit, and affords a wonderful panorama stretching eastwards as far as the Pennine Alps.

Various coloured markings lead quickly past a lonely stone shelter, then steeply down southwards through the bluffs in tight zigzags to the alp hut of **Le Grenier**, at 1744 metres in the Vallon de Cheville. Cross the stream on a wooden footbridge a few paces below, making your way down past the holiday chalets of **Les Penés** (1660 metres). The path descends into beautiful forests of larch with understorey fields of white alpine pasqueflowers *(Pulsatilla alpina)*, winding its way on down to reach the tiny summer-only village of **Derborence** at 1449 metres (see Places to Stay), 50 minutes to one hour from the Pas de Cheville.

Above Derborence is one of the Swiss Alps' classic mountain cirques, which forms a two-km-wide rock amphitheatre in which the tiny Tschiffa glacier nestles. The **Lac de Derborence**, the shallow lake beside the village, was formed by the 18th-century landslides, when rock faces of the Diablerets range collapsed down the slope to dam the Derbonne stream. The lake is gradually being filled in again by rubble washed from the slopes above after heavy downpours. A three-hour circuit walk leads through the regenerating rock debris (known as the Eboulement des Diablerets) to the small hydroelectricity reservoir at Godey.

The inaccessible forests on the slopes of L'Encorcha immediately south of Derborence have remained virtually unexploited over the past few centuries. Today many of most ancient red spruce and silver fir trees – some of which were already established at the time of the last great mountain landslide – have trunks up to 1.5 metres in diameter. This area forms a unique nature reserve which enjoys total protection.

Stage 2: Derborence to Cabane Rambert

(12 km, 4¾ to 5½ hours)
Take the signposted alp track leading south-west from the lakeshore up through slopes of low regenerating forest that grant good views back across Derborence to the area strewn with coarse rubble from the 18th-century landslides. The route moves over to meet the Derbonne, before beginning its long gradual climb through the Vallon de Derbon, a small glacial valley whose U-shaped floor is divided into several levels. Crossing the stream repeatedly, head up through attractive open meadows to pass the alp huts of **La Chaux** and **Six Long** after 1¼ to 1½ hours.

The path ascends onto another level of the valley to **Pro Fleuri**, the uppermost pastures in the Vallon de Derbou. In summer this area

of high grassland is alive with inquisitively docile cows and nervously active marmots. After recrossing to the northern bank of the stream, make your way up a small ridge towards the pyramid form of Tita Naire. Following white-red-white markings and cairns, sidle leftwards over talus fields and frequent snowdrifts before coming to a small lake in the raw moraine basin of **La Forcla** between the 2712-metre Dent de Chamosentse and Le Pacheu (2802 metres), 1¾ to 2¼ hours from Six Long.

From this point a path goes off left down to the village of Chamoson in the Rhône Valley, the wine-growers of which built this tiny reservoir as a water supply for their thirsty vineyards. The lake generally remains ice-bound well into the summer months. The Tour des Muverans route continues around the northern side of the lake, then skirts up easily over the **Glacier de la Forcla** (which is really just a broad snowfield) to the **Col de la Forcla** at 2612 metres after 25 to 30 minutes.

Drop down steeply through loose rock below the col to an obvious painted arrow on a large rock slab, then traverse south-west along the scree-slopes past a minor signposted turn-off to reach a small pass. The route sidles on quickly around into another small saddle (2504 metres), then makes a final short, steep climb to arrive at the **Cabane Rambert** (2580 metres, see Places to Stay), one to 1¼ hours from the Col de la Forcla.

The Cabane Rambert sits on a ledge beside the Plan Salentse, an arena-like cirque between the Petit Muveran (2810 metres) and the Grand Muveran, whose 3051-metre summit is only safely accessible to roped Alpine rock-climbers. The superb Alpine panorama seen from the Cabane Rambert is truly something to behold, with a stunning line-up of glistening snow-capped massifs stretching from Mont Blanc over to the south-west, the Grand Combin and Pigne d'Arolla towards the south, and the Matterhorn and Weissmies to the east. Immediately below the land falls away directly into the Rhône Valley.

Stage 3: Cabane Rambert to Cabane de Demècre

(11 km, 4½ to 5½ hours)

From the saddle below the hut drop down in tight zigzags through scree-slopes into the **Plan Salentse**. Accumulated winter snow-drifts lie long here, and the young streamlet divides into several branches as in a delta. Descend below a line of precipitous bluffs with interesting wave-like folded rock strata, following the stream down past **Plan Coppel** at 2125 metres, an alp hut in a semi-ruined state. After crossing to the right (western) bank on a steel footbridge, take a last look back through this tiny 'picture book' upper-Alpine valley towards the Grand Muveran.

The route now spirals on down beside a small ravine, recrossing the stream some distance before coming to another ruined alp hut at **Saille** (1782 metres). Here cross the stream a final time and sidle southwards high above the Rhône Valley along mountainsides scattered with yellow gentians. After passing a large alp barn you reach the restaurant and upper chair-lift station at **Bougnone** (1944 metres), 1½ to 1¾ hours from the Cabane Rambert. (Walkers can opt to begin or end the hike from here.)

Continue south-west past winter ski tows through a minor saddle (giving excellent views of the 2898-metre Grand Chavalard and other surrounding summits) to reach a disused military camp at **Petit Pré** (1995 metres). The well-trodden path rises steadily upwards through old moraines into the broad, flat hollow of the **Grand Pré de l'Euloi**. Formed when a vast funnel-like underground cavern (known as a doline) collapsed into itself, this attractive grassy-green basin drains subterraneously into the Rhône Valley. Euloi is surrounded by the Dent Favre (2916 metres), Tête Noire (2876 metres) and other interesting peaks.

Skirt the southern side of the basin to the melodic chiming of cowbells and the shrill whistle of marmots, then head south-west up the slopes of the **Combe du Fenestral** over patches of old winter snows. A last slightly steeper section cuts up diagonally leftwards over screes to arrive at the **Col de Fenestral** (2453 metres), two to 2½ hours from Bougnone. The **Cabane de Fenestral** (see Places to Stay) is a few paces around to the right. From up here you get a picturesque view down to the turquoise lake in the basin of Fully.

Traverse to the far end of a screeslide, then drop down into lovely meadows dotted with purple goblet-shaped Koch's gentians *(Gentiana kochiana)* at the head of **Lac Superior de Fully**. This natural lake is another doline formation, although the water level has been raised by several metres for producing hydroelectricity. Make your way around the western shore of the lake almost to the low dam wall, then climb away gently leftwards to meet a more prominent path. From this point the **Cabane de Sorgno** (2064 metres, see Places to Stay) is 15 to 20 minutes' walk downhill, but the route continues up to the right (ie westwards) past several small tarns to reach the **Cabane de Demècre** (see Places to Stay) at 2361 metres on the **Col du Demècre** after a final one to 1⅓ hours.

Stage 4: Cabane de Demècre to Pont de Nant

(14 km, 4½ to 5½ hours)

Drop down west as far as a line of cliffs, then double back rightwards to circle around steep talus slopes. After 20 to 25 minutes you come to a signposted junction at the Alpine pastures of **Le Dzéman**, from where a left-hand path goes down to the **Chalet Neuf** (see Places to Stay). Bear right here and sidle on upwards along the mountainside, climbing briefly beside a small stream before beginning a scenic high-level traverse north-westwards along a series of broad grassy terraces between sheer precipices.

There are exhilarating vistas to your left, where the land falls away dramatically into the deep glacial trough of the Rhône Valley. The mighty snow-capped 'teeth' of the Dents du Midi rise up directly on the adjacent side of the valley, while the Dolent – on whose 3820-metre summit Switzerland, Italy and France meet – can be made out to the south-west. The path rises over a steep spur (marking the Valais/Vaud cantonal border), before descending gently to the army barracks at **Rionda** (2156 metres), 1⅓ to 1⅔ hours from Le Dzéman.

Continue quickly along a dirt road past Rionda's several military buildings, soon after which a more uplifting view opens out towards Lake Geneva in the north-west. A short way on take a foot track leading quickly up to reach the **Cabane de la Tourche** (2198 metres, see Places to Stay) after 15 to 20 minutes. The hut enjoys more of the panoramas typical of this walk, and is the base for Alpine rock-climbers tackling the crags of the 2968-metre Dent de Morcles visible to the south.

The path leads along the right side of the ridge up in zigzags as far as the line of cliffs, then crosses over leftwards and contours around the coarse talus slopes of the **Vire aux Boeufs**. Follow the now familiar white-red-white route markings and rock cairns up through another field of scree, passing a (difficult) white-blue-white marked route going up the Dent de Morcles just before you get to the **Col des Perris Blancs** at 2544 metres after 40 to 50 minutes. This saddle overlooks the moraine-filled basin of the Les Martinets, which was formed by the receding Glacier des Martinets. At this point the Petit and Grand Muveran also reappear, although from quite a different aspect to the walk's previous stages.

Drop down in steep spirals into the upper **Vallon de Nant**, then move rightwards through boulder-strewn terrain into a gully often filled by winter snow accumulations. This small enclosed valley is being filled in by constant rockfall from the surrounding slopes. The Vallon de Nant forms a wild nature reserve with a surprisingly diverse Alpine flora and inhabited by large herds of chamois. The route descends on via a gap in the cliffs, winding its way down over slopes with stunted larches to intersect with an alp track (at point 1664 metres). Head along this dirt road across the milky-white **Torrent des Martinets** to reach the romantic little alp hut of **Nant** at 1500 metres after 1⅓ to 1⅔ hours.

The final section of the Tour des Muverans leads on down the valley through pockets of fir and spruce forest on the eastern bank of the Avançon de Nant. The route passes the **Jardin Alpin** just before arriving back at **Pont de Nant** after a final 30 to 40 minutes. This fascinating Alpine garden (entrance free, open daily from May to late October) has the most extensive collection of Alpine plants in Switzerland, with some 2500 species from mountain regions all over the world.

The Valais

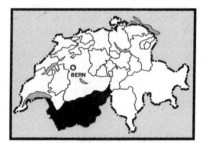

Hemmed in on its northern side by the Bernese Alps and by the Pennine Alps to the south, the canton of Valais (Wallis in German) forms Switzerland's most distinct geographical region. The Valais is the quintessential long, deep glacial valley – in fact its name originates from the Latin word *vallis* meaning simply 'valley'. The region corresponds almost exactly to the broad and fertile basin of the (Swiss) Rhône River along with its numerous lateral valleys. The Valais was shaped during the progressive glaciations by the Rhônegletscher, whose icy bulk once stretched down through the Rhône Valley as far as Lake Geneva.

Encircled by the highest mountains of the Alps, the Valais' geographical isolation is reflected in its history and culture. Once an independent state, the Valais only joined the Swiss Confederation as a separate canton in the early 1800s. Today the Valaisans remain a proud and individualistic people whose suspicion of outsiders – including other Swiss – has gradually softened as the region opened up to the outside world during the last one and a half centuries.

Most Valaisans live along the densely populated Rhône Valley. The lower half of the Valais – stretching up the Rhône Valley as far as the city of Sierre – is French-speaking, and francophone Valaisans make up around two-thirds of the canton's population. In the upper Valais live the *Oberwalliser*, a hardy German-speaking people.

Forming an almost unbroken wall of great ice-smothered summits stretching eastwards along the Swiss/Italian frontier from the Mont Blanc massif as far as the border with Uri Canton, the Pennine Alps have most of Switzerland's 4000-metre peaks, including the Grand Combin (4314 metres), the Dent d'Hérens (4171 metres), the Weissmies (4023 metres) and the classic 4477-metre Matterhorn. Half a dozen major side valleys splay out southwards deep into the Pennine Alps, while in contrast the northern side valleys of the Valais tend generally to be short and steep.

Being enclosed by the high mountains on all sides, the Valais has a decidedly continental type of climate with low precipitation levels due to a marked 'rain shadow' effect. The Valais' long periods of hot summer weather are legendary (but walkers should beware of getting too much sun). Of course the loftier summits receive considerably higher levels of precipitation – most of it falling as snow – and this nourishes the canton's astonishingly extensive areas of névés and glaciers. At last count the Valais boasted some 670 smaller and larger glaciers with combined surface area of almost 700 sq km – representing around 15% of the Valais' area and over half of the area covered by glaciers in Switzerland.

With most of Switzerland's peaks above 4000 metres, the Valais is a mountaineer's dream. You don't have to scale the peaks to enjoy them, however. With thousands of km of paths and walkways, the Valais is also prime walking country offering the most consistently spectacular scenery anywhere in the Swiss Alps.

Goms

Extending from the city of Brig right up to the Furkapass, the Goms region forms the uppermost part of the Valais. Lying mostly well above 1000 metres, Goms has a distinctly Alpine character rather different to the rest of the Rhône Valley. From its source at the Rhônegletscher, the Rhône (known locally as the Rotten) descends through this open highland valley before dropping down through a series of gorges to Brig. Goms was the homeland of the Walsers, medieval German-speaking settlers who migrated to many previous uninhabited Alpine valleys far outside the Valais. The extreme isolation of Goms was considerably reduced by the opening in 1982 of the Furka-Oberalp railway, which provides a reliable all-seasons link between Goms and Central Switzerland's Urner Oberland as well as the Surselva region of Graubünden.

WALKING BASES
Oberwald
The small tourist resort of Oberwald sits below the Furkapass in the uppermost part of Goms. The nearest *camping ground* (☎ 028-73 16 31) is at Ritzlingen. Mid-range accommodation is offered at the *Hotel Furka* (☎ 028-73 11 44), the *Sport-Hotel* (☎ 028-73 21 41), the *Hotel Tannenhof* (☎ 028-73 16 51) and the *Hotel Ahorni* (☎ 028-73 20 10). Oberwald has a tourist office (☎ 028-73 22 03).

Oberwald is the last station on the private Furka-Oberalp-Bahn (FOB) rail line from Brig via Anderatt to Disentis, which passes through Oberwald before disappearing into the Furka tunnel. Car-carrying shuttle trains run between Oberwald and Realp. From late

June until late September there are three postbus connections each day to Andermatt (via the Furkapass) and Meiringen (via the Grimselpass). Seat reservation is obligatory (call Oberwald PTT ☎ 028-73 11 41). From late May to early October there are also several daily connections across the 2478-metre Nufenenpass between Oberwald and Airolo in Ticino.

Münster
The main centre of Obergoms, the upper part of Goms, Münster is a large village of traditional Valaisan wooden houses and barns. The local church has religious works of art that demand inspection. The *Pension Spycher* (☎ 028-73 17 77) and the *Hotel Post* (☎ 028-73 11 10) are two mid-range places to stay. The *Hotel-Restaurant Landhaus* (☎ 028-73 22 73) has somewhat better rooms. Münster has a tourist office (☎ 028-73 22 54), and is on the Furka-Oberalp-Bahn (FOB) rail line.

Brig
This small city at 684 metres is the regional capital of the German-speaking Upper Valais. Brig's old centre was devastated by floods in 1993 (when the nearby Saltina River burst its banks and swept down the main street as a raging torrent), but has since been fully restored. Worth visiting is the onion-domed Stockalper Schloss, an ostentatious castle built by the notorious Kaspar Jodok von Stockalper (1609-91), who amassed a great fortune by controlling the Simplon Pass trade.

Brig has good budget-accommodation options such as the *Café Suisse* (☎ 028-23 15 33), Rhônesandstrasse 6; and the *Café la Poste* (☎ 028-24 45 54), at Furkastrasse 23. The *Campingplatz Brigerbad* (☎ 028-46 46 88) is a recommended local camping ground.

Brig is an important rail and road hub, with at least hourly trains via the tunnels of Lötschberg (to Bern), the Furka (to Central Switzerland) and the Simplon (to Domodossola in Italy, from where there are regular connections to Locarno in Ticino via the Centovalli). Through-tickets are available for this rail route and rail passes valid only for Switzerland are still accepted). The private BVZ line runs trains hourly via Visp to Zermatt. Hourly postbuses leave for Saas Fee calling at Visp and Stalden en route. Postbuses also run the winding and scenic route over the 2005-metre Simplon Pass to the village of Gondo (from where there are bus connections on to Domodossola).

The most direct route for motorists to/from the Valais and northern Switzerland are the car-carrying shuttle trains running between Kandersteg and Goppenstein via the Lötschberg tunnel. (There is no road tunnel). Cars are no longer carried by train through the Simplon tunnel to Italy.

THE GOMMER HÖHENWEG

The Gommer Höhenweg follows a middle-level route along the northern side of the Rhône (Rotten) Valley in the upper Goms, or Obergoms. This is one of the most thinly settled and isolated regions in Switzerland, and a rural Alpine lifestyle still prevails here. The walk takes you through rustic Valaisan hamlets sitting amongst lovely larch forests on the sunny slopes overlooking idyllic villages. The occasional shrill whistle of passing FOB trains well below in the valley is one of the few reminders of modernity around.

Maps

Either of two walking maps are recommended for this walk: 1:50,000 SAW/FSTP sheet *Nufenenpass (265 T)* or the 1:40,000 *Wanderkarte Obergoms* produced by the local tourist authorities. Also good is Kümmerly + Frey's walking map *Aletsch-Goms-Brig*, scaled at 1:60,000.

Walking Times & Standard

This is a moderately long day hike that traverses along the sides of the upper Rhône Valley with generally quite gentle gradients. In many places the route crosses and follows so-called alp tracks, small access roads coming up from the valley. The 'Gommer Höhenweg' signposts and the yellow

waymarkings are frequent and well positioned, so finding your way is never a problem. The route can generally be walked from at least early June until early November, but beware of black ice on the path later in the season.

The walk is rated *easy to moderate*.

Places to Stay

The only en-route accommodation is at Münster and Oberwald (see under Walking Bases above).

Getting to/from the Walk

The walk begins in Münster (1388 metres) and ends at Oberwald (1368 metres). Both of these villages are on the private Furka-Oberalp-Bahn (FOB) – see Walking Bases.

Route Directions: Münster to Oberwald (11 km, 3 to 3¾ hours)

From Münster train station (1360 metres) walk up around to the left below the old village church to the Hotel Post. Take a narrow lane leading quickly out of the village, and pick up a foot track that climbs rather steeply over grassy pastures adjacent to a tiny chapel on a hillock. Upstream is a concrete dam built to protect Münster from the devastation caused by floodwaters and alluvial debris washed down by the Minstigerbach in the summer of 1987. The path passes under a winter ski tow and across a winding farm road to reach the alp huts of **Lööwene** at 1538 metres after 30 to 40 minutes.

Now continue north-east along the Gommer Höhenweg. The route goes first along an alp track, then follows a path through ancient larch forests over a small footbridge spanning the gushing **Geschinerbach**. Head on around the low crest of **Bärg** (1542 metres) to cross another stream, then make your way along a dirt road to the farmhouse of **Nessel**, one to 1¼ hours on. At 1712 metres Nessel is the highest point on the walk, and from here there are fine views across the valley to the 3374-metre Blinnenhorn along with other high snow-topped summits on the Swiss-Italian border.

A foot track sidles around across the **Oberbach** to **Gafene**, a group of wooden cottages on a tiny hillside meadow overlooking the village of Obergesteln. Opposite you, snaking its way up through the Agenertal, is the lonely road over the 2440-metre Nufenenpass (Passo della Novena) into Ticino. Drop down a short way, then begin a traversing descent through light forest to the alp huts of **Gadestatt** at 1537 metres. The route contours ahead past the scattering of farmlets at **Hostette** (1535 metres), leaving the old mule path going up to the Grimselpass (which now serves as a hiking trail) before it crosses a footbridge over the **Milibach** upstream from another flood-control construction after 40 to 50 minutes.

Follow the yellow arrows gently down through more pleasant larch forest over the **Jostbach** footbridge to meet a road at a gas pipeline. This leads quickly down in a few hairpin curves to intersect with the main road through the valley near the **Oberwald** train station (1366 metres) after a final 50 minutes

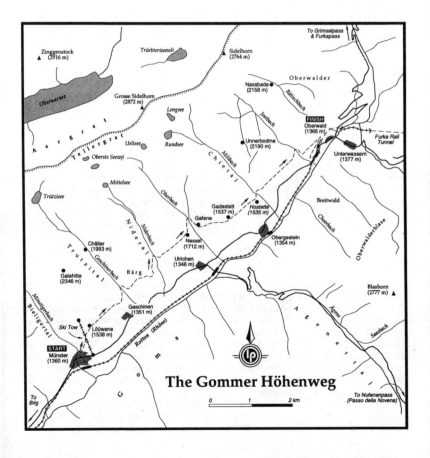

The Gommer Höhenweg

0   1   2 km

to one hour. The village itself is another 10 minutes' walk on past the station. A short distance upvalley the FOB rail line disappears into the 15-km-long Furka tunnel.

THE GROSSER ALETSCHGLETSCHER

The 22-km-long Grosser Aletschgletscher (or 'Great Aletsch Glacier') is the longest and most voluminous glacier in Europe. From its source at the Jungfraujoch, this massive stream of ice is fed by a number of other major glaciers which assures it of its enormous size. At Konkordiaplatz (around 3000 metres above sea level) the Grosser Aletschgletscher has a maximum width of some 1800 metres and depth of around 800 metres.

In the 1600s, during Europe's 'little Ice age', the icy snout of the glacier advanced menacingly down the valley, bulldozing its way through Alpine pastures and forest as it moved. For the last 150 years or so, however, the ice has been steadily retreating at an annual rate of around 20 metres, and its depth – the thickness of the ice body itself – has also diminished considerably.

On its left side the Grosser Aletschgletscher runs at right-angles to a small side valley, the Märjelental. Here the ice has dammed the small stream to create a tiny lakelet, the Märjelesee. In the past the Märjelesee was rather higher and larger than in its present form. At times the lake would rise and suddenly break through the ice wall, causing flooding farther downvalley below the glacier. The steady retreat of the great glacier, however, has now solved that problem.

The slopes fringing the lower part of the glacier are covered by the Aletschwald, a strikingly beautiful nature reserve harbouring some superb specimens of larch and ancient arolla pines – many over 1000 years old. The Aletschwald enjoys full protection, and area around the Grosser Aletschgletscher is the prime consideration for a second national park in Switzerland.

Maps

Recommended is either the 1:50,000 SAW/FSTP sheet *Jungfrau (264 T)* or the 1:25,000 *Wanderkarte Aletschgebiet und Untergoms* produced by the local tourist authorities. Kümmerly + Frey's walking map *Aletsch-Goms-Brig* scaled at 1:60,000 is a reasonable alternative.

Walking Times & Standard

This is a medium-length day walk. Although the route leads through high-Alpine terrain, it can be done by all reasonably fit walkers. Cable cars take the sweat out of the walk, and the route involves only mild climbs and descents. The walk can be shortened by an hour or so by taking the Tälli tunnel to the Restaurant Aletschstube – this is a decidedly unscenic alternative and you'll need to take a torch (flashlight). Note that before late June or after mid-October sections of the path may be snow-bound and unsafe.

The walk is rated *easy to moderate*.

Places to Stay

The cheapest places to stay in Fiesch are the *Hôtel Glacier et Poste* (☎ 028-71 13 01) and the *Pension Hirschen* (☎ 028-71 16 06). At Kühboden, the *Restaurant-Pension Kühboden* (☎ 028-71 13 77), the *Restaurant Eggishorn* (☎ 028-71 14 44) and the *Hotel Eggishorn* (☎ 028-71 14 44) all have various standards of rooms as well as good dormitory accommodation. One or two of these places stay open until mid-October. The *Restaurant Gletscherstube* (☎ 028-71 14 88, also known the *Märjelenhütte*) at 2378 metres by the Vordersee has a small dorm for walkers.

In Bettmeralp the *Touristenlager Seilbahn* (☎ 028-27 13 96) has dormitory accommodation and the *Hotel Garni Sporting* (☎ 028-27 22 52) has rooms at somewhat above average prices. There is also a *Friends of Nature hostel* (☎ 028-27 11 65) in the nearby mountain resort of Riederalp. The *Pension Bahnhof* near the train station in Betten has budget rooms.

Getting There & Away

The walk starts at Kühboden (2212 metres) and ends at Bettmeralp (2006 metres), two

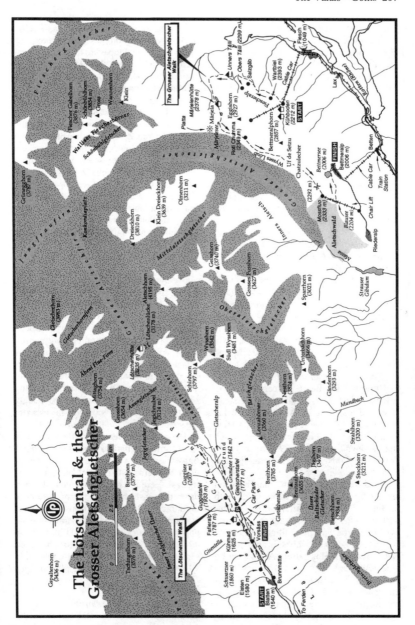

The Lötschental & the Grosser Aletschgletscher

The Grosse Aletschgletscher Walk

The Lötschental Walk

small vehicle-free mountain resorts which have cable-car access from the villages of Fiesch (1049 metres) and Betten (814 metres) respectively. Kühboden is at the intermediate station of the privately run Fiesch-Eggishorn cable car, while the cable car that brings you from Bettmeralp down to Betten is a community-run service with correspondingly cheaper tickets. The two cable cars operate at least half-hourly throughout the whole walking season. Both Fiesch and Betten are on the private FOB rail line running from Brig via Andermatt to Disentis in Graubünden.

Private cars can be left for a fee at either Fiesch by the lower cable-car station or at the train station in Betten.

Route Directions: Kühboden to Bettmeralp (via Märjelesee)

(18 km, 4 to 5 hours)

From the **Kühboden** cable-car station walk horth-east along the dirt road that contours the open mountainsides of the Fiescheralp, bearing right past the path going up to the Eggishorn and the turn-off to Märjela via the small Tälli tunnel. The route soon goes over into a broad well-graded foot track, and winds its way around the slopes high above the Fieschertal up through the grassy gully of **Unners Tälli**. Begin a steeper climb in several switchbacks leading past a small wooden cross erected on a rock platform that makes a natural viewing point granting a fine view up along the Fieschergletscher, which snakes down between the 3905-metre Gross Wannenhorn and the 4273-metre Finsteraarhorn.

Follow white-red-white markings on around westwards across rocky ledges into the tiny valley of the **Märjela**, where a signpost marks the junction of trails coming from the Fieschertal and the Tälligrat. The path continues quickly down beside an attractive lake to reach the **Restaurant Aletschstube** (2360 metres), 1½ to two hours from Kühboden. This two-storey wooden building stands below the Eggishorn on an Alpine pasture grazed by a small flock of sheep.

Head down past several little tarns, crossing the small stream at a large cairn before making your way on down through regenerating moraine slopes to the **Märjelesee** (2300 metres) after 30 to 35 minutes. Bordered by the icy edge of the **Grosser Aletschgletscher** this tiny lake presents a dramatic picture. From the polished-rock slabs above the Märjelesee you get a really tremendous view northwards across this amazingly broad, long expanse of glacial ice that stretches right up to the Jungfraujoch, where the weather station/observatory stands out on the white ridgetop. Regardless of how enticing the cool ice may appear in the heat of a summer's day, walkers are warned not to venture onto the ice.

Climb southwards around a rocky ridge and sidle up to a signposted path fork at **Roti Chumma** (2349 metres). Here take the lower right-hand way, partly following an old aqueduct along a spectacular route high above the crevassed ice along rock shelves giving spectacular views across to the great peaks dominated by the 4195-metre Aletschhorn. There are occasional fixed cables to hold onto. After coming to **Biel**, a saddle on the Greichergrat at 2292 metres, make your way on south-west along the ridge to reach the restaurant and upper chairlift station at **Mossfluo** (2333 metres) after 1⅓ to 1⅔ hours. From here the striking summit of the Matterhorn can be readily identified among the icy crags far away to the south-west.

The route continues along the ridge on a short section of marked foot track (not highlighted on some walking maps), cutting down leftwards to the tarn of Blausee (2204 metres). Here duck under the chair lift and drop down eastwards over grassy pastures to the attractive **Bettmersee**, from where a dirt road leads on across the low dam wall to the upper houses of **Bettmeralp** (2006 metres), 40 to 50 minutes from Mossfluo. The upper station of the Betten-Bettmeralp cable car is 10 minutes' walk down through the village.

OTHER WALKS
The Rhônegletscher Lehrpfad

Snaking down past the Galenstock in the

uppermost part of Goms, the Rhônegletscher is the ultimate source of the Rhône, one of Europe's largest river systems. At the height of the Ice ages the Rhônegletscher formed a colossal stream of ice that extended the whole way down through the Rhône Valley as far as Lake Geneva. Today the glacier is a comparatively meagre nine km in length, and – like glaciers the world over – has continued to creep steadily backwards over the last century and a half. The Gletscherpfad makes a very short return day walk introducing you to the interesting landscape left in the wake of recent glacial recession. Already small leafy plants are beginning to displace the primitive mosses and lichen that first colonised the moraines. The path begins from Gletsch near the historic Hotel Gletsch, which after its construction in the first half of the 19th century stood right next to the Rhônegletscher's snout!

From late June until late September there are three postbus connections each day to Gletsch from either Oberwald, Andermatt or Meiringen (via the Grimselpass). Seat reservation is obligatory (call Oberwald ☎ 028-73 11 41, Andermatt ☎ 044-6 71 88, or Meiringen ☎ 036-71 32 05). The newly renovated *Hotel Gletsch* offers rooms. No walking map seems to adequately cover the area of Rhônegletscher, so the standard 1:25,000 sheet titled *Ulrichen* is preferable.

The Griessee & the Val Corno

The Griessee is an artificial lake set in stark high-Alpine surroundings. Until very recently the Griesgletscher descended right into the icy waters of the reservoir, but the glacier has now begun to recede from the Griessee, somewhat reducing the dramatic 'Arctic' effect.

The walk starts from the postbus stop near the Gries turn-off ('Abzweigung Gries'), at 2303 metres on the Nufenenpass road, and continues to the Griessee dam wall. A path leads on south-east up to a junction on a plateau, from where there are great views across the lake to the Griesgletscher and the 3372-metre Blinnenhorn. A worthwhile side

trip can be made from here to the 2479-metre Griesspass. The route makes a steep climb over a watershed into the Val Corno then descends through this valley past Lago Corno and the SAC's Capanna Corno Gries (☎ 094-88 11 29). The walk ends at Cruina (2003 metres), a postbus stop on the Ticino side of the Nufenenpass (here called Passo della Novena) after approximately three hours.

Postbuses run (infrequently) across the Nufenenpass between Oberwald and Airolo. The walking maps covering this route are Kümmerly + Frey's 1:40,000 *Wanderkarte Obergoms* and the SAW/FSTP sheet 1:50,000 *Nufenenpass (265 T)*.

The Albunpass

The 2409-metre Albunpass (or Bocchetta Arbola) links Goms with northern Italy via the remote and fascinating Binntal, a side valley of the Rhône. Once the dangerous gorge at the lower Binntal had been negotiated, the way to the south was almost without natural hindrances, making this a favoured crossing point for trade, transport and military purposes from the early Middle Ages. In the 1840s English geologists found sulphate-based crystals in the Binntal, which exist nowhere else on earth. The first road into the Binntal was only completed in 1938, and before then the valley dwellers led a pious and spartan existence.

This easy-to-moderate walk begins at the uppermost village of Binn (also known as Schmidigehischere) at 1400 metres. The old flagged mule trail leads across the elegant arched bridge, climbing steadily up via Fäld (one of the most intact 17th-century settlements in the upper Valais) and the alp huts of Brunnebiel and Freichi to reach the pass in around four hours. There is some superb Alpine scenery on both sides, and it's well worth continuing the hike into Italy. The descent leads via the *Refugio Città di Gallarate* (1652 metres), a (CAI) club hut at Alpe Dèvero, to the village of Gòglio (1133 metres) in the Val Arbola; from here bus routes lead through the Valle Antigorio to Domodossola.

In Binn the *Café Imfeld* (☎ 028-71 45 96) has rooms, and the *Binntalhütte* (☎ 028-71 47 67), an SAC hut at 2269 metres, provides old-style mountain-hut accommodation en route. Binn is accessible by postbus from Fiesch, a station on the FOB railway. Kümmerly + Frey's 1:60,000 walking map *Aletsch-Goms-Brig* covers the route.

Simplonpass to Visperterminen

Simplonpass, a hospice originally built in 1235 and extended by Stockalper as a summer residence and guesthouse for his mule drivers, grants some wonderful views northwards over the Spitzhorli as far as the Bernese Alps, east towards the ice-bound Monte Leone (3553 metres) and southwards to the Pennine Alps.

From the Simplon Hospiz, the path heads south-west across rolling meadows, climbing over steep Alpine slopes that overlook the historic Alte Spittel to the Bistinepass (2417 metres). The route winds down to the valley floor of the Nanztal, then cuts north-west up the mountainside to the 2201-metre Gebidempass, from where there is a good view into the Mattertal. There's a rewarding side trip from the pass to the Gebidumsee, a mountain tarn. The descent to Visperterminen can be made by chair lift from Giw (1976 metres), but the path down through the forest past the Antoniuskapelle (chapel) is recommended. The Rebenweg route from Visperterminen leads down through vineyards – at some 1100 metres these are the highest in Europe – to Visp in about two hours.

This is a five to six hour moderate-standard walk, with no en-route accommodation other than the *Simplon Hospiz* (☎ 028-29 13 22) and several hotels in Visperterminen. Postbuses run every couple of hours from Brig over the Simplonpass; from Visperterminen there are buses down to Visp. Kümmerly + Frey's 1:40,000 *Rund um Visp* covers the route well.

The Mattertal & Saastal

At Stalden, just five km south of the town of Visp, the Vispatal divides into the unidentical twins of the Mattertal (western branch) and the Saastal (eastern branch) – the longest and most spectacular side-valley system in the Valais. The two 'Vispa valleys' are walled in and separated from each other by three mighty lateral ranges extending northwards from the main continental divide of the Pennine Alps. The Mattertal and Saastal have a staggering concentration of classic Alpine peaks, with some 27 of Switzerland's 34 summits over 4000 metres.

These mountains culminate – both in height and scenic splendour – in a continuous arc of heavily glaciated peaks fronting the Italian border, including the 4165-metre Breithorn, the 4634-metre Dulfourspitze (part of the Monte Rosa massif, Switzerland's highest peak) and the amazing 4477-metre rock nose of the Matterhorn. The Matterhorn so dominates the scenery of the Mattertal, that the valley is often promoted simply as the 'Matterhorn region'.

The Mattertal runs along a fault line caused by massive uplifting as the African continental plate pushed hard against the European plate, and the mountains on its western side (including the Matterhorn, Dent Blanche, Obergabelhorn, Zinalrothorn and Weisshorn) are composed of rock types of quite different origin to the mountains (such as the Breithorn, Pollux, Monte Rosa, Strahlhorn and the Rimpfischhorn) on the eastern side of the valley. The Mattertal is the only part of Switzerland where Haller's pasqueflower *(Pulsatilla halleri)*, a very rare Alpine wildflower is found.

WALKING BASES
Saas Grund/Saas Fee

Saas Grund (1559 metres) and Saas Fee (1792 metres) are two nearby villages that provide the main tourist infrastructure in the upper Saastal. Although remnants of their original rustic architecture remain, today both Saas Fee and Saas Grund are modern resorts geared to mountain sports (especially year-round skiing). The Saastaler Höhenweg and Gsponer Höhenweg routes described in this guidebook end in Saas Fee and Saas Grund respectively. An easy local walk (particularly popular in winter when the path is snow-cleared) leads up to the Stausee Mattsee, a large artificial lake at 2197 metres. A more challenging hike for experienced mountain walkers goes up past the SAC's *Almagellerhütte* (☎ 028-57 35 14) across the 3268-metre Zwischenbergenpass to the isolated village of Zwischenbergen in the Simplon region.

Saas Grund generally has the cheaper places to stay. There's a good camping ground, the *Am Kapellenweg* (☎ 028-57 29 89); and Saas Grund's *Zurbriggen Sport* (☎ 028-57 14 44) has dormitory accommodation. Two lower-budget places to stay in Saas Grund are the *Hotel Bergheimat* (☎ 028-57 20 66) and the *Hotel Roby* (☎ 028-57 12 62). Saas Grund has a tourist office (☎ 028-57 24 03).

Saas Fee's camping ground is the *Terminus* (☎ 028-57 14 57). The *Feehof* (☎ 028-57 23 08) and the *Hotel Mascotte* (☎ 028-57 27 24) have lower-budget rooms. The Saas Fee tourist office (☎ 028-57 14 57) can give other local accommodation options.

There are top mountaineering schools in both Saas Fee (☎ 028-57 23 48) and Saas Grund (☎ 028-57 14 44).

Postbuses run at least hourly from Visp in the Rhône Valley via Saas Grund to Saas Fee; there are also regular shuttle buses between the two resorts. Saas Fee itself is car-free, but there is a (fee-paying) car park at the edge of the village.

Zermatt

Situated in the upper Mattertal below the towering form of the Matterhorn – for many *the* classic mountain – Zermatt (1620 metres) is the unrivalled centre of the upper Valaisan Alps. The town has an excellent tourist infrastructure, including all classes of hotel, boutiques and outdoor equipment shops. Little remains of the original village

of Zermatt, although traditional old wooden barns can still be seen in places behind the shops and hotels along the main street. The Alpines Museum has an interesting collection covering the history of local mountaineering.

The mountains surrounding Zermatt attract tens of thousands of walkers, mountaineers and skiers each year. The Zermatt environs have countless superb walking routes. Since high peaks, large glaciers and sheer cliffs cut off the upper Mattertal on three sides, most walks are circuits that return to Zermatt. The Gornerschlucht, a small gorge of cascades just above the town, makes a easy and worthwhile short outing from Zermatt.

There is a local *camping ground* (☎ 028-66 11 81, open June to September) near the train station. Dormitory accommodation is available at the *youth hostel* (☎ 028-67 23 20), the *Friends of Nature hostel* (☎ 028-67 42 15) and the *Hotel Bahnhof* (☎ 028-67 24 06), which also has budget rooms. Zermatt has an excellent tourist office (☎ 028-66 11 81), and one of Switzerland's leading schools of mountaineering, the Bergführerbüro (☎ 028-67 34 56).

Zermatt can only be reached by the private Brig-Visp-Zermatt (BVZ) railway from Brig or Visp in the Rhône Valley. Trains run at least hourly (note that rail passes generally don't cover this privately run service). The *Glacier Express* tourist train runs between Zermatt and St Moritz. Zermatt is entirely car-free, and vehicles must be left at the large car park at the village of Täsch, some six km down the Mattertal.

THE GSPONER HÖHENWEG

The Gsponer Höhenweg is a high-level panoramic walk that traverses the eastern slopes of the Saastal from the hamlet of Gspon to Saas Grund, giving wonderful vistas of the 4000-metre peaks fringing the valley. The path follows a route at around 2000 metres, passing stands of lovely arolla and mountain pines, remote high pastures and quaint wooden houses perched high above the Saastal. At the village of Staldenried, just below Gspon, there are interesting 'earth pyramids' similar to those at Euseigne in the Lower Valais. These form in old moraine deposits where larger stone blocks shelter the earth beneath them from erosion.

Maps

The recommended walking maps are either the SAW/FSTP sheet *Visp* at a scale of 1:50,000 or Kümmerly + Frey's 1:40,000 *Wanderkarte Saastal*. Other useful K + F walking maps are the 1:50,000 *Tour Monte Rosa*, or their sheet *Visp-Zermatt-Saas Fee-Grächen* scaled at 1:60,000. Editions MPA Verlag has published a special 1:50,000 walking map titled *Zermatt/Saas Fee (5006)* which covers all of the Mattertal and Saastal.

Walking Times & Standard

This is a full day's walk that uses a cable car to gain initial height. Although the Gsponer Höhenweg is a mountain path (with the white-red-white markings), it generally involves quite moderate, gradual climbs and no really steep descents. The walk can usually be done from early June until at least the end of October, but watch out for black ice on the path in autumn.

The walk has been given an *easy to moderate* rating.

Places to Stay

In Gspon, the *Restaurant Mosji* (☎ 028-52 22 34) and the *Pension Alpenblick* (☎ 028-52 22 21) have low-budget rooms. There are also hotels in Stalden and Staldenried, in the valley below Gspon. Towards the end of the walk is the *Restaurant Heimisch Gartu* (☎ 028-57 29 20), which also offers rooms.

For places to stay in Saas Grund see Walking Bases.

Getting There & Away

The Gsponer Höhenweg begins at the car-free hamlet of Gspon (1893 metres). Gspon is only accessible by a cable car from Stalden (799 metres), a small town in the Vispertal at the confluence of the Vispa's two branches. The community-run cable car operates half-hourly until around 9 pm. Fares are relatively cheap, but the service does not run on the 2nd Monday of each month because of maintenance; at such times you will have to take a postbus from Visp to Staldenried (1154 metres) and walk up to Gspon from there. Trains on the Brig-Visp-Zermatt line as well as postbuses running from Visp to Saas Fee pass through Stalden at least hourly.

The end of the hike is Saas Grund (see Walking Bases).

Route Directions: Gspon to Saas Grund (15 km, 4 to 5 hours)

The cable car from Stalden hauls you up to **Gspon**, a tiny village at 1893 metres on a grassy shelf looking across to other isolated settlements high on the adjacent slopes of Vispertal. Walk south past wooden houses and the 17th-century village church, proceeding left at a minor fork up into the forest of Alpine conifers. Follow the broad track gently uphill for two km, then make a short, steep climb off left to pass the hamlet of **Finilu** (2039 metres) after 40 to 50 minutes. From here you get the first of many clear views up the Saastal towards the 3795-metre Balfrin; beyond lies a glistening-white expanse of snowfields and glaciers.

Sidle on around the slopes graced with beautiful old mountain and arolla pines, (whose twisted and gnarled trunks bear witness to the character-building properties of mountain living), crossing eroding gullies and following a largely disused aqueduct. After a short rise through a rocky area the path comes to **Obere Schwarze Wald**, where a lonely stone cottage sits at 2191 metres on a small lookout ridge. Make your way on across another small torrent, before contouring through lovely open meadows to reach the alp hut of **Färigen** (2271 metres), one to 1¼ hours from Finilu. Färigen is the highest point on the walk, and makes a nice spot to stop for lunch. There is a springwater fountain here and a table with chairs.

Continue down above stone animal enclosures to cross a footbridge over the Mattwaldbach, then ascend in a few quick switchbacks to the rounded grassy pasture of

Siwibode, 25 to 30 minutes on. The views up the valley now open out as you go to include the Allalinhorn. There are glimpses of the 4023-metre Weissmies up ahead to your left, while the high dam wall of the Stausee Mattmark can be made out at the head of the valley beyond the ski resort of Saas Fee. White-red-white markings lead a further 15 to 20 minutes up and down along the contour before coming to a route branching at **Lindebodu** (2230 metres). This is a grassy strip wedged between the upper line of the forest and steep rocky mountainsides.

From Lindebodu you can continue ahead to the station of the Saas Grund-Chrizbode cable car, but the recommended route to Saas Grund makes a more gradual traversing descent.

Take the prominent right-hand trail leading down into the forest to the restaurant at **Heimisch Gartu** (2110 metres, see Places to Stay). Drop quickly down beside wooden houses and the tiny chapel, then cut on down along the slope over a footbridge to join an alp track at the clustered hamlet of **Uneri Brend**. A path (signposted 'Bergwander-

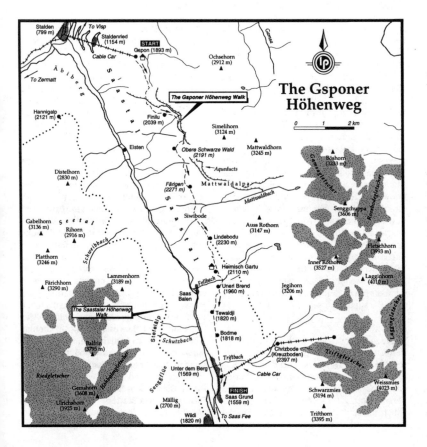

weg') soon leads off right, and crosses the dirt road several times to reach the locality of **Tewaldji** at 1820 metres, one to 1¼ hours from Lindebodu.

Follow the now broad and level foot track through more pleasant forest to the rustic dwellings of **Bodme** (1818 metres), turning off left at the next sharp road curve. An old mule trail spirals on down past two tiny chapels and jagged boulders clinging precariously to the mountainside. There are some final high views ahead across Saas Grund in the valley floor to the mighty glaciated peaks around the Allalinhorn. After crossing the **Triftbach** the route moves down to meet a bitumened laneway at the first houses of **Unter dem Berg** after 30 to 40 minutes. The nearest postbus stop is on the main road not far down to the right, but the centre of **Saas Grund** (see Walking Bases) is 10 minutes' walk on past the lower station of the Chrizbode (Kreuzboden) gondola lift.

SUNNEGGA TO RIFFELALP

This delightful short day walk from Zermatt shows the Matterhorn from some of its most classic 'chocolate-box' angles. The route passes by three of the loveliest lakes in the mountains around Zermatt, from where the Matterhorn's amazing wedge-shaped ridge known as the Hörnligrat seems to point directly towards you regardless of where you're standing. Although considered unscaleable at the time, the Matterhorn was first climbed via the Hörnligrat route by a party led by the English mountaineer Whymper on 14 July 1865. The triumph was overshadowed by tragedy, when three of the climbers fell to their deaths a short way down from the summit.

Maps

The recommended walking map for all of the Zermatt area is the *Wanderkarte Zermatt*, scaled at 1:25,000 and produced by the local tourist authorities. Editions MPA Verlag publishes a special walking map entitled *Zermatt/Saas Fee (5006)* scaled at 1:50,000, which includes the entire Mattertal-Saastal basin. Another reasonable alternative is

Kümmerly + Frey's 1:60,000 sheet *Visp-Zermatt-Saas Fee-Grächen*. Readers should also refer to the Around Zermatt map in this chapter.

Walking Times & Standard

This very short walk takes advantage of mountain transport to gain height, and makes an easier alternative to the Höhenweg Höhbalmen described below. The route dips and rises between 2200 and 2300 metres with minimal altitude differences, and can be done without further consideration by anyone with a functioning pair of legs.

The walk is rated *easy*.

Places to Stay

The *Bärghüs Findlengletscher* (☎ 028-67 25 53) at Ze Seewjinen and the *Berghotel Riffelalp* (☎ 028-67 53 33), five minutes' walk from the Riffelalp train station, both have medium-range rooms. Higher up near the Riffelberg station (2211 metres) is the *Hotel Riffelberg* (☎ 028-67 22 16). For accommodation in Zermatt itself see Walking Bases.

Getting to/from the Walk

The walk begins at the upper station of the Sennegga-Bahn, Europe's first underground funicular railway. The lower funicular station is 10 minutes on foot from Zermatt train station (walk first alongside the Gornergrat-Bahn rail lines then left after you cross the river). In summer the funicular runs at least half-hourly until around 5.30 pm.

The Riffelalp station of the Gornergrat-Bahn, a scenic cog railway that goes up from Zermatt to the 3090-metre station on a natural lookout ridge called the Gornergrat. Between the end of May and late October trains run approximately half-hourly. The last train down leaves Riffelalp at around 7.30 pm. Fares for both the funicular and cog railway are rather expensive, but most of the standard ticket concessions apply.

Route Directions: Sunnegga to Riffelalp (Train Station)

(7.5 km, 1½ to 2 hours)
The funicular takes you straight to Sun-

negga, on a sunny ridge above the treeline at 2288 metres. From here a signposted foot track drops down several minutes to the **Leisee**, a shallow and elongated tarn whose tranquil waters mirror the Matterhorn's majestic 4477-metre form. Head on around the lakeshore, turning left where you come onto a broad, well-graded walkway coming up from the hamlets of Findeln and Eggen.

Follow this path eastwards as it makes a gentle uphill traverse along the steep grassy slopes of the Findelalp high above the milky waters of the Mosjesee. After bearing right where a trail diverges to the Stellisee, continue down through stands of larch trees to reach the **Grindjisee** (2334 metres), 40 to 50 minutes on from Sunnegga. This pretty little lake is another irresistible occasion to pack out the camera for that classic shot of the Matterhorn.

For the nicest views, walk around the Grindjisee's northern bank, and cross the tiny inlet stream on a footbridge to meet a dirt road on the other side of a low lateral moraine. Here go right, tracing the roadway as it descends through a raw landscape of recent glacial deposits left by the receding Findelgletscher up to your left, and pick up a foot track off left a short way after you cross the **Findelbach** bridge. The route leads up the regenerating hillsides through a short section of easy boulder-hopping to arrive at the **Grüensee** at 2300 metres after 25 to 35 minutes. This lake lies nestled into high meadows, with the tip of the Matterhorn poking up in the background.

Make your way west across a road and down past the **Bärghüs Findlengletscher** (see Places to Stay), taking the left-hand branch at a fork a few paces on. This wide and well-built pathway quickly passes through a field of coarse glacial rubble, then dips into beautiful forests of graceful old larch and mountain pines. Contour on around slopes of Alpine heath, with airy views ahead towards the towering summits of the Ober Gabelhorn and the Zinalrothorn, to reach the train station at **Riffelalp** (2211 metres) after a final 25 to 35 minutes.

THE HÖHENWEG HÖHBALMEN

The classic Höhenweg Höhbalmen is a circuit leading up from Zermatt to the expanse of high-Alpine pastures known as Höhbalmen. Lying at over 2600 metres, these rolling terraces provide one of the finest natural lookout points in Switzerland. The looming outline of the 4477-metre Matterhorn fixes the attention of walkers for much of the way, though the quite stunning vistas include almost two dozen other 'four-thousander' peaks.

Maps

Recommended maps are as for the Sunnegga to Riffelalp walk described above. Refer also to the Around Zermatt map in this guidebook.

Walking Times & Standard

The Höhenweg Höhbalmen is one of the longest circuit day hikes in the Zermatt area. Depending on the usual snow and weather conditions, this route can normally be done from June and at least until late October. As there are some very worthwhile side trip options, the walk can be turned into an overnight outing by staying somewhere (preferably at the Trifthotel) en route. Although it presents no technical difficulties, the route is relatively tiring and is best suited to people who have done some recent (strenuous) hiking. Despite the surprisingly sporadic route markings, walkers should have little trouble finding their way on this well-trodden path.

The walk is rated *moderate to difficult* and covers a distance of 19 km.

Places to Stay

The *Pension Edelweiss* (☎ 028-67 22 36), roughly an hour from Zermatt, has a few rooms. Farther up at 2337 metres is the *Trifthotel* (☎ 077-28 18 14, open July to late September), which also has a small number of rooms as well as a dormitory for walkers. Optional off-route side trips can also be made to the *Rothornhütte* (☎ 028-67 20 43) and the *Schönbielhütte* (☎ 028-67 13 54).

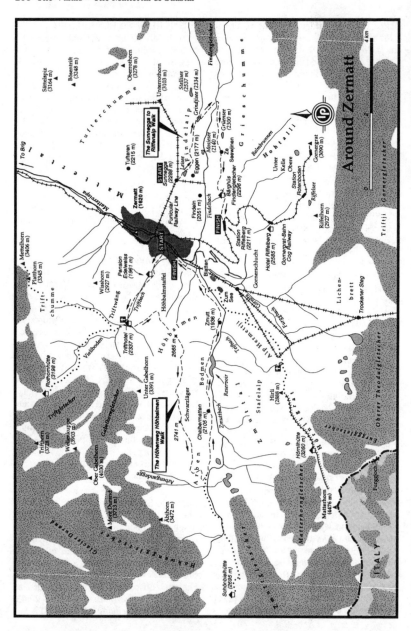

Around Zermatt

For accommodation in Zermatt see Walking Bases above.

Getting to/from the Walk

The Höhenweg Höhbalmen route begins and ends in Zermatt.

Route Directions:
Zermatt-Höhbalmen-Zermatt

(19 km, 5¼ to 6½ hours)

From Zermatt train station walk along the main street (Bahnhofstrasse) to an inconspicuous signpost at the Hotel Post, 200 metres before the village church. From here a cobbled footpath leads off to the right beside quaint old wooden barns, winding its way on more steeply up past holiday chalets and over hillside pastures. After crossing the Triftbach on a small wooden footbridge, climb on through the larch forest to reach the **Pension Edelweiss** (1961 metres, see Places to Stay) after 40 to 50 minutes. There is a restaurant here on a balcony overlooking Zermatt and the upper Mattertal.

The path rises gently to recross the stream near an (hydroelectricity) inlet tunnel, then continues up in several broad switchbacks above a gorge of the Triftbach to arrive at the **Trifthotel** (2337 metres, see Places to Stay), 50 minutes to one hour on. This cosy old three-storey mountain hotel stands near a tiny chapel at the edge of a small grassy basin under the heavily crevassed Triftgletscher. From here strenuous and lengthy side trips can be made up to the 3406-metre Mettelhorn or the Rothornhütte, an SAC hut at 3198 metres on the rugged spur descending from the Zinalrothorn.

Cross the Triftbach a final time, quickly cutting southwards across the tiny Alpine meadow and begin a diagonal, spiralling ascent up the grassy slopes. Behind you the spectacular 4221-metre Zinalrothorn comes into sight, and as you move up onto the high balcony of the **Höhbalmenstaffel** an incredible panorama unfolds. The views sweep around from the Täschhorn to the Allalinhorn, the Rimpfischhorn, the Dufourspitze – at 4618 metres Switzerland's highest peak, the Breithorn and the Klein Matterhorn, with

great highways of ice creeping down from their glacier-encrusted summits. Directly ahead stands the colossal tooth-like shape of the Matterhorn. The trail contours on through the rolling wildflower fields known as the **Höhbalmen** to reach a signpost at 2665 metres, 40 to 50 minutes from the Trifthotel.

Disregarding the left-hand path that goes back down into the upper Mattertal, make your way on westwards into the Zmuttal. The route makes a high traverse around narrowing ledges opposite the awe-inspiring north face of the Matterhorn, reaching the highest point of the walk at **Schwarzläger** (2741 metres) after 40 to 50 minutes. There are excellent views of the moraine-covered Zmuttgletscher, and more ice-bound peaks rising up at the glacier's head around the 4171-metre Dent d'Hérens.

Make a steady, sidling descent over the sparse mountainsides of **Arben** below small hanging glaciers that spill over the high craggy cliffs on your right. The path snakes down to meet a more prominent walking track leading down (from the easily reached Schönbielhütte) alongside the high lateral-moraine wall left by the receding Zmuttgletscher. Follow this down left in zigzags through the loose glacial rubble, before continuing along gentler terraces above the Zmuttbach towards mighty horned peaks to pass the restaurant at **Chalbermatten** (2105 metres), one to 1⅓ hours from Schwarzläger. These grassy slopes are grazed by Valaisan black-nosed sheep throughout the summer months.

Head on smoothly down above a small turgid-blue reservoir (whose water is diverted via long tunnels into the Lac des Dix in the adjacent Val d'Hérens), bearing right at a junction by the dam wall. This soon brings you down to the hamlet of **Zmutt** (1936 metres) with its St Katharina chapel built in 1797 and traditional old wooden buildings, from where an alp track descends on through hayfields dotted with neat farmhouses to intersect with a gravelled lane coming from Blatten and Zum See. Amble leisurely on past the Schwarzsee cable-car station, then take the next left turn-off leading up back into the thriving heart of Zermatt, 1¼ to 1½ hours from Chalbermatten.

OTHER WALKS

The Saastaler Höhenweg
The 15-km Saastaler Höhenweg goes from Grächen (1615 metres) to Saas Fee (1792 metres, see Walking Bases) and forms a section of the 10-day Monte Rosa Circuit. Following an impressive cut track above 2000 metres, the Saastaler Höhenweg leads southwards high along the western side of the Saastal, and needless to say offers some quite glorious vistas. Unlike the Gsponer Höhenweg (which runs along the opposite side of the valley – see above), however, this is a route best suited to sure-footed walkers not prone to vertigo.

The overall walking time is around seven hours, but this can be shortened by almost 1½ hours by taking the Grächen-Hannigalp gondola lift. Apart from the *Bergrestaurant Hannigalp* (☎ 028-56 23 81) at the upper gondola-lift station, which has a mattress room, there are neither restaurants nor accommodation options between Grächen and Saas Fee. Both Grächen and Saas Fee are serviced by regular and direct postbuses from Brig and Visp. Kümmerly + Frey's 1:60,000 walking map *Visp-Zermatt-Saas Fee-Grächen* is recommended. Refer also to the Gsponer Höhenweg walking map in this chapter.

Plattjen to Felskinn
This high-Alpine hike starts from Plattjen (2411 metres), accessible from Saas Fee (see Walking Bases) by gondola lift. The Saas Fee-Plattjen lift operates from late June to early October until 4.45 pm); otherwise it's 1½ hours' walk up. A well-marked path traverses the scree-slopes overlooking the upper Saastal on the eastern sides of the Mittaghorn (3144 metres) and Egginer (3367 metres), before ascending on to the *Britanniahütte* (☎ 028-57 22 88), an SAC hut at 3030 metres erected by the Alpine Club of Britain in 1912. From here the 3070-

metre Klein Allalin can be reach as a short side trip.

The way to Felskinn leads north-west over the Chessiengletscher, a broad névé with virtually no crevasses – certainly nothing at all dangerous – that can be crossed without difficulty by walkers with proper footwear. A cable car runs (between early June and mid-October) from Felskinn down to Saas Fee. Use Kümmerly + Frey's 1:60,000 walking map *Visp-Zermatt-Saas Fee-Grächen* or the SAW/FSTP sheet *Mischabel (284 T)*.

The Hörnligrat
The Hörnligrat is the craggy north-east ridge that leads up like a knife-blade to the 4477-metre summit of the Matterhorn, giving the mountain its characteristic sharply angular appearance. The upper half of the Hörnligrat is strictly mountaineer's territory, but a cut path easily good enough for fit walkers ascends from the Schwarzsee at 2552 metres (where there is a little chapel by the lake dedicated to mountain climbers) to the Hörnlihütte, an SAC hut at 3260 metres. The Hörnlihütte occupies a breathtakingly impressive site looking straight out onto the sheer rock walls of the Matterhorn's east face – with a pair of binoculars you may even be able to follow the progress of the numerous climbing parties that tackle the Matterhorn every day.

The average walking time from Zermatt to the Hörnlihütte is 4½ hours (or eight hours return), but the hike can be shortened considerably by taking the Schwarzsee cable car up or down. Hikers who go the whole way up on foot should consider staying overnight at the *Hotel Schwarzsee* (☎ 028-67 22 63), or better still the *Hörnlihütte* (☎ 028-67 68 07). Use the 1:25,000 *Wanderkarte Zermatt* walking map.

The Central Valais

The Central Valais stretches along the Rhône Valley from Sion to Visp, bridging the French/German language border. The region includes the Lötschental, the Turtmanntal, the Val Anniviers and the Val d'Hérens – larger northern and southern lateral valleys of the Rhône. The central Rhône Valley is the driest part of Switzerland, and Sion receives scarcely more than 500 mm annual precipitation – compared with around 1500 mm in Lugano and over 4000 mm on the Jungfraujoch.

Although the Central Valais accounts for a large proportion of Switzerland's wine produce, agriculture here would be severely limited without the region's intricate system of small aqueducts. Called *bisses* in French or *Suonen* in the local German dialect, these little canals divert water from mountain streams to irrigate the orchards and vineyards. In places the tiny wooden aqueducts are constructed along escarpments or fixed onto high precipices. Maintenance paths leading alongside the aqueducts serve as convenient walkways, since they have very slight inclines and usually offer excellent views. Two such routes, the Bisse de Ro near Crans-Montana and the Bisse de Clavau above Sion, are featured in this guidebook.

WALKING BASES
Sion
Sion (Sitten in German) is the capital of Valais Canton. This small and pleasant city lies at 491 metres beside the striking outcrops of Tourbillon and Valère. Historic buildings top each of these rock hills, and prehistoric inhabitants of the area built the first dwellings in the sheltered saddle between them. Sion's Notre Dame cathedral is a 12th-century construction, and the town hall dates from 1657. Other buildings of historical interest are the 'sorcerers' tower' (in a remaining section of the original city walls) and the church of St-Théodule.

The TCS has a camping ground at *Les Iles* (☎ 027-36 43 47) by the Rhône. Sion's *youth hostel* (☎ 027-23 74 70) is at Rue de l'Industrie 2. The *Auberge Relais du Simplon* (☎ 027-36 20 30) and the *Auberge des Collins* (☎ 027-36 20 80) both have lower-budget rooms. Sion's tourist office (☎ 027-22 85 86) is on the Place de la Planta.

Sion is on the main Lausanne-Brig rail route, and all trains stop here. Numerous postbus services operate out of Sion and the city even has its own airport.

Sierre
Situated amongst vineyards near where the Val d'Anniviers meets the Rhône, Sierre (540 metres) is the uppermost French-speaking centre within the main valley. Its old historic heart and dry, sunny climate give Sierre a strangely Mediterranean character. The Sentier Viticole/Rebweg route leads from Sierre through lovely terraced vineyards to the nearby German-speaking village of Salgesch in two hours, and introduces walkers to the local viticulture.

Lower-budget places to stay include the small *Auberge du Nord* (☎ 027-55 12 42), near the centre, and the *Auberge des Collines* (☎ 027-55 12 48). The *Hôtel Central* (☎ 027-55 15 66) has better standard rooms. The nearest camping is the *Bois de Finges/Pfynwald* (☎ 027-55 02 84). Sierre's tourist office (☎ 027-55 85 35) is near the train station.

Sierre is on the main Rhône Valley rail line, and is a major stop for trains between Lausanne and Brig. Postbuses from here run south into the Val d'Anniviers and up to Crans-Montana, an internationally renowned Alpine resort on the slopes immediately to the north of Sierre.

THE LÖTSCHENTAL
Enclosed on both sides by craggy glacier-hung ranges on the southern edge of the Bernese Alps, the Lötschental is the longest and most important northern side valley of the Valais. Unlike any other settled Alpine valley in Switzerland, the Lötschental is completely cut off. The only access into the valley is via a once-arduous route through the Quertalschlucht, an avalanche-prone gorge. Regular contact with the outside world was minimal, and in winter the Lötschental would remain totally isolated for months.

Despite its inaccessibility, as early as 800 BC Celtic visitors ventured into the Lötschental. This was evidently to mine its lead, as the name of both the valley and its river, the Lonza, are believed to come from *loudio*, the Celtic word for lead. The opening of the Lötschberg railway tunnel linking the Bernese Oberland with the Valais in 1913 finally broke the valley's isolation, but old customs and traditions have been upheld longer here than elsewhere. During the Fasnacht festival (Carnival or Shrovetide – 2 February to Ash Wednesday) the young men don hideous carved wooden masks, called *Scheggeten*, in a custom that may date back to pre-Christian times. Locals still carry goods around on their backs in conical baskets.

This walk explores the uppermost part of the Lötschental, an area shaped by intense glaciation. In the recent past the Langgletscher protruded much farther into the valley and has only receded to its present position over the last 150 years.

Maps

The best walking map of the Lötschental is the *Wander-und Skitourenkarte Lötschental* produced by the local tourist authorities and available in 1:25,000 and 1:50,000 versions. Almost as good is the 1:50,000 SAW/FSTP sheet *Jungfrau (264 T)*.

Walking Times & Standard

This is a day walk that takes, depending on several route options, from four to seven hours to complete. The walk follows well-marked trails to over 2000 metres, and stout footwear is necessary as there are some rocky sections. Early in the season, accumulated avalanche snows may make the route more difficult or even impassable. The Lötschental is relatively sheltered from winds, and the going can be hot on midsummer days.

The walk has an *easy to moderate* rating.

Places to Stay

The cheapest rooms in the Lötschental are offered by the *Gasthof Ferdania* (☎ 028-49

15 25) in Ferden. In Blatten the *Pension Breithorn* (☎ 028-49 14 66) has basic rooms at standard prices. The *Hotel Edelweiss* (☎ 028-40 13 63) is slightly better. Blatten's *Burgerhaus* (☎ 028-49 14 36) and the *Ferienheim* (☎ 028-49 18 32) sometimes offer dormitory accommodation for individuals. The uppermost accommodation in the Lötschental is the *Hotel Fafleralp* (☎ 028-49 14 51, open May to October), four km farther up the valley. It has a wider range of rooms and plenty of dormitory accommodation. There is a small *camping ground* (☎ 028-49 22 78) nearby at Gletscherstafel.

Getting to/from the Walk

This is a circuit walk that begins and ends in Blatten (1540 metres), the uppermost village in the Lötschental. From the train station at Goppenstein there are around 20 daily buses to Blatten; except for mountaineers, there is no other way in or out of the Lötschental. From early June until mid-October, most buses continue upvalley from Blatten via Gletscherstafel to the Hotel Fafleralp (see Places to Stay). This cuts at least two hours off the average walking time. Goppenstein is at the southern end of the Lötschberg railway tunnel on the Bern-Brig line. Trains from either direction stop at Goppenstein at least hourly; rail passengers coming from Bern will probably have to change in Spiez.

Private vehicles are best left at the large car park in Gletscherstafel, 4.5 km farther upvalley from Blatten.

Route Directions:
Blatten-Gletschertor-Blatten

(17 km, 4½ to 5¾ hours)

From the Blatten post office walk up across the bridge to the modern church, following the bitumen upvalley past typical old wooden Valaisan houses to the hamlet of **Eisten**. Here an old mule trail heads off left through pastureland dotted with occasional garden plots above the stream to reach the 18th-century church of **Kühmad** at 1625 metres after 30 to 40 minutes. Continue along the path beside the main road and cross the sidestream flowing down from hanging glaciers at the head of the Uisters Tal. The route climbs up directly over grassy slopes between sharp bends in the road then through light larch forest before coming to the **Hotel Fafleralp** (1787 metres, see Places to Stay) after a further 50 minutes to one hour.

Go on a few paces down the bitumen to where the road forks, then cut left over a flat lawn. After crossing another sidestream on a stone footbridge, make a steeper, winding ascent to **Guggistafel** at 1933 metres. These dozen-odd alp huts (most now converted into holiday cottages) sit perched on a gently sloping shelf with breathtaking views southwards across the upper valley towards the sheer 700-metre wall of the (Lötschentaler) Breithorn. Make your way up beside a little brook that flows along the base of an ancient lateral moraine, gently rising above the trees onto lovely open Alpine slopes scattered with bilberry and rhododendron bushes to reach the tiny lake known as the **Guggisee** (2007 metres), 50 minutes to one hour on.

Follow the white-red-white markings on through the rolling pastures and heathland of the **Gugginalp** towards the Langgletscher. The glacier's crevassed ice sprawls down from the narrow gap of the Lötschenlücke (3178 metres), which is also the source of the Grosser Aletschgletscher. Many other smaller hanging glaciers cling to the precipitous mountains on both sides of the enclosed upper valley. After passing through loose rockslides ease around leftwards into the tiny valley of Jegital to cross a churning little gorge on a footbridge (2108 metres). From this point a worthwhile one-hour return side trip can be made up to the **Anensee**, an Alpine tarn at around 2350 metres; the signposted path leads off left immediately after the bridge.

Head on down first alongside the stream, then move leftwards through regenerated moraine slopes to cross another bridge over the milky Lonza not far below where it emerges from the Langgletscher, 40 to 50 minutes from the Guggisee. The snout of the glacier, known as the **Gletschertor**, can be quickly reached by following rough but well-trodden trails through the rubble along the southern side of the river. Meltwaters produce interesting caves and arched forms in the debris-covered ice.

Proceed downstream across the rocky landscape left in the wake of the glacier's recession. The farther on you go the more advanced is the state of regrowth. The route leads on through stands of larch trees and attractive grassy terraces strewn with fallen boulders before crossing the outlet of the picturesque **Grundsee** (1842 metres) after 30 to 40 minutes. This shallow lake lies just off the main path, its clear, greenish waters reflect the surrounding peaks. A broad mule trail now winds its way gently on down after further 15 to 20 minutes to recross the Lonza at the hamlet of **Gletscherstafel** at 1771 metres.

Walkers not finishing the hike at Gletscherstafel, can continue along the Lonza's grassy southern banks. The foot track climbs up across pleasant forested slopes high above the river, before dropping down via the alp huts of **Vorsaas** to arrive back at **Kühmad** on the main road. From here retrace your steps as described above to reach **Blatten**, one to 1¼ hours from Gletscherstafel.

THE BISSE DE CLAVAU

Unlike other routes in this guidebook, this walk takes you into an intensively cultivated landscape along a beautiful section of the Chemin Vignoble, a long-distance trail leading through the sunny winegrowing district of the Central Valais. The Bisse de Clavau is a 500-year old aqueduct that carries water six km to the thirsty vineyards of the Rhône Valley. These steep, south-facing slopes are devoted almost entirely to the production of the fine red and white Valaisan wines known as Dôle and Fendant. Here the vines are planted on narrow terraces supported by drystone retaining walls that defy the steep gradient. Just east of Uvier, at the conclusion of the walk, is the fascinating Lac Souterrain, a 200-metre long underground lake.

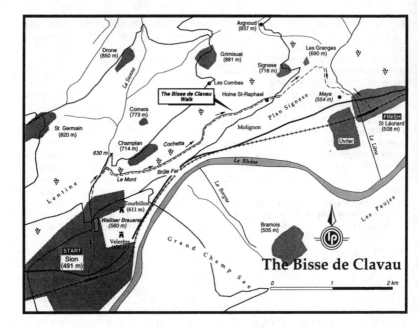

The Bisse de Clavau Walk

The Bisse de Clavau

Maps
The best walking map covering the route is the 1:50,000 SAW/FSTP sheet *Montana (237 T)*. Editions MPA Verlag has also published this sheet independently under the same title. Another good MPA walking map, *Sion-Thyon*, scaled at 1:25,000, only just includes the Bisse de Clavau. Kümmerly + Frey's 1:60,000 walking map *Val d'Anniviers-Val d'Hérens-Montana* is yet another good alternative.

Walking Times & Standard
The Bisse de Clavau is a very short half-day walk presenting no difficulties whatsoever. The going on these sun-exposed slopes can get very hot, however, so in summer wear a hat and carry liquid refreshment. Apart from the coldest days of winter, the walk can be done in virtually all seasons, although autumn is the most recommended time.

The walk is rated *easy*.

Places to Stay
For accommodation in Sion see Walking Bases.

Getting to/from the Walk
The walk begins from Sion (see Walking Bases) and ends at the village of St-Léonard. Postbuses running at approximately half-hourly intervals between Sion and Sierre call in at St-Léonard.

Route Directions: Sion to St-Léonard
(7 km, 2 to 2½ hours)
Walk 200 metres straight ahead from the train station and turn right onto the Rue des Creusets. Follow various small pedestrian laneways on up through Sion's old town, proceeding north along the Rue de Portes Nueves and Rue du Grand-Pont just past the old **Walliser Brauerei** building. Here a signpost points you off right on a pathway leading up between stone walls through the first hillside vineyards to a hairpin bend at

the start of the **Bisse de Clavau** after 40 to 50 minutes.

The route (signposted 'Chemin Vignoble') now begins an easy contouring traverse eastwards beside the tiny aqueduct amongst steeply terraced vineyards. The grape vines have been planted in closely spaced rows in order to maximise the yield of this valuable crop. Over to your right are the Tourbillon and Valère, two rounded outcrops crowned by historic fortresses. These high rock hills rise abruptly out of the built-up floor of the Rhône Valley. It seems remarkable that they survived the intense shearing action of the Rhône Glacier during past Ice ages.

Continue on above a sweeping curve of the Rhône River, enjoying views of the high mountains right along the valley. The route crosses several small roads, passing below the tiny village of Signese and the scattering of houses at Les Granges before turning down to the right away from the Bisse de Clavau. Make your way via a gravelled farm track along the edge of the vineyards above the gorge of the Liène (the waters of which are diverted subterraneously farther upstream to feed the irrigation channels), short-cutting a few curves in the road.

Yellow arrows guide you quickly down past **Maya** to a cobblestone laneway leading across the fast-flowing stream to reach the village of **St-Léonard** (508 metres), 1¼ to 1½ hours from where you first met the Bisse de Clavau. The local postbus stop is 400 metres east along the main road.

THE ILLPASS

Like the nearby Bois de Finges/Pfynwald, the Illpass forms the language border between the German and French-speaking regions of the Valais. Fronting the Rhône Valley, the mountains surrounding the pass are not especially high by Valaisan standards, but give direct views over 1500 metres down into the broad and intensively cultivated valley floor. The area around the Illpass has picturesque lakes (natural and artificial) and lonely Alpine pastures. The Illpass also has the advantage of being easily accessible without being overrun by walkers.

Maps
The SAW/FSTP 1:50,000 sheet *Montana (273 T)* covers the Illpass route. Also good is the walking map *Rund um Visp* published by Kümmerly + Frey at a scale of 1:40,000.

Walking Times & Standard
The Illpass is a medium-length day hike. Snow-melt is fairly rapid on these sunny slopes, so the walk can normally be done from June into November. Some care should be taken in routefinding, as the waymarkings are not always clear.

Carry sufficient liquids with you for the whole walk, as the path does not cross running streams close to their source so there is a slight possibility of contamination.

The walk has been given a *moderate* rating, and covers a length of 14 km.

Places to Stay
There is no accommodation on the route itself. In Chandolin, at the start of the walk, the cheapest accommodation is the *Pension du Chamois* (☎ 027-65 11 26), with rooms at somewhat above-average prices. Lower down in Vissoie, the *Auberge du Château* (☎ 027-65 13 15) offers budget rooms. There are also small local *camping grounds* at Vissoie (☎ 027-65 14 09) and St Luc (☎ 027-65 11 55). At Oberems, the *Pension Emshorn* (☎ 028-42 27 27) has standard rooms at surprisingly low rates. In Turtmann are the *Pension-Restaurant Wasserfall* (☎ 028-42 13 10) or the *Hotel Post* (☎ 028-42 13 03).

Getting to/from the Walk
The walk sets out from Chandolin (2146 metres), a ski resort high above the mouth of the Val d'Anniviers. There are some six direct postbus connections to Chandolin each day from Sierre via the village of Vissoie; the last bus from Sierre leaves at around 7 pm.

The finish of the walk is Oberems, from where the Turtmann-Oberems cable car provides public transport back into the Rhône

Valley. This community-subsidised cable car runs half-hourly to hourly at least until 8 pm. Fares are comparatively cheap. Slower regional trains running between Lausanne or Sion and Brig stop at Turtmann.

Route Directions: Chandolin to Oberems

(14 km, 4½ to 5¾ hours)

From behind the **Chandolin** tourist office (2146 metres) walk a few paces around to a winter ski lift. Short-cut up briefly through the forest to a meet an alp track and follow this uphill past a curve. Here a path goes off rightwards up across the flowery meadows of the **Alpage de Chandolin** to reach **La Grande Remointse**, a long wooden barn at 2368 metres below a chair lift, 50 minutes to one hour from the village. There are very nice views of mountaintops on the opposite side of the Val d'Anniviers and back across the Rhône Valley towards the Wildhorn.

The path continues ahead over grassed-over moraine hills, turning leftwards around into a tiny rocky valley that leads up to the unspectacular **Illpass** (2482 metres). Cross the dirt road and head east to a slight dip in the small ridge just above **Lac Noir**. This bluish lakelet is embedded in a scree-filled depression at the foot of the Rothorn and the Schwarzhorn. Drop down a short way beside a rocky gully towards the Illsee, then begin sidling leftwards below low cliffs. The route picks its way through stabilised glacial deposits, before contouring over pastures high above the lake to reach the alp huts of **Obere Illalp** at 2415 metres after 50 minutes to one hour.

Take the foot track leading down to the **Illsee** and cross the dam wall, where the land to the north falls away abruptly; far below, the village of Leuk stands out amongst the terraced vineyards. Go a short distance on around the lakeshore, then follow an eroded

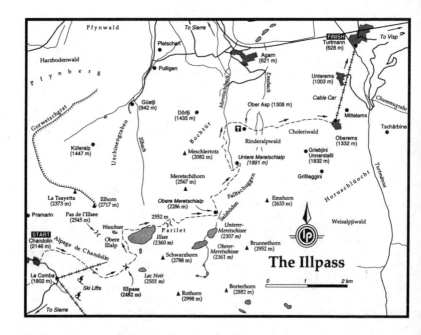

trail up in several steep switchbacks to **Parilet** (2552 metres). This col looks down to the Oberer and the Unterer-Meretschisee, two lovely emerald-green lakes sitting in a grassy basin under the 3025-metre Bella Tola. A broad mule trail now winds on gently down to the cluster of buildings at **Obere Meretschialp** (2286 metres), 1¼ to 1½ hours on.

Descend through Alpine heath towards the patchwork of intensively cultivated fields in the Rhône Valley, behind which the Balm horn rises up to 3699 metres. The white-red-white marked path continues down through scattered larch trees, edging over to the right across hillside meadows to the picturesque alp cottage of **Untere Meretschialp** at 1891 metres. At this point don't proceed straight ahead – that route is very difficult and poorly maintained – but take the foot track signposted 'Agarn'. This dips left (ie north-west) from the farmhouse into the forest, spiralling down very steeply beside the Meretschibach before coming out at the end of a dirt road after one to 1⅓ hours.

Make your way up along the road, proceeding right at a sharp bend to the hamlet and little chapel at **Ober Asp** (1308 metres). Pick up the trail marked with yellow diamonds going off left, quickly crossing two tiny branchlets of the Emsbach as you rise through the damp mossy forest to a grassy lane. The road leads into the tall larch forest of the **Choleriwald**, then on past a hydro-electric power station to arrive in the village of **Oberems**, a maze of wooden Valaisan houses and barns at 1332 metres, 40 to 50 minutes on.

The upper cable-car station is a few minutes' walk down the road. From the lower station at **Turtmann** (628 metres), the train station is 15 to 20 minutes' walk across the flat floor of the Rhône valley past the old military airstrip; follow the 'Bahnhof' signs.

OTHER WALKS
The Lötschberg Südrampe
The completion in 1913 of the Lötschberg railway with its 15-km-long tunnel provided a transport link between Bern and the upper Valais, and was a major engineering feat comparable to the construction of the Gotthard railway. The easy 5½-hour Lötschberg Südrampe (or 'southern terrace') accompanies the rail line as it makes a winding descent to the valley floor from Hohtenn (1078 metres) to Lalden (801 metres). The route leads along the steep northern sides of the Rhône through some 20 smaller tunnels and 10 avalanche galleries, in places following small aqueducts that bring water to the thirsty fields below.

The walk offers some wonderful vistas southwards towards the Pennine Alps, and can be shortened by catching a train from the en-route stations at Ausserberg or Eggerberg. Being very exposed to the sun, the Lötschberg Südrampe remains snow-free for most of the year and can normally be done from early spring until late autumn – but summer walkers will need a good hat and suncream. The 1:40,000 Kümmerly + Frey walking map *Rund um Visp* properly shows the route.

The Bois de Finges/Pfynwald
A serene little wilderness in the otherwise hectic Rhône Valley, the Bois de Finges/Pfynwald lies just two km east of Sierre. Its name originates from the Latin *ad fines*, meaning 'at the borders', and for over a thousand years the area has marked the division between the French and German-speaking regions of the Valais. The Bois de Finges/Pfynwald sits on old alluvial deposits onto which unstable mountainsides later collapsed to create this oddly scattered group of forested hillocks. Today huge blocks of rock up to 50 metres in height still lie strewn around the area.

As a large obstacle impeding movement between the two parts of the valley, this 'no man's land' was left very much to its own devices. Here the Rhône flows at whim along its ancient river bed in meandering channels past the largest stands of pine in lowland Switzerland. Shallow marshy lakes lie hidden within the forest, providing important wetlands in the dry landscape of the Central Valais. Although under official protection as a nature reserve, the Bois de Finges/ Pfynwald is seemingly threatened on all sides. In the coming years the area faces further encroachment by hydroelectric development on the Rhône and construction of a four-lane motorway through part of the reserve.

A very easy circuit walk taking several hours can be made from the public car park near the camping ground at the western end of the reserve. The route leads through the quiet woods to the lakes of Rosensee and Pfafforetsee, then returns via the stud farm of Milljere. The free tourist maps available from the Sierre tourist office probably best indicate the walking routes, but MPA's 1:25,000 sheet *Sierre-Leuk* shows the Bois de Finges/Pfynwald in more accurate topographical detail.

The Val d'Anniviers

Opening out directly south of the city of Sierre, the Val d'Anniviers is one of the Valais' major side valleys. An excellent high-level panoramic path starts at the village of Chandolin (1979 metres, see the Illpass walk), offering glorious views of the Alpine summits dominated by the mighty 4357-metre Dent Blanche at the head of the valley. The route traverses southwards along the eastern side of the Val d'Anniviers well above the treeline at between 2200 metres and 2400 metres via Tignousa, Prarion, the Hôtel Weisshorn to the pastures of Montagne de Nava. The path then makes a gradual descent to Lirec, before cutting down more steeply into the forest to Zinal (1675 metres), the uppermost village of the Val d'Anniviers.

The average walking time is six hours, which can be shortened by an hour or so by taking the funicular up the village of St-Luc (on the road to Chandolin). The scenic *Hôtel Weisshorn* (☎ 027-65 11 05) about halfway along the route offers rooms and dormitory accommodation. From Zinal there are about half a dozen postbus connections back to Sierre via Vissoire (see the Illpass walk) each day until around 6.45 pm. Kümmerly + Frey's 1:60,000 walking map *Visp-Zermatt-Saas Fee-Grächen* covers the walk;

otherwise you'll need two SAW/FSTP sheets: *Montana (273 T)* and *Arolla (283 T)*.

The Pas de Lona

The 2787-metre Pas de Lona is one of three Alpine passes linking Val d'Hérens with the Val d'Anniviers, two large southern side valleys of the Rhône. Despite the growing dependence on tourism, these Central Valaisan valleys have retained much of their rural atmosphere and charm. The special Hérens breed of cow, a descendent of the almost extinct European auerochs, originates from the Val d'Hérens. Once favoured by the Alpine herders for their hardiness in the mountains, today Hérens cows are most prized as fighting beasts for the (harmless) cow-fighting contests (or *combat de reines)* held in the French-speaking regions of the Valais throughout the summer.

From the hamlet of Eison (1650 metres) in the central Val d'Hérens, a moderate four to five-hour route climbs steeply eastwards via the alp huts of Tsalet d'Eison (2140 metres) and L'A Vieille (2368 metres) then over screeslides to the scenic Pas de Lona. From here the path sidles down north-east above lakes in the Lona basin then around the steep eastern sides of the Pointe de Lona to Bendolla (2112 metres) from a gondola lift which descends to Grimentz in the Val d'Anniviers.

Eison can be reach by some four daily postbuses from Sion (see Walking Bases) via St-Martin. From Grimnetz there are regular postbus connections to Sion via Vissoie; the last bus leaves Grimentz some time before 7 pm. There are places to stay in St-Martin and Grimentz. Use the 1:50,000 SAW/FSTP walking map *Montana (273 T)*.

The Col de Riedmatten

Connecting the Val des Dix with the village of Arolla in the neighbouring Val d'Hérens, the 2919-metre Col de Riedmatten sits amidst a stunning backdrop of high-Alpine scenery. This classic route leaves from Dixence/Le Chargeur at the mighty Lac des Dix dam wall (which for decades was the highest in the world), and follows a road around through small tunnels to the south-eastern corner of the great reservoir. A path crosses a suspension footbridge and climbs away south-east to the Col de Riedmatten. The breathtaking views include the 3869-metre Mont Blanc de Cheilon and the Glacier de Tsijiore Nouve. The descent brings you down past winter ski lifts to reach Arolla (1998 metres) after 5½ to six hours.

Although there is a good, well-marked path for virtually the whole way, this is a real mountain walk not to be taken too lightly. Unless you make a side trip to the SAC's Cabane des Dix, there is nowhere to stay en route, so it's important to get away reasonably early. For walking maps use either MPA's 1:25,000 *Val d'Hérens* or the 1:50,000 SAW/FSTP sheet *Arolla* (283 T). Dixence and Arolla are both linked with Sion by regular postbus services.

The Lower Valais

After flowing through the cantonal capital of Sion, the Swiss Rhône enters the Lower Valais. At the Coude du Rhône near the ancient city of Martigny, the river makes an abrupt right-angle turn and continues north-wards between the Muverans and the Dents du Midi massifs to mouth in Lake Geneva. The so-called 'Drance valleys' – the Val de Bagnes, the Val d'Entremont and Val Ferret – and the Val de Trient intersect with the main Rhône valley at the Coude du Rhône.

The Lower Valais occupies a zone of climatic transition between the moister environs of Lake Geneva and the almost semi-arid conditions in the central part of the Rhône Valley. The age-old trade and travel route via the Col du Grand St-Bernard passes through the Lower Valais, and this French-speaking region is rather less isolated compared to the upper Rhône Valley. At least since Roman times this trans-Alpine pass at the head of the Val d'Entremont has been the most important crossing point between Italy and northern Europe.

The Mont Blanc massif extends well into Valaisan territory, and France, Italy and Switzerland actually converge on the 3820-metre summit of the Dolent. The highest and most intensely glaciated of all Alpine ranges, the mountains of the Mont Blanc massif provide stunning backdrops that dominate the views from many lookout points in the Lower Valais. Despite its easier accessibility, this south-western corner of the canton is at least as spectacular as other parts of the Valais. Unfortunately, there is only enough space to include a few of the numerous outstanding walking routes in this region.

WALKING BASES
Martigny

Martigny (467 metres) lies at the Coude du Rhône, where the Swiss Rhône makes a sudden sweep around to the north before flowing on into Lake Geneva. Virtually surrounded by some of the very highest summits in the Alps, this small city is well situated for hikes in the Dents du Midi, Mont Blanc and Grand Muveran massifs. A short day hike from Martigny follows the Chemin Vignoble through the nearby vineyards.

Martigny was the Roman centre of the Valais, and this small city retains more than a few vestiges of its Roman past. These include the large amphitheatre, where Combat de Reines (traditional Valaisan cowfights) are held in spring and autumn, and the wide collection of Roman artefacts in the Gallo-Roman Museum. Also worth seeing are the 17th-century church and the 13th-century Château de la Bâtiaz on a hill just above town.

The local camping ground is *El Capio* (☎ 026-22 55 73). Martigny also has a cheap dormitory in the backpackers' *hostel* (☎ 026-21 22 60) in a claustrophobic old bomb shelter at Rue de Levant 66. At *Pension Poste-Bourg* (☎ 026-22 25 17), Ave du Grand St-Bernard 81, has low-budget rooms. The tourist office (☎ 026-21 22 20) is on the Place Centrale.

Martigny is the transport hub for the Lower Valais, and a major stop on the main Lausanne-Brig rail line. The *St Bernard Express* trains run from Martigny to Orsières and Le Châble, and the *Mont Blanc Express* leaves at least every two hours to the French Alpine resort of Chamonix. Buses go from Martigny via Orsières and the Grande St-Bernard tunnel to Aosta in Italy.

Orsières-Champex

Orsières (901 metres) lies at the junction of the Val d'Entremont and the Val Ferret on the road over the Col du Grand St-Bernard into Italy. The belltower of the town church dates from the 15th century. The tourist village of Champex sits above Orsières at 1472 metres beside the Lac de Champex, an idyllic lake with a superb mountain backdrop that includes the snowcapped peaks of the Grand Combin. A cable car ascends above the lake to La Breya at 2374 metres, from where a four to five-hour scenic semi-circuit leads up past the Glacier d'Orny and the Glacier Saleina to Praz de Fort.

Champex' *youth hostel* is in the Châlet Bon Ambri (☎ 026-83 12 23); the *Auberge de la Forêt* (☎ 026-83 12 78) also has dormitory accommodation and rooms. The local camping ground is *Les Rocailles* (☎ 026-83 19 79), which also offers cheaper rooms. Champex has a small tourist office (☎ 026-83 12 27), and a school of mountaineering, the L'École d'Alpinisme (☎ 026-83 29 49).

There are roughly hourly train connections to Orsières from Martigny (with a change at Sembrancher) until about 8 pm. Champex is reached by up to six daily postbuses (until around 6 pm) from Orsières. There are buses from Orsières via the Grand St-Bernard road tunnel to Aosta in Italy.

Le Châble-Bruson

These twin villages lie in the lower Val de Bagnes below the ski resort of Verbier. Le Châble (820 metres) is a more modern village but Bruson is pleasant and unspoilt, with traditional wooden chalets and *mazots* – grain storage barns built on stilts with round stone plates to keep out thieving rodents. Le Châble is the administrative centre of Val Bagnes, the largest regional council in Switzerland (whose area admit-

tedly largely consists of bare rock and glacial ice).

Popular hikes go up via Verbier (1526 metres) to the Lac des Vaux and the SAC's *Cabane Mont Fort* (☎ 026-38 13 84), but many walkers find the area excessively developed for winter sports. The Tour des Combins (a 10-day international circuit walk around the Grand Combin massif), also passes through Verbier.

The nearest camping ground is *La Prairie* (☎ 85 12 54) in Sembrancher. The local *youth hostel* (☎ 026-36 23 56) is in Bruson, and has a guests' kitchen. Le Châble has several good budget pensions such as the *Des Alpes* (☎ 026-36 14 65) and *La Poste* (☎ 026-36 11 69). A lower-budget place to stay in Verbier is the *Hôtel Rosablanche* (☎ 026-31 55 55). Le Châble has a tourist office (☎ 026-36 16 82), and nearby Verbier has one of Switzerland's leading schools of mountaineering, the École d'Alpinisme La Fantastique, CH-1936 (☎ 026-31 64 22)

There are hourly trains from Martigny to Le Châble. Regular postbuses and a cable car run from Le Châble up to nearby Verbier.

THE GLACIER DE CORBASSIÈRE

The Glacier de Corbassière is the fourth largest glacier in Switzerland. This broad river of ice rises in the extensive névés clothing the Grand Combin massif, whose main summit – despite being one of the Alps' more remote high peaks – was first climbed as early as 1857 by three local hunters using minimal equipment. Leading into this vast domain of mountaineers, this walk presents spectacular vistas of a heavily glaciated, high-Alpine landscape. The Val de Bagnes, at the end of the walk, is dominated by the Lac de Mauvoisin hydroelectricity reservoir. Although impressive, the 237-metre high dam-wall is dwarfed by the mighty rock walls of the 3703-metre Le Pleureur which towers directly above it. During extended dry periods the lake's water level drops to reveal bizarre rock formations.

Maps

The 1:50,000 SAW/FSTP sheet *Arolla (283 T)*

fully covers the route. The excellent large-format walking map *Verbier-Entremonts Champex-Lac Trient (5003)*, published at 1:50,000 by Editions MPA Verlag, also covers the walk on a single sheet. Another good walking map is Kümmerly + Frey's 1:60,000 *Val d'Anniviers-Val d'Hérens-Montana*.

Walking Times & Standard

The Glacier de Corbassière walk can be done either as a full day walk or as an overnight trip with two fairly short stages. (The latter might better suit walkers arriving at the start of the walk later in the day.) The walk involves a total ascent of almost 1400 metres (almost 1200 metres on Stage 1), and requires a good standard of physical fitness. This is a high-Alpine route almost entirely in the open – start early to avoid walking in the midday sun and be sure not to forget your waterproofs. Winter snowdrifts usually remain on the higher sections of the route at least until early July, and may make the Col des Otanes (2880 metres) harder to cross early in the season.

The walk has been given a *moderate to difficult* rating, although the total distance is just 12 km.

Places to Stay

The *Hôtel Grand Combin* (☎ 026-38 11 22) in Fionnay has rooms and dormitory accommodation for walkers.

The SAC's new *Cabane de Pannossière* (☎ 026-38 14 21) at 2645 metres beside the Glacier de Corbassière will offer modern high-Alpine hut accommodation. The old hut was destroyed by a winter avalanche in 1992, and a new and much larger hut with sleeping space for 100 people (and a controversial 'space age' design) will be roughly 600 metres north-west from where the old hut stood. Until the new Cabane de Pannossière is opened, the hut is in a temporary 32-bed structure 300 metres south-east of the old site.

At Mauvoisin the *Hôtel de Mauvoisin*

(☎ 026-38 11 30, open June to October) has rooms and a dormitory.

Getting to/from the Walk

The walk is a semi-circuit beginning at the small village of Fionnay (1490 metres) and ending at Mauvoisin (1824 metres), the last hamlet in the upper Val de Bagnes. Both places are accessible by up to four daily postbuses which run from Le Châble (see Walking Bases). At least two of these run to Fionnay all year round, but the postbuses only service the section above Fionnay as far as Mauvoisin from late June until mid to late August. Outside these times the service between Mauvoisin and Fionnay only operates on Saturday and Sunday, before stopping altogether in late September. The last bus from Le Châble to Fionnay and Mauvoisin departs at approximately 4.15 pm; the last bus from Mauvoisin back to Le Châble leaves at around 5.15 pm.

Alternatively, walkers can make a direct descent to Fionnay that takes roughly 1½ hours longer. Motorists are advised to leave their vehicles at Fionnay, then walk or take the postbus back from Mauvoisin.

Route Directions: Fionnay to Cabane de Pannossière

(6.5 km, 3 to 3¾ hours)
Although not an unattractive place, Fionnay is dominated by its power station and has mostly newly constructed houses built in traditional Valaisan style.

Cross to the western bank of the Drance de Bagnes on a road bridge, and take a foot track (signposted 'Pannossière') at the southern end of a small lake. This broad well-trodden route ascends in zigzags up the slopes between clumps of bushes, passing a right-hand turn-off at **Mardiuet** (1818 metres). Traverse on westwards below bluffs to reach a signpost at 1959 metres on a natural lookout at the end of the Corbassière ridge after one to 1⅓ hours. From here you get a great view across the valley to the peaks surrounding the 3336-metre Rosablanche, as

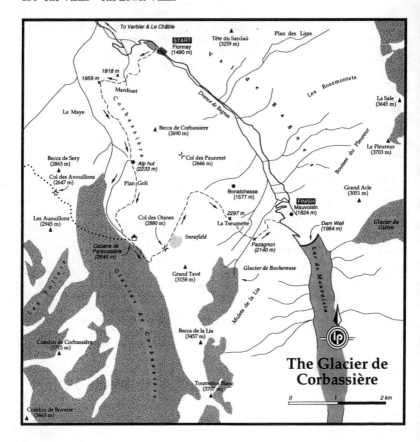

The Glacier de Corbassière

well as down the Val de Bagnes towards the skiing resort of Verbier.

Ignoring the winter route (signposted 'Chemin d'Hiver'), make your way on around south-eastwards into the Val Corbassière. The path traverses along the mountainsides high above the stream past small stone alp huts towards a broken icefall above deeply fissured cliffs at the terminus of the Glacier de Corbassière to reach a final stone shelter at 2233 metres, 50 minutes to one hour on from the Corbassière ridge. Jutting up at the head of the valley are the mighty 4000-metre peaks of the Grand

Combin, including Tsesette (4141 metres), Grafeneire (the main peak at 4314 metres) and Valsorey (4184 metres).

At this point you can either climb along the lateral-moraine ridge left by the receding glacier, or continue up around the left (eastern) side of the **Plan Goli** basin. The former route is recommended, however, and follows a path leading across the small stream before cutting diagonally upwards to a signpost on the ridgetop of stabilised moraines. From here a good path leads along the razorback-like crest beside the Glacier de Corbassière. The ice is almost completely covered by a thick layer of rock debris that is being continually pushed out of the mountains as if on an enormous slow-moving conveyor belt.

The route climbs steadily along the ridge in a broad curve to intersect with the other path near a small shallow tarn amongst grassed-over hills shortly before coming to the site of the new **Cabane de Pannossière** (2645 metres, see Places to Stay), one to 1⅓ hours from the last stone shelter. From here the vista up the broad icy belt of the Glacier de Corbassière to the ring of great summits and broad névés in the Grand Combin massif is definitely one of the finest the Swiss Alps have to offer. There is also a safe route across a crevasse-free section of the ice (marked in summer with those orange cones or 'witches' hats' used by road maintenance crews) to the Col des Avouillons.

Stage 2: Cabane de Pannossière to Mauvoisin

(5 km, 2 to 2½ hours)

From the new Cabane de Pannossière, several minor path variants lead quickly south-east through old moraines to the hut's former site. Here pick up the path and begin the steep and winding ascent north-eastwards, passing a white-blue-white marked mountain route going up right to Grand Tavé (3158 metres) just before you arrive at the 2880-metre **Col des Otanes** after 35 to 45 minutes. This point gives you a final splendid view of the Grand Combin, the northern slopes of which now appear as one unbroken mass of perpetual snow and ice.

Follow white-red-white paint splashes and marker stakes down through fields of rust-coloured talus. The route leads on across the base of a small névé on the northern side of the Grand Tavé with a few good slopes for glissading. In places large blooms of red algae appear in the snow as though an Alpine yeti with nose-bleed had just passed through. Continue down over regenerating screes and smaller snowdrifts to a signpost at 2532 metres, where a foot track departs left for Bonatchesse. Bear right here and sidle down

south-eastwards via the pastures of **Le Tseumette** (2297 metres), crossing several streamlets flowing down from the Glacier de Bocheresse to reach another route branching at **Pazagnon** (2140 metres), one to 1¼ hours from the Col des Otanes.

Just upvalley is the dam wall the glacier-fed backwaters of which form the hydroelectrity reservoir of Lac de Mauvoisin. This massive arc of solid concrete is over 200 metres high – not much lower than the dam wall of the Lac de Dix, which is less than 10 km away to the north-east on the other side of the 3703-metre Le Pleureur. Take the left-hand path and make a final serpentine descent over the slopes dotted with alpenroses, before coming onto the Val de Bagnes road a short way uphill from Mauvoisin (1824 metres, see Places to Stay) after a final 25 to 30 minutes.

THE FENÊTRE D'ARPETTE

At 2665 metres, the Fenêtre d'Arpette is a minor pass at the northern edge of the Mont Blanc massif. The hike over Fenêtre d'Arpette forms a day stage of the Tour du Mont Blanc (or Mont Blanc Circuit) and leads out of the upper Val Trient into the Val d'Arpette. These two little valleys offer contrasting high-Alpine scenery. The upper Val Trient is filled by the seven-km Glacier de Trient, whose broken ice spills down from hidden névés under the 3540-metre Aiguille du Tour in a jumbled mass of séracs. The upper Val d'Arpette is a wild little valley dominated by slopes of broken rock and talus, though the lower valley is a lovely area of highland pastures.

Maps

Recommended are two 1:50,000 walking maps: the SAW/FSTP's sheet *Martigny (282 T)* or Editions MPA Verlag's *Verbier-Entremonts Champex-Lac Trient (5003)*; the latter sheet covers a larger swathe of the lower Valais. Another good alternative is the walking map titled *Orsières – Val Ferret*, published by the local tourist authorities at a scale of 1:40,000. Kümmerly + Frey's 1:60,000 sheet *Grand St Bernard-Dents du*

Midi-Les Diablerets is yet another possibility.

Walking Times & Standard

The Fenêtre d'Arpette is essentially a longish day walk that is best done between late June and late September. There is quite a bit of loose rock, particularly on the descent from the Fenêtre, but the route presents few difficulties for fit and properly equipped hikers accustomed to mountain walking. The route is well marked in red-white-red, although old winter snows may cover upper sections earlier in the season.

The walk is rated *moderate*, and covers a total distance of 14 km.

Places to Stay

At the Col de la Forclaz, the *Hôtel de la Forclaz* (☎ 027-722 26 88) has reasonably priced rooms (of various standards) and dormitory accommodation. There are also places to stay in nearby Trient. At the scattered holiday village of Arpette is the excellent *Relais d'Arpette*, which has simple rooms, a separate walkers' bunkhouse as well as its own small camping ground.

For places to stay in Champex see Walking Bases.

Getting to/from the Walk

The walk begins the Col de la Forclaz (1526 metres). Postbuses running from Martigny (see Walking Bases) and Trient pass over the Col de la Forclaz around five times daily. The last bus leaves Martigny at around 6.15 pm.

The hike ends at Champex (see Walking Bases).

Route Directions: Col de la Forclaz to Champex

(14 km, 5 to 6¼ hours)

From the main road take the signposted vehicle track that leads south through the fir trees high above the village of Trient. This dirt road contours smoothly beside a small aqueduct (a so-called *bisse*), curving around into the tiny valley past the glacial stream shoots through a narrow gorge to reach the restaurant called the **Chalet du Glacier** at 1583 metres after 40 to 50 minutes. There is a route junction here, with a prominent path going off right to the Col de Balme (on the Franco-Swiss frontier).

A large arrow painted on a rock indicates where a foot track continues up left, climbing in zigzags away from the stream. After leaving the forest for slopes of scattered larch trees, the views towards the Glacier du Trient steadily develop. The heavily crevassed glacier tumbles down from a broad snowfield sandwiched between 3500-metre peaks, terminating in a typical snout with a milky stream emanating from an icy cavern. Traverse on up the mountainsides covered with alpenroses and other wildflowers, enjoying continual wonderful views of the glistening glacier ahead, to pass the semi-ruined old stone hut of **Vésevey** at 2096 metres, one to 1¼ hours from the Chalet du Glacier.

Follow the well-trodden path leading up left (not the fainter trail leading right alongside the glacier) and begin the final ascent. The route steepens as it gains height, avoiding an area of coarse talus to arrive at the 2665-metre **Fenêtre d'Arpette**, 1¼ to 1½ hours on. The views from the pass itself are very satisfying, but by climbing a short way south along the rocky ridge you'll get a much better idea of the surrounding Alpine scenery, including part of the Plateau du Trient and the 3540-metre Aiguille du Tour. To the north-west the mighty dam wall of the Lac d'Emosson can be identified.

Drop down over screeslides and snowdrifts into the upper Val d'Arpette, which is dominated by wide fields of shattered rock sweeping down the mountainsides. The white-red-white marked route first sidles down leftwards into the base of the gully, then picks its way on through the rocky-grassy upper valley. A short way after meeting a small stream at a stand of larches, cross over to join a small rough vehicle track. This brings you down past the scattered holiday chalets to reach the hotel at **Arpette** (1630 metres, see Places to Stay) after 1¾ to 2¼ hours. Here the Val d'Arpette broadens slightly at a pretty pasture fringed by forests, offering nice views back up the valley.

Crossing it several times on bridges, follow the stream on downhill into the trees. From a small diversion weir the route commences a gentle descent alongside a canal (which feeds the artificial Lac de Champex) to emerge near the lower station of La Breya chair lift immediately above the main road. The village of **Champex** (1472 metres, see Walking Bases) is clustered around the lake about one km on to the right, or 25 to 30 minutes from Arpette.

OTHER WALKS
Col de Grand St-Bernard to Ferret
Used as a crossing point between the Val d'Aosta in Italy and the Lower Valais since prehistoric times, the 2469-metre Col de Grand St-Bernard is one of the great Alpine passes. The busy main transport route now bypasses the Col via a long tunnel, but the less transited old road snakes its way up to the pass height. From here a wonderfully scenic walk leads north-west via the minor passes of the Col de Chevaux (2714 metres) and the Col de Bastillon (2761 metres) to the Lac de Fenêtre, several lovely highland lakes at 2456 metres. The descent leads down to the hamlet of Ferret (1707 metres) in the upper Val Ferret. (This is a stage of the 10-day Tour des Combins circuit walk.)

This is a moderate-standard route taking four to five hours. There is budget accommodation at the *hospice* on the Col de Grand St-Bernard and in Ferret. Throughout the walking season the Col de Grand St-Bernard can be reached by five daily postbuses from Orsières (see Walking Bases); two of these buses actually leave from Martigny (also see Walking Bases). Postbuses run six times daily from Ferret back to Orsières. The SAW/FSTP sheet *Courmayeur (292 T)*, the Editions MPA Verlag's *Grand Saint Bernard*

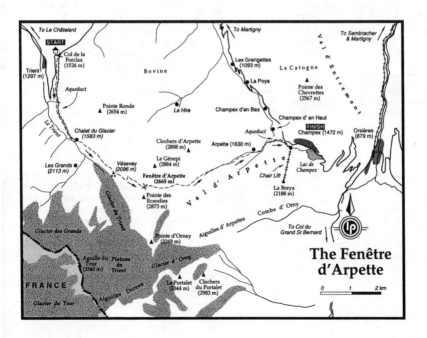

The Fenêtre
d'Arpette

(5103) 1:50,000 or Kümmerly + Frey's 1:60,000 sheet *Grand St Bernard-Dents du Midi-Les Diablerets* cover the relevant area.

The Gorges du Trient

Originating at the Glacier du Trient, the Trient river flows down through a series of ever-deeper gorges before meeting the Rhône four km downvalley from Martigny (see Walking Bases). From point 1214 metres on the road between Trient and Le Châtelard, a high-level route gently descends north-eastwards above the Gorges du Trient via the isolated hamlets of Litro, La Crêta, La Tailla and Gueuroz, before dropping down to the train station of La Verrerie in the Rhône Valley.

The walking time is three to four hours. Postbuses running between Trient and Le Châtelard pass by point 1214 metres four times daily in either direction from late June until late September; outside these times the service stops completely. Le Châtelard is accessible by roughly hourly trains from Martigny, and Trient can be reached by some five daily postbuses from Martigny. The 1:50,000 SAW/FSTP sheet *Martigny (282 T)* covers the walk.

The Col de Susanfe

Separating the Tour Sallière (3219 metres) to the south from the Dents du Midi massif, the 2494-metre Col de Susanfe is the second stage of the Tour des Dents du Midi, a popular three-day circuit. The walk over the Col makes one of the nicest hikes in the area, and is only of moderate standard. From the hamlet of Van d'En-Haut (1391 metres) head upvalley along the road to the Lac de Salanfe (1925 metres), then continue around the reservoir's northern shore. The route follows an alp track then a well-marked path leading north-west over pastures to the col. The descent leads through the tiny Val Susanfe, before dropping rather steeply to the mountain resort of Champery at 1035 metres in the upper Val d'Illiez.

There are two en-route accommodation options: the *Auberge de Salanfe* (☎ 026-61 14 38) beside Lac de Salanfe, and the *Cabane de Susanfe* (☎ 025-79 16 46), an SAC-run hut at 2102 metres on the western side of the pass. Between late June and early September postbuses run from Salvan (on the Martigny-Le Châtelard-Chamonix railway) up to Van d'En-Haut eight times daily. From Champéry there are trains via Monthey to Aigle (on the main Rhône Valley rail line) at least every hour. The SAW/FSTP sheet *St-Maurice (272 T)* is best (although it just cuts out Van d'En-Haut). Kümmerly + Frey's 1:60,000 sheet *Grand St Bernard-Dents du Midi-Les Diablerets* is also reasonable.

The Lac de Tanay

The Lac de Tanay (1408 metres) is a crystal-clear jewel embedded in the modestly high ranges of the 'Chablais' region, where the Lower Valais meets Lake Geneva. The influence of this large water body produces a moist and relatively mild local climate, and the Lac de Tanay area has a rich vegetation protected within a small nature reserve. Occupying a depression within the limestone rock, the lake drains subterraneously. The Lac de Tanay can be easily reached on foot in around two hours via a steep path leading up from the small scattered holiday resort of Miex (970 metres). A longer route possibility from the Lac de Tanay leads up through the Vallon de Tanay north across the range to St-Gingolph, an idyllic village on Lake Geneva on the border with France.

Miex is accessible by several daily postbuses all year round from Vouvry in the Rhône Valley. Vouvry is not on the main Lausanne-Brig line, so rail travellers must first journey to St-Maurice, then change to a St-Gingolph train. Lake Geneva ferries connect St-Gingolph to Montreux, Lausanne and Geneva. The best coverage of the area is given by Kümmerly + Frey's 1:60,000 sheet *Grand St Bernard-Dents du Midi-Les Diablerets*.

Ticino

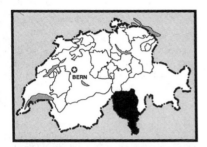

Ticino
With beautiful forests, large lakes and a warm temperate climate, Ticino includes walks from half-day to three days in duration (10 to 25 km), graded from easy to difficult. Walks include: the Val di Carassino, Passo di Cristallina and Monte Gereroso.

The Italian-speaking southern canton of Ticino (Tessin in German) is quite different to any other part of Switzerland. On their southern side the Swiss Alps rise up abruptly from altitudes of scarcely 300 metres, with long and deep valleys, most notably the Valle Leventina, stretching northwards far up into the mountains. In southern Ticino, Lago Maggiore and Lago di Lugano dominate the landscape. Created by massive Ice-age glaciers, these large elongated lakes have fiord-like arms whose watery depths sink down below sea level. Ticino's major rivers, the Maggia, Verzasca and Ticino flow into Lago Maggiore. Lago di Lugano lies farther south beyond the minor watershed of Monte Ceneri in the small but interesting region known as the Sottoceneri.

Although well within the realm of the Alps, Ticino has a decidedly warm-temperate climate. Conditions are surprisingly mild, with average winter temperatures in the valleys remaining above 0°C. Ticino's climate favours the cultivation of Mediterra-

nean species such as figs and oranges, and has produced a rich native flora. Chestnuts thrive in the mountains, often forming beautiful forests.

Many of Ticino's hiking paths originated as routes used by itinerate Alpine shepherds, who for centuries drove their animals from pasture to pasture. This practice, called *transumanza*, has now died out, but disused stone herder's cottages can still be seen throughout the Ticino Alps. Many of Ticino's Alpine valleys have experienced dramatic depopulation during the last 150 years, as industrialisation attracted people away from the hardship and isolation of the mountains.

All this makes Ticino a true paradise for hikers – in fact many northern Swiss prefer to come here to walk. This chapter features 10 of Ticino's best hikes, and gives plenty of other walking suggestions.

Northern Ticino

In its upper reaches the Ticino River flows through the Valle Leventina, whose typical 'trough' form reveals its glacial origins. This broad and fertile valley forms the heart and backbone of northern Ticino. Enclosed by the mighty Gotthard massif to the north and the arc of ranges extending from the Basodino to Pizzo Campo Tencia on its southern side, northern Ticino (or Alto Ticino to the locals) has an Alpine character less typical of the canton as a whole. The only large side branch of the Valle Leventina is the Val Blenio, which meets the main valley just above the town of Biasca.

WALKING BASES
Airolo
Airolo is situated immediately south of the Gotthard rail and motorway tunnels at 1141 metres. This attractive little town on the steep

hillsides of the upper Valle Leventina serves as a convenient base for walks in the surrounding mountains. Stepped stone laneways lead from the train station to the old centre of Airolo, built in solid Gotthard stone.

The *Hotel Airolo* (☎ 091-869 17 15) has budget rooms, and the *Ristorante Cristallina* (☎ 091-869 19 33) has cheap bunkhouse accommodation, although groups are given priority. Airolo's tourist office (☎ 091-869 15 33) is at the top of the town near the church.

Airolo is a minor transport hub on the trans-Gotthard railway, and many (but not all) trains running through the tunnel stop here. Postbuses run north over the Passo del San Gottardo to Andermatt, west over the Passo della Novena (Nufenenpass) to Ulrichen in Goms, and down the Valle Leventina to towns where the trains no longer stop.

Olivone

Lying in the upper Val Blenio at the crossroads of the Greina and Lucomagno passes is Olivone (889 metres). The charming old Gotthard-style houses of the village have painted exterior frescoes indicating contact with areas to the north. The museum is in an interesting stone and timber building dating from 1640. The San Marino church has an exterior square clock tower more typical of the Ticino style. Walking routes go off in all directions from Olivone, including marked trails to Campo (Blenio), the Val di Campo and the Bassa di Nara (to Faido), as well as the Val di Carassino (featured below) and the Plaun la Greina (see Graubünden) walks.

The *Osteria Centrale* (☎ 091-872 11 07) and the *Albergo Posta* (☎ 091-872 13 66) have rooms at slightly above average rates. Olivone has a small tourist office (☎ 091-872 14 87) near the bridge. There are several daily postbus connections from Disentis (Graubünden) via the Passo del Lucomagno, but Olivone is best accessible from Biasca in the Valle Leventina. In all seasons there are almost a dozen daily buses in either direction between Biasca and Olivone, a trip taking

around 40 minutes. (Only slower regional trains stop at Biasca, so – depending on when and where you're coming from – it may be necessary to change at Arth-Goldau, Airolo or Bellinzona.)

LAGO RITÓM CIRCUIT

Lago Ritóm lies at the heart of a nature reserve that takes in a good part of the Gotthard massif's southern slopes. Above Piora (at around 1800 metres) the steep-sided Valle Leventina opens out into a rather gentler landscape of rolling grassy highlands that shelter a dozen or so deep blue Alpine lakes. Although the Lago Ritóm area fronts one of the busiest transport thoroughfares in the Alps, visitors remain oblivious to the bustling traffic far below in the valley.

This area has a rich vegetation, including lovely forests of larch and mountain pines and over 500 species of flowering plants. Geologically it shows a diversity of rock types, with the crystalline formations of the Gotthard region converging with the gneiss rocks more typical of the Pennine Alps in the southern Valais. Originally a natural lake, Lago Ritóm was raised by seven metres for the production of hydroelectricity. Fortunately the water level is maintained at a fairly constant level, so the lake has kept its untouched appeal. This walk completely circumnavigates Lago Ritóm, exploring the landscape of the interesting valley basin that surrounds the lake.

Maps

The recommended walking map is Kümmerly + Frey's 1:50,000 *San Gottardo*, which is one of the few maps that take in the whole Gotthard region on a single sheet. Otherwise you'll need two 1:50,000 SAW/ESS sheets for this walk: *Disentis (256 T)* and *Val Leventina (266 T)*.

Walking Times & Standard

Most walkers will take two days to do the circuit, spending a night at one of the several mountain huts passed en route. (Note that the walking stages given below are merely a convenient way of breaking up the route description, and will be too short for most hikers.) The Gotthard range is one of the Swiss Alps' strongest weather divisions, and it frequently has better weather than the northern side of the mountains. While these mostly south-facing slopes often get sun-drenched, they are also very exposed in poor weather – and conditions here can deteriorate rapidly.

The Lago Ritóm Circuit has an *easy-to-moderate* rating, and covers a total distance of some 25 km.

Places to Stay

Walkers have several en-route accommodation options. The *Capanna Cadlimo* (☎ 091-869 18 33) at 2570 metres is run by the SAC. The SAT-run *Capanna Cadagno* (☎ 091-868 13 23) at 1987 metres is an attractive stone and wood construction with sleeping space for 53 walkers. It was thoroughly renovated in 1992. Overnight rates are most reasonable and good meals are served. The *Ristorante Lago Ritóm* (☎ 091-868 13 24) on the eastern side of the dam wall has pleasant rooms with shower.

In Ambrì-Piotta, the *Ristorante Vais* (☎ 091-868 15 31) right by the postbus stop has well-priced basic rooms. See also Walking Bases above for places to stay in nearby Airolo.

Getting to/from the Walk

The circuit begins from the upper station of the Piotta-Piora funicular (Funiculore Piora), Europe's steepest mountain railway. The funicular belongs to the Swiss Federal Railways (FFS in Italian), and their standard concessions apply. Departures are half-hourly.

Trains no longer stop anywhere in the Valle Leventina except Airolo, Faido and Biasca, and places between these three centres – including Piotta – are accessible only by the (roughly hourly) postbuses running between Airolo and Bellinzona. From the end of May until late September there are also several extra postbus services from Airolo right to the lower funicular station (Piotta Centrale FPR). Otherwise, the

funicular is a 10-minute signposted walk from Piotta village.

The return to Piotta can be made on the funicular (the last car down leaves soon after 6 pm), or you can walk back via the tiny mountainside village of Altanca. Postbus vans running between Lurengo and Ambrì-Piotta pass through Altanca up to six times per day; the last bus to Piotta goes just after 7 pm.

Motorists can leave vehicles at the lower funicular station or at the small car park below the Lago Ritóm dam wall. The most convenient motorway exit is at Airolo.

Stage 1: Piora (Upper Funicular Station) to Capanna Cadlimo
(6.5 km, 2¼ to 3 hours)

With a gradient of 88%, the funicular heaves you up some 850 altitude metres from the valley-floor village of Piotta to the upper station of Piora in the cooler Alpine zone at 1793 metres, thus saving your precious sweat for the higher slopes.

Follow the bitumened road up to the right to the **Lago Ritóm** dam wall, then climb gently on left around the lakeside. A signpost at **Alpe Ritóm** points you off left along a dirt track leading up through an open gully to reach the alp hut of **Alpe Tom** beside **Lago di Tom** (2021 metres) after one to 1¼ hours. This shallow lake with sandy shores lies in a broad basin enclosed by grassy hillsides.

Disregarding a walking route going eastwards to Capanna Cadagno, take a foot track around to the (often dry) inlet stream, then cross and begin climbing away to the right. The path brings you up past the **Laghetti di Taneda**, two tarns perched on a small uneven terrace, before winding its way up more steeply over the continental watershed of the **Bassa del Lago Scuro**. Here **Lago Scuro** (2451 metres) comes into sight, a deep highland lake whose outwaters flow northwards into the Rhine.

Make your way around the lake's eastern sides over persistent snowdrifts to a high signposted cairn, then dip across a stream gully to join with a more prominent path. Blending into its rocky Alpine surroundings

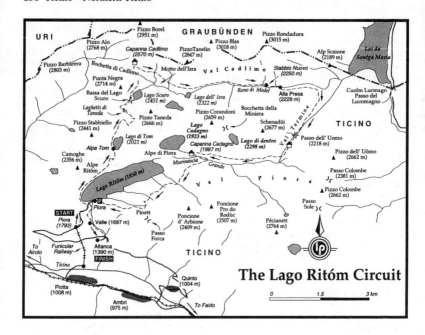

The Lago Ritóm Circuit

200 metres up to your left is the **Capanna Cadlimo**, 1¼ to 1¾ hours on from Lago di Tom. At 2570 metres the grey-stone capanna is the highest mountain hut in Ticino.

Stage 2: Capanna Cadlimo to Capanna Cadagno

(11.5 km, 2½ to 3¼ hours)

Follow a sporadic line of neat round cairns down over grassed-over moraine slopes of the **Motto dell' Isra** past the **Lago dell' Isra**, a little lake surrounded by moist grassy flats where the Val Cadlimo narrows. Soon passing a right-hand turn-off going over the Bocchetta della Miniera to Cadagno, the way leads gently down through this pretty little valley along the often snowed-over left bank of the Reno di Medel, and comes to **Stabbio Nuovo** (2250 metres) after one to 1¼ hours. Here a small herder's shelter is built against a rock block beside a meadow grazed by horses.

Head a short way on and cross the stream

at a small diversion weir called **Alla Presa** (2229 metres), following a rough vehicle track a few paces on to where another marked trail continues left. The route rises steadily away from the stream over open ridges granting clear views north-east towards the **Lai da Sontga Maria** hydro-electric reservoir, before beginning an easy descending traverse around into the **Val Termine** to meet an old dirt road running along the base of the valley. Here continue up 400 metres to recross the north-south watershed at the indistinct **Passo dell' Uomo** at 2218 metres, 45 minutes to one hour from Stabbio Nuovo. There are some alp huts here and an emergency telephone.

Walk 700 metres on down the road (just past a route going south-east towards the Passos Colombe and Sole), to where a sign-post directs you down rightwards over a concrete bridge. The track runs along the undulating northern slopes of the **Val Piora**, a wide expanse of treeless Alpine pastures into which the Murinascia Grande stream has eroded a deep a gully, falling slowly against the contour to reach **Capanna Cadagno** (1987 metres) after 50 minutes to one hour. This homy hut sits on a hillock above the Alpe di Piora in view of Lago Cadagno.

Stage 3: Capanna Cadagno to Altanca (via Pinett)

(6.5 km, 2 to 2¾ hours)

Walkers in a hurry can take the road on down around the northern shore of Lago Ritóm, but this somewhat longer alternative is nicer.

Pick up the left-hand path (signposted 'Passo Forca'), which leaves the road not far down from two barns roofed with corrugated iron and immediately crosses a stone footbridge. After bearing right at a route junction shortly on, climb around to the south-west and sidle high above the blue waters of Lago Ritóm on slopes looking out towards peaks of the main Gotthard range.

The route leads on through light forest interspersed with rhododendrons, heath and lovely patches of moor, before dropping down to **Pinett**, a small isolated Alpine pasture at around 2070 metres, a left branching goes off to Passo Forca. Continue down below a stone cottage and on past gnarled old larch trees, descending more steeply along the line of a fence to the Ristorante Lago Ritóm (see Places to Stay) at **Piora**. Follow the dirt road beneath the curved-concrete dam wall to a small car park, 1½ to two hours from the Capanna Cadagno. Your circle closes at this point, and the return to Piotta is made either by funicular, or on foot via Altanca as now described.

Steps (signposted 'Ambrì-Piotta') connect with an ancient mule trail, whose original stone paving is still largely intact and provides an excellent walkway. It brings you down via the traditional old hamlet of **Valle** (1697 metres), spirals on through the forest, then skirts above a sloping field to rejoin the road. The tiny village of **Altanca** (1390 metres) is a short way down along the bitumen, 30 to 45 minutes from Piora. There are irregular PTT minibuses back to Piotta

from here. Otherwise a steep path leads below the small church, repeatedly crossing the winding road before coming out by the lower funicular station at Piotta after 50 minutes to one hour.

THE VAL DI CARASSINO

The Val di Carassino is a charming little side valley that drains into the upper Val Blenio near Olivone. The Val di Carassino runs north-west from the 3402-metre Rheinwaldhorn, which – although the summit is shared with the neighbouring canton of Graubünden – is the highest peak in Ticino. Interesting for its long and very narrow form, this lonely Alpine valley was formed by glaciers that once descended from the Adula range. Less commonly seen wildflowers, including the rather rare Edelweiss, now grow on the valley's inaccessible and steep-sided slopes.

Maps

The 1:50,000 SAW/ESS sheet *Valle Leventina (266 T)* fully covers the route and is the recommended walking map.

Walking Times & Standard

This is a leisurely two-day walk which can easily be done as a longer day hike. Although there is some steep climbing and descending at the beginning and end of the route, the going is relatively not strenuous. The way up through the Val di Carassino itself mostly follows a dirt alp track, but access by vehicle is only permitted for the several graziers who run stock in the valley during the summer.

The walk is rated *moderate*, and covers around 16 km.

Places to Stay

Two similarly named mountain huts provide accommodation en route. There's the 70-bed *Capanna Adula (SAC)* (☎ 091-872 15 32), belonging to the Swiss Alpine Club. The resident warden/cook is only there in July and August, but otherwise it's always open. Little more than a km away and slightly off the main walking route is the somewhat larger *Capanna Adula (UTOE)* (☎ 091-872

16 75). This UTOE hut is staffed from late June to mid-September, but is also always open. (The presence of two mountain huts so close together is indicative of the historical rivalry between the nationally organised SAC and Ticino's locally strong Alpine clubs.)

There is little or nowhere to stay in the village of Dangio, at the end of the walk, but in nearby Torre is the small *Albergo Greina* (☎ 091-871 12 37). For accommodation in Olivone, see the Walking Bases section above.

Getting to/from the Walk

The walk begins in Olivone (see Walking Bases), and returns to the Val Blenio to finish at the village of Dangio. (Dangio is not to be confused with another village called Dongio farther down the valley.) All buses running between Olivone and Biasca pass through Dangio.

Stage 1: Olivone to Capanna Adula (SAC)

(11 km, 4 to 5 hours)

From the post office, follow the road to a signpost 50 metres after the Brenno bridge, then turn left up a stairway and walk on around past the village church to the trailhead. Another route here, the 'Sentiero Basso', leaves off down the valley. A short farm track brings you quickly onto a mule path, which climbs through scrubby woodland of birch and wild hazelnuts to cross a small stream. Now ascending more steeply, continue in switchbacks up the increasingly forested hillsides giving continual glimpses of the cascading Ri di Carassino.

Soon after passing an isolated cottage (1537 metres) on a high pasture overlooking Olivone, the path begins sidling along the undulating slopes, crossing the river on a footbridge just as it comes to **Compietto**, two to 2½ hours from Olivone. Occupying lawn-like river flats at 1570 metres, this charming summer-only settlement of a dozen or so old stone houses and a little church dating from the 15th century is the

perfect place to stop for a rest, a snack and a look.

Head on up the winding road to an artificial waterfall at the dam spillway, then proceed past the small reservoir to the farmhouse of **Alpe di Bolla** into the **Val di Carassino**. These open Alpine meadows sprinkled with rhododendron heaths, and the 3000-metre peaks of the Adula tower above to your right. The road leads entirely along the eastern banks of the **Ri di Carassino**, which tumbles and meanders its way down through the narrow – in places less than 200 metres wide – floor of the upper valley past the farmlets of **Alpe Carassino**, **Alpe Cassimoi** and **Alpe Bresciana** to a track division at the head of the Val di Carassino, 1¾ to 2¼ hours from Compietto.

The way to the nearby **Capanna Adula (SAC)** moves up to the right past the small chapel at **Passo Termine** (approximately 2030 metres), then cuts down leftwards over the ridgeline to arrive at the hut after just 10 to 15 minutes. The Capanna Adula (SAC) is perched on a shelf at 2012 metres looking down through the Val Soi to the villages in the Val Blenio.

The longer left-hand trail climbs steeply on up an indistinct grassy spur, before swinging rightwards across a stream in a more gentle ascent to reach the 'other' Capanna Adula run by the UTOE after 50 minutes to one hour. The UTOE hut stands at 2393 metres in the shadow of the 3402-metre Rheinwaldhorn, Ticino's highest peak. Nearby is an old lateral moraine of the Vadrecc di Bresciana, a rapidly receding glacier whose icy masses covered this site until relatively recently. Being 350 metres higher than the SAC hut, the **Capanna Adula (UTOE)** enjoys more far-ranging views that stretch out towards the mountains of the Gotthard region. Return to the main path via the ascent route.

Stage 2: Capanna Adula (SAC) to Dangio

(4.5 km, 2 to 2½ hours)

From near the hut flagpole descend rightwards (north) a short way to join the

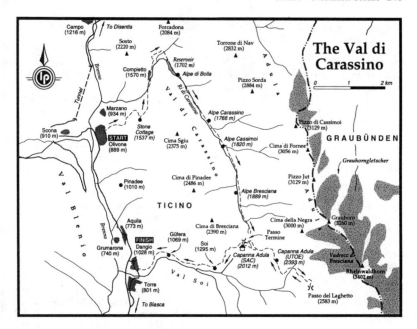

The Val di Carassino

main route coming from Passo Termine. The countless zigzags of a cut mule trail bring you down the initially extremely steep slopes above the Val Soi to the meet a rough road at the scattered locality of **Soi** (1295 metres) after one to 1¼ hours.

Follow the road on beside the rubble-choked river through the hamlet of **Güfera**, and continue on to a left-hand turn-off, just after a more prominent path going to Aquila and Olivone. A foot track leads down past houses in the forest to a chapel on the uphill side of **Dangio**, then via narrow laneways through the traditional stone village to reach the main street, a further one to 1¼ hours on. The post office (801 metres) is a short walk along to the left, directly opposite the Cima Norma chocolate factory, which shut down in 1966 and now serves as an army barracks.

CAMPOLUNGO CIRCUIT

The area around the 2714-metre summit of

Pizzo Campolungo on the southern side of the Valle Leventina forms one of Ticino's most interesting nature reserves. A curious natural feature of this reserve is Lago Tremorgio, a lake nestled in a rounded trough high above the Valle Leventina. The origins of Lago Tremorgio were something of an enigma in the past. The lake's Italian name refers to its 'funnel' form, and its water level is gradually sinking. At one time Lago Tremorgio was believed to be an ancient volcano, but the lake is more likely the impact crater of a large meteorite.

Exposed bands of white dolomite rock stand out sharply on the ridges high above Lago Tremorgio, and the Campolungo area is well known for its rock crystals, including red and blue corundums (rubies and sapphires). Farther to the south the beautiful Alpine lake of Lago di Morghirolo is the source of the Val Piumogna, whose lower valley area is a forested wilderness. The Piumogna stream enters the Valle Leventina in a spectacular waterfall that is visible from passing trains.

Maps

The best map to use on this walk is either *Valle Leventina (266 T)*, published by the SAW/ESS, or the Editions MPA Verlag sheet *Valle Maggia-Val Verzasca*, both scaled at 1:50,000. Kümmerly + Frey's 1:60,000 walking map, *Ticino Sopraceneri*, also covers the route adequately.

Walking Times & Standard

If you get a reasonably early start, the Campolungo Circuit can easily be done in a single day. As this is such a nice area it's worth stretching out the walk a bit by staying at one of the three mountain huts along the way. The best time to walk the circuit is between mid-June and mid-October. The total ascent is just 600 altitude metres, and the route is quite well marked and signposted.

The walk is rated *easy to moderate*, and covers approximately 15 km.

Places to Stay

The *Ristorante Guscetti* (☎ 091-867 12 30) down in the valley at Rodi-Fiesso has standard rooms. The *Capanna Tremorgio* (☎ 091-867 12 52) at 1851 metres on Lago Tremorgio, has a mattress room (and hot showers). The *Capanna Leit* (☎ 091-868 19 20) at 2260 metres belongs to the SAT (Società Alpina Ticinese) and is an old-style hut with self-catering only. The SAC's *Capanna Campo Tencia* (☎ 091-867 15 44), at 2140 metres is a much larger hut which offers cooked meals.

The *Albergo della Alpi* (☎ 091-867 40 24) in Dalpe-Cornone has simple rooms at very reasonable rates. The cable car at *Piano Selva* (☎ 091-867 15 46) has a dormitory. A classic place in Faido is the *Hotel Barondone* (☎ 091-866 12 44) with old-style rooms for youth-hostel prices.

Getting to/from the Walk

The Campolungo Circuit starts at Lago Tremorgio, which is accessible by a 15-minute cable-car ride from Rodi-Fiesso in the Valle Leventina. This private mountain lift offers no fare concessions and only has two small four-person cabins, so queues can build up quickly. The last upward cable car goes at 5 pm. Otherwise, Lago Tremorgio is a steep 2½-hour climb up through the forest from Rodi-Fiesso. Trains no longer stop in Rodi-Fiesso, and the village is now served by the regular postbuses that run between the train stations at Airolo and Faido. Private vehicles can be parked at the Rodi-Fiesso's little-used train station or at the cable-car station.

You can end the walk at Dalpe, from where there are five or so daily buses back to Rodi-Fiesso (the last at about 5.30 pm). Another alternative is to walk on from Dalpe to Alpe Piano, where there is a private cable car directly down to Faido that runs on demand. Slower regional trains do stop at Faido railway station.

Stage 1: Lago Tremorgio to Capanna Campo Tencia

(6.5 km, 2½ to 3½ hours)

The small cable car belonging to the local electricity company hauls you up almost 900 metres out of the sticky Valle Leventina in around 15 minutes. The **Capanna Tremorgio** (see Walking Bases) is by the lakeshore only a minute or so from where you get out.

From below the Capanna Tremorgio a well-trodden path leads around the eastern side of **Lago Tremorgio**, which sits at 1830 metres in an interesting rounded cirque enclosed by steep-sided grassy peaks. The path climbs steadily out of the forest onto open slopes above the lake, reaching a signposted intersection at the tiny Alpine valley of **Alpe Campolungo** after 30 to 40 minutes. Turn left and head up five to 10 minutes under the high-tension powerlines to **Passo Venett**, a small pass looking out towards Dalpe and Faido. Continue right, contouring along the slopes of eroding dolomite, then make your way around left over Alpine pastures to reach the **Capanna Leit** (see Places to Stay) after another 20 to 30 minutes.

Walk a few minutes on past a cross mounted on a prominent rock to **Lago Leit**. This glacial lakelet has been stocked with rainbow trout and is now a popular fishing spot. Head left around the shoreline then follow red-white paint markings which lead up steeply through the rocks to a gap on the ridge after 30 to 45 minutes. This is **Passo Leit**, from where there are nice views across the heavily forested Val Piumogna down to your left.

Sidle over to the obvious col just over to the right. The glacier-clad mountain directly to the south is the 3071-metre Pizzo Campo Tencia. The path descends gently through the grassy meadows of the **Alpe Lei di Cima**, before dropping down more steeply to reach the Ri di Piumogna. Cross the shallow stream on a row of stepping stones, then climb on quickly to a small tarn after one to 1½ hours. Here the path intersects with the trail leading up from the **Capanna Campo**

Tencia (see Walking Bases), which is a short way on down to the left.

The 1½-hour return side trip to **Lago di Morghirolo** is a highlight of this walk and not to be missed. The right-hand path continues upvalley along the rocky ridge before climbing over low mounds of moraine rubble to grassy flats near the outlet stream. Lago di Morghirolo lies at 2264 metres at the very head of the valley and is surrounded by craggy peaks.

Stage 2: Capanna Campo Tencia to Dalpe

(8 km, 1¾ hours to 2⅓ hours)

Pick up the foot track below the hut and descend across two sidestreams flowing down from the moraine slopes to the right. The path soon cuts down left to the valley floor and continues along the banks of the Ri di Piumogna to cross the small river on a footbridge after 15 to 20 minutes. Head up

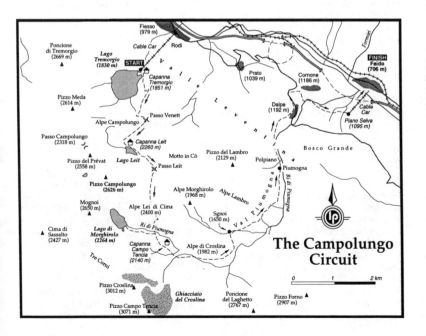

The Campolungo Circuit

over the low rhododendron-covered ridges of the **Alpe di Croslina**, then around left where stunted larch trees mark the upper forest line. Here the gradient steepens, and an old stone-laid trail brings you down to the attractive grassy clearing of **Sgnoí** at 1650 metres after 45 minutes to one hour.

Walk on down through the beautiful spruce and larch forest of the Val Piumogna. The path takes a course well away from the river, gently dropping against the contour for 30 to 40 minutes to meet a dirt road just above the hamlet of **Piumogna**. Follow the road down through birch woodland growing in a loose stony wash and continue a short way past a bridge to where a signposted foot track leaves off right. This goes down through more forest, before coming out onto a narrow cobbled lane which leads down into the quaint village of **Dalpe**, 30 to 40 minutes on from Piumogna. Postbuses leave from Dalpe post office, not far down the road. Dalpe's parish church was built in 1661 and contains old frescoes.

Walkers continuing on to the cable car at **Piano Selva** (30 to 40 minutes) or to **Faido** (one to 1½ hours) should turn right to Dalpe-Cornone, where trail markings from the Albergo della Alpi lead down onto the Piano Selva road.

PASSO DI CRISTALLINA
The Cristallina area in Ticino's north-western corner is very popular with hikers. The 2568-metre Passo di Cristallina connects the Val Bedretto (which is really just an extension of the Valle Leventina), with the Val Bavona, one of the upper branches of the Valle Maggia. The Cristallina area has scenery more typical for the northern side of the Alps, with the only significant expanse of snowfields and glaciers within Ticino. Having been extensively developed for hydroelectricity, these are some of Switzerland's most industrially productive mountains. The four or five small storage dams detract little from the magnificence of the high-Alpine scenery, however, and as engineering feats they definitely inspire admiration.

Walking Times & Standard
The Passo di Cristallina can be done as a day walk, although stretching the hike out to two days is a more leisurely option. The walk presents few difficulties for fit and properly equipped walkers accustomed to mountain conditions. The route is generally well-marked in red-white-red, with fixed cables above steep-sided sections to reassure nervous walkers. Snow is likely to cover higher sections of the route early in the season, and on the northern approach to the pass a small permanent snowfield must be negotiated.

The Passo di Cristallina walk has a total distance of around 18 km and is rated *moderate*.

Maps
The map that best covers this walk is the 1:50,000 SAW/ESS sheet *Nufenenpass (265 T)*. Other alternatives are Editions MPA Verlag's 1:50,000 *Valle Maggia-Val Verzasca*, or Kümmerly + Frey's *Ticino Sopraceneri*, scaled at 1:60,000. The 1:50,000 K + F sheet *San Gottardo* is also of use, although it only just includes the Capanna Basodino and completely cuts off San Carlo.

Places to Stay
The most convenient place to stay will probably be the *Capanna di Cristallina* (☎ 091-866 23 30 or 091-994 66 83, open early June to mid-October), roughly the midway point of the walk. This large SAC-run hut has the usual mattress rooms and excellent meals are served. The *Albergo Robièi* (☎ 091-756 50 20, open early June to early October) by the upper Robièi cable-car station has a range of nice rooms and a dormitory (with free use of showers). A short way down is the SAC's *Capanna Basodino* (☎ 093-68 26 50, open throughout the year).

No accommodation is available in Ossasco, though there is a small restaurant. See the respective Walking Bases sections for places to stay in Airolo and San Carlo.

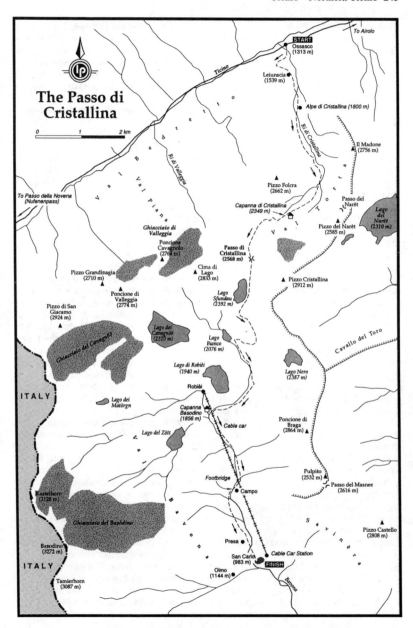

The Passo di Cristallina

Getting to/from the Walk

The walk begins at Ossasco (1313 metres), a tiny village in the Val Bedretto some 10 km by road west from Airolo (see Walking Bases). Postbuses to Ossasco run from Airolo post office (near the railway station) about a dozen times a day from late May to early October; outside this time services are far less frequent.

The walk ends in the upper Val Bavona at San Carlo (see Walking Bases). From Robièi walkers have the option of taking the cable car down to San Carlo, which cuts out the final section of Stage 2. Departures are hourly, the last at around 5 pm.

Stage 1: Ossasco to Capanna di Cristallina

(6 km, 2½ to 3½ hours)

From the postbus stop on the uphill side of Ossasco, take the signposted trail which immediately leads over the stone footbridge and alongside the gushing Ri di Cristallina. Climb steeply through mixed conifer and broadleaf forest, ignoring several track turnoffs to reach **Leiunscia** at 1539 metres after 30 to 45 minutes. A large clearwater spring flows out of the ground here, and it's a nice spot for a quick rest.

The path heads on a few paces to meet a rough road, and crosses this a number of times, cutting off sharp bends as it ascends. Continue up through open larch forest and lovely Alpine meadows scattered with martagon lilies to arrive at **Alpe Cristallina** after a further 40 to 50 minutes. This group of farm buildings lies just above the forest line at 1800 metres, and looks out north towards the mountains of the Gotthard massif.

Pick up the trail above the long barn, and follow the white-red-white paint markings that lead across slopes covered with Alpine rhododendrons. The path makes its way up beside the cascading stream, passing the memorial plaque to Mario Leonardi (a warden of the Cristallina hut who was killed here by an avalanche in 1964) before entering the pleasant **Val Torta**, where the gradient eases. Head a short way on past a signposted intersection where a side route over the Passo del Narèt leaves off left, then continue up over grassy hills to reach the **Capanna di Cristallina** (see Places to Stay), 1¼ to 1¾ hours from Alpe Cristallina; this large mountain hut lies at 2349 metres.

Stage 2: Capanna di Cristallina to San Carlo

(11.5 km, 4 to 5½ hours)

From the hut walk on towards the obvious pass at the head of the tiny upper valley, passing under the decidedly unscenic row of high-tension power lines. This is otherwise a typical glacial-recession landscape, with several small lakes among the mounds of recent moraines. Follow the path up along the right side of the gully, which invariably remains snow-covered long into the summer, to reach **Passo di Cristallina** after 40 to 50 minutes. The 2568-metre pass is the highest point on this walk and offers direct views of the Ghiacciaio del Basodino, a broad névé to the south-west. To the west are the peaks of Cima di Lago, Poncione di Valleggia and Pizzo di San Giacomo, all slightly less than 3000 metres. A tiny lake lies in the rocky basin just below the pass.

Drop down first in short switchbacks, then cut left across the slope along a graded track that quickly brings Lago Sfundau into view. Lying in a deep trough, **Lago Sfundau** (or 'sunken lake') has no visible outlet and is generally ice-chocked even during high summer. Although Lago Sfundau is a natural lake, the peculiar waterfall that spurts out of the adjacent rock wall is an artificial feeder tunnel, not a natural stream.

Continue around high above the eastern shore of Lago Sfundau (with occasional fixed cables to provide extra confidence), then climb on away from the lake to reach a cliff face, 30 to 40 minutes from Passo di Cristallina. Immediately below in the valley is Lago Bianco, a natural lake, and just to the right the impressive arched dam wall of the 2310-metre high Lago dei Cavagnöö; also visible to the south are two other hydroelectricity reservoirs, Lago di Robièi and Lago del Zött.

Following the standard white-red-white paint markings, make your way down across the open rocky slopes, passing the signposted path to Lago Nero after 20 minutes. This natural lake is an easy 15 to 20 minutes' walk away and makes a pleasant side trip. From the Lago Nero track intersection descend right for 15 to 20 minutes via a steep ridge to meet a surfaced road leading around Lago Bianco.

Walk 400 metres down to a road bridge, from where a slower route (signposted 'Lielp') follows the left side of the Barona stream to the **Capanna Basodino** (see Places to Stay). Otherwise continue 45 minutes to one hour down the road to the upper station of the Robièi cable car, then either take the cable car down to San Carlo or drop down another five to 10 minutes to the Capanna Basodino.

The well-constructed path down to San Carlo leaves from below the Capanna Basodino, descending steeply along the left side of the narrow **Bavona** stream under cliffs and cable-car wires. After passing through the hamlet of **Campo**, cross the stream on a footbridge, and continue down steeply through the forest past the historic chapel at **Presa**. The disproportionately large bell tower shows the year 1638, but the small church has frescoes of early 16th-century origin. You reach the road below the ground station of the Robièi cable car after 1½ to two hours. The nearest postbus stop is five to 10 minutes' walk on below the village of **San Carlo** (see Walking Bases).

OTHER WALKS
The Gotthard Lakes Circuit

Apart from forming a clear north-south division, the Gotthard region is a geographical centre separating the western and eastern Alps. This easy return day walk sets off from the 2191-metre Passo del San Gottardo, with its historic hospice (rooms and dorm accommodation), chapel and museum, leading through an interesting highland plateau scattered with lovely Alpine lakes and moorland. Take the Lago di Lucendro road turn-off 500 metres north of the Gotthard pass height,

then continue to about midway around the northern side of the reservoir. From here a signposted path makes its way up past the Laghi della Valletta and the Laghi d'Orsirora to Lago d'Orsino, before descending back to meet the road at the Lago di Lucendro dam wall.

From late June until late September postbuses run three times daily between Airolo and Andermatt via the Passo del San Gottardo, and there is one additional bus from Airolo terminating at the pass height. Reservations are obligatory (call PTT Andermatt on ☎ 041-887 11 88, or PTT Airolo on ☎ 091-869 13 53). The Swiss military (EMD/DMF) carries out regular shooting exercises in the Gotthard area, so it's advisable to contact the local EMD/DMF information office in Airolo on ☎ 091-869 15 70. The average walking time is five hours, but motorists can drive right to the car park at the Lago di Lucendro dam wall, thereby shortening the walk by at least one hour. The 1:50,000 Kümmerly + Frey sheet *San Gottardo* is the recommended walking map.

The Strada Alta

The 45-km-long Strada Alta runs between Airolo and Biasca along the old track used by the muleteers on the Passo del San Gottardo route. This 'high road' followed a course far up the north-eastern sides of the Valle Leventina in order to avoid the gorges, flooding and rockfalls that often made travel in the valley floor a dangerous prospect.

Gently rising and dipping at a relatively constant level of 1000 to 1400 metres, today this ancient panoramic roadway makes an ideal walking route. The Strada Alta leads through highland forests, subalpine pastures and some of northern Ticino's most picturesque mountainside villages where traditional Alpine farming methods are still widely practised. The walk is in the *easy-to-moderate* range, and can be done in two – or better three – day stages. The Strada Alta is very popular with walkers, and most of the villages you pass through on the way have good accommodation options. The 1:50,000

SAW/ESS sheet *Valle Leventina (266 T)* covers the whole of the route.

The Val di Campo

The Val di Campo is a tiny side valley of the upper Val Blenio. Unlike the adjacent Val Luzzone, the Val di Campo has not been dammed for hydroelectricity, and the upper valley area is an expanse of rolling wildflower meadows known as the Alpe di Boverina. From Campo, the uppermost village of the Val Blenio, a gently rising route leads through the Val di Campo before descending to the Passo del Lucomagno (or Cuolm Lucmagn in Romansch), a pass at 1914 metres on the Ticino/Graubünden cantonal border. A worthwhile extension to the walk is to continue around via the Passo dell'Uomo to Lago Ritóm.

The walk normally takes two days, with a night spent at the *Capanna Boverina* (☎ 091-70 16 97), a UTOE-run hut at 1870 metres, and/or the *Hospezi Santa Maria* (☎ 081-947 51 34) at the Passo del Lucomagno height; this hotel has rooms and a walkers' bunkhouse (including showers). From the Passo del Lucomagno, there are postbuses north to Disentis and south to Olivone (see Walking Bases). The walking route is covered by two 1:50,000 SAW/ESS sheets: *Valle Leventina (266 T)* and *Disentis (256 T)*.

The Valle Maggia & Val Verzasca

Although the mountains of central-western Ticino have a lower average height than the main Alpine summits farther to the north, they rise from their valley floors with surprising abruptness. The Valle Maggia and the Val Verzasca are two long valleys that drain the rugged ranges of central-western Ticino. With a catchment area that includes various wild and beautiful side valleys, this region takes in over a third of the canton. The Maggia and Verzasca rivers flow southwards from the mountains fringing the Val

Leventina to enter Lago Maggiore on either side of the city of Locarno.

Once much more densely settled, both valleys – but particularly the Val Verzasca – experienced a dramatic population drift from the mid-1800s, severely reducing their already marginal agricultural base. Left to nature, old mule tracks have overgrown, abandoned alp huts have disappeared under tangled thickets and the advancing forest has reclaimed former pastures. Today tracts of new wilderness separate the scattered villages. With low, easily crossed passes and few glaciers to block the way, this is arguably the most attractive region for walking in Ticino.

WALKING BASES

Locarno

Situated on the north-eastern shoreline of Lago Maggiore at just 197 metres, Locarno is the lowest city in Switzerland. With its grand old villas built in the Lombardic style and balmy subtropical climate, Locarno has something of a Riviera atmosphere. The city hosts the Locarno Film Festival in the first two weeks of August – when hotels are completely booked out.

One budget place to stay in Locarno is the *Albergo Montaldi/Stazione* (☎ 091-743 02 22) across the road from the train station. The cheapest rooms are in the rear annexe. Locarno's tourist office (☎ 091-751 03 33) is a short way from Piazza Grande. Locarno is not on the main Gotthard rail line, but there are trains from Bellinzona almost half-hourly. The city is also linked with Brig in the Valais by the railway route via Domodossola in Italy (which is covered by Swiss rail passes). The *Palmolino* (or *Palm Express*), a PTT-run bus service, runs from Lugano via Italy's Lago Como region to St Moritz in Graubünden; reservation is obligatory (call ☎ 091-807 95 20).

Bosco/Gurin

This interesting village lies at the end of the Valle di Bosco, a small side valley of the Valle Maggia. Apart from being the highest permanently occupied village in Ticino,

Bosco/Gurin (1503 metres) is the canton's only established German-speaking settlement. The Guriners are descendants of Walsers, colonists originally from Goms in the upper Valais who resettled from the adjacent (now Italian) Valle Formazza (Pomattal) in 1244. Bosco/Gurin's wood-based houses, such as the 18th-century Walserhaus containing the village museum, contrast with the heavy stone constructions seen elsewhere in Ticino.

The only accommodation in the village itself is the 20-bed *Hotel Edelweiss* (☎ 091-754 12 45), but there is talk of opening a youth hostel here in the not too distant future. Bosco/Gurin has a small local camping ground down across the river.

Bosco/Gurin is accessible by public (FART) bus from Locarno – you change to a postbus at the village of Cevio in the main Valle Maggia. There are up to four daily buses between Cevio and Bosco/Gurin all year round; the last leaves Cevio around 6 pm, and returns from Bosco/Gurin at about 6.30 pm.

San Carlo (Val Bavona)

Not to be confused with its namesake in the adjacent Valle di Peccia, San Carlo (938 metres) is the uppermost settlement in the wild Val Bavona. Another of Ticino's typical stone villages, San Carlo's church dates from 1595 and has interesting 17th-century frescoes. It is the only place in the Val Bavona with a permanent (ie all year-round) population and (mains) electricity – a spin-off of hydro dams in the Cristallina region at the head of the valley, which have reduced the Ri di Bavona to a pitiful trickle. San Carlo makes an excellent base for walks into the Cristallina region (quickly accessible by the Robièi cable car) as well as the rugged mountains along Ticino's western frontier with Italy.

The only accommodation is the *Ristorante Basòdino* (☎ 091-775 11 92, open June to October), with just eight beds for tired walkers. Frequent public (FART) buses run between Locarno and Bignasco, where you must change to a smaller PTT minibus for San Carlo. From early April to the end of October there are some four connections in either direction, with the last postbus leaving Bignasco not long after 4 pm, and returning from San Carlo at about 5 pm.

Sonogno

Situated at the head of the Val Verzasca, Sonogno (at 918 metres) lies well within range of central Ticino's higher peaks. Despite its remoteness, a steady stream of visitors is attracted by the village's charming stone houses and little laneways, as well as the outstanding walks into the surrounding mountains. There is a small museum, while the Casa della Lana sells locally produced wool.

Along with walks up to Passo Barone and Laghetto (included below in the Barone Circuit), some of the popular routes from Sonogno are the Forcletta di Redorta, the Bochetta di Mügaia and the Corte di Cima.

The only hotel-type accommodation in Sonogno is the *Ristorante Alpino* (☎ 091-746 11 63), which offers quite reasonably priced rooms. Also ask here about private rooms in local homes. A small store sells basic groceries.

Postbuses run between Locarno and Sonogno some six times daily in either direction throughout the year. The trip, lasting a bit over an hour, takes you right through the beautiful Valle Verzasca. The valley road is open to private traffic, and cars can be parked near the post office.

SAN CARLO TO BOSCO/GURIN

This walk introduces you to one of Ticino's wildest and most scenic corners – the spectacular mountain ranges fronting the Swiss-Italian border between the Val Bavona and the Val di Campo, two side valleys of the Valle Maggia.

No other large valley in Ticino has the dramatically enclosed features of the Val Bavona, whose sheer and unstable sides gave way in a catastrophic rock landslide in 1594. Whole forests and villages were buried under millions of tonnes of rubble, and life in the valley never fully recovered. With the steady population drift over the last century or so, mountain pastures and agricultural fields have fallen into disuse.

The relative remoteness of this region is a boon to serious walkers, who can explore a little-visited Alpine landscape of rugged peaks, crisp glacial lakes, highland heath, semi-abandoned shepherds' cottages, and rough moraine slopes. Interesting too is the area's mixture of (Germanic) Walser and Italian elements, reflected in local place names and architecture.

Maps

Most recommended is the Kümmerly + Frey sheet *Ticino Sopraceneri* at a scale of 1:60,000. Although MPA's 1:50,000 *Valle Maggia-Valle Verzasca* is actually a better map and a very good alternative, its coverage doesn't include much of the adjoining Italian territory to the west.

Walking Times & Standard

This is basically a two-day walk, the second of which is relatively long and tiring. There are two route options, a lower route (Stage 2A) and an alternative high-traverse route (Stage 2B). Both go through extensive sections of steep, loose rock, but the latter, although well marked, is extremely rugged with much clambering over rock, and is suitable only to experienced mountain walkers during fine weather. Also bear in mind that these mountains are rather prone to summer thunderstorms.

The walk is rated *difficult* and is around 17 km.

Places to Stay

The cosy 45-bed *Rifugio Piano delle Creste* (☎ 091-775 14 14) at 2108 metres is several hours up from San Carlo. Actually two huts, the rifugio is for self-caterers only, and belongs to the local ·Società Alpinistica Valmaggese (SAV). Canned drinks are on sale, but you'll have to bring all food with you; showers are available for an extra fee. Although some walkers camp at the Laghi di Formazzöö (or elsewhere), the next en-route accommodation is the *Capanna Grossalp*

(☎ 091-754 16 80, open early June to late October), a hard day's walk away at Grossalp above Bosco/Gurin. This FAT/UTOE-run hut has a restaurant and showers, and charges quite reasonable rates.

For places to stay in San Carlo and Bosco/Gurin, see Walking Bases above.

Getting to/from the Walk

The walk begins in San Carlo and finishes at Bosco/Gurin; access to both these villages is in the previous Walking Bases section.

Stage 1: San Carlo to Rifugio Piano delle Creste

(4 km, 3 to 3½ hours)

A signpost at the postbus stop (938 metres) by the road bridge just before **San Carlo** directs you into the beech forest past a small shrine dedicated to St Francis of Assissi to begin the long winding ascent on a sometimes stepped path beside the deep ravine of the **Val d'Antabia**. Ignoring unmarked trails leading off to the left, climb steeply through mountainside clearings with lonely stone cottages, then traverse up leftwards through the larch trees, crossing debris-chocked side-streams before you come to **Corte Grande** after 2¼ to 2¾ hours. This group of rustic shepherds' huts sits at 1914 metres on nettle-infested slopes looking out towards the adjacent crags of Pizzo Castello.

Make your way on up – rather more gently now – over the open rolling slopes of **Alpe di Antabia**, then move down into the basin of a tiny mountain stream. The route heads quickly across the grassy flats, before following a short ridge up to arrive at **Rifugio Piano delle Creste** (see Places to Stay), 40 to 50 minutes on. These huts are situated at 2108 metres in a beautiful upper-Alpine valley bordered by high peaks on the Swiss-Italy frontier such as the 3272-metre Basòdino, and Pizzo Solögna which lies to the south-east.

Stage 2A: Rifugio Piano delle Creste to Bosco/Gurin

(13 km, 6 to 8 hours)

Now leaving the route going on over the

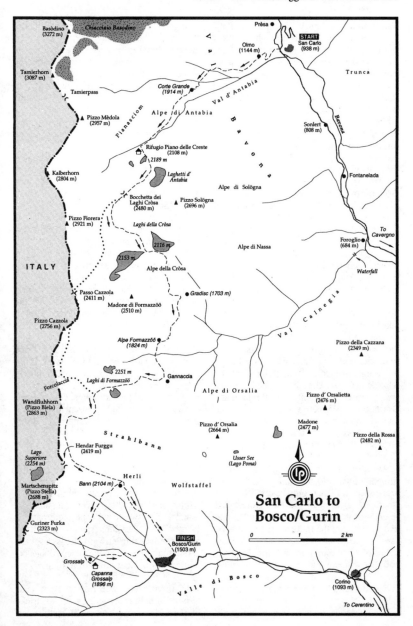

San Carlo to
Bosco/Gurin

Tamierpass into the Val Formazza in Italy, head roughly southwards through a shallow gully and up past the smaller lake of the **Laghetti d'Antabia**. Bearing right at a junction not far on, ascend via a small ridge past the larger upper lake (2189 metres), whose deep-blue waters nestle into screeslides below Pizzo Solögna. Follow the white-red-white markings on around to the right up the broken-rock slopes, finally cutting along an uneven grassy ledge – with fixed ropes for moral rather than physical support – to reach the obvious gap in the jagged ridge after one to 1¼ hours. Known to locals as the **Bocchetta dei Laghi Cròsa**, this point lies at around 2480 metres and enjoys a splendid view back into the upper Val d'Antabia.

Descend directly to a signposted route intersection at the small tarn visible from above, where the two picturesque Alpine lakes called the **Laghi della Cròsa** come into sight; Stage 2B departs from here. Continue left through more rocky terrain, then sidle along a mostly grassy ridge leading down across the stony outlet of the upper lake (2153 metres). Walk a short distance around the lower lake's steep southern side, then pick up a cairned and paint-splashed route that cuts up over the hilltop before dropping down to a derelict shelter at the Alpe della Cròsa. The path descends on very steeply through mountain heath to reach **Gradisc** at 1703 metres, 45 minutes to one hour from the bocchetta. Several stone huts stand on this grassy little shelf fringed by raspberry thickets high above the wild Val Calnegia.

Avoiding the main foot track going straight down into the valley, find a less pronounced trail that contours off to the right (southwards) through the larch forest and abandoned Alpine pastures. Although prone to overgrowing, the route is easily followed across an avalanche chute to reach the scattering of rustic buildings at **Alpe Formazzöö** (1824 metres) after 35 to 45 minutes. Small herds of adroit chamois find a favoured habitat on these remote mountainsides.

Waymarkings near the upper hut guide you gently on over pretty moors and rhododendron fields, crossing several streamlets before climbing more steeply up through tiered grassy slopes to the west. After 50 minutes to 1¼ to hours you get to the upper lake (2251 metres) of the **Laghi di Formazzöö**. With green sunny lawns around the outer shore and talus rubble edging the lake's inner sides, these crisp clear waters make a challenging spot for a (quick) dip on a hot day.

Cross the lake outlet and make your way up steeply again through a broad expanse of the granite-slab rock overlooking the lower lake to reach a yellow signpost, where a high route (Stage 2B) intersects from the right. Watching carefully for bright paint splashes on broken blocks in this bare landscape, traverse up leftwards for some distance, then double back to the right over rough moraines past a tiny grassy gap (this is a false pass, which nevertheless offers a nice overview of Grossalp). The actual ridge crossing is a little farther up across a snow gully below the 2863-metre **Wandfluhhorn (Pizzo Biela)**, one to 1⅓ hours from the upper Formazzöö lake.

Rock-hop southwards onto the poor uppermost pastures, picking up walking pads that lead down along steep and muddy ridges to meet a well-trodden international path below the Hendar Furggu. Go left here, cutting down through pleasant undulating meadows to reach the alp cottages of **Bann** at 2104 metres after one to 1¼ hours.

Walkers who still have the time and energy can take an interesting longer route to Bosco/Gurin going off left up to the Uesser See (Lago Poma), one of three well-spaced tarns on an elongated high terrace, a worthwhile route alternative taking an additional 1½ to two hours. The main path to Bosco/Gurin descends steeply into light larch forest, edging leftwards across a stream about midway to reach the upper village, 50 minutes to one hour down from Bann.

Via Capanna Grossalp Take the right-hand turn-off from Bann, crossing countless trickling brooklets as you contour along the open slopes. Where you meet a dirt track, cut down left under winter ski tows through the dozen-odd stone buildings of **Grossalp** to reach the black-stained wooden hut after 35 to 45 minutes. The **Capanna Grossalp** stands at 1896 metres and overlooks the Valle di Bosco, whose lower half is indeed heavily forested. The 40 to 50-minute walk down to **Bosco/Gurin** shortcuts bends in the road as it follows the line of chair lifts through light forest, then swings left under the wires and descends alongside a stream to the edge of the village. The unusual elongated form of a 17-stage hay barn you pass here serves as protection from avalanches.

Stage 2B: Rifugio Piano delle Creste to Bosco/Gurin via Passo Cazzola

(12 km, 6 to 7½ hours)
On the whole this high-level alternative is more scenic, but although reasonably well marked it is definitely a fine-weather route for experienced mountain-goers only.

From the small tarn below the Bocchetta dei Laghi Cròsa (see Stage 2A), follow the blue and white stripes off right, sidling around a sloping terrace high above the lakes to the **Passo Cazzola** at 2411 metres on the Swiss-Italian border. The route markings lead on southwards up the right side of the main rock range, edging over unstable scree-slopes and snowfields to a gap (identified by a large cairn) in the ridge 200 metres north-east of **Pizzo Cazzola**. Along this section there are magnificent views north-westwards to the summits of the 3235-metre Punta d'Arbola (Ofenhorn) and the 3373-metre Corno Cieco (Blinnenhorn) sticking out of extensive icefields where Italy fronts the Swiss Valais.

Drop down a short distance and begin traversing rightwards along the bare slopes to just below the pass named **Forcolaccia**. Descend 200 metres through a talus-filled couloir, then climb up to the right through a break in the rock cliffs. The route picks its way across slab mountainsides to meet the path coming up from the Formazzöö, Laghi di at an avalanche-battered signpost, where you rejoin Stage 2A.

BARONE CIRCUIT

The area around the 2864-metre Pizzo Barone is Alpine Ticino at its best. This excellent walking tour leads past two lovely highland lakes, over two mountain passes and through two wild little valleys in one of the most inaccessible parts of the canton's central-western ranges. Ironically, the seemingly pristine nature of the Barone area is due to its over-exploitation in the first half of the 19th century, when the uncontrolled clearing of its once luxuriant forests turned these highland valleys into unproductive and dangerous ravines. Having been left to recover by itself, the vegetation has now largely regenerated. In recent years a small herd of ibex has taken up residence in these mountains. Today this is a surprising wilderness that attracts a modest but increasing number of hikers.

Maps

The following walking maps cover all of the circuit's route: the 1:50,000 SAW/ESS sheet *Val Verzasca (266 T)*, Editions MPA Verlag's *Valle Maggi-Valle Verzasca* also scaled at 1:50,000, and Kümmerly + Frey's 1:60,000 walking map *Ticino Sopraceneri*.

Walking Times & Standard

The circuit is probably best done in three walking days, with a night spent at any two of the mountain huts en route. (The four walking stages in the route description may be too short for many hikers.) The red-white-red route markings are generally adequate, but the path often goes through rocky terrain. There is quite a bit of climbing and descending, so apart from stout footwear you'll need a good level of physical fitness. Also keep an eye on the weather, as these mountains tend to catch passing thunderstorms. If you don't feel like tackling such a long or difficult walk, the nearby Campolungo Circuit is a good alternative.

The Barone Circuit is rated *difficult* and covers around 28 km.

Places to Stay

Mountain huts provide the circuit's only en-route accommodation. These are the *Capanna Cògnora* (☎ 091-745 28 87); the large three-storey *Capanna Sponda* (☎ 091-745 23 52), an SAT club hut; and the small *Rifugio Barone* (☎ 091-859 07 06), which has sleeping space for 15 people. These are self-catering type huts without a resident warden but are always left open for walkers. Apart from drinks, you will have to carry supplies for the whole trip in your pack. An honesty system applies for the payment of hut fees – don't abuse it.

For places to stay in Sonogno, see Walking Bases above.

Getting to/from the Walk
The circuit's starting and finishing point is Sonogno (see under Walking Bases), at the end of the Valle Verzasca. Motoring walkers can leave their vehicles right by the trailhead, 3.5 km up from Sonogno.

Stage 1: Sonogno to Capanna Cògnora
(5 km, 3 to 4 hours)
Walk a few paces uphill from Sonogno post office and turn right at the main street. This leads north-east into the Val Vegorness, quickly leaving the village for green hay fields littered with blocks of rock that must have crashed down from the mountainsides above. Follow the road up along the narrow valley floor past clustered hamlets, crossing the Verzasca on a bridge one km before you get to a signpost indicating the trailhead, 45 minutes to one hour from Sonogno. The remains of an old stone-wall dam used to float timber can still be seen on both sides of the river.

The route heads up steeply beside a tumbling stream, which it crosses twice in quick succession before veering right to begin a long winding ascent of the very steep slopes. Higher up the gradient eases, with attractive stands of larch trees followed by meadows of Alpine rhododendrons, and after two to three hours of solid climbing you arrive at the **Alpe di Cògnora**. On this tiny grassy terrace at 1938 metres stands the **Capanna Cògnora**, gazing out to the west over the deep trough of the Val Vegorness towards the

adjacent peaks of Cimetta di Cagnoi and Corona di Redorta. Grazing stock haven't been driven up here for generations, and this neat stone hut was converted from a disused herder's shelter.

Stage 2: Capanna Cògnora to Capanna Sponda
(7 km, 3 to 4 hours)
From the hut swing up around to the left, following the well-cut foot track as it rises and dips along slanted shelves between bands of cliffs. There are some fixed cables and ladders for added security. After 50 minutes to one hour you'll come up to the flat grassy saddle of the **Passo di Piatto** (2108 metres). Immediately below lies a basin filled by the clear bluish waters of Lago di Chironico.

Drop a short way to the right, then follow the white-red-white paint markings back left through a short section of scree. The path contours on around the western rim of **Lago di Chironico** above high bluffs, before heading down a small scrubby ridge to reach the north shore after 40 to 50 minutes. Remains of an old dam wall here bear witness to previous human exploitation, though the Lago di Chironico (1763 metres) has long since returned to its former natural state. The lake's decidedly cool waters are enticing in hot weather, but swim well away from the still-functioning outlet tunnel.

Pick up the route at a broad flat rock, and continue quickly past a stone fishing cottage. Across the valley the compact little village of Cala stands out clearly on the isolated mountainside. The route now steers off leftwards to make a descending traverse into the Val Chironico, coming out of the stunted forest at an avalanche slope covered by bilberry and raspberry bushes. Cut up through this rocky area towards the powerful waterfall surging from a small gorge, where a footbridge leads you over the Ticinetto stream. No roads penetrate this intact upper valley area, and it remains a surprising wilderness so close to the Valle Leventina.

At a signposted intersection not far down the left (northern) bank of the river, take the

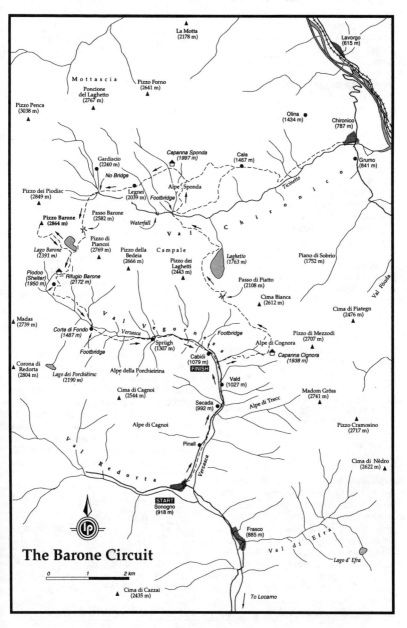

The Barone Circuit

0   1   2 km

initially vague left-hand trail. This direct route up leads past a semi-abandoned stone shelter, before climbing more steeply in zigzags first through pleasant larch forest then up over Alpine pastures. When you meet the more distinct path (coming from Cala) at two barns, proceed left for 500 metres to arrive at the **Capanna Sponda** (1997 metres, see Places to Stay), 1½ to two hours from Lago di Chironico – the lake is visible from the hut.

Stage 3: Capanna Sponda to Rifugio Barone

(5 km, 2¾ to 3½ hours)

Find the continuation of the foot track below the capanna's flagpole and start sidling along the often boggy mountainsides past lonely alp huts. The route crosses numerous streamlets coming down from the slab-rock faces higher up to reach a grassy basin at the very head of the valley. There is no bridge, but several sidestreams joining here to form the Ticinetto are easily jumped as you begin ascending southwards over the moraine-scattered slopes.

Paint markings or the odd cairn show the way up across a large permanent snowfield, then on in steep zigzags through very loose rubble. At times it's pretty hard going. A short final climb up a rocky chute brings you to the **Passo Barone** at 2582 metres, two to 2½ hours after leaving Capanna Sponda. In the rugged cirque immediately below is the kidney-shaped **Lago Barone** (2391 metres), whose deep, blue waters can stay icebound well into July.

A winding foot track now takes you back down into the watershed of the Verzasca, descending to the lakeshore over partially revegetated scree-slopes and lingering winter snowdrifts. Walk on around the grassed-over moraines at Lago Barone's southern edge to where the trail up to the 2864-metre Pizzo Barone departs. White-red-white route markings lead up in an S-bend through talus on the lake's south-eastern sides. Make your way down past where the subterraneous lake outlet emerges, following this stream a short way before

easing over to the right to reach the cosy **Rifugio Barone** (see Places to Stay) at 2172 metres after 40 to 50 minutes. In front of this converted old alp dairy the land falls away abruptly into the Val Vegorness, with the Corona di Redorta rising up behind.

Stage 4: Rifugio Barone to Sonogno

(9.5 km, 2¾ to 3½ hours)

The path picks its way through bluffs below the rifugio, dropping down in wide switchbacks past **Piodoo**, an alp hut protected from avalanches by a sizeable boulder. From here the ridge running between Pizzo Barone and the Corona di Redorta appears as a dramatic line of crags and rock turrets. Cliffs not far down from Piodoo force the route leftwards to make a traversing descent that eventually brings you into the valley floor at **Corte di Fondo** (1487 metres) after one to 1⅓ hours.

The remainder of the way through the upper Val Vegorness is easy and very pleasant. Cross over the Verzasca to a brick house, from where a broad mule track continues down along the right bank of the river through alternating patches of light forest and bilberry fields. A series of natural spillways flowing through granite pools offers intrepid bathers a cooling respite from summer heat soon before the path comes to another footbridge slightly upstream from **Cabiói**. Recross and proceed 400 metres past this clustered hamlet of stone buildings to arrive back at the trailhead up to the Capanna Cògnora after one to 1⅓ hours. Now retrace your steps as taken in Stage 1, returning to Sonogno after a further 45 minutes to one hour walk.

THE CIMA DELLA TROSA

This short high-level route leads over the rounded mountaintops immediately north of Lago Maggiore. Passing centuries-old hamlets and villages occupied only in summer and still only accessible on foot or horseback, the walk has a rustic flavour that shows how easy it can be to get off the beaten track in Ticino. Like in other parts of Ticino, many of the mountain farm cottages (called

CLEM LINDENMAYER

CLEM LINDENMAYER

Top: Running from its source at the Jungfraujoch, the 22-km-long Grosser Aletschgletscher is the longest and most voluminous glacier in Europe.

Bottom: Situated at the head of the Val Verzasca, Sonogno (918 metres) lies well within range of Ticino's higher peaks.

CLEM LINDENMAYER

CLEM LINDENMAYER

CLEM LINDENMAYER

CLEM LINDENMAYER

Top Left: Below Monte Boglia on the Monte Brè to Soragno trail.
Top Right: Monte Tamaro can be seen on the Cardada to Mergoscia trail.
Middle Left: The Laghi di Formazzöö makes a challenging spot for a (quick) dip.
Bottom: In rustic Ticino it's easy to get off the beaten track.

rustici) in the tiny Valle di Mergoscia have long been disused and are falling into ruin.

Maps

The most detailed map for this walk is the 1:25,000 sheet *Locarno/Ascona* published by Orell Füssli. Either of the following walking maps will also do: Kümmerly + Frey's *Ticino Sottoceneri* or *Ticino Sopraceneri*, both at a scale of 1:60,000; Editions MPA Verlag's 1:50,000 *Valle Maggia-Val Verzasca*; and the SAW/ESS sheet *Val Verzasca (266 T)* scaled at 1:50,000.

Walking Times & Standard

This is a day walk, though it's recommended that hikers overnight en route (see Places to Stay). Except, perhaps, on the hottest of summer days, this walk can be done from the middle of spring right through to late autumn – a few spring-fed drinking fountains spaced along the route virtually make carrying water unnecessary. Remember that you'll need protection from the elements – at least a hat and rain-jacket – regardless of when you do this walk.

The walk is rated *easy*, and covers a distance of just 10 km.

Places to Stay

Although this is short walk, spending a night 'on the mountain' is a cheaper and more scenic alternative than staying down in Locarno. At the upper cable-car station the *Albergo Cardada* (☎ 091-751 55 91) has better-standard rooms at correspondingly higher rates. The small *Albergo Ristorante Colmanicchio* (☎ 091-751 18 25), near the lower chair-lift station at Cardada, has somewhat cheaper rooms. Higher up at Alpe Cardada (1473 metres) is the recommended *Capanna Ostello Lo Stallone* (☎ 091-743 61 46), a large ski-club hut. It has small bunkrooms with hot showers, and in summer is usually open from about June to September. At the upper chair-lift station is the *Capanna-Ristorante Cimetta* (☎ 091-743 04 33) which has a plenty of dormitory space. There is a restaurant but nowhere to stay

in Mergoscia. For accommodation in Locarno, see Walking Bases above.

Getting to/from the Walk

The walk begins from the upper cable-car station at Cardada at 1332 metres, high above Locarno (see Walking Bases). To get to Cardada first take the funicular from near Locarno train station, or walk up the Via al Sasso to the famous 15th-century Madonna del Sasso sanctuary. It's worth stopping to visit the interesting pilgrim church and museum here, before taking the cable car on up to Cardada. For the less energetic, a chair lift continues up to the top of 1672-metre Cimetta.

From the little village of Mergoscia, at the end of the walk, there are about six daily postbuses back to Locarno; the last one leaves around 7 pm. From Mergoscia you could also continue walking up the Val Verzasca all the way to Sonogno (see Other Walks below).

Route Directions: Cardada to Mergoscia

(10 km, 3¾ to 5 hours)

A funicular/cable-car combination pulls you up from the muggy summer temperatures of Locarno into the crisp air of **Cardada** at 1332 metres. A short stone-laid pathway leads up around through the subalpine forest to the lower station of the chair lift, which those still too lazy to walk the final stretch to Cimetta can take. Otherwise follow the dirt track on up right, climbing around the mainly open slopes past a new panorama restaurant to reach the **Capanna Ostello Lo Stallone** in the grassy sink called **Alpe Cardada** (1488 metres, see Places to Stay) after 30 to 40 minutes.

From the Alpe, the track cuts back left up over the bracken-covered mountainsides, crossing under winter ski tows and the chairlift. It then swings up right, skirting the forest to arrive at the 1671-metre **Cimetta** (see Places to Stay) after 25 to 30 minutes. From just below the upper chair-lift station, take the left-hand path leading quickly down to a tiny saddle (1610 metres) with a springwater fountain. Make a rising traverse of the south-

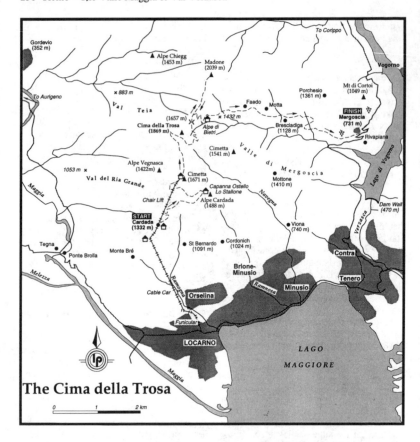

The Cima della Trosa

western slopes of the **Cima della Trosa**, doubling around right up to gain the ridge. A short side trail brings you to the large metal cross mounted on the wind-swept 1869-metre summit after a further 35 to 45 minutes. This lofty spot serves as a great lookout point giving excellent views stretching way across Lago Maggiore and including many surrounding peaks.

After signing the logbook, return to the main path. This soon begins winding down the north-eastern sides of the Cima della Trosa to a minor col at 1657 metres. From here a side trip up to the 2039-metre height of the **Madone** can be done in 1½ to two hours; the straightforward route follows white-red-white paint markings along the ridge, with some harmless rock-scrambling higher up, from where you get a another nice overview of the local scenery.

Descend in broad zigzags through brush and bilberry heath to the goat dairy of **Alpe di Bietri** (1500 metres), and continue on an old mule trail running along the northern slopes of the tiny **Valle di Mergoscia**. Dropping gently against the contour, the route passes dilapidated old houses and rustic hamlets built in local granite to reach the scattered village of **Bresciadiga** (1128 metres), 1¼ to 1¾ hours from the Cima della Trosa.

Bear right at a junction a short way on, where the path dips down into lush forest of chestnuts and beech, leading past small shrines before coming into a car park at the end of a road. Stroll 600 metres downhill to intersect with the main road, then follow the bitumen left up steep hillsides planted out with vineyards to arrive at the little square beside the large Baroque church of **Mergoscia** at 731 metres, after a final one to 1⅓ hours.

This picturesque old village sits high above the Val Verzasca, looking out to the south across stone roofs and the Lago di Vogorno reservoir towards Monte Tamaro (identifiable by the telecommunications tower). Postbuses return to Locarno from the village square. The 'Sentierone' walking route also continues from here up the Val Verzasca as far as Sonogno (see Other Walks below).

OTHER WALKS
The Sentierone (Val Verzasca)
The Sentierone follows the old mule trail up through the Val Verzasca. The walk leads past the ruins of hamlets, old stone fences and disused farm land that was gradually reclaimed by the forest as much of the valley's population migrated to the industrial centres from the mid-1800s. The Sentierone departs from Mergoscia, and leads through occasional villages to Sonogno (see Walking Bases).

The average walking time from Mergoscia to Sonogno is 6½ hours. The Val Verzasca's sunny southerly aspect tends to keep it snow-free in winter, so this walk can be generally done all year round. This is an easy route with the gentlest of inclines, and in warm weather the Verzasca River is perfect for swimming. Mergoscia can be reached from Locarno (by the city's FART line buses), and the return trip from Sonogno (or any of the other half-dozen villages en route) is made by postbus. The 1:50,000

SAW/ESS walking map *Val Verzasca (276 T)* covers the route.

The Val Bavona
At the town of Bignasco the Valle Maggia forks into two upper branches. The western branch is the Val Bavona, Ticino's deepest and most impressive glacial valley. Its sheer walls support numerous towering peaks, and huge boulders lie along the valley floor sheltering stone goatsheds and farm cottages from avalanches. Remote and wildly beautiful, the Val Bavona has a summer-only population, and in winter the valley is virtually abandoned. From Bignasco a thoroughly enjoyable walking route leads up the Val Bavona through quaint hamlets as far as the village of San Carlo (see Walking Bases). The going is easy with a relatively low gradient, but unfortunately the route follows the (often busy) valley road itself in many places. The recommended walking map is Editions MPA Verlag's *Valle Maggia-Val Verzasca* scaled at 1:50,000.

Pian Crosc
This four-hour walk from Bosco/Gurin (see Walking Bases) goes up past the Capanna Grossalp to the Passo Quadrella, a 2137-metre pass crossing leading down to the village of Cimalmotto at 1405 metres in the adjacent Val di Campo. This valley is even more densely forested than the Val di Bosco, with a wild and attractive atmosphere. The *Albergo Alpino* (☎ 091-754 12 54) in Cimalmotto has basic rooms. The recommended map is Kümmerly + Frey's 1:60,000 *Ticino Sopraceneri*.

The Sottoceneri

Known as the Sottoceneri (after the low, 554-metre watershed of Monte Ceneri situated 10 km south-west of Bellinzona) the most southerly part of Ticino forms a conical wedge that protrudes down to meet Italy's Lombardy Plain. This compact region lies in the southern Pre-Alps, an area characterised by lower limestone ranges that nevertheless rise up surprisingly abruptly. Dominated by the contorted shape of Lago di Lugano, the Sottoceneri has a somewhat confusing geography with seemingly irregular borders. The fingers of this large lake spread out through the densely forested Alpine foothills, presenting a magnificent backdrop when viewed from all over the region. Although it makes up no more than 10% of the canton's area, the Sottoceneri offers outstanding walking.

WALKING BASES

Lugano

Ticino's largest city, Lugano lies on a broad bay of Lago di Lugano surrounded by high hills. Among the pedestrian lanes and squares of Lugano's old town are the 16th-century churches of Santa Maria degli Angioli and San Lorenzo. Lugano also has several excellent museums and art galleries (including the Thyssen-Bornemisza in the Villa Favorita, Castagnola – one of the world's greatest private art collections).

There are half a dozen or so camping grounds around the shore of Lago di Lugano, of which *La Piodella* (☎ 091-994 77 88) is the best. Lugano has a *youth hostel* (☎ 091-966 27 28) at Via Cantonale 13. It's closed at the end of October for the winter. The *Hotel Montarina* (☎ 091-966 72 72), at Via Montarina 1, offers similar dormitory accommodation. The *Hotel du Midi Lac* (☎ 091-971 10 21) at Piazza E Bossi 7 in the lakeside suburb of Cassarate has rooms at quite reasonable rates by Lugano's standards. Lugano's tourist office (☎ 091-921 46 64) is at Riva Giocondo Albertolli 5.

Lugano is on the main Gotthard-Chiasso rail and road route. The *Palmolino* (*Palm Express*) bus passes through Lugano en route to St Moritz via Italy's Lago Como region.

Mendrisio

The town of Mendrisio lies at the southern tip of the Sottoceneri known as the Mendrisiotto. Along with several superb old churches the old town hub has many buildings from the 15th to the 18th century. Two

good lower-budget places to stay are the *Ristorante San Gottardo* (☎ 091-646 12 94) and the *Ristorante Grütli* (☎ 091-646 18 60). Mendrisio has a tourist office (☎ 091-646 57 61).

MONTE TAMARO TO MONTE LEMA

This is the Sottoceneri's classic ridge walk, and runs south from the 1961-metre pyramid form of Monte Tamaro to Monte Lema (1621 metres) giving wonderful views of the Ticino Alps, the Pre-Alps and Lago di Lugano. The treeless upper ridgetops are exposed to the winds and southern sun, which has produced a dry vegetation of Alpine grasses and low heath. Grazed only by flocks of hardy sheep and goats, these bare rolling ranges are strangely reminiscent the Scottish Highlands.

Maps

Recommended is the 1:25,000 *Valli di Lugano*, a walking map produced by Orell Füssli. Good alternatives are the 1:50,000 sheet *Locarno-Lugano* (5007) published by Editions MPA Verlag or *Kümmerly + Frey's Ticino Sottoceneri* scaled at 1:60,000.

Walking Times & Standard

This medium-length day hike follows rolling ridges at average heights of over 1600 metres virtually the whole way. There are relatively gentle climbs and descents, but being very exposed to the sun the going on these open ridgetops can get quite hot in summer. It's important that walkers carry plenty of liquids, since there's no running water anywhere along the route. The southerly aspect of this range makes it snow-free both early and late in the season, so the walk can generally be done from early May until late November. This is nevertheless Alpine country, and the appropriate rainwear belongs in the pack.

The walk is graded *easy to moderate* and covers 13 km.

Places to Stay

The *Capanna Tamaro* (☎ 091-946 23 03), is a UTOE-run hut at around 1928 metres with

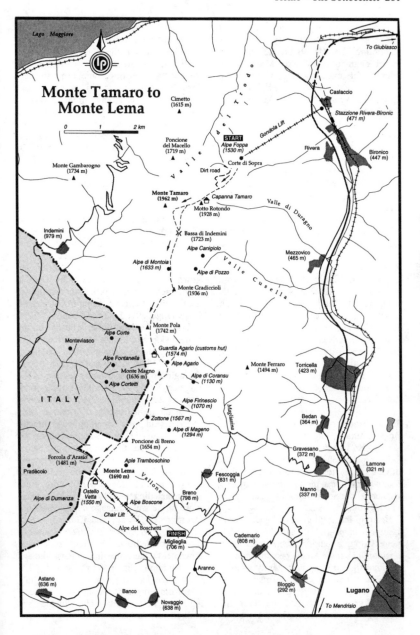

Monte Tamaro to Monte Lema

Lago Maggiore

Cimetto (1615 m)

Poncione del Macello (1719 m)

Monte Gambarogno (1734 m)

Indemini (979 m)

0   1   2 km

To Giubiasco

Caslaccio

Stazzione Rivera-Bironic (471 m)

Gondola Lift

START
Alpe Foppa (1530 m)

Corte di Sopra

Dirt road

Rivera

Bironico (447 m)

Monte Tamaro (1962 m)

Capanna Tamaro

Motto Rotondo (1928 m)

Valle di Duragno

Bassa di Indemini (1723 m)

Alpe Canigiolo

Valle Cusella

Mezzovico (465 m)

Alpe di Montoia (1633 m)

Alpe di Pozzo

Monte Gradiccioli (1936 m)

Monte Pola (1742 m)

Alpe Corte

Monteviasco

Alpe Fontanella

Guardia Agario (customs hut) (1574 m)

Alpe Agario

Monte Ferraro (1494 m)

Torricella (423 m)

Monte Magno (1636 m)

Alpe Cortetti

Alpe di Coransu (1130 m)

ITALY

Alpe Firinescio (1070 m)

Maglasina

Bedan (364 m)

Zottone (1567 m)

Alpe di Mageno (1294 m)

Gravesano (372 m)

Poncione di Breno (1654 m)

Forcola d'Arasio (1481 m)

Aple Tramboschino

Fescoggia (831 m)

Lamone (321 m)

Pradécolo

Monte Lema (1690 m)

Vallone

Breno (798 m)

Manno (337 m)

Ostello Vetta (1550 m)

Alpe Boscone

Alpe di Dumenza

Chair Lift

Cademario (808 m)

Alpe dei Boschetti

FINISH
Miglieglia (706 m)

Bloggio (292 m)

Lugano

Astano (636 m)

Banco

Aranno

Novaggio (638 m)

To Mendrisio

the typical dormitory-style accommodation. More recommendable is the *Ostello-Ristorante Vetta* (☎ 091-967 13 53), at the upper chair-lift station on Monte Lema, which offers excellent value in bunkrooms with (free) hot showers. In Miglieglia, the *Hotel San Stefano* (☎ 091-19 35) has better-standard rooms.

Getting to/from the Walk

This route takes advantage of cableways to gain and lose height at the beginning and end. Unfortunately both cableways are privately owned and offer no concessions. The gondola lift up to Alpe Foppa, the start of the walk, is 10 minutes north by foot from Rivera-Bironico train station. The last ride up goes at around 4.30 pm. Only the slower (at least hourly) regional trains running between Bellinzona and Lugano stop in Rivera-Bironico.

The walk finishes at Monte Lema, from where a chair lift takes you down to the village of Miglieglia. There are some eight postbuses each day to Lugano from Miglieglia, and postbuses running between Rivera-Bironico and Isone also pass through the village roughly every two hours until mid to late evening.

Private vehicles are best left at the car park by the lower gondola-lift station in Rivera-Bironico.

Route Directions: Corte di Sopra to Monte Lema

(13 km, 3¾ to 4½ hours)

Take the gondola lift up more than 1000 altitude metres to the **Alpe Foppa**. Fill up your water bottle at the spring fountain here, as there's precious little water along the walking route.

Head up the open grassy hillsides above the upper cable-car station/cafeteria (1530 metres) along a rough vehicular track under a winter ski tow. Many people prefer to continue right up the more gently winding road, but the white-red-white marked path follows the initially very steep spur past the upper ski-tow station and the futuristic-looking telecommunications tower on

Monte Rotondo (1928 metres) to the Capanna Tamaro (see Places to Stay).

Sidle on around the mountainside along a well-cut mule track to a small gap, then follow the main ridge quickly up to reach **Monte Tamaro**, 1¼ to 1½ hours from Alpe Foppa. The outstanding, almost 360° panorama from the 1962-metre summit includes the three main cities of southern Ticino – Lugano, Locarno and Bellinzona – as well as Lago Maggiore and Lago di Lugano. On your right a picturesque string of isolated villages stretches from Indemini along the forested slopes of the Valle Vedasca into Italy.

Drop down southwards beside an old fence to the small flattened saddle of **Bassa di Indemini** (1723 metres), before climbing on more steeply through stunted Alpine scrub to the top of **Monte Gradiccioli** (1936 metres). A smooth rolling descent brings you down past the grassy hillock of **Monte Pola** (1742 metres) to the reach **Guardia Agario**, a customs hut at a low point (1574 metres) in the range, after 1¼ to 1½ hours.

Traverse fields of bilberry bushes on the eastern slopes of **Monte Magno**, then make your way on to another minor saddle at **Zottone** (1567 metres). The path passes through a narrow and rocky section of the ridgetop, rising on over the **Poncione di Breno** (1654 metres) before it dips down to the small col of **Forcola d'Arasio** at 1481 metres. Head up the steep dirt road directly to arrive at the dome-roofed chair-lift station/hotel (see Places to Stay) just below **Monte Lema** after a final 1¼ to 1½ hours.

The short side trip up to the 1621-metre summit is recommended for more great views, including the lower part of Lago Maggiore to the west, Lugano clustered on the lakeshore far below, and Chiasso further away to the south-east. If you don't want to take the chair lift, a good foot track leads down below the cables in countless zigzags to reach **Miglieglia** in 40 to 50 minutes. It's worth having a wander through Miglieglia's lovely old laneways or visiting the interesting Santo Stefano village church which has 16th-century frescoes.

MONTE BRÈ TO SORAGNO

The 925-metre Monte Brè (not to be confused with another Monte Brè above Locarno) rises up directly from the northern sides of Lago di Lugano. Although one of the lower summits in Alpine foothills, Monte Brè offers superb views across the lake's shimmering blue waters. These porous limestone mountainsides nurture a rich vegetation that thrives in the mild climate produced by the close proximity of Lago di Lugano. Here, many plant species typical for the southern Pre-Alps find their only habitat within Switzerland.

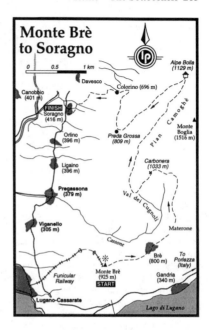

Maps

The recommended maps are the same as for the Monte Tamaro to Monte Lema walk described above.

Walking Times & Standard

This is an easy half-day walk that can be done in any season apart from mid-winter, when snow often covers the upper slopes. Midsummer weather can be uncomfortably hot, but drinking water is available and there are restaurants along the route. October and November are perhaps the best months for the walk, as the area's deciduous forests are then at their nicest and grant better views through the thinning foliage.

The Monte Brè to Soragno walk is 11 km long, and is rated *easy*.

Places to Stay

Although there are small mountain restaurants at Alpe Bolla and Preda Grossa, the only en-route accommodation is the *Albergo Brè* (☎ 091-971 47 61) in the village of Brè, which has better-standard rooms at very reasonable prices.

For suggested accommodation in Lugano see Walking Bases above.

Getting to/from the Walk

To get to the lower station of the Monte Brè funicular, catch the No 9 bus from Lugano station to Piazza Manzoni, then take the No 9 bus to the Cassarate/Monte Brè stop. Except for several weeks in January when it closes for maintenance, the funicular runs half-hourly until 6.15 pm all year round. You can also take the No 12 bus from Lugano's central post office to the village of Brè, a (less attractive) alternative that shortens the walk by 15 to 20 minutes.

The walk finishes at the small village of Soragno (416 metres), from where there are buses back to Lugano approximately every 45 minutes. The last bus to Lugano-Central passes by at around 8.30 pm.

Route Directions: Monte Brè to Soragno
(11 km, 2¾ to 3¼ hours)

The funicular leaves the stifling summer heat around the Lago di Lugano, pulling you up steeply past well-to-do residences on the cooler mountain slopes to the low 925-metre summit of **Monte Brè** in less than 15 minutes. The panoramic terrace looks out across Lago di Lugano to Monte San Salvatore and Monte San Giorgio.

A stepped walkway leads you gently up

through the light forest before dropping down to **Brè** at 800 metres. It's worth having a wander through the narrow stone-paved alleys of this lovely little village, whose parish church dates from 1591. Make your way up past the museum (Museo W Schmid), then head left across the open grassy fields. The route first follows a flagged path (signposted 'Sentiero Alpe Bolla') which crosses a winding road several times as it climbs into the woods, then continues along an old vehicle track fringed by blackberry bushes to reach **Carbonera** (1033 metres) after one to 1¼ hours. There is a water tank here for thirsty walkers.

Ascend steadily on through the beech forest (ignoring a right-hand trail branching off to Monte Boglia), then make a steep climb up to the right. The well-cut foot track sidles north-eastwards around the slope, with glimpses through the beech trees down to Lugano, finally coming out at a path junction at the edge of a small clearing. Walk on across these pretty pastures to arrive at **Alpe Bolla**, 40 to 50 minutes from Carbonera. The farm/restaurant here sits on a narrow terrace at 1129 metres and gives a pleasant view north-west towards the Val Capriasca and the round hump of Monte Gradiccioli.

Retrace your steps to the signpost and descend diagonally through the forest to the restaurant of **Preda Grossa**, in a small clearing at 809 metres. At this point double back around to the right and continue to **Colorino** (696 metres) from where a left-hand path spirals on down to meet a gravelled road. Head 600 metres left, then turn off right onto a narrow old cobbled lane between low stone walls, continuing down right via a stepped pathway that leads under a road bridge to come out at a street just above **Soragno**. The final section follows the bitumen down through the village to reach the main road after one to 1¼ hours. The local bus stop is a short way along to the right.

MONTE GENEROSO

Towering above the eastern shores of Lago di Lugano, the isolated form of Monte Generoso is the most southerly bastion of the Alps. Although at 1701 metres the mountain's height is modest compared with the Alpine summits, Monte Generoso provides a superb natural lookout with vistas stretching north across the lake and south to the plains of Italy's Po River basin. Once threatened by limestone mining for the cement industry, the forested lower slopes are now part of the Monte Generoso nature reserve. Monte Generoso is the only place in Switzerland where the wild peony *(Paeonia officinalis)* blooms.

Maps

Recommended is the Kümmerly + Frey's *Mendrisiotto Basso Ceresio* scaled at 1:25,000. A good, cheap and locally available A4-size walking map is *Monte Generoso Itinerari Consigliati*, also scaled at 1:25,000. The 1:60,000 Kümmerly + Frey sheet *Ticino Sottoceneri* is another alternative, and shows a much larger part of the southern Ticino.

Walking Times & Standard

This long but leisurely downhill walk will take up most of your day. Given suitable weather and snow-free conditions, it can generally be done from mid-May right up until the end of November. The midsummer sun can be quite penetrating, however, so carry some liquid refreshment. There are a few mountain restaurants en route.

The walk is rated *easy*, and covers 12 km.

Places to Stay

Near the train station at Capolago is the *Albergo Svizzero* (☎ 091-848 19 75) which has better rooms with mod-cons, while the *Albergo Chery* (☎ 091-648 11 37) in nearby Riva-San Vitale has standard rooms. The *Albergo Vetta* (☎ 091-649 77 22) on the summit of Monte Generoso has rooms and a bunkhouse (shower available).

Getting to/from the Walk

The walk begins from the summit of Monte Generoso, which can be reached on the historic old cog railway from the village of Capolago on Lago di Lugano. Departures are

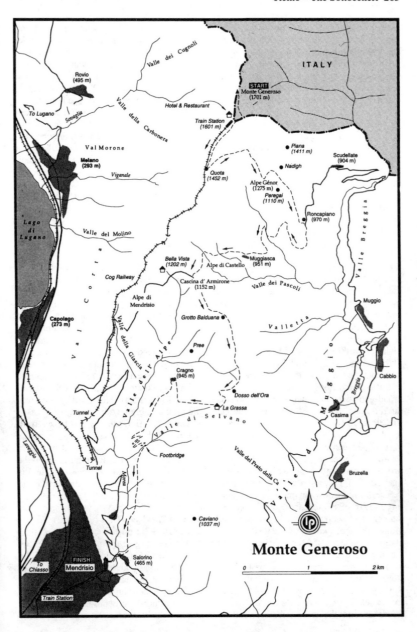

Monte Generoso

0   1   2 km

every one to 1½ hours between the beginning of May and the end of October (when the last uphill trip is at 4.45 pm), but otherwise it's a much reduced service. Various fare concessions apply. You can get to Capolago on one of the tourist ferries that ply Lago di Lugano during the tourist season, or by train via Lugano. Only regional trains stop in Capolago, so the boat may sometimes actually turn out faster.

The walk finishes at the city of Mendrisio (see Walking Bases).

Motorists can leave vehicles at the station car park in Capolago free of charge.

Route Directions: Monte Generoso to Mendrisio

(12 km, 5¼ to 6½ hours)

The cog railway heaves you up to the terminus at 1601 metres. Since it's downhill for the rest of the walk, taking the signposted foot track up the last 100 altitude metres to the 1701-metre top of **Monte Generoso** is a must. In clear weather the magnificent views stretch across the central Alps from Mont Blanc to Piz Bernina in the north. To the south the land sweeps down to the Lombardy plains of northern Italy, and with a good pair of binoculars you should even be able to make out the steeple of the Milan cathedral!

Back at the hotel/restaurant, follow the broad path over the open slopes alongside the rail lines and turn off left when you get to **Quota** at 1452 metres. Sidle on downwards around the heath-scattered slopes, passing between the rustic cottages of **Alpe Génor** (1275 metres) and below the farmhouse of **Nadigh**. The white-red-white marked trail follows a grassy-rocky spur before dropping down to the left to reach the tiny village of **Roncapiano** at 970 metres after one to 1¼ hours. Upvalley is the larger village of Scudellate (904 metres), which clings to the sides of Monte Generoso near the Italian border.

Walk down the narrow road past quaint stone houses to the church at the bottom of Roncapiano, where the road ends. A broad foot track (signposted 'Bellavista') now winds around the steep hillsides, falling gently against the contour through beech forest mixed with wild hazelnuts and gnarled old chestnut trees. When you come to a hillside paddock, climb away to the right along the edge of the trees to the meet a road just uphill from the idyllic little village of **Muggiasca**, 50 minutes to one hour on.

Continue up along the bitumen through hayfields and birch forest to intersect with another road at **Cascina d'Armirone** (1152 metres), then head southwards along the ridgetop past the **Grotto Balduana**, a scenic restaurant with a garden terrace, as far as **Dosso dell'Ora**. Here go 200 metres to the right along a narrow lane and take a signposted path down left to the farmlet/restaurant of **La Grassa**. The route makes a sidling descent around the slopes to arrive at the isolated village of **Cragno** (at 945 metres) after 1½ to two hours.

Turn left at the first road bend a few paces below Cragno, following a disused vehicle track down in repeated switchbacks under a thick cover of forest to cross a large sidestream on a footbridge. Bear left at a fork a short way and cut alongside green pastures to meet a dirt road running through the valley. Proceed 600 metres south to where a cobblestone mule trail descends past vineyards to reach **Salorino** (465 metres), one to 1⅓ hours on from Cragno. The houses of this typical southern-Ticino village have red-tile roofs and big wooden courtyard gates.

There are (infrequent) postbuses from Salorino, but the final section leads over the bridge then immediately down Via Generoso, coming out at the cathedral in the old part of **Mendrisio**. Walk on along the Via Borella to arrive at the train station after 30 to 40 minutes.

OTHER WALKS
Gazzirola & Camoghè

The two neighbouring mountains of Gazzirola (2116 metres) and Camoghè (2227 metres) stand near the southern end of the chain of mountains that stretches from the Passo della Spluga (Splügenpass) along the Swiss-Italian border as far as Monte Brè. Making easily accessible and very scenic lookout points, these are the Sottoceneri's only peaks above 2000 metres and therefore the highest in the region.

A nice route leaves from the village of Corticisaca at 1016 metres, climbing to the rounded 1816-metre top of Monte Bar. The path continues east along the open ridge to the summit of Gazzirola, then turns northwest and traverses over the Camoghè before descending steeply into the Val di Caneggio and following the valley to the village of Isone (743 metres).

The *Refugio Monte Bar*, an SAC hut at 1600 metres on the southern slopes of Monte Bar, provides basic en-route accommodation. To reach Corticiasca take a postbus from Lugano to Tesserete, then change to a postbus running via Maglio di Colla (but not via Bidogno) to Bogno; there are many daily connections. Isone has accommodation and regular postbuses to the railway station at Rivera-Bironico. The average walking time is around eight hours. The recommended walking map is Orell Füssli's *Valli di Lugano* scaled at 1:25,000.

Monte San Salvatore

Monte San Salvatore lies in Lugano's backyard, and is accessible by a funicular (closed from early November to mid to late March) from the lakeside suburb of Paradiso. From the top of this 912-metre-high mountain, the fiord-like arms of Lago di Lugano reach out into Italian territory. A popular four-hour route leads southwards past the village of Carona to Alpe Vicania (659 metres), thence descending through hillside vineyards to the

fishing village of Morcote on Lago di Lugano. There are ferries and buses from Morcote back to Lugano. The 1:60,000 Kümmerly + Frey walking map *Ticino Sottoceneri* covers the route.

Monte San Giorgio

Monte San Giorgio forms a broad and heavily forested peninsula that projects northwards between two arms of Lago di Lugano. Having been little changed by human intervention, much of the Monte San Giorgio area lies with a nature reserve. These ranges sit on a base of ancient volcanic rocks with more recent overlying sedimentary deposits containing rich saurian fossils. The small local museum in the village of Meride (not to be confused with Melide) houses a collection of 200 million year-old fossilised dinosaur bones found near Serpiano.

A short and easy day walk starts out from Meride (578 metres), and climbs up through the forest via Cassina to the 1097-metre lookout summit of Monte San Giorgio, from where there are glorious views across Lago di Lugano. After dropping to the restaurant at Alpe di Brusino, you can descend on foot directly to the small lakeside resort of Brusino-Arsizio, or detour to the nearby chair lift for a faster mechanical descent.

Meride can be reached by postbus from Mendrisio. From Brusino-Arsizio, at the end of the walk, there are buses to the train station at Capolago and ferries across the lake to Lugano. The best walking map is Kümmerly + Frey's *Mendrisiotto Basso Ceresio* at a scale of 1:25,000.

Graubünden

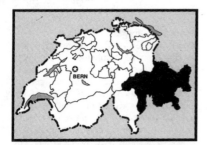

Switzerland's largest and easternmost canton of Graubünden (also known to English speakers as Grisons) makes up almost one-fifth of the county's area. This is a rugged and thinly settled region (around 70% of which lies above 1800 metres) dissected by countless remote mountain valleys that take in some of the wildest and most intact landscapes found anywhere in the Alps. The complex folding and uplifting of the Bündner Alps has brought quite varied rock types to the surface, including limestones, crystalline slates, gneiss and dolomite, giving the landscape a correspondingly varied topography.

Regional isolation is reflected in Graubünden's diverse ethnic mix; although mainly German speaking, the canton also has significant Italian and Romansch-speaking minorities. In many parts of Graubünden Germanic Walser dialects are still spoken, having been introduced from the Goms region of the upper Valais by the first settlers in medieval times.

Spread over three of Europe's major drainage systems, Graubünden's waters flow into the North, Black and Mediterranean seas, giving this pivotal Alpine canton an unusually complex geography. The northern three-quarters of Graubünden is part of the Rhine basin, with its twin upper branches, the Vorderrhein and Hinterrhein. The valley of the Engadine, in the canton's south-east, is drained by the En (or Inn) and lies within the catchment area of the Danube River. The Val Müstair, an appendage of the Engadine, and Graubünden's three most southerly valleys, the Valle Mesolcina, the Val Bregaglia and the Val Poschiavo, all flow southwards into Italy's Po River system.

With its important passes such as the Bernina, Maloja, Splügen, San Bernardino and Lucomagno; Graubünden has a history which has been dominated by the trans-Alpine trade routes. Many of the mountain valleys earned their living by servicing the pass trade, and the control of these vital communication and transport links brought political and economic power. Today, many walking routes in Graubünden follow old mule paths that not so long ago were the only means of carrying cargo across the Alps.

The Northern & Central Bündner Alps

Occupying the north-eastern half of Graubünden's Rhine basin, this region takes in the canton's heartland. Its once overwhelmingly Romansch-speaking inhabitants have gradually been assimilated by the German-Swiss language and culture, and today Romansch survives only in remoter valleys of the Central Bünder Alps.

The Northern Bündner Alps form a hub

around the cantonal capitol of Chur, extending from the Landwasser/Albula River across the Schanfingg and Prättigau valleys to the Rhätikon range on the Swiss-Austrian border. This area includes the majestic peaks around Arosa and the Weisshorn near Davos. The Northern Bündner Alps are the most developed and accessible mountains of Graubünden, but nevertheless have some great areas for hiking.

The Central Bündner Alps present a mighty barrier separating the Engadine from the rest of Graubünden. This range stretches eastwards from the Sursés (Oberhalbstein) Valley Valley as far as the Swiss-Austrian border. Forming the main continental divide, it includes major peaks such as Piz d'Err (3378 metres), Piz Kesch (3418 metres), Piz Vadret (3229 metres), Piz Buin (3312 metres) and the Silvrettahorn (3244 metres). The Central Bündner Alps are accessible by several important pass routes, with roads and/or railways crossing the Julierpass (Pass da Gülia), Albulapass (Pass d'Alvra) and the Flüelapass. These rugged ranges of Central Graubünden are especially well blessed with wild mountain valleys and sparkling glacial lakes.

WALKING BASES

Chur

The cantonal capital of Chur (600 metres) is the only place of any real size in Graubünden. The oldest city north of the Alps, Chur's origins date back to pre-Roman times. The old town has many historically interesting buildings and a very good museum of natural history. A local two-day hike goes up to the 2805-metre summit of the Haldensteiner Calanda, the highest peak of the Calanda range immediately north-west of Chur, via the SAC's *Calandahütte* (☎ 081-353 23 86).

Chur's camping ground is the *Obere Au* (☎ 081-284 22 83) by the Rhine. Accommodation is not cheap, but a reasonable mid-range hotel is the *Rosenhügel* (☎ 081-252 23 88). Chur's tourist office (☎ 081-252 18 18) is at Grabenstrasse 5.

Chur is accessible by regular direct trains from Zürich. The city is one of Switzerland's most important transport hubs, with (Rhaetian Railways) trains to Arosa, Disentis, and St Moritz/Engadine (via the lower Hinterrhein and Filisur). Numerous postbus routes operate out of Chur's imaginative hangar-design bus terminal above the train station.

Klosters

This town lies at 1206 metres in the upper valley of the Prättigau. Originally a monastic settlement, Klosters (ie 'cloisters') has developed into a winter-sports resort favoured by British royals. Of historical interest are its 13th-century church with stained-glass windows and the small local 'Nutli-Hüschi' Walser museum. A simple and rewarding excursion on foot from Klosters follows a popular walking route over the Landquart/Landwasser watershed via the hamlet of Drussetscha (1759 metres), before descending to Davoser See and continuing around the lakeshore to Davos.

Klosters' *youth hostel* (☎ 081-422 13 16) at Talstrasse 73 has dorms and rooms; the *Hotel Malein* (☎ 081-422 10 88) has rooms for low-budget travellers. Klosters is on the Rhaetian Railway's Landquart-Klosters-Filisur line, and trains run hourly.

Davos

Davos sits at 1560 metres in the upper valley of the Landwasser River. The town is divided into two western and eastern parts – Davos Platz and Davos Dorf. Davos is internationally renowned as a centre for winter sports, conferences and scientific research. The Alpinum Schatzalp, at the upper station of the Schatzalp funicular railway, has an extensive Alpine garden nurturing 800 plants from mountain regions all over the world.

The local camping ground is *Färich* (☎ 081-416 10 43). Davos' *youth hostel* (☎ 081-416 14 84) closes for the winter in November. There is a nearby *Friends of Nature hostel* (☎ 081-413 22 66) at Davos-Clavadeleralp (1980 metres). Nearby is the *Höhwaldhof* (☎ 081-416 18 77) in Wolfgang and the *Hotel Edelweiss* (☎ 081-416 10 33) in Davos Dorf have the cheapest rooms. The tourist office (☎ 081-415 21 21) is at Promenade 67.

Davos is on the Rhaetian Railway's Landquart-Klosters-Filisur line, and trains run hourly. If you are coming from Chur or Zürich change at Landquart, or from the Engadine at Filisur. Postbuses run from Davos over the scenic Flüelapass to the Lower Engadine.

St Antönien

St Antönien (1420 metres) is the highest village in the Rhätikon. Originally colonised by Walser families in the 14th century, the St Antöniental is a classic example of a scattered Walser settlement. Until the construction of grids on the surrounding slopes, this highland valley was particularly prone to avalanches, and over the centuries scores of people (and hundreds of farm buildings) in the St Antöniental were claimed by the 'white death'. St Antönien is the best base for hikes in the Rhätikon region. Walking routes such as the three-day Madrisa Circuit (see Other Walks) and the one-day Prättigauer Höhenweg from Klosters pass through or terminate in the village. The Rhätikon Höhenweg is featured in this chapter.

St Antönien also has a *youth hostel* (☎ 081-322 22 38, closed from 1 November until 25 December) not far up from the village. The *Hotel Rhätia* (☎ 081-332 13 61) and the *Haus Alpina* (☎ 081-332 15 85) offer low-budget rooms; the *Hotel Weisses Kreuz* (☎ 081-332 12 06) has better-standard rooms. The village has a small tourist office (☎ 081-332 32 33).

St Antönien is 35 minutes' ride by postbus from Küblis train station; there are up to eight buses per day, the last leaving Küblis around 7 pm. Küblis is on the Rhaetian Railway's Landquart-Davos rail line, so walkers coming from Zürich or Chur should change at Landquart. If arriving by train from the Engadine, Küblis is best reached via Filisur and Davos.

Bergün

Bergün sits at 1367 metres in the upper reaches of the Albula (Alvra) River. In Bergün the local people still speak Romansch, and their ornate houses are built in the solid-stone Bündner style. An interesting and easy two to 2½-hour walk from Bergün follows the so-called Bahnlehrpfad upvalley beside the historical mountain railway completed in 1903. The route spirals its way up via several tight tunnels to the tiny village of Preda (1792 metres). A more difficult local route goes up via an SAC hut across the 2724-metre Pass d'Ela to Tinizong in the adjacent valley of Sursés (Oberhalbstein); see also the Sertigpass walk below.

Bergün has little true budget accommodation, though there are several medium-range places to stay; one is the *Hotel Piz Ela* (☎ 081-407 11 68). Recommended in nearby Preda is the *Vegi-Pension Sonnenhof* (☎ 081-407 13 98). Bergün has a well-known tourist office (☎ 081-407 11 52).

Bergün is a stop on the Rhaetian Railway's Chur-Filisur-Samedan-St Moritz line, and there are at least hourly trains in either direction.

THE RHÄTIKON HÖHENWEG

The Rhätikon Höhenweg follows a route along the high range that runs along the Swiss-Austrian-Liechtenstein border in Graubünden's Rhätikon. With their heavily folded and upturned rock strata these magnificent limestone crags are sometimes called the 'Rhaetian Dolomites', and their resemblance to the mountains of southern Tirol is unmistakable. Alpine rockclimbers value the hard grip of the dolomite rock, yet the Rhätikon's highest peak, the 2964-metre Schesaplana, is quite accessible to non-mountaineers – as indicated by the summit crowds.

Like many parts of Graubünden, the upper valleys on both sides of the Rhätikon were first settled by Walser immigrants from Goms in the upper Valais at a time when the lower valleys were still Romansch speaking, and this is often still recognisable in the local nomenclature.

Maps

Recommended is Kümmerly + Frey's *Prättigau-Albula* scaled at 1:60,000. Two 1:50,000 SAW/FSTP sheets also cover the walk, namely: *Prättigau (248 T)* and *Montafon (238 T)*.

Walking Times & Standard

The Rhätikon Höhenweg is a relatively long three or four-day walk. The route is exceptionally well marked and getting lost is (almost) impossible. However, a high level of fitness, experience in high-Alpine walking, and stable weather conditions are essential particularly for the high-route alternative of Stages 2A and 2B. This is an international walk straddling the frontiers of three separate countries, so be sure to carry your passport with you.

The total distance is 37 km; depending on which route you choose, the walk is rated *moderate* or *difficult*.

Places to Stay

See Walking Bases for places to stay in St Antönien. Mountain club huts form the basis of all en-route accommodation. The first hut passed on the way is *Garschinahütte* (☎ 070-74 27 97), staffed from mid-June to mid-October). There are two Austrian huts both belonging to the Österreichischer Alpenverein (ÖAV) along the route. The *Douglashütte* (☎ 05559-206), at 1979 metres beside the cable-car station on the Lünersee dam wall, has a bunkhouse for walkers (hot showers and sleeping sheets cost extra) and offers simple rooms. If you're doing the high-route alternative over the Schesaplana, the *Totalphütte* (for bookings call ☎ 05447-5274, staffed from mid-June to the end of September) is a large, three-storey timber hut at 2318 metres.

The SAC's *Schesaplanahütte* (☎ 081-325 11 63) is at 1908 metres at the end of Stage 2. It's staffed from mid-June until mid-September, but is always left unlocked. At Bettlerjoch (2108 metres), roughly 3½ hours on, is the 100-berth *Pfälzerhütte* (☎ 075-263 36 79), one of the two huts in the principality run by the Liechtensteiner Alpenverein (LAV). Although it's only staffed from mid to late June until early October, a section of the Pfälzerhütte is always open. It's considerably cheaper than any club hut in Switzerland. (Swiss Francs are the currency of Liechtenstein.)

In Malbun, the *Alpenhotel Malbun* (☎ 075-263 11 81) or the *Hotel Turna* (☎ 075-263 3421) have standard rooms at average prices.

Getting to/from the Walk

The start of the walk is St Antönien-Post (see Walking Bases). If you want to terminate the walk in the middle, a cable car from the Douglashütte on the Lünersee in Austria connects with a postbus service via the (Walser) village of Brand to Brudenz.

The walk finishes in the Liechtenstein village of Malbun, from where there are roughly hourly postbuses to Vaduz between late May and mid-October; the last bus leaves around 7 pm. (The familiar yellow PTT postbuses also operate in Liechtenstein, but fares are much cheaper. A single flat fare is valid for any destination on Liechtenstein's postbus network, even if you change at Vaduz en route to Sargans in Switzerland or Feldkirch in Austria.)

Stage 1: St Antönien to Garschinahütte
(6 km, 2¼ to 3 hours)

Walk 50 metres up the turn-off behind the St Antönien post office (1420 metres), then short-cut to the right over steep pastures back to the road. Continue on up past a sharp curve, taking an old alp track going off rightwards across open slopes that overlook the village to a small telecommunications tower. From here an (unsignposted) path winds up through regenerating coniferous forest to reach the scattered wooden houses of **Älpli** (1801 metres) after 40 to 50 minutes. A small restaurant down to the left offers basic refreshments.

Follow the road on uphill past a hairpin bend, before breaking away north-eastwards onto mountainsides strewn with bilberry heath below a veritable standing army of (rather unsightly) avalanche grids guarding

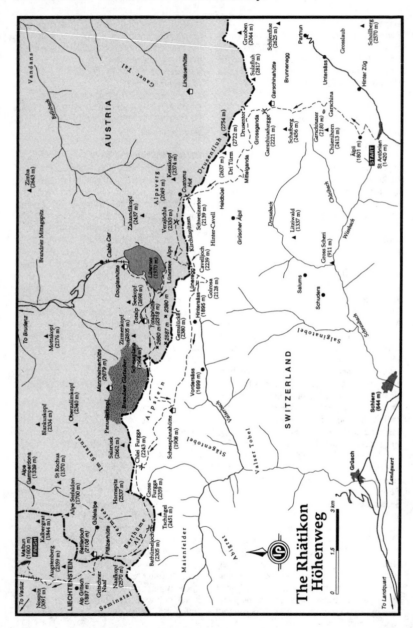

The Rhätikon Höhenweg

St Antönien. The route makes a steadily climbing traverse over rolling Alpine meadows, then cuts up left beside a brooklet to the **Garschinasee**, one to 1¼ hours on. Partially covered with reeds and water lilies, this small lake sits at 2180 metres in a shallow depression of the grassy terrace known as Garschina.

The path leads on over a gentle crest (where the 2817-metre Sulzfluh first comes into view ahead) crossing tiny streams as it rises and dips along the closely cropped slopes to arrive at the **Garschinafurgge** (2221 metres) after 40 to 50 minutes. The **Garschinahütte** (see Places to Stay) stands just east of this saddle before the spectacular backdrop of the Sulzfluh's abrupt sides. Already it will be easy to see why these mountains have been likened to the Dolomites of Italy.

Stage 2A: Garschinahütte to Totalphütte
(13 km, 3½ to 4½ hours)
Head across broken-rubble slopes towards the Drusentorpass, swinging around to the north-west at a branching just before the pass. In the distant west the snowcapped peaks of the Glarner Alps can be made out. The well-trodden path edges below fields of scree and coarse talus separated by broad grassy spurs coming off the impressive grey-white ridge known as the Drusenfluh. Sidle on alongside the sheer walls past side routes going down left towards Grüscher Älpli before beginning a short, steep climb over rock (aided by the odd fixed cable) to reach **Schweizertor** after 1¾ to 2¼ hours. This narrow gap at 2139 metres forms the Swiss-Austrian frontier.

Walk across the boggy basin to an (usually unstaffed) Austrian customs hut, then follow the grassy ridge leading westwards up over the **Verajöchle**, a minor col at 2330 metres. Descend through a tiny valley, where an interesting pinkish rock band marks the screeline along the base of the massive dolomite sides of the Kirchlispitzen range. The path leads around over slopes looking down towards the Lünersee, merging with another

route just after crossing the stream on a footbridge after one to 1¼ hours. At this point, walkers already pining for Switzerland can duck back across the border via the Cavelljoch as described below in Stage 2B/3B.

Make your way down over the meadows of the **Lünersee Alpe**, and continue westwards along the wide track running around the lakeside to the signposted Totalphütte turn-off on your left. (If you don't mind strolling with the crowds, the 30 to 40-minute return walk on around the reservoir to the restaurant/cable-car station near the **Douglashütte** (see Places to Stay) is quite pleasant.) A yellow-red marked path cuts diagonally up the hillside, climbing on first in steep loops through unstable slopes then via a rock ridge to reach the **Totalphütte** (see Places to Stay) after 45 minutes to one hour. The hut looks north across the 'dead alp' – a bare basin left behind after glacial recession – towards the crags of the Seekopf and Zirmenkopf.

Stage 3A: Totalphütte to Schesaplanahütte (via Schesaplana Summit)
(4.5 km, 3½ to 4¾ hours)
Sink down westwards into the **Totalp** and follow paint splashes across the bare moraines, then head on up steeply again through more loose rock past a route going off left to the Gemslücke to reach a tiny shelf at 2660 metres. Bearing right at the path division here, ascend through a gap in the cliffs onto a high rounded spur providing a relatively easy way up to the top of **Schesaplana**, 1¾ to 2¼ hours from the Totalphütte. The 2964-metre summit is crowned with an enormous metal cross and gives a truly superb panorama stretching in all directions; in fine weather it's standing-room only!

Go back along the spur a short way, before dropping down the Schesaplana's eroding western slopes to the broad rock backbone marking the international border. Standing out to the north-west at the far edge of the Brandner Gletscher is the Mannheimerhütte. Walk gently down alongside this sweeping icy expanse to a low point in the main ridge, from where white-blue-white markings lead off left.

The route now makes an exhilarating descending traverse along the abrupt southern side of the Alpstein range, then begins picking its way down very steeply through the crags to cross a small ravine. Although there are no really exposed places, some care is required where you have to downclimb (assisted by the usual steel cables). The final section simple follows a grassy ridge directly down to arrive at the **Schesaplanahütte** (1908 metres, see Places to Stay), 1¾ to 2½ hours from the Schesaplana summit. The hut occupies a picturesque spot right at the foot of the Alpstein, and from here various walking routes lead downvalley to Seewis, Grüsch and Schiers.

Stage 2B/3B: Garschinahütte to Schesaplanahütte (via Cavelljoch)
(16 km, 4½ to 5½ hours)

This more straightforward route variant to the Schesaplanahütte can easily be done in a single day, but – although a lovely walk – it lacks some of the spectacular high-Alpine scenery of Stages 2A and 3A.

Make your way to the route intersection above the Lünersee Alpe as in Stage 2A, then follow blue and yellow paint stripes southwards up through flowery meadows to the 2239-metre **Cavelljoch** (spelt 'Gafalljoch' in Austria). Sidle effortlessly around slopes on the Swiss side of the border, coming to a signpost on a grassy mountainside after 30 to 40 minutes.

Descend directly westwards (or walk around via the small alp restaurant on the saddle at **Golrosa** (2128 metres) not far down to the left), then begin traversing the slopes above isolated farmlets in the attractive upper valley of the Valserbach. The worn path keeps roughly to the 2000-metre contour line, rising and dipping past clumps of stunted conifers and large fields of scree that fan out below the massive rock walls of the Alpstein. The last section edges downwards across Alpine pastures to the distant

tinkling of cowbells, arriving at the **Schesaplanahütte**, 1¼ to 1¾ hours from Golrosa.

Stage 4: Schesaplanahütte to Pfälzerhütte
(9 km, 2¾ to 3¾ hours)

Head north-west around the slopes, soon passing a high-Alpine route diverging to the right. The foot track eases gently up against the contour under talus slides, then on more steeply past where a sizeable spring emerges. Here it's worth a quick climb off right to the **Chlei Furgga** (2243 metres, sometimes signposted as 'Kleine Furke') for a look down into the wild screes of Im Salaruel, before you continue sidling westwards above the tiny grassy bowl to reach the **Gross Furgga**, a larger gap at 2359 metres, after 1½ to two hours. From here you get a clear view back along the Alpstein range as far as the Sulzfluh.

Drop down into Austria and traverse leftwards along high grassy platforms formed by the rock strata at the head of a serene Alpine valley, passing just below the **Barthümeljoch** after 30 to 40 minutes. The path picks an easy route on across slab terraces as it swings around north-westwards below the 2570-metre 'borderstone' peak of the Naafkopf, before crossing over the main ridgeline into Liechtenstein. The **Pfälzerhütte** (see Places to Stay) is a short way down on the **Bettlerjoch** (2108 metres), 45 minutes to one hour on from the Barthümeljoch.

Stage 5: Pfälzerhütte to Malbun
(4.5 km, 1½ to two hours)

Follow the hut's narrow service road down over a spur to a signposted track going off right just before you come to the stone farmstead of **Alp Gritsch**. The often muddy path sidles northwards along dairy pastures high above the Saminatal, before making a short, steep ascent to a ridgetop overlooking Malbun. Descend past a group of wooden avalanche-prevention stands into the grassy basin, then move over right under winter ski lifts to meet a gravelled roadway. The route continues briefly left, before dropping down along a final section of path that brings you out to the main road through the village after 1½ to two hours. The postbus stop and tourist office are five minutes' walk downhill. First settled by Walser immigrants in 1280, **Malbun** (1600 metres, see Places to Stay) has been developed into a modern skiing resort.

THE VEREINATAL

This walk leads from near the Flüelapass over the pass of the Jöriflüelafurgge into the Vereinatal, a small highland valley at the headwaters of the Landquart River which drains the Prättigau district. Not even the Walsers – who were so often the first colonists in Graubünden's remote mountain valleys – settled in the upper Vereinatal. Having kept its wild nature up until the present day, the upper Vereinatal is inhabited by many colonies of marmots and chamois, while its lower reaches are forested with beautiful stands of arolla, mountain and dwarf pines. One of the highlights of the hike are the Jöriseen, a handful of milky-green coloured lakes lying scattered around a sparsely vegetated moraine basin at the foot of the Flüela Wisshorn, whose southern slopes are covered by extensive glaciers. In more severe winters the Jöriseen freeze completely solid, and often take until the middle of summer to thaw out completely.

Maps

The recommended walking map is the 1:50,000 *Wanderkarte Klosters-Prättigau*, produced by the local tourist authorities. Excellent alternatives are the 1:25,000 *Davos Wanderkarte* published by the Davos tourist authority, or the SAW/FSTP sheet *Prättigau (248 T)*, although both these maps show the route rather close to the edge of the sheet. Either of Kümmerly + Frey's 1:60,000 walking maps *Prättigau-Albula* or *Engadina Bassa/Unterengadin* can also be used.

Walking Times & Standard

To hike the whole way from Wägerhus to Monbiel makes a long day walk, and is best stretched out to two days by staying overnight at the Berghaus Vereina. The route can be shortened to just four hours by taking the regular private minibus service (see below) from the Berghaus Vereina to Klosters, a alternative which omits Stage 2.

Although this is a high-level mountain walk, the route is generally well marked and easy to follow. The higher parts of the route may remain snow covered until early summer, this provides minimal hindrance. After the initial rather steep ascent, the route is a long downhill walk.

The Swiss military (EMD/DMF) uses the area around Wägerhus for target practice periodically during the summer months. Army personnel stationed at the entry points will guide you through the shooting area at regular intervals. To check the current situation call the regional EMD/DMF office in Chur on ☎ 081-253 35 13.

The walk is rated *moderate* and covers a total distance of some 19 km.

Places to Stay

The *Ospiz Flüela* (☎ 081-417 17 47) on the Flüelapass height (2383 metres) 1.5 km up from Wägerhus has rooms and dormitory accommodation. The *Berghaus Vereina* (☎ 081-422 12 16, open from the beginning of July until mid to late October) about halfway along the walk, also has rooms and a walkers' dorm (showers available).

Places to stay in Davos and Klosters are covered in the Walking Bases section above.

Getting to/from the Walk

The walk begins at Wägerhus (2207 metres), a bus stop and car park on the Flüelapass road about 1.5 km north of the pass height itself. Postbuses running between Davos Platz and Susch in the lower Engadine pass by Wägerhus up to half a dozen times each day from early June until the last Sunday in October. Outside these times there is no bus service at all. Seat reservation is necessary for all services (call ☎ 081-413 66 40) and a surcharge of Sfr5 is levied.

The walk can be shortened by taking the private minibus service from the Berghaus Vereina to Klosters. Reservations are essen-

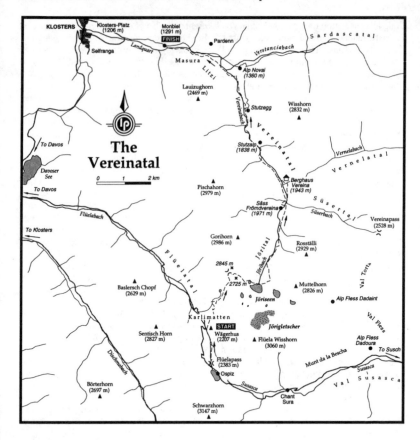

tial (call the Berghaus Vereina or Sport
Gotscha on ☎ 081-422 12 16). The minibus
runs five times daily as long as the Berghaus
Vereina remains open; the last bus leaves for
Klosters at approximately 5.30 pm.

The walk ends at the tiny village of
Monbiel, from where the local public bus
takes you down to Klosters Platz (passing the
turn-off to the youth hostel on the way).
Buses run roughly hourly year-round; the
last bus leaves Monbiel at around 7.30 pm.

Stage 1: Wägerhus to Berghaus Vereina
(9 km, 3½ to 4½ hours)

Take the signposted foot track from the lone
cottage near the PTT bus stop at **Wägerhus**
(2207 metres) and climb steadily away from
the busy Flüelapass road over stony pastures
browsed by listless cows. The broad and
well-graded path passes a side route going
off to the Winterlücke, winding its way on
up through fields of coarse broken rock
before circling around a small gully to arrive
at the **Jöriflüelafurgge** after 1½ to two
hours. This gap in the range at 2725 metres
gives the first excellent view down to the
Jöriseen.

Head a short way left below the craggy

ridge secured by fixed cables. Follow red-white-red markings down over rocky slopes covered by occasional snowdrifts, before dropping down through meadows scattered with yellow-dotted gentians to the shore of the northernmost lake of the **Jöriseen**. Unlike the others it is fed by a clearwater spring, and early in the season ice floating on the aqua-blue water gives the lake an Arctic feel. Continue through grassed-over moraine hillocks across a metal footbridge over the milky-green outlet stream of the largest lake, climbing on to reach a signposted intersection at 2519 metres after 40 to 50 minutes.

Directly to the south stands the 3060-metre Flüela Wisshorn, on whose northern slopes the icy mass of the Jörigletscher descend into the Jörisee basin, while to the north the Berghaus Vereina can be made out some four km and 600 altitude metres away. Drop down steeply into the Jörital, picking your way through regenerated glacial debris to meet the **Jöribach**. The path now leads down in staggered stages through the tiny upper valley along the eastern side of the stream, which alternatively cascades in little gorges and meanders gently beside green river flats.

After crossing the **Süserbach** on a footbridge near **Säss Frömdvereina**, make your way on through slopes of lovely Alpine heath and thickets of dwarf birch to cross another large sidestream at the gushing **Vernelabach** just before you arrive at the **Berghaus Vereina** (1943 metres, see Places to Stay), 1¼ to 1¾ hours from the Jöriseen turn-off. This homy mountain hotel is powered by a tiny hydroelectric generator, and sits on a rock outcrop below the 2979-metre Pischahorn.

Stage 2: Berghaus Vereina to Monbiel/Klosters

(10 km, 2½ to 3½ hours)
The private road through the wild and glaciated valley of the Vereinatal is closed to all traffic other than vehicles servicing the Berghaus Vereina, and therefore makes an easy walkway. Follow it smoothly down across the Vereinabach and on through

attractive riverside meadows below a long waterfall coming off the Pischahorn. After recrossing the river at a small chasm, the dirt road winds down more steeply through slopes of arolla and dwarf pines to reach a path turn-off (signposted 'Fussweg') at **Chänzeli** (1570 metres), 1¼ to 1¾ hours from the hotel.

Leave the road and descend steeply into the spruce forest, crossing sidestreams as you come out onto open pastures above the river. Head over the grassy flats and then along a levée embankment to once again cross the Vereinabach on a narrow road bridge near the farmhouse at **Alp Novai** (1360 metres), where an interesting long and narrow avalanche chute cuts straight down through the forest on the adjacent slope. The route runs along a rough farm road down the left bank of the stream past its confluence with the somewhat larger Verstanciabach, then continues close to the fast-flowing river (now called the Landquart) through occasional forest clearings of **Masura**.

When you come to **Chüenisch Boden** at 1276 metres, turn off right onto a signposted foot track leading across the Landquart on a footbridge, before climbing quickly up to arrive at the bus stop at the village of **Monbiel** (1291 metres) after a final 1¼ to 1¾ hours. If you miss the last bus, Klosters-Platz (1206 metres, see Walking Bases) is about 30 minutes' walk down the road.

THE SERTIGPASS

Marking a language division between German-speaking Davos and the predominantly Romansch Abula region, the 2739-metre Sertigpass (known in Romansch as the Pass da Sett) is one the most scenically rewarding walks in the Central Bündner Alps. The area on the southern side of the pass is a nature reserve, in which the gorgeous Lai da Ravaisch lie nestled into the grassed-over moraine mounds ringed by 3000-metre summits of grey dolomite. The Sertigpass is the highest point of the annual Swiss Alpine Marathon, a gruelling 67-km race held on the last Sunday in July. The several thousand participants can test them-

selves against the rigours of the high mountains, but walkers get to cross the Sertigpass
at a rather more leisurely and enjoyable pace.

Maps
The best map covering the route in one sheet
is *Bergün*, published by the SAW/FSTP at a
scale of 1:50,000; although Kümmerly +
Frey's 1:60,000 *Prättigau-Albula* is a reasonable option. Alternatively, you can use
two 1:25,000 walking maps: *Wanderkarte
Bergün* and *Davos Wanderkarte*, both published by local tourist authorities.

Walking Times & Standard
Unless you walk via the· Chammana digl
Kesch, this is a longish day walk (without the
option of overnighting en route). The
Sertigpass is another high-Alpine route that
can nevertheless be done by people with
reasonable fitness and ample common sense.
The best time to do the walk is from late June
until mid-October. Panting athletes training
for the big event are often encountered
throughout the early summer, but unless
you're a sports enthusiast it may be advisable
to avoid hiking over the Sertigpass close to
the Swiss Alpine Marathon in late July.

The walk is rated *moderate* and covers 15
km (or 23 km if you continue on foot from
Chants to Bergün).

Places to Stay
The *Kurhaus Sertig* (☎ 081-413 62 38, open
mid-June to mid-October) in Sertig Dörfli
has standard rooms and a small dorm. Some
hikers do the walk via the *Chammana digl
Kesch* (☎ 081-407 11 34), an SAC-run hut at
2632 metres in the Val da Tschüvel; the
chammana has the usual mattress-room
accommodation of Swiss mountain huts.
The village of Chants has a restaurant, but
nowhere to stay.

For places to stay in Davos and Bergün see
Walking Bases above.

Getting to/from the Walk
The hike begins from the Kurhaus Sertig at
the hamlet of Sand in the upper Sertigtal
(about 500 metres on from the tiny village of

Sertig Dörfli). Postbuses run almost hourly
from Davos Platz to the Kurhaus Sertig daily
all year round; it's a lovely drive taking
around 25 minutes.

The walk ends at the village of Chants in
the upper Val Tuors. Some walkers prefer to
continue on foot to Bergün (see Walking
Bases), while others are obliged to hike the
extra two hours because the local postbuses
only run from Chants to Bergün for a seven-
week period over summer. There are several
buses each day between the beginning of
July and mid to late August, but outside these
times the service stops completely. The last
bus leaves Chants at approximately 5 pm and
reservations are essential. To make a reservation call ☎ 081-407 11 84.

Route Directions: Kurhaus Sertig to Chants
(15 km, 4 to 5 hours)
First settled by Walsers, the upper Sertigtal
is a lovely basin of highland meadows bordered by old wooden fences and surrounded
by heath-covered slopes culminating in
craggy peaks. From the **Kurhaus Sertig**
(1860 metres) follow the unsurfaced road
700 metres past wooden farmhouses to
where it crosses the Sertigbach on a narrow
bridge and heads towards the Duncantal, a
side valley that ends in a waterfall spilling
over a high rock terrace. Here proceed left
along an alp track leading up into the valley
of the Chüealptal past scree fields below the
2735-metre Mittaghorn to reach the long
milking shed of **Bim Schära** at 2101 metres
after 40 to 50 minutes.

Make your way on into the upper valley,
crossing the Chüealpbach on a little footbridge just below the **Grüensee** (2197
metres). A white-red-white marked path now
ascends away from the stream past the greenish lakelet to traverse slopes of alpenroses,
before picking its way up through snowdrifts
and fields of coarse rock sprinkled with
hardy Alpine buttercups adjacent hanging
glaciers below the 3077-metre Chüealphorn.
A final climb past a shallow ice-choked tarn
brings you up to the **Sertigpass** at 2739
metres, 1½ to two hours from Bim Schära.

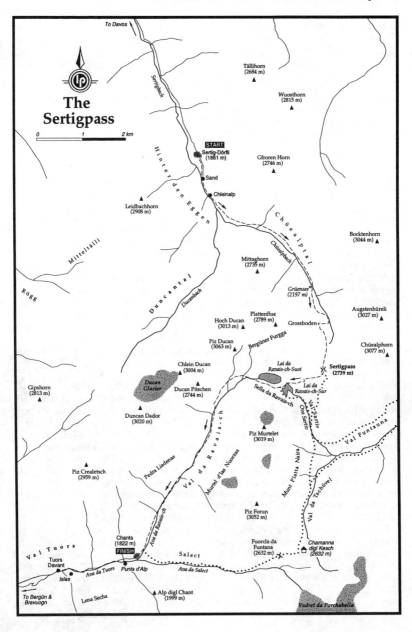

Directly to the south the majestic 3417-metre form of Piz Kesch, the highest summit in the Central Bündner Alps, rises up above the broad icy band of the Vadret da Porchabella.

Drop down leftwards from the pass over grassy mountainsides grazed by tinkling cows to the **Lai da Ravais-ch-Sur** (2562 metres), crossing ancient moraine hillocks before coming to a signposted trail intersection, where the way to the Chamanna digl Kesch departs left. Continue west towards the towering grey-rock walls of Piz Ducan (3063 metres) high above the southern shore of the beautiful **Lai da Ravais-ch-Suot** (2505 metres), a much larger and deeper glacial lake. The route heads on down into the Val da Ravaisch, a wild Alpine valley whose eastern sides are protected by a nature reserve.

Follow the well-graded path as it descends gently through open slopes abundant with herb fields and colonies of marmots, crossing the Ava da Ravais-ch stream a number of times on footbridges. In the distance more lofty summits around Piz Ela (3339 metres) can be made out beyond the mouth of the Val da Ravais-ch. The route finally leads down past haymaking fields into the scattered village of **Chants** at 1822 metres, 1¾ to 2¼ hours from the Sertigpass. Here three small valleys merge to form the Val Tuors.

Walk 500 metres down the road, then turn off left past a cluster of houses. After crossing the Ava da Tuors pick up a foot track that rises and dips along the southern side of the river to meet the road again near the hamlet of **Tuors Davant** (1704 metres). The route follows the road across another bridge near a heavily eroding chasm, then breaks away left again on a path leading past the cloudy tarn of **Igls Lajets** to the clearing of **Resgia da Latsch**.

Recross the stream and take a vehicle track winding up through forests of spruce and mountain pines. The final section follows the road or short-cut trails on down under the rail lines to arrive at **Bergün** (1367 metres, see Walking Bases), 1¾ to 2¼ hours after leaving Chants. The train station is a further 10 to 15 minutes' walk to the right down along the main street past lovely old Romansch-style buildings in the town centre.

OTHER WALKS
The Dreibundstein

Medieval Graubünden was united under the loose alliance of the Rhaetian Dreibund, or 'three leagues'. On the 2160-metre Dreibundstein, a ridgetop seven km south-west of Chur, an historic borderstone marks the point where the three leagues of the old Graubünden converged. The Dreibundstein also serves as a natural lookout with pleasant views of the surrounding mountains.

Brambrüesch (1595 metres), the start of the walk, is directly accessible by cable car from Chur. From here the route climbs up over the 2174-metre Furggabüel to the Dreibundstein, then continues via Alp dil Plaun to the village of Feldis/Veulden (1469 metres), from where a (community-run) cable car descends across the Hinterrhein to Rhäzüns on the main Chur-Filisur rail line.

The hike's average walking time is 4½ hours. Brambrüesch has a *Friends of Nature hostel* (☎ 081-252 78 72). The 1:50,000 SAW/FSTP sheet *Sardona (247 T)* is the best walking map to use.

The Madrisa Circuit

This popular three-day international walk from Klosters (see Walking Bases) circumnavigates the twin peaks of the southern Rhätikon, the 2826-metre Madrisahorn in Switzerland and the 2770-metre Madrisa on the Austrian side. The route leaves from Saaser Alp (1884 metres) at the upper station of the Madrisa cableway (Madrisabahn), and climbs northwards over the 2602-metre Rätschenjoch before dropping down to St Antönien (see Walking Bases). On the second stage the circuit ascends east over the 2379-metre St Antönier (Gärgäller) Joch, before descending to the Austrian village of Gargellen (1423 metres). The last section goes up south through the tiny valley of the Valzifenbach to the 2202-metre Schlappiner Joch, returning to Klosters either via Saaser Alp or direct along the Schlappintobel.

The route passes through steep and loose rock in places and is best suited to experienced mountain walkers. Apart from the villages of St Antönien and Gargellen, two Austrian mountain huts provide en-route accommodation: the *Madrissahütte* (1693 metres) between the Schlapiner Joch and Gargellen, and the *Rinderhütte* (2060 metres) below the St Antönier Joch. Walkers can use either 1:50,000 SAW/FSTP sheet *Prättigau (248 T) or the 1:50,000 Wanderkarte Kosters-Prättigau* produced by the local tourist authorities.

The Weissfluh

The 2843-metre Weissfluh stands immediately north-west of Davos (see Walking Bases). The range has been intensively developed for winter sports, and some walkers find the numerous ski lifts, cable cars and mountain railways a bit too much. An easy and scenic three to 3½-hour route goes north from the upper station of the Schatzalp-Strelapass gondola lift via the Wasserscheid (pass) to the Weissfluhjoch (2686 metres), where the internationally famous Eidgenössisches Institut für Schnee und Lawinenforschung (Federal Institute for Snow and Avalanche Research) is based. From here a side trip can be made on foot or by cable car to the summit of the Weissfluh. The walk continues past the Totalpsee Parsenenhütte, then follows the Panoramaweg to Gotschnagrat, from where another cable car takes you down to Klosters railway station. The most detailed and accurate walking map is the 1:25,000 *Wanderkarte Davos* which is published by the local tourist authority.

The Scalletapass

Of Graubünden's numerous trans-Alpine routes the Scalletapass had the most fearsome reputation, and in winter avalanches could wipe out whole teams of mule-drivers. Although this historic crossing is rather less dangerous today, it is no less lonely and wild. The relatively little-transited route goes north to south from Dürrboden, a tiny summer-only settlement at 2007 metres reached by (very infrequent) postbus from Davos. Dürrboden has one restaurant (with a mattress room for walkers) and 300-year-old stables, which once housed pack animals. The descent through the Val Susauna, a side valley of the Upper Engadine, leads via the small village of Sasauna to the Rhaetian Railway's station at Cinuoschel/Brail, where there is a hotel with a mattress room.

The 1:50,000 SAW/FSTP sheets *Bergün (258 T)* and *Ofenpass (259 T)* cover the route.

The Pass da Sett

The 2310-metre Pass da Sett (or Septimerpass in German) was once an important trans-Alpine trade route, but after the opening of the Gotthard railway in 1882 the old mule trail soon fell into disuse. The restoration of the route was completed for Switzerland's 700th anniversary in 1991, and today the Pass da Sett is one of Switzerland's most popular historic walkways. The start of this long day hike is the village of Bivio (1769 metres), at the foot of the main range of the Alps in the predominantly Romansch-speaking Sursés (Oberhalbstein) Valley. The name Bivio refers to the 'two ways' that lead via the Julierpass into the Engadine, and over the Pass da Sett into the Italian-speaking Val Bregaglia.

The route leads south from Bivio rising at an agreeable rate through the pastures of the Val Tgavretga to the Pass da Sett, before making a shorter and steeper descent into the Val Maroz and on to the village of Casaccia (1485 metres). Unfortunately, high-tension transmission cables accompany walkers the whole way, which detracts significantly from the otherwise marvellous scenery.

A popular (and recommended) route variant goes east from the Pass da Sett over the Pass Lunghin to Maloja (see Walking Bases) or Segl-Maria. This alterative not only avoids those unsightly cables, but allows a side trip up to Piz Lunghin, whose 2780-metre summit forms the watershed between three of Europe's major river systems (which flow into the North, Black and Mediterranean seas).

Postbuses on the long but direct route from Chur via Lenzerheide and Tiefencastel pass through Bivio (some continuing on to St Moritz) up to four times daily; seat reservation is necessary (call ☎ 081-256 31 84). The 1:50,000 SAW/FSTP sheet *Julierpass (268 T)* best covers the walking route.

Arosa to Lenzerheide/Lai

Countless marked trails lead through the mountains surrounding the winter-sports resort of Arosa (1775 metres), and some of the most popular are routes over the Parpaner range to Lenzerheide/Lai (1476 metres). One route option entails riding the cable car (Hörnlibahn) from Innerarosa to the Hörnlihütte (2513 metres), before heading west across the 2546-metre gap in the ridge known as the Urdenfürggli. The descent cuts south-west down the slopes below the Parpaner Rothorn to reach Lenzerheide/Lai in around four hours. A longer, nicer and somewhat more challenging walking route goes up past the lakes of Arosa Alp and through an enclosed and moraine-filled upper valley to the cable-car station on the Parpaner Rothorn's 2861-metre summit; the descent to Lenzerheide/Lai is made by either mechanical or pedestrian means.

Both of the suggested routes call for sturdy footwear. As this is a high-Alpine area, the walks should not be done before June or after mid-November (at the latest). There are youth hostels in both Arosa (☎ 081-377 13 97) and Lenzerheide-Valbella (☎ 081-384 12 08), as well as several en-route mountain restaurants with mattress rooms. Arosa can be reached by hourly trains from Chur and regular postbuses run between Lenzerheide/Lai and Chur. Recommended walking maps are the 1:40,000 *Wanderkarte Arosa* published by the Arosa tourist authority, or Kümmerly + Frey's 1:40,000 *Region Lenzerheide*.

Monstein to Filisur

Between Monstein and Filisur the railway runs along a deep and narrow gorge of the Landwasser River, and the completion of the line in 1909 was quite an achievement of engineering. Ducking through several long tunnels on the way, the railway has scarcely effected the natural attractiveness of the area, while the road takes an altogether different route high up the slopes on the opposite side of the valley. From Monstein train station (1346 metres) an easy and well-graded path rises and dips along the steep, forested southern slopes of the Landwasser. After passing through the hamlet of Jenisberg (1504 metres) the route descends to meet the railway at Wiesen station (1197 metres), then crosses the 90-metre high Wiesener Viadukt bridge and continues on down to Filisur (999 metres).

This is an easy day hike with an average walking time of 3½ hours. The SAW/FSTP 1:50,000 sheet *Bergün (258 T)* includes the route.

The Vorderrhein & Hinterrhein

Above the small town of Reichenau (10 km west of Chur) the valley of the Swiss Rhine divides into two upper branches. These unequal twins are the Vorderrhein (Rein Anteriur in Romansch) and the Hinterrhein (Rein Posteriur), a region taking in the whole south-western corner of Graubünden.

Rising in the Lai da Tuma, a lovely lake near the Oberalppass, the Vorderrhein is normally regarded as the true source of the Rhine. Known as the Surselva, the Vorderrhein's 60-km-long valley forms the largest Romansch-speaking region in Graubünden. Surselva means 'above the forest' in Romansch, a reference to the dense forests that once grew around the confluence of the Vorderrhein and Hinterrhein.

On its northern side the Surselva is cut off by the Alps of Central Switzerland, the Glarnerland and the St Galler Oberland, whose unbroken line of high peaks rise abruptly to over 3000 metres. To the south half a dozen or so long side valleys – whose rivers have Romansch names such as Rein da Maighels and Rein da Sumvitg indicating they are Rhine tributaries – stretch south towards the mountains on the Graubünden/Ticino cantonal border.

During the Ice ages a huge glacier smothered the whole of the Surselva under a colossal river of ice that extended right down the Rhine valley as far as Lake Constance. The Vorderrhein glacier has long since disappeared, but its effect on the landscape is obvious. Today the Surselva is a broad valley intermittently broken by gorges, including the rugged 15-km-long Ruin' Aulta along the lower section of the river.

The source of the Hinterrhein is not a lovely Alpine lake, but the extensive glaciers of the 3402-metre Rheinwaldhorn, and the river is even more dissected by gorges than the Vorderrhein. The deep Viamala and Rofla gorges divide the Hinterrhein valley into three stages: the largely Romansch-speaking Domleschg and Schons (Schams), and the uppermost area known as the Rheinwald, whose inhabitants speak German. The Rheinwald has two important trans-Alpine passes, the Splügenpass and the Passo del San Bernadino, and the valley gradually oriented itself more to the transport of goods than to dairy farming.

From medieval times Walsers migrated from Goms across the Oberalppass into the Vorderrhein and Hinterrhein, settling many upper-valley areas such as the Safiental and Rheinwald. The mix of Romansch and Germanic cultures gives this region a particularly fascinating flavour. Although rather less well known abroad than other parts of Graubünden, the Vorderrhein and Hinterrhein are a wonderland for the adventurous hiker prepared to get off the beaten track.

WALKING BASES
Thusis
The town of Thusis lies at 720 metres and divides the Domleschg and Schons regions of the once overwhelmingly Romansch-speaking lower Hinterrhein (or Rein

Posteriur). Thusis is famous for the nearby Viamala ('Bad Road'), where the Rein Posteriur flows through a deep and narrow gorge. The amazing walk through the Viamala follows short sections of the old mule path originally constructed in medieval times as part of the San Bernardino trade route. Another very popular local hike, the Burgenweg, leads down past the numerous historic castles of the Domleschg via the villages of Scharans, Almens and Tuegl/Tomils as far as Rothenbrunnen.

Thusis has a *youth hostel* (☎ 081-651 15 80) in the nearby castle of Burg Ehrenfels at Sils im Domleschg, but it generally only caters for groups. In Thusis itself, the *Turistikherberge* (☎ 081-651 49 24) offers dormitory accommodation, and the *Hotel Sternen* (☎ 081-651 18 55) has budget rooms. The local tourist office (☎ 081-651 11 34) is at Neudorfstrasse 70.

Thusis is on the Rhaetian Railway's Chur-Samedan-St Moritz line, with at least hourly through-connections from Zürich; from Davos it's often quicker travelling via Filisur. There are frequent postbuses between Thusis and Splügen/Rheinwald, from where connecting bus routes lead over the San Bernardino and Splügen passes.

Splügen
Originally a Walser settlement, Splügen (1457 metres) is the gateway to the Splügenpass and the Passo del San Bernardino, two of the most historically important passes in the Central Alps. For centuries Splügen lived well by transporting (and taxing) goods on these trans-Alpine trade routes. Splügen's early 18th-century buildings, such as the Posthotel Bodenhaus and the Schorsch-Haus (now a museum), bear witness to the town's prosperous role as a major stopping post. A short half-day walk from Splügen leads westwards along the southern banks of the river to the village of Hinterrhein at the head of the Rheinwald valley.

The local *camping ground* (☎ 081-664 14 76) is 1.5 km away. The *Wädenswilerhaus*

(☎ 081-664 13 34) usually offers dorm accommodation for individuals, but Splügen has little real other budget hotel accommodation. The *Hotel Walserhof* (☎ 081-664 16 12) in nearby Medels is somewhat less expensive than other places in town. Splügen's tourist office (☎ 081-664 13 32) is on the main square.

Postbuses run between Thusis and Splügen approximately every 1½ hours in either direction. The less frequent postbuses between Thusis and Bellinzona in Ticino (via the Passo del San Bernadino) also call in at Splügen. Reservation is necessary for some services (☎ 081-256 31 84).

Disentis/Mustér

Although quite a small place, Disentis is the main centre of the Surselva region (which is predominantly Romansch-speaking). The town's Romansch name, Mustér, refers to the enormous St Martin's Benedictine monastery founded in 750 AD, which is open to visitors (tours most days). The Senda Sursilvana walking route passes through Disentis, which makes a good base for numerous other walks in the surrounding mountains, including the Plaun la Greina and the Fuorcla da Cavardiras.

There is a TCS camping ground nearby, the *Zeltplatz Fontanivas* (☎ 081-947 44 22), 2.5 km out along the Lucomagno road (postbus). Recommended for budget travellers are the *Pension Schuoler* (☎ 081-947 52 46) 15 minutes' walk east of the train station or the *Gasthaus Brunni* (☎ 081-947 52 19). Disentis has a tourist office (☎ 081-947 58 22) and also a local school of mountaineering, the *Bergsportschule Surselva* (☎ 081-947 49 39).

Disentis can be reached on the Rhaetian Railway's direct line from Chur (trains at least once hourly), from Andermatt via the Oberalppass and on postbuses from Ticino via the Passo del Lucomagno (Cuolm Lucmagn in Romansch). The *Glacier Express* tourist trains running between Zermatt and St Moritz also pass through Disentis.

LAI DA TUMA CIRCUIT

The crystal-clear lake known to Romansch speakers as Lai da Tuma (or Thomasee to German speakers) is considered to be the ultimate source of the Rhine River. This straightforward walk leads through a highland nature reserve near the Oberalppass, which is the only Graubünden-Uri transport route and forms the cantons' common border. Here Graubünden meets the Gotthard region – the central mountain hub of the Swiss Alps. Most visiting walkers manage to glimpse the reserve's resident pair of golden eagles as these magnificent Alpine birds soar about the surrounding granite summits.

Maps

Recommended is the 1:50,000 SAW/FSTP walking map *Disentis (256 T)*. Two good alternatives are the locally produced *Wanderkarte Disentis* or Kümmerly + Frey's *San Gottardo*, both scaled at 1:50,000.

Walking Times & Standard

This is a circuit walk that returns to Oberalppass. You should have no trouble doing the circuit in five hours or less, though there's no need to rush it. Setting out from an altitude of over than 2000 metres, walkers have a relatively modest ascent of less than 700 metres to negotiate, but wearing solid footwear is essential. The top of the range around the Pazolastock is very exposed to the elements, however, so keep an eye on the weather.

The walk is just 8.5 km long, and is rated *easy to moderate*.

Places to Stay

At the Oberalppass, the *Hotel Rheinquelle* (☎ 081-949 11 12) and the *Gasthaus Piz Calmot* (☎ 041-887 12 33) offer simple rooms. The cosy SAC-affiliated *Badushütte* (☎ 01-301 48 56), built against a low cliff face at 2505 metres, is the only en-route accommodation. Simple meals and refreshments are served in season (from June to September), but the hut is always left unlocked.

Getting to/from the Walk

The walk begins and ends at the Oberalppass, the highest point on the narrow-gauge Furka-Oberalp-Bahn (FOB) mountain railway linking Graubünden's Disentis with Brig in the Valais. There are train connections in both directions (some with a change in Andermatt) almost every hour from the end of May until mid-October, with less frequent services outside these times. The scenic train known as the *Glacier Express* also passes the Oberalppass. If you're coming by train from Zürich (or any-

where else in northern Switzerland) it's quicker travelling to Oberalppass via Göschenen and Andermatt; from Ticino take a postbus from Airolo to Andermatt.

Private vehicles can be left at the car park on the Oberalppass.

Stage 1: Oberalppass to Badushütte
(4 km, 2 to 2¾ hours)

With its famous old abbey, the beautiful elongated Oberalpsee (a lake popular with anglers) and surrounding granite peaks, the Oberalppass (2044 metres) is a very pleasant

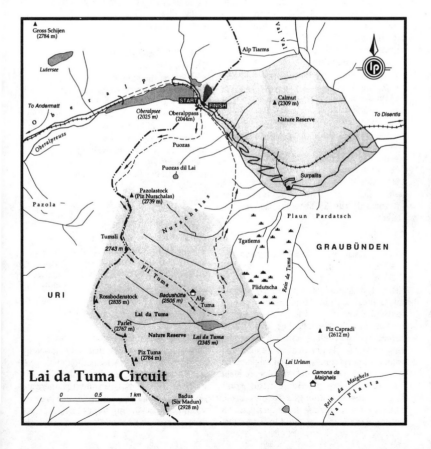

spot spoilt only slightly by the presence of a military barracks.

From the tiny train station by the lake, walk 200 metres up to the Restaurant Alpsu. Take the dirt road opposite, then cut up left over the open slopes above a cross mounted on a rock outcrop. The often steep path climbs alongside a grassy and rocky spur past lovely highland moors in the tiny upper valley of **Puozas** and makeshift stone bunkers built by wartime soldiers, coming to a signpost on the exposed ridgetop at 2571 metres after one to 1½ hours. A side route from here goes down to the village of Andermatt, now visible to the west in the valley of the Reuss. Behind Andermatt the 3500-metre summits of the Winterberg massif and Galenstock rise up on the Uri/Valais cantonal border.

The white-red-white marked route continues up the ridge past two rustic military buildings just under the 2739-metre **Pazolastock** (Piz Nurschalas), traversing the crest of the craggy range with just enough rockhopping to make the going fun and unstrenuous. At point 2743 follow the **Fil Tuma** south-eastwards, and sidle steadily down along the grassy right-hand side of the ridge to arrive at the **Badushütte** (2505 metres, see Places to Stay) after one to 1¼ hours. Built against a low cliff, the hut looks out towards the 2928-metre Badus (Six Madun).

Stage 2: Badushütte to Oberalppass (via Lai da Tuma)

(4.5 km, 1¼ to 1¾ hours)
The path descends quickly to a signposted trail leading off down to the shore of **Lai da Tuma** (2345 metres), 15 to 20 minutes from the hut. This lovely lake lies in a hollow formed by the grinding action of an extinct hanging glacier. In hot weather its snow-fed waters are good for a speedy splash, and the lush natural lawns around the inlet are ideal for that midday picnic. Cotton grass (*Eriophorum latifolium*), a species often found on waterlogged soils, thrives here; on the ungrazed slopes of the Alp Tuma just above here you can find plants that are rare on cow-trodden pastures.

While the lake outlet, the Rein da Tuma, burbles out of sight to the north-east, the walk continues northwards from the signpost above Lai da Tuma. Wind your way down the initially rocky hillside towards the multiple hairpin bends of the busy pass road, then turn left where you come onto the trail leading down from the Val Maighels. The path now sidles along slopes studded with sporadic alpenrose bushes, gradually moving around to meet the small stream flowing down from the pass. Follow the often boggy banks gently up to arrive back at the Oberalppass, just one to 1⅓ hours from the Lai da Tuma.

THE LAG SEREIN CIRCUIT

The popular walk to Lag Serein, a lovely tarn high up on the sunny mountainsides above Disentis, leads over Alpine pastures in which a great variety of Alpine wildflowers can be found. This is a high-level route that largely runs above 2000 metres and offers superb views of the Surselva valley. Glaciated peaks, precipices, snow gullies, tiny side valleys and lakelets perched on little terraces provide an ever-changing scenery.

Maps

The best map is the SAW/FSTP sheet *Disentis (256 T)* at scale of 1:50,000. Alternatively, walkers can use either the 1:50,000 *Wanderkarte Disentis*, a good locally available walking map, or Kümmerly + Frey's 1:60,000 walking map *Surselva*.

Readers should also refer to the map 'Fuorcla da Cavardiras/Lag Serein Circuit' in the Central Switzerland chapter.

Walking Times & Standard

This is a short day hike that can be done by anyone with basic fitness. Although the path is a bit rough in places, the 'artificial means of ascent' (ie cable car) ensures that there are no really strenuous sections. These are elevated and south-facing slopes that get plenty of sun – so take a hat and/or use a sunblock.

The walk has been given an *easy to moderate* rating.

Places to Stay

Apart from a small unlocked hut with four bunks at Lag Ault intended for emergency shelter only there is no en-route accommodation.

For places to stay in Disentis see Walking Bases above.

Getting to/from the Walk

This is a circuit walk from Disentis (see Walking Bases), beginning from the upper cable-car station at Caischavedra.

The lower cable-car station at Funs is 15 minutes' walk up from Disentis train station; the cable car offers most of the usual ticket concessions.

Route Directions: Caischavedra to Disentis (via Lag Crest Ault)

(10.5 km, 3 to 4½ hours)

The cable car takes you up more than 650 altitude metres to **Caischavedra**. From here take the rough alp track around above the upper cable-car station past a field of solar panels, then cut up right on a prominent path through mountain healthland. Crossing numerous sidestreams coming down from the left, sidle gently upwards over an open spur and around into the Val Acletta to reach **Lag Serein** at 2072 metres after 50 minutes to one hour. The smooth surface and transparent waters of this serene little lake contrast with the craggy range between Piz Cavardiras and Piz Ault above. Across the valley stands the striking Medels massif with several hanging ice fields blanketing its northern sides.

Ignoring an alpinists' route going up to the left, head over a footbridge and around the mountainside, then cut up left through a steep rock chute to a sloping terrace known as **Plaun Tir** dotted with bilberries and Alpine rhododendrons. A signpost here directs you on left past avalanche grids (protecting the township of Disentis far below) as you swing northwards into the Val Clavaniev. After crossing the stream at the head of this little valley, climb on via a small indistinct ridge to meet a graded path contouring the hillside. Walk a few paces left, then follow red and white markings off right through a low point to **Lag Crest Ault** (2268 metres), 50 minutes to one hour on. This tiny rock-bottom tarn is very shallow, and often dries out completely by autumn.

Continue a short distance on to a signposted intersection. (From here a return side trip up to **Lag Brit** (2361 metres) can be done a little over an hour; the good but sporadically marked trail ascends leftwards over a rock rib into the upper **Val San Placi**, where the lake lies at the base of moraine fields.) A line of paint-splashed rocks guides you diagonally down the grassy slopes of **Alp Run** to the right past the alp huts of **Catán** at 2127 metres. From here the village of Curaglia can easily be made out roughly to the south-east over in the Val Medels.

Descend on via well-trodden walking pads, making in a wide left-right curve through patches of Alpine heath into a narrow aisle at the upper edge of the forest leading down to a sealed road. A steeper path now short-cuts directly down through the spruce trees, encountering the road several more times to pass by the clearing of **Plaun Grond** (1578 metres), 40 to 50 minutes down from Lag Crest Ault.

Continue down to meet the road a final time, then steer rightwards (west) over meadows above Disentis and cross the Clavaniev stream. An old dirt track quickly brings you back across the stream through the rustic wooden barns at the hamlet of **Clavaniev** (1288 metres), from where the familiar yellow diamonds and 'Staziun' signposts indicate the way on down to Disentis train station (1142 metres), 40 to 50 minutes on.

THE PLAUN LA GREINA

The Plaun la Greina is a roughly 10 sq-km expanse of highland plains over 2200 metres above sea level and surrounded by the craggy ranges. Although it is lightly grazed by herds of sheep, during spring and early summer the Greina is resplendent with wildflowers and provides a perfect habitat for marmots and chamois. Little brooks fringed by cotton grass meander through grassy Alpine meadows and moors dotted with peaty tarns – at times the Greina is strangely reminiscent of the Scandinavian Arctic.

This is one of Switzerland's last untouched landscapes, and in the 1980s was the subject of a protracted – and ultimately successful – fight to stop the construction of a hydroelectric dam which would have flooded the whole upper valley. Local communities, which had supported the project, were compensated for the loss of income, and the Greina has now been declared a 'landscape of national significance'.

This walk takes you across the watershed dividing the Rhine basin from the catchment area of the Po River. Like many other passes in Graubünden, the gentle Passo della Greina, on the main continental divide, was a trade route used by cargo-carrying mule teams. The Plaun la Greina is also at a geological crossroads, and the green or pitch-black shale rocks typical of the Graubünden are interspersed with crystalline silicates of the Gotthard region.

Maps

One of the few walking maps that covers the whole route in a single sheet is Kümmerly + Frey's *Surselva*, scaled at 1:60,000. Better are the SAW/ESS 1:50,000 walking maps, but you'll need at least two sheets: *Val Leventina (266 T)* and *Disentis (Mustér) (256 T)*. A third SAW/ESS sheet includes the final section from Ghirone to Olivone, but is not really necessary.

Walking Times & Standard

This is basically a two-day hike, but stretching it out to three days is time well spent. Although the route is very well marked and paths are generally fairly good, remember that this is an Alpine walk and the usual considerations apply.

The walk is in the *moderate* category, and has a total distance of 27 km.

Places to Stay

In Vrin the *Hotel Pez Terri* (☎ 081-931 12 55, open May to late October), which has rooms with/without shower and WC as well as a dorm for walkers. A cheaper option is the *Ustria Tgaminada* (☎ 081-931 17 43), at the hamlet of Sogn Giusep, 2.5 km (30 minutes) up the road from Vrin. It also has rooms and a bunkhouse with a kitchen.

The most convenient place to stay en route is the SAC's 82-bed *Camona da Terri* (☎ 081-943 12 05) on the edge of the Plauna la Greina at 2170 metres. The *Capanna Scaletta* (☎ 091-609 12 85) at 2205 metres is run by the Società Alpinistica Ticinese (SAT). Originally a small mountain refuge, this hut has recently been remodelled and now has sleeping space for around 40 walkers. The SAC's *Capanna Motterascio* (☎ 091-872 16 22) is roughly 30 minutes' walk off-route beyond the 091-872 16 22) is roughly 30 minutes' walk off-route beyond the Crap la Crusch.

The *Ristorante Genziana* (☎ 091-872 11 93) 0.5 km down the road from Campo (Blenio) has rooms for standard rates. For places to stay in Olivone, see Walking Bases in the Ticino chapter.

Getting to/from the Walk

The start of the walk is the village of Vrin (1448 metres) in the upper Val Lumnezia, the largest side valley of the Surselva. Vrin can be reached by postbus from Ilanz, on the Rhaetian Railway's Chur-Disentis line; there are up to 10 daily buses, and the last departure is around 6.30 pm (or about 8.30 pm on Friday).

The walk ends at Olivone (see under Walking Bases in the Ticino chapter), although you can shorten the walk slightly by taking one of two or three daily postbus vans to Olivone from the village of Campo (Blenio), which is passed one hour beforehand.

Stage 1: Vrin to Camona da Terri

(11 km, 3 to 4 hours)
The strongly Romansch-speaking village of **Vrin** (1448 metres) is well known for its

CLEM LINDENMAYER

CLEM LINDENMAYER

Top: View of the abrupt sides of Sulzfluh (2817 metres) from the Garschinahütte, Graubünden.
Bottom: The broad icy névé of the Brunnifirn (viewed from the Cavadirashütte, Graubünden).

Top: View of the Richetlipass which connects the two main upper valleys of the Glarnerland.
Bottom: Waterfall and isolated farm on the Durnachtal (small side valley of the Linth).

The Plaun la Greina

0   2   4 km

traditional architecture, including old dark-stained wooden houses, a superb Baroque church and a charnel-house containing human skulls. From Vrin post office follow the winding road upvalley through haymaking fields past the clustered hamlets of **Cons** and **Sogn Giusep** (see Places to Stay) to reach **Puzzatsch** at 1667 metres after one to 1⅓ hours.

Walk on through the tiny village and across a bridge, then a short way on take the signposted track that continues ahead. The white-red-white marked route cuts steadily up the grassy slopes above the stream to the

herder's huts at **Alp Diesrut** (1899 metres), with nice views towards the adjacent 3149-metre Piz Terri and Piz Zamuor. Climb briefly around to the right, then sidle up westwards along the mountainside to cross the now small stream. A signpost here indicates a side trail going off to the Fil Blengias and Vanescha.

The path begins ascending more steeply beside the stream, then moves away to the left to arrive at the **Pass Diesrut** (2428 metres), 1½ to two hours from Puzzatsch. The pass, whose Romansch name means 'broken back', is the lowest point between

Piz Tgietschen and Piz Zamuor. Pass Diesrut is also the highest point on the walk and grants a view of the icy summits of Piz Vial and Piz Valdraus immediately adjacent.

Head down just right of another small stream, quickly descending past a side track that goes off leftwards to reach the valley floor. Here the broad grasslands of the **Plaun la Greina** stretch out to the south-west, drained by the **Rein da Sumvitg**, which meanders in numerous tiny channels before flowing away through a series of gushing gorges. The route now crosses the footbridge over the river, then follows markings up around the northern edge of the **Muot la Greina** ridge. After a short difficult section with a fixed rope, drop down again to reach the **Camona da Terri** (2170 metres, see Places to Stay) after 30 to 40 minutes. This timber and stone construction looks out northwards to the 3614-metre Tödi marking the Graubünden/Uri cantonal border.

Stage 2: Camona da Terri to Capanna Scaletta

(7.5 km, 1¾ to 2¼ hours)
Backtrack to the Rein da Sumvitg, then recross the footbridge and turn right (south) onto a good path running alongside the lovely river flats. Gradually rise away rightwards over regenerated moraine slopes and cross a large glacial stream to reach the gentle pass of **Crap la Crusch** at 2259 metres after 50 minutes to one hour. A prominent signposted foot track goes south from the Crap la Crusch to the Capanna Motterascio and Olivone. However the nicer route continues ahead across the Plaun la Greina.

Make your way west across the narrowing upper valley towards the mighty 3211-metre form of Piz Medel and continue on through an interesting rocky landscape, where upturned pale limestone strata contrast with brittle black shales. The route leads on past the small **Rifugio Edelweiss**, a private club hut sheltered from avalanches within a broad rock rib, to cross some way above the height of the **Passo della Greina** (Crap Greina), 40 to 50 minutes on. This watershed marks the

north-south continental divide and the Graubünden/ Ticino cantonal border.

The path traverses over loose broken shale and occasional small snowdrifts along the left side of the new valley, which has formed along the line of more quickly eroding strata of upended limestone. Where the main route crosses the stream, take the path that continues 400 metres on down to reach the **Capanna Scaletta** (see Places to Stay) after 20 to 25 minutes. This new A-frame hut rests on a round outcrop at 2205 metres, below which the land falls away abruptly into the Valle Camadra. Directly across the upper valley are the sheer walls of the 3211-metre Piz Medel.

Stage 3: Capanna Scaletta to Olivone

(8.5 km, 3 to 3¾ hours)
Jump across the stream at the main path above the hut to meet a flagged donkey track winding its way down the rocky and grassy mountainside. A fine view now opens out southwards to Campo and the interesting Sosto (2221 metres) with a steeply tilting pasture just below its pyramid-shaped summit. Farther down the route is blocked by heavily eroded slopes dropping away into a gully of accumulated snow dumped by winter avalanches. Here pick your way around to the right through the unstable rumble to reach the end of a dirt road at **Pian-Geirett**, after 25 to 30 minutes.

Walk past a utility cableway servicing the Capanna Scaletta and begin a snaking descent through the **Valle Camadra**, with occasional (poorly marked) short cuts at tight curves in the road fringed by wild raspberry bushes. Where the bitumen commences at **Daigra** (1408 metres), take a signposted path leading off left down between the hamlet's half-dozen dwellings. After briefly coming back onto the main valley road, the trail continues off rightwards along a pleasant forested track through the locality of **Ghirone**. Near a bridge over the Brenno, bear right past rustic old barns in grassy fields adjacent to the church of Baselga to arrive at **Campo** (1216 metres, see Places to Stay), 1¾ to 2¼ hours on.

Even if you have the option of taking an (infrequent) minibus from Campo, it's worthwhile continuing on foot to Olivone. Just after the bridge follow a short right-hand path above the Ristorante Genziana back to the road. Continue along the outer side of a concrete avalanche barrier to where the road enters a long tunnel, then head left along the old valley road cut into cliffs above a gorge. Although small landslides have long made this narrow carriageway quite impassable for vehicles, the walking is easy. The way leads down past a water tunnel spouting into the stream, then loops around hillsides overlooking **Olivone** to join the main road just down from the post office, 50 minutes to one hour after leaving Campo. For information on Olivone (889 metres), see Walking Bases in the Ticino chapter.

THE RUIN' AULTA
The Ruin' Aulta resulted from the largest mountain landslide that has ever occurred in Europe. As the last Ice age drew to an end around 14,000 years ago, the enormous glacier that once almost completely filled the valley of the Surselva retreated far back towards the headwaters of the Rein Anteriur (Vorderrhein). Without this icy buttress to support them, the mountains on the northern side of the valley (about where the skiing village of Flims now stands) suddenly collapsed, blocking a 15-km stretch of the river under some 15 billion cubic metres of rock and pulverised earth.

Backwaters built up behind this natural dam to create a large lake, which eventually broke through the mass of rubble, causing further devastation downstream. Over the following millennia the Rein Anteriur continued cutting its way through the deposits of debris to form this spectacular 400-metre-deep gorge. Natural erosion has produced weird pillars and columns that stand out in the chalky white cliffs, and the Ruin' Aulta is sometimes called the 'Swiss Grand Canyon'.

The local Romansch-speaking people – who have inhabited the valley for the last 1500 years – call the gorge the Ruin' Aulta,

or 'high ruin', while to the German Swiss the area is more familiar as the Vorderrhein-schlucht. Until the construction of the railway through the gorge itself, no transport route went via this rugged section of the upper Swiss Rhine. The Ruin' Aulta is still impassable for motor vehicles, and hence is an important natural sanctuary for wildlife.

Maps
Kümmerly + Frey's 1:60,000 sheet *Surselva* covers the walk. More detailed is the 1:25,000 walking map *Flims-Laax-Falera* published by the local tourist authorities, though it doesn't cover the start of the walk.

Walking Times & Standard
The walk through the Ruin' Aulta is a fairly short day hike. Although the route runs mainly along the base of the valley, markings are generally white-red-white – colours that otherwise indicate a high-Alpine route – because in places the continually eroding path calls for some sure-footedness. Keep clear of the (surprisingly busy) rail line except where the walking route itself leads over the tracks.

The walk is rated *easy to moderate* and is 12 km long.

Places to Stay
In Trin the *Gasthaus Ringel* (☎ 081-635 11 09) has rooms with private shower or budget dormitory rooms. In the lower village of Trin-Digg is the *Gasthaus Davos Crap* (☎ 081-635 11 22). Some people camp in the forest at Chli Isla, a peninsula of the river right in the Ruin' Aulta.

Getting to/from the Walk
The walk begins at Trin, a small village on the old Chur-Tamins-Flims road. Due to the opening of a bypass tunnel in 1995, not all postbuses on this route stop in Trin. The end of the walk is the Valendas-Sagogn train station on the Rhaetian Railway's Chur-Disentis line. The railway is the only transport route in the bottom of the valley, and roads both north and south of the river take a high route via villages on the high glacial terraces.

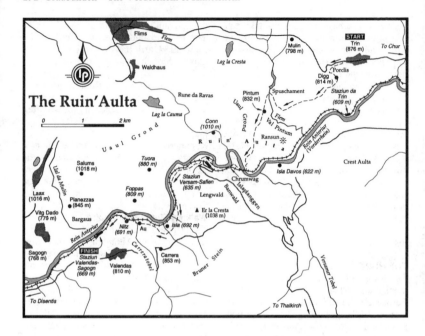

The Ruin'Aulta

Route Directions: Trin to Staziun Valendas-Sagogn

(12 km, 3¼ to 3¾ hours)

On the main road at the uphill side of **Trin** (876 metres) take the signposted footpath leading down through the lower village of **Trin-Digg**. A lonely country lane (the Senda Sursilvana marked with yellow diamonds) continues south-west through rolling pastures and pockets of beech forest on a long, broad terrace overlooking the valley of the Surselva. The impressive rock formation ahead to the right is the Crap da Flem, whose massive cliffs rise up abruptly behind the Alpine resort of Flims, giving the mountain an awesome fortress-like appearance.

After the roadway swings around northwards, follow route markings down left across the **Flem** stream and continue up a farm track to pass the houses of **Pintrun** (832 metres). Walk on up the dirt road over a slight crest (where the Senda Sursilvana departs on the right to Conn, then descend on to

Ransun, a lookout point at 805 metres above the Rein Anteriur (Vorderrhein). A white-red-white marked path now drops down quite steeply into the gorge, crossing the river on the pedestrian section of the railway bridge, 1¼ to 1½ hours from Trin.

A worthwhile 15-minute side trip to the tip of the peninsula known as **Chli Isla** can be made from 200 metres after the rail bridge, where various rough trails lead rightwards down through 'wild' camp sites. Immediately opposite, the spectacular chalky white cliffs of the Ruin' Aulta tower above the river. After climbing over a small, steep ridge past the turn-off up to Versam village, the main path drops down to the **Chrumwag** rail tunnel and makes its way upstream between the train tracks and the Rein Anteriur. In places the swift-flowing river forms whitewater rapids, and on summer days the odd inflatable raft may float past.

Where the stream makes another sweeping curve, cut straight ahead through more damp forest, rising slightly to cross over the rail tracks at the **Staziun Versam-Safien** (635 metres), 25 to 30 minutes on. The train station (for the village of Versam sitting high up on a glacial terrace at the mouth of the Safiental) looks across to another impressive cliff face of the Ruin' Aulta. Except in midsummer this part of the valley receives little direct sunlight.

Continue on above the rail lines, in places following embankments that protect the railway from landslides. Here the route leads through an interesting eroded landscape of caverns, chasms and columns formed in the unstable pulverised earth. Climb on leftwards and skirt above the farmlet of **Isla** (692 metres), from where the ski villages of Laax and Falera stand out on the slopes across the valley, then descend gently through the forest to reach the picturesque hamlet of **Au** after one to 1¼ hours. Cross the gushing Carreratobel via the rail bridge, and once again make your way upstream between the train tracks and the river. After passing final sections of chalk cliffs the path arrives at the **Staziun Valendas-Sagogn** (669 metres) after a further 15 to 20 minutes.

THE SAFIENBERG

Despite its German name, the 2486-metre Safienberg is really a pass that connects the Safiental, a remote side valley of the Surselva, with Splügen. During the early 14th century, the first Walser settlers migrated across the Safienberg into this quiet highland valley from the Rheinwald. In the lower reaches of the Safiental the Rabuisa stream runs through a deep gorge, cutting off the valley. Apart from the Safienberg itself, the Glaspass (east to Thusis) and the Tomülpass (west to Vals) were the best routes in and out of the valley. The Safiental therefore remained isolated from the Surselva until the early part of the 20th century, when the valley was penetrated by a proper road from Versam. Today the Safiental still lies well off the beaten track, and has kept much of its rural Alpine charm, with old timber houses and the traditional 'woven' wooden fences.

Maps

Best is Kümmerly + Frey's walking map *Surselva* at a scale of 1:60,000. Otherwise, two 1:50,000 SAW/FSTP sheets cover the route: *Safiental (257 T)* and *San Bernadino (267 T)*.

Walking Times & Standard

This is a day walk with an ascent of around 800 metres, so if you don't stay overnight in the Safiental you'd better arrive fairly early at Thalkirch. Despite the odd bit of loose rock or boggy ground, the route is in good condition and can easily be undertaken by all walkers with a reasonable level of fitness. The Safienberg is also quite popular with mountainbikers, and is rated *moderate*.

Places to Stay

Thalkirch's rudimentary *youth hostel* (☎ 081-647 11 07) is in an old farmhouse nearby. Check in at the next house up from the post office. It's a self-catering arrangement with no washing facilities, but is very cheap and has much rustic charm. There is no shop in Thalkirch, so hostellers will have to bring provisions with them. About 1.5 km upvalley is the *Berggasthaus Turahus* (☎ 081-651 11 85), the only other place to stay in the upper valley area. It offers rooms and (rather more expensive) dormitory accommodation.

Apart from an extremely basic shelter near the pass itself, there is no accommodation between the Turahus and Splügen. For places to stay in Splügen see Walking Bases.

Getting to/from the Walk

The walk begins in Safien-Thalkirch (or Malönja), a scattered hamlet at the end of the Safiental. Thalkirch is accessible by postbus from Versam-Safien railway station on the Chur-Disentis line. Throughout the walking season there are around 10 train/bus connections per day from Chur to Versam-Safien, with most buses going right to the Turahus. The 1¼-hour ride through the wild valley is interesting and scenic. Walkers arriving directly from the Valais or Ticino will have to travel via Disentis.

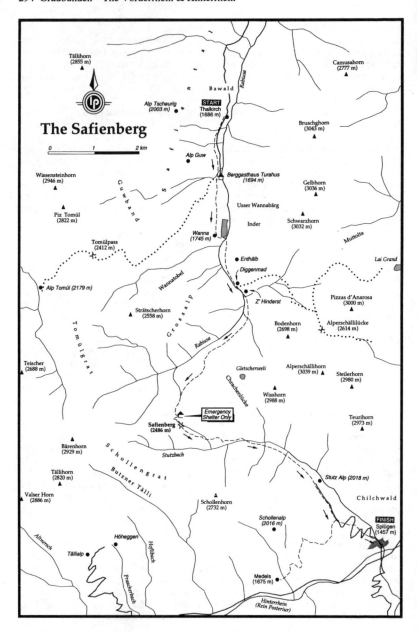

The Safienberg

0   1   2 km

START
Thalkirch
(1686 m)

Tällihorn
(2855 m)

Camusahorn
(2777 m)

Bawald

Alp Tscheurig
(2003 m)

Bruschghorn
(3043 m)

Wissensteinhorn
(2946 m)

Alp Guw

Berggasthaus Turahus
(1694 m)

Gelbhorn
(3036 m)

Piz Tomül
(2822 m)

Usser Wannabärg

Guwband

Schwarzhorn
(3032 m)

Muttolta

Inder

Wanna
(1745 m)

Tomülpass
(2412 m)

Lai Grand

Enthälb

Diggenmad

Alp Tomül (2179 m)

Wannatobel

Z' Hinderst

Pizzas d'Anarosa
(3000 m)

Strätscherhorn
(2558 m)

Grossalp

Bodenhorn
(2698 m)

Alperschällilücke
(2614 m)

Tomülgrat

Rabiusa

Gletscherseeli

Alperschällihorn
(3039 m)

Steilerhorn
(2980 m)

Teischer
(2688 m)

Chrachenlücke

Wisshorn
(2988 m)

Emergency
Shelter Only

Safienberg
(2486 m)

Teurihorn
(2973 m)

Bärenhorn
(2929 m)

Schollengrat

Stutzbach

Tällihorn
(2820 m)

Butzner Tälli

Stutz Alp (2018 m)

Chilchwald

Valser Horn
(2886 m)

Schollenhorn
(2732 m)

Schollenalp
(2016 m)

FINISH
Splügen
(1457 m)

Alfenisch

Höheggen

Hoflibach

Tällialp

Preacherbach

Medels
(1675 m)

Hinterrhein
(Rein Posteriur)

Route Directions: Thalkirch to Splügen
(13 km, 4¼ to 5¼ hours)
From Thalkirch post office (1686 metres) opposite the quaint old stone-roofed church, follow the bitumen 20 to 25 minutes upvalley past old wooden Walser-style houses and barns to the **Berggasthaus Turahus** (1694 metres, see Places to Stay). Disregarding a signposted path that branches off right up via the Tomülpass into the Valsertal, proceed past a stabilisation pond and cross the **Rabiusa** on a bridge.

The road leads on over riverside meadows scattered with small farms (from where another walking route goes up left towards the Alperschällilücke) to pass the hamlet of **Z'Hinderst**. Contrasting with the gentle grassy slopes to your right, the 3000-metre crags of the Pizzas d'Anarosa poke up from behind lower rock buttresses on the eastern side of the valley.

Continue along an old mule track past cascading rivulets, and begin climbing away to the left through a rocky gravel wash. The often steep trail brings you up beside an eroding stream, briefly follows a rounded ridge, then makes a final ascent in switchbacks past a small shelter to reach the **Safienberg**, 2½ to three hours up from the Turahus. This broad 2486-metre opening in the rocky ridge overlooks the upper Safiental, which – unlike the heavily-forested lower valley area – is characterised by broad mountain pastures. To the south-east you can make out the glaciated peaks of the Suretta group beyond Splügen.

Start descending the initially boggy grass slopes along a line of paint markings, then sidle down over to the left to cross the **Stutzbach** on a fixed-log footbridge, with the bare-rock outline of the Alpschällerhorn (3039 metres) rising up from steep talus slopes to your left. The path drops gradually against the contour above the true right bank of the stream, passing the stone alp hut of **Stutz Alp** (2018 metres) not long before coming to car park at the end of a road after one to 1¼ hours.

Follow the tarmac past a right-hand turnoff to Medels, then take well-signposted

short cuts down the steeply rolling hillsides above **Splügen** between the many hairpin bends in the road to enter the old town via an arched walkway 30 to 40 minutes on. Cobbled lanes lead either left over the bridge to the tourist office or rightwards down to the post office/bus stop (1460 metres). For more information on Splügen see Walking Bases above.

OTHER WALKS
The Senda Sursilvana
The Senda Sursilvana runs from the Oberalppass (see the Lai da Tuma walk) down through the valley of the Vorderrhein (Rein Anteriur) as far as Chur. Leading through the culturally interesting Romansch-speaking towns and villages of the Surselva. The approximately 100-km-long route forms one of the less strenuous long walks in Switzerland, taking four or five days to walk the entire length. Kümmerly + Frey has published a special 1:40,000 walking map titled *Senda Sursilvana*, which fully covers the route.

Zervreilasee to Vals
Known for its hot springs since prehistoric times (and, more recently for its bottled mineral water), the Valsertal was settled by Walsers in the 13th century. In the 1950s a dam was built in the upper Valsertal, flooding the historic summer village of Zervreila to create the Zervreilasee lake. The sharp pointed summit of the 2898-metre Zervreilahorn is the landmark peak of the upper valley. From the postbus stop at the Zervreilasee dam (1868 metres), a moderate high-level route leads up to the Guraletschsee, a lovely Alpine lake at 2409 metres. The descent is made via the Ampervreilsee and Selvasee lakes to Peil/Bodenhus, then along the road to Vals, the main village in the upper valley. This is a moderate five-hour walk. The best walking map is the SAW/FSTP sheet *Safiental (257 T)*.

The Heinzenberg Höhenweg
This scenic high traverse follows the crest of the Heinzenberg range, giving almost unbro-

ken fine views into the Safiental and the Hinterrhein valleys. Starting from Oberschappina (1571 metres), accessible by postbus from Thusis (see Walking Bases), the route first climbs up to the Glaspass (1846 metres) then leads over the Glaser Grat to the Bischolpass. From here continue along the ridgetop via the lookout summit of Tguma (2163 metres) to Präzer Höhi, thence descending via Alp Gronda to the Romansch-speaking village of Präz to catch the postbus back to Thusis.

The walking time from Oberschappina to Präz is five to six hours; recommended enroute accommodation is the *Berggasthaus Beverin* (☎ 081-651 13 23) on the Glaspass. Appropriate maps are the locally produced 1:25,000 special *Wanderkarte Thusis-Viamala-Heinzenberg*, Kümmerly + Frey's 1:60,000 *Surselva*, or the SAW/FSTP 1:50,000 sheet *Safiental* (257 T).

The Surettaseen

The Surettaseen are several sparkling blue glacial lakes perched on a high ledge overlooking the Rheinwald. This return day walk goes up directly from Splügen (see Walking Bases) to the three Alpine lakes known as the Surettaseen that sit below the 3027-metre Surettahorn on the Italo-Swiss border. All are glass-clear and reflect the magnificent surrounding mountain scenery.

From the locality of Bodmenstafel (1750 metres) on the Splügenpass road, a path climbs through open larch forest and across the broad area of highland pastures known as the Räzunscher-Alpen to Riedbödä, then on up to the lower and upper lakes at 2195 and 2266 metres. The descent leads back down via Riedbödä and the forested hillsides of Fugschtwald to Splügen (1457 metres).

The average walking time is approximately 3½ hours. From Splügen there are only two daily (morning and late evening) postbuses via Bodmenstafel to the Splügenpass. Reservation is essential (call PTT Thusis ☎ 081-651 11 85). Kümmerly + Frey's 1:60,000 sheet *Hinterrheintäler* covers the route.

The Hohenrätien & Carschenna

This easy circuit walk from Thusis (see Walking Bases) takes you up to the historically fascinating ruins of Hohenrätien, on a terrace high above the Viamala gorge at 946 metres. In prehistoric times a pagan temple existed here, but after the arrival of Christianity the site developed into a fortified settlement with a church. The castle complex stands on the old transit route of the San Bernadina and Splügen passes and presumably later served as a control and toll post. With the construction of an alternative road on the Hinterrhein's left bank in the late 15th century, the Hohenrätien fell into ruin. The site has been extensively restored since the early 1970s.

Another nearby feature of historical interest can be found 1.5 km uphill near Crap Carschenna (1180 metres), where there are ancient rock markings chiselled into smooth, glacier-polished slabs. The surprisingly intact patterns of concentric circles are believed to date back to Neolithic times, but their significance and exact origin is unknown. Visitors are requested not to stand on the rock slabs.

The descent leads down through the forest to Campi, and thence via Sils back to Thusis. The average walking time is four hours. Suitable walking maps are as for the Heinzenberg Höhenweg (see above).

Passo del San Bernadino & the Valle Mesolcina

The Passo del San Bernadino divides the Rhine basin from Graubünden's Italian-speaking Valle Mesolcina to the south. The relatively low 2065-metre pass has been a major trans-Alpine route since well before Roman times. This walk leads down from the Passo del San Bernadino through the Valle Mesolcina via Lago d'Isola and Pian San Giacomo to Mesocco (766 metres), the main town in the valley. This route is an easy five-hour walk, which largely avoids the often busy pass road. Walking maps are either the SAW/FSTP's 1:50,000 *San Bernadino (267 T)* or Kümmerly + Frey's 1:60,000 *Hinterrheintäler*.

The Engadine

The Engadine extends roughly 90 km along the valley of the En (Inn) River, from the Passo del Maloja as far as the Austrian border. Enclosed by mountain ranges that hinder the inflow of moist air masses, the Engadine has a dry climate typical for a high inner-Alpine valley, with warm, sunny summers and severe winters – similar to the Goms region of the Upper Valais. The Engadine can be divided into two fairly distinct upper and lower sections.

The 40-km section of the Upper Engadine (Engadin' Ota in Romansch) stretches northeast from the Passo del Maloja to Zernez. Here the valley floor is surprisingly broad with a very low gradient, and the upper half of the valley is filled by a chain of large highland lakes over 1800 metres above sea level. Rather than meeting the head of another valley at the Passo del Maloja, the Upper Engadine falls away abruptly southwest into the Val Bregaglia (Bergell), which together with the Val Poschiavo (Puschlav) forms one of the Upper Engadine's two Italian-speaking appendages. The Bernina massif borders the Upper Engadine on its southern side. The highest summit of this spectacular glacier-clad range, the 4049-metre Piz Bernina, is Graubünden's only 'four-thousander'.

The Lower Engadine (Engadina Bassa in Romansch) is somewhat different geographically to the Upper Engadine. Here the valley is rather lower and much narrower, repeatedly forcing the En (Inn) to flow through ravines and gorges. The Engadine's generally dry climate is particularly pronounced, and annual precipitation in the Scuol area scarcely exceeds 700 mm. The ranges surrounding the Lower Engadine are also comparatively lower, with beautiful forests of larch and mountain fir fringing the valley and interesting areas of Alpine plateaux higher up.

No other part of Switzerland has such fine walking in such a wild and undisturbed setting as the Lower Engadine. Relatively undeveloped and inaccessible, the Lower Engadine – with its large southern appendage, the Val Müstair, forms one of the last real strongholds of Switzerland's dwindling Romansch-speaking population, whose local dialect – called Ladin – is universally spoken throughout the region.

WALKING BASES
St Moritz

Spread out along the shoreline of the Lej da San Murezzan at around 1800 metres, St Moritz is the 'classic' Alpine resort. Its thermal baths were already known before the arrival of the Romans, but St Moritz experienced its first tourist boom in the Middle Ages, when pilgrims flocked here to bathe in the healing springwaters. Today St Moritz has a decidedly elitist image and caters mainly to the well-to-do, but the resort does make a good walking base for the Upper Engadine. A very scenic day hike directly from St Moritz goes up over the Pass Suvretta before descending via the Val Bever to the village of Bever in the main Engadine valley.

The *Olympiaschanze* (☎ 081-833 40 90) camping ground and the large *youth hostel* (☎ 081-833 39 69) are both in St Moritz Bad, half an hour's walk from the train station. The central *Hotel Bellaval* (☎ 081-833 32 45) has lower-budget rooms. The tourist office (☎ 081-833 31 47) is at Via Maistra 12.

There are roughly hourly trains from Chur directly to St Moritz (via Filisur). There are also regular trains via the Passo del Bernina to Tirano in Italy (with further connections to Milan). The *Palm Express* postbus service runs between Lugano and St Moritz several times per week.

Pontresina

The stretched-out village of Pontresina (1805 metres) occupies a sunny and sheltered position in the Val Bernina, the highest side valley of the Upper Engadine. Pontresina's Santa Maria chapel has medieval frescoes; also of interest is the

Ötzi, the Iceman

Throughout the Alps, 1991 is remembered as the year of the glacier bodies. By August, an unprecedented five bodies had been discovered in the melting snow. So, when Frau and Herr Simon stumbled across a sixth body, they naturally thought they had found the corpse of yet another ill-fated hiker. However, one week later incredulous scientists announced that the body was in fact that of a Neolithic hunter who had died more than 5000 years ago.

The discovery of this almost perfectly preserved body, nicknamed Ötzi because of its location near the Ötztal Alps, was in many ways miraculous. It was lying well off the normal hiking track, in a small rock hollow that protected the body from the grinding effects of the glacier. Scientists have calculated that, when found, Ötzi had only just emerged from the ice, and if not for his chance discovery, would have been reclaimed by the glacier and lost again in only a matter of days – perhaps forever!

Analysis of Ötzi's body and the accompanying artefacts continues to this day, producing fascinating evidence of life around 3200 BC. In fact, Ötzi's body is by far the oldest to have ever been retrieved from a glacier, and he ranks among the best examples of ancient mummified remains found anywhere in the world. Especially interesting are a series of tattoos decorating his body which may have been for a form of medical treatment akin to acupuncture. These tattoos make Ötzi the oldest tattooed man in history.

There is still much debate concerning who he was and what he was doing on the remote slopes. Ötzi's clothing - leggings and a coat made of deer-skin, a woven grass cape and shoes and a cap made of fur - show he was prepared for the cold weather, but the lack of any trace of food and the presence of a number of unfinished tools, especially an unfinished bow, raise a number of questions about his preparedness for the mountain conditions. One suggestion is that Ötzi was a shepherd caught by surprise by an unseasonable change in the weather. However, while his death was undoubtedly due to hypothermia, the additional fact that his ribs had been broken also suggests to some that Ötzi's trip to the mountains was unplanned – perhaps a desperate flight from the violent scenes in which he was injured.

Ironically, much of Ötzi's fame derives from the ownership dispute between the Italian and Austrian governments. Although Ötzi was rescued from the ice by Austrians, subsequent investigations revealed that his find-spot was actually (by less than 100 metres) on Italian territory. Only after weeks of political wrangling was it finally agreed that the body would remain in the possession of the University of Innsbruck until all scientific investigations had been carried out. It would then be given back into the care of the Italians. ∎

---

pentagonal Moorish tower. A classic local day walk involves taking the funicular up to Muottas Muragl (2453 metres), then hiking via the SAC hut of *Chamanna Segantini* (2731 metres) to Alp Languard (2270 metres), from where the descent continues either on foot or by chair lift to Pontresina.

Pontresina has a *camping ground* (☎ 081-842 62 85) and a 117-bed *youth hostel* (☎ 081-842 72 23) which is open from early June to mid to late October. The central *Hotel Garni Alvetern* (☎ 081-842 64 67) offers rooms as well as a bunkroom. Pontresina also has a tourist office (☎ 081-842 64 88); and its school of mountaineering, the Bergsteigerschule Pontresina (☎ 081-842 64

44), is one of the absolute best in Switzerland.

Pontresina is on the rail line from St Moritz (which continues over the Passo del Bernina to Tirano in Italy. There are also roughly half-hourly postbuses between Pontresina and St Moritz.

Maloja

The village of Maloja (1809 metres) lies just north of the Passo del Maloja. This peculiar pass plummets directly into the Italian-speaking Val Bregaglia on its western side, but drops imperceptibly to the east. There are interesting glacier mills, formed by water pressurised by ice, within easy walking distance. Maloja provides an excellent base for numerous other popular walks, including routes into the Val Bregaglia, along the Upper Engadine lakes, and over the historic Pass da Sett (Septimerpass) or the Passo de Muretto leading into Italy.

Maloja has a camping ground at *Plan Curtinac* (☎ 081-824 31 81) and a *youth hostel* (☎ 081-824 32 58). Other accommodation in Maloja is rather more expensive, with the *Hotel Longhin* (☎ 081-824 31 31) and the *Pension Bellavista* (☎ 081-824 31 95) being the least unaffordable places to stay. Maloja has a tourist office (☎ 081-824 31 88).

Depending on the season, there are up to 20 daily postbuses in either direction between St Moritz and Maloja. The *Palm Express* bus service between Lugano and St Moritz passes through Maloja several times per week in the summer season.

Poschiavo

Beyond the Bernina Pass lies the isolated Val Poschiavo, one of several Italian-speaking valleys in Graubünden. The only place of any size in the valley is the attractive town of Poschiavo itself. The small *Pensione Lario* (☎ 081-844 04 46) and the *Caffe Semadeni-Garni* (☎ 081-844 07 70) both offer budget rooms. There is excellent alternative accommodation elsewhere in the Val Poschiavo. The valley tourist office (☎ 081-844 05 71) is in Poschiavo. Poschiavo is on

the Rhaetian Railways line between St Moritz and the Italian border town of Tirano.

Zernez

Zernez (1471 metres) is situated at the upper end of the Lower Engadine near its junction with the Val da Spöl. The fire of 1871 destroyed most of the old town and today Zernez has a modern though pleasant streetscape. Significant architectural survivors are the castle of Wildenberg and the early Baroque church on the town's eastern edge. The town is an important transit point for walks into the Swiss National Park.

Zernez's local camping ground is *Cul* (☎ 081-856 14 62). Dormitory accommodation is available at the *Touristenlager* (☎ 081-856 11 41), *Hotel Bär + Post* (☎ 081-856 11 41) and the nearby *Friends of Nature hostel* (☎ 081-852 31 42). The *Hotel Adler* (☎ 081-846 12 13) has good budget rooms.

Zernez is on the Samedan-Scuol train line. There are up to eight daily postbuses via the Pass dal Fuorn (Ofenpass) to the Müstair.

Scuol

Scuol (Schuls in German) lies at 1243 metres in the lower part of the Lower Engadine and is the administrative hub of the region as well as its main tourist centre. Although the town is still largely Romansch-speaking, past fires and recent development have left a modern town centre with little of the charm of other places in the Lower Engadine. The town museum is in the Chagronda ('big house') and the nearby Tarasp castle, built on a rocky hillock that looks out over most of the valley, are worth visiting.

The local camping ground is *Gurlaina* (☎ 081-864 15 01). The *Hotel Grusaida (Alpenrose)* (☎ 081-864 14 74) and the *Hotel Quellenhof* (☎ 081-864 12 15) have lower-budget rooms. Scuol's tourist office (☎ 081-864 94 94) is in the middle of town.

If you're coming directly from northern Graubünden by train (via Chur and/or Filisur), you will have to change trains in Samedan. There are postbuses from Davos to Susch (via the Flüelapass) between early June and mid to late October, and train services to/from Scuol meet the bus in Susch. The Vereina tunnel, which is under construction and scheduled to open in the year 2000, will make Scuol directly accessible by train from Klosters.

Santa Maria/Müstair

Santa Maria (1258 metres) is a typical Romansch village in the Val Müstair, with old houses adorned with geometric and floral *sgrafitto* designs fronting the narrow main street. Several km downvalley near the Italian border is the somewhat larger village of Müstair with its historic 8th-century monastery.

Santa Maria has a *youth hostel* (☎ 081-858 50 52), but it generally only caters for groups. Two budget places to stay are the *Pensiun Crusch-Alba* (☎ 081-858 51 06) and the *Hotel Chasa Randulina* (☎ 081-858 51 24). In nearby Müstair, the *Chalavaina* (☎ 081-858 54 68) offers well-priced rooms. There are tourist offices in both Santa Maria (☎ 081-858 57 27) and Müstair (☎ 081-858 50 26).

There are up to eight daily postbus connections via the Pass dal Fuorn (Ofenpass) to Santa Maria and Müstair from Zernez between mid-June and mid to late October, sometimes with a change at the village of Fuldera. During this time there are also bus connections from Santa Maria across the scenic passes of Pass Umbrail and Passo di Stelvio (Stilfserjoch) into Italy.

THE UPPER ENGADINE LAKES

One of the region's most special features, the four highland lakes of the Upper Engadine lie strung together like a pearl necklace along the valley floor below towering craggy ranges. In the broad valley of the Upper Engadine it's easy to forget you're standing at around 1800 metres above sea level – not much less than most higher summits in the Alpine foothills! Some 10,000 years ago a single larger lake covered the Upper Engadine, but as alluvial debris was gradually washed out of the side valleys this larger lake was divided into several lakes.

In winter the lakes of the Upper Engadine

freeze over solidly, forming a one-metre layer of ice easily strong enough to support the thousands of participants in the world-famous Engadine Ski Marathon from Maloja to Zuoz. In summer countless windsurfers take advantage of the unfailingly consistent 'Majola Wind', one of the most unusual airstreams in the Alps. Quite contrary to the rules of wind dynamics in mountainous regions, the Majola Wind blows continuously in the 'wrong' direction, namely *down* through the Engadine valley, sparing the Upper Engadine from oppressively hot summer weather.

This walk takes you along the southeastern shore of the two largest of the Upper Engadine lakes, called Lej da Segl and Lej da Silvaplauna in the language of the local Romansch (or Silvaplanersee and Silsersee in the now equally widely spoken German). It leads through beautiful forests of larch, arolla pine and mountain pine, offering a continually changing perspective of Alpine and waterside scenery.

Maps

The recommended walking map is the 1:50,000 SAW/ESS sheet *Julierpass (268 T)*. Also suitable is Kümmerly + Frey's *Engadin' Ota/Oberengadin* scaled at 1:60,000.

Walking Times & Standard

This short lakeshore hike only takes several hours to complete, and can generally be done at any time of the year except winter. The nicest time is October, when the larch trees are their best autumn gold, but late in the season uncleared snow or black ice on the trail may make the walk unsafe.

The walk is 14 km long and is rated *easy*.

Places to Stay

For accommodation in Maloja and St Moritz see Walking Bases above.

Getting to/from the Walk

The walk begins in Maloja (see Walking Bases). Regular buses running between St

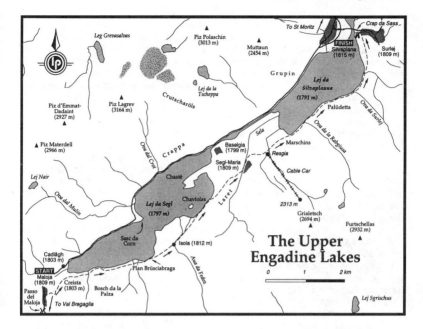

The Upper Engadine Lakes

Leg Grevasalvas

Piz Polaschin (3013 m) ▲

To St Moritz

Crap da Sass

FINISH
Silvaplana (1815 m)

Surlej (1809 m)

Muttaun (2454 m) ▲

Grupin

Lej da Silvaplauna (1791 m)

Lej da la Tscheppa

Crutscharöls

Piz d'Emmat-Dadaint (2927 m) ▲

Piz Lagrev (3164 m) ▲

Palüdetta

Ova da Surlej

Piz Materdell (2966 m) ▲

Ova dal Crot

Crappa

Sela

Baselgia (1799 m)

Marschins

Resgia

Ova da la Ratgtiusa

Lej Nair

Ova dal Mulin

Segl-Maria (1809 m)

Chastè

Cable Car

Lej da Segl (1797 m)

Chaviolas

Laret

2313 m ■

Grialetsch (2694 m) ▲

Furtschellas (2932 m) ▲

Sasc da Corn

Isola (1812 m)

Cadlägh (1803 m)

Plan Brüsciabraga

Aua da Fedoz

0   1   2 km

START
Maloja (1809 m)

Creista (1803 m)

Bosch da la Palza

Passo del Maloja

To Val Bregaglia

Lej Sgrischus

Moritz and Maloja stop in the village of Silvaplana at the end of the walk.

Route Description: Maloja to Silvaplana

(14 km, 2¾ to 3½ hours)

From the northern edge of Maloja, turn off the main road onto a minor road heading north-east. This goes across a grassy plain past a little church to meet a dirt track at the shore of the **Lej da Segl**; there is a small car park here. The well-marked route leads around the lakeside following short sections of path (or the dirt road itself) through beautiful larch forest with an alpenrose understorey. The views across the water are dominated by the 3164-metre summit of Piz Lagrev as you move out of the trees onto open grassland to reach **Isola** (1812 metres) after 45 minutes to one hour. These dozen or so rustic buildings stand at the edge of a flat alluvial fan formed by the Aua da Fedoz.

Cross this stream on a wooden footbridge, and continue on into the forest above cliffs

that fall directly into the Lej da Segl. The path passes the tiny islands of Chaviolas in front of the picturesque Chastè peninsula, gradually descending back to the shoreline before it comes to a side trail (signposted 'Laret/SeglPasso di -Maria'). Here leave off to the right away from the lake past several minor divergences to intersect with a broad road, following the bitumen down to arrive in **Segl-Maria**, 45 minutes to one hour on. This is another of the Upper Engadine's captivating old villages with Romansch-style stone houses. The German philosopher Friedrich Nietzsche spent many summers here during the 1880s, and the house in which he resided is now a museum.

Walk down the main street past the Nietzsche Haus to where a signpost points you off right. The route follows a small road over grassy fields past the lower station of the Furtschellas cable car to the southwestern edge of the **Lej da Silvaplauna**. Turn right and make your way along a broad walkway/bridle trail that traces the shoreline through more attractive open coniferous forest, with frequent clear views across the lake towards Piz Gülia (Julier) and ranges farther downvalley.

After merging into a road, the route cuts over meadows fringed by gravel beaches and past a distant thundering waterfall of the Ova da Surlej stream to meet a road near the pseudo-medieval castle of **Crap da Sass**. Here, sediments washed down by two opposing streams have gradually separated the Lej da Silvaplauna from the smaller Lej da Champfer. A short walk on across the bridge brings you up into the tourist town of **Silvaplana**, 1¼ to 1½ hours on from Segl-Maria.

THE LAKES OF MACUN

The Macun is a magical highland landscape that makes one of the most rewarding – if rather strenuous – day walks in Graubünden. Set in an impressive cirque enclosed by craggy peaks rising to over 3000 metres, this grassy bowl is sprinkled with over a dozen Alpine lakes and tarns. In the harsh climatic conditions above 2600 metres little more than a sparse vegetation of mosses, lichens and snow grasses can survive, and stock are driven up to graze in the Macun only for a very short period over the summer months. Although readily accessible on foot from the main valley of the Lower Engadine, the Macun remains a surprisingly undeveloped and wild area.

Maps

The recommended walking map is the locally produced *Wanderkarte Scuol-Tarasp-Vulpera*, scaled at 1:50,000. Kümmerly + Frey's 1:60,000 sheet *Engadina Bassa/Unterengadin* is another option.

Walking Times & Standard

This is a long day walk without the option of staying en route, so be sure to get an early start. With a total ascent/descent of around 1400 altitude metres and some rock-hopping on the higher slopes, it is reserved for the fit and agile. The highest part of the route leads along an exposed ridge at nearly 3000 metres, and the Macun area may remain snowbound into June. The Lower Engadine is known for its sunny weather, so don't forget the hat and UV cream. Carrying the appropriate wet-weather wear is also indispensable, and proper hiking boots will spare your feet in the rocky terrain.

The walk is graded *moderate to difficult* and is 16 km long.

Places to Stay

Although walkers have been known to pitch tents in the splendid seclusion of the Macun area, this is one hike with no mountain hut or restaurant anywhere en route – let's hope it stays that way! At the start of the walk in Lavin, the *Hotel Piz Linard* (☎ 081-862 26 26) on the village square, and the *Hotel Crusch Alba* (☎ 081-862 26 53) have better standard rooms. For accommodation in Zernez see Walking Bases above.

Getting to/from the Walk

The walk begins in the village of Lavin, which is serviced by trains on the St Moritz-Samedan-Scuol line. From Davos or Klosters the most direct way to reach Lavin is via the Flüelapass. Between early June and the last Sunday in October there are up to four daily postbuses from Davos over the Flüelapass to the village of Susch, on the Engadine rail line 3.5 km upvalley from Lavin. The Vereina rail tunnel, which is now under construction and scheduled to open for passenger services in the year 2000, will make Lavin (and the Lower Engadine) directly accessible by train from Klosters.

The walk ends in Zernez (see Walking Bases above).

Route Directions: Lavin to Zernez

(16 km, 6½ to 8½ hours)
From the village square just below **Lavin** train station (1412 metres), walk 250 metres down the main street to a barrel-like fountain, then proceed down left to cross the En (Inn) on a roofed wooden bridge. Continue up to the right along the gravelled road for

1.25 km past a tight bend, before leaving off left on a smaller forestry track that heads eastwards under buzzing high-tension power lines to **Plan Surücha** (1577 metres).

A broad path rises on gently up the forested slopes, turning gradually around south to cross the **Aua da Zeznina** on a small wooden bridge a short way before reaching the stone cottage at **Alp Zeznina Daidant** (1958 metres), 1½ to two hours from Lavin. These pleasant Alpine meadows look out northwards to the 3000-metre snowcapped peaks around Piz Buin, on whose southern slopes the side valleys of Val Sagliains, the Val Lavinuoz and the Val Tuoi drop steeply into the Engadine.

Make your way on into the **Val Zeznina** past a trail going off left to Murtèra, then begin climbing in numerous steep switchbacks through Alpine pastures strewn with alpenroses. The steep ascent continues via a gully filled with loose old moraines, but the gradient eventually eases as you rise up to a rustic shelter built against cliffs beside a little tarn. Cross over the streamlet and continue along its rocky western banks past a larger

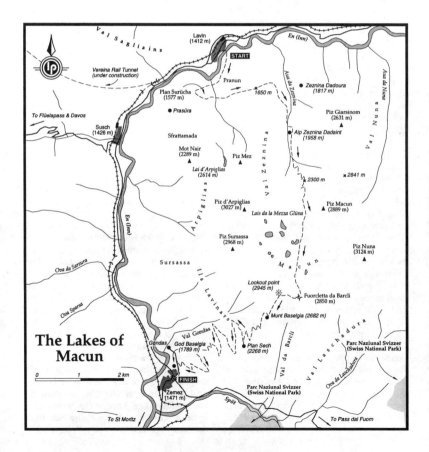

The Lakes of Macun

lake, where the upper valley opens out into the undulating plateau of **Macun**, 1¼ to 1¾ hours on.

This fascinating area of highland lakes, known in Romansch as the **Lai da la Mezza Glüna**, is worth spending an hour or two to explore. At the point where the main path recrosses the now tiny Aua da Zeznina, well-trodden walking pads lead off west to various lakes and tarns hidden amongst the grassed-over moraine mounds, the highest of which lies at 1631 metres. The Macun is enclosed on three sides by a craggy mountain cirque, and to the north the glacier-clad mountains crowned by the 3312-metre Piz Buin make a spectacular backdrop to this exceptionally scenic place.

Cross the stream and follow the white-red-white markings southwards up sparsely-vegetated ridges of glacial debris. As it gets higher the route climbs over steeper slopes of coarse, loose rock, with occasional sections of scrambling that bring you up to the **Fuorcletta da Barcli**, a gap in the range at 2850 metres. From here traverse west along the rocky ridgetop to reach a minor peak at 2945 metres after 50 minutes to 1¼ hours.

This point makes a superb lookout. To the south-west the panorama stretches up the Engadine valley from Zernez immediately below as far as the glistening white outline of 4049-metre Piz Bernina, and to the south-east across the wild valleys of the Swiss National Park to the 3899-metre Ortler in South Tirol, Italy. There is also a fine view back down into the Macun basin.

Trace a prominent spur running south-west directly from the summit, then drop away to the right through rows of avalanche grids on the open slopes of **Munt Baselgia** to meet an alp track at **Plan Sech** (2268 metres). Apart from occasional short-cuts to some of the curves the route keeps to this (gradually improving) road, making a long serpentine descent into the mixed coniferous forest via **La Rosta** and **God Baselgia**. The final stretch leads out onto grassy fields just above the town, then down past the church to arrive at the main road in **Zernez** (1471 metres, see Walking Bases) after 2½ to three

hours. The train station is a further 10 to 15 minutes' walk on to the left.

THE FUORCLA FUNTANA DA S-CHARL

The 2393-metre Fuorcla Funtana da S-charl links the Pass dal Fuorn (Ofenpass in German) with the Val S-charl, the longest side valley of the Lower Engadine. Although it lies mostly outside the Swiss National Park, the Val S-charl is a romantically wild area with the highest stands of mountain pines found in Europe. These forests were once heavily exploited to process the silver and zinc mined in the surrounding mountains from medieval times. Smelting works were built at the Pass dal Fuorn (Fuorn means 'furnace' in Romansch) and in the village of S-charl. In 1570 S-charl had some 70 houses, though today its buildings number just 13. The village is almost deserted during winter. Relics of the area's mining and smelting past include old shafts, slagheaps and kilns. While historically very interesting, they are lasting reminders of the devastating ecological damage caused by this long-abandoned industry.

Maps

The 1:60,000 Kümmerly + Frey sheet *Engiadina Bassa/Unterengadin* covers the walking route, and is useful for many other hikes in the Lower Engadine.

Walking Times & Standard

Although waymarked in the white-red-white colours of an 'Alpine route', this is a short and straightforward day hike that can be done by all walkers. Most of the Fuorcla Funtana da S-charl route is downhill so the walk has been given an *easy* rating.

Places to Stay

The *Hotel Süsom Givè* (☎ 081-858 51 82) on the Pass dal Fuorn has rooms, cabins and a backpackers' bunkroom. At S-charl (1810 metres) the *Pensiun Crusch Alba* (☎ 081-864 14 05) and the *Gasthaus Mayor* (☎ 081-864 14 12) have rooms in the mid to upper price range. S-charl also has basic dormitory accommodation.

Getting to/from the Walk

The walk begins at Süsom Givè on the 2149-metre Pass dal Fuorn. Between mid-June and mid to late October there are up to eight postbuses to Süsom Givè from Zernez (see under Walking Bases).

The walk finishes at the village of S-charl. Postbuses run between S-charl and Scuol up to four times daily from the end of May until the last Sunday in October; outside of this time there is no public transport. The last postbus leaves S-charl for Scuol shortly after 5 pm; reservation is essential (☎ 081-864 16 83).

Private vehicles are best parked at Zernez.

Süsom Givè (Pass dal Fuorn) to S-charl

(14 km, 3 to 3½ hours)

The path departs from directly opposite the Hotel Süsom Givè, first climbing slightly before contouring eastwards through the forest above the pass road to meet an alp track in the attractive Alpine meadow called the **Plaun de l'Aua** (2190 metres). To the south-east the magnificent wave-like form of the 3899-metres Ortler stands out as a solitary summit in perpetual snowfields. At the signpost a short way on (where the Senda Surova walking route through the Val Müstair continues right), follow white-red-white markings off left. The trail ascends the rolling slopes in steep switchbacks to another dirt road, and follows this over a small plain past winter ski-lifts to reach the **Fuorcla Funtana da S-charl** (2393 metres), 1½ to 1¾ hours from the Pass dal Fuorn.

Descend into the grassy basin below the pass, making your way left around a marshy flat past a large thumb-shaped boulder. After dropping down via a steep ridge above a streamlet the path comes onto a dirt road (with restricted vehicle access) at **Alp Astras** (2135 metres). This neat farmhouse sits under the eroding ranges near the junction of two pretty upper valleys. Walk on gently down above the meandering river past ruined homesteads on the adjacent eastern banks and through forests of nice old mountain pines. The route crosses the Clemgia on a small wooden bridge and leads on down

through the beautiful Val S-charl past little riverside flats with picnic tables to arrive in **S-charl** (see Places to Stay) after 1½ to 1¾ hours.

Lying at 1810 metres just east of the Swiss National Park, S-charl is a typical example of a small Engadine mountain village, and its dozen or so old stone buildings are decorated with *sgraffito* designs. S-charl's museum deals with the village's mining and smelting history. For those with the time, it's worthwhile extending the walk down through the Val S-charl to Scuol (2½ hours).

THE LAIS DA RIMS

The group of high-Alpine lakes known in Romansch as the Lais da Rims lie scattered and hidden across a rugged plateau at between 2800 and 2500 metres. Having been intensely glaciated in the recent past, the area resembles a moonscape and is extremely sparsely vegetated. The lakes are drained by the Uina stream, which flows through an amazing narrow gorge about one km in length and up to 400 metres deep. Due to their remoteness and inhospitable nature, the Lais da Rims form one of the Engadine's highland wilderness areas, receiving a modest number of hardy visitors.

Maps

The 1:50,000 sheet *Wanderkarte Scuol-Tarasp-Vulpera* produced by the local tourist authority is the most detailed walking map covering the Lais da Rims area. Kümmerly + Frey's *Engadina Bassa/Unterengadin*, scaled at 1:60,000, takes in the whole of the Lower Engadine.

Walking Times & Standard

This is essentially a two-day walk, with a night spent at either the Chamanna Lischana or the Restaurant Uina Dadaint. Although there are no great technical difficulties, this walk is physically quite demanding and crosses exposed high-Alpine country where the sun can be surprisingly intense. Depending on seasonal variation, the route may be snow-covered in places well into July or after late October. Of course you'll need sturdy

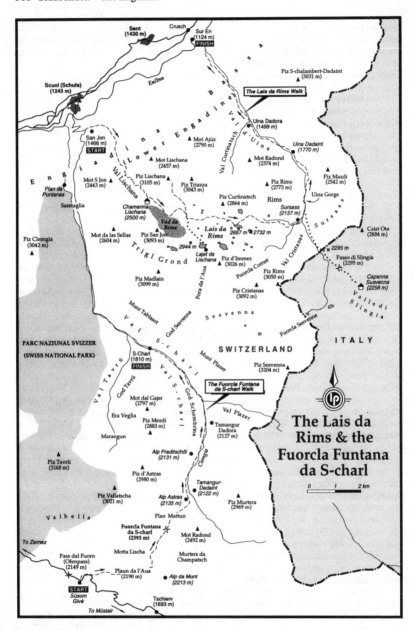

The Lais da Rims & the Fuorcla Funtana da S-charl

footwear for the rocky terrain, as well as fine and stable weather. The side trip to Piz Lischana is for experienced mountain walkers only.

The walk is rated *difficult*, and covers about 23 km.

Places to Stay

The 40-bed *Chamanna Lischana* (☎ 081-864 95 44) is a small and homy SAC-run hut at 2500 metres. It's staffed in July, August and September, but is always left open. Not far off the walking route is the *Capanna Sesvenna*, a large mountain-club hut some 1.5 km inside Italian territory across the Passo di Slingia.

The *Restaurant Uina Dadaint* (no telephone, open mid-June to early October) has a mattress room for walkers. At the end of the walk in Sur En is the *Gasthof Val d'Uina* (☎ 081-866 31 37), which has rooms and a dormitory; there's also a small *camping ground* (☎ 081-866 35 44) in Sur En.

Places to stay in Scuol are included in the Walking Bases section above.

Getting to/from the Walk

This walk starts off from the bus stop at San Jon, a short way above Scuol (see Walking Bases) on the road to S-charl. From the end of May until the last Sunday in October, postbuses from Scuol pass San Jon four times daily. The last postbus leaves Scuol train station shortly after 4 pm; reservations are essential (☎ 081-864 16 83). Otherwise it's a pleasant enough walk taking approximately one hour. There's a small car park at San Jon.

The walk ends at Sur En, from where are three daily postbuses back to Scuol via the charming Romansch village of Sent. The last scheduled departure from Sur En is around 4.30 pm. If you miss the last bus you can continue on foot to nearby Crusch on the main road, where regular postbuses running between Scuol and Martina stop.

Stage 1: San Jon to Chamanna Lischana

(5.5 km, 2¾ to 3¼ hours)
From the San Jon bus stop, walk a few paces

along the unsurfaced turn-off before heading up right along an alp track. This leads past the stud farm of San Jon at 1466 metres, then continues eastwards through a broad clearing to merge with another walking route in the trees. The path now begins a steep and tiring ascent in endless zigzags beside a small stream, leaving the forest as it leads into a small enclosed upper Val Lischana to arrive at the **Chamanna Lischana** after 2¾ to 3¼ hours.

The hut occupies a scenic position atop a prominent rock outcrop, and looks directly down towards Scuol in the main Engadine valley.

Stage 2: Chamanna Lischana to Sur En

(17 km, 5 to 6½ hours)
Ascend on over grassed-over moraines and coarse talus slides below Piz Lischana to near the end of the valley. The path cuts up leftwards between rock walls to climb rather more steeply via a scree-filled gully leading up to **point 2944 metres** on a broad, barren ridgetop, 1¼ to 1¾ hours from the Chamanna Lischana. Ahead of you lies a raw high-Alpine plateau, on which the numerous larger and smaller lakes known as the Lais da Rims lie scattered and hidden in the lunar landscape. At this point experienced walkers can opt to do the approximately one-hour return side trip to the 3105-metre summit of **Piz Lischana** by following a rough but well-trodden route northwards along the spur.

Walk a short distance along the ridge to a signpost at a track junction, where a trail continues ahead to the Lajet da Lischana. This starkly beautiful lake at 2857 metres can just be made out to the south in the direction of the 3905-metre Ortler (the unmistakable snowcapped peak in Italian South Tirol). Here head east and follow occasional red-white-red markings down through the bare terrain, slowly picking your way over mounds of glaciated rubble to pass above an attractive lake after 30 to 40 minutes. The route leads on left, rising slightly past a lone tarn before descending steadily above a rocky stream bed to **Sursass** (2157 metres), a grassy area in the valley floor, after a further 50 minutes to one hour.

Cross two little wooden bridges, then cut left across the meadows past a large boulder block to meet a foot track coming over the Passo di Slingia (2295 metres). (The Capanna Sesvenna, a mountain hut on the Italian side of the frontier, is 30 to 40 minutes' walk away. It makes a nice side trip, but the pass is not an official border crossing, so walkers who stay overnight at the Capanna Sesvenna are obliged to return to Switzerland.) Walk a short way on to where the valley narrows into the impressive **Uina gorge**. Here the path has been blasted into high cliffs; there are several short tunnels, and safety rails or steel cables securing the more dangerous sections.

Below the gorge the route enters the **Val d'Uina** proper, and goes over into a unsurfaced road (with vehicle access only by special permit). Make your way down through this lovely upper valley forested mainly with larch, soon passing the farm/restaurant of **Uina Dadaint** (see Places to Stay), a large yellow building at 1770 metres. The road descends gently on to the hamlet of **Uina Dadora** (1499 metres), which until the late 19th century was a thriving mountain village with several dozen inhabitants. You continually cross and recross the stream before arriving at the tiny village of **Sur En** (1124 metres, see Places to Stay), 2½ to three hours from Sursass.

If you missed the last postbus from Sur En, the bus stop on the main road at Crusch is 15 minutes' walk up via the quaint roofed wooden bridge across the En.

OTHER WALKS
The Val Rosegg & Fuorcla Surlej

Graubünden's mountains seldom attain the lofty heights of the Alps in the Valais or the Bernese Oberland. The exception is the Bernina massif, a superb range of glacier-smothered mountains in the Upper Engadine that touches 4000 metres. The route leads south-west from Pontresina (see Walking Bases) through lovely larch forests of the five-km-long Val Rosegg to the Hotel

Roseggletscher, then climbs diagonally up the slopes to the 2755-metre Fuorcla Surlej. From this high, narrow pass the views across to the Bernina massif include the classic knife-edge form of the Biancograt, one of the finest snow ridges in the Alps. The descent can be made by cable car from the middle station at Murel (2699 metres) or on foot via the tarn of Lej da la Fuorca.

This is a day walk that can be extended by making the long side trip to the *Chamanna Coaz* (☎ 081-852 53 06), an SAC hut at 2610 metres. The *Hotel Roseggletscher* (☎ 081-842 64 45, open June to late October) has better-standard rooms as well as a dormitory. The *Berghaus Fuorcla Surlej* (☎ 081-842 63 03, open early July to late September) on the pass height has a mattress room for walkers. The best walking map is the 1:50,000 SAW/FSTP sheet *Julierpass (268 T)*.

The Val Bregaglia Sentiero Panoramico

The Val Bregaglia (Bergell in German) is an Italian-speaking valley on the western side of the Maloja Pass. The Sentiero Panoramico is one of the nicest easy walks in the area. This well-marked 'panoramica route' has minimal gradient differences and runs downvalley through mixed forest and mountain pastures on the northern slopes of the Val Bregaglia. The path leads from Casaccia (1458 metres) via the hamlets of Braga, Rotticio, Durbegia and Parlongh to the village of Soglio at 1097 metres, from where there are postbuses back towards St Moritz.

The walking time from Casaccia to Soglio is around five hours. Casaccia's *Hotel Stampa* (☎ 081-844 31 62) has rooms and dorm accommodation. Two walking maps covering the route are the SAW/FSTP sheet *Julierpass (268 T)* and Kümmerly + Frey's 1:60,000 *Engiadin'Ota/Oberengadin*.

The Val da Camp/Poschiavo

Lying beyond the Passo di Bernina (Bernina Pass), the Val Poschiavo (Puschlav in German) is – like the Val Bregaglia – another of Graubünden's Italian-speaking valleys as well as being one of Switzerland's remotest corners. The Val da Camp (or Val Campo), a small and quite enchanting side valley of the Val Poschiavo, has an unusually rich flora with a decidedly south-eastern Alpine character.

From the small village of Sfazù, an easy and very pleasant route leads up through beautiful forests and pastures of the lower Val da Camp to Lago di Saoseo. This emerald-green lake was formed when a section of the nearby Cima di Saoseo collapsed into the valley. You can then continue up past the larger lake of Lagh da Val Viola to the 2432-metre Pass da Val Viola on the Italian frontier (six hours from Sfazù). Pass da Val is not an official border-crossing point, so you must proceed back via the Val da Camp.

There is en-route accommodation at the *Refugio Saoseo* (☎ 081-844 07 66), an SAC hut at Lungacqua (1985 metres) some way before the Lago di Saoseo, and the nearby *Ristorante Alp Camp* (☎ 081-844 04 82, June to October). The best walking map is a special sheet titled *Val Poschiavo*, scaled at 1:25,000 and produced by the local tourist authorities. Kümmerly + Frey's 1:60,000 *Engadina Bassa/Unterengadin* is a reasonable alternative.

The Swiss National Park

At the beginning of the 20th century the rugged mountain ranges that now form the Swiss National Park (Parc Naziunal Svizzer in Romansch) were an ecological disaster area. Centuries of mining, uncontrolled clearing of the Alpine forests, local smelting of silver, zinc and lime, overgrazing and the ruthless hunting of wild animals had devastated the local environment.

Although some people believed the environment would never recover, an original nature reserve was established in 1909. With the addition of small sectors since then, the Swiss National Park now totals almost 170 sq km. Today the park is one of Switzerland's few true wildernesses, whose abundant wildlife includes large herds of chamois, ibex and red deer. Extensive forests of mountain pines cover the mountainsides and large scree-slides descend from the (naturally) eroding

dolomite ranges. Even so, nature will need at least another hundred years to fully re-establish itself.

Several good hikes lead through the park. Recommended is the trail directly from Zernez (see Walking Bases) up through the Val Cluozza to the *Chamanna Cluozza* (☎ 081-856 12 35), a staffed hut open from late May to mid-October. From here there are several good route alternatives of varying difficulty. An easier and shorter option is continuing up east via Murter to Praspöl on the Zernez-Pass dal Fuorn road (postbus). A more difficult overnight route (or long day walk) from the Chamanna Cluozza leads up southwards via the Fuorcla Val Sassa into the Val Müschauns to the *Chamanna Varusch* (☎ 081-854 31 22), another hut in the Val Trupchun (accessible from S-chanf.

It is strictly prohibited to take animals, catch fish, ride mountainbikes, light fires, pick wildflowers or camp anywhere within the park. Walkers must not leave the network of marked paths, and access to some areas is therefore not possible. Having learned that humans present no danger, the herds of game are undisturbed by throngs of summer walkers and can be viewed at surprisingly close range. (During the autumn hunting season, many animals actually take refuge in the park.) The Swiss National Park attracts large numbers of walkers, and during the tourist season the paths and huts can become quite crowded.

The park headquarters (☎ 081-856 13 78) at Zernez has an interesting information centre. Kümmerly + Frey publishes a special 1:45,000 walking map titled *Parc Naziunal Svizzer*.

The Furcletta

The 2735-metre gap known as the Furcletta provides a high-level crossing route between the Val Tuoi and the Val Tasna, two lovely side valleys that descend south into the Lower Engadine from the glaciers of the Silvretta range. The walk begins from Guarda (1653 metres), arguably the most beautiful and intact Romansch-style village anywhere in the Engadine, following an alp track up to the *Chammana Tuoi* (☎ 081-862 23 22), an SAC hut at 2250 metres below Piz Buin. From here the route continues up east over the Furcletta, then drops down through the tiny Val Urezzas into the Val Tasna before descending to Ardez (1432 metres), another quaint village on the Lower Engadine rail line.

As this is a relatively strenuous route with an average walking time of eight hours, the Furcletta is best crossed as a two-stage hike. Use Kümmerly + Frey's 1:60,000 walking map *Engadina Bassa/Unterengadin*.

The Val Mora & Val Vau

Although they lie directly behind a low range just to the south of the Val M-stair, the two tiny valleys of the Val Mora and Val Vau are relatively little visited by walkers and make gentle and very pleasant walking country. The walk leads from Süsom Givè at the Pass dal Fuorn via Jufplaun up through the Val Mora. After crossing over the gentle pass of Döss Radond (2234 metres) the route descends via the narrow Val Vau to Santa Maria (see Walking Bases). A longer but worthwhile route variant goes up from Döss Radond past the Lai da Rims, a majestic Alpine lake at 2420 metres, then drops back into the Val Vau.

This easy five to six-hour walk mostly follows alp tracks with restricted vehicle access. The hike is covered by the locally produced 1:50,000 walking map *Zernez-Nationalpark-Münstertal* or Kümmerly + Frey's 1:60,000 sheet *Engadina Bassa/-Unterengadin*.

North-Eastern Switzerland

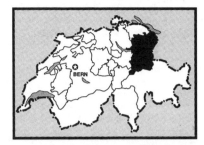

Stretching southwards from the rolling green Alpine foothills of the Swiss Mittelland and Lake Constance, the mountains of North-Eastern Switzerland – in the cantons of Glarus (the 'Glarnerland'), St Gallen and the two half-cantons of Appenzell – offer some of the most varied and interesting walking in the country. The Walensee (Lake Walen), a large Alpine lake in a long and deep glacial trough, divides the Alpstein and Churfirsten to its north from the Sarganserland and Glarner Alps region on the lake's southern side.

The Alpstein & Churfirsten Region

Dominated by the 2503-metre summit of the Säntis, the compact group of limestone ranges known as the Alpstein are the north-ernmost mountains of the Swiss Alps and form a very spectacular and interesting region. These impressive rock peaks jut up so abruptly from the more gently contoured hills of the Appenzellerland and Toggenburg that their relatively low height is not obvious.

Separated only by the valley of Obertoggenburg, the nearby Churfirsten are no less majestic. From the north this unique range appears as a serrated row of individual mountains divided by deep grassy saddles, yet when viewed from the Walensee the Churfirsten present a seemingly impenetrable barrier.

The Alpstein and Churfirsten are geologically very similar, being composed of hard limestone originating from the ancient Tethys ocean. These mountains are also of relatively recent origin, having been gradually uplifted and buckled from around 10 million years ago by tectonic forces into their remarkable form. The Alpstein and Churfirsten have perhaps the best conditions for Alpine rock-climbing in Switzerland, though humble walkers still greatly outnumber the alpinists.

WALKING BASES
Appenzell

Although very touristy, Appenzell, the tiny capital of the (Catholic) half-canton of Appenzell-Innerrhoden, makes a nice temporary walking base. The streets and lanes of this very small town are lined with quaint old Appenzeller houses, many with elaborately painted façades. Also worth a visit are the Baroque St Maurititus church, which has beautiful stained-glass, and the 16th-century town hall. A nice half-day hike from Appenzell climbs south-west along the sandstone ridges via Scheidegg to the 1652-metre lookout summit of Kronberg, from where a cable car descends to the train station at Jakobsbad.

Appenzell's local camping ground is

Camping Eischen (☎ 071-787 50 30). The *Gasthaus Hof* (☎ 071-787 22 10) offers surprisingly good-value dormitory accommodation. The *Hotel Traube* (☎ 071-787 14 07) is one of Appenzell's less expensive places to stay. The tourist office (☎ 071-87 96 41) is on Hauptstrasse in the town centre. Appenzell is most easily accessible by roughly hourly trains (the narrow-gauge Appenzeller Bahn) from St Gallen via either Herisau or Gais.

Wildhaus

Wildhaus (1090 metres) is the main tourist centre of the upper Toggenburg (or Thur Valley). Originally a Walser settlement, this scenic village lies scattered along the Nesslau-Buchs road between the Alpstein massif and the Churfirsten. Urich Zwingli, the 16th-century religious reformer, came from Wildhaus, and his birthplace, the Zwinglihaus, is one of the oldest wooden buildings in Switzerland. The 60-km-long Thurweg walking route runs from Wil through the Toggenburg to Wildhaus, and the Rheintal-Höhenweg, a 115-km walk along the Rhine Valley from Rorschach (on Lake Constance) to Sargans, passes through Wildhaus.

The *Hotel Rösliwies* (☎ 071-999 11 92) offers quite good value in rooms. There is a *youth hostel* (☎ 071-999 12 70) some two km down towards Unterwasser (ie west) from the village centre, and local camping at the *Schafbergblick* (☎ 071-999 19 34), 800 metres along the road towards Buchs. The tourist office (☎ 071-999 27 27) is 800 metres west of the village centre.

Postbuses running between Buchs (train connections to Sargans/Zürich, Altstätten/St Gallen and Chur) and Nesslau (train connections to Wil/Zürich) pass through Wildhaus approximately every hour until about 9 pm.

Walenstadt

This attractive small town is at the foot of the Churfirsten where the Seez flows into the Walensee. Of particular interest in the well-preserved historical centre of Walenstadt are the old town hall and the church dating from the 8th century. Parts of the old town walls remain.

Two good budget places to stay in Walenstadt are the *Hotel Krone* (☎ 081-735 11 70) and the *Hotel Traube* (☎ 081-735 12 59), or contact the tourist office (☎ 081-735 22 22). The local camping ground is the *Campplatz Ziegelhütte* (☎ 081-735 18 96).

Walenstadt is on the main Zürich-Chur rail line, serviced at least hourly by expresses. From the small harbour you can catch one of the ferry boats that ply the Walensee, stopping at many villages around the lakeshore.

THE SÄNTIS

The 2503-metre Säntis is a northern outpost of the Alps and the highest peak in the Alpstein. In good conditions the summit – with its prominent telecommunications tower – is clearly visible from Zürich and southern Germany. This walk takes you up through a tiny valley between the ranges of the Alpstein to the top of the Säntis, which was the main access route before the construction of the cable car from Schwägalp. For more than 100 years there has been a meteorological station on the Säntis, and the original weatherperson's house still sits on the summit.

Maps

Best for this walk is either the 1:25,000 sheet *Wanderkarte Obertoggenburg-Appenzell*, published by the Kantonal St Gallische Wanderwege, or the SAW/FSTP's 1:50,000 sheet *Appenzell (227 T)*. Other good options are Kümmerly + Frey's *Säntis-Alpstein*, a special walking/skiing map scaled at 1:40,000, or K + F's 1:60,000 sheet *St Gallen-Toggenburg Appenzellerland*, which covers a much broader swathe of North-eastern Switzerland, including the Churfirsten area to the south. Readers should also refer to the Alpstein Massif map in this chapter.

Walking Times & Standard

This is an energetic day walk requiring a

good level of fitness as it makes an often steep ascent totalling over 1600 altitude metres. Those wanting something less strenuous can do the walk in the opposite direction in rather less time, but the constant descending can be hard on the knees. The going is easier in late summer and autumn when less snow will be encountered.

The walk is rated *moderate to difficult*.

Places to Stay

The *Hotel Alpenrose* (☎ 071-799 11 33), just up from the small terminal station at Wasserauen, offers good value for rooms of various standards.

On the shore of the Seealpsee are the *Berggasthaus Forelle* (☎ 071-799 11 88) and the *Berggasthaus Seealpsee* (☎ 071-799 11 40). Both offer good value for rooms and dormitory accommodation (with showers), and are open from early May until the end of October. The *Berghaus Mesmer* (☎ 071-799 12 55, open June to October) at Unter Mesmer has bunks for walkers at reasonable rates (but no showers).

On the Säntis summit itself is the *Berggasthaus Säntisgipfel* (☎ 071-277 99 55), which offers rooms in the medium to upper price range; a few minutes down is the smaller *Berggasthaus Säntis* (☎ 071-799 11 60), with rather cheaper rooms as well as dormitory accommodation (no showers).

In Schwägalp there is the *Hotel Schwägalp* (☎ 071-364 16 03) by the lower cable-car station at 1352 metres, and just down the road you'll find the *Hotel Passhöhe* (☎ 071-364 12 43).

Getting to/from the Walk

The walk commences at Wasserauen, which is best accessible by almost hourly trains (Appenzeller Bahn) from St Gallen via Herisau and Appenzell (see Walking Bases); if you're arriving by train from Graubünden, you'll travel via Sargans and Altstätten.

The walk ends on the 1503-metre summit of the Säntis, from where there are cable cars down to Schwägalp. Between late May and mid-October the cable car operates at least half-hourly from 7.30 am until 6.30 pm (or

7 pm in July and August); various fare concessions apply. From Schwägalp there are some 10 postbuses per day to Urnäsch (train connections to Herisau/St Gallen/Zürich) and up to seven buses daily to Nesslau (train connections to Wil/Zürich). In summer the last bus in either direction leaves around 6.30 pm.

Route Directions: Wasserauen to Säntis Summit

(9 km, 4¼ to 5¼ hours)

From Wasserauen railway station (868 metres), follow the bitumen up through the narrow valley alongside the Schwendlibach stream, passing typical Appenzell-style shingled houses and a small electricity station at **Rössenaueli**. Where the stream flows through the **Schwendlibachschlucht** the road heads up through patches of light forest to reach the Seealpsee (1141 metres, see Places to Stay) after 50 minutes to one hour. With the Säntis as a backdrop, this appealing lake nestles between craggy ranges of the Alpstein and makes a delightful spot for a rest and a snack. In hot weather the Seealpsee is suitable for bathing.

Take the dirt farm road around the northern shore of the Seealpsee, continuing gently uphill across the **Seealp**. Recent landslides from the peaks above have left these lovely meadows strewn with heavy boulders that now shelter small alp huts from avalanches and further rockfall. Where the vehicle track finishes near the Seealp's south-eastern corner, a white-red-white marked path begins climbing in short spirals through a tiny steep gully fringed by abrupt bluffs. Shortly after passing a spring, where the small stream emerges from moraines, you come to the **Berghaus Mesmer** (1613 metres) at **Unter Mesmer**, 1¼ to 1½ hours from the lake.

Continue up into the **Fälalp**, an enclosed upper basin of recent glacial origin where snow often lasts well into the season. The cut path sidles along cliffs to the right of a talus-choked sink with the red and white colours of the Säntis' telecommunications tower looming ahead, before making its way up an

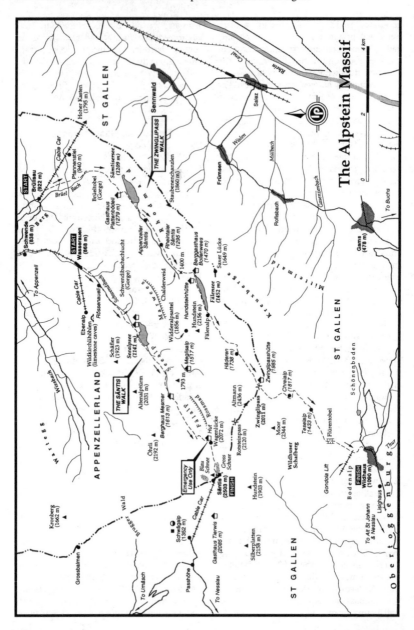

The Alpstein Massif

elongated rocky, grassy mound. A steep climb left brings you through loose slopes below a cross erected atop a rock needle on the Rossmad ridge to reach the **Wagenlücke** (2072 metres) after 1¼ to 1½ hours. There is a small stone shelter here for emergency use.

Head westwards to the left of the ridge, rising steadily against the contour, to bare-rock slopes above the Gross Schnee, one of only two small (and gradually receding) glaciers within the Alpstein massif. The route now makes a final zigzagging ascent through the rock (with sections of fixed cable to ease the nerves) to arrive at a platform immediately below the **Säntis**, after one to 1¼ hours.

As has been obvious for most of the way up, the mountaintop is crowded with the weather station, telecommunications tower, restaurant/hotel and cable-car buildings. On an average summer day this summit is teeming with cable-car visitors, but walkers can take pride that such artificial means will only be used for the descent. In clear conditions the panoramic views are stupendous in all directions, stretching southwards across the nearby peaks of the Churfirsten to the Alps, west to Zürichsee, eastwards to the mountains of Vorarlberg as well as north towards Lake Constance.

The two hour walk down to Schwägalp via the Gasthaus Tierwis is extremely steep in places and requires considerable balance surefootedness.

THE ZWINGLIPASS

This walk leads through a picturesque corner of the Alpstein massif that offers constantly changing scenery. The route passes by the Sämtisersee and Fälensee, two contrastingly idyllic mountain lakes, before crossing over the 2011-metre Zwinglipass into the Toggenburg. More apparent here than on the nearby Säntis walk are the fields of karst, a jagged greyish limestone which occurs throughout the Alpstein. On the heights of the Zwinglipass this porous rock has formed interesting sinkholes.

Maps

For the recommended walking maps see the Säntis walk above.

Walking Times & Standard

The walk from Brülisau to Wildhaus can be done by anyone with a reasonable level of fitness, either in two short stages or as a longer day walk. Robust footwear is important in this frequently rocky terrain, along with wet-weather clothing. The Zwinglipass is lower than the nearby Säntis route, and the walk can normally be undertaken from around early June until mid-November.

The walk is rated *moderate*, and covers 17.5 km.

Places to Stay

In Brülisau at an altitude of 922 metres, the *Hotel-Restaurant Krone* (☎ 071-799 11 05) offers surprisingly good value for standard rooms and dormitory accommodation. The *Gasthaus Plattenbödeli* (☎ 071-799 11 52) at Plattenbödeli near the Sämtisersee has rooms and dorms (with showers).

Recommended is the *Berggasthaus Bollenwees* (☎ 071-799 11 70, open May to October), a large mountain hotel at 1470 metres by the Fälensee. It has rooms and a dormitory, and showers are available. Higher up on the lake's northern slopes is the SAC's *Hundsteinhütte* (☎ 071-799 11 52), which is staffed from May to October but always left open.

At Fälenalp walkers can sleep in the barn during the summer months (very cheap and rustic). Farther on near the pass is the *Zwinglipasshütte* (☎ 071-988 28 02), a self-catering hut also owned by the SAC; it's staffed on weekends, but is never locked.

For places to stay in Wildhaus see the Walking Bases section above.

Getting to/from the Walk

To reach the start of the walk at Brülisau, take a Wasserauen-bound train from Appenzell (see Getting to/from the Walk section of the Säntis walk above), then disembark at the Weissbad station. From Weissbad there are at least hourly postbuses to Brülisau until roughly 6 pm.

The walk terminates at the small village of Wildhaus (see Walking Bases).

Stage 1: Brülisau to Berggasthaus Bollenwees

(7.5 km, 2¼ to 2¾ hours)

A popular alternative to Stage 1 involves taking the Hoher Kasten cable car from Brülisau, then walking south-west from the upper station (1795 metres) along the ridge via the 1860-metre Stauberenchanzlen and the saddle of Saxer Lücke (1649 metres) to the Fälensee. This route offers some wonderful views of the Rhine Valley.

From the lower Hoher Kasten cable-car station follow the signposted bitumen south-east, quickly crossing underneath the wires, past scattered wooden-shingled houses in the green fields to **Pfannenstiel** (940 metres). The quiet dirt road leads into the forested Brüeltobel gorge, rising up over a watershed to reach the quaint old **Gasthaus Platten-bödeli** (1279 metres, see Places to Stay) after one to 1⅓ hours.

Fifty metres on from the Gasthaus take a path (signposted 'Waldabstieg') down left to the **Sämtisersee**, making your way around the shoreline to meet the road again on flowery paddocks at the lake's upper side. Sandwiched between steep forested slopes, the Sämtisersee is one of the most attractive natural spots in the Alpstein massif, and in summer its shallow waters are generally warm enough for bathing.

Bear right at a fork at **Appenzeller Sämtis**, and head on towards the main peaks of the Alpstein through a charming little valley in which the stream flows through a terraced trench. The old dirt track peters out at the farmlet of **Rheintaler Sämtis** (1295 metres), and a foot track marked with red and white paint splashes continues up to the grassy flats of **Chalberweid** below impressive rock spikes of the Marwees ridge. Ignoring trails going off right to the Bogartenlücke and the Widderalpsattel ahead, ascend southwards via a steep gully

onto a tiny saddle from where the stark, elongated form of the **Fälensee** comes into view, 1¼ to 1½ hours from the Gasthaus Plattenbödeli.

The walk up to the **Hundsteinhütte** leaves off right (another 20 minutes), while the **Berggasthaus Bollenwees** (1470 metres) stands a short way ahead looking straight out across this very scenic, deep-blue lake. The Fälensee fills an enclosed glacial trough below towering craggy ranges, and is a typical karst lake which drains away subterraneously.

Stage 2: Berggasthaus Bollenwees to Wildhaus

(10 km, 3¼ to 4¼ hours)

Head around the Fälensee's northern edge, sidling across broad scree fields that slide right into the water to reach the **Fälenalp** at the lake's far end. Braving avalanches and rockfall, in season these alp huts of this romantic isolated pasture have milk for sale. Above you, spectacular needles protrude from the almost overhanging rock walls of the Hundstein (2156 metres). Continue on past marmot colonies in the tiny upper valley, before beginning quite a steep climb along a vague grassy ridge leading up to the three stone shelters of **Häderen** at 1738 metres, one to 1⅓ hours from the Bollenwees.

The route now rises more gently through long fields of karst, with good views ahead to the rounded 2436-metre Altmann, the Alpstein's second-highest summit. After passing through a dry-stone fence marking the Appenzell/St Gallen cantonal border, cross over the **Zwinglipass** (2011 metres), a rocky, grassy plateau full of depressions and sinkholes, then descend briefly leftwards to arrive at the **Zwinglipasshütte** (see Places to Stay), 40 to 50 minutes on. This hut sits at 1985 metres on a terrace that serves as a good lookout point for the adjacent Churfirsten peaks.

Drop down the grassy mountainside, moving over to the left past **Chreialp** (1817 metres) – a group of herder's huts standing below sheer cliffs opposite a prominent rock needle. The well-formed path now makes a much steeper descent in numerous switchbacks to reach the dairy of **Teselalp** (1433 metres) at the end of a farm track in a pleasant upper valley, after 50 minutes to 1¼ hours.

Follow the dirt road for 1.25 km to where a signposted foot track departs at the left. Make your way 400 metres down via the small dry chasm of the **Flürentobel**, before branching away to the right through little clearings in the spruce forest to meet another road near a gondola lift. Continue down, short-cutting the odd road curve to arrive at **Wildhaus** (see Walking Bases), 50 to 60 minutes from Teselalp. The village centre (1090 metres) is a short way down to the right along the main road.

THE CHURFIRSTEN

The Churfirsten forms one of the most striking ranges found anywhere in the Alps. Seen from the south this amazing row of horn-like peaks rises up as an abrupt barrier separating the Walensee from the Toggenburg region. This traverse route explores the high slopes between the lake and the main Churfirsten range, offering classic views of both.

Maps

Your best option is either of two 1:50,000 sheets: *Walenstadt (237 T)* published by the SAW/FSTP, or the *Wanderkarte St Galler Oberland-Toggenburg* (5015), produced by the Kantonal St Gallische Wanderwege. Another possibility is the Kümmerly + Frey walking map *St Gallen-Toggenburg Appenzellerland*, at a scale of 1:60,000.

Walking Times & Standard

This is a day walk with relatively little altitude gain. Much of the route is out of the trees on open slopes with a southerly exposure, so during the middle of the day the going may get a bit hot. The southern side of the Churfirsten is generally snow-free at least by early May, making this a good walk to do in spring.

In September and October the Schrina area is temporarily closed for army target practice. Access to all marked paths is guaranteed, but walkers may have to wait from 30 minutes to one hour before the sentry guides you through the shooting range. To check the local situation, call the regional military (EMD/DMF) information office in Sargans on ☎ 081-725 11 22.

The walk is rated *easy to moderate*, with a distance of 13 km.

Places to Stay

There are two en-route accommodation options. The *Bergrestaurant Schrina* (☎ 081-735 16 30) at Hochrugg (1290 metres, open July and August) is a large establishment offering rather basic rooms and – when not taken over by the military – dormitory accommodation at fair rates. The *Restaurant Tschingla* (☎ 081-735 21 61), at 1527 metres, has a dorm and serves simple meals and refreshments. It's open early from June to mid to late September.

For places to stay in Walenstadt, see Walking Bases at the start of this section.

Getting to/from the Walk

Walenstadt is the base for this walk, which sets out from near the Höhenklinik (sanatorium) at Knoblisbühl, high above the Walensee at some 960 metres. PTT minibuses run from Walenstadt train station to Knoblisbühl up to seven times per day, the last leaving at around 5.30 pm. One of the morning buses continues up to Hochrugg if there are enough passengers.

The walk returns to Walenstadt.

Stage 1: Knoblisbühl to Walenstadt

(13 km, 3¾ to 5 hours)

From where the postbus lets you off at **Knoblisbühl Höhenklinik** (approximately 960 metres), follow the bitumen uphill through the forest. Short-cutting occasional curves, the road climbs out onto the open hillsides scattered with holiday and farm houses before coming to the **Bergrestaurant Schrina** at Hochrugg (1290 metres, see

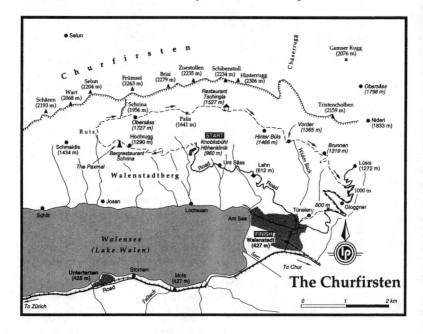

The Churfirsten

Places to Stay) after one to 1⅓ hours. A short walk from here is the Paxmal, an interesting mosaic monument dedicated to peace, which was completed by artist Karl Bickel in 1949 after 25 years of work.

Continue a further one km up the road to where a signposted path departs on your right. This brings you over the grassy pastures of **Rutz**, then spirals up along a steep cow-trodden track to a piped spring spilling into a water trough. Head on eastwards over the **Schrina** ridge, passing the stone cottage and barn at **Obersäss** (1727 metres) after 50 minutes to 1¼ hours. Far below lie the sparkling-blue waters of the Walensee, while ahead and directly above you the majestic rock walls of the Churfirsten present a dramatic outline.

Make your way along a broad, undulating balcony fringed by scree slides at the base of the Churfirsten. The trail rises gently over **Palis**, at 1641 metres on a minor spur running off the main range, then gradually

drops against the contour through light coniferous forest to meet an alp track at the **Restaurant Tschingla** (1527 metres, see Places to Stay), 50 minutes to one hour on from Obersäss.

The narrow dirt road sidles steadily around the slopes down past the picturesque isolated farmhouses of **Hinter Büls** and **Vorder Büls** to a stone cottage at **Brunnen** (1319 metres) after one to 1⅓ hours. Descend into the beech forest to intersect with the better transited road to Lüsis, which brings you down in increasingly long serpentine bends to a right-hand foot track.

This path marked with yellow diamonds drops down beside meadows and tiny vineyards on the upper slopes of Walenstadt. Laneways lead past the high-steepled church to the soldiers' memorial fountain in the old centre of Walenstadt (see Walking Bases above), one to 1⅓ hours on. The train station is 10 minutes' walk southwards along the main street.

OTHER WALKS
The Wildkirchlihöhlen

These interesting limestone caves known in German as the Wildkirchlihöhlen are situated at 1500 metres near Ebenalp above Wasserauen in the Alpstein massif. A simple dwelling, bell tower and chapel were built here by a hermit priest in the 17th century, but Wildkirchli really owes its fame to the excavations carried out in 1904, which found clear evidence that ancient Stone-Age cave dwellers lived here some 100,000 years ago.

This short half-day walk climbs up from Weissbad (near Schwende) to Wildkirchli, from where you can either descend by cable car to Wasserauen, go on foot to the Seealpsee, or even continue right along the ridge as far as the Säntis summit. For access information and maps see the Säntis walk above.

The Hinterrugg

The 2306-metre Hinterrugg is the highest peak in the Churfirsten. This route climbs the somewhat gentler northern slopes of the range and traverses the Hinterrugg before descending back into the upper Toggenburg valley. From Lisighaus near Wildhaus (see Walking Bases), take the chair lift right to the upper station at Gamsalp (1767 metres). A path ascends via the Gamser Rugg and Sattel (1944 metres) to the ridgetop terrace of Rosenboden, from where the short detour to a lookout point at 2208 metres is not to be missed. The route continues over the Chäserrugg (cable-car station) to the top of the Hinterrugg, then snakes down via Hinterlücheren to Alp Sellamatt (1390 metres). From here you can end the descent either on foot or by chair lift to the village of Alt St Johann (890 metres).

This is a *moderate* day walk taking at least six hours. There is en-route dormitory accommodation at the *Berghotel Gamsalp* (☎ 071-999 10 77), the *Berggasthaus Chäserrugg*(☎ 071-999 22 29) and the *Berggasthaus Sellamatt* ☎ 071-999 1330). The recommended walking map is the 1:25,000 *Wanderkarte Oberland-Toggenburg-Appenzell* published by the Kantonal St Gallische Wanderwege.

The Sarganserland & Glarner Alps

The small canton of Glarus essentially consists of the drainage basin of the Linthal. This long and deep Alpine valley stretches southwards from the western end of the Walensee right up to the Glarner Alps. The Sarganserland includes the fascinating Murgtal, the Weisstannental and Pizol areas.

Together the Sarganserland and Glarner Alps lie sandwiched between the Walensee (Lake Walen) and the line of high snow-capped peaks running west-to-east along the cantonal border with Graubünden, from the mighty summits of the Tödi and Clariden to the 2806-metre Calanda. At Sargans, on its eastern edge, the Sarganserland is bordered by the broad valley of Rhine, while to east the Glarner Alps converge with the slab-rock ranges of Schwyz and Uri cantons. Although it's often overlooked by walkers from abroad, this region offers some particularly fine mountain scenery and numerous classic hikes.

WALKING BASES
Sargans-Mels

These twin towns lie at around 500 metres on the flat watershed between the Swiss Rhine and the smaller Seez, the river draining the Weisstannental. Sargans was largely reconstructed after a disastrous inferno in 1811, and includes the onion-domed St Oswald church and the classic Gallatihaus, however, the prominent fortified castle overlooking the old town dates from the 13th century. Neighbouring Mels is somewhat smaller than Sargans, and has many charming old buildings clustered around the Dorfplatz. Of historical interest in Mels are the early 18th-century St Peter's parish church and the Capuchin monastery completed in 1654.

In Sargans, the *Hotel Post* (☎ 081-723 74 74), on the traffic roundabout five minutes from the station, has accommodation at a reasonable price. The *Gasthaus zum Löwen*

(☎ 081-723 12 06), opposite the post office in Mels, probably offers the best value in local accommodation. There is a tourist office in Sargans (☎ 081 723 53 30). Mels has no tourist office but there is one at nearby Wangs (☎ 081-723 33 91).

An important transport hub, Sargans is on the main Zürich-Chur rail line. You can also reach Sargans by train from Lake Constance via St Margrethen. Postbuses run from Sargans to Weisstannen and to Vaduz in Liechtenstein.

Elm

This interesting village lies in the upper Sernftal surrounded by majestic peaks. Quite a number of fine old buildings stand along the street, such as the Suworowhaus, an 18th-century stone building where the Russian general (known to English speakers as Sovorov) stayed during his campaign against Napoleon in 1799. For centuries Elm has been famous for the Martinsloch, an amazing natural hole in the Tschingelhorn ridge. Walkers who happen to be here on the morning of 1 or 2 October can witness the sun shining through the Martinsloch onto the steeple of the 15th-century village church. Plaques on the pulpit of the church are dedicated to the tragedy of 1881, when 114 Elmers lost their lives as a nearby mountainside collapsed without warning.

Several excellent pass routes leave from Elm, including the Segnaspass and the Panixerpass separating Glarus Canton from Graubünden's Vorderrhein. Walks over the Foopass and Richetlipass are featured in this guidebook.

Elm has a simple municipal camping ground at the *Zeltplatz Wisli*, 10 minutes from the village; for tent sites and dorm beds ask at the Gemeindehaus (☎ 055-642 17 41). The *Gasthaus Sonne* (☎ 055-642 12 32) and the *Hotel Elmer* (☎ 055-642 22 20) offer rooms at average rates. The *Hotel Sardona* (☎ 055-642 18 86) has more up-market accommodation.

Elm's rather basic shopping facilities include two sports stores and a small supermarket; the post office offers the only

banking services. The tourist office (☎ 058-86 60 67) is near the ground station of the Ämpachli cableway, about 1.5 km farther upvalley. Some 12 daily buses run in either direction between Elm and the town of Schwanden on the Glarus-Linthal rail line.

Linthal

Lying amongst the glorious Glarner Alps, this very small town owes its origins to the Linth. The swift-flowing waters of this river turned the first spinning mill built here in the early 1830s, and even today production of hydroelectric power and textiles support Linthal's economy. Linthal is quite a pleasant place, but has little of real historical interest. It is, however, the starting point for many excellent walks into the surrounding mountains.

The only place in Linthal that offers dormitory accommodation is the *Hotel Adler* (☎ 055-643 15 15), on the uphill side of town. For budget rooms try the *Hotel Bahnhof* (☎ 055-643 15 22) or the *Hotel Raben* (☎ 055-643 31 22) near the railway station. The post office (☎ 058-84 34 69) and the train station both give out tourist information. Linthal has one small supermarket.

Trains run roughly every 1½ hours in each direction between Linthal and Ziegelbrücke (via Schwanden and Glarus), on the main Zürich-Chur rail line.

THE FOOPASS
(Section 1 of the Alpine Pass Route)

The 2223-metre Foopass leads out of the Sarganserland's Weisstannental into the Sernftal of Glarus Canton. The upper valley area of the Weisstannental appears to have been first settled by Walsers from the Rheinwald and Safiental in Graubünden during the 14th century. For the descendants of these migrants the Foopass was the principle link with the outside world. Today the Weisstannental remains one of Switzerland's most unspoilt larger Alpine valleys, and makes a very pleasant walking route along its entire length from Mels-Sargans up to the Foopass. The much shorter descent west from the Foopass to the village of Elm takes you through the wild and lonely valley of the Raminertal.

Maps

One 1:60,000 sheet, *Glarnerland Walensee*, produced by Kümmerly + Frey, is sufficient for the whole walk, and includes all of the Sarganserland and Glarner Alps. If you're starting the walk from Weisstannen, acceptable alternatives are *Glarnerland*, published by Verlag Baeschlin or the SAW/FSTP sheet *Sardona (247 T)*, both scaled at 1:50,000.

Walking Times & Standard

This is a two-day walk that can be shortened to one day by taking the bus from Sargans to the village of Weisstannen. Stage 2 is nevertheless a long day hike, and it's important to get an early start as there's no en-route accommodation until you get to Elm. As usual, route markings are generally excellent, but until the end of June winter snows may still cover higher parts of the route. With an ascent/descent of over a 1000 altitude metres, you'll need a bit of muscle tone in your legs.

The walk has a *moderate* rating and an overall distance of 34 km.

Places to Stay

The *Gasthaus Mühle* (☎ 081-723 15 01) in Schwendi, has standard rooms. In Weisstannen village at the end of Stage 1, are the *Hotel Gemse* (☎ 081-723 17 05), which offers good value for dormitories and rooms, and the *Hotel Alpenhof* (☎ 081-723 17 63) with rooms only.

For places to stay in Sargans-Mels and Elm see Walking Bases above.

Getting to/from the Walk

Regardless of where you begin the walk, you will have to pass through Sargans.

Postbuses run around seven times daily (five times on Sunday) from Sargans train station to the village of Weisstannen at the end of Stage 1; the last bus leaves a little after 6 pm. Although the walk through the valley is quite pleasant, walkers may prefer using public transport to save a day.

Stage 1: Sargans to Weisstannen
(14 km, 3½ to 4½ hours)

From the train station in **Sargans** (see Walking Bases), follow a signposted walkway 1.25 km north-west beside the rail lines; the sheer walls of the 1829-metre Gonzen rise up from the valley floor to the right. Where you meet a busy road, head down the steps and continue through the underpass below the rail/motorway bridge. The road makes an S-bend as it brings you on to reach **Mels** (see Walking Bases) after 30 to 40 minutes.

From Mels' town square (Dorfplatz), walk rightwards along the road to cross the gushing Seez stream, then pick up a short-cut foot track just after the bridge and climb up directly back to the road. The route continues a short way up the bitumen past a small chapel at **St Martin** after 25 to 30 minutes. This attractive hamlet sits at 574 metres amongst vineyards looking north-east across Sargans to the mountains of Liechtenstein.

Not far uphill leave off left along an old flagged mule path leading up into the trees. This ascends steadily, briefly meeting the road again in several places, before coming to a signposted intersection inside the forest at **Tschess** (1020 metres), 45 minutes to one hour up from St Martin. The trail up to the right goes to Vermol and the Champfensee (1030 metres), a nearby lake within a pleasant nature reserve.

Take the left-hand branch and follow an alp track slightly downhill across sunny pastures, bearing right at another fork when you get to **Hundbüel** after 15 to 20 minutes. High peaks of the Pizol region stand on the other side of the valley, while back towards Mels the Seez flows through a deep gorge. The path now rises and dips as it gradually drops against the contour past small clearings and isolated alp huts, repeatedly crossing refreshing streamlets cascading down from the heavily wooded slopes above to the scattered farms of **Höhi**. From here a sealed road winds quickly down to arrive at **Schwendi** (see Places to Stay) at 908 metres after a further 50 minutes to one hour.

Either head directly up the main valley

road or take the gravelled farm track up right from near the **Gasthaus Mühle**. This soon leads onto a higher walking route that gently traverses field and forest – with frequent resting benches for enjoying the views of the valley and adjacent mountains – before descending again to cross the Seez on a small bridge just before you reach **Weisstannen** at 1004 metres after 45 minutes to one hour (or 30 to 40 minutes via the valley road).

This pretty little village is mostly built in the traditional wooden architecture of the St Galler Oberland. Of particular interest is the small St John the Baptist parish church erected in 1665. Weisstannen has two hotels (see Places to Stay).

Stage 2: Weisstannen to Elm

(20 km, 6 to 8 hours)

At the upper end of the village, cross the Gutelbach bridge and follow the road as it enters the upper Seez valley, passing waterfalls spilling into the sheer-sided valley before coming to another road bridge after two km. At this point take the path (signposted 'Alle Bergrichtungen') leading along the southern side of the stream, which is dry in places because the water is diverted by an aqueduct. Where the trail comes back to the road, turn right and recross the stream to reach the farms of **Vorsiez** at 1175 metres, one to 1⅓ hours up from Weisstannen.

Head left along a farm track running beside a line of telephone poles, which gradually becomes a marked trail as it makes its way through patches of spruce forest and moist meadows often grazed by deer. The route continues beside the Seez to cross the smaller Siezbach sidestream on a wooden footbridge, rising briefly to a dirt road before it descends gently to arrive at the farmstead at **Untersäss** (1361 metres) after 45 minutes to one hour.

Walk along the old alp road to an attractive stand of trees known as the **Foowäldli**, which forms both the upper limit of vehicle access and the treeline. From here the path does a spiralling ascent through glacial and avalanche rubble, passing natural lookouts offering nice views back down into the

Weisstannental. Where you enter an elongated section of the small valley covered with stunted birch scrub the gradient eases. It steepens again as you head up beside the tumbling stream to reach the alp huts of **Foo** at 1875 metres, 1¼ to 1¾ hours from Untersäss. Spectacular rock walls surround this high upper basin, whose rich pastures are ablaze with a wide variety of wildflowers in early summer.

Drop quickly down across the Foobach, and (ignoring a left-hand side trail here that goes up to Mätteli) follow white-red-white route markings that gradually veer around to the right into the tiny Alpine valley drained by the Heitelbach. Climbing at a steady pace, the path leads over rolling grassy slopes inhabited by colonies of marmots to arrive at the 2223-metre **Foopass** after 50 minutes to one hour. The Foopass lies on the St Gallen/ Glarus cantonal border, and presents quite a vista ahead towards numerous peaks of the Glarner Alps such as the Kärpf and the Hausstock.

The path makes a descent in steep zigzags to the stone farmhouse of **Raminer Matt** at 1897 metres in the lonely upper valley. From here walkers get the first real look towards the arc of craggy ranges stretching southwest from the nearby Surenstock (Piz Sardona) as far as the glacial snows of the Vorab. Make your way on along the farm track to reach the alp huts of **Mittler Staffel** at 1757 metres, 45 minutes to one hour from the pass.

Continue right across the bridge, where the first scattered conifers mark the upper limit of the forest. The road snakes down beside sloping meadows far above the deep gorge of the Raminer Bach past spectacular waterfalls plummeting off Piz Segnas on the opposite side of the valley before intersecting with a larger road at **Raminer-Stäfeli** (1248 metres) after one to 1⅓ hours.

The route descends in tight curves, passing Elm's small camping ground hidden in the forest just before departing left along a trail down beside the stream. A wooden footbridge leads over to the left bank about halfway before the much larger Sernf river is

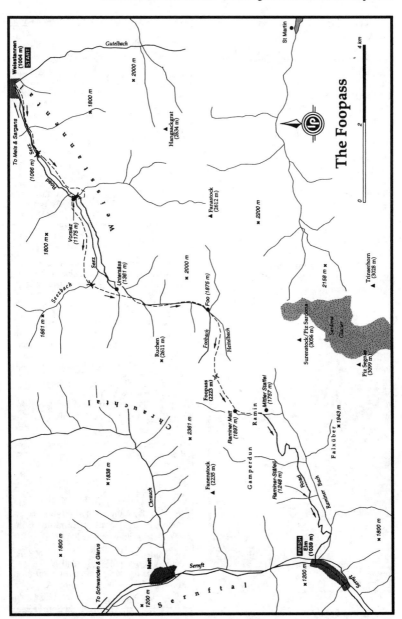

The Foopass

crossed a short way before arriving in **Elm** (see Walking Bases), 30 to 40 minutes on.

The description of the Alpine Pass Route is continùed in the Richetlipass walk (Elm to Linthal).

THE MURGTAL

The 10-km-long Murgtal has a climate milder than anywhere else in Switzerland north of the Alps. Mouthing at the Walensee (Lake Walen) near the village of Murg (448 metres) about halfway along the southern shoreline, this unique 'Föhn valley' rises up steadily to terminate at the 1825-metre Oberer Murgsee, a lovely mountain lake nestling below the ranges of the Gufelstock. The Murgtal's roughly north-south alignment and steep gradient duct warm southerly winds (known in German as the Föhn) down through the valley. This effect, together with the gently warming influence of the nearby Walensee, allows sweet chestnut trees and other species more readily associated with Mediterranean climes to thrive in the valley's lower reaches.

This wonderful walk goes over gentle

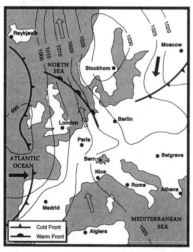

Example of a Föhn weather pattern

Föhn Winds

The word *Föhn* originates – via Romansch – from the Latin *ventus favonius* ('mild wind'). It's also standard German for 'hair drier' – an apt adaptation, as anyone who has experienced the full blast of this hot, dry wind blowing through their hair will testify.

Typical Föhn conditions arise whenever a low-pressure system lies above the British Isles with a high centred over Italy or the Balkans. The broad anti-clockwise circulation of winds around the low draw in air masses from the Alpine foothills of northern Italy. This air is sucked northwards, cooling so rapidly that its moisture soon precipitates (as often heavy rain or snow) on the Alps' southern ranges. These now relatively dry air masses continue north across the mountains, regaining some moisture as they blow across highland lakes and snowfields, then warm up quickly as they descend towards the lower Alpine foothills.

On the northern side of the Alps, the arrival of strong Föhn winds is often an indication – though not an infallible one – of approaching bad weather. The Föhn may persist for several days, however, bringing generally warm and windy conditions to the northern Alps. An interesting effect of strong Föhn conditions is the exceptionally clear skies which make the Alps appear very close and detailed even from as far away as Zürich or Bern. Despite these apparently pleasant features, few Swiss people welcome the arrival of the Föhn, blaming it for headaches, sleeplessness and irritability. Some people, however, find Föhn conditions quite invigorating – even positively uplifting. Severe storms associated with Föhn conditions are a particular threat in April or May, and can cause catastrophic flooding or flatten whole forests.

On the northern side of the Swiss Alps are certain so-called 'Föhn valleys', most notably the Murgtal by the Walensee (Lake Walen) and the Haslital in the Bernese Oberland. These Föhn valleys' south-to-north course draws in the warm southerly airstream to produce a milder local microclimate. Ticino, on the southern side of the Alps, experiences a reverse effect known as the 'north Föhn'. The north Föhn brings warm northerlies blowing down from the Alps, and often means wet weather on the northern side of the range. ■

mountain passes linking several valley heads, then descends through the wild and beautiful nature reserve of the Murgtal to the Walensee. It's recommended to all walkers who visit North-eastern Switzerland.

Maps

Best are either of the following 1:50,000 walking maps: *Glarnerland*, produced by Verlag Baeschlin; the SAW/FSTP sheet *Walenstadt (237 T)* or the *Wanderkarte St Galler Oberland-Toggenburg (5015)*, published by the Kantonal St Gallische Wanderwege. Another option is Kümmerly + Frey's *Glarnerland Walensee*, scaled at 1:60,000.

Walking Times & Standard

This walk is best done in two medium-length walking days, the second of which is a long downhill stroll. The sections of climbing are relatively short and should present few difficulties to walkers with a minimal level of physical fitness. Since the highest altitude is scarcely 2000 metres, it can generally be undertaken from the beginning of June until at least the end of October. In places there are short sections of boggy ground, but the path is otherwise quite good.

The walk's total distance is around 24 km, and it has a *moderate* rating.

Places to Stay

Accommodation in Filzbach includes the *youth hostel* (☎ 055-614 13 42) and the *Hotel Mürtschenstock* (☎ 055-614 13 59), which has standard-rate rooms. The *Restaurant Habergschwänd* (☎ 055-614 12 17, open June to mid-October), at the upper chair-lift station, has a dormitory (showers available).

Probably the most practical en-route accommodation is the *Berggasthaus Murgsee* (☎ 081-738 19 38, open mid-May to late October). Also called the Fischerhütte, this cosy little angler's hut rests on the shore of the Ober-Murgsee roughly midway along the route, and offers dormitory accommodation and better than average meals. Washing facilities are very basic, however.

In Murg, at the end of the walk, is the *Gasthaus Rössli* (☎ 081-738 11 97) with standard rooms; Murg also has a local *camping ground* (☎ 081-738 15 30).

Getting to/from the Walk

The walk is a semi-circuit, which begins and ends on the southern side of the Walensee. The setting off point is the upper station of the Filzbach-Haberschwänd chair lift, which in summer operates until 5.30 pm (no concessions). Postbuses running between Näfels-Möllis (on the Linthal rail line) and Mühlehorn (on the shore of the Walensee) pass through Filzbach. From Zürich the train/postbus connections to Filzbach are much better via Näfels-Möllis than via Mühlehorn.

Private vehicles can be left (for a fee) at the car park by the lower Filzbach-Haberschwänd chair-lift station.

Stage 1: Habergschwänd to Berggasthaus Murgsee

(10.5 km, 3½ to 4½ hours)
The chair lift from Filzbach carries you up over an all-seasons toboggan run to **Habergschwänd** (see Places to Stay), a small winter skifield at 1282 metres on a terrace high above the Walensee.

Follow the gravelled road gently eastwards down around the lightly forested hillside to a neat stone farmhouse/restaurant at **Vorder Tal**. An alp track now leads south along the eastern side of the **Talsee**, a shallow lake that sits like a puddle below chalky white crags whose sheer walls show numerous large natural cavities.

Continue past barns in the grassy pastures of **Hinter Tal** to where the road finishes at a utility cableway, 50 minutes to one hour from Habergschwänd.

Climb up to the right in steep zigzags along a well-cut old mule trail to get to the top of the ridge (1498 metres), from where a lookout ramp gives a nice view back into the head of the enclosed upper valley. Sidle on along the regenerating talus slopes under the

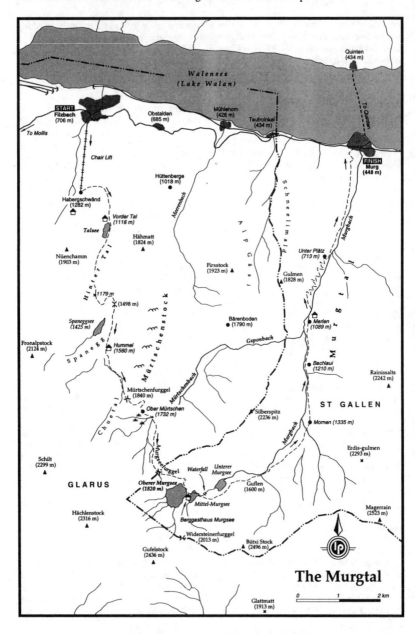

The Murgtal

0   1   2 km

almost overhanging rock sides of the Mürtschenstock, with the **Spaneggsee** (1425 metres), another small attractive lake with no direct outlet, in the undrained basin below. The path cuts up left past the alp huts of **Hummel** at 1560 metres, before steepening slightly as it ascends via the tiny valley of the Chüetal to reach the **Mürtschenfurggel**, a dip in the ridge at 1840 metres, after 1½ to two hours.

Drop down leftwards through a shallow grassy gully to a farmhouse and barn at **Ober Mürtschen** (1732 metres), a pretty, flat bowl covered by waterlogged moors and surrounded by lovely stands of scattered pines. Walk 250 metres down left, then cross the small clearwater Mürtschenbach on a halved-log bridge. White-red-white markings guide you up beside a gurgling brook to the **Murgseefurggel** (1985 metres), a little saddle on the Glarus/St Gallen cantonal border overlooking the picturesque **Oberer Murgsee**.

Descend diagonally leftwards over the snow grass slopes above a farmhouse, then follow an alp track on around the lakeshore. The route crosses a small concrete levée a short way before arriving at the **Berggasthaus Murgsee** at 1825 metres (see Places to Stay), 1¼ to 1½ hours on from the Mürtschenfurggel. Originally dammed by local iron-ore miners in the 1800s, today the tranquil shallow waters of the Oberer Murgsee draw a steady stream of anglers.

A 40-minute return walk can be made up to the 2013-metre pass to the south known as Widersteinerfurggel. Walk on around the lakeshore, then climb up through Alpine pastures to the right of a minor ridge. In clear conditions the view stretches along the Üblital as far as the Vorabfirn (Glatscher dil Vorab in Romansch), the large snowfield directly to the south.

Stage 2: Berggasthaus Murgsee to Murg/Walensee

(13 km, 3¼ to 4 hours,)

The beautiful walk through the Murgtal is fairly straightforward, following a (restricted access) road virtually the whole way down to Murg.

Take the old vehicle track on down around the northern shore of the **Mittel-Murgsee**, recrossing the Murgbach just above where the stream tumbles over cliffs in a spectacular waterfall and flows on into the **Unter-Murgsee**. The road leads on down over slopes scattered with alpenrose bushes to the grassy flats of **Guflen** (1600 metres), then continues in a steady sidling descent through beautiful mixed coniferous forests. Shortly after passing a signposted route going up right towards Flumserberg you come to **Mornen** at 1335 metres, after 1¼ to 1½ hours. The alp huts on these pastures look out westwards to the peaks of the Silberspitz.

Make your way down more gently now past **Bachlaui** to the farmlet of **Merlen** at 1089 metres, a short distance below where the Mürtschental joins the main valley. The incline steepens sharply again after the road crosses the river and begins winding down through an area of rubble left by an ancient landslide towards the serrated outline of the Churfirsten on the far side of the Walensee. Short-cut trails at many of the hairpin bends bring you quickly down to reach **Unter Plätz** (713 metres), 1¼ to 1½ hours from Mornen.

Proceed left past a fork, following the now more prominent main road down through long clearings and small stands of sweet chestnut trees. Take the last few road curves leading down to arrive in **Murg** after a final 45 minutes to one hour. This tiny industrial town is on a little peninsula (actually an alluvial fan formed by the Murgbach) which juts out into the Walensee. Taking a ferry across the lake to the adjacent village of Quinten, the only lowland settlement in Switzerland not accessible by road, makes an interesting finale to your walk.

THE RICHETLIPASS
(Section 2 of the Alpine Pass Route)

This delightful pass crossing connects the two main upper valleys of the Glarnerland, the Sernftal and the Linthal. The route passes through one of the loveliest areas of highland wildflower meadows in the Swiss Alps, the Wichlenmatt, just below the Richetlipass itself. On the other side of the pass lies the Durnachtal, a small side valley of the Linth with a stubbornly wild nature. The Durnagel stream washes large quantities of loose rock down through the Durnachtal from the slopes of the nearby Hausstock, and in the past the rich pastures of the Linthal were continually threatened by these masses of alluvial rubble. Today concrete obstructions have been built along the course of the Durnagel as part of an ambitious project to tame the stream.

Maps

Recommended for this walk is the special walking map *Glarnerland*, scaled at 1:50,000 sheet and produced by Verlag Baeschlin (Glarus) or Kümmerly + Frey's 1:60,000 sheet *Glarnerland Walensee*. The two SAW/FSTP sheets, *Sardona (247 T)* and *Klausenpass (246 T)* make good alternatives.

Walking Times & Standard

The Richetlipass is a full day's walk that requires a reasonably early start. It involves a climb of over 1250 altitude metres, with an even longer descent totalling more than 1600 metres. At Wichlen, several km upvalley from Elm, the walk passes through an area used by the Swiss army for shooting exercises (approximately one day in eight during the summer). At such times you must go via a longer but equally scenic alternative route (described below under Route Directions). For the dates of coming shooting exercises call the regional military (EMD/DMF) information office in Glarus on ☎ 055-640 57 57.

The walk is rated *moderate*.

Places to Stay

Apart from a rustic shelter at Wichlenmatt, there is no en-route accommodation between Elm and Linthal – see Walking Bases for places to stay in both villages.

Getting to/from the Walk

The walk begins in Elm and finishes in Linthal; for access details to both villages see Walking Bases above.

Route Directions: Elm to Linthal

(21 km, 6½ to 8½ hours)

At the fork 300 metres up the street from the post office in Elm, turn left along a country lane. The route soon crosses the Sernft and rises over rolling meadows before taking a right-hand path alongside the sharply sloping banks of the river to meet a gravelled farm track. Head on until you come to a sealed roadway and continue down over the bridge. A short, steep climb now brings you back up to the main road. Walk upvalley along the bitumen for 1.25 km to reach **Büel** at 1261 metres, one to 1⅓ hours up from Elm.

Follow the road on past the army canteen at **Walenbrugg**, where you enter the grassy basin at the valley head. This area, known as **Wichlen**, is dominated by the mighty 3158-metre form of the Hausstock. A signpost two km on from Büel directs you off left across a small diversion weir to another dirt road, which leads up to the barns of **Ober Stafel** at 1482 metres, after 40 to 50 minutes.

At the road branch going off to the unfriendly looking brown military barracks, turn right then break away left immediately after the bridge. Sporadic cairns and paint markings guide you up through the broken rubble to the start of an old mule track (whose initial section is impassable due to flood action). The graded trail climbs on steeply past a waterfall to rocky ridges overlooking Wichlen, crossing and following the small Mattbach to reach the lonely alp hut at **Wichlenmatt** (2037 metres), 1¼ to 1¾ hours from Ober Stafel. Wichlenmatt's gentle meadows lie nestled within a broad cirque of craggy ranges and make a lovely place to stop for a rest.

Alternative Route If the road via Wichlen is closed due to shooting practice, an alternative route leaves from Büel. Walk up the turn-off from the stone drinking fountain, and after almost one km pick up a steep short-cut trail leading through forest and

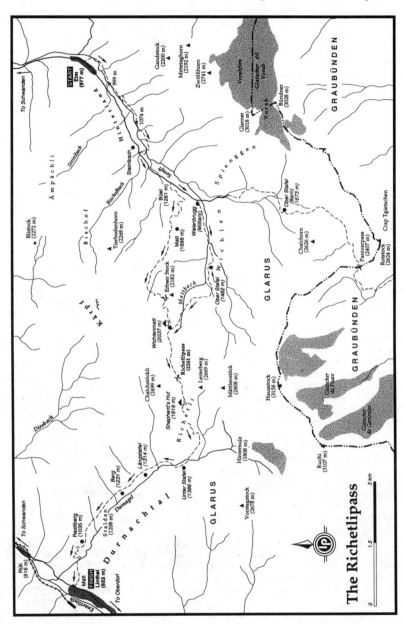

The Richetlipass

GRAUBÜNDEN

GLARUS

GLARUS

To Schwanden

START
Elm
(977 m)

Gandstock
(2200 m)

Mittetaghorn
(2192 m) ▲

Zwölfihorn
(2741 m) ▲

Glarner
(3018 m)

Bündner
(3028 m)

Gletscher dil Vorab

Vorab

Vorabfirn

Blistock
× (2272 m)

Ämpächli

Steinbach

Bischofbach

Bischof

Steinibach

Tierhotdenhorn
(2269 m) ▲

Büel
(1261 m)

Walenbrugg
(Military)

Matt
(1698 m) ●

Spienggen

Ober Stafel
(Bärn)
(1673 m) ●

Chalchorn
(2626 m) ▲

Crap Tgietschen

Panixerpass
(2407 m)

Rotstock
(2624 m)

Karpf

Diesbach

Erbser Stock
(2182 m) ▲

Mättlenbach

Ober Stafel
(1482 m) ●

Wichlen

Wichlenmatt
(2037 m) ●

Richetlipass
(2261 m)

Leiterberg
(2669 m) ▲

Mättlenstöck
(2808 m) ▲

Hausstock
(3158 m) ▲

Gletscher da Flux

Chalchtelböckli
(2499 m) ▲

Shepherd's Hut
(1916 m)

Richetli

Gletscher da Gavirola

Ruchi
(3107 m)

GRAUBÜNDEN

Längstafel
(1514 m) ●

Berg
(1231 m) ●

Hinternulz
(1808 m) ●

Vorder Stock
(2678 m) ▲

Durnagel

Unter Stafel
(1386 m) ●

Rüti
(616 m)

To Schwanden

Restiberg
(1035 m) ●

Matt

FINISH
Linthal
(653 m)

Stalden
(1208 m)

Durnachtal

Sernf

Hinter Sernftal

999 m

1074 m

To Oberdorf

Entschlttal

0   1.5   3 km

high pastures to the farmhouse of **Matt** (1698 metres). The path goes on up almost to the source of a small mountain stream, before swinging around south-west to ascend in short switchbacks to a gap in the ridge at 2161 metres, where the Richetlipass comes into view. An almost direct descent takes you on down to **Wichlenmatt**. This variant is 45 minutes to one hour longer than the main route.

The final stretch traces the meandering brook for a distance, picking its way through areas of gravel and loose earth as it steepens into an ascent of short zigzags. Even in high summer, snow covering the upper slopes may slow you down, but the 2261-metre **Richetlipass** is usually reached in 35 to 45 minutes. This neat dip between the Chalchstöckli and the Leiterberg offers excellent vistas westwards to the unmistakable hub of the Ortstock (2716 metres) at the northern end of the Jegerstöck.

The path first spirals down the steep slopes, then continues along a small spur past a shepherd's hut built in the shelter of a large boulder. Veer right here to link up with an old moraine ridge, and follow this down until it ends at a line of cliffs. At this point drop down leftwards through a rocky gully, before cutting back to the right across the open hillsides to where a wooden bridge brings you over the swift-flowing glacial waters of the Durnagel stream. Just a few paces downstream is the farmhouse of **Unter Stafel** at 1386 metres, 1¼ to 1¾ hours from the pass.

The route recrosses the river a short way on, staying on the road as it gradually falls against the contour past the remote farms of Längstafel (1314 metres) and **Berg** (1231 metres) perched high above the Durnachtal. Visible along the river's course are dozens of concrete constructions built to contain the great volumes of debris washed down from the loose mountainsides upvalley. Directly ahead is the familiar tiered form of the Orstock, while just to its right the summits of the Bächlistock and Bös Fulen have now come into sight.

Farther down, the road goes over into bitumen, passing the grassy hillsides of **Restiberg** as it begins a steeper descent in numerous hairpin bends through the forest. In midsummer aromatic wild strawberries and raspberries growing beside the way are an irresistible reason to pause for a spell. The route crosses the Durnagel a final time, and heads one km west before coming out on the main valley road at **Matt**, near the small local museum. Follow the 'Bahnhof' signposts leading down through the village and across the Linth River to reach the train station in **Linthal** (see Walking Bases), 1½ to two hours after leaving Unter Stafel.

Walkers continuing the Alpine Pass Route should refer to the Klausenpass (Linthal to Altdorf) walk in the Central Switzerland chapter.

OTHER WALKS
The Rossmatter Tal
Enclosed by the glaciated peaks of the Glärnish to the east and the rugged Silberen on its western side, the Rossmatter Tal is one of the nicest and most scenic valleys of the Glarner Alps. From Hinter Klöntal near the western shore of the Klöntaler See, an excellent route leads south up through the Rossmatter Tal via the locality of Chäseren (accommodation) to Drackloch on the cantonal border with Schwyz. From Drackloch either return to Hinter Klöntal along the high-traverse route via Alpeli (six to seven hours return) or continue up through an interesting slab-rock landscape to the Brunalpelihöchi, a pass at 2207 metres, to the SAC's *Glattalphütte* (two days). Use either of these maps: 1:50,000 *Glarnerland*, published by Baeschlin Verlag, or K + F's 1:60,000 *Glarnerland-Walensee*.

The Glarner Alps
This relatively straightforward two-day high-Alpine route traverses the eastern slopes of the Clariden and the Tödi, two of the highest peaks of the Glarner Alps. The walk gives some quite breathtakingly spectacular vistas of the mountains and glaciers around the headwaters of the Linth River.

From Argseeli, at around 1330 metres on

the Klausenpass road (postbus from Linthal), either take the small private cable car (☎ 055-643 33 73) or walk up to Vorder Orthalden (1869 metres). From here a path goes over the Fisetenpass (2036 metres), and sidles around via Friteren high above the Linthal to the *Claridenhütte* (☎ 055-643 31 21), an SAC-run hut at 2453 metres. The route continues up through the Beggilücke (2537 metres) then down across the Oberstafelbach, before climbing Bifertengrätli to the *SAC's Frindolinhütte* (2111 metres, (☎ 055-643 34 34). From here a scenic side trip can be made to the *Grünhornhütte*, an historic SAC hut built in 1863. (The descent goes via Hinterer Sand, then along an alp track to Tierfed and down the left bank of the Linth to Linthal.

The recommended walking map is the SAW/FSTP's *Klausenpass (246 T)*.

The Kistenpass

The 2714-metre Kistenpass is another outstanding high-Alpine crossing that leads over the Glarner Alps into the Surselva region of Graubünden. It passes through a superbly wild and rugged landscape formed by intense glaciation, but this hike is unsuited to inexperienced walkers.

From Linthal village (see Walking Bases) the route heads up the western banks of the river before beginning the long climb up to the *Muttseehütte* (☎ 055-643 31 67, staffed mid-June to late October), an SAC hut at 2501 metres. This section is sometimes closed due to target practice by the Swiss military; to check the situation call the EMD/DMF information office in Glarus on ☎ 055-640 57 57. The path continues up over moraine slopes to the Kistenpass, then traverses high above the Limmernsee through the basin of Cavorgia da Breil to Rubi Sura. A steep descent east leads to the Flem stream, which is followed down to the Romansch-speaking village of Breil/Brigels; from here there are postbuses to Tavanasa (on the Chur-Disentis line) until around 6.15 pm.

A faster and easier route variant involves taking the cable car from the end of the road at Tierfed (805 metres) to Ober-Baumgarten

(1860 metres), then walking through the three km tunnel to the Limmernsee reservoir, from where a good path leads up to the Muttseehütte. The cable car is operated by the local electricity company four times daily until around 4 pm; for reservations call Kraftwerke Linth-Limmern on ☎ 055-643 31 67. You'll need a headlamp or torch (flashlight) for the 50-minute walk through the tunnel.

Walkers who take the cable car can do the hike in one long day, but overnighting en route is recommended. Apart from the Muttseehütte, there is an emergency shelter on the pass itself; and the *Bifertenhütte*, a hut belonging to a small mountain club, is three km south of the Kistenpass not far off-route. The SAW/FSTP sheet *Klausenpass (246 T)* is the best walking map to use.

The Panixerpass

The 2407-metre Panixerpass (Pass dil Veptga in Romansch) is an ancient route linking the Sernftal and the Romansch-speaking Surselva region of Graubünden's Vorderrhein. The pass was crossed on 6 October 1799 by a Russian army led by General Sovorov, Napoleon's opponent. Caught in a terrible blizzard, over 200 of Sovorov's soldiers and countless pack animals fell to their deaths as they made their way along an iced-over section of narrow path cut into the mountainside 600 metres above the Alp Ranasca.

Today the way over the Panixerpass provides an ideal – and rather less dangerous – walking route, leading through an attractive landscape of moorland and karst fields on its northern side, then down above deep gorges of the Vallada de Pigniu to the south. The start of the walk is the village of Elm (see Walking Bases), from where the foot track leads upvalley along the true right bank of the Sernft stream, turning southwards where the upper valley forks and climbing to the Panixerpass. The descent from the pass goes via the Plaun da Cavals to the tiny Romansch village of Pigniu/Panix (PTT minibus to Rueun until 5.30 pm), or onward down to the railway station at Rueun.

The original old mule trail forms the path in many places, and markings and signposts are quite reliable, so there is little chance of losing your way. Less experienced walkers should note, however, that the walk involves a total climb of more than 1500 metres, and requires a good level of fitness. Apart from an emergency shelter on the pass itself, there is no en-route accommodation. The average walking time from Elm to Pigniu/Panix is 6½ hours (or 7½ hours to Rueun). Use either of these 1:50,000 walking maps: *Glarnerland* published by Verlag Baeschlin, or the SAW/FSTP sheet *Sardona (247 T)*.

The Pizol Circuit

The interesting area around the Pizol, a 2844-metre peak between the Weisstannental and the Rhine Valley, has a large colony of ibex and very appealing Alpine scenery.

The Pizol area is readily accessible by mountain cableways and can be easily visited as a day walk. A gondola/chair-lift combination from the village of Wangs near Mels-Sargans (see Walking Bases) takes you up to the *Pizolhütte* at 2227 metres. From here a four-to five-hour circuit leads west to the col of Wildseeluggen (2493 metres), then traverses around northwards past the high-Alpine lakes of Wildsee, Schottensee and Schwarzsee. The descent goes via the 2309-metre Gamidaurspitz and the Baschalvasee to the end of the walk at the middle chair-lift station at Gaffia (1823 metres), from where you return to Wangs.

The route is best after mid-July when the winter snows have mostly melted away. The best walking map to the area is the 1:25,000 *Pizolgebiet (2509)*, published by the Kantonal St Gallische Wanderwege.

Glossary

alp huts – the summer dwellings of Alpine herders

alp track – a rough access road that leads to an alp hut

alpenrose – name for the two species of Alpine rhododendron

Alpine foothills – see Pre-Alps

Alpine Pass Route – a classic route leading from Sargans to Montreux over 16 passes in the northern Swiss Alps

Alpine zone – the area above the treeline (roughly 2000 metres)

altitude metres – the vertical difference between two points measured in metres

Appenzellerland – collective name for the two half-cantons of Appenzell

avalanche gallery – a protective construction built over a mountain road or railway in places prone to winter avalanches

avalanche grids – steel or wood structures usually arranged in rows on treeless Alpine slopes to restrain winter snows and so prevent avalanches

balcony – a level or gently-sloping 'terrace' high above a valley

belvedere (Italian for 'beautiful view') – a scenic high point (often a balcony or terrace)

Berggasthaus, Berghaus – mountain inn

Bergsturz (German) – catastrophic mountain landslide

Bernese – pertaining to Bern Canton

bisse (French) – mountain aqueduct in the Valais

BL/OFT – Bundesamt für Landestopographie/Office Fédéral de Topographie (Swiss national mapping authority)

BLS – Bern-Lötschberg-Simplon, a private railway company that operates the railway running from Bern to Domodossola (in Italy) via the Lötschberg and Simplon tunnels.

Bündner Oberland – older term for Graubünden's Surselva region

Bündner – pertaining to Graubünden

BVZ intials of the Brig-Visp-Zermatt private railway in the upper Valais

cableway – a general term including chair lifts, gondola lifts and cable cars as well as the small private utility lifts used to lug goods up and down mountainsides

cairn – rocks piled into a heap to mark a route

canton – the self-governing regions (comparable to 'states' or 'provinces') within the Swiss Confederation

car-free resort – a new trend among Swiss mountain resorts is to completely ban all (private) motorised traffic in order to attract visitors who genuinely seek peace, quiet and clean Alpine air

circuit – a walk that ends back at its starting point

cirque – a rounded high precipice formed by the action of ice in the high-Alpine zone

cog (or rack) railway – a steeper railway with a rack between the tracks into which a cogwheel grips as the train climbs or descends

col – a mountain pass

contour – to move along a slope without climbing or descending appreciably

crevasse – an often dangerously deep 'crack' in the ice of a glacier

doline – a landform typically found in karst ranges where an enormous subterranean cavern formed by water seepage collapses to create a basin; if this impedes further seepage a (doline) lake may form

dolomite a hard limestone rock of calcium-magnesium composition

downclimb – to descend using your hands

EMD/DMF – the German/French initials of the Swiss defence department (Eidgenössisches Militär Departement/Departement Militaire Federal)

fixed cable – a steel cable mounted along a (potentially) dangerous section of mountain path to give walkers added confidence

334 Glossary

flagged (path) – stone-laid path, usually originally built as a mule track

Föhn – warm southerly wind

FOB – initials of the Furka-Oberalp-Bahn, a private railway running between Brig and Disentis via Andermatt

glacier 'pots' and 'mills' – formations produced by water action below glaciers

Glarnerland – Glarus Canton

Gotthard region – name of the Swiss Alps' central massif around the Passo del San Gottardo (St Gotthard Pass)

hamlet – small group of farm buildings or alps huts

haute route (French) – a high-level mountain route; also the name of a classic Chamonix to Zermatt skiing and walking route through the Valais

hayfield – a meadow mown for hay (as winter animal feed) rather than used for grazing

Helvetic – pertaining to Switzerland

high-Alpine – the upper mountains

Höhenweg (German) – see haute route

icefall – steep broken-up section of a glacier

Jura – a low chain of mountains running along and forming Switzerland's north-western border with France

K + F – Kümmerly + Frey, Switzerland's largest commercial publisher of maps and guidebooks

karst – limestone rock that forms so-called karst fields (German: *Karrenfelder)*

Lötschberg – railway and tunnel between the Bernese Oberland and the Valais (see also BLS)

massif – a high mountain range

mattress room – sleeping quarters (standard in mountain huts) with mattresses are lined up together in long rows

MOB – initials for Montreux-Oberalp-Bahn, a private railway running between Montreux and Spiez via Zweisimmen

moraine – debris left after glacial recession; lateral (ie side) and terminal (ie end) moraines

mountain hut – used in this guidebook to refer to a hut with accommodation (not be be confused with an alp hut)

mule path, mule track – old flagged paths originally built as routes for cargo-carrying mule trains

Nagelfluh (German) – a cement-like rock consisting of very coarse alluvial sediments

névé – a permanent, high-Alpine snowfield

north face – sheer, north-facing rock walls

Oberland (German) – a term used to describe the regional 'uplands' of various cantons, eg Bernese Oberland, St Galler Oberland, Bündner Oberland, Urner Oberland

postbuses – extensive network of buses run by the Swiss PTT

Pre-Alpine – pertaining to the Pre-Alps

Pre-Alps – the Alpine foothills fringing the northern and southern sides of the range

PTT – Swiss postal and telephone authority

Rhaetian Railways – the largest private railway in Switzerland, which owns and runs virtually all lines in Graubünden Canton

route – refers to the main walking route described in the route descriptions (not 'faint path' as in some walking guidebooks)

rustico/rustici (Italian, singular/plural) – 'rustic' Ticino-style cottage(s) built of stone

SAC – initials of the Swiss Alpine Club

SAW/FSTP – German/French initials of the Swiss Hiking Federation (Schweizerische Arbeitsgemeinschaft für Wanderwege/ Fédération Suisse de Tourisme Pédestre)

SBB/CFF – the German/French initials of the Swiss Federal Railways (Schweizer Bundesbahnen/Chemin de fer fédéral)

Scheidegg (Swiss German) – a watershed

scree – slopes of accumulated frost-shattered rock; often unstable and loose (screeslide)

Sennerei (German) – an Alpine cheesery

sérac – prominent block of ice typically seen on steep icefalls

sidle – to move along a slope at right-angles

skirt – see sidle

slab – smooth-surface rock, formed by glacial or water erosion (as in karst)

snowfield – a large permanent accumulation of snow

stage – an individual section of a longer walk

Suone (Swiss German) – see bisse

Surselva – the valley of the Vorderrhein (Rein Anteriur)

Swiss Mittelland – the 'plateau' between the Alps and the Jura; often divided into cantonal regions such as the Bernese Mittelland, the Fribourg Mittelland etc

switchbacks – sharp curves of a path or road that double back on themselves as they climb a slope

talus – similar to scree but generally coarser

tarn – tiny Alpine lake

terrace (see balcony)

tiers – staged levels of a range formed either by rock strata or glacial action

trans-Alpine – crossing the main north-south Alpine watershed

traverse – used in the route descriptions interchangeably with the term sidle

treeline, timberline – the uppermost (natural) level at which the forest can grow on a mountainside

Valaisan – pertaining to the Valais

vehicle track – a rough road

walking map – a map specially produced for walkers

Walsers – medieval settlers from Goms who settled numerous highland valleys in the central Alps (see also The Walser Migrations in Facts about the Country)

Index

MAPS

TEXT

Map references are in **bold** type.

PLANET TALK

Lonely Planet's FREE quarterly newsletter

We love hearing from you and think you'd like to hear from us.
When...is the right time to see reindeer in Finland?
Where...can you hear the best palm-wine music in Ghana?
How...do you get from Asunción to Areguá by steam train?
What...is the best way to see India?

For the answer to these and many other questions read PLANET TALK.

Every issue is packed with up-to-date travel news and advice including:

- a letter from Lonely Planet founders Tony and Maureen Wheeler
- travel diary from a Lonely Planet author – find out what it's really like out on the road
- feature article on an important and topical travel issue
- a selection of recent letters from our readers
- the latest travel news from all over the world
- details on Lonely Planet's new and forthcoming releases

To join our mailing list contact any Lonely Planet office.

Also available: Lonely Planet T-shirts. 100% heavyweight cotton.

LONELY PLANET ONLINE

Get the latest travel information before you leave or while you're on the road

Whether you've just begun planning your next trip, or you're chasing down specific info on currency regulations or visa requirements, check out the Lonely Planet World Wide Web site for up-to-the-minute travel information.

As well as travel profiles of your favourite destinations (including interactive maps and full-colour photos), you'll find current reports from our army of researchers and other travellers, updates on health and visas, travel advisories, and the ecological and political issues you need to be aware of as you travel.

There's an online travellers' forum (the Thorn Tree) where you can share your experiences of life on the road, meet travel companions and ask other travellers for their recommendations and advice. We also have plenty of links to other Web sites useful to independent travellers.

With tens of thousands of visitors a month, the Lonely Planet Web site is one of the most popular on the Internet and has won a number of awards including GNN's Best of the Net travel award.

http://www.lonelyplanet.com

LONELY PLANET PRODUCTS

The Lonely Planet list covers every accessible part of Asia as well as Australia, the Pacific, South America, Africa, the Middle East, Europe and parts of North America. There are eight series: *travel guides* – covering a country for a range of budgets, *shoestring guides* – with compact information for low-budget travel in a major region, *walking guides, city guides, phrasebooks, audio packs, travel atlases* and *travel literature*.

EUROPE

Austria • Baltic States & Kaliningrad • Baltic States phrasebook • Britain • Central Europe on a shoestring • Central Europe phrasebook • Czech & Slovak Republics • Dublin city guide • Eastern Europe on a shoestring • Eastern Europe phrasebook • Finland • France • Greece • Greek phrasebook • Hungary • Iceland, Greenland & the Faroe Islands • Ireland • Italy • Mediterranean Europe on a shoestring • Mediterranean Europe phrasebook • Poland • Prague city guide • Russia, Ukraine & Belarus • Russian phrasebook • Scandinavian & Baltic Europe on a shoestring • Scandinavian Europe phrasebook • Slovenia • St Petersburg city guide • Switzerland • Trekking in Greece • Trekking in Spain • Vienna city guide • Walking in Switzerland • Western Europe on a shoestring • Western Europe phrasebook

NORTH AMERICA & MEXICO

Alaska • Backpacking in Alaska • California & Nevada • Canada • Hawaii • Honolulu city guide • Los Angeles city guide • Pacific Northwest USA • Rocky Mountain States • San Francisco city guide • Southwest USA • USA phrasebook

CENTRAL AMERICA & THE CARIBBEAN

Baja California • Central America on a shoestring • Costa Rica • Eastern Caribbean • Guatemala, Belize & Yucatán: La Ruta Maya • Mexico

SOUTH AMERICA

Argentina, Uruguay & Paraguay • Bolivia • Brazil • Brazilian phrasebook • Buenos Aires city guide • Chile & Easter Island • Colombia • Ecuador & the Galápagos Islands • Latin American Spanish phrasebook • Peru • Quechua phrasebook • Rio de Janeiro city guide • South America on a shoestring • Trekking in the Patagonian Andes • Venezuela

AFRICA

Arabic (Moroccan) phrasebook • Africa on a shoestring • Cape Town city guide • Central Africa • East Africa • Egypt & the Sudan • Ethiopian (Amharic) phrasebook • Kenya • Morocco • North Africa • South Africa, Lesotho & Swaziland • Swahili phrasebook • Trekking in East Africa • West Africa • Zimbabwe, Botswana & Namibia • Zimbabwe, Botswana & Namibia travel atlas

ALSO AVAILABLE:

Travel with Children • Traveller's Tales